Encyclopedia

— *of* —

LIFE SCIENCES

Second Edition

13

Index volume

Marshall Cavendish
New York • London • Toronto • Sydney

Marshall Cavendish
99 White Plains Road
Tarrytown, New York 10591-9001

www.marshallcavendish.com

© 1996, 2004 Marshall Cavendish Corporation

Created by **The Brown Reference Group plc**

Library of Congress Cataloging-in-Publication Data

Encyclopedia of life sciences / [edited by] Anne O'Daly.—2nd ed.
    p.   cm.
Summary: An illustrated encyclopedia with articles on
agriculture, anatomy, biochemistry, biology, genetics,
medicine, and molecular biology.
Includes bibliographical references (p.   ).
    ISBN 0-7614-7442-0 (set)
    ISBN 0-7614-7455-2 (vol. 13)
    1. Life sciences—Encyclopedias. 2. Biology—Encyclopedias. [1.
Biology—Encyclopedias. 2. Life sciences—Encyclopedias.] I. O'Daly,
Anne, 1966–
    QH302.5 .E53   2003
    570'.3—dc21
                                        2002031157

Printed in Malaysia
Bound in the United States of America

07 06 05 04 03 6 5 4 3 2 1

Artworks by:
Darren Awuah, Bill Botten, Jennie Dooge, Dax Fullbrook,
and Mark Walker.

For The Brown Reference Group:
Project Editors: Caroline Beattie and Lesley Campbell-Wright
Editors: Richard Beatty, Robert Cave, Simon Hall, Rob Houston,
Jim Martin, and Ben Morgan
Designer: Joan Curtis
Picture Researcher: Rebecca Cox
Managing Editor: Bridget Giles
Design Manager: Lynne Ross
Indexer: Kay Ollerenshaw

For Marshall Cavendish:
Project Editor: Joyce Tavolacci
Editorial Director: Paul Bernabeo
Production Manager: Michael Esposito

Title page: powdery mildew *Albago* (Biophoto Associates)

CONTENTS

USEFUL INFORMATION

Use this table to convert the English system (or the imperial system), the system of units common in the United States (e.g., inches, miles, quarts), to the metric system (e.g., meters, kilometers, liters) or to convert the metric system to the English system. You can convert one measurement into another by multiplying. For example, to convert centimeters into inches, multiply the number of centimeters by 0.3937. To convert inches into centimeters, multiply the number of inches by 2.54.

To convert	into	multiply by
Acres	Square feet	43,560
	Square yards	4840
	Square miles	0.00156
	Square meters	4046.856
	Hectares	0.40468
Celsius	Fahrenheit	First multiply by 1.8 then add 32
Centimeters	Inches	0.3937
	Feet	0.0328
Cubic cm	Cubic inches	0.06102
Cubic feet	Cubic inches	1728
	Cubic yards	0.037037
	Gallons	7.48
	Cubic meters	0.028317
	Liters	28.32
Cubic inches	Fluid ounces	0.554113
	Cups	0.069264
	Quarts	0.017316
	Gallons	0.004329
	Liters	0.016387
	Milliliters	16.387064
Cubic meters	Cubic feet	35.3145
	Cubic yards	1.30795
Cubic yards	Cubic feet	27
	Cubic meters	0.76456
Cups, fluid	Quarts	0.25
	Pints	0.5
	Ounces	8
	Milliliters	237
	Tablespoons	16
	Teaspoons	48
Fahrenheit	Celsius	First subtract 32 then divide by 1.8
Feet	Centimeters	30.48
	Meters	0.3048
	Kilometers	0.0003
	Inches	12
	Yards	0.3333
	Miles	0.00019
Gallons	Quarts	4
	Pints	8
	Cups	16
	Ounces	128
	Liters	3.785
	Milliliters	3785
	Cubic inches	231
	Cubic feet	0.1337
	Cubic yards	0.00495
	Cubic meters	0.00379
	British gallons	0.8327
Grams	Ounces	0.03527
	Pounds	0.0022
Hectares	Square meters	10,000
	Acres	2.471
Horsepower	Foot-pounds per minute	33,000
	British thermal units (Btu) per minute	42.42
	British thermal units (Btu) per hour	2546
	Kilowatts	0.7457
	Metric horsepower	1.014
Inches	Feet	0.08333

To convert	into	multiply by
Inches (continued)	Yards	0.02778
	Centimeters	2.54
	Meters	0.0254
Kilograms	Grams	1000
	Ounces	35.274
	Pounds	2.2046
	Short tons	0.0011
	Long tons	0.00098
	Metric tons (tonnes)	0.001
Kilometers	Meters	1000
	Miles	0.62137
	Yards	1093.6
	Feet	3280.8
Kilowatts	British thermal units (Btu) per minute	56.9
	Horsepower	1.341
	Metric horsepower	1.397
Kilowatt-hours	British thermal units (Btu)	3413
Knots	Statute miles per hour	1.1508
Leagues	Miles	3
Liters	Milliliters	1000
	Fluid ounces	33.814
	Quarts	1.05669
	British gallons	0.21998
	Cubic inches	61.02374
	Cubic feet	0.13531
Meters	Inches	39.37
	Feet	3.28083
	Yards	1.09361
	Miles	0.000621
	Kilometers	0.001
	Centimeters	100
	Millimeters	1000
Miles	Inches	63,360
	Feet	5280
	Yards	1760
	Meters	1609.34
	Kilometers	1.60934
	Nautical miles	0.8684
Miles nautical, U.S. and International	Statute miles	1.1508
	Feet	6076.115
	Meters	1852
Miles per minute	Feet per second	88
	Knots	52.104
Milliliters	Fluid ounces	0.0338
	Cubic inches	0.061
	Liters	0.001
Millimeters	Centimeters	0.1
	Meters	0.001
	Inches	0.03937
Ounces, avoirdupois	Pounds	0.0625
	Grams	28.34952
	Kilograms	0.0283495
Ounces, fluid	Pints	0.0625
	Quarts	0.03125
	Cubic inches	1.80469
	Cubic feet	0.00104
	Milliliters	29.57353
	Liters	0.02957
Pints, fluid	Ounces, fluid	16
	Quarts, fluid	0.5

To convert	into	multiply by
Pints, fluid (continued)	Cubic inches	28.8745
	Cubic feet	0.01671
	Milliliters	473.17647
	Liters	0.473176
Pounds	Ounces	16
	Grams	453.59237
	Kilograms	0.45359
	Tons	0.0005
	Tons, long	0.000446
	Metric tons (tonnes)	0.0004536
Quarts, fluid	Ounces, fluid	32
	Pints, fluid	2
	Gallons	0.25
	Cubic inches	57.749
	Cubic feet	0.033421
	Liters	0.946358
	Milliliters	946.358
Square centimeters	Square inches	0.155
Square feet	Square inches	144
	Square meters	0.093
	Square yards	0.111
Square inches	Square centimeters	6.452
	Square feet	0.0069
Square kilometers	Hectares	100
	Square meters	1,000,000
	Square miles	0.3861
Square meters	Square feet	10.758
	Square yards	1.196
Square miles	Acres	640
	Square kilometers	2.59
Square yards	Square feet	9
	Square inches	1296
	Square meters	0.836
Tablespoons	Ounces, fluid	0.5
	Teaspoons	3
	Milliliters	14.7868
Teaspoons	Ounces, fluid	0.16667
	Tablespoons	0.3333
	Milliliters	4.9289
Tons, long	Pounds	2240
	Kilograms	1016.047
	Short tons	1.12
	Metric tons (tonnes)	1.016
Tons, short	Pounds	2000
	Kilograms	907.185
	Long tons	0.89286
	Metric tonnes	0.907
Tons, metric (tonnes)	Pounds	2204.62
	Kilograms	1000
	Long tons	0.984206
	Short tons	1.10231
Watts	British thermal units (Btu) per hour	3.415
	Horsepower	0.00134
Yards	Inches	36
	Feet	3
	Miles	0.0005681
	Centimeters	91.44
	Meters	0.9144

THE FIVE KINGDOMS

KINGDOM MONERA

The organisms in this kingdom are all prokaryotic, having cells lacking membrane-bounded nuclei. They are mainly single celled, although some multicellular forms also exist, occurring as either strings or clusters. Members of this kingdom are placed into the following two major groupings:

Subkingdom Archaebacteria
Subkingdom Eubacteria

KINGDOM PROTISTA

The organisms in this kingdom represent the most simple eukaryotic organisms, having cells with nuclei and other membrane-bound cell organelles. They include predominantly single-celled organisms or simple multicellular or colonial organisms. Protists are divided into the following three main groups:

Plantlike protists (algae)
    Phylum Pyrrophyta
    Phylum Chrysophyta
    Phylum Chlorophyta
    Phylum Phaeophyta
    Phylum Rhodophyta
    Phylum Euglenophyta

Funguslike protists
    Phylum Gymnomycota
    Phylum Oomycota

Animal-like protists
    Group Mastigophora
    Group Sarcodina
    Group Ciliophora
    Group Sporozoa

KINGDOM FUNGI

Members of this kingdom are mainly multicellular, and all are eukaryotic. They are divided into the following two divisions:

Division Zygomycota
    Subdivisions:
        Dipodascomycotina
        Endomycotina
        Dipodascopidomycotina

Division Dikaryomycota
    Subdivisions:
        Ascomycotina
        Basidiomycotina

KINGDOM PLANTAE

Members of this kingdom are complex, multicellular, eukaryotic organisms that carry out photosynthesis. They are placed in the following groupings:

Lower seedless plants
    Phylum Marchantiophyta (or Hepatophyta)
    Phylum Anthocerotophyta
    Phylum Bryophyta
    Phylum Psilotophyta
    Phylum Lycopodiophyta
    Phylum Equisetophyta
    Phylum Polypodiophyta (or Pteridophyta)

Higher seed-bearing plants
    Phylum Cycadophyta
    Phylum Ginkgophyta
    Phylum Pinophyta (or Coniferophyta)
    Phylum Gnetophyta
    Phylum Magnoliophyta (or Anthophyta)

KINGDOM ANIMALIA

Animals are complex multicellular, eukaryotic organisms that are grouped into the following 33 phyla:

    Phylum Placozoa
    Phylum Porifera
    Phylum Cnidaria
    Phylum Ctenophora
    Phylum Platyhelminthes
    Phylum Rhombozoa
    Phylum Orthonectidia
    Phylum Gnathostomulida
    Phylum Nemertea
    Phylum Gastrotricha
    Phylum Rotifera
    Phylum Kinorhyncha
    Phylum Loricifera
    Phylum Priapulida
    Phylum Acanthocephala
    Phylum Nematoda
    Phylum Nematomorpha
    Phylum Sipuncula
    Phylum Echiura
    Phylum Pogonophora
    Phylum Annelida
    Phylum Mollusca
    Phylum Phoronida
    Phylum Brachiopoda
    Phylum Bryozoa (Ectoprocta/Polyzoa)
    Phylum Entoprocta
    Phylum Arthropoda
    Phylum Onychophora
    Phylum Tardigrada
    Phylum Chaetognatha
    Phylum Hemichordata
    Phylum Echinodermata
    Phylum Chordata

GLOSSARY

abdomen In mammals, area between the rim of the pelvis and the diaphragm; in arthropods, the final division of the body.

abiotic Relating to environmental features, such as physical and chemical factors, that do not derive directly from the presence of living organisms.

abscisic acid Growth inhibitor present in plant organs; it induces dormancy in buds and seeds.

abscission layer Layer at base of leaf stalk in woody dicotyledons and gymnosperms in which cells become loosely joined. This looseness eventually allows the leaf to fall.

absorption spectrum Graph of light absorption versus wavelength of incident light. The region of the electromagnetic energy spectrum (usually visible light or ultraviolet) that is absorbed by a particular molecule or atom.

acetylcholine Neurotransmitter secreted by nerve cells that relays electrical signals in chemical form, transmitting them between nerves and between nerves and muscles. Often abbreviated to ACh.

achene Simple, dry fruit with one seed in which the fruit wall is separate from the seed coat.

acid Any substance that gives up (donates) hydrogen ions (H^+) in solution, increasing the overall hydrogen ion concentration of the solution.

acid rain Rainfall with a pH of less than 5.6. Atmospheric carbon dioxide gives rain a natural acidity. Atmospheric pollutants, such as oxides of nitrogen and sulfur, dissolve in rainwater to make acid rain.

acrosome Caplike structure that covers the head of a sperm cell.

actin Protein that is present in microfilaments, such as those that enable muscles to contract.

action potential Localized change in electric potential that travels along a nerve fiber, constituting a nerve impulse.

activation energy Energy needed to start a chemical reaction.

active transport Transport of a substance across a cell membrane—against a concentration gradient, either high to low or low to high—that requires energy.

adaptation Accumulation of inherited characteristics or a certain genetically based characteristic or behavior that makes an organism suited to its environment and way of life.

adaptive radiation Evolutionary diversification of a single species, with production of many different species adapted to different environments.

adenine Nitrogen-containing base that is present in nucleic acids such as DNA and RNA.

adenosine triphosphate (ATP) Main short-term energy storage molecule in cells.

adrenal gland Endocrine glands located just above the kidneys, consisting of an inner medulla and an outer cortex that produce steroids and hormones.

adrenocorticotropic hormone (ACTH) Hormone secreted by the pituitary gland that regulates the growth and secretions of the adrenal cortex.

adventitious root Root that grows from an unusual position on a plant, for example from a stem.

aerobic Describes a process that takes place or an organism that grows or metabolizes in the presence of gaseous or dissolved oxygen.

albinism Inability to form the pigment melanin, resulting in light-colored skin, white hair, and pink eyes.

aldosterone Hormone secreted by the adrenal cortex that controls secretion and retention of sodium and potassium ions.

algae Simple single-celled or multicellular, mostly photosynthetic organisms; present in moneran (cyanobacteria), protist (most algal species), and plant (red, green, and brown algae) kingdoms.

alkali Soluble base or a solution made up from a base.

allele Gene that determines variations of the same characteristic that is situated on corresponding position of homologous chromosomes.

allergy Hypersensitivity to some substance in the environment, such as house dust, that results in conditions such as hay fever or asthma.

allosteric enzyme Enzyme whose three-dimensional configurations alter in response to its environmental situation.

alternation of generations Life cycle that alternates between a generation that reproduces sexually and another that reproduces asexually; can also mean the alternation of two distinct cytological generations within a life cycle: that is, one is haploid and the other is diploid.

alveolus Air sac in the lung through which gaseous exchange occurs.

amino acid Organic molecule consisting of a central carbon atom, a carboxyl group (–COOH), and a side chain (–R). Amino acids are the monomers from which proteins are built.

amniocentesis Sampling of the amniotic fluid around a fetus so that information about its development and genes can be obtained.

amnion Fluid-filled sac that protects the developing embryo.

amylase Starch-digesting enzyme.

anabolism Chemical reactions in which a complex substance is made from simpler ones, which lead to storage of energy.

anaerobic Describes a process that takes place or an organism that grows or metabolizes in the absence of gaseous or dissolved oxygen.

anaphase Stage in mitosis and meiosis in which chromosomes move to opposite poles of the cell.

androgen Substance that promotes male sex hormone activity.

aneuploidy Nuclei, cells, or organisms having a chromosome number that is not an exact multiple of the usual haploid number.

angiosperm Plant that has flowers and seeds enclosed in fruits.

anion Ion with a negative charge.

annual plant Plant that completes its life cycle in one growing season.

annual ring Annual growth of secondary wood (xylem) in the stems and roots of woody plants.

anther Part of a flower's stamen that produces pollen.

antibiotic Organic compound produced synthetically or by soil microorganisms that, in dilute solutions, inhibits the growth of, or destroys, bacteria and other microorganisms. Antibiotic drugs are used mainly to treat infectious diseases in humans, other animals, and plants.

antibody Protein compound produced by vertebrate plasma cells that binds to foreign bodies (antigens), which then clump together and can be destroyed by white blood cells.

anticodon Sequence of three nucleotides on a tRNA molecule that can pair with a codon on a mRNA molecule.

antidiuretic hormone (ADH) Hormone secreted by the pituitary gland that increases blood pressure and decreases urine flow.

antigen Any molecule that can stimulate an immune response, inducing the production of a specific antibody.

anus Opening of the gastrointestinal tract to the exterior, through which excretory material may exit.

aorta Largest artery of the body, leaving the heart from the left ventricle and supplying all parts of the body with oxygenated blood.

apical dominance Effect of a terminal bud in suppressing the growth of lateral buds. In trees the effect reduces with age, thus many trees produce lateral branches.

apical meristem Growing point at the tip of the root and stem in vascular plants that originates from a single cell.

aposematic (warning) coloration Color warning other organisms of the potentially harmful effects of an animal.

atom Smallest unit of an element that retains the characteristic chemical properties of that element.

autoimmune response Pathological process in which the immune system attacks the body's own cells or tissues.

autonomic nervous system Part of the peripheral nervous system that controls the action of smooth muscle, cardiac muscle, and glands; it has overall control of homeostasis.

autotrophs Organisms that synthesize organic molecules from inorganic materials. Autotrophic organisms are the primary producers that are consumed by heterotrophs and form the base of food webs.

auxin Plant hormone that regulates growth and development.

axon Extension of neuron that transmits nerve impulses away from the cell body.

bacteria Single-celled prokaryotic microorganisms in the kingdom Monera. Most are decomposers, although some are parasites or autotrophs.

Barr body Inactivated X chromosome present in the nucleus of certain cells in female mammals.

base Substance that forms hydroxyl ions (OH^-) on dissociation in water.

basophil Type of white blood cell that stains strongly with basic dye.

Batesian mimicry Similarity in appearance of a harmless or palatable species to a dangerous or poisonous one.

B-cell Leucocyte that has migrated from the fetal liver to the bone marrow, settling in a lymph node or spleen.

benthos Organisms that live on the bottom of the ocean or lakes.

biennial plant Plant that needs two years to complete its life cycle.

bilateral symmetry Property of organisms whose anatomy is arranged symmetrically so there is just one plane in which they can be separated into two halves, which are near-mirror images of each other.

bile Fluid produced by the liver that contains digestive juices, secretory products, and excretory products.

binary fission Equal split of a cell or organism in half, a type of asexual reproduction.

biodiversity Diversity of plant and animal species in an environment.

biogeochemical cycle Process by which substances move from the living environment to the physical environment and back again. Examples include the carbon cycle and the nitrogen cycle.

biomass Total quantity of organic matter in a region or habitat.

biome Any of Earth's major ecosystems that extend over large areas and are characterized by a distinctive climate and vegetation.

biosphere Region of Earth and its atmosphere that is inhabited by living organisms.

bipedal Walking on two feet.

blastula Stage of animal embryo development at or near end of cleavage; typically, a hollow, fluid-filled, rounded cavity bounded by a single layer of cells.

blood pressure Pressure that is exerted by the blood on blood vessels.

budding Form of asexual reproduction in which a small part of the parent (a bud) becomes detached and develops into a new individual.

buffer Substance that binds with hydrogen ions (H^+) when their concentration is high and releases hydrogen ions when concentrations are low; thus, it resists pH changes.

calcitonin Polypeptide hormone produced by the thyroid gland that inhibits bone degradation and stimulates the uptake of calcium and phosphate by bone.

Calvin cycle Series of reactions in one phase of photosynthesis in which carbon dioxide is fixed and glucose is formed.

carbohydrate Compound that contains carbon, hydrogen, and oxygen in the ratio of 1:2:1.

carcinogen Any agent that causes a normal cell to become cancerous.

carpel Female reproductive organ of flowering plants.

catabolism All the enzymic breakdown processes in an organism, such as respiration and digestion.

catalyst Any substance that increases the rate of a chemical reaction, without itself being used in that reaction. Biological catalysts are usually protein molecules called enzymes.

cation Ion with a positive charge.

cecum Blind-ending structure present in the digestive system of some animals; it may house cellulose-digesting bacteria.

cell Basic unit of all living organisms.

cellulose Complex carbohydrate (a polysaccharide) that is the main constituent of plant cell walls.

central nervous system Vertebrate nervous tissue that includes the brain and spinal cord, to which sensory impulses are transmitted and from which motor impulses pass out; coordinates the activity of the entire nervous system.

centromere Chromosome region that holds together sister chromatids until the mitotic and second meiotic anaphase occur.

cerebellum Region of the vertebrate hindbrain that regulates balance, stance, and locomotion.

cerebral cortex Outer layer of the cerebrum in the brain that is made up of gray matter (nerve cells) that are closely packed together.

cerebrum Largest subdivision of the brain; it is a focus for thinking, learning, voluntary movement, and the interpretation of different sensations.

cervix Neck of mammalian uterus. It leads into the vagina.

chelicerae First paired appendages of Chelicerata (spiders, scorpions, ticks), contrasting with antennae of other groups.

chemoautotroph Organism that obtains its energy from a simple inorganic reaction.

chemoreceptor Sense organ or sensory cell that responds to chemical aspects of the internal or external environment.

chitin Nitrogen-containing complex carbohydrate (polysaccharide) present in many arthropod exoskeletons and the cell walls of many fungi.

chlorophyll Green pigment present in all algae and plants, except some saprotrophs and parasites.

chloroplast Plant cell organelle within which both the light and dark phases of photosynthesis occur.

chorionic villus sampling Test to detect genetic disorders in a fetus in which cells genetically identical to fetal cells are removed from the fetal part of the placenta.

chromatid One of the two strands of a duplicated chromosome.

chromatin Material that makes up eukaryotic chromosomes; it consists of DNA and proteins.

chromosome Long strand of coiled DNA composed of genes, the genetic information for most organisms.

chyle Milky suspension of fat droplets within the thoracic ducts and lacteals of vertebrates after absorption of a meal.

chyme Partly digested food that leaves the vertebrate stomach.

cilium (plural cilia) Short, hairlike organelle that is a tubular extension of the cell membrane. It has a capacity to beat and so propel a cell through fluid or fluid past a cell.

circadian rhythm Rhythmic changes occurring within an organism with a periodicity of approximately 24 hours.

citric acid cycle Cyclic biochemical pathway in which acetyl-CoA is completely degraded to carbon dioxide and water, releasing energy, which is stored in ATP.

class Major taxonomic grouping of organisms ranking above an order and below a phylum or division.

cleavage Series of cell divisions of a fertilized egg, resulting in a multicellular embryo.

climax community Community of organisms that has a more or less stable composition and is in equilibrium with the existing natural environment.

cloaca Common chamber into which the intestinal, urinary, and reproductive ducts open in some vertebrates.

clone Group of organisms of identical genotype produced by asexual reproduction, or a group of cells descended from the same single parent cell.

cochlea Structure located in the inner ear of mammals that contains the receptors used in hearing.

codon Group of three mRNA bases that specify an amino acid or polypeptide chain.

coelom Main body cavity of most animals.

coevolution Interdependent evolution of two or more species that occurs as a result of the way they interact over a long period of time.

collagen Structural (fibrous) protein of connective tissue. It has a high tensile strength but is not very elastic.

commensalism Relationship between two types of organisms in which one obtains food or other benefits from the other without damaging or benefiting it.

community Group of populations living in a certain area or habitat.

compound eye Eye that consists of many smaller, light-sensitive units called ommatidia; often present in insects.

cone (eyes) Cell in the retina of the eye of some vertebrates that is especially sensitive to bright light and allows color vision.

consumer Organism that cannot make its own food from inorganic materials and so must feed on other organisms as a source of energy.

convergent evolution Independent evolution of similar aspects of function or structure in two or more organisms with very different ancestors.

cornea Exposed, transparent outer layer of the vertebrate eye responsible for most light refraction.

corolla Petals of a flower.

cotyledon Seed leaf of an embryo of a plant, which may contain stored food for germination.

covalent bond Chemical bond formed by one or more pairs of electrons.

crossing over Breaking and rejoining of homologous chromatids—causing an exchange of genetic materal—during the early meiotic prophase.

cryptic coloration Coloring of an animal that helps camouflage it in its natural environment.

cytokinesis Division of cell's cytoplasm to form two daughter cells.

cytoplasm Contents of a cell, apart from the nucleus.

cytosine Nitrogen-containing pyrimidine base present in the nucleic acids DNA and RNA, as well as in nucleotides and their derivatives.

decomposer Organism that obtains the energy for all its life processes by breaking down remnants of organic materials.

dendrite Branch from cell body of nerve cell that receives electrical stimuli from other neurons.

denitrification Process in which various soil bactera convert nitrate ions into gaseous nitrogen.

diapause Inactive state of an insect during the pupal stage.

diatoms Major group of single-celled algae, important in the plankton of oceans and lakes.

dicotyledon Flowering plant that has embryo with two seed leaves.

diffusion Movement of gas, liquid, or solute particles from a region of higher to one of lower concentration.

dinoflagellate Single-celled protists that are an important constituent of plankton.

diploid Nuclei and their cells having homologous pairs of chromosomes.

divergent evolution Evolution over time of a number of different species from one species of living organism.

division Taxonomic grouping of plants belonging to similar classes; the plant equivalent of a phylum.

DNA Deoxyribonucleic acid, the nucleic acid that is the main component of chromosomes and forms the genetic material of most living organisms.

dominance In genetics, a phenomenon that is expressed equally in the homozygous and heterozygous conditions. In animal behavior, it indicates one individual's priority over another in relation to a certain resource. In ecology, it refers to the controlling influence of one particular species due to its size or population.

dominant allele Allele that is always expressed when present, regardless of whether it is homozygous or heterozygous.

dormancy Resting condition present in higher plants and animals or their reproductive bodies.

duodenum Part of the small intestine.

echolocation Used by some aquatic, nocturnal, and cave-dwelling animals to find objects by means of sound waves reflected back to the emitter by the objects.

ecology Study of relationships of organisms to their environment.

ecosystem Community of organisms and their interactions with one another, together with the environment in which they live and with which they interact.

elastin Fibrous protein in animal connective tissue; a large amount is present in the lungs and ligaments.

electron Subatomic particle with a negative charge that is located outside the atomic nucleus.

electrophoresis Technique involving the use of an electric field, used to separate and analyze molecules.

endocrine system Animal organs, tissues, and cells that secrete hormones and controls bodily functions.

endoskeleton Skeleton that is present within the body, such as the human skeleton.

endosperm Nutritive tissue surrounding the embryo of seed plants that sustains the developing embryo.

endometrium Lining of the mammalian uterus, shed during menstruation.

endorphin Neurotransmitter with pain-suppressing effects.

enzyme Protein that catalyzes chemical reactions in organisms.

eosinophil White blood cell with a coarse granular cytoplasm that stains easily when an acidic dye, such as eosin, is added to it.

epidermis Outer layer of cells that covers the body of plants and animals.

epinephrine Main hormone of the adrenal medulla; it stimulates the sympathetic nervous system.

epiphyte Plant that uses another plant for support while it grows.

epithelium Tissue that covers the body surfaces and cavities and forms glands.

epoch Subdivision of a period of geological time (See also *period*).

era One of the main divisions of geological time; one era is divided into periods.

erythrocyte Red blood cell in vertebrates.

esophagus Muscular tube in vertebrates that extends from the pharynx to the stomach.

essential amino acid Type of amino acid that an organism needs to obtain directly from its environment owing to its inability to synthesize it from other substances.

estrogen Female sex hormone produced by the ovaries.

estrus Period of heat or sexual receptivity occurring in female mammals around the time of ovulation.

ethylene Gaseous hydrocarbon, produced by many plants in small amounts; regulates growth and promotes fruit ripening.

eukaryotic cell Cell in which the chromosomal genetic material is contained within one or more nuclei and is separated from the cytoplasm by two nuclear membranes.

eutrophication Increase in the nutrients contained in a body of water; it may occur naturally or as a result of human activity (the overuse of fertilizers in agriculture).

evolution Any cumulative genetic change that occurs in a population of organisms from one generation to the next.

exoskeleton External skeleton, such as the outer covering of arthropods.

fallopian tube Paired tubes situated just behind the ovaries in female mammals; they conduct eggs from the ovary to the uterus.

family Taxonomic grouping of related organisms, ranking above a genus and below an order; consists of genera.

fatty acid Organic acid containing a long hydrocarbon chain.

fermentation Anaerobic breakdown of organic substances, usually sugars or fats, to give more simple organic products.

fetus Unborn offspring after it has completed most of its development; in humans, the term applies from the second or the third month of pregnancy to birth.

fibrin Insoluble protein in blood that aids its clotting.

flagellum (plural flagella) Long extension of a cell membrane that beats in wavelike undulations; used for locomotion.

florigen Hypothetical plant hormone that is believed to explain the transmission of flowering stimulus from the leaf, where it is perceived, to the growing point.

follicle-stimulating hormone (FSH) Hormone secreted by vertebrate pituitary gland in mammals. In females, it stimulates the ripening of follicles in the ovary that produce ova. In males, it stimulates the formation of sperm in the testes.

food chain Pattern of interactions that takes place when plants in a community convert solar energy to a stored chemical form, which is then transferred to herbivores, carnivores, and decomposers.

fossil Preserved remains of an organism, usually in materials such as rock and ice.

fruit Ripened ovary of flowering plants that encloses the seeds.

fungi Kingdom of multicellular eukaryotes lacking chlorophyll such as mushrooms, toadstools, molds, and mildews.

gamete Haploid cell used in sexual reproduction. Also called sex cell or germ cell. In plants and animals, the female gamete is the egg (ovum) and the male gamete is the sperm.

gametophyte Haploid phase in the life cycle of plants, in which gametes are produced by mitosis.

ganglion Knotlike mass of nerve cell bodies.

gastrointestinal tract Tube in which food is digested and across whose walls digestion products are absorbed; includes the stomach and intestines in vertebrates.

gastrula Stage of animal embryonic development in which the embryo is cup-shaped and has two layers.

gene Discrete unit of hereditary information present in a chromosome.

gene flow Spread of genes through populations as determined by movements of individuals and their propagating agents, such as spores.

gene pool Group of genes present in an interbreeding population.

genetic drift Random change in gene frequencies in a small and isolated population.

genome Full set of chromosomes with the genes they contain; in general, an organism's genetic material.

genotype Genetic makeup of an individual.

genus (plural genera) Taxonomic grouping of very similar organisms thought to be closely related species.

germ line Cells that become differentiated from somatic cells early in an organism's development and that later undergo meiosis (See also *somatic cell*).

gill Respiratory organ of aquatic animals.

gizzard Part of the digestive tract especially adapted for grinding food in some animals.

glucagon Hormone secreted from the pancreas that increases the glucose concentration of the blood.

glucocorticoid Adrenal cortex hormone that helps maintain the normal metabolism and resistance to stress by promoting the deposition of glycogen in the liver.

glycogen Polysaccharide made from glucose and stored temporarily in the liver.

glycolysis First stage of cellular respiration: the anaerobic degradation of glucose to yield pyruvate and the production of ATP.

granulocyte Leukocyte that has a granular cytoplasm.

greenhouse effect Shortwave radiation from the Sun enters Earth's atmosphere and is reradiated from Earth's surface in longer infrared waves. These waves are reabsorbed by components of Earth's atmosphere, so heating it up. Certain gases, such as carbon dioxide, absorb infrared wavelengths, increasing atmospheric temperature. Burning fossil fuels increases such greenhouse gases and adds to global warming.

guanine Nitrogen-containing base present in nucleic acids.

guard cell Cell in the epidermis of plant stems and leaves; a pair forms a pore (stoma) for gaseous exchange.

gymnosperm Plant whose seeds are not enclosed in an ovary; seeds are often present in cones instead.

habitat Place or environment in which a certain organism lives.

haploid Containing a single set of unpaired chromosomes.

hemoglobin Red, iron-containing pigment in red blood cells that binds with oxygen and some carbon dioxide and transports them around the body.

hemolysis Destruction of red blood cells, causing the release of hemoglobin.

hermaphrodite Plant or animal in which individuals possess both female and male sex organs.

herbaceous Nonwoody plants.

heterotrophs Organisms that cannot make their food from inorganic substances and feed at the expense of other organisms or on decaying matter.

heterozygous Term that describes a locus (position) at which the two alleles in any diploid cell are different.

histamine Substance released by mast cells in connective tissue in response to a particular antigen; it makes blood vessels dilate and causes the symptoms of allergic and inflammatory reactions.

histology Study of tissue structure.

holozoic nutrition Feeding in an animal-like way—ingesting solid organic matter, digesting and absorbing nutrients from it, and egesting undigested material.

homeostasis Those processes that help to maintain a relatively constant internal environment despite fluctuations in the external environment.

homozygous Having the two alleles at corresponding loci on homologous chromosomes identical for one or more loci.

hormone Chemical secreted directly into the blood by ductless glands and carried to specific cells or organs where they cause a physiological response.

humus Complex organic matter that forms as a result of the decomposition of dead organisms in the soil giving it a characteristic dark color.

hydrogen bond Weak attractive force between a hydrogen atom and an electronegative (electron-attracting) atom, such as oxygen.

hydrolysis Reaction in which a molecule is broken into two parts by the addition of a water molecule.

hypothalamus Area of the brain that regulates the pituitary gland and many homeostatic activities, including body temperature and water balance.

hypothesis A tentative statement that is put forward as a possible explanation for some observation and that serves as a basis for scientific experiments.

immunoglobin Antibody produced by plasma cells in response to the presence of certain antigens.

implantation Attachment of a mammalian embryo to the uterus of the mother.

imprinting Form of learning in which a young animal, such as a bird, becomes attached to an individual or an object within a few hours of birth.

inflammatory response Response of body tissue to infection or injury; it involves increased dilation of blood vessels, swelling, redness, heat, and pain.

instinct Genetically determined pattern of behavior or a response that is inherited behavior typical of the species.

insulin Hormone produced by the pancreas that lowers the level of blood glucose.

integument Outer layer of an animal, often the epidermis; also the outer layer of a plant ovule, forming the seed coat after fertilization.

invertebrate Any animal that does not possess a bony vertebral column.

ion Atom or a group of atoms with an electrical charge, either positive (cation) or negative (anion).

islets of Langerhans Groups of insulin-secreting endocrine cells that are distributed throughout the vertebrate pancreas.

isotope Any of two or more types of atoms of a chemical element with the same atomic number and nearly identical chemical behavior but with differing atomic mass or mass number and different physical properties.

karyotype Characteristics of the set of chromosomes of an individual or a cell.

keratin Tough protein that is the structural component of hair, wool, nails, feathers, claws, and horn. It also makes up the vertebrate epidermis that forms a resistant outer layer of skin.

kingdom Most inclusive taxonomic grouping.

lacteal Blind-ended vessel, part of the lymphatic system.

larynx Voice box, which contains vocal cords; present at the upper end of the trachea.

lateral line Sensory system of fish and aquatic and larval amphibians; receptors are clusters of sensory cells present on the skin or within a series of canals or grooves on the head and body.

leukocyte White blood cell.

lichen Compound organism made up of an alga and a fungus living in a symbiotic relationship.

ligament Vertebrate connective tissue that joins together bones.

lignin Substance made from polymeric molecules that makes plant stems and roots hard and rigid.

limnetic zone Open water region of a body of fresh water.

lipids Organic compounds such as fats that are insoluble in water but soluble in organic solvents, such as alcohol; a very important source of fuel for living things.

littoral zone Area of shallow water near the shore that lies between high and low tide marks.

loop of Henle U-shaped loop of the mammalian kidney tubule, which extends down into the medulla.

luteinizing hormone (LH) Hormone produced by the pituitary that stimulates the testes to produce testosterone in males and brings about menstruation in females.

lymph Clear fluid derived from the tissue fluid within vessels of the body's lymphatic system.

lymph node Structure within lymph vessels of mammals and birds that contains lymphocytes that filter lymph.

lymphocyte White blood cell that is responsible for immune responses.

lysis Process of cell destruction.

lysosome Organelle within many animal cells that contains hydrolytic enzymes.

macrophage Large phagocytotic cell that can ingest and digest bacteria.

Malpighian tubules Long, slender tubes that are used as the excretory organ of many arthropods.

mandible Lower jaw of vertebrates and an external mouthpart of certain arthropods.

mast cell Cell in connective tissue that is important in allergic reactions.

meiosis A form of nuclear division in which, after chromosome duplication in a reproductive cell, the diploid parent nucleus divides twice forming four haploid daughter cells.

menstrual cycle Monthly cycle in the human female in which an egg is released and the uterine endometrium breaks down producing bleeding.

meristem Area of mitotic cell division in plants in which new cells are formed.

messenger RNA (mRNA) RNA transcribed from DNA that specifies the amino acid sequence of a protein.

metabolism Simultaneous and inter-related chemical reactions taking place in a cell at any one time.

metaphase Stage of mitosis and meiosis during which chromosomes line up on the equatorial plane of the cell.

microorganism Organism that can be seen only under a microscope; includes protists, bacteria, and many fungi.

microvillus (plural microvilli) Small projections from the cell membrane that increase the surface area; mainly in cells responsible for absorption or secretion.

mineralocorticoid Hormone produced by the cortex of the adrenal glands that regulates salt and water.

mitochondrion Spherical or elongated organelle in which aerobic respiration occurs.

mitosis Process of nuclear division in which information from genes is distributed equally to two daughter cells.

mold Popular name for many fungi.

Mole SI unit of an amount of substance. It is equal to the amount of a substance that contains as many elementary units as there are atoms in 12g of carbon 12. These units can be atoms, molecules, ions—in fact, any specified unit. A mole of a chemical compound is equivalent to its molecular weight, which is the sum of the atomic weights.

molecule Smallest particle of a covalently bonded element or compound that has the same composition and properties as a larger part of the substance.

monocotyledon Flowering plant with embryos having one seed leaf.

morphology Study of the form and struc-

ture of living organisms, particularly their external structure.

mucus Slimy, sticky secretion that lubricates body parts and traps dirt particles.

Müllerian mimicry Mimicry of one species by another, where both are dangerous to a predator.

mutagen Agent that produces mutation or increases the rate of mutation. Mutagens include certain chemicals, X rays, gamma rays, and beta particles.

mutation Change in the chemical structure of a gene.

mycelium Tangled mass of hyphae (threads) that forms the vegetative body of a fungus.

myoglobin Protein of vertebrate muscle fibers that binds to molecular oxygen.

myosin Protein that helps the muscles to contract.

natural selection Most widely accepted theory concerning the main mechanism of evolutionary change. The genetic composition of evolutionary lineage changes over time by a nonrandom transmission of genes from one parental generation to the next. Selection of gene combinations will favor those that are best suited to a particular environment.

nekton Collective term for free-swimming animals in the pelagic zone of a sea or lake.

nematocyst Structure present in the cnidocytes (stinging cells) of cnidarians and used for defense and the capture of prey.

neoteny Slowing of the rate of growth and the development of certain body parts relative to the reproductive organs; organism reaches sexual maturity in a larval or other immature stage.

neuron Conducting cell of the nervous system, which transmits information in electrical impulses.

neutron Uncharged particle that exists in the nucleus of the atoms of elements.

niche Particular role of a certain species within a community.

nitrification Conversion of ammonium ions (NH_4^+) to nitrite and nitrate ions by soil bacteria.

nitrogen fixation Incorporation of atmospheric nitrogen into chemical compounds by certain microorganisms.

norepinephrine Type of neurotransmitter secreted by the adrenal medulla.

notochord Flexible, longitudinal rod that acts as an internal skeleton in the embryos of all chordates and is retained in the adults of some.

nucleic acid Organic compound present in living cells that is made up of a chain of nucleotides. There are two types of nucleic acid: DNA and RNA.

nucleotide Molecule that is made up from one or more phosphate groups, a 5-carbon sugar, and a nitrogenous base (purine or pyrimidine).

nutrients Chemicals in food that are used by living organisms to synthesize the materials needed to make materials and fuel.

ommatidium (plural ommatidia) Light-detecting unit of compound eye.

oocytes Cells that develop into egg cells by meiosis.

oogenesis Production of egg cells.

order Taxonomic category; a group of related families.

organ Functional unit of most multicellular organisms; consists of at least two types of tissue that are integrated so that the unit can perform a certain function or set of functions.

organ of Corti Structure within the ear that contains hair cells involved in sound detection and pitch analysis.

organelle Specialized structure within a cell that carries out particular functions.

osmoregulation Any mechanism that regulates the total volume of water within an animal's body and the concentration of solutes within its cells or body fluids.

osmosis Diffusion of water across a semipermeable membrane (permeable to water; selectively permeable to solutes) from a weak solution to a strong one.

osmotic pressure Pressure that is needed to prevent the passage of water into a solution across a semipermeable membrane.

oviduct Tube that carries ova from the ovary to the uterus.

oviparity Laying of eggs in which the embryos are only very slightly developed, if at all.

ovoviviparity Development of embryos within the mother, from whom they are nourished, but from whom they are separated by persistent egg membranes.

ovulation Release of an ovum from a mature follicle.

ovum Egg, or female gamete.

oxidation Removal of electrons from an atom or compound.

oxytocin Pituitary hormone produced by birds and mammals. It stimulates the uterus to contract and the breasts to release milk.

ozone layer Layer of ozone (O_3) at high altitude that shields Earth from much of the Sun's ultraviolet radiation.

palate Structure that separates the nasal cavity and the mouth.

parasite Any organism that obtains nutrients from the living tissue of another organism on which it lives, called the host.

parasympathetic nervous system Part of the autonomic nervous system that helps control internal organs and maintains an energy balance.

parthenogenesis Type of asexual reproduction in which an unfertilized egg develops into an adult organism.

pathogen Disease-causing organism.

pelagic Inhabiting open water, such the midocean.

peptide Compound that consists of a chain of amino acid groups.

perennial Growing year after year (of a plant).

period Interval of geological time that is the subdivision of an era.

peripheral nervous system Nerves and receptors that are present outside the central nervous system.

peristalsis Contractions of muscle that occur in the walls of hollow organs, such as parts of the digestive tract, that move the contents of the organ through the tube.

petiole Stalk that attaches a leaf to a stem.

pH Expression of the concentration of hydrogen ions in a solution. The pH scale runs from 0 through to 14, with acidic solutions having a pH of less than 7, basic solutions having a pH of more than 7, and 7 being neutral.

phagocytosis Process by which the plasma membranes of certain cells engulf particles from the surroundings.

pharynx Part of the vertebrate gut that lies between the mouth and the esophagus; in humans and other mammals, the pharynx is represented by the throat and the back of the nose.

phenotype Physical or chemical expression of an organism's genes.

pheromone Chemical that, when released into an animal's surroundings, influences the behavior or development of other individuals of the same species.

phloem Vascular tissue that transports nutrients, such as amino acids and sugars, in plants.

phospholipid Type of lipid made up of two fatty acids and a phosphorus-containing group attached to glycerol. Phospholipids are important components of cell membranes.

phosphorylation Introduction of a phosphate group into an organic molecule.

photic zone Area of water that receives sufficient light for photosynthesis to occur.

photon Particle of light.

photoreceptor Sense organ that responds to a light stimulus.

photosynthesis Metabolic process in which light energy is converted to the chemical energy stored in chemical com-

pounds; it occurs in plants and some types of bacteria, such as cyanobacteria.

phylogeny Evolutionary history of a group of organisms.

phylum Broad taxonomic grouping of organisms belonging to similar classes. The term is often restricted to the animal and protist kingdoms.

phytochrome Blue-green pigment that is sensitive to different wavelengths of light. It is present in many flowering plants and is involved in a number of responses, including initiating flowering and breaking dormancy in seeds.

phytoplankton Floating, microscopic algae present in lakes and oceans.

pinna Flap of skin and cartilage that constitutes the external, visible part of the mammalian ear.

pituitary Mass of endocrine tissue attached to the lower surface of the brain, which produces at least 10 hormones that have a variety of effects.

placenta Partly fetal and partly maternal organ of most mammals that allows materials and gases to be exchanged between the fetus and mother.

plasma Pale yellow fluid component of blood that contains proteins, salts, and other substances, and carries blood cells and platelets.

plasmid In bacteria, a small ring of DNA.

poikilotherm Organism that has a body temperature that fluctuates with the temperature of the external environment; sometimes described as a cold-blooded organism.

pollination Transfer of pollen from the male to the female part of a seed plant.

polymer Molecule that is made up of repeating units of the same type. Examples include proteins, nucleic acids, and polysaccharides.

polyploidy Having more than two sets of chromosomes in every nucleus. The condition is more common in plant cells than in animal cells.

population Group of organisms of the same species that share a particular habitat at any one time.

producers Organisms, such as plants, that manufacture food from simple inorganic substances.

profundal zone Zone of a lake that is classified as the deepest.

progesterone Hormone produced by the ovary; involved in controlling the female menstrual cycle.

prokaryote Cell that lacks a nucleus bound by a membrane and other membrane-bounded organelles. All prokaryotes are single-celled organisms.

prolactin Hormone secreted by pituitary gland that, in mammals, promotes the secretion of progesterone and is involved in lactation.

prophase First stage of mitosis and of the mitotic division of meiosis.

protein Complex compound, made of nitrogen, sulfur, carbon, hydrogen, and oxygen; consists of chemically bonded amino acids.

protist Single-celled organism containing a nucleus; may be animal-like (for example, amoeba), plantlike (diatom), or funguslike (slime molds).

proton Atomic particle with a positive electric charge.

protozoan Single-celled organism that is animal-like in its method of obtaining food and in other characteristics.

pseudocoelom Body cavity between the mesoderm (middle embryonic germ layer) and endoderm (innermost layer).

pseudopod Extension of ameboid cell used for locomotion and feeding.

punctuated equilibrium Hypothesis that the evolution of organisms takes on a pattern of periods of inactivity followed by active phases.

radial symmetry Having similar body parts regularly arranged around a central axis.

radicle Root of an embryo seed plant.

radioactivity Spontaneous emission of radiation from atomic nuclei.

rapid eye movement (REM) sleep Stage of sleep in which there is movement of the eyeballs under closed lids; the type of sleep that occurs while the sleeper is dreaming.

receptacle Upper end of the stalk of a flowering plant.

recessive (allele) Producing little or no visible effect when occurring in heterozygous condition with a contrasting allele.

recombinant DNA DNA molecules that are extracted from different sources and joined chemically.

rectum End part of the gastrointestinal tract, in which feces are stored.

redox reactions Chemical reactions involving the transfer of electrons from one reactant to another; one substance is oxidized and the other is reduced.

reduction Addition of electrons to an atom or compound.

reflex Innate, automatic, neuromuscular animal response to an internal or external stimulus.

regeneration Regrowth of parts of the body that have been lost; most common in animals such as sponges, starfish, and lizards.

reproductive isolation Reproductive factors that prevent one species from interbreeding with another.

respiration Process by which cells use oxygen, produce carbon dioxide, and store the energy of food molecules; in living organisms, respiration is the process of gaseous exchange (as by breathing).

retina Photosensitive layer of the eyes of vertebrates and certain marine mollusks.

rhizome Horizontal underground plant stem.

rhodopsin Light-sensitive pigment in rod cells of vertebrate eyes.

ribonucleic acid (RNA) Single-stranded nucleic acid that is associated with the control of cellular chemical activities (as in protein synthesis).

ribosomal RNA (rRNA) Constituent of ribosomes, the cell structures that are the sites of protein synthesis.

rod (eyes) Rod-shaped light-sensitive cell in the retina that enables monochrome vision and allows vision in dim light.

root cap Layer of cells at the tip of a root that protects the delicate tissue growing directly beneath it.

saprophyte Type of heterotrophic organism nourished by absorbing nutrients from nonliving organic material, such as leaf litter.

seed Plant reproductive body that is made from a young multicellular plant and nutritive tissue.

semen Fluid ejaculated from penis during orgasm; it is composed of sperm and various glandular secretions.

serum Pale yellow liquid that separates from the clot when blood coagulates.

sessile Description of organisms living fixed to one location. Sessile organisms include barnacles and corals.

soil Topmost layer of Earth's land surface, consisting of inorganic minerals, decaying organic material, air, water, and a variety of living organisms.

solubility Measure of the ability of a certain substance to dissolve in a particular solvent.

solute Substance that is dissolved in a solvent, forming a solution.

solvent Liquid in which other substances may be dissolved.

somatic cell Body cell that is not involved in reproduction.

somatic nervous system Part of the nervous system that keeps the body in tune with the surrounding environment; includes the sensory receptors.

speciation The process of biological species formation.

species The basic unit of biological classi-

fication; a group of actually or potentially interbreeding individuals that are reproductively isolated from other individuals.

spore Reproductive unit, usually unicellular, produced by plants, fungi, protists, and bacteria; can develop into new individual directly or after fusion with another spore.

statocyst Invertebrate sense organ, containing one or more granules, that some animals use to help them sense gravity and motion.

steroid Complex lipid molecule that contains carbon atoms in four fused rings.

stigma Part of the style in plants; the surface that receives pollen.

stoma (plural stomata) Small pore in epidermis of plants that allows the gaseous exchange with the atmosphere needed for photosynthesis.

style Column of tissue connecting the stigma to the ovary of a carpel through which the pollen tube grows.

subspecies Taxonomic category used to denote the various forms, usually geographically restricted, of a species.

symbiosis Living together, in permanent or prolonged close association, of individuals of two different species.

sympathetic nervous system Part of the autonomic nervous system that helps to release reserves of energy, particularly during stressful situations.

synapse Junction between one neuron and another or between a neuron and its effector.

tap root Prominent root in a plant that grows directly from the root tip or radicle and has smaller lateral roots.

taxis Movement of an organism in response to an environmental stimulus, such as a change of light.

taxonomy Practice of naming and classifying organisms.

telophase Final stage of mitosis and meiosis, when nuclei return to interphase.

tendon Connective tissue that joins two muscles together or a muscle to a bone.

tendril Leaf or stem that is modified for attachment to objects.

tensile strength Measure of the ability of a material to withstand a longitudinal stress; expressed as the greatest stress a material can stand without breaking.

testis (plural testes) Organ of male animal that produces sperm; in vertebrates, it also produces sex hormones (called androgens).

testosterone Vertebrate steroid male sex hormone that is produced by the testes.

thorax In vertebrates, the upper body; in arthropods, the second main division.

thymine Nitrogen-containing base (pyrimidine) found in DNA but not in RNA.

thyroid gland Vertebrate endocrine gland found in the neck region that releases hormones to regulate the metabolic rate.

T-cell or T-lymphocyte Lymphocyte that is processed in the thymus.

tissue Group of closely associated, similar cells in a multicellular organism that work together to perform a specific role.

tonsils Masses of lymph tissue in the throat region that act on pathogens entering the body through the nose and mouth.

trachea Vertebrate windpipe; in most insects and other arthropods, it is the hollow tubes of the epidermis and cuticle that conduct air from the spiracles directly to the tissues.

transfer RNA (tRNA) RNA molecules that stick to certain amino acids in protein synthesis, serving as transport molecules.

transcription Production of an RNA molecule from a DNA template.

translation Ribosomal stage of protein synthesis; the stage when information provided by mRNA is translated into a particular sequence of amino acids in a polypeptide chain.

translocation Movement of materials, such as water and dissolved salts, in a plant's vascular tissues.

transpiration Evaporation of water from the leaves of a plant, which helps draw water up the stem.

tropism Growth response to a stimulus, such as gravity or light.

tuber Thick underground stem that is adapted for the storage of food. It can also generate a new plant by vegetative reproduction.

tumor Swelling caused by the uncontrolled growth of a mass of tissue.

tundra Treeless plain between the south taiga and the northern polar ice caps. Has low temperatures, a short growing season, and frozen ground.

turgor pressure Hydrostatic pressure that develops in a walled cell, such as a plant cell, when the osmotic pressure of the cell contents is greater than that of the surrounding fluid.

uracil Nitrogenous base (pyrimidine) present in RNA.

urea Major end product of nitrogen excretion in mammals; it is a water-soluble product of protein metabolism.

uric acid End product of protein metabolism in insects, birds, and reptiles; it is the main nitrogen-containing excretory product of these organisms.

uterus Hollow, muscular organ in which an embryo develops after implantation in the endometrium (lining).

vascular tissue Type of conducting tissue found in vascular plants. It is made up of the xylem, phloem, sclerenchyma, and parenchyma cells.

vector Agent that carries disease-causing organisms but is itself unaffected by them.

vegetative reproduction Asexual reproduction in plants, occurring when part of the plant other than a spore separates from the plant body. Organs of vegetative reproduction include bulbs, corms, and tubers.

vertebrates Organisms having an endoskeleton made from bone or cartilage and a vertebral column. Vertebrata is one of the subphyla of the Chordata, and contains fish, amphibians, reptiles, birds, and mammals.

vestigial organ Organ that has become reduced in size and structure over time because it is no longer required. Vestigial organs are important to zoologists because they can show evolutionary relationships.

villus (plural villi) Tiny elongated projection from a membrane surface.

virus Minute pathogen capable of multiplication only within cells; viruses are composed of a core of nucleic acid that is usually protected by a protein case.

viviparity Reproduction in animals whose embryos develop within the female parent and who derive nourishment by close contact with her tissues.

water potential Tendency of a system to give water to its surroundings. In a plant cell, it depends on the wall pressure and the osmotic (solute) pressure inside the cell.

wood Hard water-conducting tissue (secondary xylem) present in many perennial plants and the bulk of trees and shrubs.

xylem Vascular tissue in plants that conducts water and dissolved salts.

yeasts Single-celled fungi that multiply by a budding process. Important in brewing and baking industries; certain types secrete enzymes that convert sugar into alcohol and carbon dioxide (makes bread rise).

yolk Food stored in an egg for use by an embryo that consists mainly of protein or of fats; the eggs of oviparous animals contain a relatively large yolk.

zooplankton Planktonic animals and animal-like protists.

zygote Product of the fertilization of a female gamete by a male gamete in sexual reproduction.

BIBLIOGRAPHY

AGRICULTURE

Avault, J. W. 1996. *Fundamentals of Aquaculture.* Baton Rouge, La.: Ava Publishing Company.

Benjamin, J. 2000. *Great Garden Formulas: The Ultimate Book of Mix-It-Yourself Concoctions for Your Garden.* Emmaus, Pa.: Rodale Press.

Carson, R. 2002. *Silent Spring.* Boston: Mariner Books.

Dahlberg, K. A. 1991. Sustainable agriculture— fad or harbinger? *Bioscience* 41: 337–340.

Duren, L. 2001. *Home Garden Hydroponics.* Bloomington, Ind.: 1st Books Library.

Elliott, R. J., and E. Treuille. 1998. *Planet Organic: Organic Cookbook.* London: Dorling Kindersley.

Haynes, B. N., and R. F. Kahrs. 2001. *Keeping Livestock Healthy: A Veterinary Guide to Horses, Cattle, Pigs, Goats, and Sheep.* 4th ed. North Adams, Mass.: Storey Books.

Henry Doubleday Research Association. 2001. *The HDRA Encyclopedia of Organic Gardening.* London: Dorling Kindersley.

Holmgren, D. 2002. *Sustainable Living at 'Melliodora' Hepburn Permaculture Gardens: A Case Study in Cool Climate Permaculture 1985–1995.* Reprint. White River Junction, Vt.: Chelsea Green Publishing.

Kimbrell, A., ed. 2002. *Fatal Harvest: The Tragedy of Industrial Agriculture.* Washington, D.C.: Island Press/Foundation for Deep Ecology.

Laegreid, M., et al. 2000. *Agriculture, Fertilizers, and the Environment.* New York: Oxford University Press.

Mollison, B. C. 1997. *Introduction to Permaculture.* Rev. ed. Tyalgum, Australia: Tagari Publications.

Mollison, B. C. 1997. *Permaculture: A Designer's Manual.* Reprint. Tyalgum, Australia: Tagari Publications.

Norris, R. F., E. P. Caswell-Chen, and M. Kogan. 2002. *Concepts in Integrated Pest Management.* Upper Saddle River, N.J.: Prentice Hall.

Resh, H. M. 2001. *Hydroponic Food Production: A Definitive Guidebook of Soilless Food-Growing Methods.* 6th ed. Beaverton, Oreg.: Woodbridge Press.

Smith, B. D. 1998. *The Emergence of Agriculture.* New York: W. H. Freeman and Company.

Stickney, R. R., ed. 2000. *Encyclopedia of Aquaculture.* New York: John Wiley.

Wheeler, W. B. 2002. *Pesticides in Agriculture and the Environment (Books in Soils, Plants, and the Environment.* New York: Marcel Dekker.

ANATOMY

Achord, J. L. 2001. *Understanding Hepatitis.* Jackson: University Press of Mississippi.

Bailey, J. 1994. *Animal Life: Form and Function in the Animal Kingdom.* New York: Oxford University Press.

Ballard, C. 2002. *The Lungs and Breathing.* Crystal Lake, Ill.: Heineman Library.

Bard J. 1994. *Embryos: Color Atlas of Development.* London: Wolf.

Bastian, G. 1997. *An Illustrated Review of the Skeletal and Muscular Systems.* Boston, Mass.: Addison-Wesley.

Beckingham, I. J. 2001. *ABC of Liver, Pancreas, and Gallbladder.* Philadelphia: BMJ Books.

Bier, E. 2000. *The Coiled Spring: How Life Begins.* New York: Cold Spring Harbor Press.

Bowdler, A. J. 1999. *The Complete Spleen: Structure, Function, and Clinical Disorders.* Totowah, N.J.: Humana Press.

Bradley, R.M. 1995. *Essentials of Oral Physiology.* St. Louis: Mosby Year Book.

Brusca, R.C., and G. J. Brusca. 2002. *Invertebrates.* 2nd ed. Sunderland, Mass.: Sinauer Associates.

Brynie, F. H. 2002. *101 Questions about Food and Digestion That Have Been Eating at You–Until Now.* Brookfield, Wis.: Twenty-First Century Books.

Callaghan, C. A., and B. M. Brenner. 2000. *The Kidney at a Glance.* Boston: Blackwell Scientific.

Callen, J. P., K. E. Greer, A. F. Hood, A. S. Paller, and L. J. Swinyer, eds. 1997. *Color Atlas of Dermatology.* Philadelphia: Saunders.

Chivers, D. J., and P. Langer, eds. 1994. *The Digestive System in Mammals: Food, Form, and Function.* New York: Cambridge University Press.

Cohen, B. J., and D. L. Wood. 2000. *Memler's Structure and Function of the Human Body.* 7th ed. Philadelphia: Lippincott, Williams, and Wilkins.

Dowling, J. E. 1998. *Creating Mind: How the Brain Works.* New York: W. W. Norton.

Ewer, R. F., and D. Kleiman. 1998. *The Carnivores.* Ithaca, N.Y.: Comstock Publishing.

Fleming, S., and K. Underwood. 2001. *Ferocious Fangs: 12 of Nature's Most Amazing Animals.* Charlottesville, Va: Northwood Press.

Francis, V. 1998. *The Breathing Disorders Sourcebook.* Chicago: Contemporary Books.

Freeman, S. 2002. *Biological Science.* Saddle River, N.J.: Prentice Hall Publishers.

Greenaway, T. 1995. *Tongues and Tails.* Austin, Tex.: Raintree Steck-Vaughn.

Grenberg, A., A. K. Cheung, and T. Coffman. 2001. *Primer on Kidney Diseases.* 3rd ed. New York: Academic Press.

Griffin, J. E., and S. R. Ojeda. 1996. *Textbook of Endocrine Physiology.* 3rd ed. Oxford: Oxford University Press.

Hickman B., F. 2001. *Perception: The Amazing Brain.* New York: Blackbirch Marketing.

Hickman, C. P., and L. S. Roberts. 2002. *Integrated Principles of Zoology.* 9th ed. Burr Ridge, Ill.: WCB/McGraw-Hill.

Hildebrand, M., and G. E. Goslow. 2001. *Analysis of Vertebrate Structure.* 5th ed. New York: John Wiley.

Hillson, S. 1990. *Teeth.* Cambridge: Cambridge University Press.

Kardong, K. V. 1995. *Vertebrates: Comparative Anatomy, Function, Evolution.* Dubuque, Iowa: William C. Brown.

Keefe, Emmet B. 1999. *Know Your Body: The Atlas of Anatomy.* Berkeley: Ulysses Press.

Kent, G. C. 2000. *Comparative Anatomy of the Vertebrates.* Burr Ridge, Ill.: WCB-McGraw-Hill.

Koeppen, B. M., and B. A. Stanton. 2001. *Renal Physiology.* 3rd ed. St Louis: Mosby Publishers.

Langer, G. 1999. *Understanding Disease: How Your Heart, Lungs, Blood, and Blood Vessels Function and Respond to Treatment.* Fort Bragg, Calif.: QED Press.

Levitzky, M. G. 1999. *Pulmonary Physiology.* New York: McGraw Hill Publisher.

Mackie, R. M. 1999. *Healthy Skin: The Facts.* New York: Oxford University Press.

Mackinnon, P. C. B., and J. F. Morris. 1994. *Oxford Textbook of Functional Anatomy.* Revised edition. New York: Oxford University Press.

Manohar, M., P. Panjabi, and A. White. 2000. *Biomechanics in the Musculoskeletal System.* London: Churchill Livingstone.

Parr, E. 2000. *I'm Glad You're Not Dead: A Liver Transplant Story.* 2nd ed. Carrolltown, Mass.: Journey Publisher.

Patent, D. 1995. *Why Mammals Have Fur.* New York: Cobblehill Books.

Prenzel, F. 2003. *The Hair-Pulling Problem: The Complete Guide to Trichotillomania.* New York: Oxford University Press.

Restak, R. M. 2001. *The Secret Life of the Brain.* Washington, D.C.: National Academy Press.

Rodieck, R. W. 1998. *The First Steps in Seeing.* Sunderland, Mass.: Sinauer Associates.

Schmidt-Nielsen, K. 1997. *Animal Physiology.* New York: Cambridge University Press.

Seeley, R. R., T. D. Stephens, and P. Tate. 2000. *Anatomy and Physiology.* 4th ed. Burr Ridge, Ill.: McGraw-Hill.

Seibel, M. J., et al., eds. 1999. *Dynamics of Bone and Cartilage Metabolism.* New York: Academic Press.

Siegal, I. S. 1998. *All About Bone: An Owner's Manual.* New York: Demos Medical Publishing.

Silverstein, A. 1994. *Muscular Systems.* New York: Twenty-First Century Books.

Teaford, M. F., M. M. Smith, and M. W. J.

Ferguson. 2000. *Development, Function and Evolution of Teeth*. Cambridge: Cambridge University Press.

Tortora, G. J., S. R. Grabowski, and B. Roesch. 2000. *Principles of Anatomy and Physiology*. 9th ed. New York: John Wiley.

Vander, A. J., J. H. Sherman, and D. S. Luciano. 2001. *Human Physiology: the Mechanisms of Body Function*. 8th ed. New York: McGraw-Hill.

Vonhoff, J., and J. Kozak. 2000. *Fixing Your Feet: Prevention and Treatments for Athletes*. Fremont, Calif.: Footwork Publications.

BIOCHEMISTRY AND BIOTECHNOLOGY

American College of Physicians. 1999. *Complete Home Medical Guide*. New York: DK Publishing.

Bains, W. 1998. *Biotechnology from A to Z*. New York: Oxford University Press.

Bedau, M. A., et al. 2000. Open problems in artificial life. *Artificial Life* 6: 363–376.

Berthold-Bond, A. 1999. *Better Basics for the Home: Simple Solutions for Less Toxic Living*. New York: Three Rivers Press.

Boden, M. A., ed. 1996. *The Philosophy of Artificial Life*. Oxford: Oxford University Press.

Brock, T. D. 1994. *Biology of Microorganisms*. 7th ed. Englewood Cliffs, N.J.: Prentice-Hall.

Brown, L. 2000. *Organic Living: Simple Solutions for a Better Life*. New York: Dorling Kindersley.

Burggren, W. W., K. French, and D. J. Randall. 2001. *Animal Physiology: Mechanisms and Adaptations*. 5th ed. New York: W. H. Freeman.

Byrne, P. M. 1999. *Biochemistry Made Very Easy*. London: Universal Publishers.

Carafoli, E., and C. B. Klee. 1999. *Calcium as a Cellular Regulator*. New York: Oxford University Press.

Carey, S. S. 1994. *A Beginner's Guide to Scientific Method*. Belmont, Calif.: Wadsworth Publishing.

Carr, J., and J. Brown. 2001. *Introduction to Biomedical Equipment Technology*. Upper Saddle River, N.J.: Prentice Hall.

Chadwick, J. B. 1995. *The Busy Person's Guide to Preserving Food*. Pownal, Vt.: Storey Books.

Champe, P. C., and R. A. Harvey. 1994. *Lippincott's Illustrated Reviews: Biochemistry*. 2nd ed. Lippincott-Raven Publishers.

Chow, C. K. 1992. *Fatty Acids and Their Health Implications*. New York: Marcel Dekker.

Cohen, C., and T. Regan. 2001. *The Animal Rights Debate*. Lanham, Md.: Rowman and Littlefield.

Cohen, M. R., and N. Ernest. 2002. *An Introduction to Logic and Scientific Method*. Safety Harbor, Fla.: Simon Publications.

Coombs, G. F. 1998. *The Vitamins: Fundamental Aspects in Nutrition and Health*. San Diego: Academic Press.

Dan, M. 2000. *The Doctor's Complete Guide to Vitamins and Minerals*. New York: Random House.

Dando, M. 2001. *The New Biological Weapons: Threat, Proliferation, and Control*. Boulder, Colo.: Lynne Rienner Publishers.

Enderle, J., and S. Blanchard. 1999. *Introduction to Biomedical Engineering*. San Francisco: Academic Press.

Enig, M. G. 2000. *Know Your Fats: The Complete Primer for Understanding the Nutrition of Fats, Oils, and Cholesterol*. Bethesda Press.

Erasmus, E. 1999. *Fats That Heal, Fats That Kill: The Complete Guide to Fats, Oils, Cholesterol and Human Health*. Vancouver, B.C.: Alive Books.

Fairley, Josephine. 2001. *Organic Beauty*. New York: Dorling Kindersley Publishing.

Garrett, R. H., and C. M. Grisham. 2002. *Principles of Biochemistry with a Human Focus*. Orlando, Fla.: Harcourt College Publishers.

Gould, J. L., and C. G. Gould. 1995. *The Honey Bee*. New York: W. H. Freeman.

Griffiths, P. E., and K. Sterelny. 1999. *Sex and Death: An Introduction to Philosophy of Biology*. Chicago: University of Chicago Press.

Handley, A. J., and E. R. Adlard, eds. 2001. *Gas Chromatographic Techniques and Applications*. Boca Raton, Fla: CRC Press.

Haugen, D. M. 2000. *Animal Experimentation*. San Diego: Greenhaven Press.

Hesse, M. 2002. *Alkaloids*. New York: John Wiley.

Ho, M.-W. 2000. *Genetic Engineering: Dream or Nightmare?: Turning the Tide on the Brave New World of Bad Science and Big Business*. New York: Continuum Publishing.

Holland, J. H. 1995. *Hidden Order: How Adaptation Builds Complexity*. Reading, Mass.: Helix Books.

Johnson, Steven. 2001. *Emergence: The Connected Lives of Ants, Brains, Cities, and Software*. New York: Simon and Schuster

Kauffman, S. 1995. *At Home in the Universe: The Search for the Laws of Self-Organization and Complexity*. New York: Oxford University Press.

Kostyuk, P. G., P. G. Kostiuk, and V. Verkhratsky. 1996. *Calcium Signaling in the Nervous System*. New York: John Wiley.

Lanza, R., B. Dresser, and P. Damiani. 2000. Cloning Noah's Ark. *Scientific American* (Nov.).

Lesk, A. 2001. *Introduction to Protein Architecture: The Structural Biology of Proteins*. Cambridge: Cambridge University Press.

Magner, L. 1993. *A History of the Life Sciences*. New York: Marcel Dekker.

Mandelbrot, B. 1977. *The Fractal Geometry of Nature*. New York: W. H. Freeman.

Marieb, Elaine Nicpon. 2000. *Human Anatomy and Physiology*. 5th ed. San Francisco: Benjamin/Cummings.

Mathews, C. K., K.E. Van Holde, and K. G. Ahern. 2000. *Biochemistry*. San Francisco: Benjamin Cummings.

Morrison, R. 2000. *The Spirit of the Gene*. Ithaca, N.Y.: Cornell University Press.

Nelson, D. L., and M. Lehninger Cox. 2000.

Principles of Biochemistry. 3rd ed. New York: Worth Publishing.

Oliver, R. 1999. *The Coming Biotech Age: The Business of Bio-materials*. New York: McGraw Hill.

Paul, E. F., and J. Paul, eds. 2001. *Why Animal Experimentation Matters*. New Brunswick, N.J.: Transaction Publishers.

Platt, G. C. 2002. *Fermented Foods of the World*. Boca Raton, Fla.: CRC Press.

Robyt, J. F. 1998. *Essentials of Carbohydrate Chemistry*. Berlin: Springer-Verlag.

Schecter, A., and T. Gasiewicz, eds. 2002. *Dioxins and Health*. 2nd ed. New York: Taylor and Francis.

Schrödinger, E. 1996. *Nature and the Greeks, and Science and Humanism*. Cambridge, U.K.: Cambridge University Press.

Settle, F. A., ed. 1997. *Handbook of Instrumental Techniques for Analytical Chemistry*. Upper Saddle River, N.J.: Prentice Hall.

Shephard, S. 2001. *Pickled, Potted, and Canned: How the Art and Science of Food Preserving Changed the World*. New York: Simon and Schuster.

Sparrow, G. 1999. *Carbon. The Elements*. Tarrytown, N.Y.: Marshall Cavendish.

Stewart, I., ed. 1998. *Life's Other Secret: The New Mathematics of the Living World*. New York: John Wiley.

Stick, R. V. 2001. *Carbohydrates: The Sweet Molecules of Life*. San Diego: Academic Press.

Shils, M. E., J. A. Olson, and M. Shike. 1999. *Modern Nutrition in Health and Disease*. Philadelphia: Lippincott Williams and Wilkins.

Stockholm International Peace Research Institution. 1971–1975. *The Problem of Chemical and Biological Warfare*. New York: Humanities Press.

Tanford, C., and J. Reynolds. 2001. *Nature's Robots: A History of Proteins*. Oxford: Oxford University Press.

Waldrop, M. M. 1992. *Complexity: The Emerging Science at the Edge of Order and Chaos*. New York: Simon and Schuster.

Vander, A., J. Sherman, and D. Luciano. 2001. *Human Physiology*. 8th ed. New York: McGraw Hill.

van Straten, M., and D. Lotfus. 2001. *Organic Living*. Emmaus, Penn.: Rodale Press.

Walsh, G. 2002. *Proteins: Biotechnology and Biochemistry*. New York: John Wiley.

Ward, W. 2002. *Beyond Chaos: The Underlying Theory Behind Life, the Universe, and Everything*. New York: Dunne Books.

Wright, H. 2000. *The Great Organic Wine Guide*. London: Piatkus Books.

Zilinskas, R. A. 1999. *Biological Warfare: Modern Offense and Defense*. Boulder, Colo.: Lynne Rienner Publishers.

BOTANY

Abbott, I. A. 1999. *Marine Red Algae of the Hawaiian Islands.* Honolulu, Hawaii: Bishop Museum Press.

Alcock, J. 2001. *Animal Behavior: An Evolutionary Approach.* Sunderland, Mass.: Sinauer.

Anderson, D. M. 1997. Turning back the harmful red tide. *Nature* 388, 513–514.

Armitage, A. M. 2001. *Armitage's Manual of Annuals, Biennials, and Half-Hardy Perennials.* Portland, Oreg.: Timber Press.

Attenborough, D. 1995. *The Private Life of Plants: A Natural History of Plant Behavior.* Princeton, N.J.: Princeton University Press.

Barron, G. 1999. *Mushrooms of Northeast North America: Midwest to New England.* Edmonton, Canada: Lone Pine Publishing.

Baskin, C. C., and J. M. Baskin. 1998. *Seeds: Ecology, Biogeography, and Evolution of Dormancy and Germination.* San Diego: Academic Press.

Bell, P. R., and A. R. Helmsley. 2000. *Green Plants: Their Origin and Diversity.* 2nd ed. Cambridge and New York: Cambridge University Press.

Benzing, D. H. 1990. *Vascular Epiphytes: General Biology and Related Biota.* Cambridge, U.K.: Cambridge University Press.

Bernhard, P. 2002. *The Rose's Kiss: A Natural History of Flowers.* Chicago and London: University of Chicago Press.

Bessette, A. E., et al. 2000. *North American Boletes: A Color Guide to the Fleshy Pored Mushrooms.* Syracuse, N.Y.: Syracuse University Press.

Bond, R., ed. 1985. *All about Citrus and Subtropical Fruits.* Des Moines, Iowa: Meredith Corporation/Ortho Books.

Buchmann, S. L., and G. P. Nabhan. 1997. *The Forgotten Pollinators.* Washington D.C.: Island Press and Corvallis, Calif.: Shearwater Press.

Capatti, A., G. Vaccarini, et al. 1999. *The Squash: History, Folklore, Ancient Recipes.* London, U.K.: Konemann Publishers.

Capon, B. 2001. *Botany for Gardeners: An Introduction and Guide.* Portland, Oreg.: Timber Press.

Carlile, M. J., and S. C. Watkinson. 1994. *The Fungi.* Boston: Academic Press.

Cerullo, M. M. 1999. *Sea Soup: Phytoplankton.* Gardiner, Maine: Tilbury House Publishers.

Chawla, K. K. 1998. *Fibrous Materials.* Cambridge and New York: Cambridge University Press.

Clark, L. G., and R. W. Pohl. 1996. *Agnes Chase's First Book of Grasses Explained for Beginners.* 4th ed. Washington, D.C., and London: Smithsonian Institution Press.

Cobb, B., and L. L. Foster, 1999. *A Field Guide to Ferns And Their Related Families: Northeastern and Central North America.* Boston: Houghton Mifflin.

Cullen, J. 1997. *The Identification of Flowering Plant Families: A Key to Those Native and Cultivated in North Temperate Regions.* 4th ed. Cambridge and New York: Cambridge University Press.

D'Amato, P. 1998. *The Savage Garden. Cultivating Carnivorous Plants.* Berkeley: Ten Speed Press

Damerow, Gail. 1997. *The Perfect Pumpkin.* North Adams, Mass.: Storey Books.

D'Arcy, W. G., and R. C. Keating. 1996. *The Anther: Form, Function, and Phylogeny.* Cambridge and New York: Cambridge University Press.

Duren, L. 2001. *Home Garden Hydroponics.* Bloomington, Indiana: 1st Books Library.

Ellis, B. W. 2001. *Taylor's Guide to Perennials.* Boston: Houghton Mifflin.

Evert, R. F. 1998. *Topics in Botany Lab Separates; Woody Stems.* New York: W. H. Freeman.

Facklam, H., and M. Facklam. 1994. *Bacteria.* New York: Twenty-First Century Books.

Farjon, A. 2001. *World Checklist and Bibliography of Conifers.* 2nd ed. Kew, London: Royal Botanic Gardens, Kew.

Ferguson, B., ed. 1987. *All about Growing Fruits, Berries, and Nuts.* Des Moines, Iowa: Meredith Corporation/Ortho Books.

Feughelman, M. 1996. *Mechanical Properties and Structure of Alpha Keratin Fibers: Wool, Human Hair, and Related Fibers.* Sydney: New South Wales University Press.

Garnier, E., et al., eds. 1999. *Variations in Leaf Structure: An Ecophysiological Perspective.* Cambridge and New York: Cambridge University Press.

Gelderen, D. M. van, and J. R. P. van Hoey Smith. 1996. *Conifers: The Illustrated Encyclopedia.* Portland, Oreg.: Timber Press.

Graham, L. E., and L. Warren Cox. 2000. *Algae.* Upper Saddle River, N.J.: Prentice-Hall College Division.

Greenwood, P., et al. 2000. *American Horticultural Society Pests and Diseases.* New York: Dorling Kindersley Publishing.

Grey-Wilson, C. 2000. *Annuals and Biennials. American Horticultural Society Practical Guides.* New York: Dorling Kindersley Publishing.

Gutterman, Y. 2002. *Survival Strategies of Annual Desert Plants.* Berlin: Springer-Verlag.

Hall, D. O., and K. K. Rao. 1999. *Photosynthesis.* 6th ed. New York: Cambridge University Press.

Harlan, J. R. 1998. *The Living Fields: Our Agricultural Heritage.* New York: Cambridge University Press.

Hazelton, J. W. 2000. *Summer Squash and Squash Blossoms from Seed to Supper.* St. Petersburg, Fla.: Jack's Bookshelf.

Henderson, A., et al. 1997. *Field Guide to the Palms of the Americas.* Princeton, N.J.: Princeton University Press.

Hickey, M., et al. 1997. *Common Families of Flowering Plants.* Cambridge and New York: Cambridge University Press.

Hughes, M. S. 1998. *Buried Treasure: Roots and Tubers.* Minneapolis, Minn.: Lerner Publications.

Hughes, M. S. 1999. *Spill the Beans and Pass the Peanuts: Legumes.* Minneapolis, Minn.: Lerner Publications.

Jennings, D. H. 1999. *Fungal Biology: Understanding the Fungal Lifestyle.* New York: Springer Verlag.

Jones, D. L., and J. Dransfield. 1995. *Palms Throughout the World.* Washington D.C.: Smithsonian Institution Press.

Judd, W. S., et al. 1999. *Plant Systematics.* Sunderland, Mass.: Sinauer Associates.

Kigel, J., and G. Galili, eds. 1995. *Seed Development and Germination.* New York: Marcel Dekker.

King, J. 1998. *Reaching for the Sun: How Plants Work.* Cambridge, U.K.: Cambridge University Press.

Koopowitz, H. 2001. *Orchids and Their Conservation.* Portland, Oreg.: Timber Press.

Læssøe, T., and G. Lincoff. 1998. *Dorling Kindersley Handbooks: Mushrooms.* New York: Dorling Kindersley Publishing.

Lam, K. C. (Master Lam Kam Chuen). 2002. *The Way of Tea: The Sublime Art of Oriental Tea Drinking.* Hauppauge, N.Y.: Barron's Educational Series.

Larone, D. H. 2002. *Medically Important Fungi: A Guide to Identification.* Washington, D.C.: American Society for Microbiology.

Laybourn-Parry, J. 1991. *Protozoan Plankton Ecology.* New York: Chapman and Hall.

Littler, D. S., and M. M. Littler. 2000. *Caribbean Reef Plants.* Washington, D.C.: Off Shore Graphics.

Lowell W. A. 1994. *Urban Wildlife Habitats.* Minneapolis: University of Minnesota Press.

Madgwick, W. 2000. *Flowering Plants: The Green World.* Collingdale, Pa.: Diane Publishing Company.

Malcolm, W., et al. 2000. *Mosses and Other Bryophytes: An Illustrated Glossary.* Portland, Oreg.: Timber Press.

Mathew, B. 1997. *Growing Bulbs: The Complete Practical Guide.* Portland, Oreg.: Timber Press.

McGary, J., ed. 2001. *Bulbs of North America.* Portland, Oreg.: North American Rock Garden Society/Timber Press.

Meyer, J. G., and S. Linnea. 2001. *America's Famous and Historic Trees: From George Washington's Tulip Poplar to Elvis Presley's Pin Oak.* Boston, Mass.: Houghton Mifflin.

Money, M. P. 2002. *Mr. Bloomfield's Orchard: The Mysterious World of Mushrooms, Molds, and Mycologists.* Oxford: Oxford University Press.

Nayar, N. M. 2003. *Tuber Crops.* Malden, Mass.: Blackwell Science.

Noordhuis, K. T., and S. Benvie. 2002. *Bulbs and Tubers.* New York: Booksales.

Norstog, K. J., and T. J. Nicholls. 1997. *The Biology of the Cycads.* Ithaca, N.Y. and London: Cornell University Press.

Pace, G. 1998. *Mushrooms of the World*. Toronto: Firefly Books.

Pakenham, T. 2002. *Remarkable Trees of the World*. New York: W. W. Norton and Company.

Phillips, E., and C. C. Burrell. 1999. *Rodale's Illustrated Encyclopedia of Perennials*. Emmaus, Pa.: Rodale Press.

Phillips, R., and M. E. Rix. 2002. *Perennials: The Definitive Reference with Over 2,500 Photographs*. Toronto, Ontario: Firefly Books.

Pleasant, B. 1995. *The Gardener's Guide to Plant Diseases: Earth-Safe Remedies*. Pownal, Vt.: Storey Communications.

Pridgeon, A., ed. 2000. *The Illustrated Encyclopedia of Orchids*. Portland, Oreg.: Timber Press.

Proctor, M., P. Yeo, and A. Lack. 1996. *The Natural History of Pollination*. Portland, Oreg.: Timber Press.

Raven, P. H., R. F. Evert, and S. E. Eichhorn. 1999. *Biology of Plants*. 6th ed. New York: W. H. Freeman/Worth Publishers.

Resh, H. M. 2001. *Hydroponic Food Production: A Definitive Guidebook of Soilless Food-Growing Methods*. 6th ed. Beaverton, Oreg.: Woodbridge Press.

Rickard, M. 2000. *The Plant Finder's Guide to Garden Ferns*. Portland, Oreg.:Timber Press.

Riffle, R. L., and P. Craft. 2003. *An Encyclopedia of Cultivated Palms*. Portland, Oreg.: Timber Press.

Round, F. E., R. M. Crawford, and D. G. Mann. 1990. *The Diatoms: Biology and Morphology of the Genera*. Cambridge: Cambridge University Press.

Sajeva, M., and M. Costanzo. 2000. *Succulents II: The New Illustrated Dictionary*. Portland, Oreg.: Timber Press.

Silverstein, A., V. Silverstein, and L. Silverstein Nunn. 1998. *Photosynthesis*. Science Concepts. Brookfield, Conn.: Millbrook Press.

Soderstrom, M. 2001. *Recreating Eden: A Natural History of Botanical Gardens*. Montreal: Véhicule Press.

Tate, D. 1999. *Tropical Fruit*. Singapore: Archipelago Press.

Thomas, D. N. 2002. *Seaweeds*. Washington D.C.: Smithsonian Institution Press.

Thomas, R. W. 1999. *Ortho's All About Vines and Climbers*. Des Moines, Iowa: Meredith Books.

Tomas, C. R., G. R. Hasle, B. Heimdal, and J. Throndsen, eds. 1997. *Identifying Marine Phytoplankton*. New York: Academic Press.

Vaughan, J. G., and C. A. Geissler. 1999. *The New Oxford Book of Food Plants*. Oxford and New York: Oxford University Press.

Vitale, A. T. 1997. *Leaves in Myth, Magic, and Medicine*. New York: Stewart, Tabori and Chang.

Waisel, Y., A. Eshel, and U. Kafkafi, eds. 2002. *Plant Roots: The Hidden Half*. 3rd ed. New York: Marcel Dekker.

Zuazua Jenkins, M. 1998. *National Geographic Guide to America's Public Gardens: 300 of the Best Gardens to Visit in the U.S. and Canada*. Washington, D.C.: National Geographic Society.

ECOLOGY

Aerts, R., and G. W. Heil., eds. 1993. *Heathlands: Patterns and Processes in a Changing Environment*. Geobotany Series, Volume 20. Boston: Kluwer.

Alexander, M. 1999. *Biodegradation and Bioremediation*. 2nd ed. San Diego: Academic Press.

Beck, M., and H. Garrett. 1999. *Texas Bug Book: The Good, the Bad, and the Ugly*. Austin: University of Texas Press.

Beckage, N. E. 1997. *Parasites and Pathogens: Effects on Host Hormones and Behavior*. New York: Kluwer Academic Press.

Beerling. D. J., and F. I. Woodward. 2001, *Vegetation and the Terrestrial Carbon Cycle: The First 400 Million Years*. 2001. New York: Cambridge University Press.

Berger, L. 1998. The dawn of humans: Redrawing our family tree. *National Geographic*, 194, 2: 90–99.

Berkowitz, A. R., and C. H. Nilan, eds. 2002. *Urban Ecosystems*. New York: Springer Verlag.

Bertness, M. D. 1999. *The Ecology of Atlantic Shorelines*. Sunderland, Mass.: Sinauer Associates.

Bjorn, L. O., ed. 2002. *The Science of Light and Life*. New York: Kluwer Academic Publisher.

Blackman, J. R. 2001. *Basic Hazardous Waste Management*. Boca Raton, Fla.: Lewis Publishers.

Blaustein, D. 2000. *The Everglades and the Gulf Coast*. Tarrytown, New York: Marshall Cavendish.

Bolagiano, C. 2002. *Living in the Appalachian Forest: True Tales of Sustainable Forestry*. Mechanicsburg, Pa.: Stackpole Books.

Briggs, D. E. G., and P. R. Crowther, eds. 2001. *Paleobiology II*. Oxford: Blackwell Science.

Brodo, I. M., et al. 2001. *Lichens of North America*. New Haven, Conn., and London: Yale University Press.

Bronmark, C., and L. A. Hanssin. 1998. *The Biology of Lakes and Ponds (Biology of Habitats)*. Oxford: Oxford University Press.

Byatt, A., A. Fothergill, and M. Holmes. 2001. *The Blue Planet*. London: BBC.

Carle, D. 2002. *Burning Questions: America's Fight With Nature's Fire*. New York: Praeger.

Carlile, M. J., and S. C. Watkinson. 1994. *The Fungi*. Boston: Academic Press.

Carson, R. 2002. *Silent Spring*. Boston: Mariner Books.

Cerullo, M. M. 1999. *Sea Soup: Phytoplankton*. Gardiner, Maine: Tilbury House Publishers.

Chapman, P. 1993. *Caves and Cave Life*. New York: HarperCollins.

Collinson, A. 1992. *Grasslands*. New York: Dillon Press.

Coupland. R. T., ed., 1993. *Natural Grasslands*. New York: Elsevier.

Davis, Lee A. 1998. *Environmental Disasters: A Chronicle of Individual, Industrial, and Governmental Carelessness*. New York: Facts on File Incorporated.

Day, T. 2003. *Taiga* (Biomes Atlases). Austin, Tex.: Raintree Steck-Vaughn.

De Waal, W. C., and A. R. C. Large, eds. 1999. *Rehabilitation of Rivers: Principles and Implementation*. New York: John Wiley.

Dickson, B. 1999. All change in the Arctic. *Nature*, 397: 389–391.

Douglas, A. E. 1997. *Symbiotic Interactions*. 2nd ed. New York: Oxford University Press.

Eldredge, N. 1991. *The Miner's Canary: Unraveling the Mysteries of Extinction*, New York: Prentice Hall Press.

Facklam, H., and M. Facklam. 1994. *Bacteria*. New York: Twenty-First Century Books.

Farndon, J. 2002. *Wildlife Atlas: A Complete Guide to Animals and their Habitats*. London: Readers Digest.

Fenner, D. In press. *Corals of Hawaii*. Monterey, Calif.: Sea Challengers.

Finlayson-Pitts, B. J., and J. N. Pitts. 1999. *The Chemistry of the Upper and Lower Atmosphere: Theory, Experiments, and Applications*. San Diego: Academic Press.

Flader, S. L., and J. B. Callicott, eds. 1991. *The River of the Mother of God and Other Essays by Aldo Leopold*. Madison: University of Wisconsin Press.

Furley, R. A., J. Proctor, and J. A. Ratter, eds. 1992. *Nature and Dynamics of Forest-Savanna Boundaries*. New York: Chapman and Hall.

Gibson, C. C., M. A. McKean, and E. Ostrom. 2000. *People and Forests*. Cambridge, Mass.: M.I.T. Press.

Gilmour, I., and Peter Skelton, eds. 1999. *Evolution. A Biological and Palaeontological Approach*. Wokingham, U.K.: Addison-Wesley.

Gould, S. J. 2002. *The Structure of Evolutionary Theory*. Cambridge, Mass.: Harvard University Press.

Gribbin, J., and M. Gribbin. 2001. *Ice Age*. New York: Penguin Putnam.

Griffith, B. 2001. *The Gardens of Their Dreams: Desertification and Culture in World History*. London: Zed Books.

Groombridge, B., and M. D. Jenkins. 2000. *Global Biodiversity: Earth's Living Resources in the 21st Century*. Cambridge, U.K.: World Conservation Press.

Hadidan, J., ed. 1997. *Wild Neighbours: The Humane Approach to Living with Wildlife*. Golden, Color.: Fulcrum Publishers.

Halfpenny, J. 2000. *Scats and Tracks of the Desert Southwest*. Guilford, Conn.: Falcon Publishing.

Haslett, S. K. 2001. *Coastal Systems*. New York: Routledge.

Hassett, J. J., and W. Banwart. 1997. *Soils and Their Environment*. Englewood Cliffs, N.J.: Prentice Hall.

Hawkins, B. A., and W. Sheehan. 1997. *Parasitoid Community and Ecology*. New York: Oxford University Press.

Henry, J. D., and M. Viney. 2002. *Canada's*

Boreal Forest (Smithsonian Natural History Series). Washington, D.C.: Smithsonian Institution.

Hocking, C. 1999. *Acid Rain*. Buffalo Grove, Ill.: Sargent-Welch.

Hodgson, E., and R. Kuhr, eds. 1990. *Safer Insecticides: Development and Use*. New York: Dekker.

Hogarth, P. J. 2000. *The Biology of Mangroves*. Oxford: Oxford University Press.

Holmes, H. 2001. *The Secret Life of Dust: From the Cosmos to the Kitchen Counter, the Big Consequences of Little Things*. New York: John Wiley.

Houghton, J. T. 1997. *Global Warning: The Complete Briefing*. Cambridge, Mass.: Cambridge University Press.

Humann, P., and N. Deloach. 2002. *Coral Reef Identification: Florida, Caribbean, Bahamas— Including Marine Plants*. Jacksonville, Fla.: New World Publications.

IPCC. 2001. *Climate Change 2001: The Scientific Basis*. Cambridge, U.K.: Cambridge University Press.

Juhani Keipi, K. 1999. *Forest Resource Policy in Latin America*. Washington, D.C.: Inter-American Development Bank.

Kaplan, E. H., and S. L. Kaplan. 1999. *A Field Guide to Coral Reefs: Caribbean and Florida*. Peterson Field Guides. New York: Houghton Mifflin.

Keller, R. 1999. *Levels of Selection in Evolution*. Princeton, N.J.: Princeton University Press.

Kirchman, D. L., ed. 2000. *Microbial Ecology of the Oceans*. Hoboken, N.J.: Wiley-Liss.

Knauss, J. A. 1996. *Introduction to Physical Oceanography*. 2nd ed. Englewood Cliffs, N.J.: Prentice Hall.

Korner, C. H., et al., eds. 2002. *Mountain Biodiversity*. Boca Raton, Fla.: CRC Press.

Kump, L. R., et al. 1999. *The Earth System*. Upper Saddle River, N.J.: Prentice Hall.

Lal, R., J. M. Kimble, and B. A. Stewart, eds. 1999. *Global Climate Change and Tropical Ecosystems*. Albany, Ga.: Lewis Publishing.

Lalli, C. M., and C. Lilli. 1997. *Biological Oceanography: An Introduction*. Newton, Mass.: Butterworth-Heinemann.

Lavelle, P., and A. V. Spain. 2002. *Soil Ecology*. New York: Chapman and Hall.

Lavers, C. 2001. *Why Elephants Have Big Ears: Understanding Patterns of Life on Earth*. New York: St. Martin's Press.

Laybourn-Parry, J. 1991. *Protozoan Plankton Ecology*. New York: Chapman and Hall.

Leggett, J. K. 2001. *The Carbon War: Global Warming and the End of the Oil Era*. London: Taylor and Francis Group.

Lewin, R. 1999. *Human Evolution*. Malden, Mass.: Blackwell Science.

Longman, C. 2001. *African Grasslands*. New York: Peter Bedrick Books.

Lovelock, J. E. 2001. *Gaia: The Practical Science of Planetary Medicine*. New York: Oxford University Press.

Lucas, M. 1997. *Antarctica*. New York: Abbeville Press.

Lutgens, F. K., E. J. Tarbuck, and D. Tasa. 2002. *The Atmosphere: An Introduction to Meteorology*. New York: Prentice-Hall.

MacArthur, R. H., and E. O. Wilson. 2001. *The Theory of Island Biogeography*. Princeton, N.J.: Princeton University Press.

Margulis, L., and K. V. Schwartz. 1998. *Five Kingdoms*. 3rd ed. New York: W. H. Freeman.

Marieb, E. N. 2000. *Human Anatomy and Physiology*. San Fransciso: Benjamin Cummings.

Matteson, P. 1998. *Resolving the DDT Dilemma: Protecting Biodiversity and Human Health*. Atlanta: Diane Publishing.

May, E. 1998. *At the Cutting Edge: The Crisis in Canada's Forests*. San Francisco: Sierra Club.

McCally, D. 1999. *The Everglades: An Environmental History*. Gainsville, Fla.: University Press of Florida.

McCune, B., and L. Geiser. 1997. *Macrolichens of the Pacific Northwest*. Corvallis: Oregon State University Press.

McKie, R. 2000. *Ape Man: The Story of Human Evolution*. London: BBC Books.

McMurray, J. 1995. *Chemistry*. Englewood Cliffs, N.J.: Prentice-Hall.

McNally, D., G. R. Mormino, and R. Arsenault. 2000. *The Everglades: An Environmental History*. Gainesville: University of Florida Press.

Money, M. P. 2002. *Mr. Bloomfield's Orchard: The Mysterious World of Mushrooms, Molds, and Mycologists*. Oxford: Oxford University Press.

Moore, J. 2002. *Parasites and the Behavior of Animals (Oxford Series in Ecology and Evolution)*. New York: Oxford University Press.

Morin, P. J. 1999. *Community Ecology*. Boston: Blackwell Science.

Mortimore, M. 1998. *Roots in the African Dust: Sustaining the Drylands*. New York: Cambridge University Press

Mudd-Ruth, M. 2000. *Tundra. Ecosystems of North America*. Pelham, N.Y.: Benchmark Education.

Nadakavukaren, A. 2000. *Our Global Environment: A Health Perspective*. 5th ed. Prospect Heights, Ill.: Waveland Press.

Nash, T. H., III, ed. 1997. *Lichen Biology*. New York and Cambridge: Cambridge University Press.

Nathanson, J. A. 2002. *Basic Environmental Toxicology: Water Supply, Waste Management, and Pollution Control*. Upper Saddle River, N.J.: Prentice Hall.

Nelson, J., and F. A. Sloan. 2001. *Tundra Biomes*. Austin, Tex.: Raintree Steck-Vaughn.

Nybakken, J. W. 2001. *Marine Biology: An Ecological Approach*. 5th ed. San Francisco: Benjamin Cummings.

Osbourne, P. L. 2000. *Tropical Ecosystems and Ecological Concepts*. New York: Cambridge University Press.

Parker, S. 2002. *Atlas of the World's Deserts*.

Chicago: Fitzroy Dearborn Publishers.

Pigliucci, M. 2001. *Phenotypic Plasticity: Beyond Nature and Nurture (Syntheses in Ecology and Evolution)*. Baltimore: Johns Hopkins University Press.

Pimm, S. L. 2002. *Food Webs*. Chicago: University of Chicago Press.

Postme, H., et al, eds. 1998. *Continental Shelves*. New York: Elsevier Science.

Reagan, D. P., and R. B. Waide, eds. 1996. *The Food Web of a Tropical Rain Forest*. Chicago: University of Chicago Press.

Revenga, C., ed. 1998. *Watersheds of the World: Ecological Value and Vulnerability*. Washington, D.C.: World Resources Institute.

Rhinehart, R. J., and D. Harris. 2001. *Colorado Caves: Hidden Worlds Beneath the Peaks*. Englewood, Colo.: Westcliffe Publishing.

Ricciuti, E. R. 1996. *Chaparral (Biomes of the World)*. Tarrytown, N.Y.: Benchmark Books.

Rootes, D. 2000. *The Polar Regions*. Broomhall, Pa.: Chelsea House Publications.

Round, F. E., R. M. Crawford, et al. 1990. *The Diatoms: Biology and Morphology of the Genera*. Cambridge: Cambridge University Press.

Schmidt-Nielsen, K. 1997. *Animal Physiology: Adaptation and Environment*. Cambridge, U.K.: Cambridge University Press.

Skelton, P., ed. 1994. *Evolution: A Biological and Paleontological Approach to Biology*. New York: Addison Wesley.

Silverstein, A. 1998. *Symbiosis (Science Concepts)*. Brookfield, Conn.: Millbrook Press.

Soper, T., and D. Scott. 2000. *Antarctica: A Guide to Wildlife*. Chalfont St. Peter, U.K.: Bradt Publications.

Soule, M. E., and J. Terborgh, eds. 2001. *Continental Conservation: Scientific Foundations of Regional Reserve Networks*. Washington D.C.: Island Press.

Stearns, B. P., and S. C. Stearns. 2000. *Watching, from the Edge of Extinction*. New Haven, Conn.: Yale University Press.

Stein, B. A., L. S. Kutner, and J. S. Adams, eds. 2000. *Precious Heritage: The Status of Biodiversity in the United States*. Oxford: Oxford University Press.

Stevenson, F. J., and M. A. Cole. 1999. *Cycles of Soils: Carbon, Nitrogen, Phosphorus, Sulfur, and Mircronutrients*. New York: John Wiley.

Summerhayes, C. P., and S. A. Thorpe, eds. 1996. *Oceanography*. London: Manson.

Sylvester, D. 1998. *The Environment: Global Warming, Ozone, Acid Rain, and Pollution*. San Diego: Rainbow Horizons Publishing.

Taylor, M. R., and R. C. Kerbo. 2001. *Caves: Exploring Hidden Realms*. Washington, D.C.: National Geographic Society.

Thorne-Miller, B., and S. A. Earle. 1998. *The Living Ocean: Understanding and Protecting Marine Biodiversity*. 2nd ed. Washington, D.C.: Island Press.

Tomas, C. R., G. R. Hasle, B. Heimdal, and J. Throndsen, eds. 1997. *Identifying Marine Phytoplankton*. New York: Academic Press.

Van Dyck, S. 1997. *Insect Wars*. New York: Franklin Watts.

Vitausek, P. J., L. L. Loope, and H. Anderson, eds. 1995. *Islands: Biological Diversity and Ecosystem Function*. Ecological Studies, Vol. 115. New York: Springer Verlag.

Vogt, K. A., J. C. Gordon, J. P. Wargo, and D. Vogt. 1997. *Ecosytems: Balancing Science with Managment*. Berlin: Springer Verlag.

Warner, C. F. 1997. *Air Pollution: Its Origin and Control*. 3rd ed. Boston: Addison-Wesley.

Weaver, H. D., and R. L. Walk. 1992. *The Wilderness Underground: Caves of the Ozark Plateau*. Columbia: University of Missouri.

Wetzel, R. G. 2001. *Limnology: Lake and River Ecosystems*. London and New York: Academic Press.

Wheater, C. P. 1999. *Urban Habitats (Habitat Guides)*. New York: Routledge.

Whitfield, P., P. D. Moore, C. B. Cox. 2002. *Biomes and Habitats*. Living Earth Series. New York: MacMillan Library Reference.

Wilkinson, C. 2000. *Status of Coral Reefs of the World: 2000*. Townsville: Australian Institute of Marine Science.

Wilson, E. O. 2002. *The Future of Life*. New York: Knopf.

Winner, C. 2003. *Life in the Tundra*. Minneapolis, Minn.: Lerner Publications.

Woodward, J., and R. Beatty. 2002. *Temperate Forests (Biomes Atlases)*. Austin, Tex.: Raintree Steck-Vaughn.

Wyckoff, J. 1999. *Reading the Earth: Landforms in the Making*. St. Neots, Cambs, U.K.: Adastra West.

GENETICS

Ackerman, J. 2001. *Chance in the House of Fate: A Natural History of Heredity*. Boston: Houghton Mifflin.

Alberts, B., A. Johnson, J. Lewis, M. Raff, K. Roberts, and P. Walter. 2002. *Molecular Biology of the Cell*. New York: Garland Publishing.

Altieri, M. A. 2001. *Genetic Engineering in Agriculture*. Oakland, Calif.: Food First/Institute for Food and Development Policy.

Baker, C. 1999. *Your Genes, Your Choices*. Washington, D.C.: American Association for the Advancement of Science.

Basolo, A. L. 1990. Female preference predates the evolution of the sword in the swordtail fish. *Science* 250: 808–810.

Blackford, S. L., ed. 2001. *Gale Encyclopedia of Genetic Disorders*. 2 vols. Detroit: Gale Group.

Bromage, T. G. and F. Schrenk, eds. 1997. *African Biogeography, Climate Change, and Early Hominid Evolution*. New York: Oxford University Press.

Buss, D. M. 1994. The strategies of human mating. *American Scientist* 82: 238–248.

Cantor, C. R., and C. Smith. 1999. *The Genomics: The Science and Technology behind the Human Genome Project*. New York: John Wiley.

Chervas, J., and J. Gribbin, eds. 2002. *The Human Genome*. New York: Dorling Kindersley.

Cibelli, J. B., R. P. Lanza, M. D. West, and C. Ezzell. 2002. The first human cloned embryo. *Scientific American*, **286** (January): 44–51.

Clutton-Brock, J. 1999. *A Natural History of Domesticated Animals*. Cambridge, U.K.: Cambridge University Press.

Darwin, C. 1871. *The Descent of Man, and Selection in Relation to Sex*. London: Murray.

Darwin, C., and G. Suriano, ed. 1998. *On the Origin of Species*. New York: Gramercy.

Davies, K. 2001. *Cracking the Genome Future: Inside the Race to Unlock Human DNA*. New York: Free Press.

Douglas, A. E. 1994. *Symbiotic Interactions*. Oxford: Oxford University Press.

Eggleston, D. S., C. D. Prescott, and N. D. Pearson, eds. 1998. *The Many Faces of RNA*. San Diego: Academic Press.

Evans, J. H. 2002. *Playing God? Human Genetic Engineering and the Rationalization of Public Bioethical Debate*. Chicago: University of Chicago Press.

Fisher, R. A. 1958. *The Genetical Theory of Natural Selection*. 2nd ed. New York: Dover.

Fryer, G., and T. D. Iles. 1980. *The Cichlid Fishes of the Great Lakes of Africa*. Edinburgh: Oliver and Boyd.

Futuyma, D. 1998. *Evolutionary Biology*. Sunderland, Mass.: Sinauer.

Gesteland, R. F., T. R. Cech, and J. F. Atkins, eds. 2000. *The RNA World*. 2nd ed. New York: Cold Spring Harbor Press.

Gonick, L., and M. Wheler. 1991. *Cartoon Guide to Genetics*. New York: Harper Perennial.

Griffiths, A. 2000. *An Introduction to Genetic Analysis*. New York: W. H. Freeman.

Gould, Stephen J., ed. 2001. *The Book of Life: An Illustrated History of the Evolution of Life on Earth*. New York: W. W. Norton.

Gurdon, J. B., and A. Colman. 1999. The future of cloning. *Nature*, **402**: 743–746.

Haase, A., G. Landwehr, and E. Umbach, eds. 1997. *Rontgen Centennial*. River Edge, N.J.: World Scientific Publishers.

Harold, F. M. 2001. *The Way of the Cell: Molecules, Organism, and the Order of Life*. Oxford: Oxford University Press.

Jones, S. *Introducing Genetics*. 2000. Icon Books.

Kay, L. E. 2000. *Who Wrote the Book of Life?* Stanford, Calif.: Stanford University Press.

Keller, E. F. 2001. *The Century of the Gene*. Cambridge, Mass.: Harvard University Press.

Khoury, M. J., W. Burke, and E. Thompson, eds. 2000. *Genetics and Public Health in the 21st Century: Using Genetic Information to Improve Health and Prevent Disease*. Oxford: Oxford University Press.

Klotzko, A. J., ed. *The Cloning Sourcebook*. 2001. New York: Oxford University Press.

Kresina, T. F., ed. 2001. *An Introduction to Molecular Medicine and Gene Therapy*. New York: Wiley-Liss.

Lambrecht, B. 2001. *Dinner at the New Gene Café*. New York: St. Martin's Press.

Leakey, R. E. 1996. *The Origins of Humankind*. Science Masters Series. New York: Basic Books.

Lewin, R. 1999. *Human Evolution*. Malden, Mass.: Blackwell Science.

Lively, C. M. 1996. Host-parasite coevolution and sex. *BioScience* 46: 107–114.

Marshall, E. L. 1999. *High-Tech Harvest: A Look at Genetically Engineered Foods*. London: Franklin Watt.

Mayr, E. 2001. *What Evolution Is*. New York: Basic Books.

McClafferty, C. K. 2001. *The Head Bone's Connected to the Neck Bone: The Weird, Wacky, and Wonderful X-ray*. New York: Farrar, Straus, and Giroux.

Miller, O. J., and E. Thurman. 2000. *Human Chromosomes*. New York: Springer-Verlag.

Milunsky, A. 2001. *Your Genetic Destiny*. Cambridge, Mass.: Perseus Pulishing.

Nelson, G. 2001. *Genetically Modified Organisms in Agriculture, Economics, and Politics*. San Diego: Academic Press.

Olson, S. 2002. *Mapping Human History: Discovering the Past through Our Genes*. Boston: Houghton-Mifflin.

Osborne, R., and M. Benton. 1996. *The Viking Atlas of Evolution*. New York: Viking.

Patterson, C. 1999. *Evolution*. London: Natural History Museum.

Peltonen, L., and V. A. McKusick. 2001. Dissecting human disease in the posteconomic era. *Science* 291: 1224–1229.

Price, E. O. 2002. *Animal Domestiction and Behavior*. New York: CABI Publishing.

Rantala, M. L., and A. J. Milgram, eds. *Cloning: For and Against*. 1999. Chicago and LaSalle, Ill.: Open Court.

Ridley, M. 2000. *Genome*. New York: HarperCollins.

Roca, N. B., et al. 1995. *Cells, Genes, and Chromosomes*. Broomall, Pa.: Chelsea House.

Ruse, M., and A. Sheppard, eds. 2001. *Cloning: Responsible Science or Technomadness?* Amherst, N.Y.: Prometheus Books.

Ruse, M., and E. O. Wilson. 2001. *The Evolution Wars: A Guide to the Debates*. Piscataway, N.J.: Rutgers University Press.

Skelton, P. 1994. *Evolution: A Biological and Palaeontological Approach*. Wokingham: Addison-Wesley Publishing Company.

Smith, B. D. 1999. *Emergence of Agriculture*. New York: W. H. Freeman.

Stearns, S. C., and R. F. Hoekstra. 2000. *Evolution: An Introduction*. New York: Oxford University Press.

Stock, G. 2002. *Redesigning Humans: Our Inevitable Genetic Future*. Boston: Houghton Mifflin.

Strickberger, M. W. 2000. *Evolution*. 3rd ed. Boston: Jones and Bartlett.

Sumner, A. 2002. *Chromosomes: Organization and Function*. Malden, Mass.: Blackwell Publishers.

Sykes, B. 2001. *The Seven Daughters of Eve: The Science That Reveals Our Genetic Ancestry*. New York: W. W. Norton and Company.

Tattersall, I. 1995. *The Last Neanderthal*. New York: Macmillan.

Thompson, J. N. 1994. *The Coevolutionary Process*. Chicago: University of Chicago Press.

Wood, E. J., et al. 1997. *Life Chemistry and Molecular Biology*. London: Portland Press.

Yount, L., ed. *Cloning*. 2000. San Diego: Greenhaven Press.

Zimmer, C., S. J. Gould, and R. Hutton. 2001. *Evolution: The Triumph of an Idea*. New York: HarperCollins.

Zohary, D., and M. Hopf. 2001. *Domestication of Plants in the Old World*. Oxford: Oxford University Press.

Zubay, G. L., W. W. Parson, and D. E. Vance. 1995. *Principles of Biochemistry*, vol 3. Dubuque, Iowa: William C. Brown Publishing.

MEDICINE

American Diabetes Association. 2002. *American Diabetes Association Complete Guide to Diabetes*. Alexandria, Virginia.

Anthemelli, R. M. et al. 1997. In *Substance Abuse: A Comprehensive Textbook*, edited by J. H. Lowisohn et al. 3rd ed. London: Williams and Wilkins.

Aronson , V. 2000. *How To Say No*. Philadelphia: Chelsea House.

Baird, R. M., and S. E. Rosenbaum, eds. 2001. *The Ethics of Abortion: Pro-Life vs. Pro-Choice (Contemporary Issues)*. 3rd ed. Amherst, N.Y.: Prometheus Books.

Barter, J. 2001. *Hallucinogens*. Drug Education Library. San Diego: Lucent Books.

Bauby, J.-D. 1997. *The Diving Bell and the Butterfly*. New York: Knopf.

Beauchamp, T. L., and L. Walters, eds. 1999. *Contemporary Issues in Bioethics*. 5th ed. Belmont, Calif.: Wadsworth.

Berger, W. E. 2000. *Allergies and Asthma for Dummies*. New York : John Wiley.

Bitter, C. N. 1988. *Good Enough: When Losing Is Winning and Thin Enough Can Never Be Achieved*. Penfield, N.Y.: Hopelines.

Buchanan, A., D. W. Brock, N. Daniels, and D. Winkler. 2000. *From Chance to Choice: Genetics and Justice*. Cambridge, U.K.: Cambridge University Press.

Burnell, G. 1993. *Final Choices: To Live or To Die in an Age of Medical Technology*. New York: Insight Books.

Buxton, R. 2001. *An Introduction to Functional Magnetic Resonance Imaging*. (CD-ROM). Cambridge: Cambridge University Press.

Carter, R. 1999. *Mapping the Mind*. Berkeley: University of California Press.

Chopra, D. 2001. *Perfect Health: The Complete Mind-Body Guide*. New York: Crown Publishing.

Clancy, J., Jr., ed. 1998. *Basic Concepts in Immunology: A Student's Survival Guide*. New York: McGraw-Hill, Health Professions Division.

Cobb, A. B. 2002. *The Bionic Human*. New York: Rosen Publishing.

Coiera, E. 1997. *Guide to Medical Informatics, the Internet, and Telemedicine*. New York: Oxford University Press.

Connell, E. B. 2001. *The Contraceptive Sourcebook*. New York: McGraw-Hill Professional.

Costin, C. 1999. *The Eating Disorder Sourcebook: A Comprehensive Guide to the Causes, Treatments, and Prevention*. New York: McGraw Hill-NTC.

Crule, J., ed. 2000. *The Timetables of Medicine: An Illustrated Chronology of the History of Medicine from Prehistory to Present Times*. New York: Black Dog and Leventhal.

Drews, J., and D. Kramer, trans. 1999. *In Quest of Tomorrow's Medicines*. New York: Springer Verlag.

Duo G., and B. Bernie, eds. 2001. *The Encyclopedia of Chinese Medicine*. London: Carlton Books.

Elliot, R., ed. 1995. *Environmental Ethics*. Oxford: Oxford University Press.

Evans, C., and J. Ballard. 2001. *Safe Passage: Astronaut Care for Exploration Missions*. Washington, D.C.: National Academy Press.

Finger, S. 1994. *Origins of Neuroscience*. New York: Oxford University Press.

Finn, R., R. Gree, and L. Lamb. 2000. *Organ Transplants: Making the Most of Your Gift of Life*. Cambridge, Mass.: O'Reiley and Associates.

Fontanarosa, P. B., ed. 2000. *Alternative Medicine: An Objective Assessment*. Chicago: American Medical Association.

Friedland, D. J. 1998. *Evidence-Based Medicine: A Framework for Clinical Practice*. Stamford, Conn.: Appleton and Lange.

Friedman, M., and G. W. Friedland. 2000. *Medicine's 10 Great Discoveries*. New Haven: Yale University Press.

Giddens, S., and O. Giddens. 2002. *Future Techniques in Surgery*. New York: Rosen Publishing.

Goldberg, B. 2002. *Alternative Medicine: The Definitive Guide*. 2nd ed. Berkeley: Ten Speed Press.

Goldsmith, C. 2001. *Neurological Disorder (The Amazing Brain)*. Blackbird Marketing.

Gottfried, T. 2000. *Should Drugs Be Legalized?* Brookfield, Conn.: Twenty-First Century Books.

Greenhalgh, T. 2001. *How to Read a Paper: The Basics of Evidence-Based Medicine*. 2nd ed. London: BMJ.

Griffith, H. W. *Complete Guide to Symptoms, Illness, and Surgery*. 4th ed. New York:

The Body Press/Perigee.

Grob, C. S. 2002. *Hallucinogens: A Reader*. Los Angeles: J. P. Tarcher.

Gruenwald, J. 2000. *Physician's Desk Reference for Herbal Medicines*. 2nd ed. Montvale, N.J.: Medical Economics/Thomson Healthcare.

Hall, R. 1998. *The Ultrasound Handbook: Clinical, Etiologic, Pathologic Implications of Sonographic Findings*. Baltimore: Lippincott.

Haskell, C. M. 1999. *Handbook of Cancer Chemotherapy*. Philadelphia: Lippincott Williams and Wilkins.

Heneghan, C., and D. Badenoch. 2002. *Evidence-Based Medicine Toolkit*. London: BMJ.

Hornbacker, M. 1999. *Wasted: A Memoir of Anorexia and Bulimia*. New York: HarperCollins.

Hype, M. O., and J. F. Setaro. 1999. *Alcohol 101: An Overview for Teens*. Breckenridge, Colo.: Twenty First Century Books.

Jonsen, A. R. 2000. *A Short History of Medical Ethics*. Oxford: Oxford University Press.

Katzung, B., ed. 2000. *Basic and Clinical Pharmacology*. 8th ed. Norwalk, Conn.: Appleton and Lange.

Keown, J. 1995. *Euthanasia Examined*. New York: Cambridge University Press.

Kolb, B., and I. Wishaw. 2001. *Introduction to the Brain and Behavior*. New York: Worth Publishing.

Klatt, E. C., ed. 2000. *Review of Pharmacology*. Philadelphia: W. B. Saunders.

Kuhse, H., and P. Singer, eds. 1999 *Bioethics: An Anthology*. Oxford, U.K.: Blackwell.

Levy, S. B. 2002. *The Antibiotic Paradox: How the Misuse of Antibiotics Destroys Their Curative Powers*. New York: Perseus Books.

Lilleyman, J. S. 2000. *Childhood Leukemia: The Facts*. Oxford: Oxford University Press.

Maguire, D. C. 2001. *Sacred Choices: The Right to Contraception and Abortion in Ten World Religions*. Sacred Energies Series. Minneapolis: Augsburg Fortress Publishers.

McCartney, S. 1994. *Defying the Gods: Inside the New Frontiers of Organ Transplants*. New York: Macmillan.

McGee, G. 2000. *The Human Cloning Debate*. Berkeley, Calif.: Berkeley Hills Books.

McKone, W. L. 2001. *Osteopathic Medicine: Philosophy, Principles, and Practice*. Oxford, U.K.: Blackwell Science.

Meire, H. B., D. Cosgrove, and K. Dewbury. 2000. *Clinical Ultrasound: Abdominal and General Ultrasound*. St.Louis: Harcourt.

Mills, S., and K. Bone. 1999. *Principles and Practice of Phytotherapy: Modern Herbal Medicine*. London: Churchill Livingstone.

Moe, B. 2003. *The Revolution in Medical Imaging*. New York: Rosen Publishing.

Moravec, H. 2000. *Robot: Mere Machine to Transcendent Mind*. New York: Oxford University Press.

Mucciolo, G. 2001. *Everything You Need to Know*

about Birth Control. The Need to Know Library. New York: Rosen Publishing Group.

Munson, P., et al, eds. 1997. *Principles of Pharmacology: Basic Concepts and Clinical Applications.* Oxford: Oxford University Press.

Munson, R. 2000. *Intervention and Reflection: Basic Issues in Medical Ethics.* Belmont, Calif.: Wadsworth Press.

Munson, R. 2002. *Raising the Dead: Organ Transplants, Ethics, and Society.* Oxford: Oxford University Press.

Muth, A., and K. Bellenir, eds. 2002. *Surgery Source-book: Basic Consumer Health Information about Major Surgery and Outpatient Surgeries.* Detroit: Omnigraphics.

Ninivaggi, F. J. 2001. *An Elementary Textbook of Ayurveda: Medicine With a Six-Thousand-Year-Old Tradition.* Madison, Conn.: International Universities Press.

Norris, A. 2002. *Essentials of Telelmedicine and Telecare.* New York: John Wiley.

Paoletti, L. C., and P. M. McInnes, eds. 1999. *Vaccines: From Concept to Clinic. A Guide to the Development and Clinical Testing of Vaccines for Human Use.* Boca Raton, Fla.: CRC Press.

Peacock, J., and B. Asselir. 2000. *Leukemia. Perspectives on Disease and Illness.* Mankato, Minn.: Lifematters Press.

Peakman, M., and D. Vergani. 1997. *Basic and Clinical Immunology.* New York : Churchill Livingstone.

Pool, S., and A. E. Nicogossian. 2002. *Space Physiology and Medicine.* 4th ed. Philadelphia: Williams and Wilkins.

Reese, R. E., R. Betts, and B. Gumustop. 2000. *Handbook of Antibiotics.* 3rd ed. Philadelphia: Lippincott William and Wilkins.

Reinisch, J., and R. Beasley. 1990. *The Kinsey Institute New Report on Sex: What You Must Know to Be Sexually Literate.* New York: St. Martin's Press.

Rosenberg, W., and A. Donald. 1995. Evidence-based medicine: An approach to clinical problem-solving. *British Medical Journal* 310, 1122–1126.

Rothfield, G. S. 2002. *The Acupuncture Response: Balance Energy and Restore Health—A Western Doctor Tells You How.* New York: Contemporary Books.

Sacks, O. 1999. *Awakenings.* New York: Vintage.

Sacks, T. J. 2001. *Osteopathic Medicine Careers.* New York: McGraw Hill/Contemporary Books.

Sheldon, T. 2001. Holland decriminalizes voluntary euthanasia. *British Medical Journal* **322**: 947–948.

Siegel, G. J., B. W. Agranoff, and E. Uhler, eds. 1999. *Basic Neurochemistry: Molecular, Cellular, and Medical Aspects.* Philadelphia: Lippincott, Williams, and Wilkins.

Silverman, W. A. 1998. *Where's the Evidence? Controversies in Modern Medicine.* New York: Oxford University Press.

Skeel, R. T. 2001. *Cancer Treatment.* New York: W. B. Saunders.

Slack, W. 2001. *Cybermedicine: How Computing Empowers Doctors and Patients for Better Health Care.* 2nd ed. San Francisco: Jossey-Bass.

Stoelting, R. K. and R. D. Miller. 2000. *Basics of Anesthesia.* 4th ed. Philadelphia: W. B. Saunders Publishing.

Webb, W. R., and M. G. Gotway. 2002. *Pocket Atlas of Body CT Anatomy.* Philadelphia: Lippincott, Williams and Wilkins.

Wetbrook, C. 2002. *MRI at a Glance.* Boston: Blackwell Publishers.

Williams, B. 1986. *Ethics and the Limits of Philosophy.* Cambridge, Mass.: Harvard University Press.

Wolbarst, A. B., and G. Cook. 1999. *Looking Within: How X-ray, CT, MRI, Ultrasound, and Other Medical Images Are Created, and How They Help Physicians Save Lives.* Berkeley: University of California Press.

Youngson, R. M. 1993. *The Surgery Book: An Illustrated Guide to 73 of the Most Common Operations.* New York: St. Martin's Press.

MICROBIOLOGY

Anderson, R. O., and M. Druger. 1997. *Explore the World Using Protozoa.* Arlington, Va.: National Science Teachers Association.

Bennett, J. A. 2000. *Yeasts: Characteristics and Identification.* New York: Cambridge University Press.

Biddle, W. 1996. *A Field Guide to Germs.* New York: Anchor.

Block, Seymour S., ed. 2000. *Disinfection, Sterilization, and Preservation.* 5th ed. Philadelphia: Lippincott Williams and Wilkins.

Boulton, C., and D. Quain. 2001. *Brewing Yeast and Fermentation.* Malden, Mass.: Blackwell Scientific.

Carlile, M., S. Watkinson, G. W. Gooday. 2001. *The Fungi.* 2nd ed. New York: Academic Press.

Cooke J. 1998. *Cannibals, Cows, and the CJD Catastrophe.* Sidney, Australia: Random House.

Cossart, P., ed. 2000. *Cellular Microbiology.* Washington, DC: American Society for Microbiology.

Crawford, D. H. 2000. *The Invisible Enemy: A Natural History of Viruses.* New York: Oxford University Press.

Flint, S. J., ed., et al. 2000. *Principles of Virology.* Washington, D.C.: ASM Press.

Harris D. 1999. *Prions: Molecular and Cellular Biology.* Wymondham, Norfolk, U.K.: Horizon Scientific Press.

Karlen, A. 1996. *Man and Microbes: Disease and Plagues in History and Modern Times.* New York: Touchstone Books.

Kendrick, B. 2001. *The Fifth Kingdom.* Newburyport, Mass.: Focus Publishing.

Klitzman, R. 2001. *The Trembling Mountain: A Personal Account of Kuru, Cannibals, and Mad Cow Disease.* Cambridge: Perseus Books.

Levy, S. B. 2002. *The Antibiotic Paradox: How the Misuse of Antibiotics Destroys Their Curative Powers.* New York: Perseus Books.

Marantz Hening, R. 1998. *A Dancing Matrix: How Science Confronts Emerging Viruses.* New York: Vintage Books.

Murray, P. R., E. J. Baron, M. A. Pfaller, F. C. Tenover, and R. H. Yolken. 1999. *Manual of Clinical Microbiology.* 7th ed. Washington, D.C.: ASM Press.

Oldstone, M. B. A. 2000. *Viruses, Plagues, and History.* New York: Oxford University Press.

Preston, R. 1995. *The Hot Zone.* New York: Anchor Books.

Reese, R. E., R. Betts, and B. Gumustop. 2000. *Handbook of Antibiotics.* 3rd ed. Philadelphia: Lippincott William and Wilkins.

Ridley, R., and H. Baker. 1998. *The Story of CJD, BSE and Other Prion Diseases.* Oxford: Oxford University Press.

Silverstein, A., et al. 1997. *Monerans and Protists.* Breckenridge, Co.: Twenty First Century Books.

Singleton, P. 1999. *Bacteria in Biology, Biotechnology, and Medicine.* New York: John Wiley.

Sleigh, M. A. 2003. *Protozoa and Other Protists.* 2nd ed. New York: Cambridge University Press.

Sompayrac, L. 2002. *How Pathogenic Viruses Work.* Boston: Jones and Bartlett.

Stoermer, E. F., and J. P. Smol. 2001. *The Diatoms.* New York: Cambridge University Press.

Ulloa, M., and R. T. Hanlin. 2000. *Illustrated Dictionary of Mycology.* St. Paul: American Phytopathological Society.

Walker, G. M. 1998. *Yeast Physiology and Biotechnology.* New York: John Wiley.

MOLECULAR BIOLOGY AND CYTOLOGY

Alberts, B., A. Johnson, J. Lewis, M. Raff, K. Roberts, and P. Walter. 2002. *Molecular Biology of the Cell.* New York: Garland.

Carter, G. R., and D. J. Wise. 2002. *Immunology: A Comprehensive Review.* Ames: Iowa State University Press.

Harold, F. M. 2001. *The Way of the Cell: Molecules, Organisms and the Order of Life.* Oxford: Oxford University Press.

Holland, S., K. Lebacqz, and L. Zoloth, eds. 2001. *The Human Embryonic Stem Cell Debate (Basic Bioethics),* Cambridge: MIT Press.

May, M. 2000. Mother nature's menders: Origins of a stem cell. *Scientific American* (May).

Mooney, D. J., and A. G. Mikos. 1999. Growing new organs. *Scientific American* (April): 60–73.

Nelson, D., and M. Lehninger Cox. 2000. *Principles of Biochemistry.* New York: Worth.

Rensberger, B. 1998. *Life Itself: Exploring the Realm of the Living Cell.* New York: Oxford University Press.

Rose, S. 1999. *The Chemistry of Life*. New York: Penguin Putnam.

Sompeyrac, L. 2002. *How Pathogenic Viruses Work*. Boston: Jones and Barlett Publisher.

Tortora, G. J. 2000. *Microbiology: An Introduction*. 7th ed. New York: Benjamin Cummings.

PATHOLOGY AND HISTOLOGY

Aaseng, N. 1995. *Autoimmune Diseases*. A Venture Book. Chicago: Franklin Watts.

Bayley, J. 2001. *Elegy for Iris*. New York: St. Martin's Press.

Becker, G. 2001. *The First Year Type 2 Diabetes: An Essential Guide*. New York: Marlowe.

Brown, G. I. 2001. *Invisible Rays: A History of Radioactivity*. London: Sutton Publishing.

Craighead, J. E. 1995. *Pathology of Environmental and Occupational Disease*. St Louis: Mosby Year Book.

Daniel, T. M. 1999. *Captain of Death: The Story of Tuberculosis*. Rochester, N.Y.: Boydell and Brewer.

Devinsky, O. 2001. *Epilepsy: Patient and Family Guide*. Philadelphia, Pa.: F. A. Davis.

Dolan, M., I. Murray-Lyon, and J. Tindall. 1999. *The Hepatitis C Handbook*. Berkeley, Calif.: North Atlantic Books.

Evans, C. 1998. *The Casebook of Forensic Detection: How Science Solved 100 of the World's Most Baffling Crimes*. New York: John Wiley.

Fawcett, D. W., and R. P. Jensh. 2002. *Concise Histology*. 2nd ed. Oxford: Oxford University Press.

Freeman, J. M., et al. 1997. *Seizures and Epilepsy in Childhood: A Guide for Parents*. 2nd ed. Bethesda, Md.: Johns Hopkins University Press.

Freeman, J. M. 2000. *The Ketogenic Diet: A Treatment for Epilepsy*. 3rd ed. New York: Demos Medical Publishing.

Gartner, L. P., and J. L. Hiatt. 2001. *Color Textbook of Histology*. Philadelphia: W. B. Saunders.

Gordis, L. 2000. *Epidemiology*. Philadelphia: W. B. Saunders.

Greenwood, P., et al. 2000. *American Horticultural Society Pests and Diseases*. New York: Dorling Kindersley Publishing.

Griffin, J. E., and S. R. Ojeda, eds. 2002. *Textbook of Endocrine Physiology*. 4th ed. New York: Oxford University Press.

Guillemin, J. 2001. *The Investigation of a Deadly Outbreak*. Berkeley: University of California.

Hanas, R. 1998. *Insulin-Dependent Diabetes in Children, Adolescents, and Adults*. Uddevalla, Sweden: Piara Publishing.

Hooper, E. 1999. *The River: A Journey Back to the Source of HIV and AIDS*. London: Penguin.

Hopkins, D. 2002. *The Greatest Killer: Smallpox in History*. Chicago: University of Chicago Press.

Isenberg, D., and J. Morrow. 1995. *Friendly Fire:*

Explaining Autoimmune Disease. Oxford: Oxford University Press.

Joy, J. E., and R. B. Johnston, eds. 2001. *Multiple Sclerosis: Current Status and Strategies for the Future*. Washington, D.C.: National Academy Press.

Kalichman, S. C. 1998. *Understanding AIDS: Advances in Research and Treatment*. 2nd ed. Washington, D.C.: American Psychological Association.

Kruh, G. D., and K. D. Tew, 2000. *Basic Science of Cancer*. Philadelphia: Current Medicine.

Lahita, R., N. Chiorazzi, and W. Reeves. 2000. *Textbook of Autoimmune Diseases*. Baltimore: Lippincott Williams and Wilkins.

Leal, C. 2001. *Portraits of Huntington's*. Belleville, Ontario: Essence Publishing.

Lennox, J. G. 2000. *Aristotle's Philosophy of Biology: Studies in the Origins of Life Science* (Cambridge Series in Philosophy and Biology). Cambridge, U.K.: Cambridge University Press.

Loscalo, J., and A. Schafer, eds. 2002. *Thrombosis and Hemorrhage*. Philadelphia: Lippincot, Williams and Wilkins.

Lowenthal, G., and P. Airy. 2001. *Practical Applications of Radioactivity and Nuclear Radiations*. New York: Cambridge University Press.

Marcus, P. I. 1999. *Encyclopedia of Virology*. 2nd ed. Vol. 2. San Diego, Calif.: Academic Press/Elsevier.

Nadakavukaren, Anne. 2000. *Our Global Environment: A Health Perspective*. Prospect Heights, Ill.: Waveland Press.

Parents Committee for Public Awareness. 2001. *Anthrax: A Practical Guide for Citizens*. Cambridge, Mass.: Harvard Perspectives Press.

Perry, A. R., ed. 1998. *The Essential Guide to Asthma*. Pocket Books. New York: American Medical Association.

Plaut, T. F. 1999. *Dr. Tom Plaut's Asthma Guide for People of All Ages*. Amherst, Mass.: Pedipress.

Pleasant, B. 1995. *The Gardener's Guide to Plant Diseases: Earth-Safe Remedies*. Pownal, Vt.: Storey Communications.

Schoub, B. D. 1999. *AIDS and HIV: In Perspective*. Cambridge, U.K.: Cambridge University Press.

Stine, G. J. 2000. *AIDS Update 2000*. Upper Saddle River, N.J.: Prentice Hall.

Ramakrishnan, U. 2000. *Nutritional Anemias*. New York: CRC Press.

Ramsley, J. K., J. Donelly, and N. W. Read, eds. 2001. *Food and Nutritional Supplements: Their Role in Health and Disease*. New York: Springer Verlag.

Reeves, A. G., et al., eds. 1995. *Epilepsy and the Corpus Callosum II*. New York: Plenum.

Reichman, L. B., and J. H. Tanne. 2001. *Timebomb: The Global Epidemic of Multidrug-Resistant Tuberculosis*. New York: McGraw-Hill Trade.

Ridgway, T. 2001. *Smallpox*. New York: Rosen.

Roloff, M., and T. Summer. 1999. *Against Tall Odds: Being a David in a Goliath World*. Sisters,

Oreg.: Multnomah Publishers.

Rose, N., and I. MacKay. 1998. *The Autoimmune Diseases*. San Diego: Academic Press.

Rucker, R. B., ed. 2001. *Handbook of Vitamins*. New York: Marcel Dekker Publishing.

Ruddon, R. W. 1995. *Cancer Biology*. New York: Oxford University Press.

Shilts, R. 2000. *And the Band Played On: Politics, People, and the AIDS Epidemic*. New York: St Martin's Press.

St. George-Hyslop, P. H. 2000. Piecing together Alzheimer's. *Scientific American* (December).

Strathern, P. 1999. *Marie Curie and Radioactivity*. New York: Anchor Books.

Uthman, E. 1998. *Understanding Anemia*. Jackson: University Press of Mississippi.

Vancleave, J. P. 1999. *Nutrition for Every Kid*. New York: John Wiley.

Weaver, D. F. 2001. *Epilepsy and Seizures: Everything You Need to Know*. Toronto, Ontario: Firefly Books.

Weiner, W. J., MD, L. M. Shulman MD, and A. E. Lang MD, FRCP. 2001. *Parkinson's Disease: A Complete Guide for Patients and Families*. Baltimore: Johns Hopkins Press Health Book.

PHYSIOLOGY

Abbas, A.K., and A. H. Lichtman. 2001. *Basic Immunology: Functions and Disorders of the Immune System*. Philadelphia: W. B. Saunders.

Adkinson, E. M. 1998. *Allergy: Principles and Practice*. 5th ed. St Louis: Mosby-Year Book.

Alcamo, I. E. 1996. *Anatomy and Physiology the Easy Way*. Hauppauge, N.Y.: Barrons Educational Series.

Alexander, R. M. 1999. *Energy for Animal Life*. Oxford Animal Biology Series. Oxford: Oxford University Press.

Arnett, J. J. 2001. *Adolescence and Emerging Adulthood: A Cultural Approach*. Upper Saddlebrook, N.J.: Prentice Hall.

Aronson, D., D. Clapp, and M. Hollister. 2001. *Resolving Infertility*. New York: Harper Resource.

Baskin, C. C., and J. M. Baskin. 2001. *Seeds: Ecology, Biogeography, and Evolution of Dormancy and Germination*. San Diego: Academic Press.

Beauchamp, G. K., L. Bartoshuk, and E. Carterette, eds. 1997. *Tasting and Smelling*. 2nd ed. Toronto: Academic Press.

Beck, A. T. 2000. *Prisoners of Hate*. New York: Harper Perennial.

Bellis, J. 2002. *When the Brain Can't Hear: Unraveling the Mystery of the Auditory Processing Disorder*. New York: Atria Books.

Bender, D. A. 2002. *Introduction to Nutrition and Metabolism*. 3rd ed. London: Taylor and Francis.

Berk, L. 1999. *Child Development*. 5th ed. Boston: Allyn and Bacon.

Bradshaw, S. D. 1997. *Homeostasis in Desert Reptiles (Adaptations of Desert Organisms)*. New York: Springer Verlag.

Brady, T. 1999. *Nutritional Biochemistry*.

San Diego: Academic Press.

Brown, G. C. 2000. *The Energy of Life: The Science of What Makes Our Minds and Bodies Work.* New York: Free Press.

Campbell, N., and J. Reece. 2002. *Biology.* San Francisco: Benjamin Cummings Publishers.

Carlson, B. M. 1999. *Human Embryology and Developmental Biology.* 2nd ed. St. Louis: Mosby Year Book.

Classen, C., D. Howes, and A. Synnott. 1994. *Aroma: The Cultural History of Smell.* New York: Routledge.

Cobb, N. J. 2001. *Adolescence: Continuity, Change, and Diversity.* 4th ed. Mountain View, Calif.: Mayfield Publishing Company.

Cruse, J. H., and R. E. Lewis. 2002. *Illustrated Dictionary of Immunology.* 2nd ed. Boca Raton, Fla.: CRC Press.

Dalton, K. 1999. *Once a Month: Understanding and Treating PMS.* Alameda, Calif.: Hunter House.

Davenport, P. 1995. *The Natural Way with Colds and Flu.* Rockport, Tx.: Element.

Douglas, A. 2002. *The Mother of All Pregnancy Books: The Ultimate Guide to Conception, Birth, and Everything in Between.* New York: John Wiley.

Edelson, E. 1999. *The Immune System.* New York: Chelsea House Publications.

Empson, J., and M. Wang. 2002. *Sleep and Dreaming.* New York: Palgrave MacMillan.

Farrel, J. 1998. *Invisible Enemies: Stories of Infectious Disease.* New York: Farrer, Straus, and Giroux.

Finger, T. E., D. Restrepo, and W. L. Silver, eds. 2000. *The Neurobiology of Taste and Smell.* Hoboken, N.J.: Wiley-Liss.

Frayn, K., and K. Snell. 1996. *Metabolic Regulation: A Human Perspective.* Seattle: Portland Press.

Garret, L. 1995. *The Coming Plague: Newly Emerging Diseases in a World Out of Balance.* New York: Penguin.

Garrod, A., L. Smulyan, S. I. Powers, and R. Kilkenny. 1999. *Adolescent Portraits: Identity, Relationships, and Challenges.* Boston: Allyn and Bacon.

Geisler, C. 1998. *From Sound to Synapse: Physiology of the Mammalian Ear.* New York: Oxford University Press

Gilbert, S. 2000. *Developmental Biology.* Sunderland, U.K.: Sinauer Associates.

Goddard, S. 2002. *Reflexes, Learning, and Behavior: A Window into the Child's Mind.* Eugene, Oreg.: Fern Ridge Press.

Goodenough, J., B. McGuire, and R. A. Wallace. 2001. *Perspectives on Animal Behavior.* 2nd ed. New York: John Wiley.

Griffin, J. E. and S. R. Ojeda. 1996. *Textbook of Endocrine Physiology.* 3rd ed. New York: Oxford University Press.

Guyton, A. C. 2000. *Textbook of Medical Physiology.* 10th ed. New York: W. B. Saunders.

Hall, S. S. 1998. *A Commotion in the Blood: Life, Death, and the Immune System.* Sloan Technology Series. New York: Henry Holt Publishing.

Hardie, J. 1997. *Breathing and Respiration (Body Systems Series).* Crystal Lake, IL: Heinemann Library.

Heinrich, B. 1986. *Insect Thermoregulation.* Melbourne, Fla.: Kreiger.

Hickman, C. P. 2000. *Integrated Principles of Zoology.* 11th ed. Columbus, Ohio: McGraw-Hill Higher Education.

Hobson, J. 2002. *Dreaming: An Introduction to the Science of Sleep.* New York: Oxford University Press.

Jovet, M. 1999. *The Paradox of Sleep: The Story of Dreaming.* Cambridge, Mass.: MIT Press.

Hochacka, P. W., and M. Guppy. 1987. *Metabolic Arrest and Control of Biological Time.* Cambridge, Mass.: Harvard University Press.

Holloway, M. 2001. Outbreak not contained. *Scientific American* (April): 20–22.

Honigsbaum, M. 2002. *The Fever Trail: In Search of the Cure for Malaria.* New York: Farrar, Straus, and Giroux.

Kornberg, A. 1991. *For the Love of Enzymes: The Odyssey of a Biochemist.* Cambridge, Mass.: Harvard University Press.

Kosco, M. 2000. *Mammalian Reproduction.* Clarion, Pa.: Allegheny Press.

Laflamme, L. M. 2001. *Rites of Passage: A Celebration of Menarche.* Harrisville, N.H.: Synchronicity Press.

Lawrence, J. R., K. S. Harris, and G. J. Borden. 2002. *Speech Science Primer: Physiology, Acoustics, and the Perception of Speech.* Baltimore: Williams and Wilkins.

Mann, J., ed. 1998. *Essentials of Human Nutrition.* Oxford: Oxford University Press.

McCracken, T O., and R. A. Kainer. 1999. *Spurgeon's Color Atlas of Large Animal Anatomy.* Baltimore, Md.: Lippincott Williams and Wilkins.

McDowell, L. R. 2000. *Vitamins in Animal and Human Nutrition.* 2nd ed. Ames: Iowa State Press.

McGuirk, J., and M. Elizabeth. 1991. *For Want of a Child: A Psychologist and His Wife Explore the Emotional Effects and Challenges of Infertility.* New York: Continuum Publishing Company.

Moller, A. R. 2002. *Sensory Systems: Anatomy and Physiology.* San Diego: Academic Press.

Nicholson, K. G., and Robert G. Webster. 1998. *Textbook of Influenza.* Boston: Blackwell Science.

Niehoff, D. 1999. *The Biology of Violence.* New York: Free Press.

Overy, A. 1997. *Sex in Your Garden.* Golden, Col.: Fulcrum Publishers.

Palmer, S. E. 1999. *Vision Science: Photons to Phenomenology.* Cambridge, Mass.: MIT Press.

Papathomas, T. V., ed. 1995. *Early Vision and Beyond.* Cambridge, Mass.: MIT Press.

Peoples, D., and H. Ferguson. 2000. *Experiencing Infertility.* New York: W. W. Norton

Perry, P. J. 2001. *Animals That Hibernate (Watts Library: Animals).* New York: Franklin Watts.

Raven, P. H., et al. 1999. *Biology of Plants.* 6th ed. New York: W. H. Freeman and Worth Publishers.

Resnick, S. 1999. *Blood Saga: Hemophilia, AIDS, and the Survival of a Community.* Berkeley: University of California Press.

Riordan, J. and K. G. Auerbach, eds. 1999. *Breastfeeding and Human Lactation.* Sudbury, Mass.: Jones and Bartlett Publishers.

Robbins, C. T. 1993. *Wildlife Feeding and Nutrition.* 2nd ed. San Diego: Academic Press.

Roitt, I. M., J. Brostoff, and D. K. Male. 2001. *Immunology.* St. Louis: Mosby.

Schmidt-Nielson, K. 1997. *Animal Physiology: Adaptation and Environment.* New York: Cambridge University Press.

Schulkin, J. 1999. *Neuroendocrine Regulation of Behavior.* Cambridge, U.K.: Cambridge University Press.

Schwenk, K., ed. 2000. *Feeding: Form, Function, and Evolution in Tetrapod Vertebrates.* New York: Academic Press.

Sells, S., and E. E. Max. 2001. *Immunology, Immunopathology, and Immunity.* 6th ed. Washington, D.C.: American Society of Microbiology.

Sheehy, G. *The Silent Passage: Menopause.* New York: Pocket Books, 1998.

Smith, C. U. M. 2002. *Biology of Sensory Systems.* New York: John Wiley.

Sompayrac, L. M. 2002. *How the Immune System Works.* Malden, Mass.: Blackwell Science.

Starr, D. 2000. *Blood: An Epic History of Medicine and Commerce.* New York: William Morrow.

Steidle, C., and J. Mulcahy. 1999. *Impotence Sourcebook.* New York: McGraw Hill.

Stoppard, M. 2000. *Conception, Pregnancy, and Birth.* New York: DK Publishing.

Tymoczko, J. L., L. Stryer, and J. M. Berg. 2001. *Biochemistry.* 5th ed. New York: W. H. Freeman.

Tyree, M. T., and M. H. Zimmermann. 2002. *Xylem Structure and the Ascent of Sap.* 2nd ed. New York: Springer-Verlag.

Viemont, J.-D., and J. Crabbe, eds. 2000. *Dormancy in Plants: From Whole Plant Behavior to Cellular Control.* New York: Cabi Publishing.

Vogel, S. 1999. *Vital Circuits: On Pumps, Pipes, and the Workings of Circulatory Systems.* 2nd ed. New York: Oxford University Press.

Ward, J. 2002. *Respiratory Systems at a Glance.* Malden, U.K.: Blackwell Publishers.

Watson, L. 2001. *Jacobson's Organ and the Remarkable Nature of Smell.* East Rutherford, N.J.: Plume Books.

West, J. B. 2000. *Respiratory Physiology: The Essentials.* Philadelphia: Lippincott, Williams and Wilkins.

Widmaier, E. P., H. Raff, and K. T. Strang. 2003. Vander, A. J., J. H. Sherman, and

D. S. Luciano. 2001. *Human Physiology: The Mechanisms of Body Function*. 8th ed. New York: McGraw-Hill.

Wolpert, L., R. Beddington, J. Brockes, T. Jessell, P. Lawrence, and E. Meyerowitz. 1998. *Principles of Development*. Oxford: Oxford University Press.

Wong, Dominic W. S. 1995. *Food Enzymes: Structures and Mechanism*. New York: Chapman and Hall.

Woodburne, R. T., and W. E. Burkel. 1994. *Essentials of Human Anatomy*. 9th ed. New York: Oxford University Press.

Zemlin, W. R. 1997. *Speech and Hearing Science*. Paramus, N.J.: Allyn and Bacon.

PSYCHOLOGY

Artiss, K. L. 1996. *Mistake Making*. New York: University Press of America.

Austan, S. N. 1999. *Why We Age: What Science Is Discovering about the Body and Life*. New York: John Wiley.

Badcock, C. 2000. *Evolutionary Psychology: A Critical Introduction*. Cambridge, U.K.: Polity Press.

Batshaw, M. L. 2002. *Children with Disabilities*. Baltimore: Paul H. Brookes Publishing.

Blake. T., ed. 1995. *Enduring Issues in Psychology*. San Diego: Greenhaven Press.

Bourne, J. 2001. *The Anxiety and Phobia Workbook*. Oakland, Calif.: New Harbinger Publications.

Buss, D. 1998. *Evolutionary Psychology: The New Science of the Mind*. Boston: Allyn and Bacon.

Buss, D. 1994. *Evolution of Desire: Strategies of Human Mating*. New York: Basic Books.

Carson, R., J. Butcher, and Susan Mineka. 2000. *Abnormal Psychology and Modern Life*. Boston: Allyn and Bacon.

Cavendish, R., and B. Innes, eds. 1995. *Man, Myth, and Magic*. New York: Marshall Cavendish.

Colas, E. 1998. *Just Checking: Scenes from the Life of an Obsessive-Compulsive*. New York: Pocket Books.

Comer, R. 2000. *Abnormal Psychology*. New York: W. H. Freeman.

Committee on Educational Interventions for Children with Autism. 2001. *Educating Children with Autism*. National Research Council.

Coon, D. 2000. *Introduction to Psychology: Gateways to Mind and Behavior*. Belmont, Calif.: Wadsworth.

Comer, R. 2000. *Abnormal Psychology*. New York: W. H. Freeman.

Cushman, P. 2000. *Constructing the Self, Constructing America: A Cultural History of Psychotherapy*. Boston: Addison-Wesley.

Damasio, A. 2000. *The Feeling of What Happens: Body and Emotion in the Making of Consciousness*. New York: Harvest Books.

Dennett, D. 1997. *Kinds of Minds: Towards an Understanding of Consciousness*. New York: HarperCollins.

Evans, D. 2001. *Emotion: The Science of Sentiment*. Oxford: Oxford University Press.

Evans, D., and O. Zarate. 2000. *Introducing Evolutionary Psychology*. New York: Totem Books.

Fouse, B., and M. Wheeler. 1997. *A Treasure Chest of Behavioral Strategies for Individuals with Autism*. Arlington, Tex.: Future Horizons.

Gardner, H. 2000. *Intelligence Reframed: Multiple Intelligences for the 21st Century*. New York: Basic Books.

Goleman, Daniel. 1997. *Emotional Intelligence*. New York: Bantam Books.

Hoffman, S., and P. DiBartolo, eds. 2000. *From Social Anxiety to Social Phobia: Multiple Perspectives*. Paramus, N.J.: Allyn and Bacon.

Jamison, K. 1997. *An Unquiet Mind*. New York: Random House.

Knight, P., and R. Swanwick. 1999. *The Care and Education of a Deaf Child*. Tonawanda, N.Y.: Multilingual Matters.

Kurzweil, R. 1999. *The Age of Spiritual Machines: When Computers Exceed Human Intelligence*. New York: Viking/Penguin.

LeDoux, J. E. 1994. Emotion, memory, and the brain. *Scientific American* (June), 270, 50–57.

Lord, C., and J. P. McGee, eds. 2001. *Educating Children with Autism*. Washington, D.C.: Joseph Henry.

Mesibov, G., and M. Howley. 2003. *Accessing the Curriculum for Pupils with Autistic Spectrum Disorders*. London: David Fulton Publishers.

Miller, R., and S. E. Mason, eds. 2002. *Diagnosis: Schizophrenia*. New York: Columbia University Press.

Mindell, A. 1999. *Coma: A Healing Journey: A Guide for Family, Friends, and Helpers*. Portland, Oreg.: Lao Tse Press.

Molloy, W., and Paul Cadwell. 1998. *Alzheimer's Disease*. Westport, Conn.: Firefly Books.

Moody, H. R. 2000. *Aging: Concepts and Controversies*. 3rd ed. Thousand Oaks, Calif.: Pine Forge Press.

Nasar, S. 2001. *A Beautiful Mind: The Life of Mathematical Genius and Nobel Laureate John Nash*. New York: Touchstone Books.

Pert, C. B., and D. Chopra. 1999. *The Molecules of Emotion: Why You Feel the Way You Feel*. New York: Simon and Shuster.

Pinker, S. 1999. *How the Mind Works*. New York: W. W. Norton.

Prochaska, J. O., J. C. Norcross, and C. C. Diclimente. 1995. *Changing for Good*. New York: Avon Books.

Riddick, B., J. Wolfe, and D. Lumsdon. 2002. *Dyslexia: A Practical Guide for Teachers and Parents*. London: David Fulton Publishers.

Rothschild. B. 2000. *The Body Remembers: The Psychophysiology of Trauma and Trauma Treatment*. New York: W. W. Norton.

Russell, J. A. 1997. *The Psychology of Facial Expression*. New York: Cambridge University Press.

Sapolsky, R. M. 1998. *Why Zebras Don't Get Ulcers: An Updated Guide to Stress, Stress-Related Diseases, and Coping*. New York: Freeman.

Schacter, D. 2001. *The Seven Sins of Memory*. New York: Houghton Mifflin.

Schwartz, G. E. R., W. L. Simon, and D. Chopra. 2002. *The Afterlife Experiments: Breakthrough Scientific Evidence of Life after Death*. New York: Pocket Books.

Searle, J. R. 1997. *The Mystery of Consciousness*. New York: New York Review of Books.

Secunda, V. 1998. *When Madness Comes Home: Help and Hope for the Children, Siblings, and Partners of the Mentally Ill*. New York: Hyperion.

Sexton, E. 2001. *Dawkins and the Selfish Gene*. Cambridge, U.K.: Icon Books.

Siegel, B. 1998. *The World of the Autistic Child: Understanding and Treating Autistic Spectrum Disorders*. Oxford: Oxford University Press.

Skoyles, J. R., and D. Sagan. 2002. *Up from Dragons: The Evolution of Human Intelligence*. New York: McGraw-Hill Trade.

Spock, B., et al. 2001. *Dr. Spock's The First Two Years: The Emotional and Physical Needs of Children from Birth to Age Two*. Pocket Books.

Staddon, J. E. R. 2000. *The New Behaviorism: Mind, Mechanism, and Society*. New York: Psychology Press.

Strock, M. 2000. *Depression*. Bethesda, Md.: National Institute of Mental Health.

Styron, W. 1990. *Darkness Visible: A Memoir of Madness*. New York: Random House.

Temes, R., and M. Strauss, eds. 1999. *Medical Hypnosis: An Introduction and Clinial Guide*. New York: Churchill Livingstone.

Torrey, E. F. 1995. *Surviving Schizophrenia: A Manual for Families, Consumers, and Providers*. New York: HarperPerennial.

Trefil, J. S. 1997. *Are We Unique?: A Scientist Explores the Unparalleled Intelligence of the Human Mind*. New York: John Wiley.

Wright, R. 1994. *The Moral Animal*. New York: Vintage Books.

Young, G. B. 1997. *Coma and Impaired Consciousness: A Clinical Perspective*. New York: McGraw-Hill.

ZOOLOGY

Adey, W. H., and K. Loveland. 1998. *Dynamic Aquaria: Building Living Ecosystems*. 2nd ed. San Diego: Academic Press.

Alcock, J. 2001. *The Triumph of Sociobiology*. New York: Oxford University Press.

Alcock, J. 2001. *Animal Behavior: An Evolutionary Approach*. 7th ed. Sunderland, Mass.: Sinauer Associates.

Alderton, D., and B. Tanner. 1999. *Rodents of the World*. London: Blandford Press.

Alderton, D., and B. Tanner. 1998. *Wild Cats of the World (Of the World Series)*. London: Blandford.

Allen, T. B. 1999. *The Shark Almanac*. Guildford, Conn.: Lyons Press.

Anderson, D. T. 2002. *Invertebrate Zoology*. Oxford: Oxford University Press.

Anton, M., A. Turner, and F. Clark Howell. 2000. *The Big Cats and Their Fossil Relatives*. New York: Columbia University Press.

Arnold, C. 1990. *Ostriches and Other Flightless Birds*. Minneapolis: Carolrhoda Books.

Attenborough, D. 1998. *The Life of Birds*. London: BBC Books.

Attenborough, D. 1991. *The Trials of Life*. Boston: Little, Brown, and Company.

Baratay, E., E. Hardouin-Fgier, and O. Wesh. 2002. *Zoo: A History of Zoological Gardens in the West*. London: Reaktion Books.

Barkan, J. 1991. *Creatures That Glow*. New York: Doubleday.

Barrett, P. 2001. *National Geographic Dinosaurs*. Washington, D.C.: National Geographic.

Bartlett Wright, A., and R. Tory Peterson. 1998. *Peterson First Guide to Caterpillars of North America*. Boston: Houghton Mifflin.

Bauer, H.-G., V. Westhead, and P. Berthold. 2001. *Bird Migration: A General Survey*. Oxford Ornithology Series 12. New York: Oxford University Press.

Beebee, T. 2000. *Frogs and Toads*. London: Whittet Books.

Behler, J. L., and D. A. Behler. 1998. *Alligators and Crocodiles*. World Life Series. New York: Crescent Books.

Bennett, N. C., and C. G. Faukes. 2000. *African Mole Rats: Ecology and Eusociality*. New York: Cambridge University Press.

Birkhead, T. R. 2000. *Promiscuity: An Evolutionary History of Sperm Competition*. Cambridge, Mass.: Harvard University Press.

Birkhead, T. R., and A. Pape Moller. 1998. *Sperm Competition and Sexual Selection*. Academic Press.

Bishop, N. 1997. *The Secrets of Animal Flight*. Boston, Mass.: Houghton Mifflin.

Blaxland, B. 2002. *Echinoderms*. Broomall, Pa.: Chelsea House Publishing.

Borror, D. J., and R. E. White. 1998. *A Field Guide to Insects: America North of Mexico*. Peterson Field Guides. Houghton Mifflin.

Boury-Esnault, N., and K. Rutzler, eds. 1997. *Thesaurus of Sponge Morphology*. Washington D.C.: Smithsonian Institution.

Brennan, P. 2002. *Penguins and Other Flightless Birds*. Animals of the World. New York: World Book.

Brookes, M. 2002. *Fly: The Unsung Hero of Twentieth-Century Science*. New York: Ecco Press.

Budiansky, S. 1999. *The Covenant of the Wild: Why Animals Chose Domestication*. New York: William Morrow.

Burgess, N. R. H. 1993. *A Color Atlas of Medical Entomology*. New York: Chapman and Hall Medical.

Burton, R. 2001. *The World of the Hummingbird*. Toronto: Firefly Books.

Buttfield, H. 2000. *The Secret Life of Fishes*. New York: Harry N. Abrams.

Carlson, B. 1999. *Human Embryology and Developmental Biology*. 2nd ed. St. Louis: Mosby.

Cassie, B. 2000. National Audubon Society First Field Guide. *Shells*. New York: Scholastic Books.

Castro, Peter, and Michael E. Huber. 2002. *Marine Biology*. New York: McGraw-Hill College Division.

Chapman, R. F. 1999. *The Insects: Structure and Function*. Cambridge: Cambridge University Press.

Chinery, M. 2000. *Predators and Prey*. New York: Crabtree Publishing.

Clark, W. S., and B. K. Wheeler. 2001. *Peterson Field Guides: Hawks of North America*. 2nd ed. Boston: Houghton Mifflin

Clements, J. F. 2000. *Birds of the World: A Checklist*. 5th ed. California: Ibis Publishing.

Clutton-Brock, J. 1999. *A Natural History of Domesticated Mammals*. Cambridge, U.K.: Cambridge University Press.

Cogger, H. G. and R. G. Zweisel, eds. 1998. *Encyclopedia of Reptiles and Amphibians*. San Diego, Calif.: Academic Press.

Cohen, D. 1993. *The Development of Play*. 2nd ed. New York: Routledge.

Colbert, E. H., and M. Morales. 1991. *Evolution of the Vertebrates: A History of the Backboned Animals Through Time*. 4th ed. New York: Wiley-Liss.

Corbet, P. S. 1999. *Dragonflies: Behavior and Ecology of Odonata*. New York: Cornell University Press.

Counsilman, J. E. 1994. *The New Science of Swimming*. Englewood Cliffs, N.J.: Prentice-Hall.

Cox, C. B., and P. D. Moore, eds. 2000. *Biogeography: An Ecological and Evolutionary Approach*. 6th ed. Malden, Mass.: Blackwell Scientific.

Creel, S., and N. Marusha Creel. 2002. *The African Wild Dog*. Princeton, N.J.: Princeton University Press.

Czech, B. and P. R. Krausman. 2001. *The Endangered Species Act: History, Conservation Biology, and Public Policy*. Baltimore: Johns Hopkins University Press.

Daly, H. V., J. T. Doyen, A. H. Purcell, and B. Daly. 1998. *Introduction to Insect Biology and Diversity*. 2nd ed. Oxford: Oxford University Press.

Czech, B. and P. R. Krausman. 2001. *The Endangered Species Act: History, Conservation Biology, and Public Policy*. Baltimore: Johns Hopkins University Press.

Dawkins, R. 1996. *The Blind Watchmaker: Why the Evidence of Evolution Reveals a Universe Without Design*. New York: W. W. Norton.

Dawkins, R. 1990. *The Selfish Gene*. 2nd ed. Oxford: Oxford University Press.

DeBlieu, J. 1991. *Meant to be Wild: The Struggle to Save Endangered Species through Captive Breeding*. Golden, Colo.: Fulcrum Publishing.

Decker, H. 1997. *Plant Nematodes and Their Control*. Boston: Brill Academic Publishing.

Deeming, D. C., ed. 2002. *Avian Incubation: Behaviour, Environment and Evolution*. Oxford: Oxford University Press.

Diagram Group. 1999. *Animal Anatomy on File*. New York: Facts on File.

Dingle, H. 1997. *The Biology of Life on the Move*. New York: Oxford University Press.

Dinsmore, C. E., ed. 1991. *A History of Regeneration Research*. Cambridge and New York: Cambridge University Press.

Dixon, D. 2001. *In the Sky*. (Dinosaurs.) Milwaukee: Gareth Stevens.

Drickamer, L. C., E. Jacob, and S. H. Vessey. 2001. *Animal Behavior: Mechanisms, Ecology, and Evolution*. Burr Ridge, Ill.: McGraw Hill.

Dunkle, S. W. 2000. *Dragonflies through Binoculars: A Field Guide to the Dragonflies of North America*. New York: Oxford University Press.

Dyes, J. C. 1993. *Nesting Birds of the Coastal Isles: A Naturalist's Year on Galveston Bay*. Austin: University of Texas Publishing.

Eastman, J., and A. Hansen. 1998. *Birds of Forest, Yard, and Thicket*. Mechanicsburg, Pa.: Stackpole Books.

Eckert, R. 1997. *Animal Physiology*. New York: W. H. Freeman.

Elzinga, R. J. 2000. *Fundamentals of Entomology*. 5th ed. Upper Saddle River, N.J.: Prentice Hall.

Endangered Wildlife and Plants of the World. 1993. New York: Marshall Cavendish.

Enticott, J., and D. Tippling. 1997. *The Complete Reference: Seabirds of the World*. Mechanicsburg, Pa., and U.K.: Stackpole Books and New Holland Publishers.

Ericson, A. 2001. *Whales and Dolphins*. Vero Beach, Fla.: The Rourke Book Company.

Ernst, C. H. 1992. *Venomous Reptiles of North America*. Washington, D.C.: Smithsonian Institution Press.

Ernst, C. H., J. E. Lovich, and R. W. Barbour. 2000. *Turtles of the United States and Canada*. Washington, D.C.: Smithsonian Institute.

Estes, R. 1999. *The Safari Companion: A Guide to Watching African Mammals Including Hoofed Mammals, Carnivores, and Primates*. Berkeley: University of California Press.

Evans, P. G. H. 2001. *Marine Mammals: Biology and Conservation*. New York: Plenum Publishing.

Ewer, R.F. and D. Kleiman. 1998. *The Carnivores*. New York: Comstock.

Feduccia, A. 1999. *The Origin and Evolution of Birds*. New Haven, Conn.: Yale University Press.

Feldhammer. G. A., L. C. Drickamer, et al.

1999. *Mammology: Adaptation, Diversity, and Ecology*. Boston: McGraw-Hill.

Fenner, D. *Corals of Hawaii*. In press. Monterey, Calif.: Sea Challengers.

Fenner, M. F., and C. Turk. 1998. *The Conscientious Marine Aquarist: A Commonsense Handbook for Successful Saltwater Hobbyists*. Charlotte, Vt: Microcosm.

Fenton, M. B., and M. D. Tuttle. 2001. *Bats*. 2nd ed. New York: Facts on File.

Field, L. H., ed. 2001. *The Biology of Wetas, King Crickets, and Their Allies*. London: CABI Publishing.

Findley, J. S. 1993. *Bats: A Community Perspective*. New York: Cambridge University Press.

Flokens, P. 2002. *National Audubon Society Guide to Marine Mammals of the World*. New York: Knopf.

Foelix, R. F. 1996. *Biology of Spiders*. 2nd ed. New York and Oxford, U.K.: Oxford University Press.

Forshaw, J., and D. Kirshner. 1998. *Encyclopedia of Birds*. San Diego: Academic Press.

Fortey, R. 1999. *Life: A Natural History of the First Four Billion Years of Life on Earth*. Vancouver: Vintage Books.

Gadagkar, R. 2001. *Survival Strategies: Cooperation and Conflict in Animal Societies*. Cambridge, Mass.: Harvard University Press.

Ganeri, A. 1995. *Prickly and Poisonous: The Deadly Defenses of Nature's Strangest Animals and Plants*. Pleasantville, N.J.: Reader's Digest.

Gauthreaux, S. A., Jr. 1997. *Animal Migration, Navigation, and Orientation*. San Diego, Calif.: Academic Press.

Geber, M. A. 1999. *Gender and Sexual Dimorphism in Flowering Plants*. New York: Springer Verlag.

Geist, V., and M. H. Francis. 2001. *Antelope Country: Pronghorns—The Last Americans*. Iola, Wis.: Krause Publications.

George, T. C. 2001. *Jellies: The Life of Jellyfish*. Brookfield, Conn.: Millbrook Press.

Gittleman, A. M., and O. M. Amin. 2001. *Guess What Came To Dinner?: Parasites and Your Health*. New York: Avery Penguin Putnam.

Givens, D. I., E. Owens, and R. F. E. Axford, eds. 2000. *Forage Evaluation in Ruminant Nutrition*. New York: CABI Publishing.

Glassburg, J. 2001. *Butterflies through Binoculars*. New York: Oxford University Press.

Glen, W. ed. 1993. *The Mass-Extinction Debates: How Science Works in a Crisis*. Stanford, Calif.: Stanford University Press.

Goodenough, J. et al. 1993. *Perspectives on Animal Behavior*. New York: John Wiley.

Gordon, D. G. 1996. *The Compleat Cockroach*. Berkeley, Calif.: Ten Speed Press.

Gowell, E. T. 2000. *Whales and Dolphins: What Have They in Common?* New York: Franklin Watts.

Grasshoppers and Other Leaping Insects. 2001. Animals of the World. World Book Encyclopedia. Chicago: World Book.

Green, H. W. 1997. *Snakes. The Evolution of Mystery in Nature*. Berkeley, Calif.: University of California Press.

Grenard, S. 1999. *Handbook of Alligators and Crocodiles*. Melbourne, Fla.: Krieger Publishing.

Gribbin, J. 2002. *Science: A History 1543–2001*. New York: Penguin Putnam.

Griffin, D, R. 1986. *Listening in the Dark: The Acoustic Orientation of Bats and Men*. Ithaca, N.Y.: Cornell University Press.

Groves, C. P. 2001. *Primate Taxonomy*. Washington, D.C.: Smithsonian Institution.

Halliday, T., ed. 1994. *Animal Behavior*. Norman: University of Oklahoma Press.

Hamlett, W. C., ed. 1999. *Sharks, Skates, and Rays: The Biology of Elasmobranch Fishes*. Baltimore: Johns Hopkins University Press.

Hancock, J. 2000. *Herons of North America*. New York: Academic Press.

Hansell, M. 2000. *Bird Nests and Construction Behaviour*. Cambridge, U.K.: Cambridge University Press.

Harrison, P. 1997. *Seabirds of the World: A Photographic Guide*. Princeton, N.J.: Princeton University Press.

Harvey, B. 2002. *Arthropods (The Animal Kingdom)*. Philadelphia: Chelsea House Publishing.

Hawkins, D. R. 1996. *Goodbye Scorpion; Farewell, Black Widow Spider*. Sedona, Ark.: Veritas.

Hayman, P., J. Marchant, and T. Prater. 1991. *Shorebirds: An Identification Guide*. Boston: Houghton Mifflin.

Haynes, B. N., and R. F. Kahrs. 2001. *Keeping Livestock Healthy: A Veterinary Guide to Horses, Cattle, Pigs, Goats, and Sheep*. 4th ed. North Adams, Mass.: Storey Books.

Heatwole, H. 1999. *Sea Snakes*. 2nd ed. Malabar, Fla.: Krieger.

Helfman, G. S, et al. 1997. *The Diversity of Fishes*. Oxford: Blackwell Science.

Heming, B. S. 2003. *Insect Development and Evolution*. Ithaca, N.Y.: Cornell University Press.

Hickman, C. P. 2000. *Integrated Principles of Zoology*. 11th ed. New York: McGraw-Hill.

Hildebrand, M. 1995. *Analysis of Vertebrate Structure*. 4th ed. New York: John Wiley.

Hoff, M. K. 2002. *Mimicry and Camouflage*. Buffalo, N.Y.: Creative Education.

Hofrichter, R., ed. 2000. *Amphibians: The World of Frogs, Toads, Salamanders, and Newts*. Toronto: Firefly Books.

Holldobler, B., and Wilson, E. O. 1990. *The Ants*. Cambridge, Mass.: Belknap Press of Harvard University Press.

Holmes, T. 2003. *Prehistoric Flying Reptiles: The Pterosaurs*. Berkeley Heights, N.J.: Enslow Publishers.

Hooper, J. N. A., and R. W. N. van Soest, eds. 2002. *Systema Porifera: A Guide to the Classification of Sponges*. New York: Plenum Press.

Hubbell, S. 1993. *Broadsides from the Other Orders: A Book of Bugs*. New York: Random House.

Insects and Spiders of the World. 2003. Tarrytown, N.Y.: Marshall Cavendish.

Jacobs, M. E. 1999. *Mr. Darwin Misread Miss Peacock's Mind: A New Look at Mate Selection in Light of Lessons From Nature*. Goshen, Indiana: NatureBooks.

Janda Presnall, J. 1993. *Animals That Glow*. New York: Franklin Watts.

Jordan, R., and J. Pattison. 1999. *African Parrots*. Surrey, B.C.: Hancock House Publishing.

Kaner, E., and P. Stephens. 1999. *Animal Defenses: How Animals Protect Themselves*. Tonowando, N.Y.: Kids Can Press.

Kaplan, E. H., and S. L. Kaplan. 1999. *A Field Guide to Coral Reefs: Caribbean and Florida*. Peterson Field Guides. New York: Houghton Mifflin Company.

Kardong, K. V. 2001. *Vertebrates: Comparative Anatomy, Function, Evolution*. Maidenhead, U.K.: McGraw-Hill Education.

Kaufman, K. 1996. *Lives of North American Birds*. New York: Houghton Mifflin.

Kissinge, K., and W. Kruten. 1997. *All the Colors We Are: The Story of How We Get Our Skin Color*. St. Paul: Redleaf Press.

Kitchener, A. 1998. *The Natural History of the Wild Cats*. New York: Comstock Cornell.

Laland, K., and G. Brown. 2002. *Sense and Nonsense*. Oxford, Oxford University Press.

Lambert, D., D. Naish, and L. Wyse. 2001. *Dinosaur Encyclopedia*. New York: Dorling Kindersley Publishing.

Landman, N. H., ed. 2001. *Pearls: A Natural History*. New York: Harry N. Abrams.

Langton, T. 1997. *Snakes and Lizards*. London: Whittet Books Ltd.

Lawrence, J. F., A. M. Hastings, M. J. Dallwitz, T. A. Paine, E. J. Zurcher. 1999. *Beetles of the World: Descriptions, Illustrations, and Information*. CD-Rom. Collingwood, Australia: CSIRO.

Levi, H. W., and L. R. Levi. 1996. *Spiders and Their Kin*. New York: St. Martin's Press.

Levy, C. K. 1999. *The Battle of the Species on Land, at Sea and in the Air*. New York: W. H. Freeman.

Livi-Bacci, M. 2001. *A Concise History of World Population: An Introduction to Population Processes*. 3rd ed. Boston: Blackwell Publishers.

Lohmann, K. J. 1992. How sea turtles navigate. *Scientific American* 266 (January): 100–104.

Losick, R., and D. Kaiser. 1997. Why and how bacteria communicate. *Scientific American* (Feb.).

Lovett, S. 1997. *Extremely Weird Animal Disguises*. Emeryville, Calif.: Avalon Travel.

Lowenstein, F. and S. Lechner. 1999. *Bugs: Insects, Spiders, Centipedes, Millipedes, and Other Closely Related Arthropods*. Black Dog and Leventhal Publishing.

MacDonald, David. 1995. *The Encyclopedia of Mammals*. New York: Checkmark Books.

MacDonald, G. 2001. *Space, Time and Life: The Science of Biogeography*. Somerset, N.J.: John Wiley.

MacLeod, N., and P. L. Forey, eds. 2002. *Morphology, Shape, and Phylogenetics.* Florence, Ky.: Taylor and Francis.

Madge, S., and H. Burn. 1992. *Waterfowl: Identification Guide to the Ducks, Geese, and Swans of the World.* Boston: Houghton Mifflin.

Malakhov, V. V., and W. Duane Hope, ed. 1994. *Nematodes: Structure, Development, Classification, and Phylogeny.* Washington, D.C.: Smithsonian Institution Press.

Manning, A., and M. S. Dawkins. 1998. *An Introduction to Animal Behavior.* Cambridge, U.K.: Cambridge University Press.

Margulis, L. and K. V. Schwartz. 1998. *Five Kingdoms: An Illustrated Guide to the Phlya on Earth.* New York: W. H. Freeman.

Martin, J., and J. Hamlyn. 1997. *Living Fossils.* New York: Crown Publishers.

Mattison, C. 1998. *Lizards of the World.* London: Sterling Publications.

Mauseth, J. D. 1998. *An Introduction to Plant Biology.* 3rd ed. Sudbury, Mass.: Jones and Bartlett Publishers.

Maynard, T. 1999. *Primates: Apes, Monkeys, and Prosimians.* New York: Franklin Watts.

McGavin, G. C. 2000. *Insects, Spiders, and Other Terrestrial Arthropods.* New York: DK Publishing.

McGowan, C. 1997. *The Raptor and the Lamb: Predators and Prey in the Living World.* New York: Henry Holt.

McGrew, W. C., ed. 1996. *Great Ape Societies.* New York: Cambridge University Press.

Merrick, P. 1998. *Walking Sticks.* Naturebooks. Eden Prairie, Minn.: The Child's World.

Merrick, P. *Lice.* 2000. Naturebooks. Eden Prairie, Minn.: The Child's World.

Michener, C. D. 2000. *Bees of the World.* Baltimore: Johns Hopkins University Press.

Miller, S. S. 1998. *From Flower Flies to Mosquitoes.* New York: Franklin Watts.

Miller, S. S. 1999. *Perching Birds of North America.* New York: Franklin Watts.

Miller, S. S, et al. 2002. *Rabbits, Pikas, and Hares.* London: Franklin Watts.

Miller, S. S., J. Gonzales, and S. Savage. 1999. *Horses and Rhinos: What They Have in Common.* New York: Franklin Watts.

Mitchell, R. T., A. Durenceau, and H. Spencer Moore, J., and R. Overhill. 2001. *An Introduction to the Invertebrates.* Cambridge, U.K.: Cambridge University Press.

Moss, C. 1997. *Little Big Ears: The Story of Ely.* New York: Simon and Schuster.

Moyal, A. M. 2001. *The Platypus: The Extraordinary Story of How a Curious Creature Baffled the World.* Washington, D.C.: Smithsonian Institute Press.

Moyles, J. R., ed. 1994. *The Excellence of Play.* Philadelphia: Open University Press.

Naskrecki, P. 2000. *Katydids of Costa Rica. Volume 1, Systematics and Bioacoustics of the Cone-Head Katydids.* Philadelphia: The Orthopterists Society.

Nassau, K. 2001. *The Physics and Chemistry of Color.* 2nd ed. New York: Wiley-Interscience.

Nelson, W. H., ed. 1991. *Physical Methods for Micro-organism Detection.* Boca Raton, Fla.: CRC Press.

Nowak, R. M. 1999. *Walker's Mammals of the World.* 2 vols. 6th ed. Baltimore: Johns Hopkins University Press.

Neuweiler, G. 2000. *The Biology of Bats.* Oxford: Oxford University Press.

Nybakken, J. W. 2000. *Marine Biology: An Ecological Approach.* 5th ed. New York: Benjamin/Cummings.

Opler, P. A. 1998. *Peterson First Guide to Butterflies and Moths.* Boston: Houghton Mifflin.

Owen-Smith, R. N. 2002. *Adaptive Herbivore Ecology.* Cambridge, U.K.: Cambridge University Press.

Palmer, D., et al. 1999. *Encyclopedia of Dinosaurs and Prehistoric Creatures.* New York: Simon and Schuster.

Parker, S. and A. Ganeri, Wallace, H. 2001. *Survival and Change: Life Processes.* Crystal Lake, Ill.: Heinemann Library.

Pascoe, E, and D. Kuhn. 2002. *Animals Grow New Parts.* Milwaukee, Wis.: G. Stevens.

Paten, D. H. 1999. *Prairie Dogs.* Boston: Houghton Mifflin.

Paul, G. S. 2002. *Dinosaurs of the Air: The Evolution and Loss of Flight in Dinosaurs and Birds.* Baltimore: Johns Hopkins University Press.

Pechenek, J. 2000. *Biology of the Invertebrates.* Boston: McGraw-Hill.

Pepperberg, I. M. 1999. *The Alex Studies: Cognitive and Communicative Abilities of Gray Parrots.* Cambridge, Mass.: Harvard University Press.

Pough, F. H., et al. 2001. *Herpetology.* 2nd ed. Englewood Cliffs, N.J.: Prentice Hall.

Pough, H., F. C. M. Janis, and J. B. Heiser. 2001. *Vertebrate Life.* Englewood Cliffs, N.J.: Prentice-Hall.

Prete, F. R., L. E. Hurd, P. H. Wells, and H. Wells. *The Praying Mantids.* Baltimore: Johns Hopkins University Press, 2000.

Primack, R. B. 2000. *A Primer of Conservation Biology.* Sunderland, Mass.: Sinauer Associates.

Pringle, L. 1997. *Elephant Woman: Cynthia Moss Explores the World of Elephants.* New York: Atheneum.

Prota, G. 1992. *Melanins and Melanogenesis.* San Diego: Academic Press.

Quicke, D. L. J. 1997. *Parasitic Wasps.* Boca Raton, Fla.: Chapman and Hall.

Reptiles and Amphibians. 2002. Tarrytown, N.Y.: Marshall Cavendish.

Rey, L. V. 2001. *Extreme Dinosaurs.* San Francisco: Chronicle Books.

Romer, A. S. 1997. *The Vertebrate Body.* Florence, Italy: International Thomson Publishing.

Romoser, W. S., and J. G. Stoffolano Jr. 1998. *The Science of Entomology.* 4th ed. Boston: WCB/McGraw Hill.

Ruppert, E. E., and R. D. Barnes. 1994. *Invertebrate Zoology.* 6th ed. Fort Worth: Saunders College Publishing.

Sandford, G. 2000. *Aquarium Owner's Guide: The Complete Illustrated Reference Book for the Home Aquarium.* New York: Dorling Kindersley.

Schuh, R. T. 1999. *Systematics: Principles and Applications.* Ithaca, N.Y.: Cornell University Press.

Schuh, R. T., and J. A. Slater. 1995. *True Bugs of the World (Hemiptera: Heteroptera): Classification and Natural History.* New York: Comstock Publishing Associates, Cornell University Press.

Schultz, S. A., and M. J. Schultz. 1998. *The Tarantula Keeper's Guide.* New York: Barron.

Schweid, R. 1999. *The Cockroach Papers: A Compendium of History and Lore.* Four Walls Eight Windows.

Scott, J. P., and J. L. Fuller, eds. 1998. *Genetics and the Social Behavior of the Dog.* Chicago: University of Chicago Press.

Shipman, Pat. 1998. *Taking Wing: Archaeopteryx and the Evolution of Bird Flight.* New York: Simon and Schuster.

Sibley, D. 2000. *The Sibley Guide to Birds.* New York: Knopf/National Audubon Society.

Slater, P. J. B. 1999. *Essentials of Animal Behavior.* Cambridge, U.K.: Cambridge University Press.

Soffer, R. 2002. *Mimicry and Camouflage in Nature.* Mineola, N. Y.: Dover Publications.

Stafford, P. 2000. *Snakes.* London: Natural History Museum/Washington D.C.: Smithsonian Institution Press.

Stevens, K. 2000. *Fleas.* Naturebooks. Chanhassen, Minn.: Child's World.

Taber, Stephen Welton. 2000. *Fire Ants.* College Station: Texas A&M University Press.

Tatham, B. 2002. *How Animals Shed their Skin.* London: Franklin Watts.

Thomas, J. 2002. *Echolocation in Bats and Dolphins.* Chicago: University of Chicago Press.

Thorpe, R. S., W. Wüster, and A. Malhotra. 1997. *Venomous Snakes: Ecology, Evolution, and Snakebite.* Oxford, U.K.: Clarendon Press.

Tollrian, R., and C. D. Harvell. 1998. *The Ecology and Evolution of Inducible Defenses.* Princeton, N.J.: Princeton University Press.

Tsonis, P. A. 1996. *Limb Regeneration.* New York: Cambridge University Press.

Vander Meer, R. K., et al, eds. 1998. *Pheromone Communication in Social Insects: Ants, Wasps, Bees, and Termites.* Westview Studies in Insect Biology. Boulder, Colo.: Westview Press.

Vaughn, T. A., J. M. Ryan, and N. J. Czaplewski. 2000. *Mammology.* 4th ed. Philadelphia: Saunders College Publishing.

Vogel, S., and S. T. Betty. 1996. *Life in Moving Fluids.* Princeton, N.J.: Princeton University Press.

Vrba, E. S., and G. B. Schaller, eds. 2000. *Antelopes, Deer and Relatives: Fossil Record, Behavioral Ecology, Systematics, and Conservation.* New Haven, Conn.: Yale University Press.

Waldbauer, G. 1998. *The Handy Bug Answer Book.* Detroit: Visible Ink.

Walker, E. P., and R. M. Nowak. 1999. *Walker's Mammals of the World.* Vol 1. Baltimore and London: The Johns Hopkins University Press.

Wall, R. and D. Shearer. 2001. *Veterinary Ectoparasites: Biology, Pathology, and Control.* 6th ed. Malden, Mass.: Blackwell Science.

Wallace, R. L. and W. K. Taylor. 1996. *Invertebrate Zoology: A Laboratory Manual.* 5th ed. New Jersey: Prentice Hall.

Walther, F. R., E. C. Mungall, and G. A. Grau. 2002. *Gazelles and Their Relatives: A Study in Territorial Behavior.* Norwich, N.Y.: Knovell.

Weinberg, S. 1999. *A Fish Caught in Time: The Search for the Coelacanth.* London: Fourth Estate.

White, R. E. 1998. *Beetles: A Field Guide to the Beetles of North America.* Boston: Houghton Mifflin.

Willmer, P., G. Stone, and I. Johnson. 2000. *Environmental Physiology of Animals.* Oxford: Blackwell Science.

Wilson. E. O. 2000. *Sociobiology: The New Synthesis.* 25th anniversary ed. Cambridge, Mass.: Harvard University Press.

Withers, P. C. 1992. *Comparative Animal Physiology.* Fort Worth, Tex.: Saunders.

Wright, L. 1999. *Twins and What They Tell Us About Who We Are.* Hoboken, N.J.: John Wiley.

Wyatt, T. D. 2002. *Pheromones and Animal Behavior: Communication by Smell and Taste.* Cambridge, U.K.: Cambridge University Press.

Yang, M., et al. 1999. *High School Biology: Kaplan Essential Review.* New York: Simon and Schuster.

Yaukey, D., and D. Anderton. 2001. *The Study of Human Population.* Prospect Heights, Ill.: Waveland Press.

Zim. 2001. *Butterflies and Moths: A Guide to the More Common American Species.* N.Y.: St. Martin's Press.

Zohary, D. 2001. *Domestication of Plants in the Old World: The Origin and Spread of Cultivated Plants in West Asia, Europe, and the Nile Valley.* New York: Oxford University Press.

Zug, G. R., L. J. Vitt, and J. P. Caldwell. 2001. *Herpetology: An Introductory Biology of Amphibians and Reptiles.* 2nd ed. London: Academic Press.

BIOGRAPHIES

Allen, G. E. 1978. *Thomas Hunt Morgan: The Man and His Science.* Princeton, N.J.: Princeton University Press.

Barter, J. 2003. *Jonas Salk.* Chicago: Lucent.

Baumler, Ernest. 1984. *Paul Ehrlich: Scientist for Life.* New York: Holmes and Meier Publishers.

Bertsch McGrayne, S. 2001. *Nobel Prize Women in Science: Their Lives, Struggles, and Momentous Discoveries.* 2nd ed. Washington, D.C.: Joseph Henry Press.

Bickel, L. 1996. *Florey: The Man Who Made Penicillin.* Melbourne: Melbourne University Press.

Birch, B., and F. MacDonald. 2001. *Louis Pasteur: Father of Modern Medicine* (Giants of Science). Woodbridge, Conn.: Blackbirch Marketing.

Blunt, W., et al. 2002. *The Compleat Naturalist: A Life of Linnaeus.* Princeton, N.J.: Princeton University Press.

Brooks, P. 1972. *The House of Life: Rachel Carson at Work.* Boston: Houghton Mifflin.

Darwin, F., ed. 2000. *The Autobiography of Charles Darwin.* Great Minds Series. Amherst, New York: Prometheus Books.

Defelipe, J. 1997. *Cajal on the Cerebral Cortex.* Translation of the complete writings. Oxford: Oxford University Press.

Dennett, D. C. 1996. *Darwin's Dangerous Idea: Evolution and the Meanings of Life.* New York: Touchstone Books.

Dick, S. J. 2001. *Life on Other Worlds: The 20th Century Extraterrestrial Life Debate.* New York: Cambridge University Press.

Dubos, R. J., and T. D. Brock. 1998. *Pasteur and Modern Science.* Washington: ASM Press.

Edelson, E. 2001. *Gregor Mendel and the Root of Genetics.* Oxford: Oxford University Press.

Fossey, D. 1983. *Gorillas in the Mist.* New York: Mariner Books.

Freeman, M. 1994. *Always, Rachel: The Letters of Rachel Carson and Dorothy Freeman, 1952–1964: The Story of a Remarkable Friendship.* Boston: Beacon Press.

Goujon, P. 2001. *From Biotechnnology to Genomes: The Meaning of the Double Helix.* River Edge, N.J.: World Scientific Publishing Company.

Gould, S. J. 1979. *Ever Since Darwin: Reflections in Natural History.* New York: W. W. Norton.

Harrison, A. A. 1997. *After Contact: The Human Response to Extraterrestrial Life.* Cambridge, Mass.: Perseus Press.

Hening, R. M. 2000. *The Monk in the Garden: The Lost and Found Genius of Gregor Mendel.* Boston: Houghton Mifflin.

Jakab, E. A. M. 2000. *Louis Pasteur: Hunting Killer Germs.* New York: McGraw-Hill Trade.

Kay, L. 1993. *The Molecular Vision of Life: Caltech, the Rockefeller Foundation, and the Rise of New Biology.* New York: Oxford University Press.

Koerner, L., 1999. *Linnaeus: Nature and Nation.* Cambridge, Mass., and London: Harvard University Press.

Kohler, R. 1994. *Lords of the Fly: Drosophila Genetics and the Experimental Life.* Chicago: University of Chicago Press.

Lennox, J. G. 2000. *Aristotle's Philosophy of Biology: Studies in the Origins of Life Science* (Series in Philosophy and Biology). Cambridge, U.K.: Cambridge University Press.

Maddox, B. 2002. *Rosalind Franklin and the Discovery of the Double Helix Structure of DNA.* London: HarperCollins.

Marrin, A. 2002. *Dr. Jenner and the Speckled Monster: The Search for the Smallpox Vaccine.* New York: Dutton Books.

McPherson, S. S. 2001. *Jonas Salk: Conquering Polio.* Minneapolis, Minn.: Lerner.

Medawar, J. S. 1990. *A Very Decided Preference: Life with Peter Medawar.* New York: W. W. Norton.

Medawar, P. B. 1999. *Memoirs of a Thinking Radish.* Oxford: Oxford University Press.

Mullis, K. 1998. *Dancing Naked in the Mind Field.* London: Bloomsbury.

Parker, B. R. 1998. *Alien Life: The Search for Extra-terrestrials and Beyond.* Cambridge, Mass.: Perseus.

Pasteur, L., and J. Lister. 1996. *Germ Theory and Its Applications to Medicine & on the Antiseptic Principle of the Practice of Surgery.* Great Minds. Amherst, N.Y.: Prometheus Books.

Petechuk, D. 1995. Ivan Petrovich Pavlov. In *Notable Twentieth Century Scientists*, edited by Emily McMurray. Washington, D.C.: Gale Research.

Ramón y Cajal, S. (1897) 1999. *Advice for a Young Investigator.* Cambridge, Mass.: MIT Press.

Schaller, G. B., and T. L. Matthews. 1998. *Light Shining Through the Mist: Dian Fossey.* Washington, D.C.: National Geographic Society.

Senker, C. 2002. *Rosalind Franklin (Scientists Who Made History).* Austin: Raintree/Steck Vaughn.

Shapiro, M. J. 1996 *Charles Drew: Lifesaving Scientist.* New York: Raintree/Steck Vaughn.

St. Pierre, Stephanie. 1993. *Gertrude Elion: Master Chemist (Masters of Invention).* Vero Beach, Fla: The Rourke Book Company.

Tocci, S. 2002. *Alexander Fleming: The Man Who Discovered Penicillin.* Berkeley Heights, N.J.: Enslow.

Todes, D. 2000. *Ivan Pavlov: Exploring the Animal Machine (Oxford Portraits in Science).* New York: Oxford University Press.

Tracy, K. 2001. *Barbara McClintock: Pioneering Geneticist.* Unlocking the Secrets of Science. Bear, Del.: Mitchell Lane Publishers.

Trice, L. 2000. *Charles Drew: Pioneer of Blood Plasma.* New York: McGraw-Hill Professional Publishing.

Watson, J. D. 1998. *The Double Helix: A Personal Account of the Discovery of the Structure of DNA.* Scribner Classics. New York: Simon and Schuster.

Weber, B., and A. Vedder. *In the Kingdom of Gorillas: The Quest to Save Rwanda's Mountain Gorillas.* London: Aurum Press, 2002.

Wilson, E. O. 2002. *The Future of Life.* New York: Knopf.

Zannos, Susan. 2002. *Paul Ehrlich and Modern Drug Development (Unlocking the Secrets of Science).* Bear, Del.: Mitchell Lane.

OTHER USEFUL RESOURCES

MAGAZINES

Magazines and journals often have the most current and interesting information about topics in the life sciences. This list of titles may be useful. If the magazines are not available from a local library, contact the publisher directly to obtain a subscription or single copies.

Audubon
700 Broadway
New York, New York 10003

BioScience
730 11th Street NW
Washington, D.C. 20001-4521

Canadian Geographic
39 McArthur Avenue
Vanier, Ontario K1L 8L7

Discover
Walt Disney Magazine Publishing Group
114 5th Avenue
New York, New York 10011

International Wildlife
8925 Leesburg Pike
Vienna, Virginia 22184

National Geographic
1145 17th Street NW
Washington, D.C. 20036-4688

Natural History
American Museum of Natural History
Central Park West at 79th Street
New York, New York 10024

Sea Frontiers
4600 Rickenbacker Causeway
Miami, Florida 33149

Science News
Science Service Incorporated
1719 N Street NW
Washington, D.C. 20036-2888

Scientific American
415 Madison Avenue
New York, New York 10017

Wildlife Conservation Magazine
Bronx Zoo, Wildlife Conservation Park,
Bronx, New York 10460

Museums, aquariums, and zoos

As well as places of interest to visit, many museums, aquariums, zoos, and other institutions, such as botanic gardens and arboretums (places where trees and shrubs are grown and studied), are also research institutions that have scientists or other staff who can answer questions about topics that fall within their field.

If the reader has an unanswered question, he or she might try calling their local natural history museum, aquarium, zoo, or botanic garden. Following are the addresses and telephone numbers of some of the more well known of these institutions across the country.

The East
New England Aquarium
Central Wharf
Boston, Massachusetts 02110
(617) 973-5200

American Museum of Natural History
Central Park West at 79th Street
New York, New York 10024
(212) 873-1300

Gray's Reef National Marine Sanctuary
10 Ocean Science Circle, Savannah
Georgia 31411
(912) 598-2345

Academy of the Natural Sciences
1900 Benjamin Franklin Parkway
Philadelphia, Pennsylvania 19103
(215) 299-1000

Morehead Planetarium and Science Center
Chapel Hill
North Carolina 27599
(919) 962-1236

National Aquarium in Baltimore
Pier 3, 501 E. Pratt St., Baltimore
Maryland 21202-3194
(410) 576-3800

The South
Texas Memorial Museum of Natural History
2400 Trinity Street, Austin, Texas 78705
(512) 471-1604.

National Museum of Natural History
Smithsonian Institution, Constitution Avenue at 10th Street, Washington, D.C. 20560
(202) 357-2700

Florida Keys National Marine Sanctuary
P.O. Box 500368, Marathon, Florida 33050
(305) 743-2437

The Florida Aquarium
701 Channelside Drive, Tampa,
Florida 33602-5600
(813) 273-4020

Kennedy Space Center
Cape Canaveral, Florida, Kennedy Space Center,
Florida 32899-0001
(321) 452-2121

The Living Seas
Walt Disney World Epcot Center
Lake Buena Vista, FL 32830
(407) 560-7688

The Midwest
Field Museum of Natural History
Roosevelt Road at Lake Shore Drive
Chicago, Illinois 60605
(312) 922-9410

The West
Arizona-Sonora Desert Museum
Route 9, Box 900, Tucson, Arizona 85740
(602) 883-1380

Denver Museum of Natural History
2001 Colorado Boulevard
Denver, Colorado 80205
(303) 370-6400

Colorado's Ocean Journey
700 Water Street, Denver, Colorado 80211
(303) 561-4450

The Pacific Region
The San Diego Zoo
2920 Zoo Drive
San Diego, California 92103
(619) 231-1515

Monterey Bay Aquarium
886 Cannery Row
Monterey, California 98940-1085
(408) 648-4800

Monterey Bay National Marine Sanctuary
299 Foam Street, Monterey, California 93940
(831) 647-4201

Birch Aquarium at Scripps IO, UCSD
9500 Gilman Drive, Dept. 0207
La Jolla, California 92093-0207
(858) 534-4086

Oregon Coast Aquarium
2820 SE Ferry Slip Road
Newport, Oregon 97365-9722
(541) 867-3474

The Hawaiian Islands Humpback Whale National Marine Sanctuary
Maui Office Headquarters
726 South Kihei Road, Kihei, Hawaii 96753
(808) 879-2818

Olympic Coast National Marine Sanctuary
138 West First Street,
Port Angeles, Washington 98362
(360) 457-6622

Sea Life Park Hawaii
41–202 Kalanianaole Highway, Suite 7
Waimanalo, Hawaii 96795-1897
(808) 259-7933

SeaWorld San Diego
500 Sea World Drive, San Diego
California 92109-7904
(619) 222-6363

WEBSITES

ANATOMY

Animal Anatomy and Physiology
http://www.hoflink.com/~house/Animal. html
Human Anatomy Online
http://www.innerbody.com/htm/body.html
Plant Anatomy and Glossary
http://dallas.tamu.edu/weeds/anat.html
WebAnatomy
http://www.gen.umn.edu/faculty_staff/ jensen/1135/webanatomy/

ARTIFICIAL LIFE

Artificial Life: Alife in Action.
http://www.webslave.dircon.co.uk/alife/ intro.html
Craig Reynolds' Boids
http://www.red3d.com/cwr/boids/
Game of Life
http://www.math.com/students/wonders/ life/life.html
Tierra
http://www.isd.atr.co.jp/~ray/pubs/

BIOCHEMISTRY

Glossary of Biochemistry and Molecular Biology
http://www.portlandpress.com/pp/books/ online/glick/default.htm
Metabolic Pathways of Biochemistry
http://www.gwu.edu/~mpb/
The Biology Project
http://www.biology.arizona.edu/

BIOETHICS

The American Journal of Bioethics
http://bioethics.net/
Bioethics Discussion Pages
http://www-hsc.usc.edu/~mbernste/
The Center for Bioethics and Human Dignity (CBHD)
http://www.cbhd.org/

BOTANY

Botany database, Natural History Museum, London, England
http://www.nhm.ac.uk/botany/databases/
Botany Encyclopedia of Plants and Botanical Dictionary
http://www.botany.com/

Internet Directory for Botany
http://www.botany.net/IDB/botany.html
National Museum of Natural History
http://www.nmnh.si.edu/departments/ botany.html

ECOLOGY

Ecology Center
http://www.ecocenter.org/
Ecology.com—An Ecological Source of Information
http://www.ecology.com/
The Ecology WWW Page
http://www.people.fas.harvard.edu/~brach /Ecology-WWW.html
Exploring the Environment
http://www.cotf.edu/ete/
U.S. Geological Survey
http://www.usgs.gov

EVOLUTION

Evolution
http://www.pbs.org/wgbh/evolution/
Internet History of Science Sourcebook
http://www.fordham.edu/halsall/science/ sciencesbook.html

IMMUNOLOGY

The Biology Project, University of Arizona
http://www.biology.arizona.edu/immunology /tutorials/immunology/main.html
Immunology Index
http://www.keratin.com/am/amindex. shtml
Immunology Link Home Page
http://www.immunologylink.com/
Microbiology and Immunology Online
http://www.med.sc.edu:85/book/ welcome.htm

MEDICINE

Alternative Medicine Home Page
http://www.pitt.edu/~cbw/altm.html
Institute of Medicine
http://www.iom.edu/
Health A to Z Home Page
http://www.healthatoz.com/
U.S. National Library of Medicine
http://www.nlm.nih.gov/

MICROBIOLOGY/GENETICS

Genetics Education Center
http://www.kumc.edu/gec/
Genetics Glossary
http://helios.bto.ed.ac.uk/bto/glossary/
Genetic Science Learning Center
http://gslc.genetics.utah.edu/

PSYCHOLOGY/HUMAN DEVELOPMENT/ MENTAL DISORDERS

Encyclopedia of Psychology —Psychology Websites
http://www.psychology.org/
Internet Mental Health
http://www.mentalhealth.com/
Psychology Virtual Library
http://www.clas.ufl.edu/users/ gthursby/psi/
Social Psychology Network
http://www.socialpsychology.org/

ZOOLOGY/ NATURAL HISTORY

Amphiaweb
http://www.elib.cs.berkeley.edu/aw/ index.html
Biological Sciences Education Resources (BioEd)
http://www.ciw.uni-karlsruhe.de/kopien/ bio-faq.html
Cornell University Museum of Vertebrates
http://www.cumv.cornell.edu/
ENature.com
http://www.enature.com
Insect Biology and Ecology: A Primer
http://www.nysaes.cornell.edu/ent/ biocontrol/info/primer.html
Museum of Vertebrate Zoology, University of California
http://www.mip.berkeley.edu/mvz
Natural History Museums
http://www.lib.washington.edu/sla /natmus.html
Search for Extraterrestrial Intelligence: SETI@home
http://setiathome.ssl.berkeley.edu/
Vertebrate Zoology Home Page
http://www.lions.odu.edu/~kkilburn/ vzhome.html
Welcome to BioTech
http://biotech.icmb.utexas.edu/
World Wildlife Fund Kid's Stuff
http://www.worldwildlife.org/fun/kids.cfm

SUBJECT INDEXES

■ AGRICULTURE

A

Agricultural Revolution 1:39–40
agriculture 1:37–41
  aquaculture 1:124–125
  cereal grains *see* grains
  and deforestation 4:492
  environmental diseases from 5:*626*
  fertilizers *see* fertilizers
  Green Revolution 1:40; 5:718
  and pesticides 9:1287
  history 1:*37*–40
  hydroponics 7:924–925
  livestock farming
    organic 9:1243
    use of antibiotics 9:*1245*
  organic 1:40; 9:*1242*–1243, 1246–*1247*
    see also permaculture
  and populations 1:41
  scientific developments 1:40
  seaweed farming 1:125
  shade 4:492
  sustainable 9:1279
  in the taiga 12:1590
  use of antibiotics 9:*1245*
  waste disposal 12:1697–1698
  see also pesticides
aquaculture 1:124–125
arsenic, for pest control 1:41

B

beets 8:1013; 11:1445
biological control 2:195–196;
  10:1350–1351
  using bacteria 7:960; 9:1288
  of beetles 7:960
  blight
    chestnut 9:1265; 10:1324
    corn 6:800
    potato 8:*1138*; 10:1321, *1322*
  bloat 10:1321
Botrytis cinerea (noble rot) 10:*1320*,
  1321–1322
breeding, selective *see* selective breeding

C

cereals *see* grains; grasses, cereal
chard, Swiss 8:1013–1014
clear-cutting 4:491, 492
clubroot disease 10:1321
coco 8:1014
copper carbonate 10:1323
copper sulfate 10:1323
corn (maize) 1:78; 4:*545*; 6:793
  flowers 6:758
  genetically modified 6:810
  hybrid varieties 1:40; 11:1481
  products from 9:1161
  transpiration and water economy 8:1025
crops
  frost-resistant 8:1131
  fruit 10:1328
  fungal diseases 10:*1320*, 1321–1322

genetic engineering and 6:809–*811*;
  9:1244
  Flavr Savr tomatoes 2:227; 6:765, 794,
    809
  for nitrogen fixation 9:1219
  resistance to pesticides 9:1247
leaf crops 8:1013–1014
  leguminous 9:1219; 10:1321
  new varieties 11:1481
  origins of growing 1:38; 4:545–546
  pest control 10:1346–1347
    see also biological control; pesticides
  pests of *see* pests
  root and tuber crops 11:1445–1446;
    12:1650
  rotation 1:39–40; 8:1029; 9:1219, 1243
  selective breeding 11:1481
    and polyploidy 10:1408
  squash family 11:1554
  see also agriculture; grains; grasses, cereal;
    Green Revolution

D

DDT 1:41; 3:318; 4:480–481; 5:584,
  622; 7:959; 9:1243; 10:1343–1344;
  11:1532
  biomagnification 4:481; 9:1280, 1287
  effect on birds 2:235–236; 5:584,
    622–623, 680; 9:1275, 1287;
    10:1343–1344
  for lice control 8:1033
  pest resistance 4:480–481
dieldrin 2:237
dioxins 4:532; 10:1343
ditches, permaculture and 9:1281

EF

Endothia parasitica (chestnut blight)
  9:1265; 10:1324
farming *see* agriculture
fertilizers 1:40–41; 5:717–718; 9:1219
  and algal blooms 7:*1001*
  and the environment 5:*718*; 10:1342
  organic 9:1247
foods, **organic 9:1242–1245**

G

grains 9:1161
  smuts on 8:1139
grasses
  cereal 9:1161
    see also grains
Green Revolution 1:40; 5:718
  and pesticides 9:1287

H

harvesting machines 1:*41*
herbicides
  dioxins 4:532
  genetically-modified crops resistant to
    6:810
Hoffmanseggia glauca (hog potato)
  11:1445
hydroponics 7:924–925

I

Icerya purchasi (cottony-cushion scale insect)
  2:195
insecticides *see* pesticides
Ipomoea spp. (sweet potato) 11:1445, 1446
Irish Potato Famine 10:1322, 1382

L

Lactuca sativa (lettuce) 1:*102*; 2:179
leaf crops 8:1013–1014
lettuce 1:*102*; 2:179
lightning, and nitrogen fixation 9:*1219*
livestock farming, organic 9:1243

M

maize *see* corn
manorialism 1:39
manure, green 5:718
micronutrients, and hydroponics
  7:924–925
milk production 1:40; 7:998
monocultures 9:1244

O

organic foods 9:1242–1245
organic products 9:1246–1249
organochlorines *see* DDT; dioxins
organophosphates 2:195
Ormia depleta 2:196
Oryza sativa *see* rice

P

parasitoids 2:195–196; 5:695
peanuts, growing 11:*1530*
permaculture 9:1279–1282
pesticides 1:41; 2:195; 9:1247,
  1287–1288; 11:1532
  biological/biorational (natural/organic)
    9:1244, *1247*
    neem 9:1243, *1248*
  biomagnification of 4:481; 9:1280, 1287
  harmful to birds 2:235–236, 237; 5:584,
    622–623, 680; 9:1275, 1287
  harmful to humans 5:*626*; 9:1243, 1288
  history of 9:1288
  resistance to 1:19; 4:480–481; 9:1193,
    1247
  see also DDT; herbicides
pests 10:1320–1321
  beetle 2:*178*
  cockroaches 3:*387*, 388
  control 10:1346–1347
    using viruses 12:1679
    see also biological control; pesticides
  nematode 9:1196
  phasmids as 8:1017
  resistance to pesticides 1:19;
    4:480–481
  rodent 10:*1437*

phylloxera, grapevine infestation 6:794
Phytophthora infestans (late/potato blight)
  8:*1138*; 10:1321, *1322*, 1382
plows 1:37, 39
pyrethrum 1:41; 9:*1247*

R

rice 1:40; 9:1161
  genetically modified 6:810; 9:1244
Rodolia cardinalis (vedalia beetle)
  2:195
root and tuber crops
  11:1445–1446
rots, noble 10:*1319*, 1321–1322
Roundup (pesticide) 9:1247
rye, smut 6:765

S

Secale cereale *see* rye
seed drills, invention 1:39
selective breeding 2:223; 5:659;
  11:1479–1482
  of animals 11:1480
    cattle 1:40; 11:1480, *1481*
    dogs 4:*540*–541
  of humans 7:923
  of plants 11:*1480*–1482
  polyploidy 10:1408; 11:1481
silage 9:1280
Solanum tuberosum (white/Irish potato)
  10:1321; 11:1446, 1562
spinach 8:1014
stubborn(citrus fruit disease) 10:1323
swales, permaculture and 9:1281

T

tea 4:*546*; 8:*1013*, 1014
textiles, organic 9:1248
threshing machines, development
  1:39
tobacco, cultivation 8:*1014*
tobacco mosaic diseaese 8:1130;
  10:1323, *1324*
tomatoes 6:793
  diseases 10:*1322*
  Flavr Savr 2:227; 6:765, 794, 809
  freeze-resistant 2:225; 6:765
  plants, response to attack 10:1317
tractors 1:40
Triticum *see* wheat

W

wheat 1:101
  new varieties 1:40; 4:546
  origins of 6:793
  and polyploidy 10:*1408*
  rusts of 6:800
  selective breeding 11:*1479*
Whitney, Eli 1:39

> **Bold words with bold page numbers indicate complete articles; bold numbers preceding colons are volume numbers; numbers following colons indicate page numbers; italic page numbers refer to illustrations or other graphics.**

YZ

yams 3:380; 9:1161; 11:1446
  Mexican 1:80
Zea mays (corn/maize) *see* corn

ANATOMY

A

abdomen 1:13
abomasum 11:*1452*, 1453
acini 9:1260
adenohypophysis 5:611
adrenal glands
  chromaffin cells 5:640
  hormones 4:454; 5:612, 708; 9:1201
    androgens 5:612–613; 7:906
    stress and 11:1566
  and pseudohermaphroditism 7:889
alimentary canal *see* digestive systems,
    digestive tract
alveoli 8:*1055, 1056*; 9:1253;
    10:1420–1422
amnion 10:1354
amniotic sac 10:1354
ampullae 12:1670
amygdala 2:257
anatomy 1:69–72
  plant 1:69–70; 2:253
androecium 6:758
antennae 1:105–106
  of flies 1:106
  of moths 1:*105*; 9:*1223*
antheridia 9:1166
anthers 1:78; 10:1335
antlers 2:*217*; 7:911; 11:*1486*; 12:1663
appendix 4:517, 523; 8:1065
  removal 11:1572–1573
archegonia 5:*590*; 9:1166
Aristotle's lantern 4:568
arteries 3:*375*
  coronary 7:*880*; 9:1225
  hepatic 7:894
  renal 7:989, *991*
  splenic 11:1550
atria 7:877
atrioventricular (AV) node 7:879

B

backbone *see* vertebral column
baleen 4:438; 5:*695*; 12:1708, *1709*
barbels 1:106; 6:734; 7:1001
bark, tree 12:1639
basidia 9:1186
beaks (bills) 2:230–231; 9:1274, *1275*;
    12:1606
  adaptive radiation 9:1192; 11:1541
  sensitive 12:1628
  serrations 12:1606
belly button 10:1359
berries 6:792
biceps 9:*1179*
bile duct 8:*1046*
bladder 5:671; 11:1459
blood vessels *see* arteries; capillaries; veins
blubber 11:1507
bone 2:248–250
  adaptations 2:250
  and aging 1:34
    osteoporosis 11:1502

bird 2:*229*, 250; 6:751; 11:1498, *1501*
CT scans 4:475
dermal 2:248
development 2:248, *249*; 3:319
disease and deformities 2:250
endochondral 2:248; 11:1500
formation and structure 2:*248–249*;
    11:1500–1501
fossilization of 6:781
in the human hand 7:*869*
hyaline cartilage on 3:*320*
marrow 2:249, *250*; 11:1500
  cells 8:1063
  and lymphocytes 7:*930*, 932; 11:1559
  transplants 2:249; 3:353; 4:535;
    8:1031; 11:1557; 12:*1633*
repair and remodeling 2:249–250;
    10:1402
spongy 2:248, *250*
and vitamin deficiency 4:*489*
X rays of 12:*1712*, 1713
see also horns; joints; skeletal systems
Bowman's capsule 5:668, 671; 7:990
brain 2:255–264
aging 1:35
anatomy 2:*256–259*; 9:1210–1211
blood flow 2:*264*
cerebellum 2:256, 259
cerebral cortex (neocortex) 2:257–259
  and Alzheimer's disease 1:61
  development 2:260
  and intelligence 7:967
  map (homunculus) 2:*262*; 5:637
  memory storage 8:*1104*–1105;
    11:1543–1544
cerebrum 2:257
  cerebral hemispheres 2:259, *263*–264
and circadian rhythms 2:217
and emotion 2:257; 5:604–605
evolution 2:258; 5:660
forebrain 2:257, 258
function during sleep 2:264
hindbrain 2:256
human 2:*257*, 259–263
  development and growth 2:260
  evolution 2:258
  and handedness 7:871
  learning and memory 2:261–263
imaging techniques 2:*260*
  CT scans 2:260; 4:475
  EEGs 2:*255*, 260; 5:638; 8:1090;
    11:*1509–1510*
  magnetoencephalography (MEG) 2:260
  MRI scans 2:260; 3:399–*400*; 8:*1068,
    1104*; 9:*1214*
  PET scans 2:260
injury 12:1626
  and comas 3:398
limbic system 2:257; 5:604–605
midbrain 2:256–257
neurobiology 9:1210–1211
neurons 2:255–256
nonhuman 2:259
split brain studies 2:264; 5:638
strokes 2:242, 256; 3:377; 7:902;
    12:1620
surgery 5:*639*; 11:1575
see also nervous system
branchial basket 4:552

Broca's area 11:1544
Brockman bodies 9:1261
bronchi 8:1055; 10:1420
bronchioles 8:1055; 10:1420
buds 11:1561
  and dormancy 4:547–548, *549*
bud scales 11:1560, 1561
bulbs and corms 2:265–266; 9:1277;
    11:1449
  bulbs 2:*265*–266
  corms 2:*265–266*

C

calyx 6:757, 761–762
  tubes 6:759
cambium 4:509; 11:1448, 1561
  cork 11:1561
canines 12:1603, 1605, 1606
capillaries 3:375, *376*
carapace 12:1623
cardiovascular system *see* circulatory
    systems; heart
carnassials 3:307, 321; 4:517; 12:1605
carpals (bones) 7:869
carpels 5:716; 6:758
cartilage 2:248; 3:319–320; 6:726;
    10:1376
cephalothorax 4:467
cerata 7:981
cerci 4:563, *564*
cerebellum 2:256, 259
cerebral cortex *see* brain, cerebral cortex
cerebral hemispheres 2:259, *263*–264
cerebrospinal fluid 2:259–260
cerebrum 2:257
  cerebral hemispheres 2:259, *263*–264
ceruminous glands 5:676
cervix
  cancer 3:296
    test for 4:477
  mucus 4:442; 9:1172
chelicerae 1:141
chiasma, optic 12:1685
choroid 5:685
circulatory systems 3:370–378
  closed 3:*372*–375
  CT scans 4:475
  human
    diseases of 3:376–378
    evolution of 3:378
    fetal 7:878
  lymphatic *see* lymphatic systems
  open 3:371–*372*
  role of calcium 2:278
  versus diffusion 3:370–371
  vertebrate 3:375–376
claws 7:871
clitoris 10:1413
coccyx 8:1069
cochlea 4:*560*
coelenteron 7:981
coelom, in annelids 1:98, 99;
    11:1496
colon 4:517, 523
  bacteria in 5:703
  cancer
    colon 3:295, 299; 4:523, 538
    treatment 3:353
  inflammation (colitis) 4:519

cones
  gymnosperm 3:415; 5:716
    pollination 10:*1338*
conjunctiva 5:685; 9:1172
corallite 4:452
cork 12:1639
corms *see* bulbs and corms
cornea
  grafting 12:1633, *1636*
  laser surgery 8:*1091*
corolla 6:758
corpus allata 5:612; 7:908; 8:1126
corpus callosum 2:263, 264; 5:638; 7:967
corpus cardiaca 8:1126
corpus striatum 2:259
cortex (plant) 11:1448, 1560
cotyledons 9:1160; 11:*1476*
  and germination 11:1478
crop, bird 4:521
cuticle
  arthropod 1:137, *138*; 11:1496, *1497*
  insect 11:1505–1506
  plant 8:1023; 11:1560; 12:1702
Cuverian tubules 4:570

D

dewlaps, lizard 4:459
diaphragm 8:*1057*, 1058; 10:1422
digestive systems 4:511–519
  carnivore 4:516, 520, 521
  digestive tract 4:520–523
    disorders 4:519, *523*
    herbivore 4:514–*515*, 520, 521
    human 4:*511, 516*–519, *521*–523
      bacteria in 2:172
    invertebrate 4:*512*–513
    mucosal layers 8:1065
    mucous membranes 9:1171–1172
    omnivore 4:516
    protozoan 4:511
    vertebrate 4:513–516
    see also liver; pancreas; stomach
duodenum 4:517, 522
  ulcers 1:*71*

E

ears 4:559–562
  and balance 4:560–561
  bionic 2:215
  cartilage in 3:320
  and echolocation 4:562
  fish, lateral line 4:561–562; 6:731
  human 4:*559, 562*; 7:*872*, 873–875
  and human evolution 4:561
  nonmammalian 4:*561*–562
  structure 4:*559–560*
  wax 12:1702
elbows, replacement 8:1092
elytra 4:563
embryology 1:71
embryos 5:597–601
  cryopreservation 4:472, 473
  human 3:*385*; 5:597, *600*; 10:*1352*,
    1353, 1354
    brain development 2:260
    cartilage formation 3:319–320
    for research 5:600
    stem cells 2:261; 4:497; 5:600;
      11:*1557*, 1558, 1559

transplantation **5**:711
invertebrate **5**:597–598
mammalian **8**:1074
muscle development **9**:1183
notocord **5**:597
plant **5**:597, 600–*601*; **11**:*1476*
  development **5**:*716*
  in seeds **11**:1476
transplantation (transfer)
  in animals **11**:1481
  in humans **5**:711
transplanted cells between **8**:1088
vertebrate **5**:598–600
  cartilage formation **3**:319;
    11:1500–1501
enamel **12**:1604
endocarp **6**:792, 795
endocrine systems 5:610–613
diseases **5**:613
glands of **5**:*610, 611*; **7**:903
  kidneys as **7**:990–992
  "swollen" **3**:371; **8**:*1066*
and homeostasis **7**:899–900
hormones
  adrenal **4**:454; **5**:612, 708; **9**:1201;
    11:1566
  gastrointestinal **5**:610
  hypothalamic **5**:*611*
  invertebrate **7**:908
  pancreatic **5**:612; **7**:904
  parathyroid **5**:612
  pituitary **5**:*611*
  sex hormones **1**:*26–27*; **5**:612–613
  thyroid **5**:612
and the nervous system **5**:610; **9**:1201
endometrium **8**:*1109*; **10**:1353, 1414
endosperm **5**:590, *716*; **11**:1475,
  1476, 1478
epicotyl (plumule) **11**:1476
epididymis **10**:1411
epiglottis **3**:320; **4**:516
esophagus **4**:516, 521
esthetes **12**:1595
eustachian tube **3**:320; **4**:562; **7**:874
excretory systems 1:69;
  5:664–672
countercurrent multiplication system
  7:990
in humans **5**:671–672
invertebrate **5**:666–669
protozoan **5**:666
vertebrate **5**:668, 669–671
  fish **5**:669–670
waste products **5**:*665–666*
see also kidneys
exocarp **6**:792
exocrine glands 5:673–677
embryology **5**:673
mammary **5**:676–677; **7**:997–998
oral **5**:673–675
sebaceous **5**:*673, 674*, 675–676;
  11:1508
sudiferous *see* sweat glands
exoskeletons *see* skeletal systems,
  exoskeletons
eyelids, third *see* nictitating membranes
eyes 5:685–688
compound **1**:140; **5**:*687–688*; **6**:743;
  12:1686, 1687

damage due to diabetes **4**:*506*
disorders and diseases **5**:*687*
eyelids, third (nictitating membranes)
  3:*322, 323*; **5**:*687*; **8**:1052
human **5**:*685*, 686–687
  yellowing **7**:*886*
  jaundiced **7**:*886*
lens **5**:685–686; **12**:1684
mucous membranes **9**:1172
retina **4**:*506*; **5**:686; **9**:*1202*
  implants **8**:1093
simple **5**:*685*–687; **12**:1685
surgery, laser **8**:*1091*; **11**:1575
tapetum lucidum **3**:322; **4**:464;
  10:1365
"third" (pineal; parietal body) **8**:1052;
  10:1415, 1416
eyespots **5**:685
used as mimicry **2**:271, 283

F

fallopian tubes **5**:715; **10**:*1354*, 1413
  damaged **5**:*711*, 712
and sterilization **4**:442–443
feathers **2**:*228–229*; **6**:725
feet 5:697–699
artificial **2**:213
bird
  colder than the rest of the body
    12:1618
  webbed **11**:1472
  zygodactyly **6**:775, 778
disorders **5**:*699*
of dogs **4**:539
elephant **5**:595
human **11**:1503
vertebrate **5**:697
fibers 6:725–726
collagenous **6**:*726*
fibrocartilage **3**:*319*, 320
fingernails **7**:870–871
fingers, extra (polydactyly) **4**:*525*
fins, fish **6**:729; **11**:1577
florets **6**:758
fovea **5**:687; **12**:1684
frontal lobes **2**:*259*; **11**:1544
fur **6**:725
  molting **9**:1159
  trade in **12**:*1591*
furcula **1**:141

G

gallbladder *see* liver and gallbladder
galls, plant **11**:1562
gametes **10**:1405
ganglia, nerve **2**:258
gastric pits **4**:522
gemma cups **9**:*1165*
gemmae **9**:*1165*
gills and spiracles 6:835–838
gills **10**:*1418*–1419
  book **1**:140
  caudal **4**:552
  crustacean **4**:468
  dragonfly nymph **4**:552
  fish **6**:727–728; **10**:1419
  slits **3**:364
spiracles **1**:140; **10**:*1419*
gizzard **4**:*514*, 521; **11**:1564

glands
  endocrine *see* endocrine systems,
    glands of
  exocrine *see* exocrine glands
Glisson's capsule **8**:1044
glomeruli **7**:989, 990
gonads *see* ovaries; testes
gynoecium **6**:758

H

hair **6**:*774*; **8**:1070
  defensive **4**:485
  loss (baldness) **9**:1256
  and touch **12**:1626
  see also whiskers
hairs
  leaf (trichomes) **8**:1026; **12**:*1629*
  root **11**:1447, 1448
halteres **6**:743, 744, 750
hands 7:869–871; **11**:1498, 1503
artificial **2**:212, 213; **8**:1092–1093
disorders **7**:870
evolution **7**:871
transplants **8**:1088
haustoria **10**:1321; **12**:1670
heart 3:371; **7:876–881**
and aging **1**:34
artificial **2**:214; **8**:1094; **12**:1636
  cardiac pacemakers **2**:214; **7**:879;
    8:*1039*, 1092; **12**:1636
  heart-lung machines **11**:1571–1572
  ventricular assist devices (VADs) **2**:*214*
cardiac muscle **1**:69; **7**:*879*; **9**:*1180*;
  11:*1558*
evolution **7**:876–878
heartbeat **7**:879–880
  rate **7**:880, 955; **9**:1252
mammalian **7**:878–879
muscle **7**:879
in open circulatory systems **7**:876
role of calcium **2**:278
sounds **7**:*878*
surgery, robots used in **10**:1432–1433
transplants **12**:*1635*
  heart-lung transplants **8**:1092;
    12:*1635*–1636
  see also heart, artificial
valves **7**:*876*
vertebrate **3**:375; **7**:*877–879*
heartwood **12**:1639
hemipenes **11**:1519
hemocoel **3**:371
hemolymph **1**:140; **3**:371; **7**:876
hepatic ducts **8**:1044–1045
hippocampus **2**:257
  and memory **2**:263; **8**:1105
holdfast **7**:986
hooves **5**:697; **12**:*1659*–1660
horns 7:910–911; **11**:*1528*; **12**:1663
hypocotyl **5**:601; **11**:1476
hypothalamus **2**:166, 257
  and the adrenal glands **5**:640; **7**:905
  affecting pituitary hormone release
    5:*611*, 709; **7**:900; **8**:1108

and aggression **1**:31
and blood concentration **7**:990
and body temperature **7**:901; **12**:1619
and emotion **5**:602, 604, 605
endorphin production **5**:614
and hibernation **7**:893
and lactation **7**:998
and metamorphosis **8**:1126
role in childbirth **7**:*953*
role in puberty **1**:26–27
and sex hormone release **1**:26–27;
  7:906; **8**:1108
and stress **11**:1566

I

ileum **4**:519
incisors **12**:1603, 1605
incus **4**:573
inflorescences **6**:758
intercostal muscles **8**:1058
interneurons **9**:1198
interstitial fluid **11**:1458
intestines
  carnivore **4**:*516*
  herbivore **4**:515
  human **4**:517, *521–523*
  large **4**:514, 517, 523; **9**:1172
  mucous membranes **9**:1171
  small **4**:514, 517, *521*, *522*–523; **9**:1171
  transplants **12**:1636
  smooth muscle **9**:1179
iris (of the eye) **5**:685; **12**:1685

J

Jacobson's organ **8**:1051; **10**:1416;
  11:1515, 1518; **12**:1596
jaws 4:513; **7:978–979**
of carnivores **3**:307; **7**:*978*, 979
see also teeth
joints
  fibrocartilage in **3**:320
  replacement **8**:1092
  types **11**:1501

K

kidneys 7:989–992
aging **1**:34
artificial **2**:215
blood supply **7**:*991*
Bowman's capsule **5**:668, 671; **7**:990
countercurrent multiplication system
  7:990
embryonic development **7**:992
failure **5**:672; **7**:*992*; **8**:1039–1040
fluid samples taken from **7**:990
function **7**:990
  endocrine **7**:990–992
hypertrophy **10**:1402
loop of Henle **5**:669, 670–671, *672*;
  7:990, 992
storage of **4**:472–473
structure **7**:*989*–990
transplants **4**:472; **8**:1039, 1065–1066,
  1088; **12**:*1634*, 1636

kidneys (continued)
    first 8:1088, 1092; 12:1634
    vertebrate 5:669
    see also excretory systems

L

labellae 6:745
labia 10:1413
labium 4:551; 6:743
lacteals 8:1063
larynx 1:140; 10:1420; 11:1543
lateral line 4:561–562; 6:731; 12:1628
leaves and leaf structure 8:1022–1027
    adaptations 8:1026, 1027
    cacti 8:1022
    carotenoids 3:317; 10:1306
    compound and simple 8:1026
    dicotyledon 4:509–510
    "drip tips" 12:1643
    falling leaves 8:1022, 1025
    fossil 9:1257
    fractal patterns 3:348
    hairs (trichomes) 8:1026
    leaf crops 8:1013–1014
    movements 10:1316
    palmate leaves 8:1026; 9:1258
    pinnate leaves 8:1026; 9:1258
    sclerophyllous 3:350
    sessile leaves 8:1022
    starch storage 3:297
    start of a leaf 8:1023
    tissues 8:1023–1025
    variations 8:1026–1027
    variegated 10:1323
    venation 8:1025
    see also spines; stomata
legs
    artificial 2:213; 8:1092
    bones 11:1503
    countercurrent heat exchange 7:901;
        11:1472
    regeneration 10:1400
lenses, eye 5:685–686; 12:1684
lenticels 11:1562
ligaments 3:419; 11:1501
    springing 12:1659
limbic lobes, and emotion 2:257;
        5:604–605
limbs
    artificial 8:1092–1093
    movement of paralyzed 2:213
liver and gallbladder 8:1044–1047
    gallbladder 8:1044, 1045, 1046, 1047
        removal 8:1047; 11:1575
        stones in (gallstones; bile stones) 4:523;
            8:1047
    liver
        artificial 2:215
        cancer 3:295
        detoxification in 8:1046–1047
        diseases 7:894; 8:1046
        erythrocyte destruction 8:1047
        metabolism 8:1046, 1118, 1119, 1121;
            12:1667
        regeneration 10:1401
        storage of products 3:301; 8:1044,
            1045–1046, 1047, 1118, 1124
        structure 7:894; 8:1044, 1045
        sugar regulation 8:1047, 1118

synthesis of products 8:1044–1045
transplant 4:472; 8:1046;
    12:1634–1635
loop of Henle 5:669, 670–671, 672;
    7:990, 992
lungs 8:1054–1061; 9:1253
    book 8:1060; 10:1420; 11:1547
    cancer 3:294, 295; 8:1060
        and diet 3:317
        and smoking 3:295; 8:1059–1060
        treatment 11:1575
    structure 8:1054, 1055; 10:1420–1423
    cilia 7:938
lymphatic systems 3:371; 8:1062–1066
    and cancer 8:1064, 1066
    circulation 8:1062–1063
    disease and 8:1065, 1066
    fat absorption 8:1063
    and the immune system 7:932, 942
    lymph 3:371
    obstruction 8:1065–1066
    tissues 8:1063
        age involution 8:1064
        see also lymph nodes; spleen; thymus
            gland
    lymph hearts 8:1062
    lymph nodes 3:371; 7:942; 8:1063, 1065
        and cancer 8:1064
        disorders 8:1066
        removal 8:1064
        see also lymphatic systems
    lymphoid cells 11:1559
    lymphoid tissues 8:1063

M

macrotrichia 2:267
malleus 7:873
Malpighian capsules 11:1550
Malpighian tubules 5:668–669; 7:989
mammary glands 5:676–677; 7:997–998;
    8:1070
mandibles 4:467
mantle 8:1147
marsupium 8:1077–1078
maxillae 4:467
maxillipeds 4:467
medulla (brain) 2:256, 259
    respiratory center 9:1252
megasporangium 10:1336
megaspores 5:590, 716
meibomian glands 5:676
melon (cetacean) 4:572; 12:1702
    and algal blooms 7:1001
membranes, mucous 9:1171–1172
meninges 2:259
meristems 8:1023; 11:1560
mesocarp 6:792, 795
mesogloea 7:981, 982
mesohyl 11:1552
mesonephric duct 7:992
mesonephros 7:992
metacarpals 7:869
metanephridia 5:666–667; 7:989
metatarsals 11:1503
micropyle 5:716; 10:1336; 11:1476
microsporangia 3:416
microvilli
    intestinal 4:517, 523
    on taste cells 12:1596

molars 12:1603, 1605
morphology, plant 2:254
mother-of-pearl 8:1149
mouth 4:513–514
    human 4:516
    bacteria in 2:171–172
mucosal layers 8:1065
mucous membranes 9:1171–1172
muscular systems 9:1177–1184
    and aging 1:34
    atrophy 9:1184
    capacity for new growth 9:1183
    diseases 9:1181
    and exercise
        lactic acid (lactate) accumulation 2:159;
            3:300; 5:703; 9:1183, 1252
        muscle size 9:1184
    fermentation in cells 5:703
    fibers (cells) 9:1178, 1181, 1183
    muscle blocks (myotomes) 9:1179
    muscle contraction 9:1179–1180,
        1182–1183
    muscle renewal 11:1558
    muscle structure and function
        9:1180–1183
    muscle wasting 9:1184; 11:1533
    pectoral muscles 6:748, 751
    and regeneration 10:1402
    relaxants for surgery 9:1183
    role of calcium 2:278; 9:1182
    stimulation of paralyzed 2:213
    types of muscle
        cardiac 1:69; 7:879; 9:1180; 11:1558
        skeletal 1:69; 9:1178–1179, 1180–1181
        smooth 1:69; 9:1179–1180
mushroom body 8:1105
myofibrils 9:1178, 1181
myofilaments 9:1181
myotomes 9:1179

N

nacre 8:1149
nails 7:870–871
neocortex see brain, cerebral cortex
nephridia 5:666
nephrons 5:669, 671; 7:989–990
nephrostomes 5:666
nerve cord see spinal cord
nerve nets 2:255, 258; 7:982; 9:1205
nerves see nervous systems, nerves
nervous systems 1:69; 9:1197–1205
    autonomic (ANS) 9:1197
        and the heart 9:1180
        and homeostasis 7:899
        smooth muscle contraction 9:1179
    central (CNS) 9:1197
    disorders 9:1202–1204
    and the endocrine system 5:610; 9:1201
    evolution 9:1204–1205
    and muscle contraction 9:1182
    myelin 3:362; 9:1200
    nerve cord see spinal cord
    nerve net 2:255, 258; 7:982; 9:1205
    nerves
        communication 9:1200–1201
        glossopharyngeal 12:1597
        impulses 9:1198–1200
        optic 5:687; 12:1685
        and touch 12:1626

peripheral (PNS) 9:1197
poisons 9:1203
sympathetic, epinephrine and
    norepinephrine release 5:640, 641
synapses 1:69; 9:1200–1201
see also brain
neural tube 2:260
neurohypophysis 5:611
nictitating membranes (third eyelids)
    3:322, 323; 5:687; 8:1052
nodes, leaf 8:1022, 1023
nose
    bacteria in the 2:171
    cartilage 3:320
    mucous membrane 9:1171
notochord 3:364

O

occipital lobes 2:259, 261; 12:1688
ocelli 1:140; 6:743; 12:1685
omasum 4:515; 11:1452, 1453
ommatidia 1:140; 5:688; 9:1221; 12:1686
On the Use of the Parts of the Human Body
    (Galen) 1:70
opisthosoma 1:130
organ of Corti 4:561, 562; 7:874, 875
osculum 11:1552, 1553
otoliths 4:561
ovaries 10:1412, 1413
    egg cells 5:715; 8:1108
    hormone production 5:613
    and the ovarian cycle 8:1108–1109
    plant
        angiosperm 6:759
        position 6:759
    premature ovarian failure 5:711
ovipositor 12:1592

P

pancreas 9:1260–1261
    anatomy 9:1260
    artificial 2:215
    cells 2:180
    CT scans 4:475
    endocrine function 5:612; 9:1260–1261
    evolution 9:1261
    exocrine function (digestive enzymes)
        4:518, 522; 5:677; 9:1260
    histology 7:895; 9:1261
    islets of Langerhans 5:612; 7:895, 904,
        964; 9:1260, 1261
    replacement 12:1634
    nonhuman 9:1261
    transplants 12:1634
pancreatic duct 9:1260
papillae, on the tongue 12:1597, 1621
parapineal gland 5:613
parietal lobes 2:259
pearls 8:1149
pectoralis majora 6:748
pedipalps 1:130; 11:1469, 1546, 1547
pelvic girdle 11:1503
penis
    human 10:1409, 1412
    of insects 8:1083
pericarp 6:792
pericycle 11:1448
petals 6:757
petioles 8:1022

Peyer's patches 8:1065
phalanges 11:1503
pharynx 10:1420; 12:1621–1622
phloem 4:509; 8:1024–1025; 11:1448, 1561
pineal gland
    and biorhythms 2:217–218
    in fish 6:731
    hormones 5:613
pineal/parietal eyes ("third eye") 8:1052; 10:1415, 1416
pinnae 7:872
pistils 6:758, 759, 791
pith 11:1560
pit organs 11:1518
pituitary gland 2:166, 218; 5:610, 611, 613; 7:903
    antidiuretic hormone (ADH) 5:671; 7:990
    endorphin production 5:614
    hypothalamus-pituitary connection 5:611, 709; 7:900; 8:1108
    and the menstrual cycle 8:1108
    and reproduction
        lactation 7:998
        role in childbirth 7:953
    stress and the 11:1566
placenta 8:1074; 10:1353, 1356, 1414
    choriovitelline 10:1352
    development 11:1557
    expulsion after birth 10:1359
    hormone production 5:613
plastron 12:1623
plumule 11:1476
podocarps 3:416
pollen tubes 6:760
pons 2:256
preen glands (uropygial glands) 11:1472; 12:1699
premolars 12:1603
prickles 3:380
primordia 8:1023
    leaf 11:1561
proboscis 10:1374
    of butterflies and moths 2:267, 268; 10:1337, 1374
    of mosquitoes 9:1268; 10:1374
prosoma 1:130
prostate gland 10:1412
    cancer 3:295, 352
        surgical robots used for 10:1433
    treatment of enlarged 11:1575
protocerebrums 8:1105
protoderm 11:1560
protonephridia 5:666
pseudocoelom 7:971; 9:1195, 1196
pulmonary tree 8:1055
pulvilli 6:745
pupils 12:1685
pygostyle 12:1593

R

radicle 11:1448, 1476, 1478
    development 5:601
radula 8:1147; 10:1374
recapitulation theory 1:71
rectum 4:517
    cancer 3:295; 4:523
reproductive systems 10:1409–1414
    human

female 10:1412–1414
male 10:1409–1412
respiratory systems 10:1417–1424
    of amphibians 10:1418
    of birds 10:1423–1424
    of fish
        gills 6:727–728; 10:1419
        lungfish 10:1422
    human 10:1420–1422
        bacteria 2:171
        mucus 7:928
    of insects 10:1419–1420
    of mammals 10:1423
    membranes 8:1065; 9:1171
    pigments 10:1424
    of plants 10:1424
    of reptiles 10:1422
    of spiders 10:1420
    see also gills and spiracles; lungs
rete mirabile
    in birds 11:1472
    in tuna 6:731
reticular formation 2:256–257
reticulorumen 11:1451
reticulum 4:515; 11:1451, 1452, 1453
retina 4:506; 5:686; 9:1202
    implants 8:1093
rhizoids 9:1165
rhizomes see tubers and rhizomes
rib cage, during breathing 8:1057
roots and root systems 11:1447–1450
    absorbency 8:1026
    crops 11:1445–1446
    development 11:1447–1448
    growth 11:1560
    and mycorrhizae 6:800; 9:1187–1188, 1241; 10:1321; 11:1450
    nodules 8:1029; 11:1531
    oxygen requirements 9:1253
    of plants in dry habitats and deserts 11:1449–1450
    root cap 11:1560
    root/shoot balance 11:1448
    size 8:1148; 11:1450
    storage in 11:1449
    "territorial" 12:1613
    transport by 11:1448
    tropisms 11:1449; 12:1646, 1647
    types 11:1448–1449
        adventitious 11:1449, 1450
        aerial 3:380; 11:1450
        buttresses 12:1643
        primary roots 11:1448–1449, 1476
        prop roots 11:1532; 12:1704
        tap roots 11:1449
rugae 11:1564
rumen 4:515; 11:1451, 1452, 1453, 1564
    of a cow, contents 9:1229

S

saccule 4:561
salivary glands 4:514, 516
salt glands 11:1459, 1472
sap
    in plants 12:1631, 1632
    polar 10:1332
sarcolemma 9:1181
sarcomeres 9:1181
scala tympani 4:560

scala vestibuli 4:560
scapulae 11:1503
sclera 5:685
scrotum 10:1409–1410
scutes 12:1623
sebaceous glands 5:673, 674, 675–676; 11:1508
seeds 5:716; 11:1475–1478
    ancient 11:1478
    banks 2:252; 3:427; 4:473
    coat (testa) 10:1326
    dispersal 1:79; 10:1318–1319, 1326; 11:1476–1477
        active 10:1319; 11:1477
        by animals 1:79; 10:1318, 1319; 11:1477
        by birds 1:79; 11:1477
        by water 11:1477
        by wind 1:79; 6:725; 10:1319; 11:1477
        and fruit capsules 11:1477–1478
        "splash cup" 2:274
    dormancy 4:547, 548–549; 11:1478
    evolution 5:715; 10:1325, 1326; 11:1475
    fire and 4:548
    formation 11:1475–1476
    scarification 4:547, 549
    structure 1:79
    used by man 11:1477
segmentation, metameric, in annelids 1:98, 99
sella turcica 5:611
semen (seminal fluid) 5:711; 10:1412
semicircular canals 4:560
seminal fluid see semen
seminal vesicles 10:1412
seminiferous tubules 10:1411
sensilla 12:1627
sensory cortex 2:259
sepals 6:757, 759
shells
    molluskan 8:1148–1149; 11:1497, 1506
    tortoise 12:1623
    turtle 12:1623
sinoatrial (SA) node 7:879
skeletal systems 11:1495–1504
    appendicular skeleton 11:1502
    axial skeleton 11:1502
    computer models 11:1501
    dermal skeleton 11:1501
    disorders of 11:1502
    endoskeletons 11:1498–1504
        adaptations 11:1498
        bird 11:1498, 1501
        echinoderm 4:567; 11:1499
        fetal 11:1500–1501
        fish 11:1499–1500
        human 11:1496, 1501
        invertebrate 11:1498–1499
        of sponges 7:969; 11:1498–1499
        of squid and octopuses 11:1499
        vertebrate 2:248; 3:319; 11:1499–1504
    see also bone

exoskeletons 11:1496–1498
    arthropod 1:138–139; 7:971–972; 11:1496–1497
    coral 4:452; 11:1497–1498
    insect 7:957–958; 11:1505–1506
    mollusk shells 8:1148–1149; 11:1497
human skeletons for study 11:1501
hydrostatic 11:1495–1496
somatic skeleton 11:1502
visceral skeleton 11:1501–1502
skin 11:1505–1508
    aging 1:34; 11:1507
    bacteria 2:171
    birthmarks 10:1359
    cancer 3:294, 295, 296, 317, 353; 9:1193; 12:1658
        treatment 12:1713
    collagen 6:726
    color 9:1227; 11:1507, 1508
        in caves 3:327
        loss 10:1310
    and disease 7:950; 11:1508
    excretion via 5:672
    glands 5:673, 675–676
        see also sweat glands
    grafts 8:1087, 1088; 11:1507
    human 11:1507–1508
        and touch 12:1626
    mammalian 11:1506–1507
    mucus secretion 11:1506
    renewal 11:1558
    tissue-engineered 8:1093
    vertebrate 11:1506
    see also hair
skull 11:1498
    of birds 7:978–979; 11:1498
    boring holes into 11:1570
    of Neanderthal man 7:912, 916
soredia 8:1035
spadix 6:762
spectacles (brilles) 11:1517
spermathecae 11:1547
spermatophores 4:457, 458, 551; 8:1083; 11:1456
sphincters
    anal 9:1180–1181
    cardiac 11:1564
    pyloric 4:516–517, 521; 11:1564, 1565
spinal cord 9:1201–1202
    chordate 3:364
    damaged 9:1202
    and multiple sclerosis 9:1175
spine see vertebral column
spines
    animal 4:485
    plant 2:273; 4:482; 8:1022, 1027; 10:1317
spinnerets 11:1549
spiracles see gills and spiracles
spleen 2:243; 8:1064–1065; 11:1550–1551
    accessory spleens 8:1065
    disorders of 8:1065; 11:1551
    nonhuman spleens 11:1551

Bold words with bold page numbers indicate complete articles; bold numbers preceding colons are volume numbers; numbers following colons indicate page numbers; italic page numbers refer to illustrations or other graphics.

spleen (continued)
  removal 8:1064–1065; 11:1551, 1570
  see also lymphatic systems
splenic cords 11:1550
sporangia
  in cones 10:1338
  fungal 8:1138, 1140
  in mosses and liverworts 9:1166
spores, fungal 6:798–799; 9:1186
stamens 1:78; 6:758, 759, 791; 10:1335
stapes (stirrup) 7:873, 874
  plastic 7:875
statocysts 4:469
statoliths 4:469
  in root cells 11:1449
stems and stem systems 10:1318;
    11:1560–1562
  cacti 2:273
  climbing 3:379, 380
  tropism 12:1647
  see also bulbs and corms; tubers and
    rhizomes; vascular systems
stigmas 1:79; 6:760
stirrup see stapes
stolons 5:706; 10:1405
stomach 4:514, 516, 517–518, 521–522;
    11:1563–1565
  disorders 4:523; 11:1565
  mucus 9:1171
  ruminant 4:515; 11:1451–1452, 1564;
    12:1661
  study of gastric function 4:517
  tissues of 7:894
stomata 3:415–416; 7:902; 8:1023–1024;
    10:1424; 11:1560; 12:1629–1630
  effect of water stress on 11:1567
  night-opening in desert plants 1:18–19
style 1:78
stylets 6:738, 744; 7:884
substantia nigra 9:1213
sudiferous glands see sweat glands
suprachiasmatic nucleus (SCN) 2:217, 218;
    11:1512
sweat glands 5:672, 674, 675–676;
    11:1508
swim bladders 3:405; 6:728, 729; 11:1577
swimmerets 1:13
synovia 7:869

T

tails 12:1592–1594
  chordate 3:364–365
  invertebrate 12:1592
  regeneration 10:1400; 12:1593
  shedding (autotomy) 8:1017,
    1052–1053; 10:1400; 12:1593
  vertebrate 12:1592–1593
tapetum lucidum 3:322; 4:464; 10:1365
taste buds 12:1596, 1597, 1622
tectum 2:259
teeth 4:517; 12:1603–1606
  carnassials 3:307, 321; 4:517; 12:1605
  of carnivores 3:307, 309, 310; 4:517;
    7:979; 8:1070; 12:1605
  decay 12:1604–1605
  dental formula 12:1606
  fillings 12:1605
  of herbivores 4:517; 7:979; 8:1070;
    12:1603, 1605

ungulates 12:1660–1661
  heterodont 12:1674
  human 12:1604
  hypsodont 11:1452
  mammalian 8:1070; 12:1603, 1605–1606
  milk/deciduous teeth 12:1603, 1604
  of omnivores 3:311; 7:979; 8:1072
  pleurodont 8:1051
  of rodents 10:1436; 12:1605
  wisdom 12:1604
  X rays 12:1712
temporal lobes 2:259
tendons 3:419; 6:726; 9:1178; 11:1501
tendrils 3:379–380; 8:1027; 10:1316;
    11:1554
testes 10:1409–1410
  castration 10:1414
thalamus 2:257; 5:602; 12:1627
thorax 1:13
thorns 4:482; 11:1562
thumbs, opposable 7:869
thymus gland 1:34; 7:903–904; 8:1064
  hormones 5:613; 7:904
  lymphocytes in (thymocytes) 7:930, 932;
    8:1064
  see also lymphatic systems
thyroid gland 2:166
  diseases of 2:165, 166; 7:905; 9:1227
  hormones 5:612; 7:900, 903, 907
tissues 1:69
  body, water balance 11:1459
  sampling and fixation 7:895
toes
  extra (polydactyly) 4:525
  opposable 7:697–698; 10:1365
tomentum 6:743
tongue 4:514; 12:1621–1622
  disorders of 12:1622
  and taste 12:1597, 1621
tonsils 8:1065
trachea 3:320; 8:1054–1055;
    10:1420
  arthropod and insect tracheae 1:140;
    10:1419–1420
triceps 9:1179
trichomes 4:482, 500; 8:1026, 1027
tube feet 4:567, 568, 569, 570;
    12:1670
tubers and rhizomes 11:1449;
    12:1649–1651
  crops 12:1650
  rhizomes 10:1318; 11:1560; 12:1646,
    1649, 1650–1651
  tubers 12:1649–1650
  root 11:1449; 12:1650
  stem 4:548
tubuloacinar glands 5:674
tusks 12:1606, 1663

U

umbilical cord 10:1356
  stem cells 11:1556, 1557
ureter 5:671
urethra 5:671; 9:1172; 10:1412
urogenital tracts, mucous membranes
    9:1172
uterus 10:1412, 1413–1414
  endometrial thickness 8:1109
  see also placenta

V

vagina 10:1412, 1413
  mucous membrane 9:1172
vasa deferentia 10:1411
  and vasectomy 4:443
vascular systems 12:1669–1670
  animal, in echinoderms 4:567; 12:1670
  plant 1:70; 11:1560–1561; 12:1669
    aquatic vascular plants 12:1670
    eudicot 4:509
    root 11:1448
    vascular bundles 4:509
    xylem and phloem 4:509;
      8:1024–1025; 11:1448, 1561;
      12:1631–1632, 1669
    see also stems and stem systems
veins 3:376
  hepatic portal 7:894; 8:1044
  renal 7:991
  splenic 11:1551
veins (leaf) 8:1024–1025
ventricles 7:877, 878, 879
vertebral column
  chiropractic manipulation 1:56, 57
  disks of cartilage in 3:319, 320
  mammalian 11:1498
  slipped disks 11:1502
vestibular system 4:560
villi, intestinal 4:517, 519, 521, 523;
    8:1063; 9:1171
Visible Human project 1:72
vocal cords 11:1543
vomeronasal (Jacobson's) organ 8:1051;
    10:1416; 11:1515

W

Wernicke's area 11:1544
whiskers 1:106; 8:1070; 12:1628
wings 6:747
  of bats 2:173, 175; 6:748, 750, 751
  of birds 6:747–748, 777
  of insects 7:958
    butterflies and moths 2:267–268,
      269, 271
    dragonflies 6:750
    earwigs 4:563
    flies 6:743
    grasshoppers and crickets 6:750
Wolffian duct 7:992
wool 6:725, 726

X

xylem 4:509; 8:1024; 11:1448, 1561;
    12:1631, 1669

Z

zygodactyly 6:775, 778
zygosporangia 6:799

■ BIOCHEMISTRY AND BIOTECHNOLOGY

A

acetone, from bacterial fermentation
    5:702, 703
acetyl CoA see acetyl coenzyme A
acetyl coenzyme A 2:159; 7:993, 994,
    995; 8:1118

aconitase 7:995
adenosine diphosphate see ADP
adenosine monophosphate, cyclic (cAMP)
    7:907; 8:1120
adenosine triphosphate see ATP
ADP (adenosine diphosphate) 2:158, 159;
    7:994; 9:1252; 10:1302
alanine 1:62, 63
algorithms
  evolutionary 2:151–152
  genetic 2:151, 152
ALife see artificial life
alkaloids 1:50–51; 4:481
  caffeine 8:1014
  colchicine 2:266; 3:367
  medicinal 1:51
  taste 12:1597
  toxic 1:50, 51
    from frogs 1:50; 5:677
    from fungi 1:50; 9:1188
amino acids 1:62–63; 8:1124, 1143;
    10:1375
  alpha 7:906
  breakdown 8:1119
  errors of metabolism 8:1124
  essential and nonessential 1:62; 8:1120;
    9:1226
  fermentation 5:703
  and mutations 9:1189, 1190
  properties 1:62–63
  sequencing to make proteins 4:536
  synthesis, in plants 10:1377
  testing for 1:63
  see also proteins
aminoids 6:762
analytical techniques 1:66–68
  centrifugation and ultracentrifugation
    1:67–68; 2:181; 10:1376; 12:1677
  chromatography 1:63, 66–67; 2:181
  electrophoresis see electrophoresis
  mass spectroscopy 1:68; 6:772
  microanalysis 1:68
  using radioisotopes see radioactive tagging
  X-ray crystallography 1:68; 2:182
    of viruses 12:1677
    X-ray diffraction 1:68; 6:786; 8:1146
  see also biochemistry
anthocyanins 6:761; 10:1311
anthoxanthins 6:761; 10:1311
arginase 12:1667
arginine 12:1667
argininosuccinase 12:1668
argininosuccinate 12:1667
argininosuccinate synthetase 12:1667
artificial insemination, of animals 2:224;
    5:712; 11:1481
artificial life 2:149–152
aspartic acid 12:1667
ATP (adenosine triphosphate) 2:158;
    7:993–994; 8:1117–1118;
    10:1302
  and muscle contraction 9:1181, 1182, 1183
  production 2:158–160; 5:618, 619;
    7:993; 8:1118; 9:1252
    energy for see Krebs cycle
    from chemiosmosis 5:618
    from glucose fermentation 3:299–300;
      5:702
    from photosynthesis 5:618

and oxidation-reduction reactions
5:618; 7:996
role of mitochondria 2:159–160
used in bioluminescence 2:206
ATP synthase 2:160; 7:996
automata, cellular 2:150

B

baking 12:1714–1715
beer 5:701
biochemistry 2:180–182
see also analytical techniques
bioreactors 2:223
biotechnology 2:221–227
in agriculture 2:223–225
bioremediation 2:226
DNA fingerprinting 2:224, 226; 6:773, 774
enzyme production 2:225
food production 2:225
in medicine 2:221–223
insulin production 2:225
in vitro fertilization (IVF) 2:222; 5:710, 711, 712
monoclonal antibodies 2:221, 224, 226
see also genetic engineering
boids 2:151
bonds, chemical 5:617
bovine growth hormone/bovine
somatotropin (BGH/BST) 2:224, 227; 4:545
bread 5:701
brewing 12:1715
BST *see* bovine growth hormone/
bovine somatotropin
butanol, from bacterial fermentation
5:702, 703
buttermilk 5:701
butylated hydroxytoluene (BHT) 6:764
butylate hydroxyanisole (BHA) 6:764

C

calcitonin, synthetic form 2:180–181
carbamoyl phosphate 12:1667
carbamoyl phosphate synthetase 12:1667, 1668
carbohydrates 3:297–301; 8:1143
catabolism 3:300
dietary 3:301; 9:1226, 1229
digestion 3:299; 9:1260
energy content 2:279
energy storage 3:297–298; 5:619
formation 3:298–299
glucose
and energy 3:299–301
regulation 3:301
"loading" 3:299
metabolism 2:280
errors of 8:1123–1124
without oxygen *see* fermentation
and plant structure 3:298
storage 3:297–298
in plants 3:297
types 3:297
in weight-loss diets 3:300
see also cellulose
catalysts 5:617, 629
cellulose 3:298, 341–342; 8:1143
digestion 3:342; 4:514; 9:1228

by cockroaches 3:388
by fungi 3:342
by mammals 4:514, 521; 9:1226;
10:1380, 1393; 11:1461, 1581;
12:1661
by termites 1:140; 10:1380; 11:1461,
1462; 12:1611
industrial uses 3:342, 417
in plant cell walls 3:298, 341–342
in plant fibers 3:341; 6:725
centrifugation 1:67–68
ultracentrifugation 2:181; 10:1376;
12:1677
cheese 2:225, 227; 5:700, 701;
6:763
chemical energy, stored, *see also* ATP;
FADH2; NADH; NADPH
chemiosmosis 5:618
chemiosmotic-coupling hypothesis
10:1306
cholesterol esters 5:691
chromatography 1:63, 66–67; 2:181
chromoproteins 10:1376
citrate 7:995
citric acid cycle *see* Krebs cycle
citrulline 12:1667
cloning 3:381–386; 11:1482
DNA 3:384
humans 3:385; 11:1558, 1559
sheep 3:340, 383–384; 11:1558
therapeutic 3:384–386; 11:1558, 1559
CoA (coenzyme A) 12:1691
coenzymes 9:1227
coenzyme A (CoA) 12:1691
cofactors, for enzyme activity 5:630–631
corn starch, fermentation 5:702
covalent bonds 5:617
cyclo-oxygenase 1 (COX-1) 2:182
cysteine 1:63
cytochromes 10:1377
in photosynthesis 7:973
in respiration 8:1119
similar amino acid sequences in 10:1377

D

detergents, biological 2:222
disaccharides 3:297
DNA ligases 8:1145
dyes
from lichens 8:1035
from plants 8:1029
from snails 8:1149
for microscopy 7:895

E

echolalia 2:161
electron transfer/oxidative
phosphorylation 2:159, 160; 3:300; 7:993,
996; 8:1118–1119
electrophoresis 1:67; 2:181–182
for DNA analysis 7:921, 922
gel 8:1145
electroporation 6:805–806, 807
eleostearic acid 5:690
ELISA 5:630
emergent phenomena 2:150–151
endergonic reactions 5:617
evolutionary algorithms 2:151–152
exergonic reactions 5:617

F

FAD 5:618; 7:996
FADH2 2:159–160; 7:996
fats and oils 5:689–692
absorption
by the lymphatic system 8:1063
from the digestive system 4:518–519
breakdown 8:1118
and cancer 3:295
dietary 5:690; 9:1226, 1229
digestion 8:1047; 9:1260
pollutants in 9:1244
energy content 2:279
as energy storage 5:619, 691; 8:1121
from seeds 11:1477
function 5:691–692
hydrogenation 5:692
metabolism 2:280
errors 8:1124
oil 5:690
saturated and unsaturated 5:689
monounsaturated fats 5:690
polyunsaturated fats 5:690
uses 5:691
see also fatty acids; lipids
fatty acids 5:689–690
essential 5:692
**fermentation 2:159, 225, 226; 3:301;
5:619, 700–703; 8:1117**
acetone-butanol 5:702, 703
of amino acids 5:703
discovery of action 8:1127, 1128; 9:1269
in food and drink production 2:172;
5:700, 701; 6:763; 12:1715
in the gut 5:703; 11:1452, 1453
industrial 5:702
in muscle cells 5:703
to make antibiotics 1:109
fish, shoals, computer simulation 2:151
flavone 10:1311
flavonoids 10:1311
food
GM *see* genetically modified (GM) foods
pasteurization 1:115; 2:226–227; 6:765;
8:1128; 9:1269, 1270
technology
fermented foods 5:700, 701; 12:1715
using microorganisms 8:1132
fructose-6-phosphate 5:702; 10:1304
fructose 3:297, 298, 301
fructose-1,6-biphosphate 2:159; 5:702
fumarase 7:995
fumarate 12:1667

G

Game of Life 2:150
gasoline, from seaweeds 7:988
GDP (guanosine diphosphate) 7:995
**gene therapy 2:222; 6:804–808;
8:1093; 9:1290**
for Parkinson's disease 4:497
**genetically modified (GM) foods
(GMFs) 2:223–224, 225;
6:809–811; 9:1244**

Flavr Savr tomatoes 2:227; 6:765, 794,
809
safety 2:225; 6:811
see also genetic engineering, crops
genetically modified organisms (GMOs)
see genetic engineering
genetic engineering 2:181, 221
for artificial blood 2:246
cellulose from 6:725
crops 6:809–811; 9:1244
Flavr Savr tomatoes 2:227; 6:765, 794
for nitrogen fixation 9:1219
resistant to pesticides 9:1247
ethics 2:187, 225
of farm animals 1:92
and food preservation 6:765
of growth hormone 2:224
for insulin production 2:223
recombinant DNA 2:223; 8:1143
transgenic organisms, plants 2:223;
6:809; 9:1243, 1244
using bacteria 2:170; 8:1131
versus selective breeding 11:1482
and viruses 12:1678–1679
yeasts and 12:1715
see also gene therapy
glucose 3:297, 298
alpha- and beta-glucose 3:341
blood 4:506; 7:902, 902–903;
9:1260–1261
self-monitoring 4:507
and energy 3:299–300; 8:1117, 1121
energy from 2:159
fermentation 5:701–703
regulation by the liver 8:1047
glucose-6-phosphate 3:300–301; 5:702
glutamate dehydrogenase 12:1667, 1668
glyceraldehyde-3-phosphate (GALP)
2:159; 5:702; 8:1118
glycerol 5:689; 8:1118; 12:1715
glycine 1:62, 63
glycolysis 2:159, 269–270; 5:618–619;
7:993, 994; 8:1117–1118
glycylalanine 1:63
glycylalanylcysteine 1:63
GTP (guanosine triphosphate) 7:995;
12:1668
guanine
a pigment 10:1311
a product of excretion 12:1666
guanosine diphosphate (GDP) 7:995
guanosine triphosphate (GTP) 7:995;
12:1668

H

Hatch-Slack (C4) cycle 8:1023
heme 10:1309–1310
hyaluronate 3:298
hydrogenation, of oils 5:692

I

indoloids 6:762
insemination, artificial *see* artificial
insemination

Bold words with bold page numbers indicate complete articles; bold numbers preceding colons are volume numbers; numbers following colons indicate page numbers; italic page numbers refer to illustrations or other graphics.

ionic bonds **5**:617
isocitrate **7**:995
isocitrate dehydrogenase **7**:995
isomers, of amino acids **1**:*62*, 63
isotopes, radioactive, for tagging
   see radioactive tagging

K

Kaiser, Emil **2**:180–181
ketoglutarate, alpha- **7**:995; **12**:1665,
   1668
ketoglutarate dehydrogenase, alpha-
   7:995
Krebs, Hans A. **2**:180; **7**:*994*;
   12:1666–1667
Krebs cycle (citric acid cycle;
   tricarboxylic acid cycle)
   2:*159*–160, 180; **3**:300; **5**:619,
   632; **7**:**993–996**; **9**:1252

L

lactam rings, beta- **1**:109
lactate dehydrogenase **5**:703
LD50 test **1**:93
legumin **10**:1377
life
   artificial *see* artificial life
   origins of **2**:181; **5**:651
   patenting **2**:190
lignin **12**:1639
   breakdown **11**:1462
link reaction **7**:993, 994
linoleic acid **5**:690, 692
linolenic acid **5**:*690*, 692
lipids **5**:690
   essential **9**:1226
   see also fats and oils
lipoproteins **10**:1376
liposomes **5**:691

M

macromolecules **8**:1142–1144
mass spectroscopy **1**:68; **6**:*772*
meat, preservation **5**:701
microanalysis **1**:68
monomers **8**:1142
monosaccharides **3**:297; **8**:1143
mucoproteins **10**:1376

N

NAD+ **5**:702, *703*; **7**:994, 995
NADH **2**:159–160; **5**:618–619, 702;
   7:994, 995
NADH$_2$ **2**:*159*, 160
NADP+, in photosynthesis **5**:618; **10**:1304
NADPH, in photosynthesis **5**:618; **10**:1304
ninhydrin **1**:63
nucleases, semisynthetic **2**:181
nucleoproteins **10**:1376

O

oil **5**:690
   see also fats and oils
oleic acid **5**:*689*, *691*
oligosaccharides **3**:297
opsin **12**:1685
organic molecules **3**:303
ornithine carbamoylase **12**:1667
ornithine cycle *see* urea cycle

ornithine transcarbamylase (OTC) **6**:807;
   12:1668
oxaloacetic acid/oxaloacetate **7**:995;
   10:1305
oxidation **5**:617
oxidation-reduction (redox) reactions
   5:618, 700–701; **7**:996

P

palmitic acid **5**:*689*
paraffinoids **6**:762
pasteurization **1**:115; **2**:226–227; **6**:765;
   8:1128; **9**:1269, *1270*
PCR *see* polymerase chain reaction
peptide bonds **1**:63
perfume **11**:1515
PGAL-dehydrogenase **5**:702
pH **1**:16
   optimum for enzymes **5**:631, *632*
pharming **2**:224
phenol coefficient test **1**:117
phenols **1**:116
phosphoenol pyruvate **10**:1305
phosphoenolpyruvic acid **8**:1023
phosphofructokinase **5**:702
phosphoglycerate, in carbon fixation
   10:1304
3-phosphoglyceric acid **8**:1023
phosphoproteins **10**:1376
phosphorylation
   oxidative *see* electron transfer/
      oxidative phosphorylation
   photosynthetic (photophosphorylation)
      10:1304, 1306
   substrate **8**:1118
photophosphorylation (photosyntheic
   phosphorylation) **10**:1304, 1306
pickling **5**:701
polymerase chain reaction (PCR) **3**:384;
   4:535; **6**:774; **8**:1145–1146
   invention **9**:*1173*–1174
polymers **8**:1142
polysaccharides **3**:297; **8**:1143
porcine somatotropin (PST) **2**:224
porphin **10**:1309
preservatives, chemical **6**:764
prostaglandin H synthase-1 **2**:182
prosthetic groups **10**:1376
proteins 10:1375–1378
   action-producing **10**:1377
   animal fibers from **6**:725–726
   antifreeze **4**:472; **8**:1036; **10**:1332
   breakdown **8**:1118; **9**:1226
      starvation and **8**:1120
   complete **10**:1377
   conjugated **10**:1376
   deficiency **10**:1378
      protein-energy malnutrition
         4:*487*–488; **10**:1378
   denaturization **10**:1376
   dietary **9**:1226, 1229; **10**:1377
      metabolism **2**:279, 280
   engineering **2**:180–181
      see also genetic engineering
   functions **10**:1376–1377
   metabolism, errors of **12**:1668
   microbial, in ruminants **11**:1453
   plant **10**:1377
   polymorphism **4**:524

recycled **10**:1377
   shape **8**:1143; **10**:1375–1376
   single-cell (SCP) **12**:1715
   stored **5**:619
   structure **1**:63; **8**:1143–1144; **10**:1375,
      1376
   synthesis **4**:*536*, 537; **7**:919;
      10:1377–*1378*, 1428–1430
   see also amino acids
pterins **10**:1311
purines, as pigments **10**:1311
pyrrole **10**:1309
pyruvate (pyruvic acid) **2**:159; **3**:300

QR

quercetin **10**:1311
radioactive tagging **1**:68; **2**:182
   in food webs **6**:767
   to label drugs **9**:1290
radioistope labeling *see* radioactive tagging
redox potentials **9**:1251–1252
redox reactions **7**:996; **9**:1251
reduction **5**:617
rennin **2**:225
retinal **12**:1685
rhodopsin **10**:1311
rhodopsin *see* visual purple
ribulose diphosphate (RDP) **10**:1304, 1305
robotics
   and artificial life **2**:*149*
   in medicine 10:1432–1435
      for surgery **4**:*497*; **10**:*1432*–1434
      telemedicine **8**:*1094*; **10**:*1433*–1434

S

sausages **5**:701
self-organizing systems **2**:150
single-cell protein (SCP) **12**:1715
soap **5**:*691*
somatotropin
   bovine *see* bovine growth
      hormone/bovine somatotropin
   porcine (PST) **2**:224
Southern blotting **2**:182; **4**:535
spectrography **1**:68
spermatogonia **5**:714
stearic acid **5**:*689*, 690
stereochemistry **9**:1269
subtilisin **2**:181
succinate dehydrogenase **7**:995
succinyl-CoA **7**:995
succinyl-CoA synthesase **7**:995
sugars **3**:297, *298*

T

tagging, radioactive *see* radioactive tagging
terpenoids **6**:762
tetrapyrroles **10**:1309–1310
tetrasaccharides **3**:297
Tierra (digital world) **2**:*152*
tissue culture **3**:382; **11**:1562; **12**:1676
transgenic organisms, plants **2**:223; **6**:809;
   9:*1243*, 1244
tricarboxylic cycle *see* Krebs cycle
trisaccharides **3**:297

U

ultracentrifugation **2**:181; **10**:1376;
   12:1677

"universal constructor" model **2**:150
urea cycle 12:1666–1668
   discovery **12**:1666–1667
   urea **5**:665; **12**:1666
      formation in the liver **8**:1046, *1119*
      in shark tissues **11**:1459
uric acid, as a pigment **10**:1311
use-dilution test **1**:117

V

visual purple (rhodopsin) **10**:1311;
   12:*1685*, 1687
wine **5**:701; **6**:763

X

xanthopterin **10**:1311
X rays
   X-ray crystallography **1**:68; **2**:182
   of viruses **12**:1677
   X-ray diffraction **1**:*68*; **6**:786; **8**:1146

Y

yeast artificial chromosomes (YACs)
   12:1715
yogurt **5**:701

■ BOTANY

A

Abies spp. *see* firs
acacias **1**:118–119; **3**:*390*; **4**:483; **6**:762;
   11:*1562*, 1580–1581
Aconitum spp. (monkshood) **6**:758
Acrasiomycota **8**:1139, 1140
actinomorphic flowers **6**:759
after-ripening **4**:549
agar **1**:48; **7**:988; **8**:*1131*
Agaricus spp. **9**:1185, 1187, 1188
Agathis australis (kauri) **3**:416
Agave spp. **9**:1161, 1278; **10**:1318
air plants *see* bromeliads
Aizoaceae **2**:*273*, 274
alaria **7**:987
Aleuria aurantia (orange peel fungus) **9**:*1186*
alfalfa **5**:718; **8**:1028; **10**:1322
   pests of **7**:*960*
   seeds **4**:*547*, 549
algae 1:46–49; **8**:1130; **10**:1380–1381
   benthic **1**:49
   blooms **1**:48; **7**:*1001*; **10**:*1302*
   brown **1**:47–48; **7**:985–986, 987;
      10:1381
   classification **1**:46–47; **10**:1325
   coral reef **1**:49
   distribution **1**:48–48
   epiphytic **5**:642
   euglenoids **1**:47; **10**:*1381*
   golden-brown **1**:47
   green **1**:49; **7**:987; **10**:1381
   and humans **1**:48
   prokaryotic **1**:47
   red **1**:46, 48; **7**:986, *987*; **10**:1381;
      11:1493
   reproduction in **1**:49; **5**:715–716
   symbiotic
      with corals **4**:449–450, 453; **11**:1581
      relationship with fungi *see* lichens
   see also dinoflagellates; kelps and seaweeds
Allium spp. **2**:265, 266

almonds 6:792
Aloe dichotoma (quiver tree) 12:1617
alternation of generations
  in plants 5:590; 10:1325
    ferns and fern allies 5:704–705
    flowering plants 6:759–760
    mosses, liverworts, and hornworts
      9:1165
    seaweeds 7:987
Amanita spp.
  A. muscaria (fly agaric) 9:1185,
    1186, 1187
  A. phalloides (death cap) 9:1188;
    11:1460
Ambrosia spp. (ragweed) 2:217;
    10:1317; 11:1568
Anabaena spp. 1:47
angiosperms (flowering plants)
    1:77–80; 11:1475
  drugs (medicinal) from 1:81
  embryo 5:716
  evolution 1:79, 80
    coevolution with animals 6:760
  fertilization 1:79; 5:716; 11:1475
  flowers *see* flowers and flower structure
  germination 1:79
  harmful 1:80
  number of species 5:650
  pollination 1:78–79; 6:761
    see also pollination
  seeds
    dispersal 1:79
    structure 1:79
  vegetative propagation 1:80
  vegetative reproduction 11:1562
  wood 11:1562
  see also dicotyledons; flowers and flower
    structure; monocotyledons; seeds
Angraecum sesquipedale 2:268
annual plants 1:101–102; 11:1476
Anthocerotophyta 9:1165; 10:1326
Anthophyta *see* Magnoliophyta
antipodals 5:590
Antirrhinum spp. (snapdragon) 1:78; 6:812;
    10:1337
apical dominance 8:1023
apomixis 10:1405
apples 6:794, 795
Aptenia 2:274
Araceae 10:1318
Arachis hypogaea (peanut) 8:1028
Araucaria araucana (monkey puzzle) 3:416
Araujia sericifera (cruel plant) 10:1318
Arecaceae (Palmae) 9:1258
areoles 2:273
Arisaema sp. (jack-in-the-pulpit) 7:890
aroids 10:1318
arrowroot 12:1650
artichokes, Jerusalem 4:548; 12:1650
Arum maculatum (jack-in-the-pulpit) 6:762;
    10:1318
ascomycetes 6:799–800; 8:1138–1140
Ascophyllum spp. 7:988
aspen trees, propagation 10:1405
Aspergillus spp. 8:1138–1139
  A. fumigatus 8:1139
    and lung disease 7:948
    on peanuts 11:1462
Asplenium spp. 5:706

Astracanthus gummifera (gum traganth)
    8:1029
Azolla 11:1580

B

Bacillariophora 10:1313
Bacillariophyta 1:46
balsams 11:1477
balsa trees 12:1639
bamboo 9:1160, 1161; 11:1560
banana plants 6:796; 9:1160; 10:1338;
    11:1542
  bananas 6:796
Basidiomycetes 8:1139
Basidiomycota 9:1185
basidomycetes 6:799
beans
  climbing plants 3:379
  fava/broad 8:1028
  garbanzo 8:1028
  green, germination 10:1316
  kidney 8:1029
  lima 8:1029
  mescal 8:1029
  poisonous 8:1029
  pole 12:1646
beech 12:1608
  southern 9:1255; 12:1610
Beta spp. (beet) 4:510; 11:1445
Betula spp. (birch) 9:1187
biennial plants 1:101; 2:179
bindweeds 3:379; 12:1649, 1651
birch 9:1187
blackberries 6:795
black spot 10:1321
bladderworts 3:314, 315; 12:1670
Blossfeldia minima 2:273
boletes 9:1186
Boletus spp. 9:1186
bonsai trees 11:1450; 12:1639
botanical gardens 2:251–252
botany 2:253–254; 5:582
bracken 5:706; 7:882; 10:1318
bracket fungi 9:1187
Brassica spp. 9:1229
bromeliads 5:642; 8:1027; 11:1580
broom, seed dispersal 10:1319; 11:1477
broomrape 10:1321; 12:1632
Bryophyllum spp. 8:1027
Bryophyta (bryophytes) 9:1165; 10:1326
  see also mosses, liverworts, and hornworts
**bulbs and corms 2:265–266; 9:1277;
    11:1449**
  bulbs 2:265–266
  corms 2:265–266
Bursera simaruba (gumbo-limbo tree) 5:648
buttercups 1:80; 12:1650
  in polar climates 10:1332
butterworts 3:316

C

C3 plants 10:1305
C4 plants 8:1025; 10:1305
cabbages 9:1229
**cacti and succulents 2:272–274;
    12:1630**
  cacti 2:272–274; 4:482, 499
    ball 2:273
    beavertail 2:273

cochineal 7:884
  epiphytic 5:642
  flowers 2:272
  hedgehog 2:272
  saguaro 2:273, 274; 4:499
  spines 2:273; 8:1022, 1027; 10:1317;
    11:1562
  stomata 1:18–19
  water storage 2:273
  crassulacean acid metabolism 2:273
  succulents 2:272, 274
Caesalpinioideae 8:1029
calabashes 11:1554
Calamus spp. (rattan) 9:1259
Calluna vulgaris (heather) 7:882
Calystegia spp. (bindweed) 3:379; 12:1649,
    1651
Camellia sinensis (tea) 1:51; 8:1013
Cannabis sativa see hemp
capsaicin 1:51
Capsella bursapastoris (shepherd's purse)
    5:601
Capsicum spp. (peppers) 1:51
carbonization, of plant remains 6:783
Carex spp. (sedge) 11:1477
carnauba wax 9:1259; 12:1702
carnauba wax palm 9:1259
Carnegiea gigantea (saguaro cactus) 2:273,
    274; 4:499
**carnivorous plants 3:314–316; 5:609,
    695–696; 10:1317; 12:1625**
  leaves 8:1027
  reflexes 10:1397
carob 8:1029
carotenes 3:317; 9:1227; 10:1311
carotenoids 3:317; 10:1306, 1311
Carpobrotus 2:274
carrots 11:1446
cassava 5:701; 11:1446
Castanea dentata (American chestnut)
    9:1266; 10:1324
Castanospermum australe (Moreton Bay
    chestnut) 12:1599, 1600, 1644
cellulose nitrate 3:342
Center for Plant Conservation 2:252
century flowers 9:1220
century plants 10:1319
Ceranium shuttleworthianum 7:987
Ceratophyllum spp. (hornworts) 10:1338
Chamaedorea elegans (parlor palm) 9:1259
Charophyta 1:47
chayote 11:1554
cheese plants, phototropism 10:1316
chemistry, plant 2:254
chestnuts 6:792
chestnut trees
  American 9:1266; 10:1324
  Moreton Bay 12:1599, 1600, 1644
chickpeas 8:1028
chlorella, cultivation 1:125
Chlorophyta 1:47; 10:1381
cholla, silver 2:273
Chondrus spp. (Irish moss/carragene)
    7:987, 988

chrysanthemums 2:217
Chrysophyta *see* diatoms
Chtridiomycetes 8:1137
cinchona trees 8:1103
Citrus spp. 6:792, 795
citrus fruits 6:792, 795
  prevention of scurvy 8:1095
  seedless 6:792
Cladonia spp. 8:1034, 1036, 1037
Claviceps purpurea (ergot) 1:50; 6:765, 800;
    8:1139
clematis 6:757
climbing plants 3:379–380; 11:1449
clover 8:1028; 10:1322
club mosses 5:706, 707; 10:1326–1327
Coccinia rehmanii 11:1446
cockleburs 2:217
cocoa 1:51; 12:1644
coco-de-mer 9:1259
coconut palms 6:725; 9:1160, 1259
coconuts 9:1160, 1259
Cocos nucifera (coconut palm) 6:725;
    9:1160, 1259
coir 6:725
Colchicum sp. (autumn crocus) 2:266
comfrey 7:888
coneflowers, purple 9:1277
Coniferophyta *see* conifers
**conifers 3:415–417; 10:1326,
    1327–1328; 12:1637, 1638**
  deciduous and evergreen 12:1638
  pollination 10:1338
  shape 12:1646
  timber 3:417; 12:1590, 1639
  see also gymnosperms
Conophytum 2:274
Convallaria majalis (lily-of-the-valley)
    12:1651
copal 3:417
Copernica prunifera (carnauba wax palm)
    9:1259
Corchorus spp. (jute) 3:342
cord grass 11:1493
corms *see* bulbs and corms
Corypha umbraculifera (talipot palm)
    10:1319
cotton 3:342; 4:510
  fibers 6:726
  organically grown 9:1246, 1248, 1249
  pesticide-resistant 9:1247
  pesticides used on 9:1249
Crassulaceae 2:274
Crataegus spp. (hawthorn) 4:482
creosote bushes 9:1277; 10:1319
Crocus spp. 1:80
crocuses
  autumn 2:266
  Chilean blue 2:266
  crottle lichen 8:1035
  cruel plant 10:1318
Cryptocarpus pyriformis (saltbush) 11:1459
cucumbers 3:380; 11:1554
  squirting 10:1319
Cucumis spp. 11:1554

Bold words with bold page numbers indicate complete articles; bold numbers preceding colons are volume numbers; numbers following colons indicate page numbers; italic page numbers refer to illustrations or other graphics.

Cucurbitaceae *see* squash family
Cucurbita spp. **11**:1554, *1555*
Cucurbitoideae **11**:1555
cudbear **8**:1035
"Culpepper's Herbal" **7**:888
Cupressus spp. **3**:415
Cuscuta spp. (dodder) **3**:379; **9**:1265;
 10:1321; **12**:*1632*
cuttings, plant **3**:381; **11**:1481
Cyathea spp. **5**:706
Cycadophyta (cycads) **9**:1259; **10**:1327
Cycas spp. **9**:1259
cyclamens **2**:266
Cycnoches sp. **9**:1241
Cyperus spp.
 C. congestus **11**:1446
 C. papyrus **10**:1427
cypresses **3**:415, 416; **5**:648
 bald **12**:1638
 swamp **12**:*1703*
Cypripedium spp. (lady's slipper) **9**:1240
Cystopteris spp. (bladder fern) **10**:*1327*
Cytisus spp. (broom) **10**:1319; **11**:1477

D

daffodils **6**:759
 winter **2**:266
Dahlia spp. (dahlia) **9**:*1189*; **11**:1449;
 12:1650
dandelions **1**:80; **4**:*509*; **6**:725, 791;
 10:1405
 roots **11**:1449
 seeds **11**:*1477*
Daphne spp. **1**:80
Darlingtonia spp. **8**:1027
date palms *see* palms, date
Daucus carota (carrot) **11**:1446
death cap fungus **9**:*1188*; **11**:*1460*
dendrochronology **12**:1640
Dendrosicyos socotranus **11**:1555
Deuteromycota **8**:1137
diatoms (Chrysophyta) **1**:47; **8**:*1130*;
 10:*1312*, 1313, 1380–1381
Dicentra spectabilis (Dutchman's breeches)
 10:1337
Dicksonia spp. **5**:706
dicotyledons 1:78; **4**:**509–510**;
 10:1328; **11**:1476
 anatomy of eudicots **4**:509–510
 differ from monocotyledons **9**:1161
 germination **11**:1478
 leaf veins **8**:1025
 vascular bundles **12**:1669
Digitalis spp. (foxglove) **1**:80; **2**:*179*;
 9:*1291*
Dikaryomycota **6**:799
dinoflagellates **1**:47, 48; **10**:1313,
 1347, 1380
 bioluminescence **2**:*207*
 see also zooxanthellae
Dinomastigota **10**:1313
Dionaea muscipula see Venus's-flytrap
Dioscorea spp. (yam) **3**:380; **9**:1161;
 11:1446
Diplocarpon rosae **10**:1321
Disa uniflora ('flower of the gods' orchid)
 5:609
dispersal, seed *see* seeds, dispersal
dodders **3**:379; **9**:1265; **10**:1321; **12**:*1632*

domestication, of plants **4**:545–*546*
dormancy 4:547–549
 and buds **4**:547–548, *549*
 chapparal plants **3**:350
 effect of day length on **4**:*549*
 innate and imposed **4**:547
 in perennials **4**:547
 role of hormones **4**:548
 seeds **4**:547, 548–549; **11**:1478
 see also germination
 in woody plants **4**:547–548
dormin **4**:548
"drought deciduous" plants **4**:499
drupes **6**:792, 795
dry rot fungus **6**:799; **11**:1462
duckweed **8**:1022
 pepper **7**:987
durians **10**:1318
Durio zibethinus (durian) **10**:1318
Dutch elm disease **2**:178, 184; **9**:1265,
 1294; **10**:1322; **12**:1640
Dutchman's breeches **10**:1337

E

Echballium elaterium (squirting cucumber)
 10:1318
Echinacea purpurea (purple coneflower)
 9:*1277*
Echinocactus ingens (ball cactus) **2**:273
Echinocereus engelmannii (hedgehog cactus)
 2:*272*
eelgrass (tape grass) **6**:761; **10**:1338
Elaeis guineensis (oil palm) **3**:382
elms, Dutch elm disease **2**:178, 184;
 9:1265, 1294; **10**:1322; **12**:1640
Elytrigia repens (couch grass) **12**:1651
English Physician, The ("Culpepper's
 Herbal") **7**:888
Enteromorpha spp. (green nori) **7**:987
epiphytes 5:642; **8**:1027; **12**:1643–1644,
 1670
 adaptations **5**:642
 in the Everglades **5**:*648*
 negative phototropism in **10**:1316
 orchids **9**:1161, 1240
 on underwater plants **4**:439
Equisetum spp. (horsetails) **5**:706, 707
Equisophyta (horsetails) **5**:706, 707;
 10:1327
ergot **1**:50; **6**:765, 800; **8**:1139
Erodium spp. **11**:1477
Erythronium americanum (trout lily / yellow
 adder's tongue) **2**:254
ethnobotany **2**:254; **9**:1292
eucalyptus **12**:1610
eudicots **4**:509–*510*; **10**:1328
Euglena fusca **10**:*1381*
euglenoids (Euglenophyta) **1**:47; **10**:*1381*
Eulophia **11**:1446
Eumycophyta **6**:799

F

Fabaceae *see* legumes
Fagus sylvatica (beech) **12**:1608
fairy rings **9**:*1187*, 1188
Fenestraria **2**:274, *282*
ferns and fern allies 5:704–707;
 10:1326
 classification **5**:705–706, 707

club mosses **5**:706, 707; **10**:1326–1327
ferns **5**:706–707; **10**:1327
 bladder ferns **10**:*1327*
 fork (whisk ferns) **5**:706, 707; **10**:1326
 fossilized **6**:*783*
 tree ferns **5**:*704*, 706; **12**:1637–1638
 vegetative reproduction **5**:*704*, 706
 horsetails **5**:706, 707; **10**:1327
 evolution **10**:1326
 field **12**:1651
 life cycle **5**:704–*705*
 quillworts **10**:1326–1327
feverfew **7**:*888*
Ficus spp. (fig) **12**:*1643*, 1693
fiddleheads **5**:706
figs
 pollination by wasps **12**:1693
 strangler **12**:*1643*
firs **3**:415, 416; **12**:1646
 mycorrhizae **11**:1450
 of the taiga **12**:1591
flax **3**:391; **9**:1248
"flower of the gods" orchid **5**:609
flowers and flower structure 1:79–80;
 6:**757–762**
 coevolution with animals **2**:268; **3**:389–390;
 6:757–758, 760; **10**:1337
 color **6**:761–762
 embryos **5**:601
 fragrance **6**:762
 insect-trapping **6**:*762*
 life cycle **6**:759–761
 nectar **6**:762
 nocturnal **9**:1220
 onset of flowering **6**:759
 pollen *see* pollen
 pollination *see* pollination
 structure **6**:757–759
 see also angiosperms
fly agaric **9**:*1185*, 1186, 1187
Fockea **11**:1446
fossils
 plant **6**:*783*
 living fossils **8**:1050
foxgloves **1**:80; **2**:*179*; **9**:*1291*
fruits and fruit plants 6:791–796;
 10:1328
 economically important **6**:794–796
 fertilization producing **6**:791–792
 fruits
 ancient **6**:794
 compound **6**:792, *794*
 and reproduction **6**:791
 ripening **7**:*909*
 science and **6**:793–794
 simple **6**:792, *793*
 grafting **6**:796
 and humankind **6**:793
 trees, chilling requirements **4**:549
 types of plants **6**:793
Fucus spp. **7**:988
fungi 6:797–800; **8**:1130; **12**:1601, 1670
 alkaloids from **1**:50; **9**:1188
 and aspergillosis **1**:89
 bracket **9**:1187
 breakdown of cellulose **3**:342
 club *see* Basidiomycetes
 and the colonization of land by plants
 11:1581

decomposition by **6**:797; **11**:1460–1462
drugs from, penicillin **1**:109; **2**:164;
 6:*741*–742, 799
evolution **6**:*798*; **9**:1187
farmed by termites **12**:1611
hyphae **8**:1137; **9**:1186; **12**:1670
movement of water and minerals
 12:1632
parasitic **6**:800; **12**:1670
plant diseases **10**:*1320*, *1321–1322*
propagation and dispersal **6**:798
sac *see* ascomycetes
saprophytic **6**:800; **9**:*1225*; **11**:*1460–1462*
spores **6**:798–799; **9**:1186
symbiotic *see* lichens; mycorrhizae
 see also molds and mildews; mushrooms
 and toadstools
fungusroots *see* mycorrhizae
furbelows **7**:988
Fusarium fungus **10**:1321
fuschias **6**:762

G

gametophytes **5**:590, 600–601; **10**:1325
 in algae **1**:49
 fern and fern allies **5**:*705*
 in gymnosperms **3**:416; **5**:601
 in mosses, liverworts, and hornworts
 9:1166
 in seed plants **5**:716
gardens, botanical 2:251–252
garlic **2**:266
 crow **2**:266
geotropism (gravitropism; gravity affecting
 growth) **10**:1316, *1317*; **11**:1449;
 12:1645–1646
germination 1:79; **4**:548–549; **11**:1478
 and tropisms **10**:1316, *1317*; **12**:1647
ginger **12**:1650
Ginkgo biloba see ginkgo trees
ginkgo trees **5**:659; **8**:1050; **10**:1327
ginseng **7**:888; **11**:*1445*, 1446
gladioli, corms **2**:266
Glossopteris **2**:192
Glycine max see soybeans
Gnetophyta **10**:1328
Gonyaulax spp. **1**:48; **2**:217
Gossypium spp. *see* cotton
gourds, bottle **11**:1554
grafting, in plants **6**:796; **11**:*1480*
Gramineae *see* grasses
grapefruit **6**:795
grapes **6**:794, 795
 diseases **10**:*1320*, 1321–1322
grapevines **3**:379
grasses 9:1160
 bent grass **9**:1194
 couch **12**:1651
 lawns **11**:1568
 pollination **7**:890
 rhizomes **12**:1651
growth
 plant
 acid rain and **1**:16
 determinate and indeterminate **1**:36
gumbo-limbo trees **5**:648
gum traganth **8**:1029
gymnosperms 10:1326; **11**:*1475*, 1476;
 12:1637

fertilization **5**:716
wood **11**:1562
see also conifers; Cycadophyta;
ginkgo trees

H

hawthorn **4**:482
heather **6**:800; **7**:*882*
mycorrhizae **6**:800; **7**:882
Hedera spp. **11**:1450
Helianthus spp.
H. annuus (sunflower) **1**:*101*, 102
H. tuberosus (Jerusalem artichoke) **4**:548;
12:1650
Hemerocallis spp. (day lily) **9**:*1160*
hemicelluloses **3**:298
hemlocks **3**:415
hemp **6**:726; **9**:1246, 1248
Hepatophyta **9**:1165; **10**:1326
herbaceous perennials *see* perennial plants,
herbaceous
herbals (catalogs) **2**:253; **7**:888
herbariums **2**:252
herbs, leaf crops **8**:1013
Hevea brasiliensis (rubber tree) **12**:1644
hibiscus **6**:762
hijiki **7**:987
hops **3**:*380*
hornworts **9**:1166; **10**:1326, 1338
horsetails *see* ferns and fern allies
hyacinths **1**:80
hybridization
plant **6**:794; **11**:1481
corn **1**:40
Hydrangea spp. **3**:380; **6**:761
hydrillas **5**:649
hydrophytes **12**:1703
hydrotropism **12**:1645, 1646
Hymenomycetes *see* mushrooms and
toadstools
Hymenomycotina **9**:1185

I

Iceland moss **8**:1036
iceplants **2**:274
Impatiens spp. (balsam) **11**:1477
Indigofera spp. **8**:1029
ink caps, shaggy **9**:1188
irises (plants) **12**:*1651*
seeds **10**:*1326*
Irish moss **7**:987
Isoetopsida **10**:1326–1327
ivy **3**:*380*; **4**:483; **11**:*1449*

J

jack-in-the-pulpit **6**:*762*; **7**:890; **10**:1318
Joshua trees **9**:1160
junipers **3**:415, 416
jute **3**:342

K

Kalanchoe **2**:274
kapok **6**:725
kauris **3**:416
keas, play **10**:1329
kelps and seaweeds 7:985–988
animal feed and fertilizers **7**:988
classification **7**:985
colors **7**:985–986

farming **1**:125
as food **7**:987–988
kelp **1**:*48*; **4**:439; **7**:*986*, 987, 988
translocation **12**:1632
reproduction **7**:987
on the shore **7**:986–987
structure **7**:986–987
useful products from **7**:988
see also algae
kudzu vine **3**:379

L

lady's slippers **9**:1240
Lagenieria siceraria (calabash/bottle gourd)
11:1554
Laminaria spp. **7**:987, 988
larches **3**:415, 417; **12**:1591, 1617
Dahurian **12**:1590
Larix spp. *see* larches
Larrea divaricata subsp. *tridentata* (creosote
bush) **9**:1277; **10**:*1319*
Lasallia pustulata (rock tripe) **8**:1036
Lathyrus spp. **8**:1029
Laurencia pinnatifida (pepper dulse) **7**:987
laver **7**:987
leaves and leaf structure 8:1022–1027
adaptations **8**:*1026*, *1027*
cacti **8**:1022
carotenoids **3**:*317*; **10**:1306
compound and simple **8**:1026
dicotyledon **4**:509–510
"drip tips" **12**:*1643*
falling leaves **8**:*1022*, *1025*
fossil **9**:1257
fractal patterns **3**:*348*
hairs (trichomes) **8**:1026
leaf crops 8:1013–1014
movement **10**:*1316*
palmate leaves **8**:1026; **9**:1258
pinnate leaves **8**:1026; **9**:1258
sclerophyllous **3**:350
sessile leaves **8**:1022
starch storage **3**:297
start of a leaf **8**:1023
tissues **8**:*1023–1025*
variations **8**:1026–1027
variegated **10**:1323
Lecanora esculenta (manna lichen) **8**:1036
legumes 3:380; 8:1028–1029
nitrogen fixation **5**:718; **8**:1029; **9**:1217,
1218; **10**:1322
proteins from **10**:1377
seeds **3**:297; **8**:1029
Leguminosae *see* legumes
lemons **6**:795
Lens culinaris (lentil) **8**:1028
lentils **8**:1028
leven **12**:1650
lianas **3**:379; **11**:1555; **12**:1643
liberty cap **9**:1186
lichens 6:800; 8:1034–1037; 11:1581;
12:1670
of the tundra **12**:1653
licorice **8**:1029
Licuala orbicularis **9**:1258
lilacs, dormancy **4**:547–548
Liliaceae **9**:1160–1161
lilies **2**:254; **9**:1160–1161
day **9**:*1160*

lily-of-the-valley **12**:1651
Lithops **2**:*273*, 274, *282*, 284
liverworts *see* mosses, liverworts, and
hornworts
Livistona spp. (fan palms) **9**:1259
lobelia, giant **9**:1167
locoweed **8**:1029
Lodoicea maldivica (coco-de-mer) **9**:1259
"long-day" plants **2**:217
loofahs **11**:1554
lotus **11**:*1478*
sacred **12**:1650
lucerne **2**:*227*
lupines **8**:1029
Lycoperiscon esculentum *see* tomatoes
Lycophyta *see* club mosses
Lycopodiophyta *see* club mosses
Lycopodiopsida **10**:1326–1327
Lycopodium spp. **5**:706

M

Macrocystis spp. (kelp) **1**:*48*; **7**:*986*, 987
magnolias **2**:*193*; **9**:*1257*
Magnoliophyta (Anthophyta) **1**:77;
10:1328
see also angiosperms; flowers and flower
structure
mahogany trees **5**:648
maidenhair trees *see* ginkgo trees
mangrove trees **5**:648; **11**:1494
red **12**:*1704*
Manihot esculenta (cassava) **5**:701; **11**:1446
manna lichen **8**:1036
Maranta leuconeura (prayer plant) **10**:1316
Marasmius oreades (fairy ring fungus) **9**:*1187*,
1188
Marchantia polymorpha **9**:1165
Marchantiophyta **9**:1165; **10**:1326
Medicago sativa *see* alfalfa
melaleuca **5**:649
melons (plants) **3**:380; **11**:*1554*
Mesembryanthemum crystallinum (iceplant)
2:274
mesquites, desert **4**:499
mildew *see* molds and mildews
milk, soybean **8**:1028
Mimosa pudica (sensitive plant) **10**:*1316*
Mimosoidea **8**:1029
Mimulus cardinalis (monkey flower) **3**:351;
12:1630
minerals, required by plants **2**:277
mint, rusts **10**:1321
mistletoe **9**:*1265*; **10**:1321; **11**:1477
molds and mildews 8:1137–1140
mildews
downy **8**:1138
powdery **8**:*1137*, 1138; **10**:*1321*
molds
on bread **6**:763; **8**:1138; **9**:*1225*
in cheese **6**:763
rusts and smuts **6**:800; **8**:1139; **10**:1321
slime molds and water molds
8:*1139*–1140; **10**:1381–1382
monkey flowers **3**:*351*; **12**:1630

monkey puzzle trees **3**:416
monkshood **6**:758
monocarpic plants **1**:101; **10**:1319
monocotyledons 1:78; 4:*510*;
9:1160–1161; 10:1328; 11:1476
differ from dicotyledons **9**:1161
germination **11**:1478
leaf veins **8**:1025; **9**:1160
vascular bundles **12**:1669
see also grasses; orchids; palms
Monstera tenuis (cheese plant) **10**:1316
morning glory **12**:1646
mosses, liverworts, and hornworts
9:1165–1166
hornworts **9**:1166; **10**:1326, 1338
liverworts **9**:*1165*, 1166; **10**:1326;
12:*1670*
mosses **9**:1165–1166; **10**:1326
epiphytic **12**:*1670*
sphagnum **11**:1532; **12**:1703
of the tundra **12**:1653
movement of water and minerals
12:1632, 1670
reproduction **5**:716
Mucizonia spp. **2**:274
Musa spp. (banana plant) **6**:796; **9**:1160;
10:1338; **11**:*1542*
mushrooms and toadstools 9:1185–1188
alkaloids **1**:50; **9**:1188
edible or poisionous **9**:1188
fairy rings **9**:*1187*, 1188
hallucinogenic **9**:1186
mushrooms **6**:800; **8**:1139
cap **6**:799
cultivated **9**:1185
"magic" **9**:1186
toadstools **6**:797
see also fungi
mycorrhizae **3**:389; **6**:800; **9**:1187–1188;
10:1322; **11**:1450, 1582; **12**:1590
heather **6**:800; **7**:882
orchid **9**:1241
Myxomycota **8**:1139–1140

N

National Arboretum, U.S. **2**:*252*
neem tree, extracts from **9**:1243, *1248*
Nelumbo nucifera (Oriental lotus flower)
11:*1478*
Nepenthes spp. **3**:316
Nereocystis luetkeana (bull kelp) **7**:987
nettles, stinging **4**:483
Neurospora spp. **9**:1225
Nhandiroboideae **11**:1555
Nicotiana spp. (tobacco) **1**:51, 79; **8**:*1014*;
10:1337
nightshade, deadly **1**:57, 80; **9**:1291
nitrocellulose **3**:342
Nopalea cochinillifera (cochineal cactus) **7**:884
nori **7**:987
green **7**:987
Nothofagus sp. (southern beech) **9**:*1255*;
12:1610
nuts **6**:791, 792

O

oak trees
    mycorrhizae **9**:1187–1188
    oak forests **12**:1608
    transpiration **12**:1629
Ochrolechia tartarea (cudbear) **8**:1035
oil palms **3**:382; **9**:1259
Olea europaea (olive tree) **11**:*1480*
olives **6**:795
olive trees, grafting **11**:*1480*
onions **2**:265; **8**:1013
Oomycetes **8**:1140
Oomycota **10**:1381–1382
Opuntia spp. **2**:270, 273
orange peel fungus **9**:*1186*
oranges **6**:795, 796
Orchidaceae **9**:1161, 1240
orchids 9:1161, **1240–1241**
    bee or wasp mimicry **2**:*286*; **6**:761
    endangered **5**:609, 642
    epiphytic **9**:1161, 1240
    "flower of the gods" **5**:609
    Madagascan **3**:390
    mycorrhizae **9**:1241
    pollination **3**:390; **6**:761
    root tubers **11**:1449
    saprophytic **9**:1161
orchil **8**:1035
Orobanche spp. **12**:1632
orrisroot **12**:1650

P

paleobotany **2**:254
Palmae **9**:1258
    see also palms
Palmeria palmata (dulse) **7**:987
palms 2:193; **9**:1160, *1161*, **1258–1259**;
        12:1638
    carnauba wax **9**:1259; **12**:1702
    coconut **6**:725; **9**:1160, 1259
    date **6**:758, 794; **8**:1026; **9**:*1258*, 1259
        pollen **10**:1336
    leaves **8**:1022; **9**:1258
    oil **3**:382; **9**:1259
    rattan **9**:1259
    sago **9**:1259
    talipot **10**:1318
Panax spp. (ginseng) **7**:888; **11**:*1445*, 1446
Papaver spp. **2**:*253*; **9**:*1170*
papermaking **3**:342
Papilionoidea **8**:1028–1029
Parmelia saxatilis (crottle lichen) **8**:*1035*
parsnips **11**:1449
parthenocarpy **6**:792
Parthenocissus spp.
    P. quinquefolia (Virginia creeper) **3**:*380*;
        11:1450
    P. tricuspidata (Boston ivy) **8**:*1149*
peaches, trees, diseases **10**:1321
peanuts **8**:1028
    Aspergillus on **11**:1462
    growing **11**:*1530*
pea(s) **8**:*1028*
    blackeye **8**:1028
    climbing **3**:380; **8**:1027
    germination **12**:*1647*
    and Mendelian genetics **8**:1106–1107;
        11:*1479*–1480
    see also legumes

peat
    bogs containing **11**:1532
    human remains in **9**:1166
pecans **6**:792
Pelagophycus (elk kelp) **7**:987
peppers **1**:51
    Brazilian **5**:649
perennial plants 1:101; **9**:**1277–1278**
    herbaceous **4**:548; **9**:1277
    monocarpic **9**:1278
    woody **9**:1277–1278
        dormancy **4**:547
    see also trees
perianth segments **6**:759
periphyton **5**:642
periwinkles **1**:80; **4**:483; **11**:1493
Phaeophyta **1**:47–48; **10**:1381
Phaseolus spp. **8**:1028; **10**:1316
Phoenix spp. *see* palms, date
photosynthesis 3:298–299; **5**:616, 617;
        8:1023; **10**:**1303–1306**
    anoxygenic **10**:1303
    in bacteria **3**:337
    C3 (Calvin) cycle **8**:1023; **10**:1304–1305
    C4 (Hatch-Slack) cycle **8**:1023
    and the carbon cycle **3**:303
    carbon fixation **10**:1304–1305
    and crassulacean acid metabolism (CAM)
        plants **2**:273; **10**:*1305*–1306
    cytochromes **7**:973
    dark reactions **3**:298–299; **10**:1303, *1304*
    energy pathways **5**:617–618
    equation **10**:1303
    and evolution **10**:1304
    first development of **10**:1304
    inhibited by oxygen **10**:1305
    iron-containing enzymes **7**:973
    light reactions **3**:298; **5**:617–618;
        10:1303, *1304*
    photophosphorylation **10**:1304, 1306
    pigments **5**:616; **10**:1306
        carotenoids **3**:317; **10**:1306
    for primary production **6**:767
phototropism **10**:1316, 1317; **12**:*1646*
    negative **10**:1316
Picea spp. *see* spruces
pineapples **6**:*792*
pines **3**:416
    bristlecone **12**:*1638*, 1640
    cones **3**:415
    leaves **8**:*1026*, 1027
    life cycle **3**:*416*
    lodgepole **3**:417
    mycorrhizae **11**:1450
    needles **8**:*1026*
        decay **11**:1460
    of the taiga **12**:1591
    white **4**:*492*; **12**:1639
    Wollemi **3**:417
Pinguicula spp. (butterwort) **3**:316
Pinus spp. *see* pines
Piper nigrum (pepper vine) **3**:380
Pisum sativum see pea(s)
pitcher plants **3**:316, 379; **8**:1027;
        10:1317
plagiogravitropism **12**:1646
plagiotropism **12**:1646
Plantago media (hoary plantain) **7**:*890*
plantains, hoary **7**:*890*

plants 10:**1325–1328**
    aging (senescence) **1**:36; **10**:1319
    alarm signals between **10**:1317
    alkaloids **1**:50
    anatomy **1**:69–70; **2**:253
    annual 1:**101–102**; **11**:1476
    behavior 10:**1315–1319**
        timing process **10**:1317
    biennial 1:101; **2**:179
    carnivorous *see* carnivorous plants
    cells **3**:*335*–336, *337*
    classification **10**:1326–1328
    colonization of the land by **11**:1581
    communication between **3**:404
    desert **2**:211; **4**:*499*–500; **11**:*1459*;
        12:1617
        cacti and succulents **2**:273
    diseases 10:**1320–1324**
        bacterial **10**:1322–1323
        fungal **6**:800; **10**:*1320*, *1321*–1322
        human control of **10**:1323
        mollicutes **10**:1323
        subviral **10**:1324
        viral **10**:1323–*1324*; **12**:1678, 1683
    domestication **4**:545–*546*
    economic importance **10**:*1328*
    egg cells **5**:590
    excretion in **5**:670
    gas exchange **10**:*1424*; **12**:1629
    growth
        acid rain and **1**:16
        determinate and indeterminate **1**:36
    healing of tissues **10**:1316–1317
    hormones **7**:908–909
    life cycles **10**:1325
    long-day and short-day **2**:217
    mountain **9**:1169–*1170*
    native or exotic? **2**:194
    nonvascular **12**:1670
    perennial *see* perennial plants
    as pests *see* weeds
    as primary producers **6**:766
    reflexes in **10**:1397
    senescence **10**:1319
    stress in **11**:1567
    structure, carbohydrates and **3**:298
    study of *see* botany
    in suburbia **11**:1568
    thermoregulation **12**:1617
Platanus occidentalis (sycamore) **9**:*1278*
pneumatophores **3**:416
Poaceae *see* grasses
poison ivy **1**:53
poison oak **1**:53; **4**:483
pollen **1**:78; **6**:*761*, 762; **10**:1326,
        1335–1336
    fossilized **6**:783
pollination 10:**1335–1338**, 1408
    angiosperm **1**:78–79; **6**:761
    and animal/plant coevolution **2**:268;
        3:389–390; **6**:757–758, 760;
        10:1337
    cross-pollination **1**:78; **6**:761; **10**:1335
    fertilization **6**:760
    formation of pollen grains **10**:1335–1336
    self-pollination **1**:78; **6**:761; **10**:1335
    using animals **1**:78; **6**:761, 762; **10**:1318
        bats **9**:1220
        birds **1**:78–79

    insects **6**:*761*; **7**:890; **9**:1240; **10**:*1335*,
        1336–1337; **12**:*1693*
    using mimicry, in the bee orchid **2**:*286*;
        6:761
    using water **6**:761, 762; **10**:1338
    using wind **1**:78; **6**:761; **7**:890; **9**:1241;
        10:*1338*
Polypodiophyta (Pterophyta) **10**:1327
Polystichum spp. **5**:706
pomegranates **1**:50–51; **6**:794
pomelos **6**:795
pomes **6**:792
poplars **4**:547–548; **12**:1639
    balsam **12**:1590
poppies **2**:*253*; **9**:*1170*
Populus balsamifera (balsam poplar) **12**:1590
Porphyra spp. (nori/laver) **7**:987
potatoes
    and Colorado beetles **2**:*178*
    crops **11**:1446
    defense **4**:483
    disease-resistant **2**:225
    diseases
        blight **8**:*1138*; **10**:*1321*, 1322
        common scab **10**:1322
    dormancy **4**:548
    genetically modified plants **6**:810
    hog **11**:1445
    Indian **11**:1445
    planting **12**:1651
    rhizomes **12**:*1650*
    sweet **11**:1445, 1446
    tuber formation **11**:1562; **12**:1649, *1650*
    white/Irish **12**:1649
prayer plants **10**:1316
Prosopis (mesquite) **4**:499
Protista
    movement of water and minerals
        12:1632
    see also algae; kelps and seaweeds
Protococcus **9**:1165
Psilocybe spp. **9**:*1186*
Psilophyta (fork/whisk ferns) **5**:706, *707*;
        10:1326
Psilotum spp. (fork-fern) **5**:706
Pteridium spp. (bracken fern) **5**:706; **7**:*882*;
        10:1318
Pteridophyta **5**:705; **10**:1326–1327
    see also ferns and fern allies
Pteridospermales **11**:1475
Pterophyta (Polypodiophyta) **10**:*1327*
pulses **8**:1028
pumpkins **11**:1554
Pyrrhophyta **10**:1346, 1380
    see also dinoflagellates

Q

Quercus spp. *see* oak trees
quillworts **10**:1326–1327
quiver tree **12**:1617

R

Rafflesia spp. **6**:*759*
ragweed **2**:217; **10**:1317, 1338; **11**:1568
Ramalina spp. **8**:1036
Ranunculus spp. **1**:79; **10**:*1332*
raspberry plants **10**:1405
    raspberries **6**:795
rattans **9**:1259

rayon **3**:342
redwoods **12**:1608
  coastal **3**:416; **8**:1026; **12**:1608
  dawn **3**:416
  mycorrhizae **11**:1450
reindeer moss **8**:*1036*, 1037
Rhizanthella sp. **9**:*1240*
Rhizocarpon geographicum (map lichen) **8**:1035
rhizomes *see* tubers and rhizomes
Rhizophora mangle (red mangrove) **12**:*1704*
Rhizopus spp. **8**:1138; **9**:*1225*
Rhododendron spp. (rhododendron) **1**:77
Rhodophyta **1**:46, 48; **10**:1381
Rhus spp. **1**:53
Roccella spp. **8**:1035
rock tripe **8**:1036
roots and root systems 11:1447–1450
  absorbency **8**:1026
  crops 11:1445–1446
  development **11**:1447–1448
  growth **11**:1560
  and mycorrhizae **6**:800; **9**:1187–1188, 1241; **10**:1321; **11**:1450
  nodules **8**:*1029*; **11**:1531
  oxygen requirements **9**:1253
  of plants in dry habitats and deserts **11**:1449–1450
  root cap **11**:1560
  root/shoot balance **11**:1448
  size **8**:*1148*; **11**:1450
  storage in **11**:1449
  "territorial" **12**:1613
  transport by **11**:1448
  tropisms **11**:1449; **12**:1646, *1647*
  types **11**:1448–1449
    adventitious **11**:*1449*, 1450
    aerial **3**:380; **11**:1450
    buttresses **12**:1643
    primary roots **11**:1448–1449, 1476
    prop roots **11**:1532; **12**:*1704*
    tap roots **11**:1449
Rosa spp. *see* rose family
rose family
  fruit crops **6**:794–795
  fungal diseases **10**:1321
roses **3**:*380*; **4**:482
rots
  dry **6**:799
  soft **10**:1322
rubber trees **12**:1644
Rubus spp. **6**:795
rusts **6**:800; **8**:1139; **10**:1321
  mint **10**:1321
Rutacea **6**:795

S

Saccharomyces spp. (yeasts) **5**:701; **12**:*1714*, 1715
Saccharum officinarum see sugar cane
Saccorhiza polysichoides (furbelow) **7**:988
sago palms **9**:1259
Salix sitchensis (Sitka willow) **10**:1317
saltbushes **11**:*1459*
saplings **12**:1639
Sarracenia spp. **3**:316
saxifrage, golden **6**:762
scarification, seed **4**:*547*, 549
schizocarps **2**:274

Scilla **11**:1446
sea cabbage **11**:1493
sea grasses **4**:439
sea lettuce **7**:987
seaweeds *see* kelps and seaweeds
Sechium edule (chayote/chocho) **11**:1554
sedges **11**:1477
Sedum spp. **2**:*274*
seed ferns **11**:1475
seed plants *see* angiosperms; gymnosperms
seeds 5:716; **11:1475–1478**
  ancient **11**:*1478*
  banks **2**:252; **3**:427; **4**:473
  coat (testa) **10**:1326
  dispersal **1**:79; **10**:1318–1319, *1326*; **11**:*1476–1477*
    active **10**:1319; **11**:1477
    by animals **1**:79; **10**:1318, 1319; **11**:1477
    by birds **1**:79; **11**:1477
    by water **11**:1477
    by wind **1**:79; **6**:725; **10**:1319; **11**:*1477*
  and fruit capsules **11**:1477–1478
  splash cup **2**:274
  dormancy **4**:*547*, 548–549; **11**:1478
  evolution **5**:715; **10**:1325, 1326; **11**:1475
  fire and **4**:*548*
  scarification **4**:*547*, 549
  structure **1**:79
  used by man **11**:1477
Selaginella spp. (spike moss) **5**:706
sensitive plant **10**:*1316*
Sequoiadendron giganteum (giant sequoia) **3**:*415*, 416; **12**:1608
sequoias, giant **3**:*415*, 416; **12**:1608
Sequoia sempervirens (coastal redwood) **3**:416; **8**:1026; **12**:1608
Serpula lacrymans (dry rot fungus) **6**:799; **11**:1462
shepherd's purse **5**:*601*
short-day plants **2**:217
shrubs **9**:1277–1278; **12**:1637
  development of woody stems **11**:*1561*
skydusters **9**:1258
smuts **8**:1139
snapdragons
  alleles for color **6**:812
  pollination **1**:78; **10**:1337
soybeans **8**:1028
  and acid rain **1**:17
  herbicide-resistant **6**:810
Spanish moss **5**:642
Spermatophyta (spermatophytes) **10**:1325
sphagnum mosses **11**:1532; **12**:1703
spider plants **10**:1405
spinach **2**:217; **10**:1317–1318
Spinacia oleracea (spinach) **2**:217; **8**:1014; **10**:1317–1318
sporophytes **5**:590; **10**:1325
  in algae **1**:49
  fern and fern allies **5**:704–*705*
  gymosperm **3**:416
  in mosses and liverworts **9**:1166
spruces **3**:415, 416, 417; **4**:492
spurges **2**:274
squash family 3:380; **11:1554–1555**

stems and stem systems 10:1318; **11:1560–1562**
  cacti **2**:273
  climbing **3**:379, 380
  tropism **12**:*1647*
  see also bulbs and corms; tubers and rhizomes; vascular systems
Sternbergia candida (winter daffodil) **2**:266
Sticta canariensis (canary sticta) **8**:1037
stonecrops, wall-pepper **2**:274
stoneplants **2**:285
stoneworts **1**:47
storksbill **11**:1477
stratification **4**:549
strawberry plants **6**:795
  runners **3**:*382*
  stolons **10**:1405
succulents *see* cacti and succulents
sugar beet **4**:510
sugar cane, a C4 plant **10**:1305
sunflowers **1**:*101*, 102; **10**:*1315*
Swietenia spp. (mahogany) **5**:648
sycamores **4**:547–548; **9**:*1278*
Symphytum officinale (comfrey) **7**:888
synergids **5**:590

T

tamaracks **12**:1591
Tanacetum parthenium (feverfew) **7**:*888*
tannins **3**:404; **4**:483; **11**:1562
tape grass *see* eelgrass
Taphrina deformans **10**:1321
Taraxacum spp. *see* dandelions
taxes **12**:1645, 1647
Taxodium spp. **3**:415, 416; **5**:648; **12**:*1703*
taxonomy, plant **2**:254
teak **12**:*1644*
Tecophilaea cyanocrocus (Chilean blue crocus) **2**:266
Tectaria gemmifera **5**:706
Tectona grandis (teak) **12**:*1644*
Teliomycetes *see* rusts; smuts
Teliomycotina **9**:1185
Thalassia spp. **10**:1338
thigmotropism **3**:380; **12**:1645, 1646
Tillandsia usneoides (Spanish moss) **5**:642
timber **3**:*417*; **12**:1590, 1639
  see also wood
Tmesipteris spp. (fork-fern) **5**:706
toadstools *see* mushrooms and toadstools
tobacco **1**:79; **10**:1337
tomatoes **6**:793
  diseases **10**:*1322*
  Flavr Savr **2**:227; **6**:765, 794, 809
  freeze-resistant **2**:225; **6**:765
  plants, response to attack **10**:1317
toxins, from plants **12**:1640
transpiration and translocation 12:1629–1632
  guttation **8**:1026; **12**:1632
  translocation **11**:1448, 1561; **12**:1631–1632
  transpiration **7**:902; **8**:1026; **11**:1448, 1561; **12**:*1629–1631*, 1669

see also vascular systems
trees 9:*1277–1278*; **12:1637–1640**
  age and aging of **12**:*1638*, 1640
  angiosperm (flowering) **12**:1637, 1638
  apical dominance **8**:1023
  bark **12**:1639
  bonsai **11**:*1450*; **12**:1639
  deciduous **2**:209; **8**:*1022*, 1025; **12**:1608, 1638
  decomposition of dead **11**:1460–1462; **12**:1609
  development **12**:1639
    of woody stems **11**:*1561*
  diseases **12**:1640
    Dutch elm disease **2**:178, 184; **9**:1265, 1294; **10**:1322; **12**:1640
  distribution **12**:1637
    due to glaciation **2**:194
  diversity **12**:1637
  dormancy **4**:547–548
  effects of acid rain **4**:491–492
  eudicot **4**:510
  evergreen **2**:209; **12**:1638
  fossilized **12**:1638
  fruit **4**:549
  gymnosperm **12**:1637, 1638
    see also conifers; Cycadophyta; ginkgo trees
  hardwood **11**:1562
  on island habitats **7**:977
  life in **12**:1640
  monocotyledonous *see* palms
  permaculture and **9**:1281–1282
  pests of **12**:1640
  record-breaking **12**:1608, *1638*, 1640
  rings, annual **12**:1639, *1640*
  roots **11**:1450; **12**:1640
  shade-tolerant **12**:1643
  shape **12**:*1637*, 1639
  softwood **11**:1562; **12**:1637, 1639
  structure **12**:1639–1640
  of the taiga **12**:1591
  of the tundra **12**:1653
  see also conifers; timber; wood
Trifolium spp. (clover) **8**:1028; **10**:1322
tropisms and taxes 12:1645–1647
  taxes **12**:1645, 1647
  tropisms **10**:1316; **12**:1645–1646
    geotropism (gravitropism; gravity affecting growth) **10**:1316, *1317*; **11**:1449; **12**:1645–1646
    phototropism **10**:1316, 1317
    plagiotropism **12**:1646
    thigmotropism **3**:380; **12**:1646
Tsuga spp. (hemlocks) **3**:415
tubers and rhizomes 11:1449; **12:1649–1651**
  crops **12**:1650
  rhizomes **10**:1318; **11**:*1560*; **12**:1646, *1649*, 1650–1651
  tubers **12**:1649–*1650*
    root **11**:1449; **12**:1650
    stem **4**:548

Bold words with bold page numbers indicate complete articles; bold numbers preceding colons are volume numbers; numbers following colons indicate page numbers; italic page numbers refer to illustrations or other graphics.

Tulippa spp. *see* tulips
tulips 1:*78*
  bulbs 2:*265*
  viral infections 10:*1323*

U

Ulmus spp. (elm) 2:184
Ulva spp. (sea lettuce) 7:987
Umbilicaria spp. 8:1036
Undaria pinatifida (wakame) 7:987
Urtica dioica (stinging nettle) 4:483
Ustilaginomycotina 9:1185
Utricularia spp. (bladderworts) 3:314, *315*;
  12:1670

V

Vallisneria spp. (eelgrass/tape grass)
  10:1338
vascular systems 12:1669–1670
  plant 1:70; 11:1560–1561; 12:1669
    aquatic vascular plants 12:1670
    eudicot 4:509
    root 11:1448
    vascular bundles 4:509
    xylem and phloem 4:509;
      8:1024–1025; 11:1448, 1561;
      12:1631–1632, *1669*
    see also stems and stem systems
vegetables, biennial 2:179
vegetative reproduction, plant 1:80; 2:266;
  10:1405; 11:1562; 12:1650
Venus's-flytrap 3:314, 316; 5:696; 8:*1027*;
  10:1316, 1397; 12:1625, 1646
  endangered 5:*609*; 10:1317
vetches 3:379
Vicia spp. 8:1028
Victoria amazonica 10:1318
Vigna spp. (blackeye pea) 8:1028
vines 6:795
  pepper 3:380
  woody *see* lianas
Virginia creeper 3:*380*; 11:1450
Viscum album (mistletoe) 9:*1265*; 10:1321
Vitis spp. 3:380

W

wakame 7:987
walnuts 6:792
Washingtonia spp. 9:1258
water
  storage in desert plants 2:272
  transportation in plants *see* transpiration
  water stress in plants 11:1567
water hyacinths 5:648
water lilies, Amazon 10:1318
watermelons 11:1554
water molds 8:1140; 10:1382
weeds
  genes from transgenic plants spreading to
    9:*1243*, 1244
  in suburbia 11:1568
Welwitschia mirabilis 10:*1305*
whisk ferns (fork-ferns) 5:706, *707*;
  10:1326
whistling thorns 11:*1562*
willows 1:78; 9:1292
  Sitka 10:1317
wilts, fusarium 10:1321
wisteria 3:379

witch hazel 7:887
wood 6:725
  decomposition of 11:1460–1462;
    12:1609
  development of woody stems 11:*1561*
  fossilized 12:1638
  hardwood 11:1562
  knotholes 11:1562
  softwood 11:1562; 12:1639
  see also timber; trees
woody perennials *see* perennial plants,
woody wracks 7:988

X

Xanthium strumarium (cocklebur) 2:217
xerophytes 12:1630
  at high altitude 9:1169
  see also cacti and succulents
Xerosicyos 11:1555

Y

yeasts 5:700; 12:**1714–1716**
  as animal fodder 12:1715
  baker's 5:701; 12:1715, 1716
  dietary supplements 12:1715–1716
  dried 12:1716
  fermentation by 2:159; 11:1461
  in food production 5:701; 12:1714–1715
  food spoilage 12:1716
  health problems from 12:1716
  reproduction 8:1082; 12:1714
yellowwoods 3:416, 417
yews, drugs from 3:417; 9:1290
yuccas 9:1160
  and coevolution 10:*1336*
  see also Joshua trees

Z

zooxanthellae 4:449–450, 453
Zostera marina (eelgrass) 6:761
zoysia 12:1651
zucchini 11:1554, *1555*
zygomorphic flowers 6:759
Zygomycota 6:799; 8:1137–1138

■ ECOLOGY

A

Abingdon Island 3:410; 6:770
abyssal plain 9:1231
abyssal zone 9:1231, 1237
  discovery of life in 9:1239
acid rain 1:15–17; 4:491–492; 7:1001;
  10:1340
  natural buffers against 1:16; 11:1459
adaptation 1:18–22
  to cave life 3:326–328
  and evolution 1:20–*21*; 5:650–651,
    656–657
  to high altitude 8:*1058*; 9:1169–1170;
    10:1307, *1423*
  human 1:22
  to life in the tundra 12:1653–1654
  to the parasitic mode of life 9:1267–1268
  to polar life 10:1332
  in populations 1:22
  for upright walking 1:22
adaptive radiation 11:1541–1542
  Galápagos finches 9:1192; 11:1541

Agent Orange 4:*490*, *532*
air *see* atmosphere
Alar 10:1344
Aldabra Island 4:450
Alps, Tyrol 9:*1167*
aluminum, recycling 12:1696–1697
Amazon River 2:211
ammonification 9:1218
Animal Ecology (Charles Elton) 6:769
Antarctic 9:1236; 10:1331, 1333–*1334*
  ozone hole over 2:*157*; 10:1341
  see also polar regions
Appalachians, southern, forests 12:1607
aquariums 1:*125*, 126–129; 5:*585*
Aral Sea 4:505
Arctic 10:1331, 1332–*1333*
  see also polar regions
asteroids
  collision with Earth 5:624
  and extinction of dinosaurs 5:624
atmosphere 2:154–157
  air pressure 2:155
  analysis of 2:155
  carbon dioxide 2:155; 3:*302*, 303, 306
    a greenhouse gas 2:157; 3:304, 306;
      4:492–493; 6:802; 10:1341;
      11:1542; 12:1644
  carbon monoxide 2:156
  chemical compositions 2:155
  Earth's early 2:156–157; 3:332; 5:582;
    6:801
  effect of life on 6:801
  and environmental diseases 5:*625*–626
  layers 2:154–*155*
  lead in 5:625
  models 2:155
  nitrogen 1:126
  nitrogen oxides *see* nitrogen oxides
  particulates in 2:*154*, 155–156; 5:625
  pollution *see* pollution, air
  sulfur dioxide 1:16; 5:625; 10:1340
    see also acid rain
  see also greenhouse gases and greenhouse
    effect; oxygen; ozone
atolls 4:448; 7:*974*
Australia, temperate rain forests 12:1610
autecology 12:1720
automobiles *see* vehicles
autonomous underwater vehicles (AUVs)
  9:*1233*
autotrophs 5:584, 616; 8:1117; 9:1224
  bacteria as 2:169

B

bathyal zone 9:1231, 1237
batteries, car, recycling 12:1697
beaches
  sandy 11:1494
  see also shore habitats
Bering Strait 9:1234
Bhopal, Union Carbide accident 5:628
Bikini atoll, nuclear testing 4:451
biodiversity 2:183–186
  conservation of 3:425–426
  estimation 2:183–184
  see also conservation
biogeochemical cycles 5:584
  see also carbon cycle; nitrogen cycle
biogeographic regions 5:583

biogeography 2:192–194
Biological Oxygen Demand (BOD) 7:1001
biomagnification, of pesticides 4:481;
  9:1280, 1287
biomass 6:770
  pyramid of 5:*586*
biomes and habitats 2:208–211
  biomes 2:208
    biodiversity 2:184
    see also chapparal biomes; coral reef
      biomes; desert biomes; estuaries;
      forests; grassland biomes; mountain
      biomes; shrublands; taiga biomes;
      tundra biomes
  habitats 2:208
    pathways between 12:1718
    see also cave habitats; island habitats;
      ocean habitats; shore habitats;
      suburban habitats; urban habitats
bioremediation 2:226; 11:1461; 12:1698
biosphere 2:220; 5:581–582, 583
Black Hills 9:1170
black smokers 9:1231, *1233*
BOD (Biological Oxygen Demand) 7:1001
bogs 11:1532; 12:1703
  human remains in 9:1166
  see also wetlands
bombs, nuclear 2:189; 4:*451*
buffers, environmental 1:16; 11:1459

C

calcium carbonate, forming limestone
  3:303
calcium fluorophosphate 10:1302
camouflage and mimicry 2:281–286;
  4:483
  alligator snapping turtle 2:283
  birds
    of the forest 6:775
    killdeer 2:*283*
  butterflies and moths 2:270, 271, *281*, *286*
    peppered moth 2:285
  chameleons, color change 2:282; 4:483;
    7:*908*; 10:1310
  countershading 2:283
  cryptic coloration 2:281–282; 8:*1076*
  disguise 2:283–284
  disruptive coloration 2:282–283
  evolution of camouflage 2:284–285
  frogs 6:788
  leaf insects and walking sticks 2:283, 284;
    8:*1015*–1016, *1017*
  mimicry 4:445, 484
    aggressive 2:286
    automimicry 2:270
    Batesian 2:270, 286
    eyespots 2:271, 283
    Müllerian 2:270, 285; 3:*391*
  tests of camouflage 2:284
  turning white in the snow 9:*1159*
  using bioluminescence 2:207
carbon, in the ocean 3:304–305
carbon cycle 3:302–305, 306
  and coral reefs 4:449
  see also carbon dioxide
carbon dioxide 3:306
  atmospheric 2:155; 3:*302*, 303, 306
    a greenhouse gas 2:157; 3:304, 306;
      4:492–493; 6:802; 11:1542; 12:1644

and the carbon cycle **3**:*302*, 303
and regulation of Earth temperature
6:802–803
see also carbon cycle
carbonic acid **6**:802
carbon monoxide, atmospheric **2**:156
carrying capacity **10**:1345–*1346*
cars *see* vehicles
cave habitats 3:325–328
bird sonar in **4**:574
CCNs (cloud condensing nuclei) **6**:802
CFCs *see* chlorofluorocarbons
Challenger, HMS **9**:1239
chapparal biomes 2:209; **3:350–351**
fires **3**:351; **5**:623
character displacement **12**:1711
chemoautotrophs **5**:584; **9**:1224
chemotrophs **8**:1117
Chernobyl disaster **5**:622, 626; **8**:1036;
10:*1344, 1395*
Chesapeake Bay **11**:1492
China, forests **12**:1610
chlorine, in water **5**:627
chlorofluorocarbons (CFCs) **2**:157; **5**:623;
10:*1341*
chloromethane **5**:627
CITES **2**:266; **5**:609
cities *see* urban habitats
cleaning stations, underwater **4**:450–451
Clean Water Act (1972) **12**:1706
climate
change **3**:428–429; **4**:493
recorded by fossils **9**:1257
recorded by tree rings **12**:1640
see also global warming
effect of coral reefs on **4**:449
life regulating **6**:802–803
tropical rain forests and **12**:1644
Climate Protocol, Kyoto (1997) **10**:1341
climax vegetation, in temperate forests
12:1607
clouds, role in temperature control **6**:802,
803
coal **3**:304; **6**:783
coastal waters **9**:1236–1237
see also shore habitats
coevolution 2:268; **3:389–392**; **5**:657
animals/flowers **2**:268; **3**:389–390;
6:757–758, 760; **10**:*1336*, 1337
host/parasites **3**:390; **9**:1267
of males and females **11**:1485
colonizers, plant **3**:410; **7**:974–975
coloration
of cave-dwelling animals **3**:327
change
in chameleons **2**:282; **4**:483; **7**:*908*;
10:1310
in octopuses and squid **4**:483; **7**:908
in phasmids **8**:1017
and courtship **4**:*455*
cryptic **2**:281–282; **8**:*1076*
disruptive **2**:282–283
in frogs **6**:*788*
in insects **3**:404; **7**:959–960
plant, flowers **6**:761–762
for temperature regulation **3**:397
warning **4**:483–484
see also camouflage and mimicry
Columbia River **10**:1427

comets
collision with Earth **5**:624, *653*
and extinction of dinosaurs **4**:528; **5**:624
Halley's **5**:*653*
commensalism **3**:390; **11**:1579, *1580*
communities **10**:1348
biotic **5**:583
competition 3:407–410; **11**:1484
territorial *see* territories
composting **11**:1461
conservation 2:186; **3:425–430**;
12:1724–1725
estimation of biodiversity **2**:183–184
in the Everglades **5**:649
and mountain biomes **3**:429; **9**:1168
and nesting **9**:1209
plant **2**:252, 254
reserves *see* national parks; reserves
uses of cryobiology **4**:473; **12**:1724
see also extinction
continental rise **9**:1231
continental shelves 4:437–439
continental slope **9**:1231
Convention on International Trade in
Endangered Species *see* CITES
convergent evolution 2:274; **3**:*380*;
4:444–446; **5**:656
and gliding **6**:*749*
coral reef biomes 2:211; **4:447–451**;
9:1237, *1239*
coral/alga symbiosis **4**:449–450
coral islands **4**:450
destruction **4**:*450*, 451
fish **2**:*282*; **4**:450
Great Barrier Reef **4**:447–448, *449*, 451
Coriolis force **9**:1235
corridors, wildlife **3**:429; **12**:1664, 1718

D

Daisyworld model **6**:803
dams **10**:*1426, 1427*
Darwinism **7**:912–913
neo-Darwinism **2**:202; **4**:479; **5**:654
see also evolution; natural selection
Death Valley **4**:*498*
decomposition
and the carbon cycle **3**:303
in the soil **11**:1531
of wood **11**:1460–1462; **12**:1609
defense mechanisms 4:482–486
behavioral **4**:486
bioluminescence used for **2**:206–207
chemical
in animals **3**:345; **4**:485–486
in plants **4**:482–483
feet used for **5**:698
plant **4**:482–483
safety in numbers **4**:*484*
self sacrifice **4**:486
visual *see* camouflage and mimicry
deforestation 4:490–493; **5**:623;
12:*1639*
and the carbon cycle **3**:*304*
effect on the atmosphere **4**:491–493
effect on coral reefs **4**:451, 491
rain forests **4**:493; **5**:*624*; **12**:1643
by fire **4**:*491*
causing extinctions **4**:493; **5**:*680*
slash-and-burn **4**:491

denitrification **9**:1218; **11**:1462
desert biomes 2:210–*211*; **4:498–501**
animals **2**:211; **4**:*500–501*
plants **2**:211; **4**:*499*–500; **11**:*1459*;
12:1617
cacti and succulents **2**:273
soil **11**:1530
desertification 4:502–505; **5**:624
detrivores **6**:767
developed countries **10**:1348
developing countries **10**:1348
dimethyl sulfide (DMS), and cloud
formation **6**:802
dioxins 4:532; **10**:1343
disasters, environmental *see* environmental
disasters
dispersal **2**:193–194
distribution *see* biogeography;
zoogeography
diversity, genetic **2**:183–184; **5**:589–590
downwellings **9**:1236
drought **5**:624
Dust Bowl (U.S. Midwest) **4**:*503*

E

Earth
age of **10**:1304
collision with space objects **4**:528, *529*;
5:624, 659; **8**:1073
a living organism *see* Gaia hypothesis
origins of life on **6**:801; **10**:1304
temperature *see* temperature, Earth
earthquakes **5**:624
Earth Summit **2**:183; **10**:1341
ecology and ecosystems 5:581–586
biodiversity **2**:184, 185
biogeochemical cycles **5**:584
see also carbon cycle; nitrogen cycle
biotic pyramids **5**:*586*; **6**:*768*, 769
ecology
autecology **12**:1720
behavioral **5**:643
community **5**:583
plant **2**:254
population **5**:583
restoration ecology **3**:427; **5**:*583*
ecosystems **5**:583–584; **6**:766
feedback in **7**:953
energy flow **5**:584
see also food webs
isolated ecosystems **11**:1540
see also island habitats
microecosystems **5**:585
models of **3**:348; **5**:584–585
productivity **6**:769–770
see also biomes and habitats
Edge of the Sea, The (Rachel Carson) **3**:318
Elastol **12**:*1698*
electromagnetic fields, dangers of **5**:627, 628
electronetting **12**:*1721*
El Niño events **2**:186; **4**:438
endangered species 5:606–609
categories of threat **5**:606–607
tigers **3**:323; **5**:*607–608*

cryopreservation (cold storage) **4**:473;
12:1724
elephants **5**:596
epiphytes **5**:642
giant anteater **1**:104
and humans **11**:1542
North American buffalo **5**:608–609
orchids **5**:609, 642
primates **10**:1367
Red Data Books and Red Lists **2**:186;
5:606–607
in rivers **10**:1427
Venus's-flytraps **5**:*609*
white rhinoceroses **5**:*606*, 607
whooping cranes **5**:608
zoos and **12**:1724
see also conservation; extinction
Enewetok atoll, nuclear testing **4**:451
entropy **5**:584, 615
environment, regulated by life?
6:802–803
environmental disasters 5:622–624
causing epidemics **7**:*948*
impacting space objects **5**:624
oil *see* oil, environmental
ozone layer depletion *see* ozone
power plant accidents **5**:622, 626;
10:*1344*
tidal waves and flooding **5**:624
winds, strong **5**:624
see also deforestation; desertification;
drought; environmental diseases;
fires; flooding; pollution
environmental diseases 5:625–628
Environmental Protection Agency **5**:626;
12:1696
EPA *see* Environmental Protection Agency
estuaries **2**:211; **9**:1237; **11**:1491–1492
euphotic zone **4**:437
eutrophication **9**:1280; **10**:1302, 1342;
11:1462
Everest, Mount **9**:1169
Everglades 5:647–649; **12**:*1703*
evolution 5:650–659
adaptation and **1**:20–*21*; **5**:650–651,
656–657
see also adaptation
of the animal kingdom **1**:*94*, 97
"arms races" **3**:391; **4**:482
of behavior **1**:84–85
of the brain **2**:258
chordate **3**:365
and continental drift **9**:1255
convergent *see* convergent evolution
and creationism **5**:654
Darwinian *see* Darwinism
directed **4**:546
divergent **5**:656–657
domestication and **4**:544
early **5**:651–652
fossil evidence **6**:784
and the founder effect **9**:1194
and gene flow **9**:1194
and genes **11**:1526

Bold words with bold page numbers indicate complete articles; bold numbers
preceding colons are volume numbers; numbers following colons indicate
page numbers; italic page numbers refer to illustrations or other graphics.

evolution *(continued)*
  and genetic drift **9**:1194
  and genetics **5**:653–656
  human effect on **5**:658–659
    see also endangered species; extinction
  interspecific competition and **3**:410
  on islands **7**:976
    Darwin's finches **5**:656–657; **7**:976;
      9:1192; **11**:1541
    flightless birds **7**:977
  land colonization **9**:1254
  of life **2**:167–168; **5**:651–*652*
  and living fossils **8**:1048
  mass extinctions *see* extinction, mass
  micro- and macroevolution
    9:1255–1256
  and mutation **2**:285; **5**:654–656
  by natural selection *see* natural selection
  parallel **8**:1078–1079
  plant **5**:715; **10**:1325–1326
    convergent in cacti and spurges
      2:274
  and punctuated equilibrium **1**:21; **2**:203;
    5:*654*; **9**:1255
  recapitulation theory **1**:71
  RNA and **5**:654; **9**:1254; **10**:1431
  role of oxygen **12**:1658
  saprophytes in **11**:1461
  and similarity of cytochromes **10**:1377
  speciation **1**:22; **5**:*657*; **8**:1081; **9**:1189,
    1255; **11**:1541
    sexual selection and **11**:1486
    sympatric **11**:1542
    see also adaptive radiation
  of sponges **11**:1553
  studies in **5**:652–653
  synthetic theory of (neo-Darwinism)
    2:202; **4**:479; **5**:654
  test-tube **9**:1290–1291
  theories **2**:201–203
  ultraviolet light and **12**:1658
  see also coevolution
evolutionary stable strategies (ESSs)
  1:85–86
extinction 2:185; **5**:606, 607, **678–680**;
  11:1541
  agents of **2**:156–157
  of Bachman's warbler **9**:1275
  dinosaur **2**:185; **4**:528–*529*
    due to climate change **4**:528–529
    from an impacting space object **4**:528,
      529; **5**:624, 659
  of flightless birds **6**:756; **7**:977
  human influence **2**:186; **5**:679–*680*
  on islands **2**:185; **3**:410; **7**:976, 977
    by foreign species **2**:185; **6**:770;
      7:976
    due to humans **1**:19; **6**:770
  mammoths **5**:593–594
  mass **2**:185–186; **5**:659, 679; **6**:748;
    9:1256; **11**:1541
  natural process **3**:426
  passenger pigeon **5**:659; **11**:1522
  in rain forests **4**:493
  rate **3**:426
  "vortex" **5**:607
  see also endangered species
Exxon Valdez oil spill **5**:622, *623*; **9**:1239;
  10:1342

F

filter pathways, between habitats **12**:1718
fires **5**:623
  chapparal **3**:351; **5**:623
  forest **3**:410; **4**:*491*; **5**:*622*
  moorland **7**:882
  and seeds **4**:*548*
  wildfires **5**:623
Flint Ridge Mammoth Cave **3**:326
flooding **5**:624
  deforestation and **4**:492; **12**:*1644*
  and disease **5**:*634*
food chains **6**:766–767
  Charles Elton and **6**:768, 769
  pesticide biomagnification **4**:481; **9**:1280,
    1287
  see also food webs
food webs 6:766–770
  energy flow **5**:584
  oceanic, continental shelves **4**:437–439
  see also food chains
forests
  boreal *see* taiga biomes
  mimicked by permaculturalists **9**:1281
  northern coniferous *see* taiga biomes
  organic matter decomposition
    11:1460–1462; **12**:1609
  temperate *see* temperate forest biomes
  tropical **4**:491
    rain forests *see* tropical rain forest biomes
  types **4**:490–491
fossil fuels
  and carbon **3**:304
  cutting consumption of **10**:1340
fresh water biomes **2**:211
  see also lakes and ponds; rivers and streams

G

Gaia hypothesis 2:203; **6**:801–803
Galápagos Islands **9**:1169
  finches **2**:*185*; **4**:478; **5**:656–657, 696;
    7:*976*; **9**:1192
  giant tortoises **1**:*33*; **3**:410
  goats on Abingdon Island **3**:410; **6**:770
Galápagos Rift **9**:1233
garbage, household **12**:1695, 1696
gases, greenhouse *see* greenhouse gases and
    greenhouse effect
gasoline, pollution from leaking tanks
  10:1342
glaciation **2**:194
glass, recycling **12**:1697
global warming **2**:157; **3**:306, 428–429;
  4:493, 505; **10**:1341
  and extinction **2**:186
  Gaia hypothesis and **6**:802–803
  see also greenhouse gases and greenhouse
    effect
grassland biomes **2**:210
  earthworms **1**:100
  see also savanna biomes
Great Barrier Reef **4**:447–448,
  449, 451
greenhouse gases and greenhouse effect
  2:157; **3**:304, 306; **4**:492–493;
  10:1341; **11**:1542
  carbon dioxide **2**:157; **3**:304, 306;
    4:492–493; **6**:802; **10**:1341;
    11:1542; **12**:1644

tropical rain forests and **12**:1644
  see also global warming
Greenland **10**:1331
ground cover, in temperate forests
  12:1609
growth factors, intrinsic **10**:1345
Gulf War (1991), oil disaster **12**:1698

H

habitats *see* biomes and habitats
hadal zone **9**:1231, 1237
Hawaiian islands **9**:1170
heaths and moorland habitats 7:882
"heat island" effect **12**:1665
heavy metals, environmental **12**:1696
heterosphere **2**:155
heterotrophs **8**:1117, *1124*–1126; **9**:1252
  bacteria as **2**:169
  holozoic **9**:*1224*, 1225
Himalayas **9**:1170
holoplankton **10**:1314
homeostasis, Earth in *see* Gaia hypothesis
homosphere **2**:155
humus **11**:1531
hydrocarbons, atmospheric **5**:626
hydrological (water) cycle **9**:*1235*
hydrothermal vents *see* vents, hydrothermal
hyperparasites **9**:1265

I

ice ages **3**:428
incineration, waste **12**:1696, 1697
intrinsic growth factor **10**:1345
island habitats 7:974–977
  animals change in size **7**:977
  colonization of **7**:974–975
  coral islands **4**:450
  evolution on **7**:976
    Darwin's finches **5**:656–657; **7**:976;
      9:1192; **11**:1541
    flightless birds **7**:977
  extinction of species *see* extinction,
    on islands
  number of species **2**:193
  problems facing populations on **7**:975
  variety **7**:975
  see also Galápagos Islands
isolation
  ecological **11**:1540
  geographic **11**:1541
  reproductive **11**:1540–1541
  see also island habitats
IUCN (World Conservation Union),
    Red Data Books and Red Lists **2**:186;
    5:606–607

K

Kilimanjaro, Mount **9**:1167
Kosmos (Humboldt) **2**:192
Krakatoa, explosion **2**:155
k-selection **1**:101–102; **10**:1352

L

lakes and ponds 7:999–1002
  eutrophication **9**:1280; **10**:1302;
    11:1462
  pollution *see* pollution, water
  Rift Lakes (eastern Africa) **7**:976–977
  see also rivers and streams

landfills **12**:1696
lead, environmental **5**:625, 626; **9**:1203
levees **12**:1705
life
  elements of **8**:1142
  environmental regulations **6**:802–803
  extraterrestrial 5:681–684
  molecules of **8**:1142
  origins on Earth **6**:801; **10**:1304
  prehistoric 10:1360–1364
  requirements for **5**:681
light
  energy, for photosynthesis **5**:616
  phototropism and **10**:1316, 1317;
    12:*1646*
limestone **3**:303
  acid rain and **1**:17
littoral zones **2**:211; **7**:*1000*–1001
logging **12**:1643
Lotka-Volterra model **10**:1350
lottery routes **12**:1718–1719
Love Canal community **10**:1342–1343;
  11:1532; **12**:1695

M

McKinley Park (Alaska) **2**:*208*
macroevolution **9**:1255–1256
Malawi, Lake **7**:976–977
Maldives **7**:*974*
mangroves **9**:1237; **11**:*1494*
maquis **2**:209
marble, acid rain and **1**:*17*
marshes **12**:1703–1704
  see also salt marshes
Masai Mara Game Reserve **3**:427, *430*;
  11:*1463*
matorral **2**:209
Mediterranean region, forests **12**:1610
mercury, in fish **1**:17
meroplankton (temporary marine
    zooplankton) **10**:*1313*–1314
mesosphere **2**:154, *155*
meteorites
  and extinction of dinosaurs **4**:*529*; **5**:659
  Gaia hypothesis and **6**:802
  life from Mars on **5**:682
  meteorite craters **4**:*529*; **5**:659
methane
  and the carbon cycle **3**:303–304
  as a fuel **9**:1280
  a greenhouse gas **10**:1341
  from landfills **12**:1696
  from microorganisms **5**:702
methyl isocyanate **5**:628
Michigan, deforestation **4**:*492*
Microcosmus (Lynn Margulis) **5**:585
microecosystems **5**:585
microevolution **9**:1255
Midwest, American, Dust Bowl **4**:503
mimicry *see* camouflage and mimicry
Mississippi River **10**:1427; **12**:1704–1705
  basin **10**:1426
Mojave Desert **4**:499
Monterey Bay Aquarium **1**:*129*
Monument Valley (Arizona) **2**:211
moors *see* heaths and moorland habitats
mortality, density-dependent **10**:1347
mountain biomes 9:1167–1170
  animals and plants **9**:1168–*1170*

and conservation 3:429; 9:1168
creation of mountain ranges 9:1170
mountain zones 2:209; 9:1167–1168
Mount St. Helens 1:16; 5:624
mutualism see symbiosis, mutualism

N

Namib Desert, fog harvesters 4:501
National Center for Atmospheric Research
    (NCAR) 2:155
National Oceanic and Atmospheric
    Administration (NOAA) 2:155
national parks 3:425, 426, 430
  problems with 3:428–431
  see also reserves
natural selection 1:18, 20;
    9:1191–1194
  Darwin's theory 7:912–913
    see also Darwinism
  leading to evolution 5:653, 654, 655;
    7:912–913; 10:1404
    see also evolution
  mutation and 5:653, 654, 655; 9:1191
  and sexual selection 11:1483
  see also adaptation; competition
nature versus nurture
  and animal behavior 1:83
  in child development 3:359
  in human behavior 9:1194
  in intelligence 7:968
  and twins 12:1655
NCAR (National Center for Atmospheric
    Research) 2:155
nekton 4:438; 10:1312
Ngorongoro Crater 11:1464–1465
niches, ecological 3:408, 409
nitrates
  from fertilizers 5:718
  and the nitrogen cycle 9:1217, 1218
nitric acid, in acid rain 1:16
nitrification 9:1217–1218
nitrogen cycle 9:1216–1219
  nitrogen fixation 1:17, 49; 3:352; 5:718;
    8:1132; 9:1217; 11:1531
    nonbiological 9:1219
nitrogen, in fertilizers 5:718
nitrogen oxides 2:156
  atmospheric 1:15; 10:1340
    nitrogen dioxide 5:625
    nitric oxide 2:156
NOAA (National Oceanic and Atmospheric
    Administration) 2:155
nuclear accidents see power plants, nuclear
nuclear waste 10:1344

O

ocean floor 9:1230–1233
  chemosynthetic bacteria 3:305; 5:651;
    9:1233, 1237
  mining of phosphate 10:1302
ocean habitats 9:1231, **1234–1239**
  continental shelves 4:437–439
  deep-sea 9:1230–1231, 1237–1238
  oceans
    carbon in 3:304–305
    creation 9:1237
    currents 9:1235–1236
    seawater composition 9:1237
    tides 9:1235

upwellings 4:438
  see also coral reef biomes; ocean floor;
  shore habitats
oceans, definition 9:1234
oil, environmental
  disposal 11:1461; 12:1698
  Gulf War oil disaster 12:1698
  spills 2:170; 5:623; 9:1239; 12:1698
  yeasts and 12:1715
oxygen
  atmospheric
    and combustion 9:1251, 1253
    and the origins of life on Earth 6:801;
      10:1304; 12:1658
  cycle 9:1252
  in water, Biological Oxygen Demand
    (BOD) 7:1001
ozone 2:157; 5:625; 10:1304
  depletion 2:157; 5:623, 625; 10:1341
    and coral reefs 4:449
  and evolution of life on land 12:1658
  tropospheric and ground-level 1:16;
    5:625; 10:1340

P

paleoecology 9:1254
pampas 2:210
paper, recycling 12:1696
parasites 5:695; **9:1264–1268;**
    11:1579–1580
  adaptations 9:1267–1268
  of bats 3:328
  brood 7:963
  coevoltionary response to 3:390; 9:1267
  crustaceans as 4:467–468
  disrupt instinctive patterns 7:963
  ecto- and endoparasites 9:1264–1265;
    11:1579–1580
  flies as 6:746
  fungi as 6:800; 12:1670
  in history 9:1267
  hookworms 1:90
  host-specific 9:1265
  intermediate hosts 9:1268
  kleptoparasitism 11:1472
  leeches 1:100
  lice 8:1032–1033
    carrying diseases 7:946, 950; 8:1032;
      9:1267
    fish 4:467–468
  life cycles 9:1265–1266
  nematode worms as 9:1195–1196
  neutral parasitism 9:1266
  nocturnal 9:1222
  obligate and facultative 9:1265
  of plants 9:1265
  plants as 9:1265; 10:1321; 12:1632
  self-protection 9:1268
  social, slave-making ants 1:120
parks, national see national parks
particulates, atmospheric 2:154, 155–156;
    5:625
penstocks 10:1426
permafrost 2:208; 12:1652
pH, soil 11:1531
pheromones 3:404; 5:677;
    9:1293–1294; 11:1515–1516
  alarm signals 4:485; 11:1515
  in ants 1:119

apple maggot fly 3:402
  in butterflies and moths 1:106;
    2:269–270; 4:460; 12:1596
  the silk moth 2:270; 4:460; 9:1288,
    1293
  used in pest control 9:1288
  communication with other species
    (allomones) 5:677
  courtship 4:460
  to fight Dutch elm disease 9:1294
  human 9:1294
  for pest control 2:196
  primer 9:1294
  social insect
    ant 12:1647
    honeybee 9:1294; 11:1524
phosphates, pollutants 10:1302
photoautotrophs 5:584; 9:1224
photochemical reactions 2:156
phototrophs 8:1117
pioneer plants 12:1643
plains, soils 11:1530
plastics
  environmental 10:1344
  recycling 12:1696
plate tectonics 9:1170; 12:1719
polar regions 10:1331–1334; 12:1618
  plants 10:1332
pollution 10:1339–1344
  air 2:156; 10:1340–1341; 12:1664–1665
    smog 2:156; 10:1340
    see also atmosphere
  causing global warming see global
    warming
  chemical
    by pesticides 10:1343–1344; 11:1532
    dioxins 4:532; 10:1343
    environmental hormones 5:680;
      10:1343
    and the Love Canal community
      10:1342–1343; 11:1532; 12:1695
    and the soil 11:1532
    toxic chemicals 10:1342–1343;
      11:1532
  cleaning up the community 10:1343
  and extinction 5:680
  indicator species for 8:1036
  oil see oil, environmental
  and the ozone layer see ozone, depletion
  permaculture and 9:1281
  by plastic 10:1344
  and seabirds 5:623; 11:1474
  soil 11:1532
  water 5:718; 10:1341–1342
    of lakes 7:1001
    and plankton 10:1314
  see also acid rain; waste disposal
ponds see lakes and ponds
population 5:582–583; 6:766;
    10:1345–1348
  birth and death 10:1347
  carrying capacity 10:1345–1346
  in communities see communities
  cycles, in lemmings 10:1334

density 10:1346–1347
genetics, genetic diversity 2:183–184;
    8:1135; 10:1347–1348
growth 10:1345, 1346
  bacteria in a bottle 10:1347
  Malthus's theory 4:479; 5:653;
    10:1345
  human 10:1346
    aging 1:35
  inclusive fitness 1:60
  isolation 11:1540, 1541
    see also island habitats
  size, controlled 7:953
potassium, in fertilizers 5:717
power lines, and cancer 5:627
power plants, nuclear, accidents at 5:622,
    626; 10:1344
prairies 2:210
  see also grassland biomes
predation 10:1349–1351
  cooperative hunting 1:58
    killer whales 10:1350
  defense against see defense
  human encouragement of predators
    10:1350–1351
  predator-prey relationships
    10:1349–1350
    in lakes and ponds 7:1001
  of ungulates 12:1662–1663
primary consumers 6:767
primary producers 6:767, 768; 9:1224,
    1236
productivity, ecosystem 6:769–770
pyramids, biotic 5:586
  pyramid of biomass 5:586
  pyramid of energy 5:586; 6:768
  pyramid of numbers 5:586; 6:769

R

radioactive waste 10:1344
radiotelemetry 12:1721
radon 5:626, 627
rain
  acid see acid rain
  pH 1:16
rain forests
  temperate 12:1610
  tropical see tropical rain forest biomes
  see also deforestation
rare species 5:607
  see also endangered species
recycling 10:1343, 1344; 12:1696–1697
  and composting 11:1461
Red Data Books (IUCN) 5:606
Red Lists (IUCN) 2:186; 5:606–607
red tides 10:1347
regeneration, landscape 10:1399, 1402
reserves 3:429
  see also national parks
resource partitioning 3:410
ridges, mid-ocean 9:1231
Rift Lakes (eastern Africa) 7:976–977
rivers and streams 10:1425–1427
  see also lakes and ponds

Bold words with bold page numbers indicate complete articles; bold numbers preceding colons are volume numbers; numbers following colons indicate page numbers; italic page numbers refer to illustrations or other graphics.

Rocky Mountains **9**:1167–1168
routes, lottery **12**:1718–1719
r-selection **10**:1352
   in plants **1**:101

S

Sahara Desert **4**:499, 504
Sahel Desert **4**:504, 505
Sainte-Catherine cave (Ariege) **3**:326
St. Helens, Mount **1**:*16*; **5**:624
Salt Lake City **7**:1002
salt marshes **6**:769; **9**:1237
   plant roots in **11**:1450
sampling techniques, to estimate
   biodiversity **3**:426
sand dunes **12**:*1649*, 1650
saprophytes 5:696; **9**:1224–1225;
   11:*1460–1462*
   fungi **6**:800; **9**:*1225*; **11**:*1460–1462*
   and the nitrogen cycle **9**:1217
   orchids **9**:1161
savanna biomes 2:210; **11**:*1463–1465*;
   12:*1663*
   see also grassland biomes
Sea Around Us, The (Rachel Carson) **3**:318
seabed *see* ocean floor
seamounts **9**:1231
seas, definition **9**:1234
Sea Sweep **12**:1698
seawater, composition **9**:1237
secondary consumers **6**:767
seeps, cold **9**:1233
selection
   natural *see* natural selection
   r- and k-selection **1**:101–102; **9**:1278;
      10:1352
Serengeti **3**:427; **11**:1453, 1463,
   1464–1465; **12**:1663
sewage
   disposal **12**:1695
   pollution from **10**:1342
   treatment **8**:1132; **9**:1219; **11**:1461;
      12:*1695–1696*
      permaculture and **9**:1281
shade-tolerant plants **12**:1643
shore habitats 11:*1491–1494*
   ecological zones **9**:1235
   lichens **8**:1037
   rocky **9**:1236–1237; **11**:*1493–1494*
   seaweed **7**:986–987
   see also estuaries; wetlands
shrublands **2**:209
   see also chaparral biomes
Silent Spring (Rachel Carson) **1**:41; **3**:318;
   4:481; **5**:584, 680; **9**:1288
sky, color **2**:155
smog **10**:1340
   photochemical **2**:156
soil ecology 11:*1529–1532*
   acid rain and **1**:17
   aeration **11**:1532
   and conservation **11**:1532
   contamination **11**:1532
   desert soils **11**:1530
   and disease **11**:1531
   erosion **11**:1530–1531; **12**:1640
   formation **11**:1529–1530
   hydric soils **12**:1703
   life in **11**:1531–*1532*

ants **11**:1531–1532
earthworms **1**:99, 100; **11**:1532
nematodes **9**:1195; **11**:1531
permaculture and the **9**:1281
pH **11**:1531
and plants **11**:1530
profiles and horizons **11**:1530
in savannas **11**:1464
urban soils **12**:1664
wetland soils **12**:1703
speciation *see* evolution, speciation
species 11:*1539–1542*; **12**:1600
   adaptive radiation **11**:1541–1542
      Galápagos finches **9**:1192; **11**:1541
   biodiversity **2**:185
   classification limitations **11**:1539–1540
   distribution **9**:1257
   early ideas about **11**:1539
   emergent **5**:658
   endangered *see* endangered species
   extinction *see* extinction
   and geographic isolation **11**:1541
   introduced **2**:195, *196*; **3**:*410*; **5**:607
   keystone **2**:184
   mutation **11**:1542
   names **8**:1042
   new *see* evolution, speciation
   number on islands **2**:193
   number of **2**:185; **5**:650; **9**:1255
   plant **2**:253
   ranges and geographical barriers
      12:1717–1718
   recognition **3**:402–403; **4**:456
   and reproductive isolation **11**:1540–1541
   ring **5**:657
Species Survival Plan (SSP) **12**:1724
steppes **2**:210
stratosphere **2**:154, 155
streams *see* rivers and streams
submersibles **9**:1233, 1238
subsoil **11**:1530
suburban habitats 11:*1568–1569*
succession
   plant **3**:428, *429*; **10**:1402
      in lakes and ponds **7**:999
      in tropical rain forests **12**:1643
sulfur dioxide
   atmospheric **1**:*16*; **5**:625; **10**:1340
   see also acid rain
sulfuric acid **1**:16
sulfur oxides, as pollutants **2**:156
sunsets **2**:*154*
swamps **12**:1704
symbiosis 9:1264; **11**:*1579–1582*
   between plant and animal **9**:1252
   commensalism **3**:390; **11**:1579, *1580*
   endosymbiosis, prokaryotes as organelles
      2:203; **3**:332, 392; **5**:585; **10**:1380
   mutualism **3**:390; **11**:*1579*
      ant/acacia tree **1**:118–119; **3**:*390*;
        4:483; **11**:1580–1581
      ant/aphid **4**:483; **11**:*1581*
      bird/herbivore **4**:485
      clams/bacteria **9**:1233
      cockroaches/protozoa **3**:388
      and coevolution **3**:*390*–391
      cooperative hunting **1**:58
      corals/single-celled algae **1**:49;
        4:449–450, 453

evolution **11**:1581
   facultative **11**:1579, 1581–1582
   honeyguides **3**:403; **11**:1582
   legumes/soil-bacteria **8**:*1029*; **9**:1217,
      1218
   lichens **8**:1034; **11**:1581
   microorganisms in the gut **4**:517;
      9:*1226*, 1228; **12**:1611
   mycorrhizae **3**:389; **6**:800;
      9:1187–1188; **10**:1322; **11**:1450,
      1582; **12**:1590, 1640
   obligatory **11**:1579, 1581
   vestimentiferan worms/bacteria
      9:1233
parasitism *see* parasites
symbiotic luminous bacteria **2**:205

T

taiga biomes 2:208; **4**:490–491;
   12:*1589–1591*
   animals **2**:208, 210; **12**:*1591*
      birds **6**:776–777; **12**:1591
   farming in **12**:1590
   light taiga **12**:1590
Taj Mahal **1**:*17*
taxon cycle **12**:1711
TCDD **4**:532
temperate forest biomes 2:209;
   12:*1607–1610*, 1637
   animals and birds **6**:777; **12**:*1609*
   deciduous **2**:209; **12**:1608
   epiphytes **5**:642
   evergreen **2**:209; **12**:1610
   growth and renewal **10**:1402; **12**:1609
   layers **12**:1608–1609
   mixed **4**:491
   rain forests **12**:1610
temperature
   Earth **6**:802, *803*
   see also global warming
territories 12:*1613–1615*
   a counterproductive stategy **12**:1615
   limiting population density **10**:1346
   territorial behavior **3**:402
      aggression **1**:29–30, 85
   see also competition
thermocline **7**:1002
thermosphere **2**:154–155, *155*
Three Mile Island **5**:626; **10**:1395
tidal zones *see* littoral zones
tides **9**:1235
timberline **9**:1168
topsoil **11**:1530
tourism, in savannas **11**:1464
trenches, deep-sea **9**:1231
trophic levels **5**:586; **6**:768
tropical rain forest biomes 2:*209*–210;
   5:*581*; **12**:*1641–1644*
   animals **5**:694; **12**:1642
      birds **6**:777–778; **12**:1642
   biodiversity **2**:184; **12**:1637, 1641–1642
   commercial yield **12**:*1644*
   conservation **3**:426
   deforestation **4**:492, 493; **12**:1643
   effects on global climate **12**:1644
   layers **12**:1642–1643
   plants **5**:642; **12**:*1643*–1644
   regeneration **10**:1402
   soils **11**:*1529*

troposphere **2**:154, *155*
tundra biomes 2:*208*; **10**:1332–1333;
   12:1590, **1652–1654**
   Alpine and Arctic **12**:1653
   animals **2**:208, 210; **12**:*1653–1654*
   lichens **12**:1653
   plants **12**:1653

U

Union Carbide accident **5**:628
United Nations, Conference on
   Environment and Development
   (UNCED) **2**:183
upwellings **4**:438; **9**:1236
urban habitats 12:*1664–1665*
   cities by lakes **7**:1002

V

vehicles, and pollution **10**:*1340*
veld **2**:210
vents, hydrothermal **5**:651, 681; **9**:1230,
   1232–*1233*, 1237, 1239
Victoria, Lake, new species of fish
   11:1486
volcanoes **5**:624
   islands **9**:1231
      life on the Galápagos Islands **9**:1169
vulnerable species **5**:606
   see also endangered species

W

warnings *see* coloration, warning
waste disposal 12:*1695–1698*
   agricultural **12**:1697–1698
   algae and **1**:48
   animal waste for fertilizers **5**:718
   oil spills *see* oil, environmental
   radioactive **10**:1344; **12**:1697
   recycling **10**:*1343*, 1344; **12**:*1696*–1697
      and composting **11**:1461
   see also pollution; sewage
water cycle (hydrological cycle) **9**:*1235*
weather changes **5**:624
   see also global warming
wetlands 2:*184*; **12**:*1703–1706*
   coastal **12**:*1704*, 1706
   Everglades 5:647–649; **12**:*1703*
   sewage treatment in **12**:1696
   see also bogs; mangroves; shore habitats
winds
   as an energy source **10**:1340–1341
   and environmental disasters **5**:624
woodlands, English **4**:493

YZ

Yellowstone National Park **3**:*425*, 426;
   5:623
Yucca Mountain (Nevada) **10**:1344;
   12:1697
zoogeography 12:*1717–1719*

■ **GENETICS**

A

albinism **9**:*1191*; **10**:*1310*
alleles **5**:653
   and adaptations **1**:18
   codominant **6**:812
   dominant and recessive **6**:812

formation of new *see* mutation
frequencies **5**:655
and polymorphism **4**:524
aneuploidy **3**:369
autosomes **3**:368

B
backcrossing, of plants **10**:1323
breakage-fusion-bridge cycles **8**:1086

C
chromosomes 3:333, *366*–369; **7**:*919*;
　10:1403
abnormalities, and genetic diseases **3**:369;
　6:812–813
bacterial **3**:367
chromatids **3**:*338, 339,* 340, *366*
deletions and duplications **7**:921
extra **9**:1190
　and aggression **1**:30
　see also aneuploidy; polyploidy
genes on **3**:367
　see also genes
haploid and diploid **3**:368
homologous **3**:339–340, 368; **5**:588
karyotyping **3**:*367*
"lampbrush" **5**:589
loss **3**:369; **9**:1190
lymphocytic, and leukemia **8**:1030
maps **7**:920–*921*
mutations *see* mutation
numbers **3**:367–368; **6**:812; **7**:918
prokaryotic **3**:366–367
recombination (crossing over) **3**:368;
　7:919–920
　and mutations **9**:1190
sex **3**:368; **6**:812; **7**:906, 918
　and X-linked characteristics **9**:1164
　and X-linked disorders **8**:1107;
　　10:1358
structure **3**:366
translocation, and leukemia **8**:1030
XYY combination **1**:30
see also genes
crossing over (recombination) **3**:368;
　7:919–920
and mutations **9**:1190

D
demes **9**:1194
DNA 3:366; **4**:**533–538**; **8**:1144; **10**:1428
cloning **3**:384
discovery **8**:1142
effects of chemotherapy on **3**:353
and evolution **5**:654
fingerprinting **2**:224; **4**:*535*; **6**:*773*, 774;
　9:*1174*
the genetic code **4**:536
"junk" (noncoding) **4**:534; **7**:922–923
mapping **7**:920–921
markers **7**:920
in mitochondria (mtDNA) **2**:168; **3**:385
　and human origins **7**:917
mutation **4**:538
prokaryotic **2**:167; **3**:331
and protein synthesis **4**:*536*, 537; **10**:1378
radioactive tagging **2**:182
recombinant **2**:170, 223; **8**:1143, 1145
repair **6**:806
replication **4**:*534*–536
scientific (polymerase chain reaction)
　3:384; **4**:535; **6**:774; **8**:1145–1146
see also meiosis; mitosis
sequencing **7**:*920*, 921–*922*; **8**:*1146*
splitting **8**:1145
structure **4**:*533*–534; **7**:918–919
　discovery **4**:461–462, 537; **8**:1142
transcription **4**:537; **9**:1189; **10**:1378,
　1428, *1429*
transposons (transposable elements;
　jumping genes) **1**:110; **7**:922–923;
　8:1086; **9**:1190
typing **2**:182
viral **12**:1681
X-ray crystallography **6**:786
Dolly (sheep) **3**:*340, 383*–384; **11**:1558

EF
exons **4**:538; **6**:805; **7**:920; **10**:1429
F_1, F_2, and F_3 generations **8**:1107

G
genes **3**:367; **4**:534; **7**:918, *919*
activation by hormones **7**:*906*
and aggression **1**:30
cancer-associated (oncogenes) **1**:35;
　3:294
　silencing **10**:1430
closing down **10**:1430, *1431*
co-dominant **6**:812
dominant and recessive **6**:812
evolution and **11**:1526
exons **4**:538; **6**:805; **7**:920; **10**:1429
expression **4**:536; **6**:805, 807–808;
　11:1558
fitness **1**:59
　inclusive **1**:60
flow (migration) **5**:656; **9**:1194
introns **4**:538; **6**:805; **7**:920; **10**:1429
"jumping" *see* transposons
linked **12**:1597
mutation *see* mutation
numbers in the human genome **7**:920
patenting **7**:923
promoters **6**:807–808
regulatory (control genes) **4**:538; **5**:599
repairing **6**:806
sex-linked **9**:1164; **12**:1688
site on DNA, identifying *see* Human
　Genome Project
structural **4**:538
switched on and off **5**:632
　by TCDD **4**:532
transgenic **6**:809; **9**:*1243*, 1244
tumor-suppressor **3**:294
see also alleles; chromosomes; Human
　Genome Project
genetic drift **1**:18; **5**:656; **9**:1194
genetics 12:1721
biochemical **12**:1598
dominant and recessive genes **6**:812
and evolution **5**:653–656
Mendelian **8**:*1106*–1107
　and selective breeding **11**:1479–1480
plant **2**:254
population, Hardy-Weinberg law **5**:655
use of colchicine **3**:367
see also heredity
genomes, mapping *see* Human Genome
　Project
genotypes, genotypic polymorphism **4**:525
good-gene hypothesis (handicap hypothesis)
　11:1485

H
handicap hypothesis (good-gene hypothesis)
　11:1485
haploid cells **10**:1404
heredity **6**:812
and intelligence **7**:968
and Mendel's experiments **8**:1106–1107
see also genetics
heterosis (hybrid vigor) **4**:546; **11**:1480, 1541
heterozygotes **6**:812; **9**:1193
heterozygous advantage **11**:1482
homozygotes **6**:812; **9**:1193
Human Genome Project (HGP)
　2:222; **6**:808; **7**:**918–923**
hybrid vigor (heterosis) **4**:546; **11**:1480, 1541

I
inbreeding **11**:1480, 1482; **12**:1724
inheritance *see* heredity
inheritance, chromosome theory of **6**:746
introns **4**:538; **6**:805; **7**:920; **10**:1429

L
let-7 gene **10**:1430
linebreeding **11**:1482

M
meiosis **3**:*339*–340, *368*; **10**:1403–1404
in egg cells **5**:587–588, 589–590
see also DNA, replication
Mendel, Gregor 2:202, 227; **5**:653;
　8:**1106**–1107; **11**:1479–1480
Law of Segregation **8**:1106
mitosis **3**:*338*–339
blocked by drugs **3**:353
interruption leading to polyploidy **2**:266
see also DNA, replication
mutation 1:*19*; **4**:538; **9**:**1189–1190**
adaptive **11**:1542
bacterial **2**:170
and cancer **3**:294–295, 333; **9**:1190;
　12:1658
causes **9**:1189, 1190
　radiation **10**:1394–1395
　X rays **12**:1713
and evolution **2**:285; **5**:654–656; **7**:913
frameshift **9**:1190
in fruit flies **5**:599; **6**:746
and genetic variation **1**:20
homeotic **6**:746
and jumping genes **8**:1086; **9**:1190
and natural selection **5**:653, 654, 655;
　9:1191
plant **9**:*1189*
　and selective breeding **11**:1481–1482
point **9**:1190
and polymorphism **4**:524
somatic **9**:1189, 1190

NO
nondisjunction, chromosomal **3**:369
nuclear transfer (nuclear transplantation;
　NT) technique **3**:383, *385*;
　11:1558
oncogenes **1**:35; **3**:294
silencing **10**:1430

P
phenotypes, polymorphism **4**:524–525
Polly (sheep) **3**:384
polydactyly **4**:*525*
polyploidy **2**:266; **3**:369; **9**:1190; **10**:*1408*;
　11:1481, *1542*

S
Segregation, Law of **8**:1106
sex-linkage
of disorders **8**:1107; **9**:1181; **10**:1358;
　12:1688
of traits **9**:1164
sheep, cloning **3**:*340, 383*–384;
　11:1558
simian crease **3**:369
single nucleotide polymorphisms (SNPs)
　7:922

T
transposons (transposable elements;
jumping genes) **1**:110; **7**:922–923; **8**:1086;
　9:1190
trisomy-21 **3**:369

▮ MEDICINE
A
abortion 1:14
ethics **1**:14; **2**:188, 191
and *Listeria* **6**:765
and multiple births **12**:1656
spontaneous (miscarriage) **1**:14; **10**:1354
acupressure **1**:57
acupuncture **1**:*54*, 55, 76; **3**:*360*, 361;
　5:614
acyclovir (Zovirax) **7**:898; **12**:1678
addiction 1:**23–24**
biochemistry of **1**:24; **4**:556
treatment **1**:24; **4**:558
see also drugs; hallucinogens
African Americans, equal rights **8**:1101
Ageless Body, Timeless Mind (Deepak Chopra)
　7:944
alcohol
for antisepsis **1**:116
dependence **1**:*24*
a depressant **1**:24; **4**:556
alcoholism
and cirrhosis **8**:1046
symptoms **10**:1389
allergies 1:**52–53**, 114; **5**:*627*–628;
　7:931
and anaphylaxis **1**:53, 110
to antibiotics **1**:110
and asthma **2**:153

allergies *(continued)*
　blood cells and **2**:240, 241
　immune response **1**:52–53; **7**:941–942
　treatment **4**:454; **5**:641
alternative medicine 1:54–57; 8:1094
　acupuncture **1**:*54*, 55, 76; **3**:*360*, 361;
　　5:614
　aromatherapy **1**:56
　Chinese medicine 1:55; **3:360–361**
　crystal therapy **1**:57
　and endorphin release **1**:55; **5**:614
　homeopathy **1**:*55–56, 57*
　Indian medicine 7:887–888, **943–944**
　iridology **1**:56
　light or color therapy **1**:57
　massage and manipulation **1**:*56*, 57
　　chiropractic **1**:*56*, 57
　　osteopathy 1:57; **9**:*1250*
　　reflexology **1**:57; **5**:614
　see also herbal medicine
aluminum, dietary, and Alzheimer's disease
　1:61
amphetamines **1**:24; **4**:555
　and schizophrenia **9**:1212
　and sleep **11**:1512
amphotericin B **1**:109
ampicillin **6**:742
amyl nitrate (poppers) **9**:1174
anaphylaxis **1**:53, 110
anesthesia 1:*75–76*; **11**:1571, *1573*
　epidural **11**:1573
　general **1**:75–76
　history of **1**:*76*; **8**:*1102*; **11**:1570
　local **1**:*75*, 76
angiograms **7**:*880*; **8**:*1090*; **12**:*1620*
angioplasty
　balloon **7**:881
　percutaneous transluminal coronary
　　(PTCA) **11**:1574
animal experimentation 1:91–93;
　2:189–190
　for aggression **1**:31
anosmia **11**:1516
antacids **11**:1565
antibiotics and antimicrobials
　1:108–110
　in agriculture **9**:*1245*
　allergic reactions to **1**:110
　discovery **2**:*180*; **6**:741–742, 799;
　　8:1103, 1131
　and hearing **7**:875
　manufacture **1**:109
　mode of action **1**:108–110; **5**:630
　natural antibiotics **6**:764
　on plants **10**:1323
　resistance to **1**:*19*, 109–*110*; **6**:811;
　　9:1245, 1291
　side effects **1**:109; **12**:1622
　and surgery **11**:1571
anticonvulsants **5**:639
antimetabolites **1**:108
antimicrobials *see* antibiotics and
　　antimicrobials
antipsychotics **11**:1466
antisepsis 1:115–117; 8:*1128*
　Lister and **1**:115; **8**:1043, 1102,
　　1128–1129
　Pasteur and **8**:1101, 1128
　Semmelweiss and **8**:1101

antivirals **12**:1678
Apgar scoring system **1**:123
appendectomy **11**:1572–1573
arginosuccinic aciduria **12**:1668
arms
　artificial **2**:212–213; **8**:*1093*
　bones **11**:1503
　paralyzed, movement **2**:213
aromatherapy **1**:56
arsenic
　poisoning **9**:1203
　in water **5**:627
arsphenamine (salvarsan) **5**:592; **8**:1103;
　　9:1289
Atropa belladonna (deadly nightshade) **1**:57, 80
atropine **1**:51; **11**:1573
audiometers **7**:874
autoclaves **1**:115
autotransplantation **8**:1092
ayurveda **7**:887–888, 944
azathioprine **8**:1088; **12**:1634, 1635
azidothymidine *see* zidovudine
AZT (azidothymidine) *see* zidovudine

B

bacitracin **5**:630
back pain **3**:320
　treatment **1**:57
bactericides **1**:108
bacteriostatic agents **1**:108
barbiturates **4**:556; **11**:1512
barium X rays **11**:1565; **12**:1712
Barr body **2**:191
BCG vaccine **7**:935; **12**:1648
"beating-heart" donors **12**:1636
benzodiazepines **11**:1512
Betafactin **12**:*1715*
Billings method, of ovulation prediction
　　4:442
bioethics 2:187–191, 204
　abortion **1**:14; **2**:188, 191
　allocation of limited resources **2**:190–191
　cloning **3**:386
　contraception **4**:443
　embryo research **5**:600
　embryo transplantation **5**:711
　euthanasia **5**:646
　and experimentation
　　animal **1**:92; **2**:189–190; **5**:603
　　on humans **2**:189
　genetic engineering **2**:225
　and immunization **7**:934
　and life support **8**:1040
　medical confidentiality **2**:190
　patenting life **2**:190
　prenatal diagnosis and therapy
　　2:*191*
　stem cell research **11**:1559
　surrogate motherhood **5**:712
　utilitarianism **2**:188
　zoos **12**:1726
bioglas **2**:212
biomedical engineering (bioengineering)
　　see bionics
biomedical ethics *see* bioethics
bionics 2:212–215
　prostheses **2**:212–215; **7**:875;
　　8:1092–1093
　see also implants

biopsies **4**:475; **7**:895
birth control *see* contraception
bleomycin **3**:353
Botox **9**:1203
bromocriptine **5**:709, 712
bronchodilators **2**:153; **8**:1059
bronchoscopes **8**:1091
bypass surgery **7**:881; **12**:1620
　robots used for **10**:1432–1433; **11**:1572

C

caffeine **1**:24, 51; **4**:555; **8**:1014; **11**:1512
calcium antagonists **2**:278
cannabis (marijuana) **4**:557
caps, cervical **4**:440–*441*
carbolic acid **8**:1043, 1129
carbon monoxide, poisoning **5**:625;
　　10:1420
carcinogens **3**:294–295; **9**:1190
　Ames test **3**:295
　and leukemia **8**:1031
　tobacco *see* smoking, and cancer
carpal tunnel syndrome **5**:628
case reports **5**:635
castration **10**:1414
catatonia **3**:398; **11**:1466
catheterization
　balloon-tipped catheters **11**:1574
　bladder **11**:1574
CAT scanning *see* CT scanning
Centers for Disease Control and
　　Prevention (CDC) **5**:634
cephalosporins **1**:109
　allergy to **1**:110
cesarean sections **10**:1357, 1359;
　　11:1574
chemotherapy 2:219; **3**:296, **352–353**;
　　8:1130–1131
　for leukemia **8**:*1031*
　and taste **12**:1597
chi (Qi) **1**:55; **3**:360, 361
Chinese medicine 1:55; **3:360–361**
　see also acupuncture
chiropractic **1**:*56*, 57
chloral **9**:1215
chlorine, a disinfectant **1**:116
chloroform **1**:76; **8**:1102
chlorpromazine **9**:1212, 1215
　Thorazine **11**:1466
choking, prevention **8**:1059
cholecystectomy **8**:1047; **11**:1575
cigarettes *see* smoking
cimetidine **7**:898
ciprofloxacin **2**:196
circumcision **10**:1412
citrullinaemia **12**:1668
clomiphene citrate **5**:709, 711
cocaine **1**:24; **4**:*555*, 556; **8**:1014
　crack **1**:24
　during pregnancy **2**:260
cochicine **1**:136
cochlear implants **2**:215; **7**:874; **8**:1093
codeine **1**:51
cold turkey **1**:24; **4**:558
color therapy **1**:57
comas 3:398–400; **5**:644
complementary therapies *see* alternative
　　medicine
computed axial tomography *see* CT scanning

computed tomography *see* CT scanning
condoms **4**:*440*
confidentiality, medical **2**:190
continuous subcutaneous insulin infusion
　　(CSII) **4**:507
contraception 4:440–443; 8:1111
coronary artery bypass grafting (CABG)
　　7:881; **11**:1572
　see also bypass surgery
corticosteroids
　　treatment **4**:454
　　for asthma **2**:153
crack **1**:24
croup **5**:641
cryosurgery **4**:473
crystal therapy **1**:57
CSII (continuous subcutaneous insulin
　　infusion) **4**:507
CT scanning 1:72; **2**:260; **4:474–475**;
　　8:1090
Curacin A **9**:1290
curare **9**:1183, 1203
　in medicine **9**:1183, 1203; **11**:1571
Cyborg (Caidin) **2**:215
cyclophosphamide **3**:353
cycloserine **5**:630
cyclosporine **8**:1088; **12**:1635
cystitis **5**:671
cytotoxic drugs, effects of **2**:240

D

D5W, intravenous **8**:1039
Darwinian medicine **4**:479
da Vinci (surgical robot) **10**:1432–1433
deafness **7**:*874–875*
　and bionic ears **2**:215
　and communication **7**:873; **11**:*1545*
　hearing restoration **7**:875
　and learning **11**:*1537*, 1538
death
　assisted *see* euthanasia
　brain **3**:399; **12**:1636
　criteria **8**:1040
　and forensic science **6**:746, 772–773;
　　9:1183
　and organs for transplants **12**:1636
deep brain stimulation **4**:497
defibrillators, ventricular **2**:214
dental procedures, anesthetic **1**:75
deontological theories **2**:188
deprenyl **9**:1204
depressants **1**:23–24
dermatitis **1**:*53*
detergents **1**:117
De Usu Partium (Galen) **2**:*200*
dialysis **7**:992; **8**:1039–1040
diaphragms (contraceptives) **4**:440–*441*
diarrhea **4**:519, 523
　"traveler's" **7**:949
diazepam (Valium) **9**:1215
diethylstilbestrol (DES) **3**:352
digitoxin **9**:*1291*
digoxin **9**:*1291*
dissection **1**:*70*, 72
diuretics, urea as **12**:*1667*
dizziness **4**:561
"doctrine of signatures" **7**:887
donepezil **4**:496
drips, intravenous **8**:1039; **11**:1571

drugs
  affecting the emotions **5**:603
  antibacterial **5**:630
  anticonvulsant **5**:639
  antiviral **12**:1678
  automated dispensing systems
    10:*1434*–1435
  calcium antagonists **2**:278
  for cancer treatment (chemotherapy)
    2:219; **3**:296, 352–353
  computer modeling **1**:*93*
  corticosteroid *see* corticosteroids
  curare-type **9**:1183, 1203; **11**:1571
  delivery **8**:*1092*
  dependency on *see* addiction
  depressants **4**:556
  design **7**:898
  fertility **5**:709, 711
  from fungi *see* penicillin
  from plants **1**:80; **4**:483
    ethnobotanical search for **9**:1292
    see also herbal medicine
  illegal
    cannabis (marijuana) **4**:557
    during pregnancy **2**:260
    ecstasy **4**:556, *557*
    emotion manipulation **5**:603
    heroin **1**:*23*–24; **4**:556–557, *558*
    LSD **4**:557
    see also cocaine; hallucinogens
  immunosuppressive **12**:1635
  medicinal **4**:555, 557
  mind-altering **1**:*23*; **4**:555–557
  mode of action **9**:1291
  opiates **4**:556–557
  origins of treatment **9**:1289, 1291
  psychedelic **4**:557
  radioactively labelled **9**:1290
  resistance to **3**:353
  sleeping pills **11**:1512
  stimulants **4**:555–556
  study of (**pharmacology**) **8**:1090;
    9:**1289–1292**
  sulfa **9**:1290
  synthetic **9**:1290
  testing and approval **9**:1291–1292
  test-tube evolution **9**:1290–1291
  use and abuse 4:555–558
  see also addiction; antibiotics

E

eating, compulsive **4**:566
eating disorders 4:565–566; 8:1114
ecstasy **4**:556, *557*
EEGs *see* electroencephalograms
electrocardiograms (EKGs; ECGs) **7**:*881*;
  8:1090
electroencephalograms (EEGs) **2**:*255*, 260;
  5:638; **8**:1090
  and sleep **11**:*1509–1510*
electromyography **4**:496
endoscopy **1**:71–72; **7**:895; **8**:1091;
  10:1433; **11**:1574
  see also surgery, keyhole
endotracheal tubes **11**:1573
ephedrine **1**:50
epidemics **7**:*948*
  influenza **7**:951
  models of **3**:348

epidemiology 5:633–635
erythromycin **1**:109
esthesiometers **12**:1626
ethanol, for antisepsis **1**:116
ether **8**:1102; **11**:1570
ethics *see* bioethics
euthanasia 2:_188_**; 5:645–646**
Expanded Program on Immunization (EPI)
  7:936

F

face-lifting, using Botox **9**:1203
feticide, selective **12**:1656
filtration, for sterilzation **1**:115
fluconazol **1**:109
fluoride **12**:1604
  in water **5**:627; **12**:1604
fluoxetine (Prozac) **9**:1215
food
  allergies to **1**:53
  cravings **8**:1121
  diseases carried in **7**:949
fractures, osteoporosis and **11**:1502
Framingham Heart Study **5**:635

G

gamete intrafallopian transfer (GIFT) **5**:710
gastroscopes **8**:1091; **11**:1575
GIFT (gamete intrafallopian transfer) **5**:710
Glasgow Coma Score **3**:399
glycosuria **4**:506
grafting **12**:1633
  corneal grafts **12**:1633, *1636*
  skin grafts **8**:1087, 1088; **11**:1507
  see also transplants

H

hallucinogens **4**:557; **9**:1186
  see also addiction
Haro (robot) **10**:*1435*
Health Interview Surveys **5**:635
heartburn **11**:1563, 1565
Heimlich maneuver **8**:1059
hemodialysis **2**:215; **8**:1040
hemorrhoids **4**:519
hemostasis **11**:1573
herbal medicine 1:56**; 7:887–888;**
  8:1103
  Chinese **3**:*361*; **7**:887
  see also drugs, from plants
heroin **1**:*23*–24; **4**:556–557, *558*
hip dysplasia, in cats and dogs **1**:90
hip joint replacement **8**:1092
Hippocratic Oath **2**:189
Holter monitors **7**:881
homeopathy **1**:*55*–56, 57
homocystinuria **5**:630
hormone replacement therapy (HRT)
  1:61; **2**:250; **8**:1110
HRT *see* hormone replacement therapy
"humors," Greek **7**:888; **8**:1099
Humulin **2**:227
hyperammonaemia **12**:1668
hyperbaric oxygen therapy (HBOT) **3**:400;
  9:1176
hypoxia **3**:398
hysterectomy, laser treatment as an
  alternative to **11**:1575
hysteroscopes **11**:1575

I

ileus, paralytic **11**:1574
imaging, medical
  CT scans 1:72; **2**:260; **4:474–475**;
    8:1090
  ECGs **7**:*881*; **8**:1090
  EEGs **2**:*255*, 260; **5**:638; **8**:1090;
    11:*1509–1510*
  MRI *see* magnetic resonance imaging
  PET **2**:*260*; **8**:1090–1091
  ultrasound 8:1090; **12**:**1657**
  see also X rays
immunization 7:933–936
  active and passive **1**:112; **7**:934
  against viral diseases **12**:1677–1678
  history of **7**:933–934, *936*, *984*
  vaccines **5**:*635*; **7**:934–935; **8**:1102
    from attenuated (live) organisms **7**:935
    from biotechnology **2**:227
    cancer **3**:296
    genetic **7**:935
    from inactivated organisms **7**:935
    schedules **7**:935–936
    subunit **7**:935
    testing **7**:934
    toxoid **7**:935
immunology 7:937–942; 8:1130
  blood typing **2**:243, *244*–245; **6**:774
immunotherapy **3**:296
implants
  cochlear **2**:215; **7**:874; **8**:1093
  drug **8**:1092
  retinal **8**:1093
incubators **8**:1040
Indian medicine 7:887–888, **943–944**
indigestion **11**:1565
Industrial Revolution **8**:1101; **10**:*1339*, 1340
infection, prevention *see* antisepsis
injections, drug **8**:1092; **9**:1291, *1292*
intensive care *see* life support
interferon **2**:222; **3**:395; **7**:929, 930
  and multiple sclerosis **9**:1176
intravenous therapy **8**:1039
iodine **1**:116
iridology **1**:56
iron lungs **8**:1039
IUDs (interuterine devices; coils) **4**:440,
  441–*442*, 443
IUSs (interuterine systems) **4**:442

J

Jarvik-7 heart **2**:214; **8**:1094
Jarvik-2000 heart **8**:1094

K

keratoplasty (corneal grafting) **12**:1633, *1636*
keratotomy, radial **5**:687
Koch's postulates **8**:1129

L

laparoscopes and laparoscopy **8**:1091;
  11:*1574*
laparotomy **11**:1573
laryngoscopes **8**:1091

laser surgery **8**:*1091*; **11**:1574, *1575*
Lasik **5**:687
laudanum **1**:23
L-dopa **8**:1092; **9**:1204
lead, poisoning **5**:625, 626; **9**:1203
life support 8:1038–1040
  and euthanasia **5**:646
light therapy **1**:57
limbs, artificial **2**:212–213
lithium **9**:1215
lithotripsy, extracorporeal shockwave
  (ESWL) **8**:1091
lovastatin **3**:363
LSD **4**:557; **8**:1139
lumbar punctures (spinal taps) **11**:1573
lymphadenectomy **8**:1064

M

magainins **9**:1290
magnetic resonance imaging (MRI)
  1:72; **2**:260; **3**:*399*–400;
    8:**1067–1068**, 1091, *1104*; **9**:*1214*
  functional (fMRI) **2**:260; **8**:1091
magnetoencephalography (MEG) **2**:260
marijuana *see* cannabis
mastectomy **3**:296
MDMA (ecstasy) **4**:556, *557*
medical technology 8:1089–1094
  see also bionics; imaging, medical;
    pharmacology; transplants
medication, preoperative **11**:1573
medicine
  alternative *see* alternative medicine
  Darwinian **4**:479
  and diagnosis, remote **10**:1434
  evidence-based (EBM) 8:1095–1098
  genetic **8**:1093–1094
  history of 8:1099–1103
    anatomy and dissection **1**:*70*–71
    anesthesia **1**:76; **8**:1102; **11**:1571
    antibiotics **2**:*180*; **6**:741–742, 799;
      8:1103
    antisepsis **1**:115; **8**:1043, 1101,
      1102
    discovery of blood circulation **1**:71;
      8:*1100*
    discovery of insulin **4**:508; **7**:*965*;
      8:1103
    the first MRI scanner **8**:1068
    Greek medicine **8**:*1099*
    herbal drugs **8**:1103
    immunization **1**:110–111; **7**:933–934,
      936, 984; **8**:1130; **11**:1513
    nursing **8**:*1102*
    surgery **11**:1570–1571
    transplants **8**:1087–1088, 1103
  robotics in 4:497**; 10:1432–1435**
  telemedicine **8**:1094; **10**:*1433*–1434
  veterinary **1**:88, *90*
medicines *see* drugs
6-mercaptopurine **7**:898
mercy killing *see* euthanasia
metanalysis **8**:1098
methadone **4**:558

methotrexate **3**:353
methyldopa **2**:164
micropuncture, kidney **7**:990
microsurgery **11**:*1572*
miscarriage **1**:14; **10**:1354
morality *see* bioethics
morphine **9**:1215
motion sickness **4**:561
in astronauts **11**:1534
MRI *see* magnetic resonance imaging
mustard gas **3**:352
myoclonus **11**:1511

N

nalidixic acid **1**:109
nanobots **10**:1434
narcotics **1**:23
nausea **4**:519; **11**:1565
Nd-YAG lasers **11**:1575
neurobiology **9**:1210–1211
Ramón y Cajal and **10**:1396
neurochemistry **9**:1212–1213
neuroscience 9:1210–1215
nicotine **1**:51; **4**:555; **8**:1061
patches **8**:1092
nitrofurans **1**:108
nitrogen mustard **3**:352
nitrogen oxides, nitrous oxide, for
anesthesia **1**:76; **8**:1102
nonoxynol-9 **4**:441
nuclear magnetic resonance *see* magnetic
resonance imaging
Nuremberg (Nürnberg) Code **2**:189
nursing **8**:*1102*
nystatin **1**:109

O

operating rooms **11**:*1571*
"smart" **10**:1433
ophthalmoscopes **8**:1102
opiates **1**:23
opium **1**:23; **4**:*556*; **9**:1291
organ networks, in Chinese medicine
3:360
organs, cryopreservation **4**:472–473
oscilloscopes **12**:1627
osteopathy 1:57; 9:1250
see also chiropractic

P

pacemaker, artificial **2**:214; **7**:879; **8**:*1039*,
1092; **12**:1636
pain **12**:1627
back **3**:320
treatment **1**:57
natural painkillers **5**:614
reflex **10**:1398
pandemics, influenza **7**:951
paralytic ileus **11**:1574
paternity testing, blood groups
2:245
Patient Self-determination Act (1991),
U.S. **5**:646
penicillin **1**:108; **2**:164; **6**:742, 799;
11:1571
allergy to **1**:110
bacteria resistant to **1**:*110*
discovery **1**:*108*; **6**:*741*–742; **8**:1103,
1131, 1138; **9**:*1290*; **11**:1461

manufacture **1**:109
mode of action **1**:109; **5**:630; **6**:799;
9:1291
percutaneous transluminal coronary
angioplasty (PTCA) **11**:1574
peroxides **1**:116–117
persistent vegetative state (waking coma)
3:399; **5**:646; **8**:1038, 1040
PET *see* positron emission tomography
pharmacology 8:1090; 9:1289–1292
see also drugs
phenylketonuria (PKU) **8**:*1123*, 1124;
10:1358
phosphonomycin **5**:630
photoradiation therapy **11**:1575
phytotherapy *see* herbal medicine
pill, the **4**:441, 443
PKU (phenylketonuria) **8**:*1123*, 1124;
10:1358
placebo effect **9**:1292
PMS (premenstrual syndrome)
8:1110–1111
positron emission tomography (PET)
2:*260*; **8**:1090–1091
postvegetative state **3**:399
premenstrual syndrome (PMS)
8:1110–1111
prontosil **9**:1290
propanolol **7**:898
prostheses **2**:212–215; **7**:875;
8:1092–1093
see also implants
Prozac (fluoxetine) **9**:1215; **10**:*1390*
PTCA (percutaneous transluminal coronary
angioplasty) **11**:1574
ptosis **1**:72

Q

Qi (chi) **1**:55; **3**:360, 361
quaternary ammonium compounds (quats)
1:117
quinine **1**:51; **2**:164; **6**:744; **8**:1103

R

**radiation and radiation sickness
10:1394–1395**
dangers to humans **5**:626; **10**:1395
causing leukemia **8**:1031
radiation sickness **10**:1395
and use of robots **10**:1432
ionizing radiation **10**:1395
for microbial sterilization **1**:116
radiation therapy **3**:296
photoradiation **11**:1575
radioactive tagging, for drugs **9**:1290
see also X rays
radiotherapy **3**:296; **8**:1031, 1091
radium **10**:1394
reflexology **1**:57; **5**:614
reiki **1**:57
repetitive motion injury **5**:628
reserpine **1**:51
respirators **8**:*1038*–1039
Retin A **12**:1691
rifampin **1**:109; **12**:1648
Ringer's solution, lactated **8**:1039
robotics, **in medicine 4**:497;
10:*1432–1435*
ROBOT-RX **10**:*1434*–1435

S

salvarsan (arsphenamine) **5**:592; **8**:1103;
9:1289
sanitization **1**:115
SBGM (self-blood-glucose monitoring)
4:507
scans *see* imaging, medical
scopolamine **1**:51
self-blood-glucose monitoring (SBGM)
4:507
shiatsu **1**:57
shock **3**:378
anaphyactic **1**:53
siddha **7**:944
SIDS (sudden infant death syndrome)
12:1691
silver nitrate **1**:116
Six Million Dollar Man, The (television
series) **2**:215
sleeping pills **11**:1512
slipped disk **11**:*1502*
smelling salts **11**:1516
smoking **4**:555
and cancer **3**:*295*; **8**:1059–1060;
12:1622
and free radicals **1**:*34*
historical development **8**:1014
and the lungs **8**:*1061*
and Parkinson's disease **4**:497
passive **8**:1061
snakebite, inactivation **7**:934
soap, and antisepsis **1**:117
Socrates **2**:187
space medicine 11:1533–1534
space sickness **11**:1533
spermicides **4**:440, 441
sphygmomanometers **3**:374
spinal taps (lumbar punctures) **11**:1573
splenectomy (removal of the spleen)
8:1064–1065; **11**:1551, 1570
split-brain syndrome **5**:638
sponges (contraceptives) **4**:440–441
sterilization (fertility), human **4**:442–442
stethoscopes, invention **8**:*1101*, 1102
stimulants **1**:24
streptomycin **6**:742
stress tests **7**:881
strokes **2**:242, 256; **3**:377; **7**:902; **12**:1620
learning to move after **10**:1435
Sudden Infant Death Syndrome (SIDS)
12:1691
sulfa drugs **9**:1290
sulfones **1**:108
sulphonamides **1**:108
surgery 11:1570–1575
anesthesia for **1**:75–76; **8**:1102; **11**:1571,
1573
and antisepsis **8**:1043
biopsies **4**:475
brain **5**:*639*; **11**:*1575*
cryosurgery **4**:473
development **11**:1570–1571
see also medicine, history of
elective and nonelective **11**:1572–1573
eye **11**:1575
heart **8**:1101; **11**:1571–1572
keyhole (minimally invasive surgery;
MIS) **10**:1433; **11**:*1574*–1575
see also endoscopy

laser **8**:*1091*; **11**:1574, *1575*
microsurgery **11**:*1572*
minimal access *see* surgery, keyhole
plastic **11**:1572
remotely controlled **8**:1094
robots used in **4**:497; **10**:*1432*–1434
spare-part **8**:1092
transplantation *see* transplants
use of microscopes **8**:*1089*
surrogate motherhood **5**:712
sutures **11**:1573
syringes, needle-free **8**:*1092*

T

tacrine **4**:496
THA **1**:61
tamoxifen **3**:353
taxol **3**:417; **9**:1290
Teddy (robot) **10**:1435
telemedicine **8**:*1094*; **10**:*1433–1434*
tetracycline **1**:109
thalidomide **5**:698; **8**:1090
thermometers, history **8**:1102
thoracoplasty **11**:1570–1571
Thorazine (chlorpromazine) **11**:1466
tine test **12**:1648
tissue engineering **8**:1093
toxoid vaccines **7**:935
transfusions
blood **2**:*244*–245; **11**:1571
Charles Drew and **4**:*553*–554
transplants 8:1092; 12:1633–1636
abdominal viscera **12**:1636
small bowel **12**:1636
autotransplants and allotransplants
8:1092; **12**:1633
bone marrow **2**:249; **3**:353; **4**:535;
8:1031; **11**:1557; **12**:*1633*
drawbacks **3**:384–385
embryo **5**:711
hand **8**:1088
heart **7**:*940*; **8**:1088
from animals **12**:1634
heart-lung **8**:1092; **12**:1635–1636
history of **8**:1088; **12**:*1633–1636*
and the immune response **7**:932,
940–941; **8**:1087–1088
kidney **4**:472; **8**:1039, 1065–1066,
1088; **12**:*1634*, 1636
the first **8**:1088, 1092; **12**:1634
liver **4**:472; **8**:1046; **12**:*1634*–1635
Medawar (Peter) and **8**:1087–1088,
1103; **12**:*1633*–1634
multivisceral "cluster" **12**:1636
pancreas **12**:1634
and rejection **12**:1635
supply of organs **12**:1636
and therapeutic cloning **3**:384–385;
11:1558
using stem cells **5**:600; **11**:1557
xenotransplants **2**:189, 225; **8**:1092;
12:1634
see also grafting
trephining **11**:1570
tretinoin cream **12**:1691
trials
blind and double-blind **8**:1096
fertility **7**:896
randomized controlled **8**:1096, 1097

trimethoprim 1:108
tubal ligation 4:442–443
tuberculin skin test 12:1648
Tuskegee Syphilis Study 2:189

U

ultrasound 1:72; **12:***1657*
  Doppler 8:1090
  for prenatal screening 12:*1657*
unani 1:044
urea, medical uses 12:*1667*
urine
  examination 5:671
  retention 11:1574
utilitarianism 2:188

V

vaccines *see* immunization, vaccines
VADs (ventricular assist devices) 2:*214*
Valium (diazepam) 9:1215
vancomycin 5:630
vasectomy 4:443
vedic medicine 7:944
vegetative state 3:399, 400; 5:646; 8:1038, 1040
ventilation, mechanical 8:1038–1039
ventricular assist devices (VADs) 2:*214*
vertigo 4:561
vicodin 4:557
vinblastine 7:887
vincristine 7:887
vitamins 9:1229; **12:1689–1691**
  absorption from the gut 4:519
  attacking free radicals 3:294
  biotin 12:1691
    deficiency 4:488
  as coenzymes 9:1227; 12:1691
  deficiency 4:488–*489*; 9:1227
  fat-soluble 4:488–489, 519;
    12:1689–1690
  folic acid 12:1691
    deficiency 4:488; 12:1691
  in foods 9:1226–1227
  medical uses of 12:1691
  megadoses 12:1691
  stored in the liver 8:1046
  supplements 12:1691
  vitamin A (retinol) 3:317; 10:1311;
    12:1689
    absorption 4:519
    deficiency 4:488–489; 9:1227, 1291;
      12:1689
  vitamin B, from yeast 12:1715
  vitamin B$_1$ (thiamine) 4:488; 12:1690
    deficiency 9:1227
  vitamin B$_2$ (riboflavin) 10:1310;
    12:1690
    deficiency 12:1690
  vitamin B$_3$ (niacin) 5:630
    deficiency 4:488
  vitamin B$_5$ (pantothenic acid)
    12:1690–1691
  vitamin B$_6$ (pyridoxine) 5:630–631;
    12:*1689*, 1691
    deficiency 4:488; 12:1691
  vitamin B$_{12}$ (cobalamine) 4:519;
    12:1690, 1691
    deficiency 1:74; 2:246, 247; 4:488;
      12:1691

vitamin C (ascorbic acid) 3:294, 395;
    12:1691
  absorption 4:519
  deficiency 4:488; 6:764; 8:1095;
    9:1227; 12:*1691*
vitamin D 12:1658, 1689
  absorption 4:519
  and calcium absorption 2:278; 12:1691
  deficiency 2:250; 4:*489*; 9:*1227*;
    11:1502; 12:1689
vitamin E (alpha tocopherol) 3:294;
    12:1690, 1691
  absorption 4:519
  deficiency 4:489
vitamin K 12:1690
  absorption 4:519
  for babies 4:519
  deficiency 2:242; 4:489
  water-soluble 4:488, 519; 12:*1689*,
    1690–1691
Vomit Comet 11:1534
vomiting 4:519; 11:1565
  induced 11:1565

W

waking coma (persistent vegetative state)
    3:399; 5:646; 8:1038, 1040
warfarin 8:1096–1097
water
  diseases carried in 5:627; 7:948–949
  need, in humans 8:1120
weightlessness, effects on the body
    11:1533
World Health Organization (WHO)
    5:634

X

xenotransplantation 2:189, 225; 8:1092
X rays 5:626; **12:1712–1713**
  dangers of 12:1713
    mutations 6:746; 12:1713
  discovery 8:1090, 1102; 10:*1395*;
    12:*1713*
  imaging using 1:72; 10:*1394*
    of the chest 12:*1648*
    in CT scanning 4:474–475
    of the stomach 11:*1563*, 1565
  see also radiation and radiation sickness

YZ

yin and yang 3:360
ZEUS (robotic surgical system) 10:*1432*,
    1433
zidovudine (azidothymidine, AZT) 1:44,
    109; 9:1292; 12:1678
ZIFT (zygote intrafallopian transfer) 5:710
zygote intrafallopian transfer (ZIFT) 5:710

■ MICROBIOLOGY

A

Actinomyces spp. 2:172
adenoviruses 6:806–807
aerotolerant organisms 5:700
Agrobacterium tumefaciens 6:*809*
algae, blue-green *see* cyanobacteria
amoebas 10:*1379*, 1382
  digestion by 4:511
  diseases from 8:*1132*

feeding 5:693
  pseudopods 5:693, 698; 11:1578
arboviruses 7:946, 947
archaea 2:167
archebacteria 5:582
Azobacter 9:1217

B

Bacillus spp.
  B. *anthracis* 1:88–89, *107*, *117*; 2:170
  B. *cereus* 2:170
  B. *popilliae* 7:960
  B. *thuringiensis* 6:810; 8:1132; 9:1288
bacteria 2:167–172; 8:1130
  anaerobic 8:1117; 9:*1253*
    first forms of life 6:801
  ATP production 2:158
  attachment 2:*167*, 168, 169
  autotrophic 2:169
  and bioremediation 11:1461; 12:1698
  blooms 5:*584*
  capsule 2:169
  cave-dwelling 3:325
  cell walls 2:168–169; 3:298
    and antibiotics 5:630
  chemosynthetic
    at the seafloor 3:305; 5:651; 9:1233,
      1237
    in caves 3:325
    and the nitrogen cycle 9:1217–1218
  cytoplasmic membrane 2:168
  in the digestive tract 2:172
  endospores 2:170–171
  evolution 2:167–168
  feeding 2:169
  first forms of life 2:168
  first observed 2:169
  flagella 2:*167*, 168, 169; 3:338
  fossils 2:168; 6:784; 10:1380
  frost-resistant 8:1131
  gas vesicles 2:169
  and genetic engineering 2:170; 8:1131
  genetic material 2:169
    chromosomes 3:367
    transfer 1:110
  gram-positive and gram-negative
    2:168–169, *171*
  green 10:1303, 1306
  heterotrophic 2:169
  illnesses from 2:172
  industrial uses 2:172
  infecting plants 10:1322
  iron 7:973
  lactic acid 5:700, 701, 703
  lithoautotrophic 2:169
  luminescent 2:205, 207
  methanobacteria 5:702
  motion 2:*167*, 168, 169
  mutations 2:170
  oral 2:171–172
  photosynthetic 3:337
  pili 2:170
  population growth curve 10:1347
  purple 2:168; 10:1303, 1306

reproduction 2:*169*–170
  resistance to antibiotics 1:*19*, 109–110,
    110; 8:1129; 9:1291
    penicillin 1:*110*
  saprophytic 11:1460, *1462*
  on the skin 2:171
  soil 11:1531
  spores 2:170; 11:1531
  staining 2:168–169
  structure 2:*168*–169
  sulfur 9:1239; 10:1303
  symbiotic, in the gut 4:517; 9:*1226*,
    1228
  toxins 2:169, 172
  types 2:*170*–171
  used in biological control 7:960; 9:1288
  viruses of *see* bacteriophages
  for waste management 8:1132
  and waterborne diseases 5:627;
    7:948–949
  see also microbiology; prokaryotes
bacteriological warfare *see* biological
    warfare
bacteriophages 1:110; 4:537; 12:1675,
    1681
Bacteroides spp. 2:172
baculoviruses 12:1679
binary fission 3:338
  by bacteria 2:*169*–170; 3:338; 10:*1404*
bioleaching 8:1132
biological warfare 2:197–199
  anthrax for 1:107; 2:198, 199
  nerve gases 9:1183
  smallpox and 2:198; 11:1513; 12:1679
Bordetella pertussis 7:948
Borrelia burgdorferi 7:946, 949
brewer's yeast 12:1715
budding
  by bacteria 2:170
  by yeasts 12:1714

C

Candida spp.
  C. *albicans* 12:*1716*
  C. *utilis* 12:1715
capsid 12:1680
Caulimovirus 10:1323
Chlamydia psittaci 1:89
choanoflagellates, evolution of sponges
    from 11:1553
ciliates (Ciliophora) 10:1382
Clostridium spp. 5:700, 702, 703; 9:1217
  C. *botulinum* 6:764, 765; 8:1117; 9:*1253*;
    11:1462
    toxins 9:1203; 11:1462
  C. *perfringens* 6:765; 9:1253
  C. *tetani* 9:1203
  and food poisoning 6:765
coal, desulfurization 8:1132
conjugation, bacterial 1:110; 8:1082
corynebacteria 2:171
cosmids 12:1679
cultures, of microorganisms
    8:1131–1132

Bold words with bold page numbers indicate complete articles; bold numbers preceding colons are volume numbers; numbers following colons indicate page numbers; italic page numbers refer to illustrations or other graphics.

cyanobacteria **1**:47, 49; **3**:332; **5**:*651*;
 6:801
 are prokaryotes *see* prokaryotes
 evolution into chloroplasts **2**:168; **3**:392
 nitrogen fixing **9**:1217
cyanophytes *see* cyanobacteria
cytoprocts **4**:511

DE
Dictyostelium discoideum **9**:1293
endospores, bacterial **2**:170–171
Entameba histolytica **3**:388
Enterococcus spp. **2**:172
Epstein–Barr virus **3**:295; **8**:1066
Epulopiscium bacteria **2**:170; **3**:331
Escherichia coli **1**:*19*; **4**:517, 519; **5**:703
 binary fission **3**:338
 discovery **2**:226
 in genetic engineering **2**:222, 223, 246
 saprophytes **11**:1460, *1462*
 vitamin production **2**:172
exotoxins, bacterial **2**:172

F
filoviruses **12**:1683
fimbriae **2**:167, *168*, 169
flagellates (Mastigophora) **10**:1382
 swimming **11**:1578
flaviviruses **12**:1683

GH
germ warfare *see* biological warfare
Gymnomycota *see* slime molds
Haemophilus influenzae **2**:171
Helicobacter pylori **4**:516, 523; **11**:1565
HEPA filter masks **2**:198
herpes simplex **7**:949
herpesviruses **12**:1682, 1683
herpes zoster **7**:948
HTLV-I and HTLV-II **8**:1031
hyaluronidase **2**:172

KL
Kirby-Bauer test **8**:1129
Lactobacillus spp. **2**:172
 L. bulgaricus **6**:763
Legionella pneumophila **5**:627
Lipomyces spp. **12**:1714
lipopolysaccharide (LPS) **2**:169
Listeria spp. **6**:765; **10**:*1404*
Lithotrops spp. **6**:767
lysogenic cycle **12**:1681

M
Mastigophora *see* flagellates
methanobacteria **5**:702
microbiology 8:1127–1132
 environmental **8**:1132
 famous microbiologists **8**:*1127–1129*
 industrial **8**:1132
 medical **8**:1132
Micrococcus spp. **2**:171
Micrographia (Hooke) **3**:*330*
microorganisms **8**:1130
 ecological role **5**:585
 immune system and **7**:928–929
 mating in **8**:1082
 study of *see* microbiology
 see also bacteria; protozoa; viruses

mining industry, bacteria used in **8**:1132
mollicutes **10**:1323
Monera **10**:1380; **12**:1601
Mononegavirales **12**:1682
murein **2**:169
Mycobacterium tuberculosis **5**:591; **7**:948;
 8:1059, 1066; **12**:1648
Mycoplasmas (mollicutes) **10**:1323

N
Nitrobacter **9**:1217, 1218
Nitrococcus **9**:1217–1218
Nitrosomonas **9**:1217–1218
Norwalk viruses **7**:948

O
ore, extraction **8**:1132
orthomyxoviruses **7**:*951*
Oscillatoria bacteria **2**:*169*

P
Paramecium spp. **10**:*1382*
 competition **3**:408
 digestion **4**:511
paramyxoviruses **12**:1683
parvoviruses **6**:807; **12**:1683
Penicillium spp.
 in cheesemaking **6**:763
 and penicillin **1**:109, *110*; **6**:799; **8**:1138;
 9:1290; **11**:1461
peptidoglycan **3**:298
phages *see* bacteriophages
phagocytosis **2**:240; **3**:336, *337*; **5**:693;
 7:929, 938
Photobacterium **2**:205
phytoplasmas **10**:1323
picornaviruses **12**:*1682*, 1683
pili **2**:170
Plasmodium spp. **7**:946
 and malaria **5**:621; **6**:744; **9**:1265
pospiviroids **10**:1324
poxviruses **12**:1681, 1682, 1683
prions (proteins) 10:1371–1373
prokaryotes **2**:167; **3**:331
 aerobic respiration **8**:1118
 become eukaryote organelles **2**:168, 203;
 3:332, 392; **10**:1380; **11**:1581
 DNA **2**:167; **3**:331
 flagella **3**:338
 and origins of life **2**:168; **3**:332; **10**:1380
 prokaryotic algae **1**:47
 see also bacteria; cyanobacteria
protists 8:1130; 10:1379–1382;
 12:1601
 animal-like **10**:*1382*
 see also protozoa
 funguslike **10**:1381–1382
 plantlike **10**:1380–*1381*
protozoa
 chemoreception **12**:1595, 1625
 digestion by **4**:511
 in digestive systems
 cockroach **3**:388
 termite **11**:*1461*; **12**:1611
 estuarine **11**:1492
 excretion **5**:666; **7**:902
 feeding **5**:693
 infections by **7**:949
 carried by ticks **7**:947

 see also Paramecium spp.; *Plasmodium*
 spp.; *Trypanosoma* spp.
 movement **11**:1578
pseudopodia (pseudopods) **4**:511; **5**:693,
 698; **11**:1578

R
radiolarians **4**:438; **10**:1382
retroviruses **4**:537; **6**:806; **10**:1431;
 12:1681–1682, 1683
 causing leukemia **8**:1031
 causing mutation **9**:1189
 genetic engineering and **12**:1679
 HIV as **1**:43
rhinoviruses **3**:395
Rhizobium **11**:*1531*
 leghemoglobin **7**:973
 nitrogen fixation **8**:*1029*; **9**:1217, *1218*
Rhodospirillum spp. **2**:171
rickettsias **7**:946, 947; **9**:1267

S
Salmonella spp. **5**:703
 and food poisoning **6**:765
 from cockroaches **3**:388
 S. typhi **7**:948
 as a terrorist weapon **2**:199
sarcodines (Sarcodina) **10**:1382
 see also amoebas; radiolarians
satellites (subviral agents) **10**:1324
Shigella **5**:703
simian immunodeficiency viruses (SIVs)
 1:42, 43
SIV virus **1**:42, 43
slime molds (Gymnomycota)
 8:*1139*–1140; **10**:1381; **12**:1647
 communication **9**:1293
spiroplasmas **10**:1323
spontaneous generation **1**:116; **2**:202;
 5:652; **8**:1127; **9**:1269
spores, bacterial **2**:170; **11**:1531
sporozoans (Sporozoa) **10**:1382
 see also Plasmodium
Staphylococcus spp. **2**:171
 S. aureus **2**:171; **6**:765
 S. epidermidis **2**:171
sterilization (microbial) **1**:116
streak plating **8**:1131
Streptococcus spp. **2**:172
 in food making **6**:763
 S. mutans **2**:171, 172; **12**:1605
 S. pneumoniae **2**:171; **11**:1551
stromatolites **3**:332
sulfur, desufurization of coal **8**:1132

T
T4 phages **12**:*1681*
Thiobacillus spp.
 T. denitrificans **9**:1218
 T. ferrooxidans **7**:973
Tobamovirus **10**:1323
toxins, bacterial **2**:169, 172
transduction **1**:110; **2**:170
transformation **1**:110; **2**:170
Treponema pallidum **2**:171
Trichomonas spp.
 T. hominis **9**:1266
 T. vaginalis **7**:950
Trichonympha spp. **11**:*1461*, 1462

Trychonympha **10**:1380
Trypanosoma spp. **9**:1265; **10**:1382
 T. brucei **7**:946
 T. cruzi **7**:885, 946

V
vaccinia virus **12**:1679
Vibrio spp. **2**:171, 205
 V. cholerae **2**:197; **5**:633; **7**:*935*, 948
viroids **10**:1324
virology 12:1675–1679
viruses 8:1130; **12**:1680–1683
 attacking cells **12**:1681–1682
 bacteriophages **1**:110; **4**:537; **12**:1675,
 1681
 and cancer **3**:295
 coat **12**:1680
 culturing **12**:1676
 diseases **12**:1682–*1683*
 common cold 3:395
 fighting **12**:1677–1678
 of plants **10**:1323–*1324*; **12**:1678,
 1683
 DNA **12**:1681
 extraction and purification
 12:1676–1677
 families **12**:1681
 for gene therapy **6**:806–807, *808*
 genetic engineering and **12**:1678–1679
 genetic material **3**:367; **12**:1681
 identifying **12**:1677
 mosaic
 cauliflower **10**:1323
 tobacco (TMV) **8**:1130; **10**:1323, *1324*
 origins **12**:1682
 orthomyxoviruses **7**:*951*
 RNA **10**:1430–1431; **12**:1681
 see also retroviruses
 size **12**:1680–1681
 structures analyzed **12**:1677
 types **12**:1680–1681, 1683
 waterborne diseases **5**:627; **7**:948
 as weapons **12**:*1679*
 see also microbiology; prions (proteins)

W
World War I
 biologial weapons **2**:198
 lice **8**:1033
World War II
 biologial weapons **2**:198
 lice **8**:1033

Y
Yersinia pestis **6**:740; **7**:950; **8**:1063

■ MOLECULAR BIOLOGY AND CYTOLOGY

A
acrosomes **5**:713–714
adenine **4**:533, 535, 537; **5**:654; **10**:1428
amniocentesis **3**:367; **4**:477; **10**:*1358*
amyloplasts **12**:1646
apoptosis **3**:353
axons **2**:255; **9**:1183, 1198; **12**:1626
 terminal buttons **9**:*1198*, 1200

B

bacteriochlorophyll 3:337; 10:1306
blastoderm 5:598
blastula 5:597, *598, 599*
blind spot 5:687

C

cell biology 3:329–340
  aging 1:33–34
  animal cells 3:*336*
  apoptosis 3:353
  ATP production 2:*158*–160; 3:299–300;
    5:*618*; 7:993
  autolysis 3:334–335
  cell differentiation 3:330; 7:894;
    10:1400; 11:1556
  cell division
    cytokinesis 3:339
    DNA replication 4:*534*–536
    see also meiosis; mitosis
  cell theory 2:202; 3:330–331
  circadian rhythms 2:217
  cytology 4:476–477
  cytosol 2:159
  electrical potential of cells 10:1308
  endoplasmic reticulum 3:334
  evolution 3:332
  flow cytometry 4:476–477
  freezing of cells 4:471–472
  Golgi complex 3:334
  life span of cells 1:36
  lysosomes 3:334–335; 4:511; 7:929
  membranes *see* plasma membranes
  mitochondria *see* mitochondria
  muscle cells, fermentation by 5:703
  nucleus *see* nuclei
  organelles 3:333–335, *336*
  and osmosis 11:1458–1459
  peroxisomes 3:335
  plant 3:*335*–336, *337*; 4:*476*
    cell walls 3:298, 341–342
    vacuoles 3:*335*, 336; 8:1023
  pluripotent cells 3:340; 11:1557,
    1558–1559
  position of molecules within cells
    8:1144–1145
  prokaryotes and eukaryotes 10:1380
  ribosomes *see* ribosomes
  structure, and freeze-etch microscopy
    4:*473*
  totipotent cells 3:340; 6:809; 11:*1557*
  types 3:330
  unipotent cells 11:1557–1558
  vacuoles 3:336–337
  walls
    bacterial 2:168–169; 3:298; 5:630
    of plants 3:298, 336
central dogma 10:1429–1430
centriole 3:338–339
centromere 3:338, 366
chiasmata 3:339–340
chlorobium chlorophyll 10:1306
chloroplasts 3:332, *335*; 8:1023;
  10:1303–1304
  bundle sheath 10:1305
  evolution from symbiotic bacteria 3:392
  mesophyll 10:1305
chorionic villus sampling (CVS) 3:367;
  4:477; 10:1358

chromatids 3:*338, 339*, 340
chromatin 3:333
chylomicrons 3:362–363
cilia 3:338; 11:1578
codons 4:*536*, 537; 10:1378
contractile vacuoles 3:336–337; 5:666
CVS *see* chorionic villus sampling
cytokinesis 3:339
cytology 4:476–477
  clinical 4:477
  plant 2:254
cytosine 4:533, 535, 537; 5:654; 10:1428

D

dendrites 2:255; 9:1198; 12:1626
DICER enzyme 10:1430, *1431*
DNA 3:366; 4:533–538; 8:1144; 10:1428
  cloning 3:384
  discovery 8:1142
  effects of chemotherapy on 3:353
  and evolution 5:654
  fingerprinting 2:224; 4:*535*; 6:*773*, 774;
    9:*1174*
  the genetic code 4:536
  "junk" (noncoding) 4:534; 7:922–923
  mapping 7:920–921
  markers 7:920
  in mitochondria (mtDNA) 2:168; 3:385
    and human origins 7:917
  mutation 4:538
  prokaryotic 2:167; 3:331
  and protein synthesis 4:*536*, 537;
    10:1378
  radioactive tagging 2:182
  recombinant 2:170, 223; 8:1143, 1145
  repair 6:806
  replication 4:*534*–536
    scientific (polymerase chain reaction)
      3:384; 4:535; 6:774; 8:1145–1146
    see also meiosis; mitosis
  sequencing 7:920, 921–*922*; 8:*1146*
  splitting 8:1145
  structure 4:*533*–534; 7:918–919
    discovery 4:461–462, 537; 8:1142
  transcription 4:537; 9:1189; 10:1378,
    1428, *1429*
  transposons (transposable elements;
    jumping genes) 1:110; 7:922–923;
    8:1086; 9:1190
  typing 2:182
  viral 12:1681
  X-ray crystallography 6:786
DNA polymerase 3:353; 4:535;
  8:1146

E

electrical potential, of cells 10:1308
endocytosis 3:336, *337*
endoplasmic reticulum 3:334
euchromatin 3:367

F

flagella 3:338; 11:1578
  of bacteria (prokaryotes) 2:*167, 168*,
    169; 3:338
flow cytometry 4:476–477

G

gastrulation 5:597–599

GenBank 8:1145
glycolipids 3:298
glycoproteins 3:298
Golgi complex 3:334
grana 3:335; 10:1304
guanine 4:533, 535, 537; 5:654, *665*;
  10:1428

H

heterochromatin 3:367
high-density lipoproteins (HDLs) 3:363
histones 3:366
hydroxyapatite (hydroxylapatite) 3:319;
  10:1302

I

intracellular fluid 10:1307
islets of Langerhans 5:612; 7:*895*, 904,
  964; 9:1260, *1261*
  replacement 12:1634

KL

karyotyping 3:*367*
LDLs (low-density lipoproteins) 3:363
liposomes, used in gene therapy 6:807
low-density lipoproteins (LDLs) 3:363
lysosomes 3:334–335; 7:929
  of protozoans 4:511

M

macrofibrils 3:341
meiosis 3:339–340, 368;
  10:1403–1404
  in egg cells 5:587–588, 589–590
  see also DNA, replication
membranes, cell *see* plasma membranes
microfibrils 3:341
mitochondria 3:332, *333*, 335; 8:1118,
  1119
  DNA (mtDNA) 2:168; 3:385
    and human origins 7:917
  evolution of 2:168; 3:392; 5:585
  Krebs cycle and ATP production
    2:159–160; 3:300, 335; 5:619;
    7:996
  link reaction in 7:994
  and the urea cycle 12:1667
mitosis 3:*338*–339
  blocked by drugs 3:353
  interruption leading to polyploidy
    2:266
  see also DNA, replication
molecular biology 8:1141–1146
  DNA
    structure discovered 4:461–462,
      533–534, 537; 7:918–*919*;
      8:1142
    see also DNA
  karyotyping 3:367
  monoclonal antibodies 1:113; 2:*221*,
    224, 226
  RFLP analysis *see* restriction fragment
length polymorphisms
myeloblasts 2:243

N

neural plate 5:599
neurulation 5:597, *599*
nucleic acids 8:1144; 10:1428
  discovery 4:537
  see also DNA; RNA
nucleoid 3:331, 366
nucleoli 4:*476*
nucleoplasm 3:333
nucleosomes 3:366
nucleotides 4:535
nucleus 3:333–334
  freeze-etch microscopy of 4:*473*
  polar nuclei 5:601
  synergids 5:590

O

oogenesis 5:587, *588*
oogonia 5:587–588
organelles, cytoplasmic 3:333–335, *336*
  evolution from prokaryotes 2:168, 203;
    3:332, 392; 10:1380; 11:1581
organogenesis 5:599–600
osteoblasts 2:248, 249; 3:319
osteoclasts 2:249, 250

P

Pap smear test 4:477
peroxisomes 3:335
phospholipids 5:690–691
  in the plasma membrane 3:*331*
  see also plasma membranes
pinocytosis 3:336, *337*
plasma membranes
  electrical potential across 10:1308
  inhibition of function of 1:108–109
  structure 3:*331*–332, 362
plasmids 1:109–110; 3:337; 8:1145
  and genetically modified foods 6:*811*
plasmodesmata 8:1025; 12:1631, 1683
polar body 5:589
primitive streak 5:598–599, 600
proplastids 10:1306
protochlorophyllide 10:1306
purines
  in DNA 4:533
  in RNA 10:1428
pyrimidines
  in DNA 4:533
  in RNA 10:1428

R

restriction fragment length polymorphisms
  (RFLPs) 6:774; 7:920; 8:1146
RFLPs (restriction fragment length
  polymorphisms) 6:774; 7:920; 8:1146
Rh blood typing *see* rhesus (Rh) system
rhesus (Rh) system 2:244, 245; 6:774;
  7:941
ribonucleoproteins, small nuclear
  (snRNPs) 10:1429
ribosomes 3:334
  and amino acid/protein synthesis 4:537;
    9:1189; 10:*1378*, 1429, 1430

Bold words with bold page numbers indicate complete articles; bold numbers preceding colons are volume numbers; numbers following colons indicate page numbers; italic page numbers refer to illustrations or other graphics.

ribosomes (continued)
  bacterial 2:169
  structure 10:1429
ribozymes 10:1431
RNA 8:1144; **10:1428–1431**
  and evolution 5:654; 9:1254; 10:1431
  interference (RNAi) 10:1430
  messenger (mRNA) 3:333; 4:536, 537;
    7:919, 920; 10:1378, 1428–1429
    and mutations 9:1189, 1190
  and the origins of life 2:181
  and protein synthesis 4:536, 537;
    10:1378, 1428–1430
  ribosomal (rRNA) 10:1429, 1431
  structure 10:1428
  transfer (tRNA) 4:536, 537; 9:1189;
    10:1378, 1429, 1430
RNA polymerase 1:109; 4:537; 10:1378,
    1428–1429

S

smear tests 4:477
somites 5:599
spindle, action of colchicine 3:367

T

thylakoids 3:335; 10:1304
  membranes 10:1306
thymine 4:533, 535, 537; 5:654; 10:1428
transcription 4:537; 9:1189; 10:1378,
    1428, 1429
translation, in protein synthesis 4:537;
    9:1189; 10:1378, 1429–1430

U

uracil 4:536; 10:1428
vacuoles, cell 3:335, 336–337; 5:666;
    8:1023
VLDLs (very low-density lipoproteins)
    3:363

Y

yolk 5:588–589
zona pellucida 5:589

■ **PATHOLOGY AND**
HISTOLOGY
A
acne 5:676; 11:1508
acromegaly 7:905
actin 6:726, 772; 9:1178, 1181, 1182;
    10:1377
Addison's disease 2:165; 4:454; 5:612;
    7:905
adipocytes 3:420
adipose tissue 3:420
AIDS 1:42–45
  epidemic 1:45
  and HIV 1:42, 43–44; 3:298; 7:932,
    940; 8:1129
    hemophilics infected with 1:45
    origins 1:42–43
    test for 5:630; 12:1676
    types 1:42–43
  and the immune response 1:43; 7:940
  infections associated with 1:42
  Mullis and Duesberg's theories
    9:1174

prospects for a vaccine 1:45
  stages 1:44
  transmission 1:44–45
  treatment 1:44
albuminous cells 12:1631
Alzheimer's disease 1:61; 4:494–497;
    9:1204, 1213; 10:1389; 11:1558
amebiasis 7:949
Ames (mutagenicity) test 3:295
amyotrophic lateral sclerosis (ALS;
    Lou Gehrig's disease) 9:1181, 1202
anemia 1:73–74
  aplastic 1:74
  hemolytic 1:73–74; 2:164
  iron-deficiency 1:73; 2:246; 4:489;
    7:973
  macrocytic 2:246–247
  megaloblastic 1:73, 74
  pernicious 1:74; 4:488, 519
  sickle-cell 1:74; 2:191, 247; 4:538;
    5:656
    gene therapy 6:806
    and malaria 2:247; 4:525; 9:1266
    and the spleen 8:1065; 11:1551
    stable polymorphism 4:525
angina 7:881; 9:1225
animal diseases 1:87–90
  veterinary medicine 1:88, 90
anthracosis (anthrasilicosis; black lung)
    5:628
anthrax 1:88–89, 107, 117; 11:1531
  for biologial warfare 1:107; 2:198, 199
  treatment 2:198
appendicitis 4:523
archeocytes 10:1400; 11:1558
arteriosclerosis, cerebral 10:1389
artery disease 3:363
  see also atherosclerosis
arthritis 1:136; 2:250; 11:1502
  osteoarthritis 1:136; 7:870
    in cats and dogs 1:90
  prevention 1:136
  rheumatoid 1:136; 2:165; 5:690; 7:870,
    931, 942
  treatment 1:136
asbestos, diseases from 5:628
asbestosis 5:628
aspergillosis 1:89
astereognosis 12:1626
asthma 2:153; 5:628, 690; 8:1059
  treatment 2:153; 8:1059
astigmatism 5:687
atheroma 3:362; 9:1225
atherosclerosis 1:35; 3:363, 376–377
athlete's foot 5:699
autoimmune disorders 2:164–166;
    5:613; 7:931, 942
  and aging 1:34
  anemia, hemolytic 1:73–74; 2:164
  diabetes mellitus 2:165; 5:613
  of the endocrine system 5:613
  and mouth ulcers 12:1622
  multiple sclerosis 9:1175
  myasthenia gravis 9:1181
  rheumatoid arthritis 1:136
  scleroderma 2:164
  treatment 11:1557
autopsies (post-mortem investigations)
    6:773; 7:896

  see also forensic science
autoradiography 7:895–896

B
babesiosis 7:947
basophils 1:53, 114; 2:239, 240–241
B-cells see lymphocytes, B-cells
bends, the 9:1238; 10:1422
beriberi 4:488; 9:1227; 12:1690, 1715
beta cells 7:964; 9:1261
bile stones see gallstones
birth defects see congenital defects
birthmarks 10:1359
Black Death 7:950; 8:1063
blackheads 5:676
black lung' (anthracosis; anthrasilicosis)
    5:628
blastocysts 5:598, 600; 10:1353;
    11:1557
blastomycosis 7:948
blindness 5:687
  and Braille 11:1538; 12:1628
  color 5:687; 12:1687–1688
  devices to aid in 2:213
  night 9:1291; 12:1687
  snow 12:1658
blood 2:238–247; 3:376
  amount in the human body 2:238
  artificial 2:246
  basophils 1:53, 114; 2:239, 240–241
  carbon dioxide in 3:306
  cell manufacture 2:242–243;
    11:1558–1559
  circulation, first described 1:71; 8:1100
  clotting 2:241–242, 278; 7:937; 12:1620
    disorders 2:242
    drugs to prevent 12:1620
    vitamin K and 12:1690
  components 2:238–243
  diseases and disorders 2:246–247
    thalassemias 1:73; 2:247
  eosinophils 2:239, 240
  erythrocytes (red blood cells)
    2:238–239; 8:1056
    effect of high altitude on numbers of
    10:1307
    manufacture 2:243; 11:1558–1559
    natural destruction 2:243; 8:1047
    in the spleen 8:1064; 11:1550–1551
  erythropoietin 2:239; 10:1307
  glucose regulation 4:506; 7:902,
    904–905; 9:1260–1261
  haptoglobin (Hp) 6:774
  HIV-contaminated 1:45
  iron in 7:973
  leukocytes 2:239, 240, 243
    granulocytes 2:239, 243
    mononuclear cells 2:239
  megakaryocytes 2:243
  monocytes 2:241, 243
  neutrophils 2:239–240; 7:929
  nonmammalian 2:241
  phosphoglucomutase (PGM) 6:774
  plasma 2:238, 241; 4:554
  platelets 2:241, 243
    and blood clotting 2:241–242; 12:1620
    disorders 2:247
  screening 1:45
  storage 4:472

  blood banks 2:245; 4:471, 554;
    11:1571
  tested for freshness 2:206
  transfusions 2:244–245; 11:1571
    Charles Drew and 4:553–554
    types (groups) 2:243, 244–245; 6:774
    in Australian aborigines 9:1194
botulism 2:172; 6:765; 7:949; 9:1203,
    1253; 11:1462
bronchitis 8:1059
brown lung (byssinosis) 5:628
brucellosis 1:89
BSE (bovine spongiform encephalitis; mad
    cow disease) 1:89; 3:337; 7:949;
    10:1372
bunions 5:699
Burkitt's lymphoma 8:1066
bursitis 2:250
byssinosis 5:628

C
CAD see coronary artery disease
café au lait spots 11:1504
cancer 3:293–296; 8:1094; 12:1625
  and African Americans 3:296
  and the Ames test 3:295
  and antioxidants 3:294
  brain tumors 3:333, 398, 399; 8:1089
  breast 3:293, 295
    chemotherapy 3:353
    surgery for 2:219; 3:296
  causes 3:294–295; 9:1190
    diet 5:690
    environmental 5:627
  cervical 3:296
    test for 4:477
  colon 3:295, 299; 4:523, 538
    treatment 3:353
  diagnosis 4:477; 7:896; 8:1064
  digestive system 3:317
  in the elderly 1:35
  genes associated with 3:293, 294
  Hodgkin's disease 3:353; 8:1066
  liver 3:295
  lung 3:294, 295; 8:1060
    and diet 3:317
    and smoking 3:295; 8:1059–1060
    treatment 11:1575
  and the lymphatic system 8:1064
  lymphomas 3:294; 8:1066
    Burkitt's 8:1066
    non-Hodgkin's 3:371; 8:1066
  metastases 3:294; 8:1064
  poverty and 3:296
  prostate 3:295, 352
  rectal 3:295; 4:523
  skin 3:294, 295, 296, 317, 353; 9:1193;
    12:1658
    treatment 12:1713
  staging 4:477; 8:1064
  stomach 11:1565
  of the testis 7:896
  tongue 12:1622
  treatment 3:296
    with drugs (chemotherapy) 2:219;
    3:296, 352–353; 8:1031,
    1130–1131; 12:1597
    radiotherapy 3:296; 8:1091
    using stem cells 11:1557

using X rays **12**:1713
vaccines **3**:296
tumor growth **3**:352–353
types **3**:294
see also leukemia
candidiasis **12**:1716
canker sores (aphthous ulcers) **12**:1622
carcinoma(s) **3**:294
bronchogenic **8**:1060
see also cancer
caries, dental (tooth decay) **12**:1604–*1605*
carotenemia **3**:317
carpal tunnel syndrome **7**:870
cartilage 2:248; **3**:*319–320*; **6**:726;
10:1376
cataracts **5**:*687*; **12**:1658
celiac disease **4**:519
Chagas' disease **7**:885, 946
chemoreceptors, and heart rate **9**:1252
chicken pox **7**:948; **12**:*1683*
childbed fever **8**:1101
chitin **3**:298, 342; **6**:726; **8**:1143
choanocytes **11**:1552, 1553
cholera **5**:627, 633, *634*; **6**:746; **7**:948
for biological warfare **2**:*197*
in chickens **7**:934–935
vaccine **7**:*934–935*
chondroblasts **3**:319
chondrocytes **3**:319–320
chromaffin cells **5**:640
chromophores **10**:1309, 1310
chromoplasts **6**:761
cirrhosis **7**:894; **8**:1046
clubfoot **5**:699
cnidoblasts **7**:980
coal, dust **5**:*628*
coast disease **9**:1227
coccidiomycosis **7**:948
colds, common 3:395; **7**:929; **8**:1059
colitis **4**:519
collagen **3**:298, 319, 419; **6**:*726*; **8**:1142;
10:1376
and aging **1**:34
and bone formation **2**:277
in connective tissue **10**:*1377*
disorder of **3**:420
in tendons **6**:*726*
and wounds **10**:1402
collenchyma **8**:1025; **11**:1560
color blindness **5**:687; **12**:*1687*–1688
companion cells **12**:1631
congenital defects
clubfoot **5**:*699*
congenital adrenogenital syndrome
7:889
prenatal diagnosis **2**:191
see also genetic diseases
congestive heart failure **10**:1308
connective tissue 3:298, **418–420**
fibroblasts **3**:419; **10**:1402
see also collagen
constipation **4**:519
coronary artery disease (CAD) **3**:362, 363;
7:881; **9**:1225
and ultrafast scanning **4**:475
see also heart disease
coronary thrombosis **12**:1620
corpus luteum **8**:1109, 1110; **10**:*1413*,
1414

cowpox **7**:933–934, *936*; **8**:1100–1101,
1130
Creutzfeldt-Jakob disease (CJD) **1**:89;
4:495; **7**:949; **9**:1202; **10**:1371,
1372, 1373
new variant (vCJD) **10**:1371, 1372
prion causing **3**:*371*
Crohn's disease **4**:519
cryptosporidiosis **7**:948, 949
crypts of Lieberkuhn **5**:674
Cushing's syndrome **4**:454
cystic fibrosis (CF) **2**:191; **6**:805, *812*;
8:1061; **9**:1172
effect on the pancreas **9**:1261
gene therapy **6**:806

D

Daltonism *see* blindness, color
decompression sickness (the bends)
9:1238; **10**:1422
deficiency-related diseases 4:487–489
malnutrition **4**:*487*–488, 489; **9**:1227;
10:1378
mineral deficiency **4**:489
vitamin deficiency **4**:488–*489*
**degenerative brain diseases
4:494–497**
Alzheimer's disease 1:61; **4**:*494*–497;
9:1204, 1213; **10**:1389; **11**:1558
Creutzfeldt-Jakob disease (CJD) **1**:89;
4:495; **7**:949; **9**:1202; **10**:1371,
1372
new variant (vCJD) **10**:1371, 1372,
1373
prion causing **10**:*1371*
Huntington's chorea **4**:495–*496*; **6**:805;
9:1202
motor neurone disease **4**:495, 496, 497
Parkinson's disease **2**:261; **4**:*494–497*;
8:1092; **9**:1204, 1213; **11**:1558
delta cells **9**:1261
dengue fever (breakbone fever) **7**:947
dermatitis **7**:870
dermis **11**:1506, 1508
diabetes 4:506–508; **9**:1261
bronze **4**:508
diabetes insipidus **4**:506
diabetes mellitus **2**:165; **4**:506–507;
5:612
types I and II **4**:507; **7**:905, 965
and dioxins **4**:532
insulin **4**:*507*; **7**:965
from genetic engineering **2**:222; **7**:965;
8:1131
in pregnancy **4**:507–508
self-monitoring **4**:507
and transplants **12**:1634
diphtheria **5**:592
vaccine **7**:935
diseases
of animals *see* animal diseases
autoimmune *see* autoimmune disorders
coevolution and **3**:391–392
environmental 5:625–628
epidemiology 5:633–635
germ theory **1**:117; **2**:202; **8**:1128;
9:1269; **11**:1570
hereditary *see* genetic diseases
incidence rate **5**:634

infectious 7:945–950
of animals **1**:*88*–90
prevalence **5**:634
respiratory *see* respiratory diseases
vectors **7**:945
distemper **1**:89–90; **8**:1061
diverticular disease **9**:1225
Down syndrome **3**:*369*; **6**:812–813;
10:1358; **11**:1536
testing for **4**:477
dropsy, treatment **9**:1291
dwarfism **5**:613
dysentery, amoebic **3**:388
dystrophia myotonica **9**:1181

E

eczema **11**:*1508*
treatment **12**:1667
edema **8**:1065; **12**:*1667*
Edwards' syndrome **3**:369
effector cells **7**:938
eggs 5:587–590
excretion within **5**:665
meiosis **5**:587–588, 589–590
nurse cells and follicle cells **5**:589
oogenesis **5**:587, *588*
of plants **5**:*590*
sperm penetration **5**:*713–714*
Ehler's Danlos syndrome **3**:420
ehrlichiosis **7**:949
elastin **3**:419; **10**:1377
elephantiasis **7**:946; **8**:1065; **9**:1267
Elephant Man **11**:*1504*
embolisms **3**:377
pulmonary **11**:1573
emphysema **2**:153; **8**:1059
encephalitis
bovine spongiform *see* BSE
from smallpox vaccine **11**:1513
endocrine diseases **5**:613
environmental diseases 5:625–628
eosinophils **1**:53; **2**:239, *240*
epidermis (plant) **8**:*1023, 1024*; **11**:1560
epidermis (skin)
of invertebrates **11**:1505
of vertebrates **11**:1506, *1507*
humans **11**:1507–1508
epilepsy 2:263–264; **5:636–639**
epiphyseal plates **2**:248; **3**:319
ergotism **6**:800; **8**:1139
erythroblasts, basophilic **2**:243
erythrocytes *see* blood, erythrocytes
erythroleukemia **8**:1030
extracellular fluid **10**:1307

F

farsightedness (hyperopia) **5**:687
fatal familial insomnia (FFI) **10**:1371, 1373
favism **8**:1028
fibroblasts **3**:419; **10**:1402
filariasis **7**:946; **8**:1065; **9**:1196
fixation, of tissues **7**:895
flame cells **7**:970, 989
flu *see* influenza

follicle cells **5**:589; **10**:1413
food poisoning **6**:765
and cockroaches **3**:388
foot and mouth disease (hoof and mouth
disease) **1**:88; **7**:949
forensic science 6:771–774
cause of death **6**:773
collecting evidence **6**:*771–772*
flies and **6**:746
and the polymerase chain reaction **9**:*1174*
serology **6**:774
blood typing **2**:243, *244*–245; **6**:774
DNA fingerprinting **2**:224; **4**:*535*;
6:*773*, 774; **9**:*1174*
time of death **6**:773; **9**:1183

G

galactosemia **8**:1123
gallstones (bile stones) **4**:523; **8**:*1047*
gangrene **3**:377
gastroenteritis **7**:948
genetic diseases 6:812–815
albinism **9**:*1191*
asthma as **2**:153
autosomal recessive traits **6**:*812*
chromosome abnormalities **6**:812–813
color blindness **5**:687; **12**:*1687*–1688
of connective tissues **3**:420
Down syndrome **3**:*369*; **6**:812–813;
10:1358; **11**:1536
testing for **4**:477
errors of metabolism **8**:1123
phenylketonuria (PKU) **8**:*1123*, 1124;
10:1358
gene therapy **6**:805
genetic counseling **4**:496
hemophilia **2**:222, 242; **6**:805; **8**:1107
Huntington's disease (Huntington's
chorea) **4**:495–*496*; **6**:805; **9**:1202
Marfan's syndrome **3**:420, *421*
multiple sclerosis **9**:1175
neurofibromatosis **11**:1504
screening for **2**:191, 222; **8**:1093–1094;
10:1358
sickle-cell anemia *see* anemia, sickle-cell
single nucleotide polymorphisms (SNPs)
7:922
Tay-Sachs disease **4**:477
thalassemias **1**:73; **2**:247
X-linked **8**:1107
see also cystic fibrosis; muscular dystrophy
German measles *see* rubella
germ cells, primordial **5**:587
Gerstmann-Straussler-Scheinker disease
(GSS) **10**:1371, 1373
gigantism **5**:613
gingivitis **12**:1605
glands, swollen **3**:371; **8**:*1066*
glaucoma **5**:687
treatment **11**:1575
glial cells **2**:255; **9**:1200
gliomas **3**:294
goiter **2**:166; **7**:*905*; **9**:1227
gonorrhea **1**:116; **5**:710; **7**:949

Bold words with bold page numbers indicate complete articles; bold numbers preceding colons are volume numbers; numbers following colons indicate page numbers; italic page numbers refer to illustrations or other graphics.

granulation tissue 3:419
granulocytes 2:239, 243; 8:1109
granulomatosus, chronic 2:240
granulosa cells 8:1108
Graves' disease 2:166
ground meristem cells 11:1448
guanophores 10:1310, 1311
guard cells 7:902; 12:1630
gum disease 12:1605

H

Hashimoto's thyroiditis 2:165, 166
Haversian system 2:248; 11:1500
hay fever (allergic rhinitis) 1:53; 5:628;
    9:1172; 10:1338
heart, rheumatic fever and 2:164
heart attacks 7:881; 9:1225
    and atherosclerosis 3:363, 376
    clots causing 2:242
    and ultrafast scanning 4:475
heart disease 8:1094; 9:1225
    in cats and dogs 1:90
    see also coronary artery disease
heart failure, congestive 10:1308
hemangiomas, strawberry 10:1359
hemophilia 2:222, 242; 6:805; 8:1107
    and HIV-infected blood 1:45
hemorrhages, cerebral 3:377
hepatitis 7:886; 8:1046
    hepatitis A 7:886, 948; 8:1046
    hepatitis B 3:295; 7:886; 8:1046
    vaccines against 7:886
histology 7:894–896
histoplasmosis 2:176
HIV (Human Immunodeficiency Virus)
    see AIDS
hives 1:53
Hodgkin's disease 3:353, 371
hoof and mouth disease (foot and mouth
    disease) 1:88; 7:949
Hunter's syndrome 8:1123–1124
Huntington's disease (Huntington's chorea)
    4:495–496; 6:805; 9:1202
Hurler's syndrome 8:1123–1124
hybridomas 12:1677
Hyman, Flo 3:420
hyperglycemia 4:506
hyperopia 5:687
hypersensitivity 7:931, 941–942
hypersensitivity response (HR), in plants
    7:932
hypersplenism 11:1551
hyperthyroidism 7:905
hypoglycemia 4:506, 507
hypostasis 6:773
hypothroidism 7:905

I

icterus see jaundice
immunodeficiency 7:931, 942
    severe combined immunodeficiency
disease (SCID) 6:804, 808
    see also AIDS
immunohistochemistry 7:895
infection, and "swollen glands" 8:1066
infectious diseases 7:945–950
    of animals 1:88–90
inflammation 3:419; 7:930, 937
    effect of corticosteroids on 4:454

influenza 7:951–953; 8:1059
    equine 1:89
    vaccines 7:936, 951
    virus, evading the immune system 7:929
integuments
    invertebrate 11:1505–1506
    plant 11:1475–1476

JK

jaundice (icterus) 7:886; 8:1046, 1047
Kaposi's sarcoma 1:42, 44; 9:1174
keratin 2:228; 6:725–726, 774; 7:910;
    10:1375, 1377; 11:1506
keratinocytes 11:1558
ketacidosis 2:165
kidney disease, in cats and dogs 1:90
Kupffer cells 8:1047
kuru 10:1371
kwashiorkor 4:487; 9:1227; 10:1378

L

lamina propria 9:1171
Lassa fever 10:1438
Legionnaire's disease 5:627; 7:948
leishmaniasis 7:946
leukemia 2:247; 3:294; 8:1030–1031
    causes 8:1031
    treatment 8:1031; 11:1557
leukocytes 2:239, 240, 243
    granulocytes 2:239, 243
    mononuclear cells 2:239
leukoplakia 12:1622
Lincoln, Abraham 3:420
listerosis 6:765; 7:949
loop of Henle 5:669, 670–671, 672;
    7:990, 992
Lou Gehrig's disease (amyotrophic lateral
    sclerosis) 9:1181, 1202
Lyme disease 1:131; 7:947, 949
lymph 7:942; 8:1062
    buildup in the tissues 8:1065–1066
    circulation 3:371; 8:1062–1063
lymphadenitis see swollen glands
lymphadenopathy 8:1066
lymphangiosarcomas 8:1066
lymphedema 8:1065
lymphocele 8:1066
lymphocytes 2:241; 7:927, 941, 942;
    8:1063
    B-cells 1:43–44, 52, 53; 2:241, 243;
        7:934, 938
    and the immune response 1:112;
        7:929, 930, 939–940
    memory B-cells 1:114; 7:929
    becoming memory cells 7:929, 932
    CD-4 1:43, 44
    development 2:243; 7:932; 11:1559
    and the lymphatic system 7:932
    natural killer (NK) 7:929, 938
    T-cells 1:52–53; 2:241, 243; 7:934, 938,
        939–940
    and aging 1:34
    cytotoxic (killer T-cells) 1:44; 7:930,
        931, 938
    inducer 7:931–932
    suppressor 7:932
    T-helper cells 2:241; 7:929, 934, 938,
        940
    and the thymus 7:930, 932; 8:1064

lymphomas 3:294; 8:1066
    Burkitt's 8:1066
    non-Hodgkin's 3:371; 8:1066

M

macroglossia 12:1622
macrophages 1:52; 2:241; 3:420; 5:592;
    7:937, 938; 8:1059
    and acquired immunity 7:929, 931
    chemotaxis 12:1647
    and natural immunity 7:928, 929
    and wound healing 10:1402
mad cow disease see BSE
malaria 5:621; 6:744; 7:946; 9:1265,
    1266, 1268
    and sickle-cell anemia 2:247; 4:525;
        9:1266
    treatment 6:744; 8:1103; 9:1266
malnutrition see deficiency-related diseases
mange 1:90
marasmus 4:487; 9:1227; 10:1378
Marfan's syndrome 3:420, 421
mast cells 1:53, 114; 3:420; 7:941
mastitis 1:89
mechanoreceptors
    and breathing 8:1058–1059
    and touch 12:1626
megakaryocytes 2:243
melanocytes 10:1310; 11:1507
melanomas, malignant 3:295;
    9:1193
melanophores 2:282; 10:1310
melanophore-stimulating hormone
    (MSH) 10:1310
memory cells 7:929, 932, 939
Ménière's disease 4:561
meningitis 9:1202
    tuberculous 12:1648
mesophyll 8:1024
mesothelioma 5:628
metastases 3:294; 8:1064
Milroy's disease 8:1065
Mongolian spots 10:1359
monocytes 2:241, 243
mononuclear cells 2:239
motor neurone disease 4:495, 496, 497
mucin 9:1171
mucosa-associated lymphoid tissue
    (MALT) 8:1065
mucous membranes 9:1171–1172
mucus 9:1171, 1172
    cervical 4:442; 9:1172
    respiratory-tract 7:928; 9:1171
multinucleated cells 5:592
multiple sclerosis (MS) 2:165;
    9:1175–1176, 1202–1204
muscular dystrophy 2:222; 7:895;
    9:1181
    Duchenne 7:921; 9:1181
mutagenicity (Ames) test 3:295
myasthenia gravis 9:1181
myeloid cells 11:1559
myeloid tissue 2:249
myocardial infarction see heart attacks
myofibroblasts 10:1402
myopia 5:687
myosin 6:726, 772; 9:1178, 1181, 1182;
    10:1377
myxoma virus 3:391–392

N

NANB ("non-A non-B") 7:886
natural killer (NK) cells 7:929, 938
nearsightedness (myopia) 5:687
nematocysts 7:970, 980
nephritis, in cats and dogs 1:90
nerve cells see neurons
neurofibromatosis 11:1504
neurons (nerve cells) 9:1197–1201;
    10:1308
    association (interneurons) 9:1198
    function 9:1198–1201
    motor 9:1198
    myelination 3:355–356
    receptor 9:1198
        primary 12:1595
    sensory 9:1198; 12:1627
    structure 2:255–256; 9:1198
    see also synapses
neutrophils 2:239–240; 7:928, 929,
    937–938
nevi 10:1359
night blindness 9:1291
NK (natural killer) cells 7:929, 938
nocireceptors 12:1626
"non-A non-B" (NANB) 7:886
    enteric 7:886
non-Hodgkin's lymphoma 3:371; 8:1066
nucellus 11:1475
nurse cells 5:589

O

oocytes 5:587, 588–589
osteoarthritis 1:136; 7:870
    in cats and dogs 1:90
osteocytes 2:248–249, 250; 11:1500
osteomalacia see rickets
osteons 2:248
osteoporosis 2:250, 277, 278; 8:1110;
    11:1502
    in astronauts 11:1533
osteosarcomas 3:294
otosclerosis 7:875
ova 5:587
ovarian failure, premature 5:711

P

Pacinian corpuscles 12:1626
Paget's disease 2:181
palisade layer 8:1024
pancreatitis 9:1261
paralysis
    infantile see poliomyelitis
    movement of paralyzed limbs 2:213
parenchyma 8:1024; 11:1448, 1560
parkinsonism 4:495
Parkinson's disease 2:261; 4:494–497;
    8:1092; 9:1204, 1213; 11:1558
Patau syndrome 3:369
pellagra 4:488
pelvic inflammatory disease 5:712
perichondrium 2:248, 249; 3:320
peridontitis 12:1605
periosteum 2:248, 249
pertussis (whooping cough) 7:948
    vaccine 7:935
phagocytes 7:937–938; 11:1551
    chemotaxis 12:1647
    see also macrophages; neutrophils

photocytes **2**:205

photoreceptors **5**:685, *688*

  in the retina **5**:686; **12**:1685

plague **10**:1438

  and biological warfare **2**:198

  bubonic **6**:740; **7**:950; **8**:1063; **11**:1569

    fleas and **6**:740

    pneumonic **7**:950

plasma **2**:238, 241; **4**:554

plasma cells **7**:938

plastids **8**:1023

  evolution **2**:168

platelets **2**:241, 243

  and blood clotting **2**:241–242

  disorders **2**:247

pleuropneumonia **1**:88

pneumonia **8**:1059

poliomyelitis (polio; infantile paralysis) **3**:388

  vaccines **1**:92; **5**:*635*; **7**:934; **8**:*1129*; **11**:1457

    causing polio **7**:935

  virus **8**:*1129*; **12**:1682

polyarthritis **1**:*136*

Pontiac fever **5**:627

port-wine stains **10**:1359

postmortem investigations *see* autopsies

prenatal testing *see* genetic diseases, screening for

pressure receptors **12**:1626

procambium **11**:1560

progeria **1**:34

proprioceptors **4**:469; **12**:1626

protanopia **12**:1688

proteus syndrome **11**:1504

pseudohermaphroditism **7**:889

psittacosis **1**:89

psoriasis

  and arthritis **1**:136

  treatment **12**:1667

puerperal fever **8**:1101

pus **7**:937

QR

Q fever **7**:947; **8**:1061

rabies **1**:90; **9**:1202

  and bats **2**:176

  vaccine **9**:1270; **11**:1569

Raynaud's disease **3**:377–378

receptors , sensory **12**:1626, 1627

  see also chemoreceptors; mechanoreceptors

relapsing fevers **1**:131; **7**:946

respiratory diseases **8**:1059–1061

  in animals **8**:1061

  see also asthma

retinitis pigmentosa **5**:687

rheumatic fever **1**:136; **2**:164

rheumatism **7**:870

rhinitis, allergic *see* hay fever

rhinotracheitis **8**:1061

rickets **2**:250, 278; **4**:*489*; **9**:*1227*; **11**:1502

rinderpest **1**:89

Rocky Mountain spotted fever **1**:*131*; **7**:947; **9**:*1264*

rods and cones **5**:686–687; **12**:1685, 1687

  and night vision **9**:1221; **12**:1687

rubella **7**:875, 950; **10**:1354

S

salmon patches **10**:1359

sarcomas **3**:294

scabies **1**:131

scabs **7**:937; **10**:1401, 1402

schistosomiasis **6**:*736*; **10**:1438

Schwann cells **3**:362; **9**:1200

SCID (severe combined immunodeficiency disease) **6**:804, 808; **9**:1290

sclereids **11**:1448, 1560

sclerenchyma cells **11**:1448, 1560

scleroderma **2**:*164*, 165

sclerosis

  amyotrophic lateral (ALS; Lou Gehrig's disease) **9**:1181, 1202

  multiple *see* multiple sclerosis

scrapie **1**:89; **10**:1371, 1373

screening, genetic **2**:191, 222; **8**:1093–1094; **10**:1358; **11**:1482

scrofula **8**:1066

scrub disease **1**:131

scurvy **4**:488; **6**:764; **8**:*1095*; **9**:1227; **12**:1605, *1690, 1691*

seizures, epileptic *see* epilepsy

serology **6**:774

  blood typing **2**:243, *244–245*; **6**:774

  DNA fingerprinting **2**:224, 226; **6**:*773*, 774

severe combined immunodeficiency disease (SCID) **6**:*804*, 808; **9**:1290

sexually transmitted infections (STIs) **7**:949–950

  and infertility **5**:710

shingles **7**:948

sickle-cell disease *see* anemia, sickle-cell

sieve tubes **12**:1631, 1632, 1669

silicosis **5**:628

Sjögren disorder **2**:165

skin corrosion test **1**:93

sleeping sickness **1**:88; **7**:929, 946

smallpox 11:**1513**; **12**:*1677*, 1682

  biological warfare and **2**:198; **11**:1513; **12**:1679

  immunization **7**:933–934, *936*, 984; **8**:1100–1101, 1130; **11**:1513

snow blindness **12**:1658

sores, canker (aphthous ulcers) **12**:1622

sperm **10**:*1410*, 1411–1412

  "competition" **8**:1083

  egg penetration **5**:*713–714*

  formation of **5**:714–715; **10**:*1411*

  and infertility **5**:710–711

  survival **4**:442

spermatids **5**:715; **10**:1411

spermatocytes **5**:714–715; **10**:1411

splenomegaly **11**:1551

spongy layer **8**:*1024*

staining techniques **7**:895

starvation **8**:1120; **9**:1227

  see also deficiency-related diseases

stem cells 11:**1556–1559**

  adult **11**:1557–1558

  evolution **11**:1558

  hematopoietic (blood) **2**:242–243; **3**:330; **11**:1559

  human embryonic **2**:261; **4**:497; **5**:600; **11**:*1557*, 1558, 1559

  medical uses of **11**:1557

    and gene therapy for SCID **6**:804

  and regeneration of body parts **10**:1400

  therapeutic cloning **3**:385, 386; **11**:1558

  multipotent **3**:340

  pluripotent **3**:340; **11**:1557, 1558–1559

  research **3**:334; **9**:1204

  unipotent **11**:1557–1558

stones, bile *see* gallstones

sunburn **12**:*1658*

swollen glands **3**:371; **8**:*1066*

synapses **1**:69; **12**:1626

  discovery **10**:1396

  nerve impulses across **9**:1200–1201

  pruning **2**:260

syphilis **7**:949

  cure for **5**:*591*, 592

  Tuskagee Syphilis Study **2**:189

systemic lupus erythematosus (SLE) **2**:164, 165

T

T4 cells *see* T-helper cells

TB *see* tuberculosis

T-cells *see* lymphocytes, T-cells

tetanus **2**:172; **9**:1203; **11**:1531

  vaccines **9**:1203

tetany **2**:278; **5**:612

thalassemias **1**:73; **2**:247

T-helper cells **2**:241; **7**:*929*, 934, 938

  AIDS and **7**:940

thermoreceptors **12**:1626

thrombi **12**:1620

thrombocytopenia **2**:247

thrombophlebitis **12**:*1620*

thrombosis 12:**1620**

  cerebral **3**:377

  coronary **12**:1620

  deep vein (DVT) **12**:1620

    post-operative **11**:1573

  prevention **12**:1620

thrush (candidiasis) **12**:1716

thymidine **7**:896

thymocytes **8**:1064

thymomas **8**:1064

tinnitus **7**:875

toxocariasis **9**:*1266*

tracheae (plant cells) **12**:1631

tracheids **12**:1631

transmissible spongiform encephalopathies (TSEs) **10**:1371

traveler's disease *see* dysentery, amoebic

trench fever **7**:946, 950

trichinosis **9**:1196

trichomoniasis **7**:950

tritanopia **12**:1688

trumpet cells **12**:1632

trypanosomiasis

  African *see* sleeping sickness

  American *see* Chagas' disease

  host response **9**:1267

tuberculosis 5:591–592; **7**:948; **8**:1059; **12**:**1648**

  bovine **1**:88

  renal **5**:671

  treatment **12**:1648

  vaccine **7**:935; **12**:1648

  X rays to show **12**:*1648*, 1713

tularemia **2**:198; **7**:947

tumors **3**:294

  hormone-secreting **5**:613

  in the spleen **11**:1551

  see also cancer

typhoid (typhoid fever) **5**:627, *634*; **7**:948

typhus **9**:1267

  tick **7**:947

typing, blood **2**:243, *244–245*; **6**:774

U

ulcers

  mouth **12**:1622

  peptic **4**:516, 519, 523

    duodenal **1**:*71*

    stomach (gastric) **9**:1172; **11**:*1565*, 1567

uremia **7**:992

urinary tract diseases, in cats and dogs **1**:90

V

varicocele **5**:711

verrucae **5**:699

vitiligo **2**:165; **10**:*1310*

W

warts

  genital **7**:949

  plantar (verrucae) **5**:699

Werner's syndrome **1**:34

West Nile virus **7**:947

whooping cough *see* pertussis

wounds **7**:*937*

  healing **3**:419; **10**:1401–1402

  see also inflammation

XY

xerophthalmia **12**:1689

yellow fever **7**:947; **9**:*1268*; **12**:1678

  and the Panama Canal **9**:1267

  and the Suez Canal **8**:1126

Z

zinc

  and Alzheimer's disease **1**:61

  deficiency **4**:489

Z lines **9**:*1181*

zoonoses **1**:90

■ PHYSIOLOGY

A

2,4-D **1**:41; **7**:909

ABA *see* abscisic acid

abscisic acid (ABA) **4**:548; **7**:909

abscission **8**:1025

absorptive and postabsorptive states **8**:1124

acetylcholine **1**:61; **9**:1182, 1201, 1213

acetylcholinesterase **5**:632; **9**:1182

ACTH *see* adrenocorticotrophic hormone

ADCC **1**:114

adhesion molecules 2:240
adrenalin *see* epinephrine and
    norepinephrine
adrenocorticotrophic hormone (ACTH)
    5:614; 7:905, 907; 9:1158
aflatoxin 11:1462
aging 1:33–36
    antiaging vitamin 12:1690
    plant senescence 1:36; 10:1319
    skin 1:34; 11:1507
albumin 2:241
alcohol dehydrogenase 5:632
aldosterone 2:219; 4:454; 5:672; 7:901, 990
alginic acid 1:48
allomones 5:677
altitude sickness 8:1058; 10:1423
amenorrhea 8:1110
ammonia
    the urea cycle and 12:1667, 1668
    waste product 5:665
ammonotelic organisms 12:1666
amylases 3:342
    pancreatic 9:1260
    salivary 4:516, 517; 11:1564
amyloid 1:61
amylopectin 3:297
amylose 3:297
anabolism 8:1116, 1119–1120, 1121
androgens 5:612–613; 7:906; 10:1410
    see also testosterone
anestrus 8:1111
angiotensin 7:990
anovulation 8:1110
antibodies 1:52, 111–114; 2:241
    antibody-antigen complexes 1:*114*
    chimeric 1:113
    in milk 7:*934*
    monoclonal 1:113
        from biotechnology 2:*221*, *224*, *226*
    production 11:1551
    structure 1:*111–112*, *113*
    used as chemotherapy 3:353
    used to identify viruses 12:1677
    see also immunoglobulins
antibody-dependent cellular cytotoxicity
    (ADCC) 1:114
antidiuretic hormone (ADH; vasopressin)
    5:611, 671, 672; 7:903, 990
"antifreeze"
    in animals 4:472; 10:1332
    in GM potato seedlings 6:810
    in lichens 8:1036
antioxidants 1:34; 3:*294*, 317; 12:1691
appetite 8:1120, 1123
appositional growth 3:320
arachidonic acid 5:692
aspirin 9:1292
    and hearing 7:875
    for heart-attack or stroke victims 8:1098
    mode of action 9:1291
atrial natriuretic factor (ANF) 7:880
atrophy, muscular 9:1184
auxins 7:908–909; 10:1316; 11:1561;
    12:1645

B

baroreceptors 7:880
basal metabolic rate (BMR) 2:280;
    8:1121–1122

batrachotoxin 4:485
beta-carotene 3:294; 12:1691
bile 3:362; 4:522; 8:1044–1045, *1046*,
    1047
    bile salts 8:1044
bilichromes 10:1310
bilirubin 8:1047; 10:1310
biliverdin 10:1310
biological clocks 2:217–218; 9:1159, 1223
    and molting 9:1159
bioluminescence 2:205–207; 5:686
    and courtship 4:457
    fireflies 2:178, *206*
    in fish 5:686
    in jellyfish 7:982
biorhythms 2:216–219
    biological clocks 2:217–218; 9:1159,
        1223
    human 2:217–219
    in plants 2:217
biosynthesis *see* anabolism
blood pressure 3:374; 7:880
    control 7:902
    during shock 3:378
    measurement 3:374
BMR *see* basal metabolic rate
bombykol 4:460; 9:*1293*
brain hormone (BH) 5:612; 7:1005
brain waves 2:*255*
breathing *see* respiration, breathing
buffers, of biological fluids 11:1459
bufotenine 1:*51*

C

cacolytic acid 9:1294
calcitonin 2:278
calcium 2:277–278
    absorption 2:278
    deficiency 4:489
    pump 2:277
    regulation in the body 2:278; 5:612
    role in muscles 2:278; 9:1182
calmodulin 2:277
calories 2:279–280
    reduction, and life span 1:36
calorimetry 2:279–280
CAM (crassulacean acid metabolism)
    2:273; 10:*1305–1306*
carbamino-hemoglobin 8:1056
carbon dioxide 3:306
    in the body 3:306
        gas exchange 9:1253
    elimination from organisms 5:665;
        8:1056–1057
carbonic anhydrase 5:629
carboxypepsidase 5:630; 9:1260
cardiac cycle 7:879
catabolism 5:618–619; 8:1116,
    1117–1119
cellulases 3:342; 11:1451, 1452,
    1461–1462
chilling, requirements of plants 4:549
chlorophyll 3:335; 5:616; 10:*1303*
    chlorophyll a 10:1304, *1306*
    chlorophyll b 10:*1306*
    chlorophyll c 10:1306
    chlorophyll d 10:1306
    P_{680} 5:617–618
    P_{700} 5:618; 10:1306

cholecystokinin (CCK) 8:1047; 9:1260
cholesterol 3:362–363; 5:691
    and artery disease 3:362, 363, 377;
        7:881; 9:1225
    bile derived from 8:1044, 1047
    and the menopause 8:1110
    transport 3:362–*363*
cholesterol esterase 9:1260
chondrin 3:319
chyle 8:1063
chyme 4:522; 11:1564
chymotrypsin 4:518; 5:*632*; 9:1260
clotting, blood 2:241–*242*, 278; 7:937
coagulation cascade 12:1620
cobalt
    deficiency 4:489
        in livestock 9:1227
coffee 3:295
colchicine 2:266; 3:367
colostrum 5:676; 7:998
complement 1:114; 7:929 930, 938
conception 5:708
contact inhibition 12:1625
control systems *see* feedback systems
copper
    deficiency 4:489
    and metabolism 8:1124
corticoids *see* corticosteroids
corticosteroids 2:240; 4:454; 5:612
    glucocorticoids 4:454
    mineralocorticoids 4:454
corticosterone 4:454
corticotropin releasing factor (CRF)
    7:905
cortisol *see* hydrocortisone
countercurrent systems
    in gills 6:728
    heat exchange 7:901; 11:1472, 1488;
        12:1618
    in the kidney 7:990
    oxygen exchange 10:1424
crassulacean acid metabolism (CAM)
    2:273; 10:*1305–1306*
crop milk 7:997
cryonics 4:472
cryopreservation 4:472
cucurbitacins 11:1555
cybernetics 7:952
cyclosis 3:371
cytokines 1:53
cytokinins 7:909; 10:1316, 1317

D

dark adaptation 12:1687
daylength
    plants and 2:217; 6:759
        dormancy 4:*549*
deamination 5:665
dehydroepiandrosterone (DHEA) 1:36
detoxification, in the liver 8:1046–1047
DHEA (dehydroepiandrosterone) 1:36
diapause 2:269; 7:1005
    in the housefly 6:745
diastole 7:879
diestrus 8:1111
diets, reducing 3:300
diffusion
    circulatory systems versus 3:370–371
    passive 9:1252

    in plants 9:1252
    for respiration 10:1418
digestion 4:511, 520–521
    absorption of nutrients 4:518–519
    chemical processes 4:517–518
    enzymes *see* enzymes, digestive
    extracellular 4:511, 512
    of fats, and bile 8:1047
    fermentation in the gut 4:515
    intracellular 4:511, 512
    in the stomach 4:516, 517–518
dopamine 1:24; 4:494, 556; 8:1092;
        9:1204, 1213
    and aggression 1:33
    dopamine-producing tissue 2:261
    and schizophrenia 9:1212
dysmenorrhea 8:1110
dystrophin 7:895

E

ecdysis *see* molting
ecdysone 7:908, 1005; 8:1126
ectothermy 3:396; 12:1617–1618
ejaculation 10:1411, 1412
    retrograde 5:710
electro-osmosis 12:1631
endochondral ossification 3:319
endometrial cycle 8:*1109*–1110
endometriosis 8:1110
endonucleases, restriction *see* enzymes,
    restriction
endorphins 1:55; 5:614
endothermy 3:396; 7:900–901; 12:1617
energy 5:615–619
    activation 5:617, 631
    from aerobic respiration 5:618–619
        **Krebs cycle 2:*159*–160; 3:300;
            5:619, 632; 7:*993–996*; 9:1252**
        see also respiration
    alternative 10:1340–1341
    from anaerobic respiration 8:1117
    chemical 5:*616*
    in humans, need for 8:1120–1121
    laws of thermodynamics 5:*615*
    light 5:616
        see also photosynthesis
    potential and kinetic 5:616
    pyramid of 5:586; 6:*768*
    solar 5:616
    storage 5:619
        in animals 5:619
        as fats and oils 5:619
        in plants 5:619
    thermal 5:616
enkephalin 5:614
enzymes 5:629–632; 8:1116, 1118
    allosteric 5:632
    are catalysts 5:617, 629
    bacterial 2:172
        disruption by antibiotics 1:109
    cofactors 5:630–631
    designer 5:631
    in detergents 2:222
    digestive 4:517–518, 520
        pancreatic 4:518; 5:677
    discovery 5:629–630
    inhibition 5:630, 632
    in Krebs cycle 7:995
    in medical diagnostic tests 5:630

mode of action **5**:630
nomenclature **5**:630
nucleases
 semisynthetic **2**:181
 see also enzymes, restriction
optimum temperatures **3**:396
pH range for **5**:631, *632*
reaction rates **5**:631–632
regulation of **5**:632
restriction **2**:181; **8**:1145, 1146
semisynthetic **2**:180
structure **5**:630; **10**:1377
to break up chromosomes *see* enzymes, restriction
epinephrine and norepinephrine 5:612, **640**–**641**
 epinephrine (adrenalin) **3**:301; **5**:*603*, 605; **7**:904
 and heart rate **7**:880
 and horn development **7**:910
 stress and **11**:1566
 and temperature regulation **12**:1618
 norepinephrine (noradrenalin) **1**:33; **3**:301
 stress and **11**:1566
erythropoiesis **8**:1047
erythropoietin **2**:239; **10**:1307
estradiol **7**:998
estrogen **5**:612, 613
 in the contraceptive pill **4**:441
 effect on cervical mucus **4**:442; **9**:1172
 endometriosis treatment **8**:1110
 environmental **10**:1343
 in HRT **2**:250; **8**:1110
 in the menstrual cycle **2**:219; **8**:1109, 1110; **10**:1413–1414
 protects against bone loss **1**:34; **11**:1502
 and puberty **1**:*27*; **10**:1413
estrus **8**:*1111*
 estrus cycle **5**:714; **10**:1414
 signs of **5**:715
 see also menstrual cycle
ethylene, plant hormone **7**:*909*
exercise
 carbohydrate loading **3**:*299*
 and endorphin release **5**:614
 and heart rate **7**:880; **9**:1252
 lactic acid accumulation in the muscles **2**:159; **3**:300; **5**:703; **9**:1183, 1252

F
Factor VIII **2**:225, 242
Factor IX **2**:242; **3**:384
fasting **8**:1124
feedback systems **7**:*900*, 952–953
 life regulates the environment? **6**:*802–803*
 negative **7**:900, 953; **8**:1116; **10**:1308
 blood concentration and volume **7**:990
 blood glucose **4**:506; **7**:902, 953
 blood pressure **7**:902
 hormone production **7**:*900*
 temperature control **7**:900–901
 positive **7**:900, 953
 childbirth **7**:*953*; **10**:1308
 milk production **7**:998
 see also cybernetics; homeostasis
ferredoxins **7**:973
fertility 5:**708**–**712**

infertility **5**:710–712
 animal **5**:*712*
 drugs for **5**:709
 in vitro fertilization (IVF) **2**:223; **5**:*710*, 711, 712
 trials **7**:896
 see also menstrual cycle; ovulation; reproduction
fertilization 5:**713**–**716**
 animal **5**:*713–715*
 artificial insemination **2**:224; **5**:712; **11**:1481
 the estrus cycle **5**:714; **10**:1414
 see also menstrual cycle
 external **8**:*1081–1082*; **10**:1406, 1409
 in frogs **5**:*715*
 human **5**:*713*, 714–715; **10**:1353, *1354*
 see also menstrual cycle
 internal **8**:*1081*, 1082; **10**:1406, 1409
 plant **5**:715–716; **6**:791–792
 avoidance of self-fertilization **6**:761
 double **6**:760
 self, versus cross-fertilization **7**:889
 in vitro (IVF) **2**:223; **5**:*710*, 711, 712
 embryo storage **4**:473
fevers **7**:901, 938
fiber, dietary **3**:299, 342; **9**:1225
fibrin **2**:242, 278; **12**:1620
fibrinogen **2**:242, 278; **12**:1620
fibroids **8**:1110
fibroin **10**:1375; **11**:1549
fight-or-flight reaction **5**:641; **7**:905; **11**:1566
flavins **10**:1310
flavors **12**:1597
florigen **2**:217
folic acid
 antimetabolites and **1**:108
 deficiency **1**:74; **2**:246
follicle-stimulating hormone (FSH) **5**:708, 709, 712; **7**:906; **8**:1108, 1109, 1110; **10**:1410, 1413
 and twins **12**:1655
fractures, repair **2**:249
free radicals **1**:*34*, 35, 36; **3**:294, 317
fucoxanthin **7**:986

G
galactose **3**:297
gamma-aminobutyric acid (GABA) **5**:639; **9**:1212
gas exchange
 in the lungs **8**:*1055–1056*
 in plants **10**:*1424*; **12**:1629
 see also respiration, breathing
gastric juice **11**:1564
gastrin **5**:610
gibberellins **4**:548; **7**:909
globulins **2**:241
glucagon **3**:301; **5**:612; **7**:902, *904*, 953, 964; **9**:1261
glucocorticoids **4**:454, 487
glutamate **9**:1212
glycogen **2**:277; **8**:*1143*
 and exercise **3**:299
 as glucose storage **3**:298, 300–301; **5**:619, 641; **7**:902, 904, 964
 in the liver **3**:*301*; **8**:1047, *1118*, 1124

GnRH (gonadotropin-releasing hormone) **5**:708, 709; **8**:1108, 1111; **10**:1410
gonadotropin-releasing hormone *see* GnRH
gonadotropins (gonadotrophins) **7**:907; **8**:1108
 FSH *see* follicle-stimulating hormone
 human chorionic (HCG) **2**:224; **5**:613; **8**:1110; **10**:1353
 LH *see* luteinizing hormone
"goose bumps" **7**:*901*
gout **2**:266; **3**:300; **8**:1124
growth
 appositional **3**:320
 in children **3**:358
 and hormones **7**:905–906
 interstitial **3**:320
growth hormone (GH; somatotropin) **2**:219, 222; **7**:906; **8**:1120
 genetically engineered **2**:224
 and lactation **7**:998
 over/under secretion **5**:613
gustation *see* taste
guttation **8**:1026; **12**:1632

H
haptoglobin (Hp) **6**:774
helicase **4**:534
hematopoiesis **11**:1559
hemerythin **7**:973
hemocyanin **10**:1310, 1376, 1424
hemoglobin **1**:73; **2**:239; **10**:*1375*, 1377, 1424
 in animals at high altitudes **1**:18; **8**:*1058*
 artificial **2**:246
 broken down **8**:1047
 and carbon monoxide **10**:1420
 carrying oxygen **7**:973; **8**:1056; **9**:*1252*, 1253
 fetal **10**:1355
 in sickle-cell anemia **1**:74; **4**:538; **9**:1266
 structure **2**:*239*
heparin **3**:420
hermaphrodites 7:**889**–**890**; **10**:*1407–1408*
hibernation induction trigger (HIT) **7**:892
histamines **1**:53; **2**:153, 241; **3**:420; **4**:454; **7**:937, 941
homeostasis 7:**899**–**902**; **10**:*1307*
 blood glucose levels **3**:301; **7**:902
 for blood pressure **7**:902
 for body temperature **7**:900–*901*
 and the excretory system **5**:664, 669; **7**:*902*
 feedback **7**:*900*
 see also feedback systems
 for fluid balance **7**:901–902
 from endocrine and nervous systems **7**:899–900
 and osmosis **11**:1458
 plant **7**:902
 see also cybernetics
homeotherms **3**:396; **7**:891; **8**:1122; **12**:1616
 endothermic **7**:900–901

hormones 7:**903**–**909**
 chemical composition **7**:906–907
 classification **7**:903
 in contraceptives **4**:441, 442
 corticosteroid *see* corticosteroids
 effects on the cell **7**:907
 endocrine
 adrenal **5**:612
 gastrointestinal **5**:610
 hypothalamic **5**:*611*
 invertebrate **7**:908
 pancreatic **5**:612; **7**:904
 parathyroid **5**:612
 pituitary **5**:*611*
 sex hormones **1**:*26–27*; **5**:612–613
 thyroid **5**:612
 environmental **5**:680
 from tumors **5**:613
 gastrointestinal *see* cholecystokinin; gastrin; secretin
 gonadotropic *see* gonadotropins
 growth *see* growth hormone
 and heartbeat **7**:880
 hormonal diseases **7**:905
 invertebrate **7**:908
 molting **7**:908
 and metamorphosis **7**:908, 1005
 molting **7**:908; **9**:1158
 in mammals **9**:1159
 negative-feedback control **7**:*900*
 neurohormones **5**:611
 parapineal **5**:613
 peptide **7**:907
 pineal **5**:613
 plant **7**:908–*909*
 and dormancy **4**:548
 protein **7**:907; **10**:1377
 receptors, adrenergic **5**:640–641
 role in metabolism **8**:1120
 sex hormones **1**:*26–27*; **5**:612–613
 steroid *see* steroids
 stress **5**:641
 of the thymus **5**:613
 and tumor growth **3**:352
 used in blood glucose regulation *see* glucagon; insulin
 vertebrate **7**:907–908
hot flashes **8**:1110
human chorionic gonadotropin (HCG) **2**:224; **5**:613; **8**:1110; **10**:1353
humoral immune response **7**:930–931
hydrocortisone (cortisol) **2**:219, 240; **4**:454; **7**:905; **11**:1566
 effect on the immune system **11**:1567
hydrogen peroxide, to kill bacteria **2**:240
hypertension **3**:374
hypertrophy, kidney **10**:1402
hypotension **3**:374

I
immune systems 7:**927**–**932**
 and aging **1**:34
 AIDS and **1**:*43*
 development and organization **7**:932

Bold words with bold page numbers indicate complete articles; bold numbers preceding colons are volume numbers; numbers following colons indicate page numbers; italic page numbers refer to illustrations or other graphics.

immune systems (continued)
  evasion by microorganisms 7:929
  evolution 7:928
  immunity
    acquired (adaptive) 7:929, 930–932,
      938–941
    active and passive 7:939
    cell-mediated 7:931–932, 939
    humoral 7:930–931, 938–939
    natural (innate) 7:927–930, 937–938
  and the lymphatic system 7:932, 942
  memory cells 7:929, 932, 939
  MHC see major histocompatibility
    complex
  of plants 7:932
  primary and secondary immune
    responses 7:939
  recognition of self-nonself 2:164;
    7:939–940
immunoglobulins 7:931
  IgA 1:111, 114; 7:931, 998
  IgD 1:114; 7:931
  IgE 1:52, 53, 111, 114; 7:931
    and asthma 2:153
  IgG 1:52, 66, 111, 114; 7:931
  IgM 1:52, 111, 113, 114; 7:931
  see also antibodies
implantation, of fertilized eggs, delayed
  10:1353
indoleacetic acid (IAA) 7:909; 12:1645
induced fit hypothesis 5:631
infertility see fertility, infertility
insulin 2:222; 4:507; 5:612; 7:964–965
  in blood glucose regulation 3:301; 4:506;
    7:902, 904, 953, 964–965; 9:1261
  continuous subcutaneous insulin infusion
    (CSII) 4:507
  discovery 4:508; 7:965; 8:1103
  from genetic engineering 2:223
  manufacture 2:223
  structure 7:903
interleukins
  IL-1 7:929, 931, 938; 11:1508
  IL-2 7:929
  IL-4 7:929
intermedin see melanocyte-stimulating
  hormone
intrinsic factor of Castle 4:519
iodine, dietary 9:1227
  and goiter 2:166; 9:1227
iron 7:973
  and iron-deficiency anemia 1:73; 2:246;
    4:489; 7:973
  stored in the spleen 11:1551

J

jasmolic acid 10:1317
jet lag 2:219
juvenile hormone (JH) 7:908, 1005; 8:1126

K

ketone bodies 8:1124
ketones 3:300; 4:506–507
ketosis 3:300; 4:506–507
kilocalories 2:279

L

labor 10:1357–1358, 1414
  premature 8:1098

lactamases, beta- 9:1291
lactase 9:1225
  deficiency 8:1124; 12:1715
lactation 7:997–998; 10:1414
lactic acid 2:159; 3:300; 5:703; 8:1122;
  9:1183
lectins 7:928
leghemoglobin 7:973
LHRF (luteinizing hormone releasing
  factor) 4:442
LHRH see GnRH
light, and photoperiodism 2:217; 6:759;
  10:1317
lipase 2:172; 4:517
  pancreatic 9:1260
lock and key hypothesis
  for enzyme action 5:631
  for olfaction 11:1514–1515
luciferase 2:205, 206
luciferin 2:205, 206
lupulin 3:380
luteinizing hormone (LH) 5:708; 7:906;
  8:1108, 1109, 1110; 10:1410, 1413
luteinizing hormone releasing factor
  (LHRF) 4:442
luteinizing hormone releasing hormone
  (LHRH) see GnRH
lyochromes (flavins) 10:1310
lysozome 6:741
lysozyme 7:928

M

macronutrients 5:717; 9:1226
  plant 11:1447
magnesium, deficiency 4:489
major histocompatibility complex (MHC)
  7:931, 932, 940
maltose 3:299; 4:517
manganese, deficiency 4:489
meat eating, versus vegetarianism 9:1228
melanin 9:1193; 10:1310; 11:1507;
  12:1658, 1689
  absence 10:1310
melanocyte-stimulating hormone
  (MSH/intermedin) 5:611; 7:907–908
melatonin 2:218, 219; 5:613
menarche 1:28; 7:906; 8:1111
Menkes syndrome 8:1124
menopause 8:1110
  osteoporosis and 11:1502
  in primates 8:1111
menorrhagia 8:1110
menstrual cycle 2:219; 7:906;
  8:1108–1111; 10:1414
  and cervical mucus 4:442; 9:1172
  cessation see menopause
  disorders of 8:1110
  menstruation 8:1108, 1109–1110
    and iron loss 1:73
  and natural methods of contraception
    4:442
  premenstrual syndrome (PMS)
    8:1110–1111
  and puberty 1:27–28; 8:1111
  synchronized 9:1294
  see also fertilization; ovulation
mercury, compounds 1:116
metabolism 8:1116–1124
  anabolism 8:1116, 1119–1120, 1121

basal metabolic rate (BMR) 2:280;
  8:1121–1122
catabolism 5:618–619; 8:1116, 1117–1119
crassulacean acid (CAM) 2:273;
  10:1305–1306
  and enzymes 8:1118
  see also enzymes
  and hormones 8:1120
  see also hormones
  human 8:1120–1124
  inborn errors of 8:1123
  metabolic oxygen consumption
    2:279–280
  metabolic rate and heart rate 7:880
  respiratory quotient (RQ) 2:280
  role of the liver in 8:1118, 1119, 1121
  and starvation 8:1120
  see also energy; homeostasis
metestrus 8:1111
methionine 5:630
MHC see major histocompatibility complex
micelles 4:519
micronutrients 5:717; 9:1226–1227
  plant 11:1447–1448
  and hydroponics 7:924–925
  see also minerals; trace elements
milt 6:732
mineralocorticoids 4:454
minerals, deficiency 4:489
molting 1:139; 7:908; 8:1126;
  9:1157–1159; 11:1497, 1506
  in insects 7:1005; 8:1126
monestrus animals 8:1111
morphine 1:51; 4:556; 5:614
musth 5:595–596
myelin 3:362; 9:1200
myelination 3:355–356
myelin basic protein (MBP) 9:1175
myoblasts 9:1183
myogenic contraction 9:1179–1180
myoglobin 7:913–914, 973; 9:1183;
  10:1375, 1424

N

1-naphthaleneacetic acid 7:909
nerve gases 9:1183
neurohormones 5:611
neurotransmitters 2:277–278; 9:1182,
  1183, 1200–1201
  and aggression 1:31, 32, 33
  in the brain 9:1212–1213
  mind-altering drugs like 1:24; 4:556
  peptide (neuropeptides) 9:1212–1213
  and PMS 8:1111
  see also acetylcholine; dopamine
nitrogenase 9:1217
noradrenalin see epinephrine and
  norepinephrine
norepinephrine see epinephrine and
  norepinephrine
nutrients
  absorption by digestion 4:518–519
  plant 11:1446–1447
nutrition 8:1117; 9:1224–1229
  amino acids 9:1226
  antioxidants 3:294; 12:1691
  ß-carotene 3:317
  autotrophism and heterotrophism 5:584;
    9:1224–1226

a balanced diet 9:1229
calories 2:279–280
carbohydrates 3:301; 9:1226, 1229
  loading 3:299
colostrum 5:676; 7:998
dioxins in food 4:532
fats and oils 5:690
  and atherosclerosis 3:377
  fish oils 5:690
fiber 3:299, 342; 9:1225
food coloring, carotenes 3:317
iodine 9:1227
iron 7:973
macronutrients 9:1226
micronutrients 9:1226–1227
  and organic foods 9:1244
poor 9:1225
reducing diets 3:300
and root crops 11:1446

O

olfaction see smell
oligomanose 1:111
opioid peptides 5:614
osmoregulation 5:671–672
  in fish 5:669
osmosis 11:1458–1459
  fish and 5:669; 6:732; 7:902
  and water flow in plants 12:1631, 1670
ossification, endochondral 3:319
ovarian cycle 8:1108–1109
ovulation 2:219; 5:715; 8:1109, 1111;
  10:1413
  and cervical mucus 9:1172
  disorders 8:1110
  induced 10:1352
  prediction 4:442
oxyhemoglobin 8:1056; 9:1253
oxyradicals 1:34
oxytocin 7:903, 906, 953, 998; 10:1414

P

pacemaker, biological (sinoatrial node)
  7:879; 9:1180
pancreozymin 4:522
parathyroid gland, hormones 2:278; 5:612;
  7:903
parathyroid hormone (parathormone)
  2:278; 5:612; 7:903
pathophysiology 10:1308
PBN (phenylbutyl nitrone) 1:36
pepsin 4:516, 517, 518, 522; 11:1564
pepsinogen 4:517, 518
peptides, opioid 5:614
periods see menstrual cycle, menstruation
peristalsis 4:513, 517, 521; 9:1179;
  11:1564
phenylalanine 8:1123, 1124
phenylbutyl nitrone (PBN) 1:36
phenylthiocarbamide, tasting 12:1597
phosphoglucomutase (PGM) 6:774
phosphoglycerate kinase 5:618
phospholipase 9:1260
photoperiodism 2:217
  plant 6:759; 10:1317
photosynthesis 3:298–299; 5:616, 617;
  8:1023; 10:1303–1306
  anoxygenic 10:1303
  in bacteria 3:337

C3 (Calvin) cycle 8:1023; 10:1304–1305
C4 (Hatch-Slack) cycle 8:1023
and the carbon cycle 3:303
carbon fixation 10:1304–1305
and chloroplasts 10:1303–1304
and crassulacean acid metabolism (CAM)
    plants 2:273; 10:1305–1306
cytochromes 7:973
dark reactions 3:298–299; 10:1303, 1304
energy pathways 5:617–618
equation 10:1303
and evolution 10:1304
first development of 10:1304
inhibited by oxygen 10:1305
iron-containing enzymes 7:973
light reactions 3:298; 5:617–618;
    10:1303, 1304
photophosphorylation 10:1304, 1306
pigments 5:616; 10:1306
    carotenoids 3:317; 10:1306
for primary production 6:767
phycobilins 10:1306
phycocyanin 7:986
physiology 10:1307–1308
    plant 2:253
phytoalexins 1:117; 7:932
phytochromes 2:217; 6:759; 10:1317
pimagedine 1:36
plasmin 2:242
plasminogen 2:242
poikilotherms 3:396; 7:891; 8:1122–1123;
    10:1415; 12:1616–1617
poisons 1:51
    from legumes 8:1029
polyestrus animals 8:1111
polypeptides 10:1375
    pancratic 9:1261
porphyrins 10:1310
potassium
    deficiency 4:489
    and nerve impulses 9:1198–1199, 1200
prednisone 2:240
proestrus 8:1111
progesterone 5:613; 8:1109
    challenge test 5:712
    in the contraceptive pill 4:441
    effect on cervical mucus 4:442
    and the menstrual cycle 10:1413–1414
    and milk production 7:998
    and puberty 1:27
prolactin 2:219; 5:611, 712; 7:998
prostaglandins 5:692; 7:938, 990–992;
    8:1109
    and aspirin 9:1291
proteolysis (protein catabolism) 8:1119,
    1120
prothoracicicotropic hormone 8:1126
prothrombin 2:242
pruning, of axons and synapses 2:260–261
ptyalin 11:1564
purines, metabolism, errors of 8:1124

QR
"quickening" 10:1355
regeneration 10:1399–1402, 1404
    of body parts 10:1399–1401
        limb generation in phasmids 8:1017
    in planarians 6:735, 737
relaxin 10:1354

releasing factors 1:26, 27
renin 7:901, 990
rennin 11:1564
reproduction 10:1403–1408
    asexual 10:1403, 1404–1405, 1406
        in plants 1:80; 2:266; 10:1405;
        11:1562
        in vertebrates 10:1405
    asexual or sexual, in the same animal
        10:1407
    in dual-sex organisms see hermaphrodites
    hermaphrodites 7:889–890;
        10:1407–1408
    k- and r-selection 1:101–102; 10:1352
    pair bonding 4:456
    plant
        apomixis 10:1405
        sexual 10:1408
        vegetative 1:80; 2:266; 10:1405;
        11:1562
    reproductive cycles 8:1111
        see also estrus; menstrual cycle
    sexual 10:1403, 1405–1406
        benefits to evolution 10:1404
        evolution of 3:390
    sexual versus asexual 10:1406
    strategies 10:1406
    theories of 2:202
    see also fertility; fertilization
resilin 1:138; 6:738, 739
respiration
    aerobic 7:993; 9:1252
        efficiency 8:1121
        electron transfer/oxidative
            phosphorylation 2:159, 160; 7:993,
            996; 8:1118–1119
        energy from see energy, from aerobic
            respiration
        glycolysis 2:159, 269–270; 5:618–619;
            7:993; 8:1117–1118
        Krebs cycle 2:159–160; 3:300;
            5:619, 632; 7:993–996; 9:1252
    anaerobic 2:159; 5:619; 8:1117
        in muscles 9:1252
    breathing 3:306; 8:1057–1059; 10:1398,
        1420
        at high altitudes 8:1058; 9:1170
        in birds 10:1423
    and the carbon cycle 3:303
    cutaneous 6:789
    gaseous exchange 9:1252–1253
    in the human body 3:306
    respiratory quotient (RQ) 2:280
    resting potential 9:1199
    restriction enzymes see enzymes, restriction
    retinoic acid 5:676
    reverse transcriptase (RT) 1:44; 6:806;
        12:1679, 1682
    rigor mortis 6:772; 9:1183
    RQ (respiratory quotient) 2:280
    runner's high 5:614

S
saliva 3:299; 11:1564
    human 4:516, 521
    ruminant 4:515; 11:1452
salt, concentration in the blood 5:672
salts 11:1458–1459
sebum 7:870; 11:1508

secretin 4:518, 522; 5:610, 612; 9:1260
selenium 3:294
serotonin 3:420; 4:556; 9:1213
    and aggression 1:32
sex hormones 7:904
    and animal behavior 1:84
sight see vision
smell 8:1070; 11:1514–1516
    disorders of 11:1516
    in mammals 11:1515
    in nocturnal animals 9:1223
    and taste 11:1516; 12:1597
    see also taste
sodium
    and nerve impulses 9:1198–1199, 1200
    pump 9:1198; 11:1458–1459
somatostatin 5:612; 9:1261
somatotropin, in humans
    see growth hormone
squalene 6:728
steroids 3:362; 7:906, 907
    gene activation 7:906
    treatment for cancer 3:352
    see also corticosteroids
strychnine 1:51
suberin 8:1025; 11:1561
sucrose 5:619
superoxide 2:240
sweat 5:672, 675–676; 12:1619
    night sweats 8:1110
symplastic pathways 8:1025
systemic acquired resistance (SAR) 7:932
systole 7:879

T
T3 see triiodothyronine
T4 see thyroxine
taste 8:1070; 11:1516; 12:1595–1597,
    1621
    disorders 12:1597
    see also smell
Tay-Sachs disease 4:477
temperature 5:616
    affecting sex of crocodilians 4:466
    body 5:641
        basal body (BBT), at ovulation 4:442
    regulation see thermoregulation
temperature-dependent sex determination
    (TSD) 4:466; 10:1416
testosterone 5:708
    and aggression 1:31
    and castration 10:1414
    daily rhythm 2:219
    and puberty 1:26, 27; 7:906; 10:1410
    secretion 5:612, 613
tetraiodothyronine see thyroxine
tetrodotoxin 1:50; 4:485
thelarche 8:1111
thermoregulation (temperature
    regulation) 7:900–901;
    12:1616–1619
    in bats 2:175–176
    behavioral 8:1051
    in butterflies and moths 2:271

in cold-blooded animals 3:396–397;
    8:1122; 12:1616–1618
    under water 3:397
    in vertebrates 11:1506
    in warm-blooded animals 12:1616, 1617,
    1618–1619
thrombin 2:278
thromboplastin 2:242, 278
thromboxanes 5:692
thymopoietin 11:1508
thymosin 7:904
thyroid-stimulating hormone (TSH) 2:166;
    5:612; 7:900; 8:1120; 9:1159
thyrotropin-releasing hormone (TRH)
    2:166
thyroxine (tetraiodothyronine; T4) 2:166;
    7:907; 8:1126; 12:1618
touch 8:1071; 12:1625–1628
    communication by 3:405
    nerves and 12:1626
trace elements
    deficiency 4:489; 9:1227
    plant 9:1227
translocation (plant) see transpiration and
    translocation
transpiration and translocation
    12:1629–1632
    guttation 8:1026; 12:1632
    translocation 11:1448, 1561;
    12:1631–1632
    transpiration 7:902; 8:1026; 11:1448,
    1561; 12:1629–1631, 1669
triglycerides 5:641, 689, 690, 691
triiodothryronine (T3) 2:166; 8:1126
trimethylamine oxide (TMAO; TMO)
    5:665, 670; 11:1459
tropomyosin 9:1182
troponin 9:1182
trypsin 4:518, 522; 9:1260
    optimum pH for 5:631
tumor promoters 3:295
tyrosine 10:1310

U
ultradian rhythms 2:219
undernutrition 9:1227
ureotelic organisms 12:1666, 1667, 1668
uric acid
    causing gout 8:1124
    waste product 5:665; 12:1666
uricotelic organisms 12:1666

V
vasopressin 5:611
vegans 9:1228
vincoleukoblastine 1:51
vision 8:1071; 12:1684–1688
    and aging 1:35
    artificial 12:1688
    binocular/stereoscopic/three-
        dimensional 3:322; 5:687; 12:1687
    bioluminescence used for 2:205
    in cats 3:322
    color 12:1686, 1687

Bold words with bold page numbers indicate complete articles; bold numbers preceding colons are volume numbers; numbers following colons indicate page numbers; italic page numbers refer to illustrations or other graphics.

vision *(continued)*
and the compound eye **1**:140;
5:*687–688*; **6**:743; **12**:1686
daytime/photopic **12**:1686–1687
in fish **6**:731; **12**:*1688*
human **12**:1684–1685, 1687
the brain and **2**:*263*; **12**:*1684*
in invertebrates **5**:688; **12**:1685–1686
night/scotopic **9**:*1221–1222*; **10**:1311;
12:*1686*, 1687
and the simple eye **5**:*685–687*; **12**:1685
von Willebrand's factor **2**:242

W

waste products, animal **5**:*665–666*
water, balance in the body **11**:1459
Wilson's disease **8**:1124
wilting
plant **12**:1630, *1631*
prevention **8**:1026; **12**:1670

X

xanthophylls **3**:317

■ Psychology

A

16PF (16 Personality Factor Questionnaire)
9:1283
aggression 1:*29–32*, 84, *85–86*; **5**:661
competitive **1**:30
defensive **1**:30; **4**:486
hostile **1**:29
instrumental **1**:29
sexual **1**:29
territorial **1**:29–30, 85
agoraphobia **10**:*1301*
altitude, high, adaptation to **8**:*1058*;
9:1169–1170; **10**:1307, *1423*
altruism 1:*58–60*, 86; **11**:1526–1527
reciprocal **1**:59, 60; **11**:*1526–1527*
American Society for Psychical Research
(ASPR) **9**:1263
Ames room **3**:*394*
amnesia **8**:1105, 1114
animal behavior 1:*81–86*
aggressive *see* aggression
behaviorism **1**:82; **3**:423; **5**:660;
10:1383–1384
causes **1**:83–84
conditioned *see* conditioning
defensive **4**:486
development **1**:84
ethology 1:*82–83*; **5**:*643–644*
and evolution **1**:84–85
fixed action patterns **1**:83
function **1**:*85–86*
and genetics **1**:83
instinctive *see* instinct
intelligent **7**:968
social *see* social organization
territorial **1**:29–30, 85
see also communication; courtship;
emotions; play; psychology
animals, training **3**:413
anorexia nervosa **4**:565–566; **8**:1114
anthropomorphism **5**:644
antisocial personality disorder (ASPD)
8:1115; **9**:1284

anxiety 1:*121–122*; **5**:*662–663*; **8**:1113
applied behavior analysis (ABA) **2**:163
arachnophobia **3**:*414*; **5**:*663*
attachment theory **5**:604
attention deficit hyperactivity disorder
(ADHD; attention deficit disorder
[ADD]) **8**:1115; **11**:1536
autism 2:*161–163*; **8**:1113;
11:1536–1537
autistic savants **2**:162
autoganzfeld **9**:1263
aversion therapy **3**:414; **10**:1387
avoidant personality disorder **9**:1285

B

Babinski's sign **5**:697; **10**:1398
Bedlam (Bethlehem Hospital) **9**:*1215*
bed wetting **8**:1115
behavior
animal *see* animal behavior
human
and autism **2**:161–162
evolutionary theory and **2**:203–204;
9:1194
behaviorism **1**:82; **3**:423; **5**:660;
10:1383–1384
behavior therapy **3**:414; **10**:1301, 1387
bipolar affective disorder (manic
depression) **8**:1113; **10**:1390
blushing **5**:605
body language **3**:404, 406
borderline personality disorder (BPD)
9:1284
Braille **11**:*1538*; **12**:1628
bulimia nervosa **4**:*565*, 566; **8**:1114

C

Calvin cycle (C3 cycle) **8**:1023;
10:1304–1305
channeling **9**:1263
child development 3:*354–359*
attention span **3**:358
cognitive development **3**:354–355, *359*,
394
differences between the sexes **3**:359
imitation **3**:358
importance of stimulation **3**:356–357
memory development **3**:358
motor skills **3**:356
nature versus nurture **3**:359
nervous system development **3**:355–356
newborn babies **3**:355
physical growth **3**:358
and play **10**:1330
pruning of axons and synapses **2**:260–261
reading and writing **3**:358
social contacts **3**:358–359
speech **3**:357–358
children
emotional and behavioral problems
11:*1536*, 1537–1538
mental disorders **8**:1115
see also special educational needs
chromesthesia **11**:1516
circadian rhythms **2**:216, 217, 218, 219
and sleep **11**:1511–1512
circalunar cycles **2**:216
cognition 3:*393–394*
cognitive development **3**:*359*, 394

stages **3**:354–355
see also child development
and intelligence, *see also* intelligence
see also learning; memory; perception;
problem solving
collective unconscious **10**:1385
communication 3:*401–406*
decoding **3**:401
methods **3**:404–406
using the tail **12**:1594
plant-to-animal **10**:1318
plant-to-plant **10**:1317
primate **3**:*406*
uses **3**:402–404
for courtship *see* courtship
for danger **3**:403–404
for dominance or submission **3**:*402*
see also parapsychology
concepts, learning **8**:1021
conditioning 3:*411–414*
classical **3**:411–412; **8**:*1020*
conditioned reflexes **3**:*411*; **9**:*1271*, 1272
counterconditioning **10**:1301
operant **10**:1387
operant/instrumental **3**:*412–413*;
8:1020
the Skinner box **3**:*412*, 413; **8**:1020
consciousness 3:*421–424*; **5**:662
cooperative behavior **1**:58, 86
see also altruism
counterconditioning **10**:1301
courtship 4:*455–460*; **11**:1540
an innate behavior pattern **1**:*82*
by nocturnal species **4**:457
communal **4**:460
evolution **4**:458
flehmen behavior **4**:*460*
functions **4**:455–456
gift giving **4**:459; **8**:1084
and sexual selection **11**:*1483–1484*
using bioluminescence **2**:206; **4**:457
using pheromones **4**:460
vocal communication **4**:458–459
songs **4**:459
creativity **10**:1329
cyclothymia **10**:1390

D

danger signals **3**:403–404
death, playing dead **2**:*206*; **8**:1017, 1080
deception **3**:404
delirium **10**:1389
delusions **10**:1388; **11**:1466
dementia **10**:1389
dependent personality disorder **9**:1285
depression **5**:663; **10**:1390
manic **8**:1113; **10**:1390
desensitization (exposure therapy) **1**:122;
10:1301
development, cognitive *see* child
development
*Diagnostic and Statistical Manual of Mental
Disorders* (DSM) **9**:1283; **10**:1389
discrete trial teaching (DTT) **2**:163
discrimination **8**:1021
displacement activities **11**:1566–1567
displays
courtship
in birds **1**:*82*, 84–85

in dolphins **4**:*456*
see also courtship
threat **8**:1072–1073
dissociation, double **9**:1212
dissociative disorders **8**:1114–1115
dominance **8**:1072; **11**:*1522*
signals **3**:*402*
dreaming **2**:264; **11**:*1512*
*DSM (Diagnostic and Statistical Manual of
Mental Disorders)* **9**:1283; **10**:1389
dyslexia **11**:1536
dyspraxia **11**:1536

E

ECT (electroconvulsive therapy) **8**:1113;
10:1390
ectomorphs **10**:1385
Edwin Smith papyrus **9**:1213–1214
electric shock treatment *see* shock
treatment
electroconvulsive therapy (ECT) **8**:1113;
10:1390
emotions 5:*602–605*
in animals **5**:603–*604*
brain areas involved **2**:257; **5**:604–605
expression **5**:605
love **5**:*602*
manipulation for pleasure **5**:*603*
physiology of **5**:605
endomorphs **10**:1385
ESP (extrasensory perception) **9**:1262
ethology 1:*82–83*; **5**:*643–644*
etiolation **10**:1306
evisceration, a defense mechanism **4**:570
evolutionary psychology 5:*660–663*
excretion, in plants **5**:670
exposure therapy (desensitization) **10**:1301
Expression of the Emotions in Man and Animals
(Charles Darwin) **5**:605
extinction principle (behavioural) **3**:413,
414; **8**:1021
extrasensory perception (ESP) **9**:1262
extroverts **10**:1385

F

facial expressions
in apes **10**:1368–1369
and emotions **5**:*605*
and play **10**:1329
fighting *see* aggression
fixed action patterns **1**:83; **7**:962
flehmen behavior **4**:*460*
flooding (psychology) **10**:1301
fugue, psychogenic **8**:1114

G

game theory **1**:32, 85–86
ganzfeld technique **9**:1263
generalization **8**:1021
generalized anxiety disorder (GAD) **1**:122;
8:1113
genius **7**:967
Gestalt psychology **10**:1384
grooming **3**:405; **8**:1072; **10**:*1370*
group therapy **10**:*1384*

H

habit **1**:23
habituation **8**:1020; **12**:1627

hallucinations **10**:1388
  with schizophrenia **8**:*1112*; **11**:1466;
    12:1597
handedness, left- and right- **7**:*871*
handwashing, compulsive **8**:*1114*
hawk-dove game **1**:32
Head Start program **7**:967
helping behavior **5**:644
  see also altruism
histrionic personality disorder **9**:1285
hunger, and animal behavior **1**:84
hypnosis 1:57; **3**:*421*; **7**:*926*; **9**:*1213*
  hypnotherapy **10**:1387
hypomania **10**:1390
hysteria **9**:*1213*

I

imprinting **7**:962; **8**:1019
inferiority complex **10**:1385
inkblot tests, Rorschach **9**:*1211*
insight **8**:1021
insomnia **11**:1510
instinct 7:**961–963**; **8**:1019
  fixed action patterns **1**:83; **7**:962
  see also reflexes
intelligence 7:**966–968**
  artificial (AI) **3**:424; **7**:967
  see also cognition
introverts **10**:1385
IQ tests **7**:966

L

language **3**:394; **11**:1544, 1545
  body **3**:404, 406
  development in the child **3**:357–358;
    11:1544
  dolphins and **12**:1710
  evolution of **5**:662
  sign language **7**:873; **11**:*1545*
    taught to apes **3**:406
  see also speech
Law of Effect, Thorndike's **3**:412
learning 2:261–262; **8**:**1019–1021**
  of aggressive behavior **1**:30–31
  associative **8**:1020
  of birdsong **3**:402–403; **8**:1021
  of concepts **8**:1021
  conditioned *see* conditioning
  difficulties **11**:1535–1538
  experimental psychology and
    10:1386
  habituation **8**:1020
  insight and problem solving **8**:1021
  laboratory experiments **8**:1020
  in octopuses **8**:1149
  perceptual **8**:1021
  role of play **10**:1330
  sensitization **8**:1020
  see also cognition; intelligence
long-term potentiation (LTP) **2**:263
Lovaas therapy **2**:163
love **5**:*602*

M

mania **5**:663; **8**:1113; **10**:1388
memory 8:**1104–1105**; **9**:1211
  declarative (explicit) **2**:261–263
  development in the child **3**:358
  and emotions **5**:604
  and experimental psychology
    8:1020–1021
  and forgetting **8**:1105
    see also amnesia
  immediate/sensory **8**:1104, *1105*
  improvement **8**:1105
  long-term **2**:262–263; **8**:1104, *1105*;
    11:1543
  nondeclarative (procedural/implicit)
    2:262
  short-term/working memory **2**:262,
    263; **8**:1104, *1105*; **11**:1543–1544
  storage **2**:257; **8**:*1104*–1105
  see also cognition; conditioning; learning
mental disorders 8:**1112–1115**
  difficult diagnosis of **10**:1389
  see also phobias; psychology; psychoses;
    psychotherapy; schizophrenia
mesomorphs **10**:1385
mind-body problem **3**:422, 423
mnemonics **8**:1105
mood disorders **8**:1113
Moro reflex **10**:1397–1398
motivation **1**:83–84; **10**:1386
multiple personality disorder (MPD)
    8:1114, 1115

N

narcissistic personality disorder (ASPD)
    9:1284–*1285*
narcolepsy **11**:1511
neural networks **9**:1214
neuropsychiatry **9**:1213, 1215
neuropsychology **3**:424; **9**:*1211*–1212
neuroses **8**:1113–*1114*; **10**:1389
nightmares **8**:1115
night terrors **8**:1115

O

obsessive-compulsive disorders (OCDs)
    1:*122*; **8**:*1114*; **9**:1285
optimization problems **1**:86
Ouija boards **9**:*1262*

P

pair bonding **4**:456
panic attacks **1**:122; **10**:1301
panic disorder (PD) **8**:1113
paranoid personality disorder (paranoia)
    9:1284; **10**:1388
parapsychology 9:**1262–1263**
parasomnias **8**:1115
parental care **10**:1352
  altruism **1**:58
pecking-order **11**:1523
perception **3**:393–394; **10**:1386
  see also cognition; intelligence
personality **10**:1385, 1386
personality disorders 8:1115;
    9:**1283–1286**
  obsessive-compulsive **1**:*122*; **8**:*1114*;
    9:1285
phi phenomenon **10**:1384
phobias 1:121–122; **8**:1113–1114;
    10:1301
  agoraphobia **10**:*1301*
  arachnophobia **3**:*414*; **5**:*663*
  social **8**:1114; **10**:1301
  treatment **1**:122; **3**:*414*; **10**:1301

photorespiration **10**:1305
phrenology **5**:662; **9**:1214
Piaget's theory **3**:354–355
play 3:359; **10**:**1329–1330**
"playing dead" **2**:*206*; **8**:1017, 1080
posthypnotic suggestion **7**:926
post-traumatic stress disorder (PTSD)
    1:*122*; **8**:1114, *1115*; **11**:1567
posture
  upright **11**:*1503*
  see also body language
potentiation, long-term (LTP) **2**:263
Prisoner's Dilemma **1**:59
problem solving **3**:394
  and insight **8**:1021
  see also cognition; intelligence
profiling, psychological **6**:773
prosopagnosia **9**:1211
psychiatry **5**:662–663; **9**:1213
  difficult diagnoses in **10**:1389
  psychiatrists **10**:1384
Psychical Research, Society for (SPR)
    9:1263
psychoanalysis **10**:*1383*, 1384–1385
psychoanalysts **10**:1384
psychologists **10**:1384, *1386*
psychology 10:**1383–1387**
  abnormal **10**:1386
  applied **10**:1386–1387
  cognitive **3**:393, 423; **5**:661–662;
    9:1211; **10**:1385
    see also cognition
  evolutionary 5:**660–663**
  experiments **10**:1385–1386
  Gestalt **10**:1384
  personality types **10**:1385
  psychological profiling **6**:773
  schools of thought **10**:1383–1384
  social **5**:661; **10**:1386
  see also behavior; conditioning; learning;
    parapsychology; psychotherapy
psychopaths *see* antisocial personality
    disorder
psychoses 8:1112–1113; **10**:**1388–1390**
psychotherapy **10**:*1387*, *1388*, 1390
  group therapy **10**:*1384*
  for personality disorders **9**:*1286*
  for phobias **10**:1301
  psychoanalysis **10**:*1383*, 1384–1385
PTSD *see* post-traumatic stress disorder
punishment **3**:413; **8**:1020

R

rage, sham **1**:31
reading, development **3**:358
reductionism **3**:423
reflexes 7:961–962; **9**:*1204*;
    10:**1397–1398**
  in babies **3**:355; **5**:697; **10**:*1397*–1398
  brain-stem **10**:1398
  conditioned, *see also* conditioning
  conditioned (acquired) **3**:*411*; **9**:*1271*,
    1272; **10**:1398
  knee-jerk **10**:1397

milk-ejection **7**:998
plantar **10**:1398
pupillary **10**:1397
  the reflex arc **9**:*1204*; **10**:1397
  simple and complex **10**:1398
reinforcement
  negative **3**:413; **8**:1020
  positive **8**:1020
  theory of **3**:412
REM (rapid eye movement) sleep **2**:264;
    11:*1510*–1511, 1512

S

SAD (seasonal affective disorder) **2**:218
schizoaffective disorder **10**:1390
schizoid personality disorder **9**:1284
schizophrenia 3:398; **8**:**1112**–1113;
    9:1212; **10**:1388, 1389–1390;
    11:*1466*
  disorganized **11**:1466
  and taste **12**:1597
schizotypal personality disorder **9**:1284
seances **9**:1263
seasonal affective disorder (SAD) **2**:218
selfish behavior **11**:1525–1526
self-sacrifice **4**:486
sensitization **8**:1020
sensory deprivation **12**:1626
serial killers **9**:*1284*
shock treatment
  for mental disorders **8**:1113
  for nervous diseases **9**:*1212*
sign stimuli **1**:83
Simon-Binet test **7**:966–967
skills, learning **3**:394
Skinner boxes **3**:*412*, 413; **8**:1020
sleep 11:**1509–1512**
  brain function during **2**:264;
    11:*1509*–1510
  cycle (stages of sleep) **2**:219;
    11:*1510*–1511
  deprivation **11**:1510
  disorders **8**:1115; **11**:1511
  dreaming **2**:264; **11**:1512
sleep apnea **11**:1511
sleep talking **8**:1115; **11**:1511
sleepwalking **8**:1115; **11**:1511
slow learners **11**:1535–1536
smiling **5**:*605*
snakes, phobia of **1**:122
social contacts, and child development
    3:358–359
social organization 11:**1521–1524**
  and altruism **1**:59–60, 86
  in cnidarians **11**:1524
  communal feeding **11**:1522
  and communication **3**:402; **11**:1524
    see also communication
  defending food **11**:1523
  in dogs **4**:540
  dominance **8**:1072; **11**:*1522*, 1523
  grooming **8**:1072; **10**:*1370*
  in insects **2**:203; **7**:958–959; **11**:*1524*;
    12:1611

Bold words with bold page numbers indicate complete articles; bold numbers
preceding colons are volume numbers; numbers following colons indicate
page numbers; italic page numbers refer to illustrations or other graphics.

social organization (continued)
in mammals **8**:1072–1074
modeling **3**:349
phenotypic variation **4**:524
in primates **10**:1369–1370
problems associated with **11**:1524
related individuals **11**:1523–1524
in rodents **10**:1437–1438
safety reasons **11**:1521–1522
sociogenesis **3**:349
see also sociobiology
sociobiology 5:644; **11**:1525–1528
sociopaths see antisocial personality disorder
**special educational needs
11**:1535–1538
for autism **2**:162–163; **11**:1536–1537
speech 11:1543–1545
the brain and **2**:264; **11**:1543–1544
child development and **3**:357–358;
11:1544
child-directed (CDS) **3**:356–357
stuttering **11**:1545
teeth and **12**:1604
therapy **11**:*1544*, 1545
the tongue and **12**:1622
see also language
spontaneous recovery, and conditioning
8:1021
stimuli, sign stimuli **1**:83
stress 11:1566–1567
and the immune system **7**:942
post-traumatic stress disorder (PTSD)
1:122; **8**:1114, *1115*; **11**:1567
stress hormones **5**:641
Study of Instinct, The (Tinbergen) **1**:84
stuttering **11**:1545
submission, signals **3**:402
synesthesia **11**:1516

T

TEACCH program **2**:162–163
teaching machines **3**:414
telekinesis **9**:1262
thermophilic and thermophobic behavior
3:397
thoughts, organization of **3**:394
torpor **12**:1618

UW

unconscious **3**:422
collective **10**:1385
Weschler-Bellevue Scale **7**:967
writing, development **3**:358

Z

zeitgebers **2**:216–217
Zener cards **9**:1262

■ **ZOOLOGY**

A

aardvarks **4**:445
aardwolves **3**:312
Abralia **2**:207
Abraliopsis **2**:207
Acanthaster planci (crown-of-thorns starfish)
4:*450*, 451, 453, 568
Acanthocephala **1**:95–96; **9**:1267

acanthodians **6**:730; **7**:978
Acanthophis antarcticus (death adder) **2**:286;
11:1520
Accipitridae **2**:235–236
Achatina fulica (giant African snail) **2**:185,
196
Acinonyx jubatus see cheetahs
acoelomates **9**:1196
acorn worms **1**:97; **7**:*1006*
Acronicta psi (dagger moth) **2**:284
Actinopterygii **6**:730; **12**:*1672*
Actinopyga spp. **4**:570
Actophilornis africanus (African jacana)
8:*1083*
Adapidae **7**:871
adders, death **2**:286; **11**:1520
adolescence 1:25–28
see also puberty
Aedes spp. **7**:947; **8**:1126; **9**:*1268*
Aegolius acadius (saw-whet owl) **9**:*1220*
Aepyornis titan (elephant bird) **6**:755
Aesthna mixta (hawker migrant dragonfly)
4:*550*
Afropavo congensis (Congo peacock) **6**:778
Agalychnis calcarifer **6**:788
Agama agama (agama lizard) **3**:396; **8**:*1053*
Agapornis spp. (lovebirds) **4**:459
Agelena republicana **11**:1548
Agnatha see fishes, jawless
Ailuropoda melanoleuca see pandas, giant
alates **1**:119; **12**:1612
albatrosses **4**:456; **11**:1473, 1474
black-browed **6**:*752*
royal **2**:232; **5**:*658*
soaring **6**:*752*; **11**:*1473*
Alca (Pinguinus) impennis (great auk) **6**:*754*;
12:1654
Alcedo atthis (kingfisher) **2**:*230*
Alces alces (elk/moose) **8**:1084; **10**:1350;
12:1591, *1619*
allelopathy **3**:350
Alligator mississippiensis (American alligator)
4:459, 464, *466*; **5**:647
alligators see crocodilians, alligators
Allosaurus **4**:528
Alopex lagopus (Arctic fox) **9**:*1159*; **12**:1619
Alopias vulpinus (thresher shark) **11**:1488
Alosa sapidissima (American shad) **4**:573
Alouatta spp. (howler monkey) **10**:1368;
12:1594, 1615, 1640
alpacas **4**:545
Alpheus spp. (snapping shrimp) **4**:470
alternation of generations, in jellyfish and
hydroids **7**:980–981
Alytes obstetricans (midwife toad) **6**:*790*
Amazona amazonica (Amazon parrot) **12**:*1642*
amber, fossils preserved in **6**:*781*, 782
Amblyrhynchus cristatus (marine iguana)
8:*1052*
Ambystoma spp. **9**:*1256*; **10**:1418; **11**:*1454*,
1455
ammonites **4**:446; **6**:*784*
amphibians 1:64–65; **12**:*1673*
brain **2**:258
circulatory system **3**:373–374; **7**:*877*
courtship **4**:458–459
eggs **5**:587–588
embryo development **5**:*598*, 599
evolution **1**:*65*; **6**:*790*; **11**:1456

excretion **5**:666, 670
first known **6**:790
fossils **11**:1456
hibernation and estivation **7**:892, *893*
jaws **7**:978
life cycles
metamorphosis **7**:1005; **8**:1125, 1126
nesting **9**:1206
molting **9**:1158
pancreas **9**:1261
regeneration of body parts **10**:1400
respiration
gills **10**:1418
lungs **8**:1060; **10**:1423
sense of taste **12**:1596
sense of touch **12**:1628
tails **12**:1592, *1593*
temperature regulation **3**:397
see also frogs and toads; salamanders
and newts
amphicyonids **3**:310
amphioxus (lancelet) **3**:*364*, 365; **7**:*972*
circulatory system **3**:371; **7**:877
Amphiprion spp. (clownfish/anemone fish)
1:126; **3**:*389*, 390; **4**:450; **7**:890,
970; **11**:1580
amphiumas (Amphiumidae) **11**:1454
Anableps **6**:731
anacondas **11**:1518, 1519
anagenesis **5**:678
Anas spp. **4**:*524*; **5**:695
anchovies, Peruvian **4**:438
anemones, sea see jellyfish, sea anemones,
and hydras
Anemonia sulata **9**:*1237*
angelfish **2**:283; **6**:*731*
Angiostrongylus cantonensis **9**:1265
angwantibos **10**:1366
animal kingdom 1:94–97; **12**:1601
animals, selectively bred, welfare **11**:1480
Anisoptera **4**:550
ankylosaurs **4**:531
annelids 1:96, 98–100; **7**:971
excretory systems **5**:666–667
mucus **9**:1172
see also earthworms; leeches; polychaetes
Anolis spp. (anole lizard) **4**:459
Anomalops katoptron (flashlight fish) **5**:686
Anopheles spp. (mosquito) **6**:744; **7**:946,
1004; **9**:1265, 1268
Anoplura (sucking lice) **8**:1032, 1033
Anseriformes **12**:1700–1701
Anser rossii (Ross's goose) **8**:1134
**anteaters, sloths, and armadillos
1**:103–104
anteaters **1**:103–104
giant **1**:*103*, 104; **4**:*445*; **12**:*1621*
silky **1**:103
spiny see echidnas
tongue **12**:*1621*, 1622
armadillos **1**:104; **4**:486
sloths **1**:*104*
hands **11**:1498
Antedon sp **4**:*569*
antelopes **3**:403; **4**:460; **7**:910
Anthias **9**:*1236*
Anthonomus grandis (boll weevil) **2**:178
Antilocapra sp. (pronghorn antelope) **3**:403;
7:910

antipatharians (black corals) **4**:453
ant lions **5**:695; **9**:1208
ants 1:118–120
army/driver **1**:119, 120; **3**:404; **11**:1580
black **1**:*119*
brain and nervous system **2**:*258*
carpenter **1**:118
castes **1**:119
colonies **1**:119; **7**:958–959
modeling **3**:349
communication **3**:404; **12**:1647
alarm secretions **9**:1293
defense
chemical **1**:*118*, 119
self-sacrifice **4**:486
feeding **1**:119–120
fire **1**:119, 120; **2**:196
harvester **1**:120; **4**:486
leaf-cutting **1**:*59*–60, 120; **12**:*1645*
nests **1**:118–119
parasitized **2**:196
sense of smell **11**:1515
slave-making **1**:120
in the soil **11**:1531–1532
stings **1**:119
symbiosis
with acacia trees **1**:118–119; **3**:*390*;
4:483; **11**:*1562*, 1580–1581
with aphids **4**:483; **7**:884; **11**:*1581*
with caterpillars **2**:271
with *Cecropia* trees **11**:1581
with silverfish **11**:1580
vampire **1**:120
weaver **1**:118
"white" see termites
wood **1**:*118*
Anura **1**:64; **6**:787
see also frogs and toads
Apatosaurus **4**:*528*, 529–530
apes
"aquatic" **7**:913
great **10**:1368–*1369*
see also chimpanzees; gorillas;
orangutans
hands **7**:869, *870*
see also primates
Aphelocoma coerulescens (Florida scrub jay)
1:*58*
aphids
agricultural pests **7**:885
feeding on sap **12**:1632
honeydew (sugary milk) from **1**:*120*;
4:483; **7**:884; **11**:*1581*
peach **7**:*885*
protected by ants **1**:*120*; **4**:483; **7**:884
reproduction **10**:*1407*
rose **10**:*1407*
Apis mellifera see honeybees
Aplacophora **8**:1150
Aplodontia rufa (mountain beaver) **10**:1438
Aplysia **2**:261; **10**:1397
Apocrita **12**:1692, 1693
Apodiformes **2**:231
Aptenodytes forsteri (emperor penguin)
6:754; **11**:1473
Apterygota **7**:960
Apteryx spp. (kiwis) **6**:*756*
arachnids 1:130–133, 141
diseases carried by **1**:*131*; **7**:945, *946*–947

see also arthropods; mites; scorpions; spiders; ticks
Arachnocampa luminosa (fungus gnat) **3**:328
Araneus diadematus (garden spider) **12**:*1627*
Archaeocetes **12**:1708
archaeopteryx 1:*134*; **2**:233; **4**:529; **5**:653; **6**:749; **9**:1254, 1274
Archilochus colubris (ruby-throated hummingbird) **9**:*1275*
Architeutis sp. (giant squid) **4**:574
architomy **10**:1400
archosaurs **4**:*530*
Arctocebus calabarensis (angwantibo) **10**:1366
Ardipithecus ramidus **7**:914, 915
Arenicola marina (lugworm) **12**:1592
Argiope spp. **5**:*663*; **11**:1548
Argulus spp. **4**:467–468
Argyroneta spp. (water spiders) **11**:1549
Arixenia spp. **4**:564
Arixeniina **4**:563, 564
armadillos **1**:104; **4**:486
arrow worms **1**:97
Arthropleura **3**:346
arthropods 1:96–97, **137–142**
  circulatory systems **3**:371–372
    heart **7**:876
  classification **1**:138
  digestion by **1**:140
  evolution **1**:138
  exoskeleton **1**:138–139; **7**:971–972; **11**:*1496–1497*
  eyes **1**:140; **12**:1686
  legs **1**:139
  molting **9**:1157–1158; **11**:1497
  nervous system and senses **7**:971
  number of species **2**:184
  tails **12**:1592
  and touch **12**:1627
  see also arachnids; centipedes and millipedes; chelicerates; crustaceans; insects
Artiodactyla *see* ungulates, even-toed
Ascaris lumbricoides **9**:1196
asses, Somali wild **12**:*1659*
Asteroidea **4**:569–570
Ateles spp. (spider monkeys) **10**:*1368*
Athene cunicularia (burrowing owl) **9**:1206
Atta spp. **1**:59–60; **12**:*1645*
Attacus atlas (atlas moth) **9**:*1223*
Auchenorrhyncha **7**:883, 884
auks **6**:751; **11**:1472, 1473, 1474, 1578
  great **6**:*754*; **12**:1654
Aurelia aurita (moon jelly) **7**:*981*, 982
Auriparus flaviceps (verdin) **2**:273
Australopithecus spp. **2**:258
  A. afarensis **7**:871
    "Lucy" **6**:784; **7**:*914*, 915
  A. africanus **7**:915
  A. boisei **7**:915
  A. robustus **7**:871, 915
  relationship to *Homo* **7**:915
  skin color **9**:1227
Austrophlebia spp. **4**:552
Automeris io (bull's eye-moth) **2**:271
automimicry **2**:270
autotomy (self-amputation) **10**:1400
  in lizards **8**:*1052–1053*; **10**:1400
  in phasmids **8**:1017
Avicularia spp. (bird-eating spider) **11**:*1548*

avocets **2**:230–231; **12**:*1699*, 1700
axolotls **9**:*1256*; **10**:1418; **11**:1455
aye-ayes **10**:1366
Azteca spp. **11**:1581

B

babies
  birthweight, optimal **9**:1193
  brain **2**:260
  conception **5**:708
  development **3**:354–357
  immunity **7**:*934*, 998
  incubators **8**:1040
  jaundiced **8**:1047
  newborn **3**:355
    Apgar scoring system **1**:123
    PKU test **8**:*1123*
  premature **10**:*1359*
  reflexes **3**:355; **10**:*1397–1398*
    Babinski's sign **5**:697; **10**:1398
  sense of smell **11**:1514
  sleep **11**:1511
  speech development **11**:1544
  teeth **12**:1604
  vitamin K given to **4**:519
baboons **1**:*86*; **10**:1368
  estrus **8**:*1111*
  heart transplanted from **12**:1634
  male-female bonds **10**:1369
  movement **10**:1370
  reciprocal altruism **1**:59
backswimmers **7**:885; **11**:1577
badgers **10**:1353
  honey **11**:1582
baijis **12**:1709
Balaena mysticetus (bowhead whale) **12**:1709
Balaenoptera musculus (blue whale) **3**:405; **4**:438; **8**:1069
balloonfish **4**:486
bandicoots **8**:1080
barnacles **4**:445, 470
  acorn **11**:1493
  goose **4**:*470*; **11**:1493
  stalked **7**:*889*
  on whales **11**:1580
barracudas **4**:450
basket stars **2**:206; **4**:570
bats 2:**173–176**
  altruism **1**:*60*
  Azorean **6**:747
  Bechstein's **2**:*173*
  big brown **4**:573
  cave-dwelling **3**:*325*, 328
  communication **2**:175
  ears **4**:562
  echolocation **2**:*174–175*; **4**:562, 572–574; **7**:*873*; **9**:1222
    detected by moths **7**:873
  evolution **2**:174; **6**:749
  and evolution of butterflies **2**:268
  flight **2**:*173*, 175; **6**:748; **12**:1593
  greater horseshoe **2**:*174*, 175; **3**:*325*
  hands **11**:1498
  human conflict **2**:176
  insectivorous **2**:174; **4**:573–574
  little brown **4**:*573*
  long-eared **4**:*571*, 574
  Old World fruit bats **2**:173–174
  parasites **3**:328

  pest control by **2**:176
  pipistrelle **2**:*176*; **7**:*873*
  pollination by **9**:1220; **10**:1338
  reproduction **2**:176; **10**:1353
  southern blossom bat **2**:173
  tail **12**:1593
  thermoregulation **2**:175–176
  tube-nosed fruit bat **2**:173
  vampire **2**:*173*, 174; **4**:574
    altruism **1**:*60*; **11**:*1526–1527*
  Wahlberg's fruit **2**:*175*
  wings and flight **2**:*173*, 175; **6**:748, 750, 751
bear-dogs **3**:310
beard worms **1**:96
bears **3**:308–309
  black **12**:1609, 1655–1656
  dawn **3**:309
  diet **5**:695
  grizzly **2**:*183*
  polar **3**:309; **5**:*692*; **10**:*1330*
  speciation **11**:1541
  teeth **3**:307
  winter lethargy **7**:891–892
beavers **5**:659
  American **10**:*1438*
  dams **9**:*1207*
  family groups **10**:1437
  fur **10**:1436
  lodges **9**:*1207*
  mountain **10**:1438
  swimming **11**:1578
  tail **12**:1593, 1594
  teeth **8**:1070, *1071*; **10**:*1438*
beetles 2:**177–178**
  bark **2**:178
  biodiversity **2**:184
  blister **2**:178
  bombardier **4**:485; **5**:677
  cave-dwelling **3**:327
  click **2**:178
  Colorado potato **2**:*178*
  death-watch **2**:178
  diving **10**:1420; **11**:1578
  dune **4**:501
  dung **11**:*1464*
  elm-bark **9**:1294; **12**:1640
  fog harvesters **4**:501
  ground **3**:327
  hercules **2**:*177*
  ironclad **4**:485
  Japanese **7**:960
  jewel **2**:283
  ladybug *see* ladybugs
  lily **8**:*1081*
  oil **3**:404
  parasitic **7**:963
  as pests **2**:*178*
  pollination by **6**:760; **10**:1318, 1337
  rove **7**:963
  scarab **2**:177
  stag **2**:177–178; **11**:1483
  stink **12**:1647
  tiger **9**:1208

  vedalia **2**:195
  whirligig **2**:284
Bering Land Bridge **10**:1363
Beroe spp. **7**:982
Betta splendens (Siamese fighting fish) **9**:*1206*
bichirs **6**:734
Bilateria **9**:1196
binturong **3**:312
biosonar **4**:571
bipedalism **1**:22; **7**:871, 914, *916*; **10**:1360, 1361
  and the aquatic ape **7**:913
  and the skeleton **11**:*1503*
birds 2:**228–233**; **12**:1673, 1674
  banding of **8**:1136
  beaks (bills) **2**:230–231; **9**:1274, *1275*; **12**:1606
    adaptive radiation **9**:1192; **11**:1541
    sensitive **12**:1628
    serrations **12**:1606
  bones **2**:229, 250; **6**:751; **11**:1498, *1501*
  brain **2**:*257*, 259
  as brood parasites **7**:963
  bursa of Fabricius **7**:930
  calls **2**:233; **6**:776
    modified **7**:*962*
    see also birds, songs
  camouflage **6**:775
  circulatory system **3**:*373*, 375
  colonies **9**:1209; **11**:1474
  courtship **1**:*82*, 84–85; **4**:*459–460*; **8**:1084; **9**:1276
    dances **4**:460
    nuptial feeding **8**:1084
    songs **2**:232; **4**:459
  crop **2**:230
  digestive systems **4**:*514*, 521; **11**:1564
  ears **4**:561
  echolocation **9**:*1222*
  eggs **2**:231–232; **10**:1413
    camouflaged **2**:284
    effects of DDT **2**:235–236; **4**:481; **5**:622–623; **9**:1275; **10**:1343–1344
    hatching together **3**:405
    incubation **1**:83–84
    retrieval by gulls **1**:83
  egg tooth **2**:232
  embryo development **5**:*598–599*
  evolution **2**:233, 235; **4**:529; **9**:1274
    convergent **4**:446
  excretion **2**:230; **5**:670; **7**:989
  fat storage **5**:619
  feathers **2**:228–229; **6**:725
  feet **2**:231; **5**:697, 698; **9**:1273; **11**:1472
    zygodactyl **6**:775, 778
  flight **6**:747–749, 751–752
    adaptations for **6**:751
    evolution **9**:1254–1255
    soaring **6**:*752*; **8**:1134; **11**:*1473*
    see also flight
  flightless 2:230; **6**:751, **753–756**
    at risk **6**:756
    cormorants **6**:754; **9**:1169; **11**:1473
    evolution **7**:977

birds *(continued)*
  extinction **6**:756; **7**:977
  swimmers **6**:*753, 754*
  see also penguins
  terrestrial **6**:755–756
flocks **3**:402; **4**:*484*
  computer simulation **2**:*151*
  mixed-species **6**:778
  forest 6:775–778
   communication **6**:776
   rain forest **6**:777–778
   of the taiga **6**:776–777
   temperate forests **6**:777; **12**:*1609*
  heart **2**:230; **7**:877–878
  and high altitude **9**:1169
  imprinting **8**:1019
  instincts **7**:*961*, 962
  jaws **7**:978–979
  of mangroves **11**:1494
  migration **2**:210; **5**:619; **6**:776–777;
   8:1135–1136; **10**:1333; **11**:1474;
   12:1700
   Arctic tern **8**:*1133*; **11**:1474
   to the tundra **12**:1654
   white storks **8**:1134
  molting **2**:229; **9**:*1158*–1159
  nervous system **2**:230
  nests **2**:231; **9**:1208–*1209*
   communal **9**:1209
   forest birds **6**:775–776
   seabirds **9**:1209; **11**:1473
   of swiftlets **3**:*328*
  nocturnal **9**:1220, 1221–*1222*
  orders of **2**:232
  pancreas **9**:1261
  perching 5:697; **9**:**1273–1276**
  plant pollination by **10**:*1337*–1338
  play **10**:1329
  preening **5**:676; **12**:1699
  of prey 2:234–237
   effects of DDT on **2**:235–236;
    5:622–623; **9**:1287; **10**:1343–1344
   evolution **2**:235
   in the suburbs **11**:*1569*
   vision **12**:1686–1687
  respiration **10**:1423–1424
   lungs **2**:230; **8**:*1060*; **10**:1424
  salt glands **11**:1459, 1472
  seabirds 5:*623*; **11**:**1471–1474**
   nests **9**:1209; **11**:1473; **12**:1614–1615
  skeleton **2**:229–230
  skull **7**:978–979; **11**:1498
  social **11**:1522
  songbirds **9**:1273, 1274
  songs **2**:232, 233; **3**:402; **4**:459; **9**:1274;
   12:1614, 1615
   learning **3**:402–403; **8**:1021
  sounds **2**:232–233
   sonar **4**:574
  species **2**:228
  in the suburbs **11**:*1569*
  swimming **11**:1578
  tail **12**:*1592*, 1593
  taste receptors **12**:1596
  temperature regulation **12**:*1618*
  territories **1**:29–30; **12**:1613–1615
  and song **9**:1274; **12**:1614, 1615
  tongue **12**:1621
  of the tundra **12**:1654

in urban areas **12**:1665
uropygial glands **5**:676
vision **12**:1686–1687
waterbirds and waders
  12:1699–1701
weight reduction **2**:229–230
wings **6**:747–748
  claws on **6**:777
  penguin **6**:*753*, 754
young
  altricial **11**:1474
  nidifugous (precocial) **6**:776; **11**:1474
birds of paradise **8**:1084
Birgus latre (coconut crab) **4**:469
birth *see* pregnancy and birth
Bison bison (bison/American buffalo) **5**:*583*,
  608–609; **12**:*1660*
Biston betularia (peppered moth) **2**:285
Bitis gabonica (gaboon viper) **2**:282
bivalves (Bivalvia) **8**:1150
  foot **5**:698
  shell **11**:1497
blackbirds **9**:*1274*
blackflies, pupae **7**:1006
Blastophaga psenes (fig wasp) **12**:*1693*
Blatella spp. **5**:655; **9**:1193
blennies
  coral **2**:282
  sabre-toothed **4**:445
blowflies **6**:746, 773
bluebirds, eastern, decline **3**:*410*
boar, wild **12**:1606, *1610*
boas **11**:1519
  boa constrictors **11**:*1518*, 1519
  tree **11**:1519
bobcats **3**:322, 324
boids **11**:1519
bollworms, cotton **2**:270
Bombyx mori (silk moth) **5**:677; **6**:*725*;
  9:1288, *1293*
boobies **11**:1472–1473, 1474
boomslangs **11**:1518
Bos spp. **1**:18; **4**:545
  see also cattle
botflies **6**:746
Bothriuridae **11**:1470
Bothus lunatus (peacock flounder) **2**:282
Bovicola spp. (lice) **8**:1033
bowerbirds, courtship **4**:*459*–460; **8**:1084;
  9:*1208*; **11**:1540; **12**:*1614*
bowfins **6**:734
brachiation **10**:1368
Brachinus spp. (bombadier beetle) **4**:485;
  5:677
brachiopods **1**:96
Brachiosaurus **4**:530, 531
Brachycera **6**:743
Bradypus spp. (three-toed sloths) **1**:*104*
Branchiopoda **4**:470
Branchiostoma lanceolatum see amphioxus
Branta spp. (goose) **11**:*1482*, 1521
breeding, captive *see* captive breeding
  programs
bristle worms **1**:96, *98*
brittle stars **2**:206; **4**:568, 570; **9**:1232
Brontosaurus see Apatosaurus
Bronx Zoo, New York City **12**:1725
Brookesia minima (stump-tailed chameleon)
  8:1051

browsers **5**:694
Bryozoa **1**:96
budding **10**:1400, 1404, *1405*
  by coral polyps **4**:449, 453
buffaloes **4**:485
  African **4**:514
  American **5**:*583*, 608–609
  water **4**:545; **12**:1662
Bufonidae **6**:787
Bufo spp. **6**:790
  B. americanus (American toad) **3**:403
  B. marinus (cane toad) **1**:*51*; **2**:196
bugs
  ambush **7**:885
  assassin (kissing bugs) **7**:*884*, 885, 946
   mimicry by **3**:*391*
  bodyguard **4**:483
  green shield **7**:*883*
  lygus **7**:885
  red **1**:132
  see also Hemiptera
bullfrogs **1**:64; **5**:666; **6**:787, 790
Bungarus spp. (krait) **9**:*1203*
buntings, Lapland **10**:1333
buoyancy, fish **6**:*728*–729; **11**:1577
Buphagus spp. (oxpecker bird) **11**:*1579*
burrows **9**:1207
  fossilized **6**:783
bush babies **9**:1294; **10**:1366
Buteo spp. **2**:234, 235
Buthidae **11**:1470
butterflies and moths 2:267–271
  beneficial **2**:270
  butterflies
   apollo **2**:186
   blue chalkhill **10**:*1403*
   Cairns birdwing **1**:*137*
   cloudless sulfur **2**:269
   courtship **4**:457
   European large blue **2**:271
   glasswing **2**:271
   hairstreak **2**:*271*
   leaf **2**:271, 283
   monarch **2**:269, 270; **4**:484;
    6:810–811; **7**:959–960, 1003;
    8:*1125*, 1135
   purple emperor **2**:268
   stomach **11**:1563
   swallowtail **2**:*267*, 269, 283, 284;
    4:483
   viceroy **4**:484
   wings **6**:750
   Xerxes blue **2**:267
  camouflage and mimicry **2**:270, 271,
   281, 286
  caterpillars **2**:268–269; **7**:*1003*, 1006;
   8:1125; **10**:*1308*
   false eyes **1**:19
   frozen **4**:472
   spiracles **10**:1420
   woolly bear **4**:472
  colors and patterns **2**:270–*271*
  communication, chemical (pheromones)
   1:106; **2**:269–270, *270*; **4**:460;
   9:1288; **12**:1596
  differences **2**:268
  evolution **2**:268
  feeding **2**:267, 268
  flight **9**:1180

life cycle **2**:*268*–269
metamorphosis **7**:1006; **8**:*1125*; **10**:1308
migration **2**:*269*; **8**:*1135*
mimicry by **2**:270
moths
  antennae **1**:*105*, 106; **9**:*1223*
  atlas **9**:*1223*
  bat avoidance **4**:574; **7**:873
  for biological control **2**:270
  brown-tail **2**:270
  bull's-eye **2**:271
  coevolution with plants **3**:390
  corn earworm **2**:269
  dagger **2**:284
  gypsy **2**:196, 268–269, *270*; **10**:*1346*
  hawk **1**:19; **2**:268
  herald **3**:328
  hornet **2**:*286*
  peppered **2**:285
  silk **2**:270; **5**:677; **6**:*725*; **9**:1288, *1293*
  tiger **4**:574
  tissue **3**:328
  tussock **2**:269
  vampire **2**:267
  yucca **2**:269; **10**:*1336*
  as pests **2**:*270*
  plant pollination **10**:*1336*, 1337
  proboscis **2**:267, 268; **10**:*1337*
  relationship with ants **2**:271
  temperature **2**:271; **12**:*1617*
  wings **2**:267–268, 269, *271*
by-the-wind sailor **7**:983

C

Cacajao spp. (uakaris) **10**:1368
Cacatua spp. **7**:*962*
cacomistles **3**:311
Cactoblastis cactorum **2**:270
caecilians 1:64; **2**:**275–276**
Caenorhabditis elegans **10**:1430
Calcarea **11**:1553
Calcarius lapponicus (Lapland bunting)
  10:1333
Callianassa spp. (ghost shrimps) **4**:467
Callibaetes spp. **4**:552
Callimico goeldii (Goeldi's monkey) **10**:1368
Callithrix argentata (white-eared marmoset)
  5:694
Callitrichidae **10**:1367–1368
calls
  alarm **3**:403; **11**:1522
  bird **2**:233; **6**:776
   modified **7**:*962*
  frog and toad **4**:458–459; **6**:790
Calpe eustrigata (vampire moth) **2**:267
Calthrop spp. **2**:282
camels **4**:*501*
  milk **7**:998
Camelus spp. (camels) **4**:*501*
Camposcia retusa **2**:282
Campylorhynchus brunneicapillus (cactus
  wren) **2**:273; **9**:1206
canaries **9**:1273
Cancer pagurus (edible crab) **4**:467
Canidae **3**:309; **12**:1601
  see also dogs
Caniformia **3**:308–311
Canis spp.
  C. dingo (dingo) **4**:*542*

C. familiaris (domestic dog) **4**:*540–541*, 544
C. latrans (coyote) **4**:*539*, 540; **11**:1569
C. lupus (gray wolf) **3**:309; **4**:539; **10**:1350; **11**:*1522*, 1524
C. lupus lycaon (timber wolf) **3**:*428*
C. rufus (red wolf) **4**:542
C. simensis (Ethiopian wolf) **4**:541–542
cannibalism **8**:1076
human, and kuru **10**:1371
Caprimulgus sp. (whippoorwill) **2**:216; **6**:776; **9**:*1221–1222*
Capris hircus (goat) **4**:544
captive breeding programs **11**:*1482*; **12**:1725, *1726*
capybaras **10**:1436, 1437; **11**:1465
carapace **4**:*467*
Carausius morosus (laboratory stick insect) **8**:*1017*
Carcharhiniformes **11**:1487
Carcharhinus spp. **11**:1488, 1489; **12**:*1672*
Carcharias falciformis (silky shark) **11**:*1490*
Carcharodon spp. (great white shark) **4**:450; **11**:1489
Carduelis hornemanni (Arctic/hoary redpoll) **10**:*1333*
caribou **8**:1135; **10**:1333; **12**:*1590*, 1654, 1663
European (reindeer), diet **8**:*1036*; **12**:1654
ptarmigan and **11**:1580
carnivores 3:307–313; 5:694–695; 8:1071–1072
anatomy **3**:307
cats *see* cats
digestive system **4**:*516*, *520*, 521; **11**:1563
dogs *see* dogs
evolution **3**:*310*
in food webs **6**:767, 768
jaws **3**:307; **7**:*978*, 979
nonmammalian **3**:308
nutrition **9**:1228
teeth **3**:*307*, 310; **4**:517; **7**:979; **8**:1070; **12**:1605
carp **4**:545
Carthartes aura (turkey vulture) **2**:235
cassowaries **5**:698; **6**:756, 775
Castor spp. *see* beavers
Castoroides **10**:1438
Casuarius spp. (cassowaries) **5**:698; **6**:756, 775
Catarrhini **10**:1365, 1367, 1368–1369
caterpillars *see* butterflies and moths, caterpillars
catfish
barbels **1**:106
eggs **6**:733
farming of **1**:*124*
gills **10**:1419
walking **6**:728
Cathartidae **2**:236
cats 3:321–324; 5:694
black-footed **3**:313
camouflaged **2**:*284*
and civilization **3**:323
classification **3**:323–324; **12**:1600
diseases **1**:89–90; **8**:1061
domestic **3**:322, 323, 324
Manx **12**:*1593*

as predators **10**:*1350*, 1351
Siamese **3**:*324*
territories **12**:1614, 1615
endangered **3**:323
evolution **3**:324
the feline body **3**:322–323
feral **11**:1569
fleas **6**:738; **9**:*1288*
hearing **3**:322
lice **8**:1033
as predators **3**:322–323
purring and roaring **3**:*321*
saber-toothed *see* tigers, saber-toothed
sense of smell **3**:321–322
sight **3**:322
tail **12**:1593
teeth **3**:321; **12**:1605
tongue **12**:1622
whiskers **3**:322; **12**:1628
see also carnivores
cattle
cows **1**:39
licking newborn **12**:*1625*
mammary glands **5**:676
milk composition **7**:998
milk production **4**:545; **9**:1193
digestion by **5**:*694*; **11**:*1453*
diseases **1**:88–89
coast disease **9**:1227
mad cow disease **1**:*89*
domestic **4**:545
lice **8**:1033
saliva **11**:1452
see also ruminants
Caudata *see* salamanders and newts
Cavea porcellis (guinea pig/cavy) **4**:545
cavernicoles **3**:325
Cebidae **10**:1368
Cebuella pygmaea (pygmy marmoset) **10**:1367
Cebus spp. (capuchin monkeys) **3**:402; **10**:1368
Centengraulis mysticetus (Peruvian anchovy) **4**:438
centipedes and millipedes 3:343–346
centipedes **1**:142; **3**:*343*–345
millipedes **1**:142; **3**:*344*, 345–346; **4**:485
Centrocercus urophasianus (sage grouse) **4**:460
Centruroides spp. **11**:1470
Cepaea spp. **4**:525
Cephalocarida **4**:470
Cephalochordata **3**:364
see also amphioxus
cephalopods (Cephalopoda) **8**:1150
foot **5**:698
see also mollusks; octopuses; squid
Cephalopus spp. (West African duiker) **5**:694
Ceramornis **12**:1701
Ceratina spp. **12**:*1693*
Ceratophylloidea **6**:740
ceratopsians **4**:531
Ceratotherium simum (northern white rhinoceros) **5**:606, 607
cercariae **9**:1265
Cercocebus spp. (African mangabey) **3**:406
Cercopithecus aethiops (vervet/African green monkey) **3**:403; **11**:1523

Cervus spp.
C. canadensis (wapiti) **5**:656; **8**:1084, 1133
C. elaphus (red deer) **3**:*409*; **4**:460
Cestoda **6**:737
see also tapeworms
cetaceans *see* whales, porpoises, and dolphins
Cetorhinus maximus (basking shark) **6**:732; **11**:1487
Chactidae **11**:1470
Chaerilidae **11**:1470
Chaetodon spp. (butterfly fish) **2**:283; **6**:732; **11**:*1576*
Chaetognaths **1**:97
chameleons **8**:1053
color change **2**:282; **4**:483; **7**:*908*; **10**:1310
feeding and diet **5**:694–695; **10**:1351
stump-tailed **8**:1051
chamois **9**:*1169*
Charadriidae *see* plovers
Charadriiformes **11**:1471; **12**:1699–1700
Charadrius vociferus (killdeer) **2**:232, *283*; **3**:404
cheetahs **3**:307, 313, 324
speed **3**:322; **8**:1069
chelicerates **1**:97, 141
Chelonia **10**:1415
see also tortoises and turtles
Chelonia mydas (green sea turtle) **4**:*437*; **8**:1134; **11**:*1492*; **12**:*1624*
chickens
domestic **4**:544
pecking order **11**:1523
lice **8**:1033
permaculture **9**:*1280*
prairie **4**:459
chiggers **9**:1264
chigoes **6**:738
childbirth *see* pregnancy and birth
children, growth **3**:358
Chilopoda **3**:343–345
Chimaera (ratfish) **6**:734
chimpanzees **10**:1368–1369
adolescence **1**:28
brain **2**:260
communication **3**:406
with man **3**:406
grip **7**:869
grooming **10**:1370
hunting by **10**:1370
intelligence **7**:967
movement **10**:1370
nests **9**:1206
play **10**:*1329*
pygmy **10**:1368–1369
territories **12**:1615
tools **10**:1369–1370
understanding language **3**:406
chipmunks
eastern **12**:*1608*
winter lethargy **7**:891–892
Chiropotes sp. (bearded sakis) **10**:1368

Chiroptera **2**:173
chitons **8**:*1148*
Chlamydosaurus kingii (frilled lizard) **8**:1052
Chlamyphorus truncatus (lesser fairy armadillo) **1**:104
Choloepus spp. (two-toed sloths) **1**:104
Chondrichthyes **6**:730; **11**:1487; **12**:1671
see also fishes, cartilaginous
Chondrostei **6**:734
chordates 1:97; 3:364–365; 7:972; 12:1671
chrysalids **2**:268, 269
Chrysemys picta (painted turtle) **4**:459
Chrysina spp. (jewel beetles) **2**:283
chuckwallas **4**:486
cicadas **2**:216
cichlids, parental care **6**:733
Cicindela campestris (tiger beetle) **9**:1208
Ciconia ciconia (white stork) **8**:1134
Cimolestes **3**:310
Cimolopteryx **12**:1701
Ciona intestinalis **3**:365
civets **3**:311–312
Cladoselache **11**:1489
clams **3**:371; **8**:*1148*
deep-sea **8**:1149; **9**:1233
farming of **1**:124
gills **10**:1418–1419
Clarias mossambicus (African catfish) **10**:1419
Cliona spp. **11**:1553
clownfish (anemone fish) **1**:126; **3**:*389*, 390; **4**:450; **7**:890, *970*; **11**:1580
Cnemidophorus unipareus (whiptail lizard) **10**:1405
Cnidaria (cnidarians) **1**:94–95
characteristics **7**:980–981
digestion **4**:512; **7**:969–970
nervous system **9**:1204–1205
radial symmetry **7**:969–970
social **11**:1524
stinging cells, used by sea slugs **7**:981
undifferentiated cells **10**:1400
see also corals; jellyfish, sea anemones, and hydras
coatis (coatimundis) **3**:310, 311; **12**:*1725*
cobras **9**:1203; **11**:1518, 1520
tooth structure **11**:*1519*, 1520
Coccinella spp. (ladybug) **7**:*957*; **10**:1351
cockatoos, pink **7**:962
cockroaches 1:*18*, **139; 3:387–388; 5:655; 8:1076; 12:1612, 1665**
resistance to insecticides **9**:1193
cod **12**:*1599*
coelacanths **6**:734; **8**:1048–1049, 1050; **12**:1673
coelenterates *see* Cnidaria
coelomates **9**:1196
cold-blooded animals 3:396–397
dinosaurs as **4**:531
ectothermy **5**:*632*; **12**:1617–1618
enzymes in **5**:631
metabolism **8**:1122–1123
see also amphibians; fish; reptiles
Coleoptera **2**:177

> Bold words with bold page numbers indicate complete articles; bold numbers preceding colons are volume numbers; numbers following colons indicate page numbers; italic page numbers refer to illustrations or other graphics.

Coleorrhyncha 7:884
Collocalia spp. (cave swiftlets) 3:328;
    4:574; 9:*1222*
colonies
    ant 1:119; 7:958–959
    bird 9:1209; 11:1474; 12:1614–1615
Coluber constrictor (racer) 11:1518
Colubridae 11:1519–1520
comb jellies (sea gooseberries) 1:95; 2:207;
    7:969–970
Concentricycloidea 4:569–570
condors 6:752
    California 2:236, 237; 5:607; 12:1725
Condylactis gigantea (pink-tipped anemone)
    7:983
Condylura cristata (star-nosed mole) 7:955
Connochaetes taurinus (wildebeest)
    8:1134–1135, *1136*; 12:1662
Conraua goliath (goliath frog) 6:787;
    12:1642
cooties (human body lice) 8:*1032*, 1033
copepods 1:*141*; 10:1314
    estuarine 11:1492
copperheads 11:1520
coprophagy *see* feces, consumption
Corallus spp. 11:1519
corals 4:452–453
    black 4:*453*
    bleaching 2:*186*; 11:1581
    blue 10:1310
    hard (stony) 4:449, *452*, 453
    reproduction 4:453
    skeleton 4:452; 11:1497–*1498*
    symbiosis with algae 4:449–450, 453;
        11:1581
    see also Cnidaria
cormorants 11:1472, 1473, 1474, 1578;
    12:1701
    flightless (Galápagos cormorant) 6:754;
        9:1169; 11:1473
Corythosaurus 4:531
cottonmouths (water moccasins) 11:1520
cougars 3:323, 324
countershading 2:283
Covenant of the Wild, The (Stephen
    Budiansky) 4:544
cowbirds, brown-headed 4:445; 9:1274
cows *see* cattle
coyotes 4:*539*, 540, 541; 11:1569
coypus (nutrias) 10:*1436*; 11:1465;
    12:*1705*
crabs
    blue 11:1492
    camouflage 2:282
    edible 4:*467*
    fiddler
        biorhythms 2:*218*
        claw waving 4:457; 7:962
        feeding 4:467
    hermit 4:450, 468, *469*; 11:1581
    horseshoe/king 1:93, 130, *140*, 141;
        5:650; 8:*1049*
    molting 9:1158
    movement 1:139
    spider 1:137; 4:484
    see also crustaceans
crabs (lice) 8:1033
cranes 12:1701
    whooping 5:607, 608; 12:1701

Craniata 12:1671
Cratena pilata (striped nudibranch) 7:981
crayfish 3:327, 371
creodonts 3:310
Crepidula fornicata (slipper limpet) 7:890
crickets *see* grasshoppers and crickets
Crinoidea 4:570
crocodiles *see* crocodilians, crocodiles
crocodilians 4:463–466; 8:1050
    alligators
        American 4:459, *463*, 464, *466*; 5:647
        circulatory system 3:374–375
    circulation 4:465
    crocodile or alligator 4:465
    crocodiles
        American 5:*649*
        Indopacific 4:464
        Nile 4:464
        saltwater 4:465
        swimming 11:1578
    distribution 4:463–464
    evolution 4:464; 9:1255
    excretion 5:665
    eyes 4:464
    hearing by 4:562
    and humans 4:464
    movement 4:465
    nutrition 4:466
    physiology 4:465
    reproduction 4:*466*
    senses 4:464–465
Crocodylus spp. 4:463–464; 5:*649*
Crocuta crocuta (spotted hyena) 3:*312*;
    10:1414
Cro-Magnon man 7:917
Crossopterygii 12:1673
Crotalus spp. 3:351; 9:1207, 1222; 11:*1520*
crustaceans 1:97, 141; 4:467–470
    anatomy 4:467–468
    antennae 1:*106*
    chemoreception 12:1595
    courtship 4:457
    excretory systems 5:668
    gas exchange 4:468
        gills 4:468
    hormones 5:612
    larvae 4:469; 10:1314
    limbs 1:139
    locomotion 4:468
    migration 4:469
    nervous system and sensory organs
        4:468–469
        touch receptors 12:1627
    parasitic 4:467–468
    reproduction 4:469
    tail 12:1592
    waste removal 4:468
    see also barnacles; crabs; lobsters; shrimps
Cryptobranchidae 11:1454, 1456
Cryptocercus spp. 3:388; 12:1612
Ctenophora *see* comb jellies
cuckolding 8:1083
cuckoos 1:58–59; 4:445
Cuclotogaster heterographus (chicken-head
    louse) 8:1033
Cuculus spp. (cuckoo) 1:58–59; 4:445
cuds 4:515, 521; 11:*1453*
Culex spp. (mosquitoes) 7:1004; 10:*1419*
    diseases carried by 7:946, 947

culture, human 7:917
Cuon alpinus (dhole) 3:309; 4:540
curlews 2:230; 12:1628
cushion stars 4:569
cuttlefish
    courtship 4:458
    see also mollusks
Cyanea capillata (lion's mane jellyfish)
    7:982
Cyclopes didactylus (silky anteater) 1:103
Cyclorrhapha 6:743
Cyclostomata 12:1671
Cygnus spp. 12:1701
Cylindroiulus punctatus 3:346
Cynomys spp. (prairie dog) 5:694; 9:1207;
    12:1614
Cyprinus carpio (carp) 4:545
Cystophora cristata (hooded seal) 7:998

D

Dactylopius coccus (cochineal scale insect)
    7:884
damselflies
    common blue 12:*1719*
    see also dragonflies and mayflies
Danaus plexippus (monarch butterfly) 2:269,
    270; 4:484; 6:810–811; 7:959–960,
    1003; 8:*1125*, 1135
Daphnia spp. 4:467; 7:1001
Dasypus spp. (long-nosed armadillos) 1:104
Daubentoniidae 10:1366
deer
    antlers 12:1663
        growth and shedding 2:*217*; 7:911
    feet 5:697
    migration 2:210
    mule 3:*350*, 351
    muntjac 12:1663
    musk 12:1606, 1663
    red 2:210; 4:460
        intersexual competition 3:*409*
        strutting 8:1084
    in urban areas 12:1665
    vocal communication 8:1083–1084
Deima 9:1232
Deinonychus 4:531
Demospongiae 11:1553
Dendroaspis polylepis (black mamba)
    11:1518, 1520
Dendrobates spp. (poison-dart/poison-arrow
    frogs) 4:483–484; 5:677; 6:*788*
Dendrocopus major (great spotted
    woodpecker) 2:232
Dendrocygna bicolor (fulvous tree duck)
    4:460
Dendroica pennsylvanica (chestnut-sided
    warbler) 3:402
Dermanector spp. (wood tick) 1:*131*; 9:*1264*
Dermaptera 4:563
Dermochelys coriacea (leatherback turtle)
    11:1492
Desmana moschata (Russian desman) 7:955
desmans 7:955
Desmodus rotundus (common vampire bat)
    1:60; 2:174; 4:574; 11:*1526*–1527
deuterostomes 7:972
dholes 3:309; 4:540, 541
Diadema antillarium 3:403–404
Diatrymas 6:755

Diceros bicornis (black rhinoceros) 11:*1579*
Dicrostonyx spp. (lemming) 10:1334;
    12:1654
Didelphis virginiana (Virginian/Northern
    opossum) 5:*650*; 8:1080; 11:*1541*
Digenea 6:736–737
    see also flukes
dikdiks 12:*1662*, 1663
**dimorphism and polymorphism
    4:524–525**
    polymorphism in cnidarian colonies
        7:981
    sexual dimorphism 4:458, *524*–525
    in birds 4:459, *524*
dingos 4:*542*
dinosaurs 4:526–531
    classification 4:529–531
    eggs 4:*526*, 528
    evolution, coevolution 3:391
    evolution of birds from? 4:529
    extinction 2:185; 4:528–529
        due to an impacting space object 4:528,
        529; 5:624, 659
        due to climate change 4:528–529
    fossils 4:*527*
        see also fossils
    life of 4:527–528
    warm- or cold-blooded 4:531
Diomedea spp. 2:232; 4:456; 5:*658*; 6:*752*
Diplocentridae 11:1470
Diplodocus 4:530
Diplopoda 3:345–346
Dipodomys spp. (kangaroo rat) 4:501;
    5:669, *670*, 699; 9:1207; 10:1436
Diptera *see* flies
Dismorphia amphione 2:286
Dispholidus typhus (boomslang) 11:1518
Ditylenchus dipsaci 10:1321
dodos 1:19; 5:*678*; 7:977
dogfish 6:734; 11:1489
    embryos 5:*597*
    piked 11:1490
dogs 3:309; 4:539–542
    African wild 3:307, 309; 4:540, 542
        breeding 11:1524
        communication 3:404; 4:542
        dominance 11:1524
        hunting 7:979
    breeding, selective 4:*540*–541
    bush 4:540, *541*
    characteristics 4:539–540
    feet 4:539
    classification 4:542; 12:1601
    conditioning experiments on 3:411, 412
    diseases 1:89–90
    dog-wolf hybrids 4:541–542
    domestic 1:37–38; 4:*540*–541, 544
    dominance and submission signals 3:402
    endangered 4:541
    evolution 4:540
    feet 5:697
    feral 11:1569
    fleas 6:738
    lice 8:1033
    nose, wet 12:1622
    panting 11:1506; 12:*1622*
    Pavlov's, and conditioned reflexes
        9:*1271*, 1272
    sense of smell 11:1515

sheepdogs 1:*83*
social behavior 4:540
in space 11:1534
training 3:*413*
dolphins *see* whales, porpoises, and dolphins
domestication 1:38; **4:543–546**; 5:659
of cats 3:323
of dogs 4:*540–541*
of ungulates 12:1662
dormice 7:*891*; 8:*1069*
doves 6:776
dragonflies and mayflies 4:550–552
dragonflies
northern limit 12:1718
wings 6:750
mayflies 1:*142*
see also damselflies
dragons, Komodo 7:977; 8:1051; 12:1717
Dromaius novaehollandiae (emu) 5:698;
6:756
dromedaries 4:501
drones, honeybee 12:1694
Drosera spp. (sundew) 3:*314–316*; 5:696
Drosophila spp. (fruit fly)
circadian clocks 2:218
courtship 3:402; 4:455, 456–457; 7:962
early genetic studies on 9:1164, 1193
embryo development 5:597–598
memory 8:1105
mutation 5:599; 6:746
nurse cells 5:589
reproduction 7:958
for scientific research 1:93; 6:746
speciation 5:657
Dryopithecus see Proconsul
ducks 12:1701
communication in the egg 3:405
countercurrent heat-exchange system
7:901
courtship 1:85
ruddy 12:1700
sea 11:1472
shoveler 5:695
steamer 6:754
torrent 12:1701
see also tree ducks
Dugesia 5:685; 6:735
duikers, West African 5:694
Dynastes hercules (rhinoceros/hercules
beetle) 2:*177*

E

eagles
bald 2:235
effects of DDT 2:235–236; 4:481;
5:680; 9:1287; 10:1343–1344
territories 12:1614
harpy 2:234
earthworms 1:96
aortic arches (hearts) 3:372; 7:876
clones 3:382
excretion 5:667; 7:989
feeding and digestion 4:512–513
reproduction 10:1407–1408
respiration 10:1418
skeleton 11:1496
and the soil 1:99, 100; 11:1532
touch receptors 12:1627
see also annelids

earwigs 4:563–564
earworms, corn 2:270
echidnas 4:445; 9:*1162–1163*
echinoderms 1:97; 4:567–570; 7:972
bioluminescence 2:206
classification 4:569–570
endoskeleton 4:567; 11:1499
evolution 4:568
locomotion 4:567–568
nervous system 4:569; 9:1205
tube feet 4:567, *568*, 569, *570*
water vascular system 4:567; 12:1670
Echinoidea 4:570
Echinus spp. 4:*570*; 8:*1126*; 11:*1499*
Echis spp. (saw-scaled vipers) 11:1518
Echiura 1:96
echolocation 4:562, 571–574; 12:1657
by bats 1:19; 2:*174–175*; 4:562,
572–573; 7:873; 9:1222
by birds 9:*1222*
by mammals 8:1071
by shrews 8:1071
by whales and dolphins 4:572; 7:873;
8:1135; 12:1708
Ectopistes migratorius (passenger pigeon)
5:659; 11:1522
Ectoprocta 1:96
Edentata 1:103–104
eels 12:1592
electric 4:485; 6:728
European, migration 2:210
moray 11:1576
Elaphe obsoleta (rat snake) 11:*1517*
Elasmobranchii 11:1487; 12:1671
elasmobranchs 6:734
uterine milk 7:997
see also rays; sharks; skates
electricity, in fish 4:485; 6:728, 734
Electrophorus electricus (electric eel) 4:485
Eledone cirrhosa 11:*1577*
elephant birds 6:755
elephants and mammoths 5:593–596
elephants 5:593, 594–596
African 4:514; 5:*593*, 595; 8:1074
Asian 5:593, 595, *596*
differences between African and Asian
5:595
duels 4:460
effect on the environment 5:594
evolution 5:593
feeding 5:696
gestation 8:1074
heartbeat 7:880
teeth and tusks 5:594–595; 12:1605
trunk 5:595; 10:*1374*
young 10:*1348*
mammoths 5:593; 6:764, 782; 9:1256
elephant snouts 3:405
Elephantus rufescens (rufous elephant shrew)
7:*956*
Elephas maximus (Asian elephant) 5:593,
595, *596*
elk (moose) 8:1084; 10:1350; 12:1591,
1619
emus 5:698; 6:756
Enaliornis 6:754
Enallagma cyathigerum (common blue
damselfly) 12:*1719*
Enhydra lutris (sea otter) 3:*308*; 4:439

Enterobius vermicularis 9:1265
entomology 5:620–621
see also insects
Entoprocta 1:96
eolids 7:981
Eoraptor lunensis 4:530
Ephemera spp. 4:*551*
Ephemeroptera 4:550
Epinephelus spp. (groupers) 6:732
Epipristis nelearia 2:*281*
Epomophorus wahlbergi (Wahlberg's fruit bat)
2:*175*
Equus spp. 2:194
E. burchelli (Burchell's zebra) 3:391, *392*,
407; 8:*1074*
E. przewalski (Przewalski's horse) 5:*712*;
12:*1603*
E. somalicus (Somali wild ass) 12:*1659*
see also horses
Erasipteron larischi 4:552
Eretmochelys imbricata (hawksbill turtle)
12:1624
Erithacus spp.
E. rubeculaare (Eurasian robin) 12:1614
E. rubecula (robin) 1:29–30; 8:1136
ermines 9:1159; 12:*1591*
Erythrocebus patas (patas monkey) 3:406
Eschrichtius robustus (gray whale) 8:1134;
10:*1417*
Essay on the Principle of Population (Malthus)
4:479; 5:653; 10:1345
estivation *see* hibernation, estivation
Eubalaena spp. (right whales) 12:1709
Eudimorphodon 10:1391
Euglandina spp. 2:185, 196
Euglossa sp. 9:*1240*
Eugomphodus taurus (gray nurse shark)
11:*1500*
Eunectes spp. (anacondas) 11:1518, 1519
Eupagurus spp. (hermit crab) 4:450, 468
Europelma mesomelas (bird-eating spider)
11:*1548*
Eurymylus 10:1393
Eurypelma smithi (red-kneed tarantula)
11:*1546*
eurypterids 1:132, 141
eutherians (Eutheria) 8:1074; 12:1674
placenta 8:1074
evisceration 4:570
Exallias brevis (coral blenny) 2:282
Exatosoma tiaratum 8:*1018*
excrement *see* feces
Exocetidae 6:750
extremophiles 5:681–682, *683*

F

Falconidae 2:235
Falconiformes 2:235–236
falconry, history 2:237
falcons 2:234
peregrine 2:235, 236, 237; 12:1665
Falco spp.
F. peregrinus (peregrine falcon) 2:235,
236, 237; 12:1665

F. sparverius (American kestrel) 11:1569
F. tinnunculus (common kestrel) 11:*1569*
Fannia spp. (housefly) 5:699
Fasciola spp. (common fluke) 6:*735*
feather stars 4:568, *569*, 570
feces 4:519
consumption (coprophagy) 4:515–516;
9:1229; 10:1393; 11:1453, 1564
elephant 5:594
elimination 5:665
feeding 5:693–696
behavior for survival 1:86
cannibalism 8:1076
carnivores *see* carnivores
communal 11:1522
deposit 4:439
filter 4:439; 5:695
by crustaceans 4:467
by sharks 10:*1314*
herbivores *see* herbivores
heterotrophism 8:1117, *1124–1126*;
9:1252
omnivores *see* omnivores
by phagocytosis 2:240; 3:336, *337*;
5:693; 7:929, 938
prenuptial 8:1084
scavengers 5:695
and territoriality 12:1613
Felidae 3:312–313
see also cats
Feliformia 3:311–313
Felis spp. 3:313, 324
F. lynx (lynx) 3:324; 10:1350
F. serval (serval cat) 3:321; 4:445
F. silvestris catus see cats, domestic
fennecs 4:*500*, 501, 539; 9:1220
Fennecus zerda (fennec) 4:501, 539; 9:1220
feral animals 4:543; 11:1569
fetalization *see* paedomorphosis
fetus 10:1355
accepted by mother's immune system
7:941
bone development 2:248, *249*
brain development 2:260
circulatory system 3:375; 7:878
effects of rubella on 7:950
exocrine gland development 5:673
fetal tissue to treat Parkinson's disease
2:261
fishlike characteristics 12:1594
screening 2:191, 222
amniocentesis 3:367; 4:477; 10:*1358*
chorionic villus sampling (CVS) 3:367;
4:477; 10:1358
karyotyping 3:367
X rays 12:1713
spleen 8:1064
filarial worms, parasitic 8:1065
finches
cactus ground 2:*185*
Galápagos 2:*185*; 5:656–657, 696
and Darwin 4:478; 9:1192
fireflies 2:178, *206*, 217; 3:404
courtship 4:457

fireworms **2**:216
fish 6:*727–734*; **12**:1671
  Age of **12**:1672
  alarm signals **3**:403
  anemone **7**:890
  angler **6**:729
  antifreeze proteins **4**:472; **10**:1332
  aquarium **1**:*125*, 128
  bioluminescent **2**:205; **6**:729
  body shapes **6**:727, *731*
  bony **6**:727, 734; **12**:1672–1673
  brain **2**:257, 258, 259
  buoyancy **6**:*728–729*; **11**:1577
  butterfly **2**:282; **6**:732; **11**:*1576*
  camouflage **2**:283
  cartilaginous **3**:319; **6**:727, 733–734;
    11:*1499–1500*; **12**:1671, *1672*
    see also rays; sharks; skates
  cave-dwelling **3**:*326*, 327
  circulatory system **3**:*373*
    heart **7**:*877*
  classification **6**:733–734
  coloration **6**:*732*
  communication **3**:405
  courtship **4**:457, 458
  deep sea **6**:729
    bioluminescence **6**:729
    floor **9**:*1232*
    jaws **7**:979
  effect of acid rain on **1**:17
  eggs **5**:587–588
  electricity **4**:485; **6**:728, 734
  embryo development **5**:598
  evolution **6**:*730*; **7**:978
    to amphibians **1**:*65*; **6**:790; **11**:1456
  excretion **5**:669–670; **6**:732; **12**:1666
    and osmosis **5**:669; **6**:732
  eyes **5**:685–686; **12**:*1688*
  feeding and digestion **6**:732
  fins **6**:729; **11**:1577
  flashlight **2**:205
  flying **6**:730, 750
  four-eyed **6**:731
  freshwater **11**:1459
  frog **6**:730
  fusiform **11**:1576
  hermaphrodite **7**:890
  jawless **6**:727, 730, 733; **7**:978;
    12:1671, 1672
    and evolution of the pancreas **9**:1261
    skeleton **11**:1499–1500
  jaws **6**:730; **7**:978, 979
  labyrinth **9**:1206
  lateral line **4**:*561–562*; **6**:731
  light perception and sight **6**:731
  lobe-finned (fleshy-finned) **6**:734;
    11:1456; **12**:1672–1673
  of mangroves **11**:1494
  man-of-war **11**:1580
  marine **11**:1459
  migration **10**:1426
  molting **9**:1158
  movement **6**:729–730
    see also fish, swimming
  nesting **9**:*1206*
  nocturnally active **9**:1220
  pancreas **9**:1261
  parrot **4**:451, 453
  puffer, poisons **1**:50; **4**:485

rat-tail **9**:*1232*
ray-finned **6**:734; **12**:*1672*
reproduction **6**:732–733
respiration **6**:727–728
  gills **6**:727–728; **10**:1419
river **10**:1426, *1427*
sargasso **2**:282
schooling **3**:402; **6**:729, 730–731
scorpion **2**:*282*
sexual selection in **11**:1486
Siamese fighting, nests **9**:*1206*
sounds **3**:405
structure **6**:*727*
sweetlip, lined **6**:729
swim bladders **3**:405; **6**:728, 729
swimming **6**:729–730; **9**:1178–1179;
  11:*1576–1577*
  sharks **11**:1500, 1577
tail **12**:1592
taste organs **12**:1596
teeth **6**:732
temperature **6**:731
territories **12**:*1613*, 1615
thermotaxis **12**:1647
tongue **12**:1621
tripod **9**:1232
warm-blooded or warm-bodied
  6:*731*; **11**:1488
Fissipedia **3**:307–308
flamingos **12**:1700
  color **10**:*1311*
  courtship **4**:460
  crop milk **7**:997
  feeding **5**:695
  greater **12**:*1699*
flatworms 1:95; **6**:*735–737*
  digestive system **4**:*512*
  excretion **5**:666; **7**:989
  nervous system **7**:970; **9**:*1205*
  planarian **6**:735, 737
    eyespots **5**:685
  regeneration by **6**:735, 737;
    10:*1400*
  see also flukes; tapeworms
fleas 6:*738–740*
  and the Black Death **6**:740; **9**:1287
  cat **6**:738; **9**:*1288*
  human **6**:740
  jumping **6**:*738, 739*
  as parasites **6**:738–739
  water *see* water fleas
flickers, yellow-shafted, decline
  3:410
flies 6:*743–746*
  antennae **1**:106; **6**:743
  apple maggot **3**:402
  chemoreception/taste **12**:*1595*
  economic importance **6**:746
  eyes **6**:*743*
  flesh flies **6**:773
  flight **6**:744, 750
  and forensic science **6**:746
  fruit **6**:746
  fruit/vinegar *see* **Drosophila** spp.
  houseflies **6**:743, 745
    DDT resistant **4**:480
    feet **5**:699; **6**:745
    flight **9**:1180
    potential populations **10**:1345

larvae (maggots) **6**:744–*745*
  phototaxis **12**:1647
life cycle **6**:744–745
mouthparts **6**:743–744, 745
parasitic **2**:196
plant pollination **10**:1337
robber **6**:744
sand **7**:946
scorpion **8**:1084
spreading disease **6**:*744, 746*
swatting **12**:1627
tsetse, and sleeping sickness **1**:88; **7**:946
vision **5**:688
warble **6**:746
wings **6**:743
see also mosquitoes
flight 6:*747–752*
  adaptations **6**:750–751
  advantages and disadvantages **6**:749–750
  in bats **2**:*173*, 175; **6**:748; **12**:1593
  in birds *see* birds, flight
  evolution **9**:1254–1255
  human attempts **6**:*751*
  in insects **9**:1180
    butterflies and moths **9**:1180
    dragonflies and mayflies **4**:550–551
    flies **9**:1180
  parachuting and gliding **6**:*749*
  soaring **6**:*752*; **8**:1134
flightless birds *see* birds, flightless
flounders **2**:282; **4**:483
  Arctic, and tomatoes **2**:225
flukes **3**:390–391; **6**:*735*, 736–737;
  9:*1267*, 1268
  blood **6**:736, 737
  excretion **7**:970
  life cycle **9**:1265–1266
  see also flatworms
flycatchers, spotted **6**:750
flying foxes, common **2**:174
fog harvesters **4**:501
foraminiferans **9**:1232; **10**:1314
forests, birds *see* birds, forest
Forficula auricularia (common earwig)
  4:*563*, 564
Forficulina **4**:563
Formica spp. **1**:*118*; **4**:483; **7**:963
fossas **3**:313
fossils 6:*781–784*
  amphibian **11**:1456
  annelid **1**:99
  bacteria **2**:168; **6**:784; **10**:1380
  body fossils **6**:781
  complete preservation **6**:782–783
  dating **6**:783–784
  diatom **10**:1313
  dinosaur **4**:*527*
  earliest **3**:332
  earwig **4**:564
  formation **6**:781–782
  fossil, lagerstätten **9**:1256
  horses **9**:1256
  human
    "Lucy" **6**:784; **7**:*914*, 915
    Piltdown Man hoax **6**:782; **7**:917
  lagomorph **10**:1393
living 8:*1048–1050*
  and paleobiology **9**:1254–1257
  petrifaction **6**:*782*; **12**:1638

preserved in amber **6**:*781*, 782
of pterosaurs **10**:*1391*
and the study of evolution **6**:784
to map extinction **5**:678–679
trace fossils **6**:781, 783; **9**:1257
founder effect **9**:1194
foxes **4**:540
  Arctic **9**:*1159*; **12**:1619
  bat-eared **4**:540
  desert sand **4**:501
  fennec **4**:*500*, 501, 539; **9**:1220
  kit **4**:501
  red **11**:1523; **12**:*1671*
Fratercula cirrhata (tufted puffin) **11**:*1471*
Fregata spp. **4**:455
frigate birds **2**:250; **4**:455; **11**:1473, 1474
Fringilla teydea (canary) **9**:1273
frogmouths **6**:776
frogs and toads 6:*787–790*
  adaptations **6**:789
  avoiding predators **6**:*788*
  body shape **6**:787
  calls **4**:458–459; **6**:790
  courtship **4**:*458–459*
  distribution **6**:788
  ears **6**:789
  estivation **7**:892
  evolution **6**:790
  excretion **5**:666
  eyes **6**:788–789
  feeding **6**:790
  frogs
    breathing **10**:1422
    clawed **9**:1290
    common **5**:*715*
    crab-eating **6**:788
    eggs **5**:*589*
    embryo formation **5**:599
    external fertilization by **5**:*715*
    flying **5**:699
    goliath **6**:787; **12**:1642
    leopard **6**:787
    mating behavior **11**:*1527–1528*
    nests **9**:1206
    poison arrow (poison dart frogs)
      4:483–484, 485; **5**:677; **6**:*788*, 790
    swimming **11**:1578
    tree **5**:699; **6**:787, 790; **11**:*1527*
  lungs **8**:*1060*
  metamorphosis **8**:1125; **10**:1308
  molting **9**:1158
  reproduction and development **6**:*790*
    direct development **6**:789
  spleen **11**:1551
  tadpoles **3**:403; **5**:696; **6**:*789*, 790;
    7:1005; **8**:1125
    change into frogs **3**:335; **10**:1308
    phototaxis **12**:1647
    respiratory system **10**:1418
  temperature regulation **3**:397; **6**:789
  toads
    American **3**:403
    cane **1**:*51*; **2**:*196*
    estivation **7**:892
    Malayan/Asian horned **6**:*787*
    midwife **6**:*790*
    spadefoot **4**:458–459, 500–501; **5**:699;
      6:790; **7**:892; **12**:*1673*
    Surinam **6**:789

tongue **12**:1621
see also amphibians
fulmars **11**:1474
fungus gnats *see* glowworms
"fuzzy raptor" **4**:529

G

Gadus morrhua (cod) **12**:*1599*
galagos (bush babies) **9**:1294; **10**:1366;
  12:*1686*
Galago senegalensis (lesser northern galago)
  9:1294; **12**:*1686*
Galenys pyrenaicus (Pyrenean desman)
  7:955
Gallinago gallinago (common snipe)
  12:*1593*
Gallodactylus svevicus **10**:*1391*
gannets **2**:*231*; **11**:*1472–1473*, 1474
garpike (long-nosed pike) **7**:978
Gasterosteus aculeatus (three-spined
  stickleback) **4**:456, 485; **7**:*1002*
gastropods **8**:1150
  feet **5**:698
  mucus **9**:*1172*
gastrotrichs **1**:95
gaurs **4**:545
Gavialis gangeticus (gharial) **4**:446, 463–464
gavials (gharials) **4**:446, 463–464
Gazella thomsoni (Thomson's gazelle) **4**:460;
  12:*1662*, 1663
gazelles **12**:*1726*
  Thomson's **4**:460; **12**:1662, 1663
geckos **5**:699; **8**:1052, 1053; **9**:1221
geese **12**:1701
  Canada **11**:*1521*
  communication **3**:404
  fixed action patterns **1**:83; **7**:962
  flocks **3**:402
  greylag **7**:962
  Hawaiian nene **11**:*1482*
  migrating **2**:216; **8**:1134
    flight **6**:752
genets **3**:311–312
Geospiza scandens (cactus ground finch)
  2:185
Geospiza spp. (finches) **2**:185
Geotrupes spp. (dung beetles) **11**:*1464*
Gerardia savaglia (black coral) **4**:453
gestation **10**:1352
gharials (gavials) **4**:446, 463–464
gibbons **3**:406; **10**:1368, 1370
gifts, during courtship **4**:459; **8**:1084
gila monsters **8**:1053
Giraffa camelopardalis see giraffes
giraffes
  blood pressure **3**:*374*
  evolution of long neck **1**:20
    Lamarck's theory **1**:21; **9**:*1191*
  feeding by **5**:694; **11**:*1451*, 1452
  horns **7**:910, *911*
  mating **8**:*1084*
  neck vertebrae **11**:*1498*
  nerve cells **3**:329
  tongue **12**:1622
Glaucidium brasilianum (cactus ferruginous
  pygmy owl) **2**:273
Glaucomys spp. (flying squirrels) **6**:*749*;
  12:*1591*
gliders **8**:1080

gliding **6**:*749*
Globodera rostochiensis (golden nematode)
  9:1195
glochidia (immature mussels) **8**:1149
Glossinia spp. (tsetse fly) *see* flies, tsetse
glowworms (fungus gnats) **2**:205; **3**:328
gnathostomes **6**:730
Gnathostomulida **1**:95
gnats
  fungus (glow-worms) **2**:205; **3**:328
  larvae **11**:1577–1578
goats
  domestication **4**:544
  saliva **11**:1452
  see also ruminants
godwits **12**:1628
Gorilla gorilla see gorillas
gorillas **1**:*28*; **10**:*1365*, 1368–1369
  albino **9**:*1190*
  endangered **10**:1367
  grip **7**:869
  mountain, Dian Fossey and **6**:779–780;
    10:1367
  movement **10**:1370
  sense of smell **8**:1070
  social groups **10**:1369; **11**:1523
  threat displays **8**:1073
goshawks **2**:235
grasshoppers and crickets 7:*958*
  circulatory system **3**:371–*372*
  coloration **12**:1618
  crickets
    biological control of **2**:196
    cave **3**:325
  grasshoppers, temperature regulation
    12:1618
  life cycle **7**:1004–1005
  molts **8**:1126
  nervous system **9**:*1205*
  wings **6**:750
grazers **5**:693–694
  and desertification **4**:503
  on grasslands **11**:1464–1465
grebes **11**:1471, 1472, 1473, 1578
groupers **6**:732; **12**:*1688*
grouse
  sage **4**:460
  of the taiga **12**:1591
Gruiformes **12**:1701
Grus spp. **5**:607, 608; **12**:1701
Guara rubra (scarlet ibis) **10**:1311
guenons **10**:1369
guillemots **11**:1474
guinea pigs **4**:545
gulls **11**:1471
  egg incubation **1**:83–84
  glaucous-winged **11**:*1458*
  herring **5**:*657*; **11**:1471
    instincts **7**:*961*
  lesser black-headed **5**:657
  as pests **11**:1474
  ring species **5**:657
Gulo gulo (wolverine) **12**:*1654*
guppies **1**:*127*
Gymnogyps (*Vultur*) *californianus* (California
  condor) **2**:236; **5**:607
Gymnophiona **1**:64; **2**:275
Gynaephora groenlandica (woolly bear
  caterpillar) **4**:472

Gyps ruppellii (Ruppell's griffon vulture)
  2:*237*
Gyrinusis spp. **2**:284

H

hadrosaurs **4**:530–531
Haemotopinus vituli (long-nosed cattle louse)
  8:1033
hagfish **6**:733; **11**:1499
  excretion **6**:732
  splenic tissue **11**:1551
  tongue **12**:1622
Haliaeetus leucocephalus (bald eagle)
  2:235–236; **4**:481; **5**:680; **12**:1614
Halichondria panicea **11**:*1553*
Haliplanella luciae (striped anemone) **7**:983
hamsters **7**:880
  molting **9**:1159
  pheromones **9**:1294
Haplochromis spp. **11**:1486
Haplorhini **10**:1365
Hardy-Weinberg law **5**:655
harems *see* mating, polygyny
hares *see* rabbits and hares
Harpia harpyja (harpy eagle) **2**:234
harvestmen **1**:141
hawkmoths, five-spotted **4**:483
hawks **2**:*234*, 235; **5**:687
  fish *see* ospreys
hearing 7:872–875; **8**:1070–1071
  and aging **1**:35
  colored (chromesthesia) **11**:1516
  in humans **7**:*872*, 873–875
  loss and deafness **7**:873, *874*–875
  measurement **7**:874
  see also echolocation
hedgehogs **7**:955–956
  hibernation **7**:892
Heleomyza serrata **3**:328
Heliconius spp. **2**:286; **9**:1293
Helicoverpa spp. **2**:270
Heliopora caerulea (blue coral) **10**:1310
Helix aspersa (common snail) **8**:*1150*
hellbenders **11**:1454
Hemichordata **1**:97; **3**:365; **7**:*1006*
Hemimerina **4**:563, 564
Hemiptera 7:883–885
herbivores **5**:693–694; **8**:1071, *1072*;
  9:1228–1229
  cellulose digestion **9**:1228; **10**:1380,
    1393; **12**:1661
  digestive systems **4**:514–*515*, 520, 521;
    11:1563
  in the food web **6**:767
  teeth **4**:517; **7**:979; **8**:1070; **12**:*1603*,
    1605
  see also ruminants
herds **2**:284; **12**:1662–1663
herons, black **12**:*1701*
Herpestes spp. (mongoose) **3**:313; **11**:1520
Herpestidae **3**:313
Hesperiidae **2**:268
Hesperornis **12**:1701
Heteractis magnifica **7**:970

Heterocephalus glaber (naked mole rat) **1**:60;
  4:*486*; **10**:1438; **11**:*1523*
Heteroptera **7**:883, 884
Hexactinellida **11**:1553
hibernation 3:396, 420; **7**:891–893;
  8:1072
  estivation **7**:892; **8**:1072
    desert animals **4**:500, 501
    frogs and toads **7**:892, *893*
  heart rate during **7**:880
Hilara sartor **4**:459
Hippocampus spp. (sea horse) **6**:729–730, *733*
Histrio histrio (sargasso fish) **2**:282
hoatzins **1**:134; **6**:777
Holocephali **12**:1671
Holostei **6**:734
Holothuria spp. **4**:570
Holothuroidea **4**:570
hominines **10**:1360–1361
Homoptera **7**:883, 884
Homo spp.
  H. erectus (Java man) **3**:293; **7**:*915*, 916;
    10:1361
    migration **7**:917; **10**:1361, 1363
    skin color **9**:1227
  H. habilis **2**:258; **7**:916; **10**:1361
  H. neanderthalensis (Neanderthal man)
    7:*912*, 917; **10**:1362
  H. sapiens **10**:1362–1364
    migration **10**:1363
    prehistoric creativity **10**:*1363*–1364
  H. sapiens sapiens **7**:916
    Cro-Magnon man **7**:917
Homotherium **3**:310
honeybees **12**:1693–*1694*
  antennae **1**:106
  beeswax **12**:*1702*
  comb cells **12**:*1702*
  communication **3**:402, *403*; **12**:1694
  defense **4**:484
  drones **12**:1694
  honey from **12**:*1694*
  metamorphosis **7**:1006
  pheromones **9**:*1294*
  pollination by **10**:1336–1337
  queen **9**:*1294*; **11**:*1524*; **12**:1694
  royal jelly **12**:1694
  social groups **11**:*1524*
  swarms **12**:1694
  temperature regulation **3**:397
  vision **12**:1687
honeycreepers **11**:1542
honeyguides **3**:403; **6**:761; **11**:1582
hookworms **1**:90
hornets **4**:484; **12**:1692–1693
horsehair worms **1**:96
horses
  courtship **4**:460
  digestion by **9**:1228
  distribution **2**:194
  domestication **4**:545
  evolution **5**:659; **6**:784; **9**:1255
  fighting **4**:457
  fossil **9**:1256

horses *(continued)*
  hooves **5**:697
  lactation **7**:998
  Przewalski's **5**:*712*
  tail **12**:1594
  teeth **12**:*1603*, 1604
  vision **12**:1687
horseshoe worms **1**:96
human evolution 4:479; **7**:**912–917**
  Australopithecus see Australopithecus spp.
  bipedalism **1**:22; **7**:871, 914, *916*;
     10:1360, 1361
    and the aquatic ape **7**:913
  continuing **9**:1193
  and culture **7**:917
  ears as indicators of **4**:561
  first humans **7**:915–917
  fossil skeletons
    "Lucy" **6**:784; **7**:*914*, 915
    Piltdown Man hoax **6**:782; **7**:917
  from apes **7**:913–915
  Homo see Homo spp.
  Proconsul (Dryopithecus) **7**:914–915
  Ramapithecus **7**:916
  sites of **7**:917
humans
  adaptations for upright walking **1**:22
  altruism **1**:60
  evolution *see* human evolution
  life expectancy **10**:1348
  preserved **6**:782–783
  sexual selection in **11**:1486
  sociobiology **11**:1528
hummingbirds
  bill **9**:*1275*
  feet **2**:231
  intraspecific competition **3**:*408*
  migration **8**:1136
  nests **9**:1208
  pollination by **1**:78–79; **10**:*1337*–1338
  ruby-throated **12**:1718
  rufous **3**:*408*
  territories **12**:1614
hunter-gatherers, ancient **10**:1362
hunting
  by prehistoric humans **10**:1364
  cooperative **1**:58
Hyaena spp. **3**:312
Hyaenidae **3**:312
Hyalophora cecropia (cecropia silkmoth) **2**:270
hybridization
  animal **11**:1480
    dog-wolf **4**:541–542
    donkey-horse (mules) **4**:546; **11**:1480,
     1540, 1541
    sheep-goat **11**:1540
hydras **7**:981–*982*; **10**:*1405*
Hydrochoerus hydrochoeris (capybara)
  10:1436, 1437; **11**:1465
Hydrodamalis gigas (Steller's sea cow) **2**:186
hydroids **7**:980, 982
Hydrozoa **7**:981–982, *983*
Hydrurga leptonyx (leopard seal) **10**:*1334*
hyenas **3**:*312*; **9**:1223; **10**:1414
Hylobates spp. **3**:*406*
Hylobatidae **10**:1368
Hylobittacus spp. **8**:1084
Hymenoptera **12**:1611
  see also ants; wasps and bees

Hympolimnas misippus **2**:270
Hynobiidae **11**:1456
Hyperchiria nausica **2**:284
hypermetamorphosis **2**:178
hypodonts **11**:1489
hyraxes, related to elephants **5**:*594*
Hystricognathi **10**:1437, 1438

I

ibises **5**:648; **12**:1700
  scarlet **10**:1311
ice worms **9**:1233
Ichthyophiidae **2**:275–276
Ichthyostega **6**:790; **11**:1456
iguanas **8**:1053
  at high altitude **9**:1169
  marine **8**:*1052*
Iguanodon **4**:527
Indicator indicator (honeyguide) **3**:403
Indriidae **10**:1366
Indri indri (indris) **9**:1221
indrises **9**:1221
insectivores 7:**954–956**; **8**:1072
insects 1:142; **7**:**957–960**
  anatomy **7**:*957–958*
  antennae, types **1**:105
  bioluminescence **2**:178, 205, *206*; **4**:457
  brain **1**:140
  in caves **3**:327
  circulatory system **3**:371–*372*
  classification **7**:960
  coloration **7**:959–960
    butterflies and moths **2**:270–*271*
    in phasmids **8**:1017
  communication **12**:1647
  courtship **4**:456–457
  diapause **2**:269; **6**:745; **7**:1005
  diseases carried by **7**:945–946, *947*
    lice **7**:946, 950; **8**:1032; **9**:1267
  endocrine glands **5**:612
  entomology 5:**620–621**
  evolution **7**:958
  excretion **5**:668–669; **7**:989
  exoskeleton **7**:957–958; **11**:1505–1506
  eyes **5**:687–*688*
    and night vision **9**:1221
  flight **4**:550–551; **9**:1180
  hearing **7**:872, 873
  hemimetabolous **8**:1126
  and humans **7**:960
  memory **8**:1105
  molting (ecdysis) **7**:1005; **8**:1126;
    9:1157–1158
  nesting **9**:*1208*
  numbers **7**:958
  pollination by **6**:*761*; **7**:890; **9**:1240;
    10:*1335*, 1336–1337; **12**:*1693*
  reproduction **7**:959
  respiration **10**:*1419*–1420
  social **2**:203; **4**:524; **7**:958–*959*; **11**:*1524*
    pheromones **11**:*1524*
    torpor **12**:1618
  swimming **11**:1577–1578
  taste **12**:*1595*
  temperature regulation **3**:397
  touch receptors **12**:1627
  wings **7**:958
International Species Information System
  (ISIS) **12**:1724

invertebrates 7:**969–972**
  abdomen **1**:13
  asymmetrical **7**:969
  circulatory systems **3**:372–373
  courtship **4**:456–458
  digestive systems **4**:*512*–513
  embryo development **5**:597–598
  endocrine glands **5**:612
  excretory systems **5**:666–669; **7**:989
  feet **5**:698
  hormones **7**:908
  immunity **7**:928
  integuments **11**:1505–1506
  memory storage **8**:1105
  molting (ecdysis) **7**:1005; **9**:1157–1158
  mucous membranes **9**:1172
  protostomes **7**:971–972
  pseudocoelomates **7**:971; **9**:1196
  regeneration of body parts
    10:1399–1400, *1401*
  success compared with vertebrates
    12:1674
  symmetry
    bilateral **6**:735; **7**:970–971
    radial **7**:969–970
  tails **12**:1592
  taste **12**:1595
  vertebrates are larger than **12**:1673
  vision **5**:688; **12**:1685–1686
Isoptera **12**:1611
Ixodes spp. **1**:131, 132

J

jacanas **8**:*1083*; **12**:1700
jackals **4**:540
  simien *see* wolves, Ethiopian
jackrabbits **4**:500
  antelope **10**:1392
Jaculus spp. (African jerboa) **4**:501
jaguars **2**:284; **3**:324
Java man *see Homo* spp, *H. erectus*
jays, scrub **1**:58
jellyfish, sea anemones, and hydras
  7:**980–983**
  hydras **7**:981–*982*
    budding **7**:982; **10**:*1405*
    feeding and digestion **4**:*512*; **7**:981
    nerve net **7**:982; **9**:*1205*
    skeleton **11**:1495
    see also Cnidaria
  hydroids **7**:980, 982
  hydrozoans
    by-the-wind sailor **7**:983
    Portuguese man-of-war **7**:*983*; **9**:1182;
     11:1580
    stem cells (interstitial cells) **11**:1558
  jellyfish **7**:*981*
    bioluminescence **7**:982
    cannonball **7**:982
    compass **11**:*1495*
    differences in **7**:982
    lion's mane **7**:982
    skeleton **11**:1495–1496
    touch receptors **12**:1628
  sea anemones **7**:982–983; **9**:1232, *1237*
    reproduction **3**:*381*, 382; **7**:983
    stinging structures **7**:*970*
    symbiosis **3**:389, 390; **4**:*469*
jerboas, African **4**:501

jiggers **6**:738
juncos **8**:1134
June bugs **2**:178

K

kakapos **6**:755
Kalahari desert, bushmen **9**:1227
Kallima inachus (leaf butterfly) **2**:283
Kampecaris tuberculata **3**:346
kangaroos **8**:1080
  gray **11**:*1465*
  lactation **7**:998
  red **11**:1465
  reproduction **8**:*1078*, 1079;
    10:1352–1353
  tail **12**:*1594*
Kanzi (chimpanzee) **3**:406
kestrels **11**:*1569*; **12**:*1592*
killdeer **2**:232; **3**:404
  camouflage **2**:*283*
kingfishers **2**:230; **5**:699
kinkajous **3**:310, 311
kinorhynchs **1**:95
kin selection **1**:58, 60; **11**:1524, *1525*
kites, snail **2**:234, 237
kittiwakes **11**:1474
kiwis **6**:*756*
kleptoparasitism **11**:1472
koalas **8**:*1077*, 1080
kobs **11**:1521; **12**:1613
Kobus kob (African kob) **11**:1521
  K. kob thomasi (Uganda kob) **12**:1613
Komodo dragons **7**:*977*; **8**:1051; **12**:1717
krait **9**:1203
krill **4**:467

L

Labroides dimidiatus (cleaner wrasse)
  4:450–451
ladybugs **7**:957, 960; **10**:1351
lagomorphs *see* rabbits and hares
Lagopus spp. **10**:1333
Lagothrix spp. (woolly monkeys) **10**:1368
Lama spp. **4**:545
lampreys **6**:733; **11**:1499, 1500
  mouth **6**:732
  splenic tissue **11**:1551
Lampropeltis spp. **4**:484
lamp shells **1**:96
Lampyridae **2**:206
lancelets *see* amphioxus
Laniarius aethiopicus (boubou shrike) **3**:402
Lanius spp. (shrikes) **9**:1274
lantern eyes **2**:205
lapwings **11**:1580
Larus spp.
  L. argentatus (herring gull) **5**:*657*;
    11:1471
  L. glaucescens (glaucous-winged gull)
    11:*1458*
larvae and pupae 7:**1003–1006**; **9**:1158
  larvae **7**:959, 1003–1004, 1005
    permanent **7**:*1006*
  marine larvae
    of echinoderms **4**:569; **8**:*1126*
    nauplius **4**:469
    pedogenesis **7**:1006
  pupae **7**:959, *1005*–1006
    see also chrysalids

Lasius spp. (black ant) **1**:*119*, 120; **4**:483
Lates niloticus (Nile perch) **2**:186
Latimeria (coelacanth) **6**:734;
    8:1048–1049, 1050; **12**:1673
Latrodectus mactans (black widow spider)
    1:*133*, *139*; **11**:1547
Lazerta galloti **7**:977
leafhoppers **10**:1323
leaf insects and walking sticks
    8:**1015–1018**
    camouflage **2**:283, 284; **8**:*1015–1016*,
      1017
leeches **1**:96, *100*
Leipoa ocellata (mallee fowl) **2**:232
lemmings **10**:1334; **12**:1654
Lemmus spp. (lemming) **10**:1334; **12**:1654
Lemuridae **10**:1366
lemurs
    gentle **9**:1221
    mouse **10**:1366
    nocturnal **9**:1221
    plant pollination by **10**:1338
    ring-tailed **10**:*1366*
    sportive **10**:1366, 1369
    tail **12**:1594
    true **10**:1366
leopards **2**:284; **3**:*313*, 324
    clouded **3**:313, 324
    snow **3**:*323*, 324; **7**:*997*
Lepas spp. **4**:*470*; **7**:*889*
Lepidochora discoidalis (dune beetle) **4**:501
Lepidoptera *see* butterflies and moths
Lepilemuridae **10**:1366
Lepisosteus osseus (garpike/long-nosed pike)
    7:978
Leptinotarsa decemlineata (Colorado potato
    beetle) **2**:*178*
Lepus spp. **10**:1393
    L. alleni (jackrabbit) **4**:500; **10**:*1392*
    L. americanus (snowshoe hare)
      2:281–282; **9**:1159; **10**:1392
    L. mandshuricus (Manchurian hare)
      10:1393
    L. timidus (Arctic/mountain hare) **9**:1159
Leuconia spp. **11**:1552
Lialis spp. (snake lizard) **8**:1052
lice 8:**1032–1033**
    carrying diseases **7**:946, 950; **8**:1032;
      9:1267
    controlled by DDT **8**:1033
    fish **4**:467–468
life expectancy, human **10**:1348
life spans **1**:33, 36
Lilioceris lilii (lily beetle) **8**:*1081*
Limosa spp. (godwit) **12**:*1628*
limpets **3**:408; **4**:445
    slipper **7**:890
    vision **12**:1685
Limulus spp. *see* crabs, horseshoe/king
Linognathus vituli (long-nosed cattle louse)
    8:1033
linsangs, spotted **3**:312
Liolaemus **9**:1169
lions **1**:*81*; **3**:321, *322*; **5**:*643*
    Asiatic **3**:324
    feeding **5**:*693*; **9**:*1224*, 1228
    kin selection **11**:*1525*, 1526
    male lions killing young **11**:1526
    mating **10**:*1406*

teeth **3**:*307*
territories **12**:*1615*
Litoria citropa (Blue Mountain tree frog)
    11:*1527*
living fossils 8:**1048–1050**; **9**:1255
lizards 8:**1051–1053**
    agama **3**:*396*; **8**:*1053*
    anole **4**:459
    asexual reproduction **10**:1405
    beaded **8**:1053
    courtship **4**:459
    defenses **8**:1052
    dewlaps **4**:459
    exocrine gland secretions **5**:677
    flat **8**:1052
    frilled **8**:1052
    iguanid *see* iguanas
    monitor **7**:977; **8**:1053
    night **8**:1053
    parapineal gland **5**:613
    self-amputation and regeneration
      8:*1052–1053*; **10**:1400
    side-blotched, mating strategies **11**:*1485*
    snake **8**:1053
    in suburbia **11**:1569
    tail **12**:1593
    temperature regulation **3**:396, 397;
      8:*1122*
    thorny devil **4**:*485*
    tongue **12**:1622
    tuatara **8**:*1050*; **11**:1581–1582
    whiptail **10**:1405
    see also chameleons; geckos; gila
      monsters; iguanas; reptiles; skinks
llamas **1**:18; **4**:545; **8**:*1058*; **9**:1169
lobsters **4**:468
    antennae **1**:106
    larvae **10**:1314
    spiny **1**:*13*; **4**:469
locusts
    pheromones **9**:1293–1294
    swarms **5**:*620*; **7**:959; **9**:1294
Loligo vulgaris (common squid) **2**:*205*
loons **9**:1209; **11**:1471, 1472, 1473, 1578
Loricifera **1**:95
lorises
    slender **9**:1223
    slow **10**:1366, *1367*
Loris tardigradus (slender loris) **9**:1223
lovebirds **4**:459
Loxodonta africana (African elephant) **5**:*593*,
    595; **8**:1074
Loxosceles spp. (recluse spiders) **1**:133;
    11:1547
"Lucy" (*Australopithecus afarensis*) **6**:784;
    7:*914*, 915
lugworms **12**:1592
lungfish **6**:734; **8**:1060; **12**:1672–1673
    African **10**:*1422*
    excretion **6**:732
    estivation **7**:*892*; **12**:1672–1673
    respiration **6**:728
    splenic tissue **11**:1551
Luridae **11**:1470
Lycaon pictus see dogs, African wild
Lygus spp. (lygus bugs) **7**:885, *960*
Lymantria dispar (gypsy moth) **2**:196,
    268–269, 270; **10**:1346, *1347*
lynxes **3**:324; **10**:1350

lyrebirds **6**:778; **9**:*1276*
Lysandra coridon (blue chalkhill butterfly)
    10:*1403*

M

Macaca spp. **1**:*19–20*; **3**:*405*; **5**:*604*;
    10:1368
macaques *see* monkeys, macaque
macaws **6**:778
mackerel **6**:732; **10**:1424
    California **4**:481
Macroclemys temmincki (alligator snapping
    turtle) **2**:283; **12**:1623–1624
Macropanesthia rhinoceros (giant burrowing
    cockroach) **3**:387
Macropodus opercularis (labyrinth fish)
    9:1206
Macropus spp. (kangaroo) **11**:*1465*
Madoqua spp. (dikdik) **12**:*1662*, 1663
maggots *see* flies, larvae
Magicicada spp. (cicadas) **2**:216
magpies, nests **9**:1208
Maiasaura **4**:528
Malacopsylloidea **6**:740
Malacosama spp. **2**:269
Malacostraca **4**:469–470
mallards, sexual dimorphism **4**:*524*
mallee fowl **2**:232
Mallophaga (chewing lice) **8**:1032, 1033
mambas, black **11**:1518, 1520
mammals 8:**1069–1074**; **12**:1674
    anatomy and characteristics **8**:1069–1070
    armor **4**:485
    at high altitude **9**:1169
    brain **2**:258
    circulatory system **3**:*373*, 375
    courtship **4**:*460*
    digestive system **4**:*520*, 521
    dwellings **8**:1072
    ears **7**:872
    embryos
      development **5**:*598–599*
      similarity **8**:1074
    endothermy **7**:900–901; **8**:1069
    evolution **8**:*1073*; **12**:1672
    excretion **5**:670–671
    feeding **8**:*1071–1072*
      insectivores 7:**954–956**; **8**:1072
      see also carnivores; herbivores
    feet **5**:697
    hair 6:*774*; **8**:1070
    heart **7**:877–879
      heart rates **7**:880
    hibernation and estivation **7**:892–893
    jaws **7**:979
    lactation **7**:997–998
    licking skin of newborn **12**:*1625*, 1626
    lungs **10**:1423
    mammary glands **5**:*676–677*;
      7:997–998; **8**:1070
    marine *see* whales, porpoises, and
      dolphins
    migration **8**:1072
    molting **9**:1159

    nesting **9**:1206–*1207*
    nocturnal **9**:1220–1221
    orders of **8**:1071
    pancreas **9**:1261
    plant pollination by **10**:1338
    in polar regions **10**:1333; **11**:1507
    regeneration in **10**:1401
    reproduction **8**:1074, 1083
    sense of touch **12**:1626
    senses **8**:1070–1071
    skin **11**:1506–*1507*
    sleep **11**:*1511*
    social behavior **8**:1072–1074
    of the taiga **12**:*1590*, *1591*
    tail **12**:1593, *1594*
    taste receptors **12**:1596
    teeth **8**:1070; **12**:1603, 1605–1606
    toothless **1**:103
    see also marsupials; monotremes;
      ruminants
mammoths **5**:593–594, 679–680
Mammuthus spp. *see* mammoths
mandrills **10**:1368; **12**:1594
mangabeys, African **3**:406
Manta birostris (manta ray) **6**:734
mantids 4:483; **8**:**1075–1076**
    mantises
    Chinese **8**:1075
    orchid **2**:286
    praying **8**:*1075*, 1084
Mariopteris nervosa **6**:*783*
Marmosa spp. (mouse opossum) **7**:997;
    8:1077
marmosets **5**:694; **10**:1367–1368
    pygmy **10**:1367
marmots, Alpine **10**:1437
marsupials 5:656; **8**:**1077–1080**;
    12:1674
    American **8**:1077
    birth and development **8**:1078;
      10:1352–1353
    evolution and distribution **8**:1078–1079;
      11:1541; **12**:1717
    convergent evolution **4**:446
martens **12**:1591
Martes spp., of the taiga **12**:1591
martins, nests **9**:1209
Masai people **9**:*1194*; **11**:1465
mastodons **5**:679–680
Mastomys natalensis (multimammate rat)
    10:1438
mating 8:**1081–1084**
    attracting a mate **8**:1083–1084; **11**:1540
    and cannibalism **8**:1076
    cuckolding **8**:1083
    differences between the sexes
      8:1082–1083
    females choosing a mate **11**:*1527*–1528
    and intersexual selection **11**:1485
    and intrasexual selection **11**:1484
    monogamy **10**:1406
    nonrandom **5**:656
    polyandry **3**:409; **8**:*1083*
    polygamy **3**:409; **10**:1406

mating *(continued)*
  polygyny (harem breeding) **3**:409; **4**:460;
    8:1084; **11**:1523
  postcopulatory mate guarding **8**:1083
  and sperm "competition" **8**:1083
  and territories **12**:1613–*1614*
Maxillopoda **4**:470
  see also barnacles
mayflies *see* dragonflies and mayflies
Mayotis bechsteric (Bechstein's bat) **2**:*173*
medusae **7**:980
meerkats **1**:*58*; **3**:313; **11**:1522
Megachiroptera **2**:173–174; **9**:1222
Megalosaurus **4**:527
Meganeura **4**:552; **6**:748
Megaptera novaeangliae (humpback whale)
    1:*97*; **3**:405; **4**:*438*, 460; **11**:1580
Megazostrodon **7**:954
Megophrys nasuta (Asian horned toad) **6**:*787*
Melanerpes uropygialis (Gila woodpecker)
    2:273
Meloe franciscanus **2**:178
Melospiza melodia (song sparrow)
    3:402–403, 408
Menacanethus stramineus (chicken-body
    louse) **8**:1033
Menura spp. (lyrebirds) **6**:778; **9**:*1276*
Mephitis spp. (skunk) **4**:486; **11**:*1516*
mermaid's purses **11**:*1489*
Merostomata **1**:141
Mesosaurus **2**:192; **9**:1255
Mesothelae **11**:1546
metamorphosis **7**:1004; **8**:**1125–1126**;
    10:1308
  complete **7**:1005–1006; **8**:1126
    in butterflies and moths **7**:1006
    in fleas **6**:739–740
    in flies **6**:743
    in insects **7**:959; **9**:1158
    pupae **7**:959, *1005–1006*
  hormonal control **7**:908, 1005; **8**:1126
  incomplete **7**:1004–1005; **8**:1126
    in amphibians **7**:1005
    in dragonflies and mayflies **4**:551
    in earwigs **4**:564
    in grasshoppers and crickets
      7:1004–1005; **8**:1126
    in insects **7**:959; **9**:1157–1158
    in phasmids **8**:1018
  purpose **8**:1125
  tracheal system during **10**:1420
  see also larvae and pupae
Metatheria *see* marsupials
mice
  chemical signals **3**:404
  harvest **1**:79
  house **10**:1437; **11**:1569
  pheromones **9**:1294
  pygmy **10**:1436
Micrathene whitneyi (elf owl) **2**:236
Microcebus murinus (mouse lemur)
    10:1366
Microchiroptera **9**:1222
Microtus ochrogaster (prairie vole)
    10:1437
microwhip scorpions **11**:1469
Micrurus spp. **4**:484
midges **7**:1001
  gall **7**:1006

migration **2**:210; **8**:**1133–1136**
  an adaptive behavior **1**:19
  bird **2**:210; **5**:619; **6**:776–777;
      8:1135–1136; **10**:1333; **11**:1474;
      12:1700
    Arctic tern **8**:*1133*; **11**:1474
    to the tundra **12**:1654
    white storks **8**:1134
  butterflies and moths **2**:269
  caribou **8**:1135; **10**:1333; **12**:1654
  eel **2**:210
  elephant **5**:594
  and genetic diversity **8**:1135
  mammalian **8**:1072
  navigation **8**:1135–1136
  salmon **8**:*1133–1134*, 1135; **10**:1426
  spiny lobster **4**:469
  squid **8**:1136
  vertical **8**:1136
  whale **8**:1135; **12**:1710
milk
  antibodies in **7**:*934*
  and bovine somatotropin/growth
      hormone **4**:545
  crop milk **7**:997
  fermentation **6**:763
  mammalian
    composition **7**:998
    purpose **7**:998
  uterine **7**:997
Miller-Urey experiment **5**:651, *652*, 682
millipedes *see* centipedes and millipedes
Mimus polyglottos (mockingbird) **9**:1274
mink **10**:*1351*; **12**:1591
minnows, fathead **6**:733
miracadia **9**:1265, 1268
Mirounga spp. (elephant seals) **1**:*85*; **3**:311
mites **1**:90, 132, 141
  carrying disease **1**:131
  cockroach **3**:388
  flour **1**:132
  follicle **1**:132
  house **2**:153; **5**:*627*
  spider **10**:1320
  velvet **1**:*132*
mockingbirds **9**:1274
Moeritherium **5**:593
molecular clock theory **5**:654
moles **7**:*954*, 955; **11**:1532
  golden **7**:956
  marsupial **8**:1079–1080
  star-nosed **7**:955
mollusks **1**:96; **7**:972; **8**:**1147–1150**
  anatomy **8**:1147–1149
  aquaculture **1**:125
  bivalve *see* bivalves
  circulatory system **3**:371, 372–373;
    8:1148
  classification **8**:1150
  courtship **4**:458
  epidermis **11**:1506
  evolution **8**:1148
  excretion **5**:667
  exoskeletons **11**:1497
  and humans **8**:1149
  mucus **9**:*1172*; **11**:1506
  nervous system **8**:1147; **9**:1205
  range **8**:1149–1150
  reproduction **8**:1150

  shell **8**:*1148*–1149; **11**:1497, 1506
  see also octopuses; snails; squid
Moloch horridus (thorny devil) **4**:*485*
Molothrus ater (brown-headed cowbird)
    4:445; **9**:1274
Monachus spp. **5**:*655*
mongooses **3**:313; **11**:1520
monkeys **10**:1368
  capuchin **3**:402; **10**:1368
  colobus **10**:1368
  dominance hierarchy **8**:1083
  feet **5**:697
  Goeldi's **10**:1368
  grip **7**:869
  howler **10**:1368; **12**:1594, 1615, 1640
  macaque **1**:19–*20*; **3**:*405*; **10**:1368, 1369
  mating **8**:1083
  New World **10**:1367–*1368*
  Old World **10**:1367, 1368
  patas **3**:406
  play **10**:1329–1330
  proboscis **10**:1374
  rhesus **3**:*405*; **5**:*604*
  spider **12**:1594
    marimonda **10**:*1368*
  squirrel **8**:*1070*
  tail **12**:1594
  titi **3**:405
  vervet/African green **3**:403; **11**:1523
  washing food **1**:19–*20*
  woolly **10**:1368
  see also primates
monogamy **10**:1406
Monogenea **6**:736
Monoplacophora **8**:1049, 1150
monotremes **8**:1074; **9**:**1162–1163**;
    11:1541; **12**:1674
  mammary glands **5**:*676–677*; **7**:997
moon jellies **7**:*981*, 982
moose (elk) **8**:1084; **10**:1350; **12**:1591, *1619*
Morpho spp. (morpho butterfly) **12**:1642
mosquitoes **7**:1004
  antennae **1**:106
  control, using microorganisms **8**:1132
  diseases from **6**:*744*; **7**:946, *947*
  larvae and pupae **7**:*1004*; **10**:*1419*;
      11:1577–1578
  nocturnally active **9**:1222
  pitcher plant **3**:316
  and threadworms **9**:1222
moths *see* butterflies and moths
mouse *see* mice
mud puppies **10**:1418; **11**:1454
mudskippers **6**:*728*, 730
mudsuckers **6**:728
muggers **4**:463–464
mules **4**:546; **11**:1480, *1540*, 1541
mullet **11**:1492
Murex spp. **8**:1149
murres (guillemots) **11**:1474
Mus spp. (mouse) **10**:1436, 1437; **11**:1569
Musca domestica (housefly) **4**:480; **5**:699;
    6:745; **12**:*1647*
Muscardinus avellanarius (common
    dormouse) **8**:*1069*
Muscicapa striata (spotted flycatcher) **6**:750
musk ox **10**:1333; **12**:*1653*, 1654
muskrats **10**:1351; **12**:1593
  nests **9**:1206–1207

mussels **8**:*1147*; **11**:1493
  freshwater **8**:1149–1150; **10**:1427
Mustela spp. **3**:308; **9**:1159; **10**:1351;
    12:*1591*
Mustelidae **3**:308
Muttaburrasaurus **4**:*527*
Mycteria americana (American wood stork)
    12:1700
Mylabris tiflensis (toxic oil beetle) **3**:404
Myocastor coypus (coypu/nutria) **10**:*1436*;
    11:1465; **12**:*1705*
Myotis spp. **4**:*573*, 574
myriapods, evolution **3**:346
Myripristis violaceous (squirrelfish) **3**:403
Myrmecophaga tridactyla (giant anteater)
    1:*103*, 104; **4**:445; **12**:*1621*
mysticetes (Mysticeti) **12**:1707, 1708
Mytilus spp. (mussel) **8**:*1147*; **11**:1493

N

Naja naja (hooded cobra) **9**:1203
Nannopterum harrisi (Galápagos cormorant)
    6:754; **9**:1169
narwhals **12**:1606
Nasalis larvatus (proboscis monkey)
    10:1374
nasutes **12**:*1612*
Natrix natrix (grass snake) **9**:*1157*
Nautilus **4**:446; **5**:687; **8**:*1048*
Neanderthals **7**:*912*, 916–917; **10**:1362
Nectarinia reichenovi (golden-winged
    sunbird) **5**:696
Necturus maculosus (mud puppy) **10**:1418
Negaprion brevirostris (lemon shark) **11**:1490
Nematocera **6**:743
Nematoda (Nemata; Nemalthelminthes)
    9:1196
nematode worms **1**:90, 96; **7**:971;
    9:**1195–1196**
  causing disease **7**:946; **9**:1196, *1266*
  molting **9**:1157, 1195
  as plant pests **9**:1196; **10**:1321
  in the soil **9**:1195; **11**:1531
Nematomorpha **1**:96
Nemertea **1**:95
nemertines **1**:95; **7**:970–971
neo-Darwinism **2**:202; **4**:479; **5**:654
Neofelis nebulosa (clouded leopard) **3**:313, 324
Neopilina **8**:1049
neoteny *see* paedomorphosis
Neotoma spp. (wood rat) **10**:1437
Nephila clavipes **11**:1549
nesting **9**:**1206–1209**
  in birds *see* birds, nests
newts *see* salamanders and newts
nighthawks **6**:775, 776
nightjars **6**:775
nits **8**:1032–1033
nocturnal life **9**:**1220–1223**
  courtship **4**:457
  echolocation and hearing **9**:*1222*–1223
  flowers opening at night **9**:1220
  forest birds **6**:776
  phasmids **8**:1017
  sense of smell **9**:1223
  vision **9**:*1221*–1222; **12**:*1686*, 1687
Notomis mantelli (takahe) **6**:756
Notophthalmus viridescens (red-spotted newt)
    11:1456

Notoryctes spp. **4**:446

   N. typhlops (pouched mole) **8**:1079

nudibranchs (sea slugs) **4**:484; **7**:981

Numenius spp. (curlew) **12**:1628

nuthatches **12**:*1609*

nutrias *see* coypus

Nycticebus coucang (slow loris) **10**:1366, *1367*

Nyctimene albiventer (tube-nosed fruit bat) **2**:173

Nygmia phaeorrhoea (brown-tail moth) **2**:*270*

nymphs

   dragonfly and mayfly **4**:551–552

   grasshopper and cricket **7**:1004–1005

   mantid **8**:1076

   see also metamorphosis, incomplete

O

Obelia spp. **11**:1524

ocelots **3**:323, 324

octopuses **8**:*1149*

   "brain" **2**:255

   color change **4**:483; **7**:908

   larvae **8**:1150; **10**:1313–1314

   learning by **8**:1149

   movement **11**:1499, *1577*

   reproduction **8**:1150

   skeleton **11**:1499

   see also cephalopods; mollusks

Octopus vulgaris (common octopus) **8**:1149

Odobenus rosmarus (walrus) **3**:311

Odocoileus hemionus (mule deer) **3**:*350*, 351

Odonata **4**:550

odontocetes (Odontoceti) **12**:1707, 1708

Odontosyllis spp. **2**:216

   bioluminescence **2**:206

oilbirds **4**:*574*

Oligochaeta **1**:99

olms **11**:1454

omnivores **5**:695; **6**:767; **8**:1072

   digestive system **4**:516

   jaws and teeth **3**:311; **4**:517; **7**:979

Oncorhynchus spp. **8**:1133–1134; **10**:1426, *1427*

Ondatra zibethicus (muskrat) **9**:1206–1207; **10**:1351

ontogeny

   and behavior **1**:84

   recapitulates phylogeny **5**:597

Onychophora **1**:97; **7**:972; **8**:1049; **12**:*1602*

Onymacris unguicularis **4**:501

Oparin-Haldane theory **5**:651

Ophiophagus hannah (king cobra) **11**:1518

Ophiuroidea **4**:570

Opisthocomus hoazin (hoatzin) **1**:134; **6**:777

opossums **8**:1080; **11**:1569

   mouse **7**:997; **8**:1077

   Virginian/Northern **5**:*650*; **8**:1080; **11**:*1541*

optimality theory **4**:458

orangutans **7**:*870*; **10**:1367, 1368–*1369*, 1370

orcas (killer whales) **10**:1350; **12**:1707, *1708*, 1709, 1710

Orcinus orca (killer whale) **10**:1350; **12**:1707, *1708*, 1709, 1710

Orconectes **3**:327

Ornithischia **4**:530–531

Ornithorhynchus anatinus see platypuses, duckbill

Orphyrys apifera (bee orchid) **2**:286

orthogenesis **7**:912

Orthonectida **1**:95

Orthoptera, *see also* cockroaches; grasshoppers and crickets; mantids

Oryctolagus cuniculus (European rabbit) **3**:391–392; **8**:*1072*; **10**:*1353*, 1392

oryxes, Arabian **12**:1725

Oscines **9**:1273

ospreys **2**:*236*

   effects of DDT **4**:481

   feet **5**:698

   nests **2**:236

Osteichthyes **6**:730, 734; **12**:1672–1673

   see also fish, bony

ostracoderms **6**:730; **12**:1672

ostriches **5**:698; **6**:755

Otariidae **3**:311

Otocyon megalotis (bat-eared fox) **4**:540

otters **11**:*1578*

   sea **4**:439; **7**:*988*

      cracking shells **3**:*308*

ovenbirds **6**:776

Ovibos moschatus (musk ox) **10**:1333; **12**:*1653*, 1654

Ovis spp. (sheep) **4**:460, 544

owl parrots **6**:755

owls **2**:234, *235*, 236–237

   barn **2**:237; **9**:*1158*, 1222

   burrowing **9**:1206

   elf **2**:236

   feet **5**:*698*

   forest **6**:776

   great horned **2**:237

   hearing **2**:235

   little **11**:1569

   nocturnal **9**:*1220*, 1221, 1222

   saw-whet **9**:*1220*

   songs **3**:402

   suburban **11**:1569

   tawny **3**:402; **9**:1221

   vision **2**:234–235; **12**:1687

oxen, musk oxen **10**:1333; **12**:*1653*

oxpeckers **11**:*1579*

Oxyura jamaicensis (ruddy duck) **12**:1700

Oxyuranus microlepidotus (taipan) **11**:1518

oystercatchers **12**:1700

oysters

   farming of **1**:124, 125

   fishing for **8**:1149

P

Pachycephalosaurs **4**:531

paddlefish **6**:734

paddle worms **7**:*971*

paedogenesis *see* paedomorphosis

paedomorphosis **4**:544; **7**:1006; **9**:*1256*; **11**:1455

   in cave-dwelling animals **3**:327

   and dog breed selection **4**:541

paintings, cave **10**:*1363*–*1364*

Palaemonias ganteri (Kentucky cave shrimp) **3**:326

Palaeocoma egertoni **6**:*784*

Palaeotringa **12**:1701

paleobiology 9:1254–1257

Palpigradi **11**:1469

pandas

   giant **3**:308–309; **5**:656; **12**:1609

      captive breeding **12**:1725

      fertility **5**:712

   red **3**:309

Pandinus spp. **1**:133; **11**:*1469*

Pandion heliaetus (osprey) **2**:*236*; **4**:481; **5**:698

Pandionidae **2**:236

Pandulus borealis (deep-sea prawn) **1**:*106*

pangolins **1**:103; **4**:445, 486

Panorpa spp. **8**:1084

panspermia, theory of **5**:651–652

Pan spp. *see* chimpanzees

Panthera spp. **3**:313, 323–324

   P. atrox **3**:324

   P. leo see lions

   P. pardus (leopard) **3**:313, 324

   P. tigris see tigers

   P. uncia (snow leopard) **3**:*323*, 324; **7**:997

panthers, Florida **3**:323, **10**:1343

Panulirus argus (spiny lobster) **1**:*13*; **4**:469

Papilio machaon (common swallowtail) **2**:267, 284

Papio spp.

   P. hamadryas (hamadryas baboon) **1**:*86*

   P. sphinx (mandrill) **10**:1368; **12**:1594

Parabuteo unicinctus (Harris's hawk) **2**:235

parakeets **3**:401

Parasaurolophus **4**:531

Paratrechina longicornis **7**:976

Parnassius apollo (apollo butterfly) **2**:186

parrots **6**:778; **12**:*1642*

   feet **5**:698

parthenogenesis **4**:469; **10**:1407

   in insects **4**:552; **8**:1018; **10**:*1407*

   in rotifers **10**:1313

Parus major (great tit) **1**:*29*, 85; **9**:1274

Paruvoctus mousiness **9**:1223

Passer domesticus (house sparrow) **9**:1274–1275

Passeriformes *see* birds, perching

passerines *see* birds, perching

Patella cochlear (limpet) **3**:408

Pavo cristatus (Indian peacock) *see* peacocks

peacocks **4**:459; **5**:656

   tail **2**:*228*; **4**:525; **11**:*1483*–1484

peanut worms **1**:96

Pedetes capensis (African spring hare) **10**:1437

Pediculus spp. (body louse) **7**:946, 950; **8**:*1032*, 1033

pedogenesis *see* paedomorphosis

Pelecaniformes **11**:1471–1472

Pelecanus spp. *see* pelicans

pelicans **11**:1472–1473, 1494

   brown **12**:*1706*

penguins **1**:*22*; **6**:754; **11**:1473, 1474

   countercurrent heat exchange system **12**:1618

   emperor **6**:754; **11**:1473, 1474

   swimming **6**:*753*; **11**:1578

perch, Nile **2**:186

perching birds 5:697; 9:1273–1276

Periophthalmus barbarus (mudskipper) **6**:*728*

Peripatopsis spp. **12**:*1602*

Peripatus **8**:1049–1050

Perissodactyla *see* ungulates, odd-toed

Perodicticus potto (potto) **10**:1366, 1370

Petaurista elegans (spotted giant flying squirrel) **10**:1436–1437

petrels **11**:1473

   blue **11**:1473

   flight **6**:752

   Wilson's storm **11**:1474

phalangers, flying **4**:*446*

phalaropes **5**:656; **12**:1700

Pharomachrus mocino (quetzal) **6**:777

Phascolarctos cinereus see koalas

Phoca hispida saimensis (Saimaa ringed seal) **3**:311

Phocidae **3**:311

phoebe, eastern **2**:193; **12**:*1718*

Phoenicopterus spp. *see* flamingos

Phoronida **1**:96

Photinus spp. **3**:404

Photoblepharon palpebratus **2**:205

photophores **2**:205, 206, 207

Photuris spp. **2**:206, 217; **3**:404

Phthiraptera **8**:1032

Phthirus pubis (pubic louse; crabs) **8**:1033

Phycodurus eques (sea dragon) **6**:732

phyletic change **6**:784

Phyllidae (leaf insects) *see* leaf insects and walking sticks

Phyllium bioculatum (Japanese leaf insect) **8**:*1015*

Phyllobates spp. (poison dart frog) **6**:788

Phyllodactylus marmoratus (marbled gecko) **8**:1052

Phyllodoca lamelligera (paddle worm) **7**:*971*

Phyllophaga spp. (June bug) **2**:178

phylogeny, from DNA **5**:654

Physalia physalis (Portuguese man-of-war) **7**:*983*; **9**:1182; **11**:1524, 1580

Physeter catodon (sperm whale) **4**:572

pigeons **6**:776; **11**:1569

   crop milk **7**:997

   digestive system **4**:*514*

   passenger **5**:659; **11**:1522

   in towns **12**:1665

pigs

   diseases **1**:*88*

   genetically modified **1**:*92*

   stressed **11**:*1567*

   teats **7**:998

   wild **12**:1606, *1610*

pike **6**:732

   long-nosed (garpike) **7**:978

Piltdown Man hoax **6**:782; **7**:917

Pinguinus (Alca) impennis (great auk) **6**:*754*; **12**:1654

Pinnipedia **3**:308, 311

Pipa pipa (Surinam toad) **6**:789

pipefish **11**:1484

Bold words with bold page numbers indicate complete articles; bold numbers preceding colons are volume numbers; numbers following colons indicate page numbers; italic page numbers refer to illustrations or other graphics.

Pipistrellus pipistrellus (pipistrelle bat) **2**:*176*; **7**:*873*

piranhas **3**:*401*; **6**:732

placoderms **6**:730

Placozoa **1**:94

plagues, of locusts **5**:*620*; **7**:959; **9**:1294

planarians *see* flatworms, planarian

Platalea spp. (spoonbills) **5**:648; **10**:1311

Platanista minor (Indus River dolphin) **12**:1709

Plateosaurus **4**:529–530

platyfish **11**:1485–1486

Platyhelminthes **1**:95; **5**:715; **7**:970

   see also flatworms; flukes; tapeworms

platypuses

   duckbill **2**:204; **8**:1050; **9**:1162, *1163*

     mammary glands **5**:676–677; **7**:997

Platyrrhini **10**:1365, 1367–1368

Platysaurus intomedius (flat lizard) **8**:1052

Pleocotus auritus **4**:*571*

Plethodontidae **11**:1455

plovers **11**:1471, 1580; **12**:1699

   black-bellied **12**:1654

    golden **12**:*1700*

     migration **8**:1136; **12**:*1700*

   see also killdeer

Pluvialis spp. **8**:1136; **12**:*1700*

Poecilia reticulata (guppy) **1**:*127*

pogonophores **1**:96

polyandry **3**:409; **8**:*1083*

polychaetes **1**:100

   bristle worms **1**:96, *98*

   ice worms **9**:1233

   proboscis **10**:1374

Polyergus spp. **1**:120

polygamy **3**:409; **10**:1406

polygyny (harem breeding) **3**:409; **4**:460; **8**:*1084*; **11**:1523

polymorphism *see* dimorphism and polymorphism

Polyplacophora **8**:1150

polyps **7**:980

   coral **4**:447, 448–449, 452, 453; **11**:1497–1498

Polyxenus spp. **3**:345, 346

Polyzoa **1**:96

Pomacanthus spp. (angelfish) **2**:283

Pongo pygmaeus see orangutans

poorwills **6**:776

Popillia japonica (Japanese beetle) **7**:960

porcupines, tail **12**:1594

Porifera **11**:1552

Porifera *see* sponges

porpoises *see* whales, porpoises, and dolphins

Portuguese man-of-war **7**:*983*; **9**:1182; **11**:1524

   commensal fish **11**:1580

possums, American **8**:1078

Potos flavus (kinkajou) **3**:310, 311

pottos **10**:1366, 1370

poultry, lice **8**:1033

prairie dogs **5**:694; **9**:1207; **12**:1614

prawns, antennae **1**:*106*

pregnancy and birth 10:1352–1359

   birth **3**:355; **10**:*1357*–1359, 1414

    cesarean sections **10**:1357, 1359; **11**:1574

    a positive feedback system **7**:*953*

premature labor **8**:1098

   see also babies

pregnancy

   diabetes in **4**:507–508

   ectopic **5**:711; **10**:1359

   fetus *see* fetus

   human timetable **10**:1353–1357

   and illegal drugs **2**:260

   iron deficiency in **7**:973

   kits to test for **10**:1353

   miscarriage **1**:14; **10**:1354

   multiple births *see* twins and multiple births

   problems of **10**:1359

   "quickening" **10**:1355

   Rh typing **2**:245

   tests **2**:224

   see also fetus

Prepona spp. **2**:271

priapulids **1**:95

primates 10:1365–1370

   adolescence **1**:*28*

   defense **4**:484–485

   emotions **5**:603–*604*

   gestation time **10**:1369

   grooming **10**:*1370*

   hunting **10**:1370

   movement **10**:1370

   opposable fingers or toes **5**:697–698; **10**:1365

   prosimians **9**:1223; **10**:1365–1367

   simians **10**:1367–1369

   social organization **10**:1369–1370

   tail **12**:1594

   teeth **12**:1605–1606

   tree shrews as **7**:955

   see also apes; monkeys

Principles of Humane Animal Experimentation, The (Russell and Burch) **1**:92

Priodontes maximus (giant armadillo) **1**:104

Prionace glauca (blue shark) **11**:1488

Prionodon pardicolor (spotted linsang) **3**:312

prions (birds) **11**:1473

proboscis worms **1**:95

Procavia capensis (rock hyrax) **5**:*594*

Proconsul **7**:871, 914–915

Procyonidae **3**:310–311

Procyon spp. *see* raccoons

Prodoxus y-inversus (yucca moth) **2**:269; **10**:1336

progeny testing **11**:1480

Propalaeotherium **9**:1256

Propithecus verreauxi (Verreaux's sifaka) **9**:1221

prosimians **9**:1223; **10**:1365–1367

Proteidae **11**:1454

Proteles cristatus (aardwolf) **3**:312

Proteus spp. **3**:*327*; **11**:1454

Protoceratops **4**:*526*, 529, 531

Protopterus spp. (African lungfish) **10**:*1422*

protostomes **7**:971–972

Prototheria *see* monotremes

Psammechinus miliaris (purple-tipped sea urchin) **4**:*439*

Psammomys obesus (North African sand rat) **4**:501

Psephotus pulcherrimus (paradise parrot) **6**:778

Pseudaelurus **3**:312, 324

pseudocoelomates **7**:971; **9**:1196

Pseudocreobota ocellata (orchid mantis) **2**:286

pseudoscorpions **11**:1469

Psittacosaurus **4**:531

Psittacus erithacus (gray parrot) **6**:*778*

Psyllophryne didactyla **6**:787

ptarmigan **11**:1580

   rock **10**:1333

Pteranodon **10**:1391

Pterocnemia spp. (rheas) **6**:755, 756

pterodactyls **10**:1391

Pteropus vampyrus (common flying fox) **2**:174

pterosaurs 4:530; 6:748; 10:1391; 12:1593

Pterygota **7**:960

Ptilonorhynchus violaceus (satin bowerbirds) **4**:459; **12**:1614

puberty **1**:*25, 26*; **5**:708

   in animals **8**:1111

   hormones **5**:708; **8**:1108

    female **7**:906; **10**:1412–1413

    male **7**:906; **10**:1410

   and the menstrual cycle **1**:27–28; **8**:1111

   see also adolescence

puffins **11**:*1471*

Pulicoidea **6**:740

pupae *see* larvae and pupae

puparia **6**:745

pupfish, Devil's Hole **2**:186

pythons **11**:1519

   overcoming prey **11**:1518

   reticulated **11**:1518

   warming their eggs **3**:397

Q

queleas, red-billed **9**:1275

Quercusia quercus (great purple hairstreak) **2**:*271*

Quetzalcoatlus **10**:1391

quetzals **6**:777

R

rabbits and hares 10:1392–1393

   digestion by **4**:515–516; **9**:1228–1229; **11**:1453, 1564

   hares

    Arctic/mountain **9**:1159; **10**:1392–1393

    breeding **10**:1352

    European **10**:*1393*

    jackrabbits **4**:500

    Manchurian **10**:1393

    rock **10**:1393

    snowshoe **2**:281–282; **9**:1159; **10**:1350, 1392

   rabbits **8**:*1072*

    breeding **10**:1352, *1353*

    cottontail **10**:*1392*

    European **10**:1393

    fleas **6**:739

    and the myxoma virus **3**:391–392

    tail **12**:1594

    teeth **5**:694

raccoons **3**:*309*, 310, 311; **5**:695; **12**:1609

   fishing **12**:1628

   in suburban habitats **11**:*1568*–1569

racers **11**:1518

Ramapithecus **7**:916

Ramphastos sulfuratus (keel-billed toucan) **6**:*777*

Rana spp.

   R. cancrivora (crab-eating frog) **6**:788

   R. catesbeiana (bullfrog) **1**:64; **5**:666; **6**:787, 790

   R. pipiens (leopard frog) **6**:787

   R. temporaria (common frog) **5**:*715*

Rangifer tarandus (Arctic caribou) **8**:1135; **10**:1333; **12**:*1590*, 1654, 1663

Ranidae **6**:787

Raphus cucullatus (dodo) **1**:19; **5**:*678*; **7**:977

ratfish **6**:734

ratites, *see also* birds, flightless

rats

   black/ship/roof **10**:1437; **11**:1569

   brown/Norway **10**:*1437*; **12**:*1664*

   fleas **6**:740

   kangaroo

    burrows **9**:1207

    drumming with feet **5**:699

    water conservation **4**:501; **5**:669, *670*; **10**:1436

   learning experiments with **8**:1020

   mole **1**:60; **4**:*486*; **10**:1437–1438

   naked **11**:*1523*

   multimammate **10**:1438

   pheromones **9**:1294

   and plague **6**:740; **7**:950

   sand **4**:501; **7**:*990*

   whiskers **12**:1628

   wood **10**:1437

rattlesnakes

   courtship **4**:459

   diamondback **9**:1207

   heat detectors **9**:1222

   rattle **11**:1519

   tooth structure **11**:*1519*

   venom **11**:1518

Rattus spp. (rat) **10**:1437; **11**:1569; **12**:*1664*

ravens, play **10**:1329

rays **6**:732, 734; **11**:1500

   excretion **5**:670; **6**:732

   spleen **11**:1551

Recurvirostra spp. **2**:231; **12**:*1699*

redpolls, Arctic/hoary **10**:*1333*

reindeer *see* caribou

Remipedia **4**:470

remoras **11**:1490

repletes **1**:119

reptiles 10:1415–1416; 12:1673

   anatomy **10**:1416

   brain **2**:257, 258

   circulatory system **3**:*373*, 374–375

   courtship **4**:459

   eggs **10**:1413, 1416

   embryo development **5**:598–599

   evolution **10**:*1416*

   excretion **5**:670; **7**:989; **12**:1673

   eyes **5**:685–686

   hearing **4**:562

   heart **7**:877; **10**:1416

   hibernation **7**:893

   jaws **7**:978

   locomotion **10**:1416

   molting **9**:1158

   nesting **9**:1207

   respiration **10**:1422

    lungs **8**:*1060*; **10**:1416, 1423

salt glands 11:1459
skin 11:1506
stomach 11:1563–1564
tail 12:1592–1593
temperature regulation 3:397; 10:1415;
   12:1617
vision 10:1416
see also crocodilians; dinosaurs; snakes;
   tortoises and turtles
Reticulitermes lucifugus 11:1461; 12:1611
Rhacophorus spp. (flying frog) 5:699; 6:749
Rhagioletis pomonella (apple maggot fly)
   3:402
Rhea americana (gray/common rhea) 6:755
rheas 6:755–756
Rhinatrematidae 2:276
Rhincodon typus (whale shark) 10:1314,
   1418; 11:1487, *1488*
rhinoceroses
   black 11:*1579*
   horns 7:911; 12:1663
   white
     endangered 5:*606*
     hunting of 11:1464
   woolly 5:679–680; 6:782
Rhinolophus ferrumequinum (greater
   horseshoe bat) 2:*174, 175*; 3:*325*
Rhombozoa 1:95
Rhynchocephala 10:1415
   see also tuataras
Rhynchops spp. (skimmer) 11:1473
rhyncocoels 1:95
ribbon worms 1:95; 7:970–971
Riftia pachyptila 5:651
ringtails 3:310
Riopa fernandi (Fernand's/fire skink)
   8:*1051*
roadrunners 4:501
robins 1:29–30; 8:1136; 12:1614
   American 11:1569
rodents 10:1436–1438
   coprophagy 11:1564
   and disease 10:1438
   evolution 10:1438
   teeth 10:*1436*; 12:1605
Rostrhamus sociabilis (snail kite) 2:234, 237
rotifers 1:95; 10:1313, 1407
roundworms *see* nematode worms
Ruminantia 11:1451
ruminants 11:1451–1453
   digestion by 3:342; 4:*515*, 521; 8:1071,
     1128; 9:*1226*; 11:1453, 1581;
     12:1661–1662
   feeding behavior 11:1453
   saliva 4:515; 11:1452
   stomach of 4:515; 11:1451–*1452*, 1564
   teeth 11:1452
   see also cattle; goats; sheep; ungulates
Rupicapra rupicapra (chamois) 9:*1169*

S

sable 12:1591
Sagittariidae 2:236
Sagittarius serpentarius (secretary bird) 2:236
Saimiri sciureus (squirrel monkey) 8:*1070*
salamanders and newts 11:1454–1456
   cave-dwelling 3:*327*
   leg regeneration 10:1400
   lungs 8:*1060*

metamorphosis 8:1125
nervous system 9:*1205*
newts
   fat store 7:892
   palmate 11:*1456*
   red-bellied 4:458
   red-spotted 11:1456
   tail 12:*1593*
paedomorphosis 11:1455
poisonous 11:1454
reproduction 11:1456
respiration 11:1455
salamanders 1:*64*
   fire 11:*1455*
   giant 11:1454, 1455
   lungless 10:1423; 11:1455
   mole 11:1454, 1455
   molting 9:1158
   tiger 11:1454, 1455
   torrent 11:1455
temperature regulation 3:397
see also amphibians
Salamandra salamandra (European fire
   salamander) 11:*1455*
Salmo spp. 1:124; 8:*1082, 1134*; 11:1492
salmon
   Atlantic, fertilization 8:*1082*
   farmed 1:124
   migration 6:733; 8:1133–*1134*, 1135;
     10:*1427*
   nests 9:1206
   Pacific 10:1426
   and salinity changes 11:1492
   sockeye 6:731; 8:1133–1134; 10:*1427*
sand dollars 4:568, 570
sanderlings 11:1494
sandfish, long belted 7:890
sandpipers 11:1471; 12:1699–1700
   broad-billed 12:1700
   curlew 12:1700
   nests 9:1209
Sarcophilus harrisii (Tasmanian devil) 8:*1079*
Sarcopterygii 6:730; 12:1672–1673
Sarracenia spp. (pitcher plants) 3:316;
   8:*1027*; 10:1317
Saurischia 4:529–530
Saurolophus 4:530–531
sauropods 4:529–530
Sayornis phoebe (eastern phoebe) 2:193;
   12:*1718*
scale insects 2:*195*; 7:885
scallops 8:1149; 11:1497
Scaphiopus spp. (spadefoot toad)
   4:*458*–459, 500–501; 6:790
Scaphopoda 8:1150
Scarus spp. (parrot fish) 4:451, 453
scavengers 5:695
Schistocera spp. (locusts) 9:1294
Schistosoma spp. (blood fluke) 6:*736*, 737;
   9:1265; 10:1438
schooling, fish 3:402; 6:*729*, 730–731
scissor bills (skimmers) 11:1473; 12:1700
Sciurognathi 10:1437, 1438
Sciurus spp. (squirrels) 2:194; 9:1206;
   12:*1665*
Sclerospongiae 11:1553
Scolecomorphidae 2:276
Scoliopteryx libatrix (herald moth) 3:328
Scolopacidae *see* sandpipers

Scolopendra spp. 3:343
Scolytus scolytus (elm-bark beetle) 2:178
Scomber sp. (mackerel) 6:732
scorpion flies 8:1084
Scorpionidae 11:1470
scorpions 1:*133*; 11:1469–1470
   coloring 11:1470
   courtship 4:457
   feeding 1:141; 11:1470
   imperial 11:*1469*
   reproduction 11:*1470*
   sand 9:1222–1223
   true and false 1:133
   venomous 11:1470
   whip scorpions 11:1469
   see also arachnids
screamers 12:1701
Scyphozoa *see* jellyfish
sea anemones *see* jellyfish, sea anemones,
   and hydras
seabirds *see* birds, seabirds
sea cows 2:186
sea cucumbers 4:568, 570; 9:*1230*, 1232
sea dragons 6:732
sea gooseberries *see* comb jellies
sea hares 2:217
sea horses 6:729–730, *733*; 11:1484
sea lilies 4:568, 569, 570; 9:1232
sea lions 2:210; 3:*311*; 8:1124; 12:1615
seals 3:311; 10:1334
   elephant 1:*85*; 3:311; 11:*1484*
   flippers 5:699
   leopard 10:*1334*
   migration 2:210
   milk 7:998
   monk
     Hawaiian 3:311
     Mediterranean 5:*655*
   swimming 11:1578
sea pens 9:1232
sea scorpions 1:132
sea slugs *see* nudibranchs
sea spiders 1:130, 141
sea squirts 3:*365*, 371
sea urchins 4:570
   alarm signals 3:403–404
   endoskeleton 4:567; 11:*1499*
   feeding 4:568
   larvae 4:569; 8:*1126*; 10:1314
   metamorphosis 7:1005; 8:*1126*
   purple 4:439
   purple-tipped 4:*439*
   reproduction 4:569
   spines 4:568
   tube feet 4:567, 569, *570*
   see also echinoderms
secretary birds 2:236
Seiurus aurocapillus (ovenbird) 6:776
Selasphorus rufus (rufous hummingbird)
   3:*408*
selection
   kin 1:58, 60; 11:1524, *1525*
   sexual *see* sexual selection
Sepia spp. 4:458; 7:978

Sergestes 2:207
servals 3:321; 4:445
Sesia apiformis (hornet moth) 2:*286*
sex
   change in 7:890
   of crocodilians depends on temperature
     4:466
   differences between, in child
     development 3:359
sexual selection 4:458, 524–525;
   11:1483–1486
   and horns 12:1663
   the peacock's tail and courtship display
     4:525; 11:*1483*–1484
shads 4:573
sharks 11:1487–1490
   basking 6:732; 11:1487
   behavior 11:1490
   benthic and deep-sea 9:1232;
     11:1488–1489
   blue 11:1488
   body form 11:1488–1489
   bull 11:1488
   buoyancy 6:728; 11:1577
   cat 11:1488
   chemical reception 12:1596
   distribution 11:1488
   evolution 11:1489
   excretion 5:670; 6:732; 7:*902*
   feeding 11:1489
   fossil 11:1489
   goblin 9:1232
   great white 4:450; 11:*1487*, 1489, 1490
   Greenland 9:1232
   ground 11:1487
   hammerhead 6:733; 11:1489, 1490
   hunting of 11:1490
   lemon 11:1490
   mackerel 11:1488
   megamouth 11:1489
   nurse, gray 11:*1500*
   osmotic regulation 11:1489
   reef 12:*1672*
   reproduction and life cycle 6:733;
     11:*1489*–1490
   and salts 11:1459
   silky 11:*1490*
   skeleton 11:1489, *1500*
   spiny 7:978
   spleen 11:1551
   swell 11:*1489*
   swimming 11:1500, 1577
   teeth 6:732, 733–734; 12:*1606*
   thermotaxis 12:1647
   thresher 11:1488
   tiger 11:1489
   vision 6:731
   "warm-bodied" 11:1488; 12:1617
   whale 10:*1314, 1418*; 11:1487,
     1488
   see also dogfish
shearwaters 11:1473, 1474
sooty 11:1582
sheathbills 11:1471

Bold words with bold page numbers indicate complete articles; bold numbers
preceding colons are volume numbers; numbers following colons indicate
page numbers; italic page numbers refer to illustrations or other graphics.

sheep
  in Australia **11**:1465
  bighorn **4**:500; **7**:*910*, 911; **11**:*1528*
    behavior **4**:*460*
  clones of Dolly the **3**:*340*, *383*–384;
    11:*1558*
  crossbred **11**:1480
  diseases, coast disease **9**:1227
  domestication **4**:544
  lice **8**:1033
  protection from predators **4**:545
  saliva **11**:1452
  see also ruminants
shelducks **12**:1700–1701
shipworm **8**:1149
shoebills **12**:1701
shorebirds (waders) **12**:1699–*1700*
shrews **7**:880, 954, 955
  echolocation **8**:1071
  elephant **7**:*956*
  tree **7**:955
shrikes **9**:1274
  boubou **3**:402
shrimp
  brine **12**:1592
  fairy **1**:106; **12**:1592
  ghost **4**:467
  Kentucky cave **3**:326
  larvae **10**:1314
  mud **4**:467
  snapping **4**:470
  see also crustaceans
Sialia sialis (eastern bluebird) **3**:*410*
sidewinders **11**:*1520*
sifakas **9**:1221
silkworms **6**:*725*
  diseases of **9**:1269–1270
silverfish **11**:1580
simians **10**:1367–1369
Sinosauropteryx **9**:1254
Siphonaptera **6**:738
Sipuncula **1**:96
sirens (Sirenidae) **11**:1455
Sistrurus spp. **4**:459
Sitta europea (nuthatch) **12**:*1609*
skates **6**:734
skimmers (scissor bills) **11**:1473; **12**:1700
skinks **8**:1053
  Fernand's/fire **8**:*1051*
  tail **12**:*1593*
  tongue **12**:1622
skippers (Hesperiidae) **2**:268
skunks **4**:486; **11**:*1516*
sloths **1**:*104*
  hands **11**:1498
sludge worms **1**:*128*
slugs
  foot **5**:698
  mucus **9**:*1172*
Smilodon (saber-toothed tiger) **3**:310, 312,
    324; **5**:678; **10**:*1349*
snails
  common **8**:*1150*
  giant African **2**:185
  land, lungs **8**:1060
  mucus **9**:1172
  polymorphism **4**:525
  radula **10**:1374
  shell **8**:*1148*; **11**:*1497*

slime **5**:699
  see also mollusks
snakes 11:1517–1520
  advanced **11**:1519–1520
  blind **11**:1518, 1519
  brown tree **2**:186
  coral
    instinctive avoidance of **7**:961
    mimics of **2**:*285*; **4**:484
  courtship **4**:459
  ears **11**:1517
  eyes **11**:1517
  "flying" **11**:1519
  garter **10**:1351; **11**:1519, 1520
  grass **9**:*1157*
  jaws **5**:695; **7**:978, 979
  mating and reproduction **11**:1519
  milk **4**:484
  mimicry **2**:*285*, 286
  molting **9**:*1157*
  pipe **11**:1519
  primitive **11**:1519
  rat **11**:*1517*
  record-holding **11**:1518
  respiration **10**:1422
  sea **10**:1422; **11**:1520
  sense of smell and taste **10**:1416;
    11:*1515*, 1518; **12**:*1596*
  skin **11**:1518
  sunbeam **11**:1519
  tail **12**:1592
  teeth **11**:*1519*; **12**:1606
  tongue **10**:1416; **12**:*1596*, 1622
  venomous **4**:485; **7**:*939*; **11**:1518;
    12:1606
  vine **11**:1519
  see also reptiles
snipe, common **12**:1593
solenodons **7**:956
Solifugae **11**:1469
Solpugida **11**:1469
sonar **4**:574
  for underwater exploration **9**:1238
songbirds **9**:1273, 1274
songs, bird *see* birds, songs
Sotalia fluviatilis (tucuxi) **12**:1710
sounds
  caterpillar **1**:119
  signals **3**:404–405
    courtship **4**:457, 458–459
  see also echolocation
sow bugs **4**:468
sparrows
  house **9**:1274–1275
  song sparrows **3**:402–403, 408
  white-crowned **3**:402
  white-throated **8**:1136
Spartina spp. (cord-grass) **11**:1493
Speothos venaticus (bush dog) **4**:540, *541*
Spermophilus spp.
  S. parryi (Arctic ground squirrel) **12**:1654
  S. richardsoni (Richardson's ground
    squirrel) **11**:*1532*
Spheniscus humboldti (Humboldt penguin)
    6:754
Sphenodon spp. (tuatara lizard) **8**:*1050*;
    10:*1415*; **11**:1581–1582
Sphyma lewini (scalloped hammerhead)
    11:1490

spiders 1:*130*, 131–132; **11:1546–1549**
  anatomy **11**:*1547*
  "ballooning" **11**:1548
  bird-eating **11**:*1548*
  black widow **1**:133, *139*; **11**:1547
  bolas/angling **1**:131–132
  camouflage **1**:131
  catching prey **11**:1548
  courtship **4**:457; **11**:1548–1549;
    12:1628
  crab **1**:96, 131; **11**:1548, 1549
  digestion by **1**:140
  excretion **7**:989; **12**:1666
  eyes and vision **11**:1547; **12**:1687
  feet **5**:699
  funnel-web **1**:133, 139
  garden **1**:131; **11**:1548; **12**:*1627*
  habitats **11**:1548
  jumping **4**:457; **9**:1169; **11**:1547,
    1548–1549
  legs **1**:139
  movement coordination **11**:1547
  nocturnal, vision **12**:1687
  nursery web **11**:1549
  recluse **1**:133
    brown **11**:1547
  redback/button **1**:133
  reproduction **11**:1547–1548
  respiration **11**:1547
  silk produced by **1**:131; **6**:726; **11**:1549
  spitting **1**:132
  tarantula **11**:1548
    red-kneed **11**:*1546*
  trap-door **11**:1548
  true **11**:1546
  underwater **1**:131
  venomous **1**:133, *139*, 141; **4**:485;
    11:1547
  waste products **5**:*665*
  water **11**:1549
  web-building **1**:131, 141; **11**:1547,
    1548, *1549*; **12**:*1627*–1628
    courtship **4**:457
  wolf **11**:1548
  see also arachnids
sponges 1:*94*; **11:1552–1553**
  asconoid **11**:1552
  boring **11**:1553
  bread-crumb **11**:*1553*
  colored **11**:1552
  diffusion in **3**:371
  evolution **11**:1553
  feeding and digestion **7**:969
  leuconoid **11**:1552
  regeneration **10**:1400
  skeleton **7**:969; **11**:1498–1499
  vegetable (loofahs) **11**:1554
spoonbills **5**:648; **10**:1311; **12**:1700
spoon worms **1**:96
spring hare, African **10**:1437
springtails **1**:141; **8**:1126
  distribution **12**:1719
Squalus acanthias (piked dogfish) **11**:1490
Squamata **10**:1415; **11**:1517
squid **8**:*1148*
  bioluminescence **2**:*205*, 207
  color change **4**:483; **7**:908; **10**:1310
  common **2**:*205*
  eyes **5**:685–686; **8**:1149

giant **4**:574; **8**:1149; **11**:1499
  "jaws" **7**:978
  movement **11**:1499, 1577
  skeleton **11**:1499
  vertical migration **8**:1136
  see also cephalopods; mollusks
squirrelfish **3**:403; **12**:*1613*
squirrels
  desert **8**:1072
  flying **6**:749; **10**:1436–1437; **12**:1591
  gray **2**:194; **12**:*1665*
  ground **7**:891, 892; **11**:*1532*; **12**:1654
  red **2**:194
  tree **7**:891–892; **9**:1206
starfish **4**:568, 569, *569*–570
  crown-of-thorns **4**:*450*, 451, 453, 568
  endoskeleton **11**:1499
  regeneration **10**:1399–1400, *1401*, 1404
  reproduction **10**:1400
  structure **4**:567
  sunflower **9**:*1230*
  tube feet **4**:567
  see also echinoderms
starlings **3**:401, 410; **9**:*1273*, 1275
  communication **3**:402
  introduction to the United States **3**:410
Steatornis caripensis (oilbird) **4**:*574*
Stegosaurus **4**:528, 531; **12**:*1593*
Stenonychosaurus **4**:529
stereotypes, behavioral **12**:1725
Sterna spp.
  S. albifrons (little tern) **11**:*1474*
  S. hirundo (common tern) **11**:*1472*
  S. paradisaea (Arctic tern) **8**:*1133*;
    12:1654
  S. sumatrana (black-napped tern) **1**:*82*
Sternorrhyncha **7**:883–884
Stichopus spp. **4**:570
stick insects **4**:483
  see also leaf insects and walking sticks
sticklebacks **6**:733; **9**:1206; **12**:1615
  three-spined **4**:456, 485; **7**:*1002*
stilts **12**:1700
stints, little **12**:1700
Stomolophus meleagris (cannonball jellyfish)
    7:982
Stone Age man **10**:1362, 1364
storks **6**:752; **8**:1134; **12**:1700
  whale-headed **12**:1701
Strepsirhini **10**:1365
stridulation **3**:405
Strigidae **2**:236–237
Strigiformes **2**:236–237
Strigops habroptilus (owl parrot/kakapo)
    6:755
Strix spp. **3**:402; **9**:1221
Strongylocentratus franciscanus (purple sea
    urchin) **4**:439
Struthio camelus (ostrich) **5**:698; **6**:*755*
sturgeons **6**:734; **11**:1492
Sturnus vulgaris (starling) **3**:401, 410;
    9:*1273*, 1275
suckerfish **11**:1490
suckling **7**:998
Suiformes **11**:1451
Sula spp. **2**:*231*
sunbirds, golden-winged **5**:696
Suncus etruscus (Savi's pygmy shrew) **7**:954
sundews **3**:*314*–316; **5**:696

superfetation 10:1353

superregenerators 10:1399–1400

surfperches 6:733

Suricata suricatta (gray meerkat) 1:*58*; 3:*313*; 11:1522

suricates 3:313

suspension feeders, on the ocean floor 9:1232

Sus scrofa (wild boar) 12:1606, *1610*

swallows

  nests 9:1209

  parasites of 11:1524

swans 12:1701

swiftlets, cave 3:*328*; 4:574; 9:*1222*

swifts 2:231

swimming 11:1576–1578

  fish 6:729–730; 9:1178–1179; 11:*1576–1577*

    sharks 11:1500, 1577

  in humans 11:1577

  babies 3:*356*

Syconycteris australis (southern blossom bat) 2:173–174

Sylvilagus spp. (cottontail rabbits) 10:*1392*

Symphata 12:1692, 1693

Systema Naturae (Carolus Linnaeus) 5:621; 8:1041, 1042; 12:1600

T

Tachyglossus aculeatus (short-beaked echidna) 9:1162–1163

Tadorna tadorna (shelduck) 12:1701

tadpoles *see* frogs and toads, tadpoles

Taenia spp. (tapeworms) 6:737; 9:1268

tagging, of animals 12:*1720*, 1721

taipans 11:1518

takahes 6:756

Takifugu rubripes (Japanese puffer fish) 1:50; 4:485

tamanduas 1:103–104

tamarins 10:1367–1368

  golden lion 10:1367; 12:1718, 1725

Tamias striatus (eastern chipmunk) 12:*1608*

tapeworms 1:90; 3:390–391; 6:736, *737*; 9:1267–1268

  excretion 7:970

  self-fertilization 7:890

tapirs 9:1257

tarantulas 4:485; 11:*1546*, 1548

Tardigrada 1:97

Taricha rivularis (red-bellied newt) 4:458

tarsiers 9:*1221*, 1222; 10:1367

Tarsiidae 10:1367

Tarsius spp. 9:*1221*

Tasmanian devils 8:*1079*

Tasmanian tigers (Tasmanian wolves/thylacines) 4:446; 8:1079

Teleostei 6:734

Telicomys 10:1438

Tenebrio spp. 2:178

Tenodera aridifolia (Chinese mantis) 8:1075

tenrecs 7:*955*, 956; 9:1221

termitaria 12:1612

termites 12:1611–1612

  castes 12:1611

  cellulose digestion 1:140; 10:1380; 11:*1461*, 1462; 12:1611

  evolution 12:1612

  nests 7:*959*; 9:*1208*; 12:1612

touch receptors 12:1627

terns 11:*1472, 1474*

  Arctic, migration 8:*1133*; 12:1654

  black-napped 1:*82*

terrapins 12:1624

  river 12:1623

Testudo elephantopus (Galápagos tortoise) 1:*33*; 12:*1623*

Tetracanthella arctica (springtail) 12:1719

tetras 1:*125*

Thamnophis spp. (garter snake) 10:1351; 11:1520

Thaumatogyllus 3:326

thecodonts 4:530

therapods 4:529

thrushes, song 4:459; 9:1274

Thylacinus cynocephalus (Tasmanian wolf/Tasmanian tiger) 4:446; 8:1079

Thyone spp. 4:570

tick birds 4:485

ticks 1:132, 141

  diseases from 1:*131*; 7:*946*–947, 949; 9:*1264*

  northern deer 7:*946*

  wood 1:*131*; 9:*1264*

tigers 1:*32*; 2:*284*; 3:313, *321*, 324; 5:607–*608*, 694

  saber-toothed 3:310, 312, 324; 5:678; 9:*1254*; 10:*1349*

tits, great 1:*29*, 85; 9:1274

toadfish 3:405

toads *see* frogs and toads

Tollund man 6:782–783

tongue worms 1:97

tools

  ancient man and 10:*1361*, 1362–1363

  chimpanzees and 10:1369–1370

Torosaurus 4:531

tortoises and turtles 12:1623–1624

  armor 4:485; 12:1623

  and humans 12:1624

  movement 12:1623

  respiration 12:1623

  tortoises, giant 3:410; 12:*1623*, 1624

  turtles 11:*1492*

    alligator snapping 2:283, 286; 12:*1623*–1624

    courtship behavior 4:459

    eggs 12:1624

    feeding by 12:1623–1624

    green 4:*437*; 8:1134; 11:*1492*; 12:1624

    hawksbill 11:1492; 12:1624

    jaws 7:978; 12:1606

    leatherback 11:1492

    loggerhead 11:1492

    map 12:1623

    migration 8:1134

    nest holes 9:1209

    painted 4:459

    reproduction 12:1624

    sea 12:1623, *1624*

    soft-shelled 12:1623

    terrapin 12:1623, 1624

toucans 6:777

toxins 1:51

Toxocara canis 9:*1266*

Trachurus symmetricus (California mackerel) 4:481

tracks, fossilized 6:783

transformist theory, of Lamarck 5:652

Trechus micros (ground beetle) 3:327

tree ducks, fulvous 4:460

treehoppers 2:283

Trematoda 6:735; 9:1265

Triadobatrachus 6:790

Triatoma spp. 7:885

Triceratops 4:528, 531

Trichinella spiralis 9:1196

Trichodectes oris (sheep-biting louse) 8:1033

Trichoplax adhaerens 1:94

trilobites 1:138; 6:783

Triphosa dubitata (tissue moth) 3:328

triplets 12:1656

Triturus helveticus (palmate newt) 11:1456

triungulins 2:178

troglodytes 3:325

trogons 6:777

Trombidium spp. 1:*132*

tropic birds 11:1472–1473

trout

  farmed 1:124

  population densities 3:408

tsetse flies *see* flies, tsetse

tuataras 8:*1050*; 10:*1415*; 11:1581–1582

tubenoses 11:1474

Tubifex spp. 1:*128*

tucuxis 12:1710

tuna 10:1424; 12:1617

  skipjack 6:731

Tunga penetrans (chigger/chigoe/jigger) 6:738; 9:*1264*

Tunicata (Urochordata) 3:*365*

Turbellaria 6:735–736

Turdus spp. 9:1274; 11:1569

Tursiops truncatus (bottlenose dolphin) 4:572

turtles *see* tortoises and turtles

twins and multiple births 5:590; 12:1655–1656

  identical twins 3:383, *384*; 12:*1655*, 1656

  nonidentical/fraternal twins 12:1655, *1656*

    and skin grafts 8:1087, 1088

  Siamese twins 12:1656

Tylopoda 11:1451

Tympanuchus spp. (prairie chicken) 4:459

Typhlonectidae 2:276

Tyrannosaurus 4:528, 529, 531

Tyto alba (barn owl) 2:237; 9:*1158*, 1222

Tytonidae 2:237

U

uakaris 10:1368

Uca spp. (fiddler crab) 2:*218*; 4:457, 467

Umbonia spinosa (treehopper) 2:283

ungulates 12:1659–1663

  defense 4:484–485

  domestic 12:1662

  even-toed (Artiodactyla) 12:1659, *1660*, 1661

  evolution 12:*1661*

  feet 5:697; 12:1659–*1660*

  on grasslands 11:1453, 1464–1465; 12:*1663*

  mammary glands 5:*676*

  odd-toed (Perissodactyla) 12:1659, *1660*, 1661

  see also ruminants

Uniramia 1:97

uniramians 1:141–142

Upogebia spp. (mud shrimp) 4:467

Uraeotyphidae 2:276

Uria aalge (common guillemot) 11:1474

Urochordata 3:365

Urodela 1:64

Uropygi 11:1469

Ursavus elmensis (dawn bear) 3:309

Ursidae 3:308–309

  see also bears

Ursus spp. 3:308–309

  U. americanus (American black bear) 12:1655–1656

  U. arctos (European bear) 11:1541

  U. maritimus see bears, polar

  U. spelaeus (cave bear) 11:1541

V

vaquitas 12:1709

Varanus komodoensis (Komodo dragon) 7:*977*; 8:*1051*; 12:1717

Vargula spp., bioluminescence 2:206

Vejovidae 11:1470

Velella velella (by-the-wind-sailor) 7:983

Velociraptor 4:528, 529

velvet worms 1:97, 138; 8:1049–1050; 12:*1602*

venom 4:485

  snake 7:*939*; 11:1518

  spider 1:133, *139*, 141; 4:485

  see also toxins

verdins 2:273

Vermivora bachmanii (Bachman's warbler) 9:1275

vertebrates 1:94, 97; 12:1671–1674

  abdomen 1:13

  are chordates 3:365

  are larger than invertebrates 12:1673

  brain 2:257, 258, 259

  circulatory systems 3:373–376

  cloning 3:382–383, 385

  colonizing the land 12:1674

  digestive systems 4:513–516

  embryo development 5:598–600

  evolution 12:1672

  excretory systems 7:989–990

  heart 3:375; 7:877–879

  immune system 7:928

  molting 9:1158–1159

  skeleton 11:1499–1504

  skin 11:1506

  success 12:1674

  tails 12:1592–1593

  taste 12:1596

  see also amphibians; birds; chordates; fish; mammals; reptiles

Vespa spp. (hornets) 12:1692–1693

Vespula vulgaris (common wasp) **12**:*1692*
vinegaroons **11**:1469
viperfish **7**:979
vipers **11**:1520
 Gaboon **2**:282
 pit **11**:1518, 1520
 saw-scaled **11**:1518
 see also rattlesnakes
Viverridae **3**:311–312
viviparity, *see also* gestation
voles, prairie **10**:1437
Vombatus ursinus (wombat) **4**:446; **5**:656;
 8:*1080*
vomit, fossilized **9**:1257
Vulpes spp.
 V. macrotis (kit fox) **4**:501
 V. rupelli (desert sand fox) **4**:501
 V. vulpes (red fox) **11**:1523; **12**:*1671*
vultures **2**:235, 236, *237*
 flight **6**:750, 752
 Old World and New World **4**:446

W

waders *see* waterbirds and waders
walking sticks *see* leaf insects and
 walking sticks
wallabies **8**:1080
walruses **3**:311
wapiti **5**:656; **8**:1084, 1133; **12**:1609
warblers
 Bachman's **9**:1275
 chestnut-sided **3**:402
 reed **1**:*59*
 resource partitioning **3**:410
warm-blooded animals
 dinosaurs as **4**:531
 endothermy **7**:900–901; **8**:1069
 fish as **6**:731; **11**:1488
 pterosaurs as **10**:1391
Washoe (chimpanzee) **3**:406
wasps and bees 12:1692–1694
 bees **12**:1692, *1693–1694*
  Africanized **12**:1693
  bumblebees **7**:893
  carpenter **12**:*1693*
  cuckoo **12**:1693
  hibernation **7**:893
  mimics of **2**:*286*
  orchid **9**:1240
  pollen baskets **6**:*761*
  pollination by **6**:*761*; **9**:1240;
   10:1336–1337; **12**:*1693*
  sting **1**:53
  temperature regulation **3**:367; **12**:1618
  vision **12**:1687
  see also honeybees
 wasps **12**:*1692–1693*
  common **12**:*1692*
  ichneumon **12**:1692
  parasitic **12**:1692
  pollination by **6**:761; **12**:1693
  social **12**:1692–1693
  sting **1**:53
waterbirds and waders 12:1699–1701
water boatmen **11**:1577
water bugs, giant **7**:885
water dogs **11**:1454
water fleas **4**:467, 468
waterfowl **12**:1699, 1700–1701, 1706

water scorpions **7**:885
water striders/water skippers **7**:885
weasels **3**:308; **9**:1159; **10**:1353
weavers, nests **9**:1208–*1209*
weevils **7**:969
 boll **2**:178
whales, porpoises, and dolphins
 12:1707–1710
 anatomy **12**:1707–1708
 behavior **12**:*1707*, 1709
 blowholes **10**:*1417*, 1423; **12**:1707,
  1708, *1710*
 distribution **12**:1710
 dolphins
  bottlenose **4**:572, 573; **12**:1707
  Chinese river (baiji) **12**:1709
  communication **3**:*404*, 405
  courtship displays **4**:456
  endangered **12**:1709
  Indus River **12**:1709, 1710
  intelligence **12**:1709–1710
  sonic weapons **4**:574
  swimming **11**:1578
  teeth **12**:1606
  testes **10**:1410
 echolocation **4**:572; **7**:873; **8**:1135;
  12:1708
 endangered **12**:1709
 evolution **12**:1708
 feeding **12**:1709
 intelligence **12**:1709–1710
 navigation and strandings **12**:1710
 porpoises, endangered **12**:1709
 reproduction **12**:1709
 senses **12**:1708–1709
 whales
  baleen **4**:438; **5**:*695*; **12**:1606, 1708,
   1709, 1710
  beaked **12**:1606
  blue **3**:405; **4**:438; **8**:1069; **12**:1707,
   1708, 1709, 1710
  bowhead **12**:1710
  bryde's **12**:1710
  diving **10**:1423
  fin whales **12**:1709, 1710
  gray **8**:1134; **10**:*1417*; **12**:1709, 1710
  humpback **1**:97; **3**:405; **4**:*438*, 460;
   11:1580; **12**:1709, 1710
  killer (orcas) **10**:1350; **12**:1707, *1708*,
   1709, 1710
  migrations **8**:1135; **12**:1710
  minke **12**:1710
  northern bottlenose **12**:1709
  pilot **12**:1707
  respiration **10**:1423
  right **12**:1709, 1710
  rorqual **12**:1710
  sei **12**:1710
  "skyhopping" **8**:1135
  sounds **3**:405; **12**:1709
  spermaceti **12**:1702
  sperm whales **4**:572, 574; **12**:1707,
   1708, 1709, 1710
  swimming **11**:1578; **12**:1593
  toothed **4**:572, 574; **12**:1606,
   1707–1708, 1710
  whaling and **12**:1710
wheel animals *see* rotifers
whippoorwills **2**:216; **6**:776; **9**:1221–1222

whip scorpions **11**:1469
widow birds, long-tailed **11**:1486
wildcats **3**:324
wildebeest
 grazing **12**:1662, 1663
 migration **8**:1134–1135, *1136*
wildfowl **11**:1578
wolverines **12**:*1654*
wolves **4**:*539–540*
 dog-wolf hybrids **4**:541–542
 domesticated **4**:541
 dominance interactions **3**:*402*; **11**:*1522*
 Ethiopian **4**:541–542
 howling **4**:542
 maned **4**:445
 red **4**:541, 542
 social behavior **4**:540
 territories **12**:1613
 timber/gray **3**:309, *428*; **4**:*539*, 541;
  10:1350; **11**:*1522*, 1524
wombats **4**:446; **5**:656; **8**:*1080*
wood lice, molt **9**:1158
woodpeckers **6**:*775*
 competition **3**:410
 drumming **4**:459
 feet **5**:698; **9**:1273
 Gila **2**:273
 great spotted **2**:232
 nests **9**:1209
 tongue **12**:1621, 1622
worms
 parasitic
  in cats and dogs **1**:90
  see also hookworms; nematode worms;
   tapeworms
wrasse **4**:445, 450–451; **11**:*1582*
wrens
 cactus **2**:273; **9**:1206
 flightless **6**:756
 nests **9**:1206, 1208
Wucheraria **9**:1222
Wyeomyia smithii **3**:316

X

Xanthopan morgani praedicta (hawk moth)
 2:268
xenacanths **11**:1489
Xenicus lyalli (flightless wren) **6**:756
Xenopsylla cheopis (rat flea) **6**:740
Xestobium rufovillosum (death-watch beetle)
 2:178
Xiphophorus spp. (platyfish) **11**:1485–1486
Xysticus sp. **11**:1549

Y

yaks **1**:18; **4**:545; **8**:1058
yellow jackets **12**:1692–1693

Z

Zaglossus spp. (echidnas) **9**:1162–1163
Zalophus californianus (California sea lion)
 3:*311*; **8**:1124
zebras **3**:391, *392*; **8**:*1074*
 communication **3**:401
 competing males **3**:*407*
 courtship **4**:460
 grazing **12**:1663
 plains/Burchell's **12**:1663
  social groups **11**:1523

Zonotrichia spp. **3**:402; **8**:1136
zooids **11**:1524
zoology 12:1720–1721
zoos 12:1722–1726
zorros, small-eared **4**:539
Zygoptera **4**:550

■ PEOPLE INDEX

A

Addison, Thomas **5**:612; **7**:905
Adler, Alfred **10**:1385
Aldrovandi, Ulisse **5**:620
Alexander of Tralles **5**:637
Alvarez, Luis and Walter **5**:679
Alzheimer, Alois **4**:495
Ames, Bruce **3**:295
Anaximander **2**:200; **5**:652
Apgar, Virginia 1:123
Appert, Nicholas **6**:765
Araneomorphae **11**:1546
Aristotle 1:70, 135; 2:207; 5:620, 652;
 9:1214; **11**:*1539*; **12**:1721
 and logic **11**:1467
Arrhenius, Svante **5**:651–652
Artedi, Petrus **8**:1041
Asfaw, Berhane **7**:915
Assicott, F. T. **4**:548
Avery, Oswald **2**:227; **4**:537;
 8:1141–1142

B

Bacon, Francis **2**:201
Baer, Karl von **2**:202
Baker, Henry **2**:207
Bakewell, Robert **11**:1479
Ballard, Dr. Robert **9**:1238
Banks, Joseph **2**:254; **8**:1042
Banting, Frederick Grant **4**:*508*; **7**:*965*;
 8:1103
Barbier, Charles **12**:1628
Bard, Philip **5**:602
Barnard, Christiaan **8**:1088; **12**:1635
Barr, M. L. **2**:191
Basalo, A. F. **11**:1485
Bauhin, Caspar **2**:253
Beadle, George 8:1085; 12:1598
Beattie, John **4**:553
Beaumont, William **4**:517
Behring, Emil Adolf von **1**:112; **5**:592
Bender, Hans **9**:1263
Benzer, Seymour **12**:1676
Berg, Paul **2**:227
Bernard, Claude **1**:91; **7**:*899*; **10**:1307;
 12:1721
Bernoulli, Daniel **6**:751
Bertram, E. G. **2**:191
Best, Charles **4**:508; **7**:965; **8**:1103
Billingham, R. **8**:1087
Binet, Alfred **7**:966
Black, James Whyte **7**:898
Bleuler, Eugen **9**:1212
Bloch, Felix **8**:1068
Bonnet, Charles **2**:202
Bonpland, Aimé **2**:192
Bordet, Jules **2**:244
Boyer, Herbert **2**:227
Boyer, Paul **2**:160
Boyle, Robert **5**:637

Braid, James **7**:926
Braille, Louis **11**:1538; **12**:*1628*
Briggs, Robert **3**:383
Broca, Paul **9**:1214
Brown, William L. **12**:1711
Buchheim, Rudolph **9**:1289
Buchner, Eduard **5**:630
Buckland, Rev. William **4**:527
Budiansky, Stephen **4**:544
Buffon, Georges-Louis Leclerc,
    Comte de **2**:201
Burch, Rex L. **1**:92
Burnet, Macfarlane **8**:1088

C

Calvin, Melvin **10**:1304
Cannon, W. B. **5**:602, 641; **10**:1307
Carlsson, Arvid **9**:1215
Carson, Rachel Louise 1:41; **3**:**318**;
    4:481; **5**:584, 680; **9**:1288
Catesby, Mark **5**:621
Cattell, Raymond B. **9**:1283
Caventou, Joseph Bienaimé **8**:1103
Cayley, George **6**:751
Chain, Ernst **6**:742, 799
Charaka **7**:887
Charcot, Jean-Martin **9**:*1213*, 1214;
    12:1658
Chargaff, Erwin **4**:537
Chase, Martha **4**:537
Chauliac, Guy de **5**:*637*
Chomsky, Noam **5**:662
Chopra, Deepak **7**:943–944
Cohen, P. P **12**:1667
Cohen, Stanley **2**:227
Colle, Giovanni **2**:244
Collins, Francis **7**:919, *923*
Collip, James Bertram **4**:508
Collip, John **7**:965
Conway, John **2**:150
Cormack, Allan **4**:474
Correns, Karl **8**:1107
Cortés, Hernán **12**:1723
Cottam, Clarence **4**:481
Crick, Francis, and James Watson
    2:202, 221, 227; **4**:**461–462**, 537;
    7:918
Cruveilhier, Jean **9**:1175, *1176*
Culpepper, Nicholas **7**:888
Curie, Marie **8**:1091; **10**:1394, 1395
Curie, Pierre **8**:1091; **10**:1395
Cuvier, Georges **2**:201, 202; **5**:652, 679;
    10:1391

D

Damadian, Raymond B. **8**:1068
Dart, Raymond **7**:915
Darwin, Charles 2:192; **4**:**478–479**;
    5:585
  and animal experimentation **1**:91
  and the bombardier beetle **5**:677
  and carnivorous plants **3**:314
  and coral reefs **4**:448
  Descent of Man **7**:913
  and facial expressions **5**:605
  and Galápagos finches **4**:478; **9**:1192
  and insect/flower coevolution **2**:268;
    3:389–390
  and instinct **7**:963

On the Origin of Species **4**:479; **5**:653;
    7:912–913; **9**:1192, 1193
  and phototropism **12**:1645, *1646*
  and seed dispersal **1**:79
  and sexual selection **11**:1483
  theory of evolution **4**:479; **5**:652–653;
    7:912–913; **9**:1192–1193; **11**:1479;
    12:1721
  survival of the fittest **4**:444–445;
    10:1345
Darwin, Erasmus **7**:912
Darwin, Francis **12**:1645, *1646*
David, Père **3**:309
da Vinci, Leonardo *see* Leonardo da Vinci
Dawson, Charles **6**:782; **7**:917
Deane, John **9**:1238
Deere, John **1**:39
Descartes, René **3**:*422*–423
Dioscorides **2**:253
Dobzhansky, Theodosius **9**:1193
Domagk, Gerhard **8**:1103
Donald, Anna **8**:1096, 1097, 1098
Donald, Ian **8**:1090
Donkin, Bryan **6**:765
Drew, Charles 2:*245*; **4**:**553–554**
Dubois, Eugene **7**:916, 917
Duesberg, Peter **9**:1174

E

Ebbinghaus, Hermann **10**:1383
Ehrlich, Paul 2:239; **5**:**591–592**; **8**:1103,
    1131; **9**:1289
Einstein, Albert **5**:*703*; **7**:*967*; **10**:1394
Einthoven, Willem **8**:1090
Eldredge, Niles **1**:21; **2**:203; **5**:654
Elion, Gertrude *see* **Hitchings, George,
    and Gertrude Elion**
Elton, Charles **6**:768, 769
Emerson, Rollins **8**:1085, 1086
Erikson, Erik **1**:28
Erwin, Terry **2**:184
Eysenck, Hans J. **9**:*1283*

F

Fabre, Henri **7**:963
Fabricius, Johann **5**:621; **8**:1042
Fallopius, Gabriele **4**:560
Faraday, Michael **8**:1102
Fischer, Emil **5**:*629*, 631
Fisher, Ronald Aylmer **5**:654; **11**:*1468*, 1485
Fleming, Alexander 1:*108*; **2**:227;
    6:**741–742**, 799; **8**:1103, 1131,
    1138; **9**:*1290*; **11**:1461, 1571
Flor, H. H. **3**:391
Florey, Howard **6**:742, 799
Flourens, Marie-Jean-Pierre **7**:874
Forbes, Edward **9**:1239
Fossey, Dian 6:**779–780**; **10**:1367
Francis, Thomas **11**:1457
Franklin, Rosalind 2:202, 221; **4**:462,
    537; **6**:**785–786**
Frere, John **7**:912
Freud, Sigmund **1**:*30*, *121*, 122; **3**:422;
    4:556; **10**:*1383*, 1384–1385
  and phobias **10**:1301
Fromm-Reichmann, Frieda **9**:1212

G

Galdikas, Dr. Birute **10**:1367

Galen **1**:70, 71; **2**:200, *201*; **8**:1099;
    9:1214, 1289
Gall, Franz Joseph **9**:1214
Gallaudet, Thomas Hopkins **7**:873
Galton, Francis **7**:966, 967
Gause, G. F. **3**:408
Gebhart, Gerald **1**:92
Gericke, Dr. William F. **7**:924
Ghini, Luca **2**:251
Gibbon, John **11**:1572
Gilbert, Walter **7**:919
Glenny, A. **7**:935
Glidden, J. F. **1**:40
Goldman, Emma **4**:*443*
Goldschmidt, Richard **8**:1086
Golgi, Camillo **3**:334
Goodall, Jane **10**:1370
Gorgas, William **9**:1267
Gorham, Eville **1**:15
Gosling, Raymond **6**:786
Gosse, Philip **1**:126
Gould, Stephen Jay **1**:21; **2**:*203*; **5**:654;
    11:1525
Gram, Hans Christian **2**:168
Grant, Peter R. **9**:1192
Greengard, Paul **9**:1215
Griffin, Donald R. **4**:573
Gurdon, John **3**:383

H

Haeckel, Ernst **1**:71; **3**:320; **5**:581
Hagenback, Carl **12**:1723
Hahnemann, Samuel **1**:*55*
Haldane, J. B. S. **2**:181; **5**:654
Halsted, William **3**:296
Hansen, James **10**:1341
Hanson, Joseph **5**:585
Hardy, Alister **7**:*913*
Harlow, Harry **5**:604
Harris, Thaddeus **5**:621
Harvey, William **1**:71; **2**:201; **3**:*378*;
    8:*1100*
Heath, Dr. R. G. **5**:604–605
Helmholtz, Hermann von **8**:1102
Henseleit, Hans **12**:1666–1667
Henseleit, Kurt **7**:994
Henslow, John Stevens **4**:478
Herophilus **1**:70
Hershey, Alfred **4**:537
Hertwig, Oscar **4**:476
Hertz, Heinrich **12**:1713
Hess, W. R. **1**:31
Hill, William **8**:1091
Hippocrates **2**:187, 200; **3**:293;
    5:636–637; **8**:*1099*; **9**:1214
**Hitchings, George, and Gertrude
    Elion 7**:**897–898**; **8**:1088
Holland, John **2**:151
Holmgren, David **9**:1279
Hooke, Robert **2**:226; **3**:*330*; **4**:476;
    8:1100; **12**:1721
Horsley, Victor **5**:638
Horwitz, Susan **9**:1290
Hounsfield, Godfrey **4**:474

Huggins, Charles Brenton **3**:352
Humboldt, Alexander von **2**:192
Hunter, John **7**:984; **12**:1633
Huntington, George **4**:495
Huxley, Thomas **5**:653
Hyatt, John W. **3**:342

I

Ibn An-Nafis **2**:201; **8**:1100
Ivanovsky, Dmitri **12**:1675
Iwanowski, Dmitri **8**:1130

J

Jackson, John Hughlings **5**:637–638
James, William **10**:1383
Janssen, Zacharias **2**:226
Jarvik, Robert Koffler **8**:1094
Jeffreys, J. Gwen **9**:1239
Jenner, Edward 7:933, 934, *936*, **984**;
    8:1100, 1130; **11**:1513; **12**:1678
Johanson, Donald **6**:784; **7**:*914*
Jones, Drs. H. and G. **5**:*708*
Jung, Carl **10**:1385
Jurine, Charles **4**:573

K

Kalm, Pehr **8**:1042
Kandel, Eric **9**:1215
Kanner, Leo **2**:*162*
Kevorkian, Dr. J. **5**:645
King, Thomas **3**:383
Kircher, Athanasius **2**:207
Kitasato, Shibasaburo **1**:112; **5**:592
Kleinman, Devra **10**:1367
Knoop, Franz **7**:994
Koch, Robert **1**:107, 117; **5**:591; **8**:1102,
    1129
Koestler, Arthur **9**:*1263*
Kohler, Georges **1**:113; **2**:224
Köhler, Wolfgang **8**:1021
Kolff, Willem Johan **2**:*212*
Kornberg, Arthur **4**:534
Koss, Leopold **4**:477
Kraepelin, Emil **9**:1212
Kuhne, Fredrich **5**:629
Kurzweil, Raymond **3**:*424*

L

Laennec, René T. H. **8**:*1101*, 1102
Laing, R. D. **9**:1212
Lamarck, Jean Baptiste de **1**:20–*21*; **5**:652;
    7:912; **9**:*1191*–1192; **12**:1721
Landsteiner, Karl **2**:*243*, 244; **4**:554;
    8:1092
Langdon, John **3**:369
Langerhans, Paul **7**:904, 965
Langton, Christopher **2**:149
Leakey, Louis **6**:779; **7**:915–916
Leakey, Mary **6**:784; **7**:915
Leakey, Richard **7**:916
Leeuwenhoek, Antonie van **1**:71; **2**:169,
    201, 207; **8**:1100, 1127; **12**:1715
Lenard, Philipp E. A. **12**:1713
Leonardo da Vinci **2**:201; **7**:*871*; **9**:1214

Bold words with bold page numbers indicate complete articles; bold numbers
preceding colons are volume numbers; numbers following colons indicate
page numbers; italic page numbers refer to illustrations or other graphics.

Leopold, Aldo 5:582, 586
Lilienthal, Otto 6:*751*
Lind, James 8:*1095*; 12:*1690*
Lindenmayer, Aristid 3:349
Linnaeus, Carolus 2:201, 253, 276;
    5:621, 652; 7:*912*; **8:1041–1042**;
    11:1539; 12:1600, 1721
Linné, Carl von *see* Linnaeus, Carolus
Lister, Joseph 1:116; 5:701; **8:1043**,
    1102, 1128–1129
Locard, Edmond 6:771
Long, Crawford 1:76
Lorenz, Edward 3:347
Lorenz, Konrad 1:30, 31–32, 84; 5:604,
    643; 7:*963*
Loret, Erwann 8:*1142*
Lovelock, James 2:203; 6:801, *802*, 803
Lyell, Charles 4:478; 5:653

M

McCarthy, Maclyn 8:1141–1142
McClintock, Barbara 8:**1085–1086**;
    9:1190
McCormick, Cyrus 1:*39*
McDougall, William 9:1262
MacLeod, Colin 8:1141–1142
Macleod, John J. R. 4:508; 7:*965*
Mairan, Jean-Jacques d'Ortous de 2:216
Malpighi, Marcello 1:71; 2:201, 202;
    3:378; 5:621, *671*; 8:1100
Malthus, Thomas 4:479; 5:653; 9:1192;
    10:*1345*
Mandelbrot, Benoît 3:347
Mantell, Dr. Gideon 4:527
Mantell, Mary Ann 4:527
Margulis, Lynn 2:*202*, 203; 3:332; 5:585
Marsh, George Perkins 4:490
Marsh, Pete 9:1166
Martins, Carl 7:994
Maupertuis, Pierre Louis Moreau de 2:202
May, Robert 3:348
Medawar, Peter 8:1087–1088, 1103;
    12:1633–1634
Mege-Mouries, Hippolyte 5:692
Mendel, Gregor 2:202, 227; 5:653;
    8:1106–1107; 11:**1479–1480**
  Law of Segregation 8:1106
Merriam, C. Hart 9:1167
Meselson, Matthew 4:534
Mesmer, Franz Anton 7:926
Miescher, Friedrich 4:537
Miller, Frederick Robert 4:508
Miller, Stanley 2:181, 202; 5:651, *652*, 682
Milstein, Cesar 1:113; 2:224
Minkowski, Oskar 7:965
Mitchell, Peter 2:*160*
Mode, C. J. 3:389
Mollison, Bill 9:1279, 1280
Montezuma 12:1723
Morgan, Thomas Hunt 6:746; 8:1085,
    1107; 9:**1164**; 12:1721
Morris, Robert 9:1263
Morton, W. T. G. 1:*76*
Muir, John 3:426
Müller, Fritz 3:391
Muller, Hermann J. 2:202; 6:746; 9:1190
Müller, Johannes 2:276; 9:1214
Müller, Paul 4:480, *481*
Mullis, Kary 9:**1173–1174**

Murray, Joseph 8:1088
Mygalomorphae 11:1546

N

Nageli, Karl von 8:1107
Needham, John Turberville 2:202
Nelson, Ridley 4:503
Newell, Allen 7:967
Newton, Isaac 9:1235
Nicolson, Garth 3:*331*
Nightingale, Florence 8:*1102*

O

Oparin, Alexander 2:181, 202
Ostrom, John 4:529
Owen, Richard 4:527; 5:653

P

Papanicolaou, George 4:477
Paracelsus 8:1100; 9:1289
Paré, Ambroise 8:1099–1100; 11:1570
Parkinson, James 2:261; 4:497
Pasteur, Louis 9:**1269–1270**
  and antisepsis 8:1101, 1128
  and diseases of silkworms 9:1269–1270
  and fermentation 2:226; 5:629; 8:*1127*,
    1128; 9:1269; 12:1715
  and germ theory 8:1128; 9:1269
  and the origins of microorganisms 1:*116*;
    2:202; 5:652; 8:1127–1128
  and pasteurization 1:115; 2:226–227;
    6:765; 8:1128; 9:1269
  and vaccines/immunization 1:107;
    7:934–935; 8:1102; 9:1270;
    12:1678
Pauling, Linus 4:462
Pavlov, Ivan 2:261; 3:*411*–412; 7:961;
    8:*1020*; 9:**1271–1272**; 10:1383, *1398*
Payen, Anselme 5:629
Pelletier, Pierre-Joseph 1:50–51; 8:1103
Penfield, Wilder 5:637
Persoz, François 5:629
Perutz, Max 2:246
Pete Marsh 9:1166
Piaget, Jean 3:354, 356, 394
Pinker, Stephen 5:662
Pitts, H. and J. 1:39
Plato 3:422
Pliny the Elder 2:200; 5:637
Plutchik, Robert 5:603
Poincaré, Henri 3:347
Popper, Karl 11:1467
Prusiner, Stanley 1:89; 10:1371
Purcell, Edward M. 8:1068

R

Ramón y Cajal, Santiago 10:**1396**
Ratner, S. 12:1667
Ray, John 11:1539
Ray, Tom 2:152
Redi, Francesco 2:202
Reed, Walter 5:621
Rensselaer Potter II, Van 2:187
Reynolds, Craig 2:151
Rhine, J. B. and Louisa 9:1262
Rhoades, Marcus 8:1085
Ringer, Sydney 2:278
Roentgen *see* Röntgen, Wilhelm
Rohm, Otto 2:222

Röntgen (Roentgen), Wilhelm 8:1090,
    1102; 10:*1395*; 12:1712, *1713*
Rosenberg, William 8:1096, 1097, 1098
Ross, Ronald 5:621
Russell, William M.S. 1:92

S

Sabin, Albert 1:92
Sachs, Julius von 7:924
Sackett, David 8:1098
Sacks, Oliver 9:1211
Sagan, Carl 5:*684*
Sagan, Dorian 5:585
Salk, Jonas 8:1103, *1129*; **11:1457**
Sanger, Frederick 7:*920*, 921, 965
Sanger, Margaret Higgins 4:443
Savage-Rumbaugh, Dr. S. 3:406
Say, Thomas 5:*621*
Schachter, Stanley 5:602–603
Schiaperelli, Giovanni 5:682
Schindler, Robert 7:874
Schjelderup-Ebbe, T. 11:1523
Schleiden, Matthias 3:330–331; 4:476
Schmiederberg, Oswald 9:1289
Schwann, Theodor 1:71; 2:202; 3:331;
    4:476; 5:629
Scopes, John Thomas 7:913
Scudder, John 4:554
Seacole, Mary 8:1102
Seba, Albertus 2:276
Semmelweis, Ignatz P. 1:115; 8:1101
Shannon, Claude 7:952
Sharpey-Schafer, Edward 7:965
Sheldon, William 10:1385
Shên Nung 7:887, 987; 8:1014
Sherrington, Charles Scott 9:1215
Simon, Herbert A. 7:967
Simon, Theodore 7:966
Simpson, James 1:76; 8:1102
Singer, Jonathan 3:*331*
Singer, Peter 1:91
Skinner, B. F. 1:82; 3:412–413, 414;
    8:*1020*; 10:1383
Smith, Robert Angus 1:15
Smith, Susan 7:961
Snow, John 5:*633*, 634
Soal, Samuel 9:1262
Solander, Daniel 2:254
Southern, Edwin 2:182; 4:535
Spallanzani, Lazzaro 2:202; 4:572–573;
    5:652; 8:1127
Spearman, Charles 7:967
Sperry, Roger 2:264
Stadler, Lewis 8:1086; 9:1190
Stahl, Franklin 4:534
Stanley, Wendell 8:1130
Stern, William 7:966–967
Steward, F. C. 3:382
Still, Andrew Taylor 9:1250
Suwa, Gen 7:915
Svedberg, The 10:1376
Swammerdam, Jan 5:621
Sydenham, Thomas 8:1100
Szent-Györgi, Albert 7:994

T

Takaki, Kanehiro 12:1690
Tansley, Arthur 5:582
Tatum, Edward 8:**1140**; 12:*1598*

Taylor, Edwin 2:276
Tenhaeff, W. H. C. 9:1263
Terman, Lewis M. 7:967
Thomson, Charles Wyville 9:1239
Thorndike, E. L. 3:412
Tinbergen, Nikolaas 1:83, 84; 5:643,
    644; 7:*963*
Tradescant, John 2:*254*
Tradescant, John the younger 2:*254*
Treviranus, Gottfried 2:200
Trivers, Robert 11:1527
Tschermak, Erich 8:1107
Tull, Jethro 1:39

U

Ulam, Stanislaw 2:150
Uloboridae 11:1547
Urey, Harold 2:181; 5:651, *652*, 682

V

Venter, Craig 7:*923*
Vesalius, Andreas 1:71; 2:201;
    8:1099
von Neumann, John 2:150
Voronoff, Serge 12:1633
Vries, Hugo de 8:1107

W

Walker, John 2:160
Wallace, Alfred Russel 2:192; 4:479;
    5:653; 9:*1192*–1193
Wareing, P. F. 4:548
Warwick, Kevin 2:215
Watson, James *see* Crick, Francis,
    and James Watson
Watson, John B. 1:82; 3:423; 7:963;
    10:1383
Weaver, Warren 7:952
Wegener, Alfred 2:192
Weizmann, Chaim 5:*703*
Wells, Horace 8:1102
Went, F. W. 12:1645
Wepfer, Johann Jacb 9:1214
Wernicke, Carl 9:1214
Wertheimer, Max 10:1384
Weschler, David 7:967
Whipple, Allen 4:554
White, Tim 7:915
Wiener, Norbert 7:952
Wilkins, Maurice 6:785–786
Williams, Cicely 10:1378
Williams, Daniel Hale 8:1101
Willis, Thomas 9:1214
Wilmut, Ian 3:340, 383, 385
Wilson, Edward O. 5:644, 661, *680*;
    11:1525; 12:1647, **1711**
Wilson, Ernest Henry "Chinese" 2:254
Withering, William 9:1291
Wright, Orville and Wilbur 6:751
Wright, Sewell 5:654
Wundt, Wilhelm 3:423; 10:1383

Y

Yersin, Alexandre 7:950

Z

Zasloff, Michael A. 9:1290
Zener, Karl 9:1262
Zion, Elie de 9:1271

COMPREHENSIVE INDEX

A

2,4-D **1**:41; **7**:909

16PF (16 Personality Factor
Questionnaire) **9**:1283

aardvarks **4**:445

aardwolves **3**:312

ABA *see* abscisic acid

abdomen 1:13

Abies spp. *see* firs

Abingdon Island **3**:410; **6**:770

abomasum **11**:*1452*, 1453

aborigines, Australian **7**:917; **9**:1194

abortion 1:14

ethics **1**:14; **2**:188, 191

Listeria and **6**:765

and multiple births **12**:1656

spontaneous (miscarriage) **1**:14;
10:1354

Abralia **2**:207

Abraliopsis **2**:207

abscisic acid (ABA) **4**:548; **7**:909

abscission **8**:1025

absorptive and postabsorptive states
8:1124

abyssal plain **9**:1231

abyssal zone **9**:1231, 1237

discovery of life in **9**:1239

acacias **1**:118–119; **3**:*390*; **4**:483; **6**:762;
11:*1562*, 1580–1581

Acanthaster planci (crown-of-thorns
starfish) **4**:*450*, 451, 453, 568

Acanthocephala **1**:95–96; **9**:1267

acanthodians **6**:730; **7**:978

Acanthophis antarcticus (death adder) **2**:286;
11:1520

Accipitridae **2**:235–236

accommodation **12**:1684

acetone, from bacterial fermentation
5:702, 703

acetylcholine **1**:61; **9**:1182, 1201, 1213

acetylcholinesterase **5**:632; **9**:1182

acetyl CoA *see* acetyl coenzyme A

acetyl coenzyme A **2**:159; **7**:993, 994,
995; **8**:1118

Achatina fulica (giant African snail) **2**:185,
196

acid rain 1:15–17; **4**:491–492; **7**:1001;
10:1340

natural buffers against **1**:16; **11**:1459

acini **9**:1260

Acinonyx jubatus see cheetahs

acne **5**:676; **11**:1508

acoelomates **9**:1196

aconitase **7**:995

Aconitum spp. (monkshood) **6**:758

acorn worms **1**:97; **7**:*1006*

Acrasiomycota **8**:1139, 1140

acromegaly **7**:905

Acronicta psi (dagger moth) **2**:284

acrosomes **5**:713–714

ACTH *see* adrenocorticotrophic hormone

actin **6**:726, 772; **9**:1178, *1181*, 1182;
10:1377

actinomorphic flowers **6**:759

Actinomyces spp. **2**:172

Actinopterygii **6**:730; **12**:1672

Actinopyga spp. **4**:570

Actophilornis africanus (African jacana)
8:*1083*

acupressure **1**:57

acupuncture **1**:*54*, 55, 76; **3**:*360*, 361;
5:614

acyclovir (Zovirax) **7**:898; **12**:1678

Adapidae **7**:871

adaptation 1:18–22

to cave life **3**:326–328

and evolution **1**:20–*21*; **5**:650–651,
656–657

to high altitude **8**:*1058*; **9**:1169–1170;
10:1307, *1423*

human **1**:22

to life in the tundra **12**:1653–1654

to the parasitic mode of life
9:1267–1268

to polar life **10**:1332

in populations **1**:22

for upright walking **1**:22

see also camouflage and mimicry;
evolution; natural selection

adaptive radiation **11**:1541–1542

Galápagos finches **9**:1192; **11**:1541

ADCC **1**:114

adders, death **2**:286; **11**:1520

addiction 1:23–24

biochemistry of **1**:24; **4**:556

treatment **1**:24; **4**:558

see also drugs; hallucinogens

Addison, Thomas **5**:612; **7**:905

Addison's disease **2**:165; **4**:454; **5**:612;
7:905

adenine **4**:533, 535, 537; **5**:654;
10:1428

adenohypophysis **5**:611

adenosine diphosphate *see* ADP

adenosine monophosphate, cyclic (cAMP)
7:907; **8**:1120

adenosine triphosphate *see* ATP

adenoviruses **6**:806–807

adhesion molecules **2**:240

adipocytes **3**:420

adipose tissue **3**:*420*

Adler, Alfred **10**:1385

adolescence 1:25–28

see also puberty

ADP (adenosine diphosphate) **2**:158, 159;
7:994; **9**:1252; **10**:1302

adrenal glands

chromaffin cells **5**:640

hormones **4**:454; **5**:612, 708; **9**:1201

androgens **5**:612–613; **7**:906

stress and **11**:1566

see also corticosteroids; epinephrine
and norepinephrine

and pseudohermaphroditism **7**:889

adrenalin *see* epinephrine and
norepinephrine

adrenocorticotrophic hormone (ACTH)
5:614; **7**:905, 907; **9**:1158

Aedes spp. **7**:947; **8**:1126; **9**:*1268*

Aegolius acadius (saw-whet owl) **9**:1220

Aepyornis titan (elephant bird) **6**:755

aerotolerant organisms **5**:700

Aesthna mixta (hawker migrant dragonfly)
4:*550*

aflatoxin **11**:1462

African Americans, equal rights **8**:1101

Afropavo congensis (Congo peacock)
6:778

after-ripening **4**:549

Agalychnis calcarifer **6**:788

Agama agama (agama lizard) **3**:396;
8:*1053*

Agapornis spp. (lovebirds) **4**:459

agar **1**:48; **7**:988; **8**:*1131*

Agaricus spp. **9**:1185, 1187, 1188

Agathis australis (kauri) **3**:416

Agave spp. **9**:1161, 1278; **10**:1318

Agelena republicana **11**:1548

Ageless Body, Timeless Mind (Deepak
Chopra) **7**:944

Agent Orange **4**:490, *532*

aggression 1:29–32, 84, *85*–86;
5:661

competitive **1**:30

defensive **1**:30; **4**:486

hostile **1**:29

instrumental **1**:29

sexual **1**:29

territorial **1**:29–30, 85

see also territories

aging 1:33–36

antiaging vitamin **12**:1690

plant senescence **1**:36; **10**:1319

skin **1**:34; **11**:1507

Agnatha *see* fish, jawless

agoraphobia **10**:*1301*

Agricultural Revolution **1**:39–40

agriculture 1:37–41

aquaculture 1:124–125

cereal grains *see* grains

and deforestation **4**:492

environmental diseases from **5**:*626*

fertilizers *see* fertilizers

Green Revolution **1**:40; **5**:718

and pesticides **9**:1287

history **1**:*37–40*

hydroponics 7:924–925

livestock farming

organic **9**:1243

use of antibiotics **9**:*1245*

organic **1**:40; **9**:*1242*–1243,
1246–*1247*

see also permaculture

and populations **1**:41

scientific developments **1**:40

seaweed farming **1**:125

shade **4**:492

sustainable **9**:1279

in the taiga **12**:1590

use of antibiotics **9**:*1245*

waste disposal **12**:1697–1698

see also biological control; crops;
genetic engineering; pesticides;
selective breeding

Agrobacterium tumefaciens **6**:*809*

AIDS 1:42–45

epidemic **1**:45

and HIV **1**:*42*, 43–44; **3**:298; **7**:932,
940; **8**:1129

hemophilics infected with **1**:45

origins **1**:42–43

test for **5**:630; **12**:*1676*

types **1**:*42–43*

and the immune response **1**:*43*; **7**:940

infections associated with **1**:42

Mullis and Duesberg's theories **9**:1174

prospects for a vaccine **1**:45

stages **1**:44

transmission **1**:44–*45*

treatment **1**:44

Ailuropoda melanoleuca see pandas, giant

air *see* atmosphere

air plants *see* bromeliads

Aizoaceae **2**:*273*, 274

alanine **1**:*62, 63*

Alar **10**:1344

alaria **7**:987

alates **1**:119; **12**:1612

albatrosses **4**:456; **11**:1473, 1474

black-browed **6**:*752*

Bold words with bold page numbers indicate complete articles; bold numbers
preceding colons are volume numbers; numbers following colons indicate
page numbers; italic page numbers refer to illustrations or other graphics.

albatrosses (continued)
    royal 2:232; 5:658
    soaring 6:752; 11:1473
albinism 9:1191; 10:1310
albumin 2:241
albuminous cells 12:1631
Alca (Pinguinus) impennis (great auk) 6:754;
    12:1654
Alcedo atthis (kingfisher) 2:230
Alces alces (elk/moose) 8:1084; 10:1350;
    12:1591, 1619
alcohol
    for antisepsis 1:116
    a beverage 6:763
    dependence 1:24
    a depressant 1:24; 4:556
alcohol dehydrogenase 5:632
alcoholism
    and cirrhosis 8:1046
    symptoms 10:1389
Aldabra Island 4:450
aldosterone 2:219; 4:454; 5:672;
    7:901, 990
Aldrovandi, Ulisse 5:620
Aleuria aurantia (orange peel fungus)
    9:1186
Alexander of Tralles 5:637
alfalfa 5:718; 8:1028; 10:1322
    pests of 7:960
    seeds 4:547, 549
algae 1:46–49; 8:1130; 10:1380–1381
    benthic 1:49
    blooms 1:48; 7:1001; 10:1302
    blue-green see cyanobacteria
    brown 1:47–48; 7:985–986, 987;
        10:1381
    classification 1:46–47; 10:1325
    coral reef 1:49
    distribution 1:48–48
    epiphytic 5:642
    euglenoids 1:47; 10:1381
    golden-brown 1:47
    green 1:49; 7:987; 10:1381
    and humans 1:48
    phytoplankton see plankton,
        phytoplankton
    prokaryotic 1:47
    red 1:46, 48; 7:986, 987; 10:1381;
        11:1493
    reproduction in 1:49; 5:715–716
    symbiotic
        with corals 4:449–450, 453; 11:1581
        relationship with fungi see lichens
    see also dinoflagellates; kelps and
        seaweeds
alginates, from seaweeds 7:988
alginic acid 1:48
algorithms
    evolutionary 2:151–152
    genetic 2:151, 152
aliens 5:684
ALife see artificial life

alimentary canal see digestive systems,
    digestive tract
alkaloids 1:50–51; 4:481
    caffeine 8:1014
    colchicine 2:266; 3:367
    medicinal 1:51
    taste 12:1597
    toxic 1:50, 51
        from frogs 1:50; 5:677
        from fungi 1:50; 9:1188
alleles 5:653
    and adaptations 1:18
    codominant 6:812
    dominant and recessive 6:812
    formation of new see mutation
    frequencies 5:655
    and polymorphism 4:524
allelopathy 3:350
allergies 1:52–53, 114; 5:627–628;
    7:931
    and anaphylaxis 1:53, 110
    to antibiotics 1:110
    and asthma 2:153
    blood cells and 2:240, 241
    immune response 1:52–53; 7:941–942
    treatment 4:454; 5:641
Alligator mississippiensis (American alligator)
    4:459, 464, 466; 5:647
alligators see crocodilians, alligators
Allium spp. 2:265, 266
allomones 5:677
Allosaurus 4:528
almonds 6:792
Aloe dichotoma (quiver tree) 12:1617
Alopex lagopus (Arctic fox) 9:1159;
    12:1619
Alopias vulpinus (thresher shark) 11:1488
Alosa sapidissima (American shad) 4:573
Alouatta spp. (howler monkey) 10:1368;
    12:1594, 1615, 1640
alpacas 4:545
alpha particles 5:626; 10:1394
Alpheus spp. (snapping shrimp) 4:470
Alps, Tyrol 9:1167
alternation of generations
    in jellyfish and hydroids 7:980–981
    in plants 5:590; 10:1325
        ferns and fern allies 5:704–705
        flowering plants 6:759–760
        mosses 9:1165
        seaweeds 7:987
alternative medicine 1:54–57; 8:1094
    acupuncture 1:54, 55, 76; 3:360, 361;
        5:614
    aromatherapy 1:56
    Chinese medicine 1:55; 3:360–361
    crystal therapy 1:57
    and endorphine release 1:55; 5:614
    homeopathy 1:55–56, 57
    Indian medicine 7:887–888,
        943–944
    iridology 1:56

light or color therapy 1:57
    massage and manipulation 1:56, 57
        chiropractic 1:56, 57
        osteopathy 1:57; 9:1250
        reflexology 1:57; 5:614
        reiki 1:57
    see also herbal medicine
altitude, high, adaptation to 8:1058;
    9:1169–1170; 10:1307, 1423
altitude sickness 8:1058; 10:1423
altruism 1:58–60, 86; 11:1526–1527
    reciprocal 1:59, 60; 11:1526–1527
    see also predation, cooperative hunting;
        symbiosis, mutualism
aluminum
    dietary, and Alzheimer's disease 1:61
    recycling 12:1696–1697
Alvarez, Luis and Walter 5:679
Alvin (submersible) 9:1238
Alytes obstetricians (midwife toad) 6:790
Alzheimer, Alois 4:495
Alzheimer's disease 1:61; 4:494–497;
    9:1204, 1213; 10:1389; 11:1558
Amanita spp.
    A. muscaria (fly agaric) 9:1185, 1186, 1187
    A. phalloides (death cap) 9:1188; 11:1460
Amazona amazonica (Amazon parrot)
    12:1642
Amazon River 2:211
amber, fossils preserved in 6:781, 782
Amblyopsidae 3:327
Amblyrhynchus cristatus (marine iguana)
    8:1052
Ambrosia spp. (ragweed) 2:217; 10:1317;
    11:1568
Ambystoma spp. 9:1256; 10:1418;
    11:1454, 1455
amebiasis 7:949
amenorrhea 8:1110
American Society for Psychical Research
    (ASPR) 9:1263
Ames, Bruce 3:295
Ames room 3:394
Ames (mutagenicity) test 3:295
amino acids 1:62–63; 8:1124, 1143;
    10:1375
    alpha 7:906
    breakdown 8:1119
    errors of metabolism 8:1124
    essential and nonessential 1:62; 8:1120;
        9:1226
    fermentation 5:703
    metabolism see Krebs cycle; urea cycle
    and mutations 9:1189, 1190
    properties 1:62–63
    sequencing to make proteins 4:536
    synthesis, in plants 10:1377
    testing for 1:63
    see also proteins
aminoids 6:762

ammonia
    industrial manufacture 9:1217
    the urea cycle and 12:1667, 1668
    waste product 5:665
ammonification 9:1218
ammonites 4:446; 6:784
ammonotelic organisms 12:1666
amnesia 8:1105, 1114
amniocentesis 3:367; 4:477; 10:1358
amnion 10:1354
amniotic sac 10:1354
amoebas 10:1379, 1382
    digestion by 4:511
    diseases from 8:1132
    feeding 5:693
    pseudopods 5:693, 698; 11:1578
amphetamines 1:24; 4:555
    and schizophrenia 9:1212
    and sleep 11:1512
amphibians 1:64–65; 12:1673
    brain 2:258
    circulatory system 3:373–374; 7:877
    courtship 4:458–459
    eggs 5:587–588
    embryo development 5:598, 599
    evolution 1:65; 6:790; 11:1456
    excretion 5:666, 670
    first known 6:790
    fossils 11:1456
    hibernation and estivation 7:892, 893
    jaws 7:978
    life cycles
        metamorphosis 7:1005; 8:1125, 1126
        nesting 9:1206
        molting 9:1158
    pancreas 9:1261
    regeneration of body parts 10:1400
    respiration
        gills 10:1418
        lungs 8:1060; 10:1423
    sense of taste 12:1596
    sense of touch 12:1628
    tails 12:1592, 1593
    temperature regulation 3:397
    see also frogs and toads; salamanders
        and newts
amphicyonids 3:310
amphioxus (lancelet) 3:364, 365; 7:972
    circulatory system 3:371; 7:877
Amphiprion spp. (clownfish/anemone fish)
    1:126; 3:389, 390; 4:450; 7:890,
    970; 11:1580
amphiumas (Amphiumidae) 11:1454
amphotericin B 1:109
ampicillin 6:742
ampullae 12:1670
amygdala 2:257
amylases 3:342
    pancreatic 9:1260
    salivary 4:516, 517; 11:1564
amyl nitrate (poppers) 9:1174
amyloid 1:61

amylopectin **3**:297

amyloplasts **12**:1646

amylose **3**:297

amyotrophic lateral sclerosis (ALS; Lou Gehrig's disease) **9**:1181, 1202

Anabaena spp. **1**:*47*

Anableps **6**:731

anabolism **8**:1116, 1119–1120, 1121

anacondas **11**:1518, 1519

anaerobes

    obligate and facultative **5**:700

    see also bacteria, anaerobic

anagenesis **5**:678

analytical techniques 1:66–68

    centrifugation and ultracentrifugation **1**:67–68; **2**:181; **10**:1376; **12**:1677

    chromatography **1**:63, 66–67; **2**:181

    electrophoresis *see* electrophoresis

    mass spectroscopy **1**:68; **6**:*772*

    microanalysis **1**:68

    using radioisotopes *see* radioactive tagging

    X-ray crystallography **1**:68; **2**:182

        of viruses **12**:1677

        X-ray diffraction **1**:*68*; **6**:786; **8**:1146

    see also biochemistry; forensic science; scientific method

anaphylaxis **1**:53, 110

Anas spp. **4**:*524*; **5**:695

anatomy 1:69–72

    plant **1**:69–70; **2**:253

Anaximander **2**:200; **5**:652

anchovies, Peruvian **4**:438

androecium **6**:758

androgens **5**:612–613; **7**:906; **10**:1410

    see also testosterone

anemia 1:73–74

    aplastic **1**:*74*

    hemolytic **1**:73–74; **2**:164

    iron-deficiency **1**:73; **2**:246; **4**:489; **7**:973

    macrocytic **2**:246–247

    megaloblastic **1**:*73*, 74

    pernicious **1**:74; **4**:488, 519

    sickle-cell **1**:74; **2**:191, *247*; **4**:538; **5**:656

        gene therapy **6**:806

        and malaria **2**:247; **4**:525; **9**:1266

        and the spleen **8**:1065; **11**:1551

        stable polymorphism **4**:525

anemones, sea *see* jellyfish, sea anemones, and hydras

Anemonia sulata **9**:*1237*

anesthesia 1:75–76; 11:1571, *1573*

    epidural **11**:1573

    general **1**:75–76

    history of **1**:76; **8**:1102; **11**:1570

    local **1**:*75*, 76

anestrus **8**:1111

aneuploidy **3**:369

angelfish **2**:283; **6**:*731*

angina **7**:881; **9**:1225

angiograms **7**:*880*; **8**:*1090*; **12**:*1620*

angioplasty

    balloon **7**:881

    percutaneous transluminal coronary (PTCA) **11**:1574

angiosperms (flowering plants) 1:77–80; 11:1475

    drugs (medicinal) from **1**:81

    embryo **5**:*716*

    evolution **1**:79, 80

        coevolution with animals **6**:760

    fertilization **1**:79; **5**:*716*; **11**:1475

    flowers *see* flowers and flower structure

    germination **1**:79

    harmful **1**:80

    number of species **5**:650

    pollination **1**:78–79; **6**:761

        see also pollination

    seeds

        dispersal **1**:79

        structure **1**:79

    vegetative propagation **1**:80

    vegetative reproduction **11**:1562

    wood **11**:1562

    see also dicotyledons; flowers and flower structure; monocotyledons; seeds

Angiostrongylus cantonensis **9**:1265

angiotensin **7**:990

Angraceum sesquipedale **2**:268

angwantibos **10**:1366

animal behavior 1:81–86

    aggressive *see* aggression

    behaviorism **1**:82; **3**:423; **5**:660; **10**:1383–1384

    causes **1**:83–84

    conditioned *see* conditioning

    defensive **4**:486

        see also defense

    development **1**:84

    ethology 1:82–83; 5:643–644

    and evolution **1**:84–85

    fixed action patterns **1**:83

    function **1**:*85*–86

    and genetics **1**:83

    instinctive *see* instinct

    intelligent **7**:968

    social *see* social organization

    territorial **1**:29–30, 85

    see also communication; courtship; emotions; play; psychology

animal diseases 1:87–90

    veterinary medicine **1**:88, *90*

Animal Ecology (Charles Elton) **6**:769

animal experimentation 1:91–93; 2:189–190

    for aggression **1**:31

animal kingdom 1:94–97; 12:1601

    animals

        selectively bred, welfare **11**:1480

        training **3**:*413*

    Anisoptera **4**:550

    ankylosaurs **4**:531

annelids 1:96, **98–100; 7:**971

    excretory systems **5**:*666–667*

    mucus **9**:1172

    see also earthworms; leeches; polychaetes

annual plants 1:101–102; 11:1476

Anolis spp. (anole lizard) **4**:459

Anomalops katoptron (flashlight fish) **5**:686

Anopheles spp. (mosquito) **6**:744; **7**:946, 1004; **9**:1265, 1268

Anoplura (sucking lice) **8**:1032, 1033

anorexia nervosa **4**:565–*566*; **8**:1114

anosmia **11**:1516

anovulation **8**:1110

Anseriformes **12**:1700–1701

Anser rossii (Ross's goose) **8**:1134

antacids **11**:1565

Antarctic **9**:1236; **10**:1331, 1333–*1334*

    ozone hole over **2**:*157*; **10**:1341

    see also polar regions

anteaters, sloths and armadillos 1:103–104

    anteaters **1**:103–104

        giant **1**:*103*, 104; **4**:*445*; **12**:*1621*

        silky **1**:103

        spiny *see* echidnas

        tongue **12**:*1621*, 1622

    armadillos **1**:104; **4**:486

    sloths **1**:*104*

        hands **11**:1498

Antedon sp **4**:*569*

antelopes **3**:403; **4**:460; **7**:910

antennae 1:105–106

    of flies **1**:106

    of moths **1**:*105*; **9**:*1223*

antheridia **9**:1166

anthers **1**:78; **10**:1335

Anthias **9**:*1236*

Anthocerotophyta **9**:1165; **10**:1326

anthocyanins **6**:761; **10**:1311

Anthonomus grandis (boll weevil) **2**:178

Anthophyta *see* Magnoliophyta

anthoxanthins **6**:761; **10**:1311

anthracosis (anthrasilicosis; black lung) **5**:*628*

anthrax 1:88–89, 107, *117*; **11:**1531

    for biologial warfare **1**:107; **2**:198, 199

    treatment **2**:198

anthropomorphism **5**:644

antibiotics and antimicrobials 1:108–110

    in agriculture **9**:*1245*

    allergic reactions to **1**:110

    discovery **2**:*180*; **6**:741–742, 799; **8**:1103, 1131

    and hearing **7**:875

    manufacture **1**:109

    mode of action **1**:108–110; **5**:630

    natural antibiotics **6**:764

    on plants **10**:1323

    resistance to **1**:*19*, 109–*110*; **6**:811; **9**:1245, 1291

    side effects **1**:109; **12**:1622

    and surgery **11**:1571

antibodies 1:52, **111–114; 2:**241

    antibody-antigen complexes **1**:*114*

    chimeric **1**:113

    in milk **7**:*934*

    monoclonal **1**:113

        from biotechnology **2**:*221*, *224*, 226

    production **11**:1551

    structure **1**:*111–112*, *113*

    used as chemotherapy **3**:353

    used to identify viruses **12**:1677

    see also immunoglobulins

antibody-dependent cellular cytotoxicity (ADCC) **1**:114

anticonvulsants **5**:639

antidiuretic hormone (ADH; vasopressin) **5**:611, 671, 672; **7**:903, 990

antifreeze

    in animals **4**:472; **10**:1332

    in GM potato seedlings **6**:810

    in lichens **8**:1036

antigens

    and the allergic response *see* allergies

    pollen **6**:761

    on red blood cells **2**:243, *244*, 245

        see also blood, types

    shifting (variation) **7**:929

    see also infection

Antilocapra sp. (pronghorn antelope) **3**:403; **7**:910

antimetabolites **1**:108

antimicrobials *see* antibiotics and antimicrobials

antioxidants **1**:34; **3**:*294*, 317; **12**:1691

antipatharians (black corals) **4**:453

antipodals **5**:590

antipsychotics **11**:1466

Antirrhinum spp. (snapdragon) **1**:78; **6**:812; **10**:1337

antisepsis 1:115–117; 8:*1128*

    Lister and **1**:115; **8**:1043, 1102, 1128–1129

    Pasteur and **8**:1101, 1128

    Semmelweiss and **8**:1101

antisocial personality disorder (ASPD) **8**:1115; **9**:1284

antivirals **12**:1678

antlers **2**:*217*; **7**:911; **11**:*1486*; **12**:1663

ant lions **5**:695; **9**:1208

ants 1:118–120

    army/driver **1**:119, 120; **3**:404; **11**:1580

    black **1**:*119*

    brain and nervous system **2**:*258*

Bold words with bold page numbers indicate complete articles; bold numbers preceding colons are volume numbers; numbers following colons indicate page numbers; italic page numbers refer to illustrations or other graphics.

ants (continued)
  carpenter 1:118
  castes 1:119
  colonies 1:119; 7:958–959
    modeling 3:349
  communication 3:404; 12:1647
    alarm secretions 9:1293
  defense
    chemical 1:118, 119
    self-sacrifice 4:486
  feeding 1:119–120
  fire 1:119, 120; 2:196
  harvester 1:120; 4:486
  leaf-cutting 1:59–60, 120; 12:1645
  nests 1:118–119
  parasitized 2:196
  sense of smell 11:1515
  slave-making 1:120
  in the soil 11:1531–1532
  stings 1:119
  symbiosis
    with acacia trees 1:118–119; 3:390;
      4:483; 11:1562, 1580–1581
    with aphids 4:483; 7:884; 11:1581
    with caterpillars 2:271
    with Cecropia trees 11:1581
    with silverfish 11:1580
  vampire 1:120
  weaver 1:118
  white see termites
  wood 1:118
Anura 1:64; 6:787
  see also frogs and toads
anxiety 1:121–122; 5:662–663; 8:1113
Apatosaurus 4:528, 529–530
apes
  "aquatic" 7:913
  great 10:1368–1369
    see also chimpanzees; gorillas;
      orangutans
  hands 7:869, 870
  see also primates
Apgar, Virginia 1:123
Apgar scoring system 1:123
Aphelocoma coerulescens (Florida scrub jay)
  1:58
aphids
  agricultural pests 7:885
  feeding on sap 12:1632
  honeydew (sugary milk) from 1:120;
    4:483; 7:884; 11:1581
  peach 7:885
  protected by ants 1:120; 4:483; 7:884
  reproduction 10:1407
  rose 10:1407
apical dominance 8:1023
Apis mellifera see honeybees
Aplacophora 8:1150
Aplodontia rufa (mountain beaver) 10:1438
Aplysia 2:261; 10:1397
Apocrita 12:1692, 1693
Apodiformes 2:231

apomixis 10:1405
apoptosis 3:353
Appalachians, southern, forests 12:1607
appendectomy 11:1572–1573
appendicitis 4:523
appendix 4:517, 523; 8:1065
  removal 11:1572–1573
Appert, Nicholas 6:765
appetite 8:1120, 1123
apples 6:794, 795
  crab 6:791
applied behavior analysis (ABA) 2:163
appositional growth 3:320
Aptenia 2:274
Aptenodytes forsteri (emperor penguin)
  6:754; 11:1473
Apterygota 7:960
Apteryx spp. (kiwis) 6:756
aquaculture 1:124–125
aquariums 1:125, 126–129; 5:585
Araceae 10:1318
arachidonic acid 5:692
Arachis hypogaea (peanut) 8:1028
arachnids 1:130–133, 141
  diseases carried by 1:131; 7:945,
    946–947
  see also arthropods; mites; scorpions;
    spiders; ticks
Arachnocampa luminosa (fungus gnat) 3:328
arachnophobia 3:414; 5:663
Aral Sea 4:505
Araneomorphae 11:1546
Araneus diadematus (garden spider) 12:1627
Araucaria araucana (monkey puzzle) 3:416
Araujia sericifera (cruel plant) 10:1318
arboviruses 7:946, 947
archaea 2:167
Archaeocetes 12:1708
archaeopteryx 1:134; 2:233; 4:529;
  5:653; 6:749; 9:1254, 1274
archebacteria 5:582
archegonia 5:590; 9:1166
archeocytes 10:1400; 11:1558
Archilochus colubris (ruby-throated
  hummingbird) 9:1275
Architeutis sp. (giant squid) 4:574
architomy 10:1400
archosaurs 4:530
Arctic 10:1331, 1332–1333
  see also polar regions
Arctocebus calabarensis (angwantibo)
  10:1366
Ardipithecus ramidus 7:914, 915
Arecaceae (Palmae) 9:1258
Arenicola marina (lugworm) 12:1592
areoles 2:273
arginase 12:1667
arginine 12:1667
argininosuccinase 12:1668
argininosuccinate 12:1667
  lyase 12:1667
  synthetase 12:1667

arginosuccinic aciduria 12:1668
Argiope spp. 5:663; 11:1548
Argulus spp. 4:467–468
Argyroneta spp. (water spiders) 11:1549
Arisaema sp. (jack-in-the-pulpit) 7:890
Aristotle 1:70, 135; 2:207; 5:620, 652;
  9:1214; 11:1539; 12:1721
  and logic 11:1467
Aristotle's lantern 4:568
Arixenia spp. 4:564
Arixeniina 4:563, 564
armadillos 1:104; 4:486
arms
  artificial 2:212–213; 8:1093
  bones 11:1503
  paralyzed, movement 2:213
aroids 10:1318
aromatherapy 1:56
Arrhenius, Svante 5:651–652
arrowroot 12:1650
arrow worms 1:97
arsenic
  for pest control 1:41
  poisoning 9:1203
  in water 5:627
arsphenamine (salvarsan) 5:592; 8:1103;
  9:1289
Artedi, Petrus 8:1041
arteries 3:375
  coronary 7:880; 9:1225
  hepatic 7:894
  renal 7:989, 991
  splenic 11:1550
arteriosclerosis, cerebral 10:1389
artery disease 3:363
  see also atherosclerosis
arthritis 1:136; 2:250; 11:1502
  osteoarthritis 1:136; 7:870
    in cats and dogs 1:90
  prevention 1:136
  rheumatoid 1:136; 2:165; 5:690; 7:870,
    931, 942
  treatment 1:136
Arthropleura 3:346
arthropods 1:96–97, 137–142
  circulatory systems 3:371–372
    heart 7:876
  classification 1:138
  digestion by 1:140
  evolution 1:138
  exoskeleton 1:138–139; 7:971–972;
    11:1496–1497
  eyes 1:140; 12:1686
  legs 1:139
  molting 9:1157–1158; 11:1497
  nervous system and senses 7:971
  number of species 2:184
  tails 12:1592
  and touch 12:1627
  see also arachnids; centipedes and
    millipedes; chelicerates; crustaceans;
    insects

artichokes, Jerusalem 4:548; 12:1650
artificial insemination
  of animals 2:224; 5:712; 11:1481
  see also captive breeding programs
artificial life 2:149–152
Artiodactyla see ungulates, even-toed
Arum maculatum (jack-in-the-pulpit) 6:762;
  10:1318
asbestos, diseases from 5:628
asbestosis 5:628
Ascaris lumbricoides 9:1196
ascomycetes 6:799–800; 8:1138–1140
Ascophyllum spp. 7:988
Asfaw, Berhane 7:915
aspartic acid 12:1667
aspen trees, propagation 10:1405
aspergillosis 1:89
Aspergillus spp. 8:1138–1139
  A. fumigatus 8:1139
  and lung disease 7:948
  on peanuts 11:1462
asphalt pools 6:783
aspirin 9:1292
  and hearing 7:875
  for heart-attack or stroke victims 8:1098
  mode of action 9:1291
Asplenium spp. 5:706
asses, Somali wild 12:1659
Assicott, F.T. 4:548
astereognosis 12:1626
Asteroidea 4:569–570
asteroids
  collision with Earth 5:624
  and extinction of dinosaurs 5:624
  and iridium in sediments 4:528
asthma 2:153; 5:628, 690; 8:1059
  treatment 2:153; 8:1059
astigmatism 5:687
Astracanthus gummifera (gum traganth)
  8:1029
Ateles spp. (spider monkeys) 10:1368
Athene cunicularia (burrowing owl) 9:1206
atheroma 3:362; 9:1225
atherosclerosis 1:35; 3:363, 376–377
athlete's foot 5:699
atmosphere 2:154–157
  air pressure 2:155
  analysis of 2:155
  carbon dioxide 2:155; 3:302, 303, 306
    a greenhouse gas 2:157; 3:304, 306;
      4:492–493; 6:802; 10:1341;
      11:1542; 12:1644
  carbon monoxide 2:156
  chemical compositions 2:155
  Earth's early 2:156–157; 3:332; 5:582;
    6:801
  effect of life on 6:801
  and environmental diseases 5:625–626
  layers 2:154–155
  lead in 5:625
  models 2:155
  nitrogen 1:126

nitrogen oxides *see* nitrogen oxides

particulates in 2:*154*, 155–156; 5:625

pollution *see* pollution, air

sulfur dioxide 1:*16*; 5:625; 10:1340

see also acid rain

see also greenhouse gases and greenhouse
effect; oxygen; ozone

atolls 4:448; 7:*974*

ATP (adenosine triphosphate) 2:158;
7:993–994; 8:1117–1118; 10:1302

and muscle contraction 9:1181, 1182,
1183

production 2:158–160; 5:*618*, 619;
7:993; 8:1118; 9:1252

energy for *see* Krebs cycle

from chemiosmosis 5:618

from glucose fermentation 3:299–300;
5:702

from photosynthesis 5:618

and oxidation-reduction reactions
5:618; 7:996

role of mitochondria 2:159–160

used in bioluminescence 2:206

ATP synthase 2:160; 7:996

atria 7:877

atrial natriuretic factor (ANF) 7:880

atrioventricular (AV) node 7:879

Atropa belladonna (deadly nightshade) 1:*57*, 80

atrophy, muscular 9:1184

atropine 1:51; 11:1573

Atta spp. 1:59–60; 12:*1645*

attachment theory 5:604

Attacus atlas (atlas moth) 9:*1223*

attention deficit hyperactivity disorder
(ADHD; attention deficit disorder
[ADD]) 8:1115; 11:1536

Auchenorrhyncha 7:883, 884

audiometers 7:874

auks 6:751; 11:1472, 1473, 1474, 1578

great 6:*754*; 12:1654

Aurelia aurita (moon jelly) 7:*981*, 982

Auriparus flaviceps (verdin) 2:273

Australia, temperate rain forests 12:1610

Australopithecus spp. 2:258

A. afarensis 7:871

"Lucy" 6:*784*; 7:*914*, 915

A. africanus 7:915

A. boisei 7:915

A. robustus 7:871, 915

relationship to *Homo* 7:915

skin color 9:1227

Austrophlebia spp. 4:552

autecology 12:1720

autism 2:161–163; 8:1113;
11:1536–1537

autistic savants 2:162

autoclaves 1:115

autoganzfeld 9:1263

autoimmune disorders 2:164–166;
5:613; 7:931, 942

and aging 1:34

anemia, hemolytic 1:73–74; 2:164

diabetes mellitus 2:165; 5:613

of the endocrine system 5:613

and mouth ulcers 12:1622

multiple sclerosis 9:1175

myasthenia gravis 9:1181

rheumatoid arthritis 1:136

scleroderma 2:*164*

treatment 11:1557

automata, cellular 2:150

Automeris io (bull's eye-moth) 2:271

automimicry 2:270

automobiles *see* vehicles

autonomous underwater vehicles (AUVs)
9:1233

autopsies (post-mortem investigations)
6:773; 7:896

see also forensic science

autoradiography 7:895–896

autosomes 3:368

autotomy (self-amputation) 10:1400

in lizards 8:1052–*1053*; 10:1400

in phasmids 8:1017

autotransplantation 8:1092

autotrophs 5:584, 616; 8:1117; 9:1224

bacteria as 2:169

auxins 7:908–909; 10:1316; 11:1561;
12:1645

aversion therapy 3:414; 10:1387

Avery, Oswald 2:227; 4:537;
8:1141–1142

Avicularia spp. (bird-eating spider) 11:*1548*

avocets 2:230–231; 12:*1699*, 1700

avoidant personality disorder 9:1285

axolotls 9:*1256*; 10:1418; 11:1455

axons 2:255; 9:1183, 1198; 12:1626

terminal buttons 9:*1198*, 1200

aye-ayes 10:1366

ayurveda 7:887–888, 944

azathioprine 8:1088; 12:1634, 1635

azidothymidine *see* zidovudine

Azobacter 9:1217

Azolla 11:1580

AZT (azidothymidine) *see* zidovudine

Azteca spp. 11:1581

B

babesiosis 7:947

babies

birthweight, optimal 9:1193

brain 2:260

conception 5:708

development 3:354–357

immunity 7:*934*, 998

incubators 8:1040

jaundiced 8:1047

newborn 3:355

Apgar scoring system 1:123

PKU test 8:*1123*

premature 10:*1359*

reflexes 3:355; 10:*1397*–1398

Babinski's sign 5:697; 10:1398

sense of smell 11:1514

sleep 11:1511

speech development 11:1544

teeth 12:1604

vitamin K given to 4:519

Babinski's sign 5:697; 10:1398

baboons 1:*86*; 10:1368

estrus 8:*1111*

heart transplanted from 12:1634

male-female bonds 10:1369

movement 10:1370

reciprocal altruism 1:59

Bacillariophora 10:1313

Bacillariophyta 1:46

Bacillus spp.

B. anthracis 1:88–89, *107*, *117*; 2:170

B. cereus 2:170

B. popilliae 7:960

B. thuringiensis 6:810; 8:1132; 9:1288

bacitracin 5:630

backbone *see* vertebral column

back crossing, of plants 10:1323

back pain 3:320

treatment 1:57

backswimmers 7:885; 11:1577

Bacon, Francis 2:201

bacteria 2:167–172; 8:1130

anaerobic 8:1117; 9:*1253*

first forms of life 6:801

see also fermentation

ATP production 2:158

attachment 2:*167*, *168*, 169

autotrophic 2:169

and bioremediation 11:1461; 12:1698

blooms 5:*584*

capsule 2:169

cave-dwelling 3:325

cell walls 2:168–169; 3:298

and antibiotics 5:630

chemosynthetic

in caves 3:325

and the nitrogen cycle 9:1217–1218

at the seafloor 3:305; 5:651; 9:1233,
1237

cytoplasmic membrane 2:168

in the digestive tract 2:172

endospores 2:170–171

evolution 2:167–168

feeding 2:169

first forms of life 2:168

first observed 2:169

flagella 2:*167*, *168*, 169; 3:338

in food *see* food, preservation

fossils 2:168; 6:784; 10:1380

frost-resistant 8:1131

gas vesicles 2:169

and genetic engineering 2:170;
8:1131

genetic material 2:169

chromosomes 3:367

transfer 1:110

Gram positive and Gram negative
2:168–169, *171*

green 10:1303, 1306

heterotrophic 2:169

and humans 2:171–172

illnesses from 2:172

industrial uses 2:172

see also biotechnology

infecting plants 10:1322

iron 7:973

lactic acid 5:700, 701, 703

lithoautotrophic 2:169

luminescent 2:205, 207

methanobacteria 5:702

motion 2:*167*, *168*, 169

mutations 2:170

oral 2:171–172

photosynthetic 3:337

pili 2:170

population growth curve 10:1347

purple 2:168; 10:1303, 1306

reproduction 2:*169*–170

resistance to antibiotics 1:*19*, 109–110,
110; 8:1129; 9:1291

penicillin 1:*110*

saprophytic 11:1460, *1462*

on the skin 2:171

soil 11:1531

spores 2:170; 11:1531

staining 2:168–169

structure 2:*168*–169

sulfur 9:1239; 10:1303

symbiotic, in the gut 4:517; 9:*1226*,
1228

toxins 2:169, 172

types 2:*170*–171

used in biological control 7:960;
9:1288

viruses of *see* bacteriophages

for waste management 8:1132

and waterborne diseases 5:627;
7:948–949

see also microbiology; prokaryotes

bactericides 1:108

bacteriochlorophyll 3:337; 10:1306

bacteriological warfare

see biological warfare

bacteriophages 1:110; 4:537; 12:1675,
1681

bacteriostatic agents 1:108

Bacteroides spp. 2:172

baculoviruses 12:1679

badgers 10:1353

honey 11:1582

Baer, Karl von 2:202

baijis 12:1709

Bold words with bold page numbers indicate complete articles; bold numbers
preceding colons are volume numbers; numbers following colons indicate
page numbers; italic page numbers refer to illustrations or other graphics.

Baker, Henry **2**:207
Bakewell, Robert **11**:1479
baking **12**:1714–1715
Balaena mysticetus (bowhead whale) **12**:1709
Balaenoptera musculus (blue whale) **3**:405; **4**:438; **8**:1069
balance **4**:560–561; **7**:953
baleen **4**:438; **5**:*695*; **12**:1708, *1709*
Ballard, Dr. Robert **9**:1238
balloonfish **4**:486
balsams **11**:1477
balsa trees **12**:1639
bamboo **9**:1160, 1161; **11**:*1560*
banana plants **6**:796; **9**:1160; **10**:1338; **11**:*1542*
bandicoots **8**:1080
Banks, Joseph **2**:254; **8**:1042
Banting, Frederick Grant **4**:*508*; **7**:*965*; **8**:1103
barbels **1**:106; **6**:734; **7**:1001
Barbier, Charles **12**:1628
barbiturates **4**:556; **11**:1512
Bard, Philip **5**:602
barium X rays **11**:1565; **12**:1712
bark, tree **12**:1639
barnacles **4**:445, 470
  acorn **11**:1493
  goose **4**:*470*; **11**:*1493*
  stalked **7**:*889*
  on whales **11**:1580
Barnard, Christiaan **8**:1088; **12**:1635
baroreceptors **7**:880
Barr, M.L. **2**:191
barracudas **4**:450
Barr body **2**:191
basal metabolic rate (BMR) **2**:280; **8**:1121–1122
Basalo, A.F. **11**:1485
basidia **9**:1186
Basidiomycetes **8**:1139
Basidiomycota **9**:1185
basidomycetes **6**:799
basket stars **2**:206; **4**:570
basophils **1**:53, 114; **2**:239, 240–241
bathyal zone **9**:1231, 1237
bathyscapes **9**:1238
batrachotoxin **4**:485
bats 2:173–176
  altruism **1**:*60*
  Azorean **6**:*747*
  Bechstein's **2**:*173*
  big brown **4**:573
  cave-dwelling **3**:*325*, 328
  communication **2**:175
  ears **4**:562
  echolocation **2**:*174–175*; **4**:562, 572–574; **7**:873; **9**:1222
    detected by moths **7**:873
  evolution **2**:174; **6**:749
  and evolution of butterflies **2**:268

flight **2**:*173*, 175; **6**:748; **12**:1593
greater horseshoe **2**:*174*, 175; **3**:*325*
hands **11**:1498
human conflict **2**:176
insectivorous **2**:174; **4**:573–574
little brown **4**:*573*
long-eared **4**:*571*, 574
Old World fruit bats **2**:173–174
parasites **3**:328
pest control by **2**:176
pipistrelle **2**:176; **7**:*873*
pollination by **9**:1220; **10**:1338
reproduction **2**:176; **10**:1353
southern blossom bat **2**:173
tail **12**:1593
thermoregulation **2**:175–176
tube-nosed fruit bat **2**:173
vampire **2**:173, 174; **4**:574
  altruism **1**:*60*; **11**:*1526–1527*
Wahlberg's fruit **2**:*175*
wings and flight **2**:*173*, 175; **6**:748, 750, 751
batteries, car, recycling **12**:1697
Bauhin, Caspar **2**:253
B-cells *see* lymphocytes, B-cells
BCG vaccine **7**:935; **12**:1648
beaches
  sandy **11**:1494
  see also shore habitats
Beadle, George 8:1085; **12**:1598
beaks (bills) **2**:230–231; **9**:1274, *1275*; **12**:1606
  adaptive radiation **9**:1192; **11**:1541
  sensitive **12**:1628
  serrations **12**:1606
beans
  climbing plants **3**:379
  fava/broad **8**:1028
  garbanzo **8**:1028
  green, germination **10**:1316
  kidney **8**:1029
  lima **8**:1029
  mescal **8**:1029
  poisonous **8**:1029
  pole **12**:1646
bear-dogs **3**:310
beard worms **1**:96
bears **3**:308–309
  black **12**:1609, 1655–1656
  dawn **3**:309
  diet **5**:695
  grizzly **2**:*183*
  polar **3**:309; **5**:*692*; **10**:*1330*
  speciation **11**:1541
  teeth **3**:307
  winter lethargy **7**:891–892
"beating-heart" donors **12**:1636
Beattie, John **4**:553
Beaumont, William **4**:517
beavers **5**:659
  American **10**:*1438*
  dams **9**:*1207*

family groups **10**:1437
  fur **10**:1436
  lodges **9**:*1207*
  mountain **10**:1438
  swimming **11**:1578
  tail **12**:1593, 1594
  teeth **8**:1070, *1071*; **10**:*1438*
Bedlam (Bethlehem Hospital) **9**:*1215*
bed wetting **8**:1115
beech **12**:1608
  southern **9**:*1255*; **12**:1610
beer **5**:701; **6**:763
beeswax **12**:*1702*
beetles 2:177–178
  bark **2**:178
  biodiversity **2**:184
  blister **2**:178
  bombardier **4**:485; **5**:677
  cave-dwelling **3**:327
  click **2**:178
  Colorado potato **2**:*178*
  death-watch **2**:178
  diving **10**:1420; **11**:1578
  dune **4**:501
  dung **11**:*1464*
  elm-bark **9**:1294; **12**:1640
  fog harvesters **4**:501
  ground **3**:327
  hercules **2**:*177*
  ironclad **4**:485
  Japanese **7**:960
  jewel **2**:283
  ladybug *see* ladybugs
  lily **8**:*1081*
  oil **3**:404
  parasitic **7**:963
  as pests **2**:*178*
  pollination by **6**:760; **10**:1318, 1337
  rove **7**:963
  scarab **2**:177
  stag **2**:*177–178*; **11**:1483
  stink **12**:1647
  tiger **9**:1208
  vedalia **2**:195
  whirligig **2**:284
beets **8**:1013; **11**:1445
behavior
  animal *see* animal behavior
  human
    and autism **2**:161–162
    evolutionary theory and **2**:203–204; **9**:1194
behaviorism **1**:82; **3**:423; **5**:660; **10**:1383–1384
behavior therapy **3**:414; **10**:1301, 1387
Behring, Emil Adolf von **1**:112; **5**:592
belly button **10**:1359
Bender, Hans **9**:1263
bends, the **9**:1238; **10**:1422
Benzer, Seymour **12**:1676
benzodiazepines **11**:1512
benzoquinones **3**:345; **5**:677

Berg, Paul **2**:227
beriberi **4**:488; **9**:1227; **12**:1690, 1715
Bering Land Bridge **10**:1363
Bering Strait **9**:1234
Bernard, Claude **1**:91; **7**:*899*; **10**:1307; **12**:1721
Bernoulli, Daniel **6**:751
Beroe spp. **7**:982
berries **6**:792
Bertram, E.G. **2**:191
Best, Charles **4**:508; **7**:965; **8**:1103
beta-carotene **3**:294; **12**:1691
beta cells **7**:*964*; **9**:*1261*
Betafactin **12**:*1715*
beta particles **10**:1394
Beta spp. (beet) **4**:510; **11**:1445
Betta splendens (Siamese fighting fish) **9**:*1206*
Betula spp. (birch) **9**:1187
Bhopal, Union Carbide accident **5**:628
biceps **9**:*1179*
bichirs **6**:734
biennial plants 1:101; **2**:179
Bikini atoll, nuclear testing **4**:451
Bilateria **9**:1196
bile **3**:362; **4**:522; **8**:1044–1045, *1046*, 1047
  bile salts **8**:1044
  bile duct **8**:*1046*
  bile stones *see* gallstones
bilichromes **10**:1310
bilirubin **8**:1047; **10**:1310
biliverdin **10**:1310
Billingham, R. **8**:1087
Billings method, of ovulation prediction **4**:442
binary fission **3**:338
  by bacteria **2**:*169–170*; **3**:338; **10**:*1404*
bindweeds **3**:*379*; **12**:*1649*, 1651
Binet, Alfred **7**:966
binturong **3**:312
biochemistry 2:180–182
  see also analytical techniques
biodiversity 2:183–186
  conservation of **3**:425–426
  estimation **2**:183–184
  see also conservation
bioethics 2:187–191, 204
  abortion **1**:14; **2**:188, 191
  allocation of limited resources **2**:190–191
  cloning **3**:386
  contraception **4**:443
  deontology **2**:188
  embryo research **5**:600
  embryo transplantation **5**:711
  euthanasia **5**:646
  and experimentation
    animal **1**:92; **2**:189–190; **5**:603
    on humans **2**:189
  genetic engineering **2**:225
  and immunization **7**:934

and life support 8:1040

medical confidentiality 2:190

patenting life 2:190

prenatal diagnosis and therapy 2:191

stem cell research 11:1559

surrogate motherhood 5:712

utilitarianism 2:188

zoos 12:1726

biogeochemical cycles 5:584

see also carbon cycle; nitrogen cycle

biogeographic regions 5:583

biogeography 2:192–194

bioglas 2:212

bioleaching 8:1132

biological clocks 2:217–218; 9:1159,
1223

and molting 9:1159

biological control 2:195–196;
10:1350–1351

of beetles 7:960

using bacteria 7:960; 9:1288

Biological Oxygen Demand (BOD) 7:1001

biological warfare 2:197–199

anthrax for 1:107; 2:198, 199

nerve gases 9:1183

smallpox and 2:198; 11:1513; 12:1679

biology, history and philosophy of
2:200–204

bioluminescence 2:205–207; 5:686

and courtship 4:457

fireflies 2:178, 206

in fish 5:686

in jellyfish 7:982

biomagnification, of pesticides 4:481;
9:1280, 1287

biomass 6:770

pyramid of 5:586

biomedical engineering (bioengineering)
see bionics

biomedical ethics see bioethics

biomembranes 1:93

biomes and habitats 2:208–211

biomes 2:208

biodiversity 2:184

see also chapparal biomes; coral reef
biomes; desert biomes; estuaries;
forests; grassland biomes; mountain
biomes; shrublands; taiga biomes;
tundra biomes

habitats 2:208

pathways between 12:1718

see also cave habitats; island habitats;
ocean habitats; shore habitats;
suburban habitats; urban habitats

bionics 2:212–215

prostheses 2:212–215; 7:875;
8:1092–1093

see also implants

biopsies 4:475; 7:895

bioreactors 2:223

bioremediation 2:226; 11:1461;
12:1698

biorhythms 2:216–219

biological clocks 2:217–218; 9:1159,
1223

daily see circadian rhythms

human 2:217–219

in plants 2:217

biosonar 4:571

biosphere 2:220; 5:581–582, 583

biosynthesis see anabolism

biotechnology 2:221–227

in agriculture 2:223–225

bioremediation 2:226

DNA fingerprinting 2:224, 226; 6:773,
774

enzyme production 2:225

food production 2:225

in medicine 2:221–223

insulin production 2:225

in vitro fertilzation (IVF) 2:222; 5:710,
711, 712

monoclonal antibodies 2:221, 224, 226

see also genetic engineering

bipedalism 1:22; 7:871, 914, 916;
10:1360, 1361

and the aquatic ape 7:913

and the skeleton 11:1503

bipolar affective disorder (manic
depression) 8:1113; 10:1390

birch 9:1187

birds 2:228–233; 12:1673, 1674

banding of 8:1136

beaks (bills) 2:230–231; 9:1274, 1275;
12:1606

adaptive radiation 9:1192; 11:1541

sensitive 12:1628

serrations 12:1606

bones 2:229, 250; 6:751; 11:1498, 1501

brain 2:257, 259

as brood parasites 7:963

bursa of Fabricius 7:930

calls 2:233; 6:776

modified 7:962

see also birds, songs

camouflage 6:775

circulatory system 3:373, 375

colonies 9:1209; 11:1474

courtship 1:82, 84–85; 4:459–460;
8:1084; 9:1276

dances 4:460

nuptial feeding 8:1084

songs 2:232; 4:459

crop 2:230

digestive systems 4:514, 521; 11:1564

ears 4:561

echolocation 9:1222

eggs 2:231–232; 10:1413

camouflaged 2:284

effects of DDT 2:235–236; 4:481;
5:622–623; 9:1275; 10:1343–1344

incubation 1:83–84

retrieval by gulls 1:83

egg tooth 2:232

embryo development 5:598–599

evolution 2:233, 235; 4:529; 9:1274

convergent 4:446

excretion 2:230; 5:670; 7:989

fat storage 5:619

feathers 2:228–229; 6:725

feet 2:231; 5:697, 698; 9:1273; 11:1472

zygodactyly 6:775, 778

flight 6:747–749, 751–752

adaptations for 6:751

evolution 9:1254–1255

soaring 6:752; 8:1134; 11:1473

see also flight

flightless 2:230; 6:751, 753–756

at risk 6:756

cormorants 6:754; 9:1169; 11:1473

evolution 7:977

extinction 6:756; 7:977

swimmers 6:753, 754

see also penguins

terrestrial 6:755–756

flocks 3:402; 4:484

computer simulation 2:151

mixed-species 6:778

forest 6:775–778

communication 6:776

rain forest 6:777–778

of the taiga 6:776–777

temperate forests 6:777; 12:1609

heart 2:230; 7:877–878

and high altitude 9:1169

imprinting 8:1019

instincts 7:961, 962

jaws 7:978–979

of mangroves 11:1494

migration 2:210; 5:619; 6:776–777;
8:1135–1136; 10:1333; 11:1474;
12:1700

Arctic tern 8:1133; 11:1474

to the tundra 12:1654

white storks 8:1134

molting 2:229; 9:1158–1159

nervous system 2:230

nests 2:231; 9:1208–1209

communal 9:1209

forest birds 6:775–776

seabirds 9:1209; 11:1473

of swiftlets 3:328

nocturnal 9:1220, 1221–1222

of prey 2:234–237

effects of DDT on 2:235–236;
5:622–623; 9:1287; 10:1343–1344

evolution 2:235

in the suburbs 11:1569

vision 12:1686–1687

orders of 2:232

pancreas 9:1261

perching 5:697; 9:1273–1276

plant pollination by 10:1337–1338

play 10:1329

preening 5:676; 12:1699

respiration 10:1423–1424

lungs 2:230; 8:1060; 10:1424

salt glands 11:1459, 1472

seabirds 5:623; 11:1471–1474

nests 9:1209; 11:1473; 12:1614–1615

skeleton 2:229–230

skull 7:978–979; 11:1498

social 11:1522

songbirds 9:1273, 1274

songs 2:232, 233; 3:402; 4:459; 9:1274;
12:1614, 1615

learning 3:402–403; 8:1021

sounds 2:232–233

sonar 4:574

species 2:228

in the suburbs 11:1569

swimming 11:1578

tail 12:1592, 1593

taste receptors 12:1596

temperature regulation 12:1618

territories 1:29–30; 12:1613–1615

and song 9:1274; 12:1614, 1615

tongue 12:1621

of the tundra 12:1654

in urban areas 12:1665

uropygial glands 5:676

vision 12:1686–1687

waterbirds and waders
12:1699–1701

weight reduction 2:229–230

wings 6:747–748

claws on 6:777

penguin 6:753, 754

young

altricial 11:1474

nidifugous (precocial) 6:776; 11:1474

birds of paradise 8:1084

Birgus latre (coconut crab) 4:469

birth see pregnancy and birth

birth control see contraception

birth defects see congenital defects

birthmarks 10:1359

Bison bison (bison/American buffalo)
5:583, 608–609; 12:1660

Biston betularia (peppered moth) 2:285

Bitis gabonica (gaboon viper) 2:282

bivalves (Bivalvia) 8:1150

foot 5:698

shell 11:1497

Black, James Whyte 7:898

blackberries 6:795

blackbirds 9:1274

Black Death 7:950; 8:1063

blackflies, pupae 7:1006

blackheads 5:676

Bold words with bold page numbers indicate complete articles; bold numbers preceding colons are volume numbers; numbers following colons indicate page numbers; italic page numbers refer to illustrations or other graphics.

Black Hills **9**:1170

"black lung" (anthracosis; anthrasilicosis) **5**:*628*

black smokers **9**:1231, *1233*

black spot **10**:1321

bladder **5**:671; **11**:1459

bladderworts **3**:314, *315*; **12**:1670

blastocysts **5**:598, 600; **10**:1353; **11**:*1557*

blastoderm **5**:598

blastomycosis **7**:948

Blastophaga psenes (fig wasp) **12**:1693

blastula **5**:597, *598, 599*

Blatella spp. **5**:655; **9**:1193

blennies

  coral **2**:282

  sabre-toothed **4**:445

bleomycin **3**:353

Bleuler, Eugen **9**:1212

blight

  chestnut **9**:1265; **10**:1324

  corn **6**:800

  potato **8**:*1138*; **10**:1321, *1322*

blindness **5**:687

  and Braille **11**:*1538*; **12**:1628

  color **5**:687; **12**:*1687–1688*

  devices to aid in **2**:*213*

  night **9**:1291; **12**:1687

  snow **12**:1658

blind spot **5**:687

bloat **10**:1321

Bloch, Felix **8**:1068

blood 2:**238–247**; **3**:376

  amount in the human body **2**:238

  artificial **2**:246

  basophils **1**:53, 114; **2**:239, *240*, 240–241

  carbon dioxide in **3**:306

  cell manufacture **2**:242–243; **11**:1558–*1559*

  circulation, first described **1**:71; **8**:*1100*

  clotting **2**:241–242, 278; **7**:937; **12**:1620

    disorders **2**:242

    drugs to prevent bleeding **12**:1620

    vitamin K and **12**:1690

    see also embolisms; hemophilia; strokes; thrombosis

  components **2**:238–243

  diseases and disorders **2**:246–247

    thalassemias **1**:73; **2**:247

    see also anemia; leukemia

  eosinophils **2**:239, *240*

  erythrocytes (red blood cells) **2**:*238–239*; **8**:1056

    effect of high altitude on numbers of **10**:1307

    manufacture **2**:243; **11**:1558–*1559*

    natural destruction **2**:243; **8**:1047

    in the spleen **8**:1064; **11**:1550–1551

  erythropoietin **2**:239; **10**:1307

  glucose regulation **4**:506; **7**:902, 904–905; **9**:*1260–1261*

    see also glucagon; insulin

haptoglobin (Hp) **6**:774

HIV-contaminated **1**:45

iron in **7**:*973*

leukocytes **2**:239, *240*, 243

  granulocytes **2**:239, 243

  mononuclear cells **2**:239

lymphocytes *see* lymphocytes

megakaryocytes **2**:243

monocytes **2**:241, 243

neutrophils **2**:239–*240*; **7**:929

nonmammalian **2**:241

oxygen transport, *see also* hemoglobin

phosphoglucomutase (PGM) **6**:774

plasma **2**:238, 241; **4**:554

platelets **2**:241, 243

  and blood clotting **2**:241–242; **12**:1620

  disorders **2**:247

  screening **1**:45

  storage **4**:472

    blood banks **2**:245; **4**:*471*, 554; **11**:1571

  tested for freshness **2**:206

  transfusions **2**:*244–245*; **11**:1571

    Charles Drew and **4**:553–554

  types (groups) **2**:243, *244–245*; **6**:774

    in Australian aborigines **9**:1194

blood pressure **3**:374; **7**:880

  control **7**:902

  during shock **3**:378

  measurement **3**:374

blood vessels *see* arteries; capillaries; veins

Blossfeldia minima **2**:273

blowflies **6**:746, 773

blubber **11**:1507

bluebirds, eastern, decline **3**:*410*

blushing **5**:605

BMR *see* basal metabolic rate

boar, wild **12**:1606, *1610*

boas **11**:1519

  boa constrictors **11**:*1518*, 1519

  tree **11**:1519

bobcats **3**:322, 324

BOD (Biological Oxygen Demand) **7**:1001

body language **3**:404, 406

bogs **11**:1532; **12**:1703

  human remains in **9**:1166

  see also wetlands

boids **2**:*151*; **11**:1519

boletes **9**:1186

Boletus spp. **9**:1186

bollworms, cotton **2**:270

bombs, nuclear **2**:*189*; **4**:*451*

bombykol **4**:460; **9**:*1293*

Bombyx mori (silk moth) **5**:677; **6**:*725*; **9**:1288, *1293*

Bonaparte, Napoleon, and scurvy **6**:764

bonds, chemical **5**:617

bone(s) 2:**248–250**

  adaptations **2**:250

  and aging **1**:34

    osteoporosis **11**:1502

bird **2**:*229*, 250; **6**:751; **11**:1498, *1501*

  CT scans **4**:475

  dermal **2**:248

  development **2**:248, *249*; **3**:319

  disease and deformities **2**:250

  endochondral **2**:248; **11**:1500

  formation and structure **2**:*248–249*; **11**:1500–1501

  fossilization of **6**:781

  in the human hand **7**:*869*

  hyaline cartilage on **3**:*320*

  marrow **2**:249, *250*; **11**:1500

    cancer of *see* leukemia

    cells **8**:1063

    and lymphocytes **7**:*930*, 932; **11**:1559

    transplants **2**:249; **3**:353; **4**:535; **8**:1031; **11**:1557; **12**:*1633*

  repair and remodeling **2**:249–250; **10**:1402

  spongy **2**:248, *250*

  and vitamin deficiency **4**:*489*

  X rays of **12**:*1712*, 1713

  see also horns; joints; skeletal systems

Bonnet, Charles **2**:202

Bonpland, Aimé **2**:192

bonsai trees **11**:*1450*; **12**:1639

boobies **11**:1472–1473, *1474*

boomslangs **11**:1518

borderline personality disorder (BPD) **9**:1284

Bordetella pertussis **7**:948

Bordet, Jules **2**:244

Borrelia burgdorferi **7**:946, 949

Bos spp. **1**:18; **4**:545

  see also cattle

botanical gardens 2:**251–252**

botany 2:**253–254**; **5**:582

botflies **6**:746

Bothriuridae **11**:1470

Bothus lunatus (peacock flounder) **2**:282

Botox **9**:1203

Botrytis cinerea (noble rot) **10**:*1320*, 1321–1322

bottling, food **6**:764–765

botulism **2**:172; **6**:765; **7**:949; **9**:1203, 1253; **11**:1462

Bovicola spp. (lice) **8**:1033

bovine growth hormone/bovine somatotropin (BGH/BST) **2**:224, 227; **4**:545

bowerbirds, courtship **4**:*459–460*; **8**:1084; **9**:1208; **11**:1540; **12**:*1614*

bowfins **6**:734

Bowman's capsule **5**:668, 671; **7**:990

Boyer, Herbert **2**:227

Boyer, Paul **2**:160

Boyle, Robert **5**:637

brachiation **10**:1368

Brachinus spp. (bombardier beetle) **4**:485; **5**:677

brachiopods **1**:96

Brachiosaurus **4**:530, 531

Brachycera **6**:743

bracken **5**:706; **7**:*882*; **10**:1318

bracket fungi **9**:1187

Bradypus spp. (three-toed sloths) **1**:*104*

Braid, James **7**:926

Braille **11**:*1538*; **12**:1628

Braille, Louis **11**:1538; **12**:*1628*

brain 2:**255–264**

  aging **1**:35

  anatomy **2**:*256–259*; **9**:1210–1211

  blood flow **2**:264

  cerebellum **2**:256, 259

  cerebral cortex (neocortex) **2**:*257–259*

    and Alzheimer's disease **1**:61

    development **2**:260

    and intelligence **7**:967

    map (homunculus) **2**:*262*; **5**:637

    memory storage **8**:*1104*–1105; **11**:1543–1544

  cerebrum **2**:257

  cerebral hemispheres **2**:259, *263*–264

  and circadian rhythms **2**:217

  degenerative diseases *see* degenerative brain diseases

  electrical activity

    see electroencephalograms

  and emotion **2**:257; **5**:604–605

  evolution **2**:258; **5**:660

  forebrain **2**:257, 258

  function during sleep **2**:264

  hindbrain **2**:256

  human **2**:*257*, 259–263

    development and growth **2**:260

    evolution **2**:258

    and handedness **7**:871

    learning and memory **2**:261–263

  imaging techniques **2**:260

    CT scans **2**:260; **4**:475

    EEGs **2**:255, 260; **5**:638; **8**:1090; **11**:*1509*–1510

    magnetoencephalography (MEG) **2**:260

    MRI scans **2**:260; **3**:*399–400*; **8**:*1068*, *1104*; **9**:*1214*

    PET scans **2**:260

  injury **12**:1626

    and comas **3**:398

  limbic system **2**:257; **5**:604–605

  midbrain **2**:256–257

  neurobiology **9**:1210–1211

  neurons **2**:255–256

  nonhuman **2**:259

  split brain studies **2**:264; **5**:638

  strokes **2**:242, 256; **3**:377; **7**:902; **12**:1620

  study of *see* neuroscience

  surgery **5**:*639*; **11**:*1575*

  see also mental disorders; nervous system

brain hormone (BH) **5**:612; **7**:1005

brain waves **2**:*255*

branchial basket **4**:552

Branchiopoda **4**:470

Branchiostoma lanceolatum see amphioxus

Branta spp. (goose) **11**:*1482, 1521*

Brassica spp. **9**:*1229*

bread **5**:701

breakage-fusion-bridge cycles **8**:1086

breathing *see* respiration, breathing

breeding

    captive *see* captive breeding programs

    selective *see* selective breeding

brewer's yeast **12**:1715

brewing **12**:1715

Briggs, Robert **3**:383

bristle worms **1**:96, *98*

brittle stars **2**:206; **4**:568, 570; **9**:1232

Broca, Paul **9**:1214

Broca's area **11**:1544

Brockman bodies **9**:1261

bromeliads **5**:*642*; **8**:1027; **11**:*1580*

bromocriptine **5**:709, 712

bronchi **8**:1055; **10**:1420

bronchioles **8**:1055; **10**:1420

bronchitis **8**:1059

bronchodilators **2**:153; **8**:1059

bronchoscopes **8**:1091

Brontosaurus see Apatosaurus

Bronx Zoo, New York City **12**:1725

Brookesia minima (stump-tailed chameleon) **8**:1051

broom, seed dispersal **10**:1319; **11**:1477

broomrape **10**:1321; **12**:1632

brown lung (byssinosis) **5**:628

Brown, William L. **12**:1711

browsers **5**:694

brucellosis **1**:89

Bryophyllum spp. **8**:1027

Bryophyta (bryophytes) **9**:1165; **10**:1326

    see also mosses, liverworts, and hornworts

Bryozoa **1**:96

BSE (bovine spongiform encephalitis; mad cow disease) **1**:*89*; **3**:337; **7**:949; **10**:1372

BST *see* bovine growth hormone/bovine somatotropin

Buchheim, Rudolph **9**:1289

Buchner, Eduard **5**:630

Buckland, Rev. William **4**:527

budding **10**:1400, 1404, *1405*

    by bacteria **2**:170

    by coral polyps **4**:449, 453

    by yeasts **12**:1714

Budiansky, Stephen **4**:544

buds **11**:1561

    and dormancy **4**:547–548, *549*

bud scales **11**:1560, 1561

buffaloes **4**:485

    African **4**:514

    American **5**:*583*, 608–609

    water **4**:545; **12**:1662

buffers

    of biological fluids **11**:1459

    environmental **1**:16; **11**:1459

Buffon, Georges-Louis Leclerc, Comte de **2**:201

Bufonidae **6**:787

Bufo spp. **6**:790

    B. americanus (American toad) **3**:403

    B. marinus (cane toad) **1**:*51*; **2**:196

bufotenine **1**:*51*

bugs

    ambush **7**:885

    assassin (kissing bugs) **7**:*884*, 885, 946

        mimicry by **3**:*391*

    bodyguard **4**:483

    green shield **7**:*883*

    lygus **7**:885

    red **1**:132

    see also Hemiptera

bulbs and corms 2:265–266; **9**:1277; **11**:1449

    bulbs **2**:265–266

    corms **2**:265–266

bulimia **4**:*565*, 566; **8**:1114

bullfrogs **1**:64; **5**:666; **6**:787, 790

Bungarus spp. (krait) **9**:*1203*

bunions **5**:699

buntings, Lapland **10**:1333

buoyancy, fish **6**:728–729; **11**:1577

Buphagus spp. (oxpecker bird) **11**:*1579*

Burch, Rex L. **1**:92

Burgess Shale **9**:1256, 1257

Burkitt's lymphoma **8**:1066

Burnet, Macfarlane **8**:1088

burrows **9**:1207

    fossilized **6**:783

Bursera simaruba (gumbo-limbo tree) **5**:648

bursitis **2**:250

bush babies **9**:1294; **10**:1366

butanol, from bacterial fermentation **5**:702, 703

Buteo spp. **2**:*234*, 235

Buthidae **11**:1470

buttercups **1**:80; **12**:1650

    in polar climates **10**:*1332*

butterflies and moths 2:267–271

    beneficial **2**:270

    butterflies

        apollo **2**:186

        blue chalkhill **10**:*1403*

        Cairns birdwing **1**:*137*

        cloudless sulfur **2**:269

        courtship **4**:457

        European large blue **2**:271

        glasswing **2**:271

        hairstreak **2**:*271*

        leaf **2**:271, 283

        monarch **2**:*269*, 270; **4**:484; **6**:810–811; **7**:959–960, 1003; **8**:*1125, 1135*

        purple emperor **2**:268

        stomach **11**:1563

        swallowtail **2**:*267*, 269, 283, 284; **4**:483

        viceroy **4**:484

        wings **6**:750

Xerxes blue **2**:267

    camouflage and mimicry **2**:270, 271, *281, 286*

    caterpillars **2**:*268–269*; **7**:*1003*, 1006; **8**:1125; **10**:*1308*

        false eyes **1**:19

        frozen **4**:472

        spiracles **10**:1420

        woolly bear **4**:472

    colors and patterns **2**:270–*271*

    communication, chemical (pheromones) **1**:106; **2**:269–270, *270*; **4**:460; **9**:1288; **12**:1596

    differences **2**:268

    evolution **2**:268

    feeding **2**:267, 268

    flight **9**:1180

    life cycle **2**:268–269

    metamorphosis **7**:1006; **8**:*1125*; **10**:1308

    migration **2**:*269*; **8**:*1135*

    mimicry by **2**:270

    moths

        antennae **1**:*105*, 106; **9**:*1223*

        atlas **9**:*1223*

        bat avoidance **4**:574; **7**:873

        for biological control **2**:270

        brown-tail **2**:270

        bull's-eye **2**:271

        coevolution with plants **3**:390

        corn earworm **2**:269

        dagger **2**:284

        gypsy **2**:196, 268–269, 270; **10**:1346, *1347*

        hawk **1**:19; **2**:268

        herald **3**:328

        hornet **2**:*286*

        peppered **2**:285

        silk **2**:270; **5**:677; **6**:*725*; **9**:1288, *1293*

        tiger **4**:574

        tissue **3**:328

        tussock **2**:269

        vampire **2**:267

        yucca **2**:269; **10**:1336

    as pests **2**:*270*

    plant pollination **10**:*1336*, 1337

    proboscis **2**:267, 268; **10**:1337

    relationship with ants **2**:271

    temperature **2**:271; **12**:*1617*

    wings **2**:267–268, 269, *271*

buttermilk **5**:701

butterworts **3**:316

butylated hydroxytoluene (BHT) **6**:764

butylate hydroxyanisole (BHA) **6**:764

bypass surgery **7**:881; **12**:1620

    robots used for **10**:1432–1433; **11**:1572

byssinosis **5**:628

by-the-wind sailor **7**:983

C

C3 plants **10**:1305

C4 plants **8**:1025; **10**:1305

cabbages **9**:*1229*

Cacajao spp. (uakaris) **10**:1368

Cacatua spp. **7**:*962*

cacolytic acid **9**:1294

cacomistles **3**:311

cacti and succulents 2:272–274; **12**:1630

    cacti **2**:272–274; **4**:*482*, 499

        ball **2**:273

        beavertail **2**:273

        cochineal **7**:884

        epiphytic **5**:642

        flowers **2**:272

        hedgehog **2**:272

        saguaro **2**:273, 274; **4**:499

        spines **2**:273; **8**:1022, 1027; **10**:1317; **11**:1562

        stomata **1**:18–19

        water storage **2**:273

    crassulacean acid metabolism **2**:273

Cactoblastis cactorum **2**:270

CAD *see* coronary artery disease

caecilians 1:64; **2:275–276**

Caenorhabditis elegans **10**:1430

Caesalpinioideae **8**:1029

café au lait spots **11**:1504

caffeine **1**:24, 51; **4**:555; **8**:1014; **11**:1512

Cajuns **12**:1704

calabashes **11**:1554

Calamus spp. (rattan) **9**:1259

Calcarea **11**:1553

Calcarius lapponicus (Lapland bunting) **10**:1333

calcitonin **2**:278

    synthetic form **2**:180–181

calcium 2:277–278

    absorption **2**:278

    deficiency **4**:489

    pump **2**:277

    regulation in the body **2**:278; **5**:612

    role in muscles **2**:278; **9**:1182

calcium antagonists **2**:278

calcium carbonate, forming limestone **3**:303

calcium fluorophosphate **10**:1302

calcium phosphate, in bone **3**:319; **10**:1302; **11**:1500

Callianassa spp. (ghost shrimps) **4**:467

Callibaetes spp. **4**:552

Callimico goeldii (Goeldi's monkey) **10**:1368

Callithrix argentata (white-eared marmoset) **5**:694

Callitrichidae **10**:1367–1368

calls

alarm **3**:403; **11**:1522

bird **2**:233; **6**:776

modified **7**:*962*

frog and toad **4**:458–459; **6**:790

Calluna vulgaris (heather) **7**:882

calmodulin **2**:277

calories 2:279–280; **5**:616

reduction, and life span **1**:36

calorimetry **2**:279–280

Calpe eustrigata (vampire moth) **2**:267

Calthrop spp. **2**:282

Calvin, Melvin **10**:1304

Calvin cycle (C3 cycle) **8**:1023; **10**:1304–1305

Calystegia spp. (bindweed) **3**:*379*; **12**:*1649*, 1651

calyx **6**:757, 761–762

tubes **6**:759

CAM (crassulacean acid metabolism) **2**:273; **10**:*1305*–1306

cambium **4**:509; **11**:1448, 1561

cork **11**:1561

Camellia sinensis (tea) **1**:51; **8**:*1013*

camels **4**:*501*

milk **7**:998

Camelus spp. (camels) **4**:*501*

camouflage and mimicry 2:281–286; **4**:483

alligator snapping turtle **2**:283

birds

of the forest **6**:775

killdeer **2**:*283*

butterflies and moths **2**:270, 271, *281*, *286*

peppered moth **2**:285

chameleons, color change **2**:282; **4**:483; **7**:*908*; **10**:1310

countershading **2**:283

cryptic coloration **2**:281–282

in insects **8**:*1076*

disguise **2**:283–284

disruptive coloration **2**:282–283

evolution of camouflage **2**:284–285

frogs **6**:788

leaf insects and walking sticks **2**:283, 284; **8**:*1015*–1016, *1017*

mimicry **4**:445, 484

aggressive **2**:286

automimicry **2**:270

Batesian **2**:270, 286

eyespots **2**:271, 283

Müllerian **2**:270, 285; **3**:*391*

tests of camouflage **2**:284

turning white in the snow **9**:*1159*

using bioluminescence **2**:207

Camposcia retusa **2**:282

Campylorhynchus brunneicapillus (cactus wren) **2**:273; **9**:1206

canaries **9**:1273

cancer 3:293–296; **8**:1094; **12**:1625

and African Americans **3**:296

and the Ames test **3**:295

and antioxidants **3**:*294*

brain tumors **3**:*333*, 398, 399; **8**:*1089*

breast **3**:293, 295

chemotherapy **3**:353

surgery for **2**:219; **3**:296

causes **3**:294–295; **9**:1190

diet **5**:690

environmental **5**:627

see also carcinogens

cervical **3**:296

test for **4**:477

colon **3**:295, 299; **4**:523, 538

treatment **3**:353

diagnosis **4**:477; **7**:*896*; **8**:*1064*

digestive system **3**:317

in the elderly **1**:35

genes associated with **3**:293, 294

Hodgkin's disease **3**:353; **8**:1066

liver **3**:295

lung **3**:294, *295*; **8**:1060

and diet **3**:317

and smoking **3**:*295*; **8**:1059–1060

treatment **11**:1575

and the lymphatic system **8**:*1064*

lymphomas **3**:294; **8**:1066

Burkitt's **8**:1066

non-Hodgkin's **3**:371; **8**:1066

metastases **3**:294; **8**:*1064*

poverty and **3**:296

prostate **3**:295, 352

rectal **3**:295; **4**:523

skin **3**:294, 295, 296, 317, 353; **9**:*1193*; **12**:1658

treatment **12**:1713

staging **4**:477; **8**:*1064*

stomach **11**:1565

of the testis **7**:*896*

tongue **12**:1622

treatment **3**:296

with drugs (chemotherapy) **2**:219; **3**:296, 352–353; **8**:*1031*, 1130–1131; **12**:1597

radiotherapy **3**:296; **8**:1091

using stem cells **11**:1557

using X rays **12**:1713

vaccines **3**:296

tumor growth **3**:352–353

types **3**:294

see also leukemia

Cancer pagurus (edible crab) **4**:*467*

candelilla wax **12**:1702

Candida spp.

C. albicans **12**:*1716*

C. utilis **12**:1715

candidiasis **12**:1716

Canidae **3**:309; **12**:1601

see also dogs

Caniformia **3**:308–311

canines **12**:1603, 1605, 1606

Canis spp.

C. dingo (dingo) **4**:*542*

C. familiaris (domestic dog) **4**:*540*–541, 544

C. latrans (coyote) **4**:*539*, 540; **11**:1569

C. lupus (gray wolf) **3**:309; **4**:539; **10**:1350; **11**:*1522*, 1524

C. lupus lycaon (timber wolf) **3**:*428*

C. rufus (red wolf) **4**:542

C. simensis (Ethiopian wolf) **4**:541–542

canker sores (aphthous ulcers) **12**:1622

cannabis (marijuana) **4**:557

Cannabis sativa see hemp

cannibalism **8**:1076

human, and kuru **10**:1371

canning, food **6**:764–765

Cannon, W.B. **5**:602, 641; **10**:1307

capillaries **3**:375, *376*

Caprimulgus sp. (whippoorwill) **2**:216; **6**:776; **9**:1221–1222

Capris hircus (goat) **4**:544

caps, cervical **4**:440–*441*

capsaicin **1**:51

Capsella bursapastoris (shepherd's purse) **5**:*601*

Capsicum spp. (peppers) **1**:51

capsid **12**:1680

captive breeding programs **11**:*1482*; **12**:1725, *1726*

capybaras **10**:1436, 1437; **11**:1465

carapace **4**:*467*; **12**:1623

Carausius morosus (laboratory stick insect) **8**:*1017*

carbamino-hemoglobin **8**:1056

carbamoyl phosphate **12**:1667

carbamoyl phosphate synthetase **12**:1667, 1668

carbohydrates 3:297–**301**; **8**:1143

catabolism **3**:*300*

dietary **3**:301; **9**:1226, 1229

digestion **3**:299; **9**:1260

energy content **2**:279

energy storage **3**:297–298; **5**:619

formation **3**:298–299

glucose

and energy **3**:299–301

regulation **3**:301

"loading" **3**:*299*

metabolism **2**:280

errors of **8**:1123–1124

without oxygen *see* fermentation

see also Krebs cycle

and plant structure **3**:298

storage **3**:297–298

in plants **3**:297

types **3**:297

in weight-loss diets **3**:300

see also cellulose

carbolic acid **8**:1043, 1129

carbon

compounds **3**:303

life based on **5**:681

in the ocean **3**:304–305

radiocarbon dating **3**:305; **6**:784

carbon cycle 3:302–305, 306

and coral reefs **4**:449

see also carbon dioxide; photosynthesis; respiration

carbon dioxide 3:**306**

atmospheric **2**:155; **3**:*302*, 303, 306

a greenhouse gas **2**:157; **3**:*304*, 306; **4**:492–493; **6**:802; **11**:*1542*; **12**:1644

in the body **3**:306

gas exchange **9**:1253

and the carbon cycle **3**:*302*, 303

elimination from organisms **5**:665; **8**:1056–1057

"missing" **3**:305

and regulation of Earth's temperature **6**:802–803

see also carbon cycle

carbonic acid **6**:802

carbonic anhydrase **5**:629

carbonization, of plant remains **6**:783

carbon monoxide

atmospheric **2**:156

poisoning **5**:625; **10**:1420

carboxypepsidase **5**:630; **9**:1260

Carcharhiniformes **11**:1487

Carcharhinus spp. **11**:1488, 1489; **12**:*1672*

Carcharias falciformis (silky shark) **11**:*1490*

Carcharodon spp. (great white shark) **4**:450; **11**:1489

carcinogens **3**:294–295; **9**:1190

Ames test **3**:295

and leukemia **8**:1031

tobacco *see* smoking, and cancer

carcinoma(s) **3**:294

bronchogenic **8**:1060

see also cancer

cardiac cycle **7**:879

cardiovascular system *see* circulatory systems; heart

Carduelis hornemanni (Arctic/hoary redpoll) **10**:*1333*

Carex spp. (sedge) **11**:1477

caribou **8**:1135; **10**:1333; **12**:*1590*, 1654, 1663

European (reindeer), diet **8**:*1036*; **12**:1654

ptarmigan and **11**:1580

caries, dental (tooth decay) **12**:1604–*1605*

Carlsson, Arvid **9**:1215

carnassials **3**:307, 321; **4**:517; **12**:1605

carnauba wax **9**:1259; **12**:1702

carnauba wax palm **9**:1259

Carnegiea gigantea (saguaro cactus) **2**:273, 274; **4**:499

carnivores 3:307–313; **5**:694–695; **8**:1071–1072
  anatomy **3**:307
  cats *see* cats
  digestive system **4**:*516, 520, 521*; **11**:1563
  dogs *see* dogs
  evolution **3**:*310*
  in food webs **6**:767, 768
  jaws **3**:307; **7**:*978*, 979
  nonmammalian **3**:308
  nutrition **9**:1228
  plants *see* carnivorous plants
  teeth **3**:*307*, 310; **4**:517; **7**:979; **8**:1070; **12**:1605
carnivorous plants 3:314–316; **5**:609, 695–696; **10**:1317; **12**:1625
  leaves **8**:*1027*
  reflexes **10**:1397
carob **8**:1029
carotenemia **3**:317
carotenes 3:317; **9**:1227; **10**:1311
  beta-carotene **3**:294; **12**:1691
carotenoids **3**:317; **10**:1306, 1311
carp **4**:545
carpals (bones) **7**:869
carpal tunnel syndrome **5**:628; **7**:870
carpels **5**:716; **6**:758
Carpobrotus **2**:274
carrageenan, from seaweeds **7**:988
carrots **11**:1446
carrying capacity **10**:1345–*1346*
cars *see* vehicles
Carson, Rachel Louise 1:41; **3**:318; **4**:481; **5**:584, 680; **9**:1288
Carthartes aura (turkey vulture) **2**:235
cartilage 2:248; **3**:319–320; **6**:726; **10**:1376
casein, vegetable **10**:1377
case reports **5**:635
cassava **5**:701; **11**:1446
cassowaries **5**:698; **6**:756, 775
Castanea dentata (American chestnut) **9**:1266; **10**:1324
Castanospermum australe (Moreton Bay chestnut) **12**:1599, *1600*, 1644
Castor spp. *see* beavers
Castoroides **10**:1438
castrati **10**:1414
castration **10**:1414
Casuarius spp. (cassowaries) **5**:698; **6**:756, 775
catabolism **5**:618–619; **8**:1116, 1117–1119
catalysts **5**:617, 629
  see also enzymes
cataracts **5**:*687*; **12**:1658
Catarrhini **10**:1365, 1367, 1368–1369
catatonia **3**:398; **11**:1466
caterpillars *see* butterflies and moths, caterpillars
Catesby, Mark **5**:621

catfish
  barbels **1**:106
  eggs **6**:733
  farming of **1**:*124*
  gills **10**:1419
  walking **6**:728
Cathartidae **2**:236
catheterization
  balloon-tipped catheters **11**:1574
  bladder **11**:1574
cats 3:321–324; **5**:694
  black-footed **3**:313
  camouflaged **2**:*284*
  and civilization **3**:323
  classification **3**:323–324; **12**:1600
  diseases **1**:89–90; **8**:1061
  domestic **3**:322, 323, 324
    Manx **12**:1593
    as predators **10**:*1350*, 1351
    Siamese **3**:*324*
    territories **12**:1614, 1615
  endangered **3**:323
  evolution **3**:324
  the feline body **3**:322–323
  feral **11**:1569
  fleas **6**:738; **9**:*1288*
  hearing **3**:322
  lice **8**:1033
  as predators **3**:322–323
  purring and roaring **3**:*321*
  saber-toothed *see* tigers, saber-toothed
  sense of smell **3**:321–322
  sight **3**:322
  tail **12**:1593
  teeth **3**:321; **12**:1605
  tongue **12**:1622
  whiskers **3**:322; **12**:1628
  see also carnivores
CAT scanning *see* CT scanning
Cattell, Raymond B. **9**:1283
cattle
  cows **1**:39
    licking newborn **12**:*1625*
    mammary glands **5**:*676*
    milk composition **7**:998
    milk production **4**:545; **9**:1193
  digestion by **5**:*694*; **11**:*1453*
  diseases **1**:88–89
    coast disease **9**:1227
    mad cow disease **1**:*89*
  domestic **4**:545
  lice **8**:1033
  saliva **11**:1452
  see also ruminants
Caudata *see* salamanders and newts
Caulimovirus **10**:1323
Cavea porcellis (guinea pig/cavy) **4**:545
cave habitats 3:325–328
  bird sonar in **4**:574
Caventou, Joseph Bienaimé **8**:1103
cavernicoles **3**:325

Cayley, George **6**:751
CCNs (cloud condensing nuclei) **6**:802
Cebidae **10**:1368
Cebuella pygmaea (pygmy marmoset) **10**:1367
Cebus spp. (capuchin monkeys) **3**:402; **10**:1368
celiac disease **4**:519
cell biology 3:329–340
  aging **1**:33–34
  animal cells **3**:*336*
  apoptosis **3**:353
  ATP production **2**:*158*–160; **3**:299–300; **5**:*618*; **7**:993
  autolysis **3**:334–335
  cell differentiation **3**:330; **7**:894; **10**:1400; **11**:1556
  cell division
    cytokinesis **3**:339
    DNA replication **4**:*534*–536
    see also meiosis; mitosis
  cell theory **2**:202; **3**:330–331
  circadian rhythms **2**:217
  cytology 4:476–477
  cytosol **2**:159
  electrical potential of cells **10**:1308
  endoplasmic reticulum **3**:334
  evolution **3**:332
  flow cytometry **4**:476–477
  freezing of cells **4**:471–472
  Golgi complex **3**:334
  life span of cells **1**:36
  lysosomes **3**:334–335; **4**:511; **7**:929
  membranes *see* plasma membranes
  mitochondria *see* mitochondria
  muscle cells, fermentation by **5**:703
  nerve cells *see* neurons
  nucleus *see* nuclei
  organelles **3**:333–335, *336*
  and osmosis **11**:1458–1459
  peroxisomes **3**:335
  plant **3**:*335*–336, *337*; **4**:476
    cell walls **3**:298, 341–342
    chloroplasts *see* chloroplasts
    vacuoles **3**:*335*, 336; **8**:1023
  pluripotent cells **3**:340; **11**:1557, 1558–1559
  position of molecules within cells **8**:1144–1145
  prokaryotes and eukaryotes **10**:1380
    see also eukaryotes; prokaryotes
  ribosomes *see* ribosomes
  structure, and freeze-etch microscopy **4**:*473*
  totipotent cells **3**:340; **6**:809; **11**:*1557*
  types **3**:330
  unipotent cells **11**:1557–1558
  vacuoles **3**:336–337

walls
  bacterial **2**:168–169; **3**:298; **5**:630
  of plants **3**:298, 336
cellulases **3**:342; **11**:1451, 1452, 1461–1462
celluloid **3**:342
Cellulon **6**:725
cellulose 3:298, **341–342**; **8**:1143
  digestion **3**:342; **4**:514; **9**:1228
    by cockroaches **3**:388
    by fungi **3**:342
    by mammals **4**:514, 521; **9**:*1226*; **10**:1380, 1393; **11**:1461, 1581; **12**:1661
    by termites **1**:140; **10**:1380; **11**:*1461*, 1462; **12**:1611
  industrial uses **3**:342, 417
  in plant cell walls **3**:298, 341–342
  in plant fibers **3**:*341*; **6**:725
cellulose nitrate **3**:342
Centengraulis mysticetus (Peruvian anchovy) **4**:438
Center for Plant Conservation **2**:252
Centers for Disease Control and Prevention (CDC) **5**:634
centipedes and millipedes 3:343–346
  centipedes **1**:142; **3**:*343*–345
  millipedes **1**:142; **3**:*344*, 345–*346*; **4**:485
central dogma **10**:1429–1430
centrifugation **1**:67–68
  ultracentrifugation **2**:181; **10**:1376; **12**:1677
centriole **3**:338–339
Centrocercus urophasianus (sage grouse) **4**:460
centromere **3**:338, 366
Centruroides spp. **11**:1470
century flowers **9**:1220
century plants **10**:1319
Cepaea spp. **4**:525
Cephalocarida **4**:470
Cephalochordata **3**:364
  see also amphioxus
cephalopods (Cephalopoda) **8**:1150
  foot **5**:698
  see also mollusks; octopuses; squid
Cephalopus spp. (West African duiker) **5**:694
cephalosporins **1**:109
  allergy to **1**:110
cephalothorax **4**:467
Ceramornis **12**:1701
Ceranium shuttleworthianum **7**:*987*
cerata **7**:981
Ceratina spp. **12**:*1693*
Ceratophylloidea **6**:740
Ceratophyllum spp. (hornworts) **10**:1338

Bold words with bold page numbers indicate complete articles; bold numbers preceding colons are volume numbers; numbers following colons indicate page numbers; italic page numbers refer to illustrations or other graphics.

ceratopsians 4:531

Ceratotherium simum (northern white rhinoceros) 5:*606*, 607

cercariae 9:1265

cerci 4:563, *564*

Cercocebus spp. (African mangabey) 3:406

Cercopithecus aethiops (vervet/African green monkey) 3:403; 11:1523

cereals *see* grains; grasses, cereal

cerebellum 2:256, 259

cerebral cortex *see* brain, cerebral cortex

cerebral hemispheres 2:259, *263–264*

cerebrospinal fluid 2:259–260

cerebrum 2:257

cerebral hemispheres 2:259, *263–264*

Certocystis ulmi 9:1294

see also Dutch elm disease

cerumen 12:1702

ceruminous glands 5:676

cervix

cancer 3:*296*

test for 4:477

mucus 4:442; 9:1172

Cervus spp.

C. canadensis (wapiti) 5:656; 8:1084, 1133

C. elaphus (red deer) 3:*409*; 4:460

cesarean sections 10:1357, 1359; 11:1574

Cestoda 6:737

see also tapeworms

cetaceans *see* whales, porpoises, and dolphins

Cetorhinus maximus (basking shark) 6:732; 11:1487

CFCs *see* chlorofluorocarbons

Chactidae 11:1470

Chaerilidae 11:1470

Chaetodon spp. (butterfly fish) 2:283; 6:732; 11:*1576*

Chaetognaths 1:97

Chagas' disease 7:885, 946

Chain, Ernst 6:742, 799

Challenger, HMS 9:1239

Chamaedorea elegans (parlor palm) 9:1259

chameleons 8:1053

color change 2:282; 4:483; 7:*908*; 10:1310

feeding and diet 5:694–695; 10:1351

stump-tailed 8:1051

chamois 9:*1169*

channeling 9:1263

chaos, order, and complexity 3:347–349

chapparal biomes 2:209; 3:350–351

fires 3:351; 5:623

character displacement 12:1711

Charadriidae *see* plovers

Charadriiformes 11:1471; 12:1699–1700

Charadrius vociferus (killdeer) 2:232, *283*; 3:404

Charaka 7:887

Charcot, Jean-Martin 9:*1213*, 1214; 12:1658

chard, Swiss 8:1013–1014

Chargaff, Erwin 4:537

Charophyta 1:47

Chase, Martha 4:537

Chauliac, Guy de 5:*637*

chayote 11:1554

cheese 2:225, 227; 5:*700*, 701; 6:763

cheese plants, phototropism 10:1316

cheetahs 3:307, 313, 324

speed 3:322; 8:1069

chelicerae 1:141

chelicerates 1:97, 141

Chelonia 10:1415

see also tortoises and turtles

Chelonia mydas (green sea turtle) 4:*437*; 8:1134; 11:*1492*; 12:*1624*

chemical energy, stored, *see also* ATP; FADH$_2$; NADH; NADPH

chemicals, as defense *see* defense mechanisms

chemiosmosis 5:618

chemiosmotic-coupling hypothesis 10:1306

chemistry, plant 2:254

chemoautotrophs 5:584; 9:1224

chemoreceptors, and heart rate 9:1252

chemotaxis 12:1647

bacterial 2:169

chemotherapy 2:219; 3:296, 352–353; 8:1130–1131

for leukemia 8:*1031*

and taste 12:1597

chemotrophs 8:1117

Chernobyl disaster 5:622, 626; 8:1036; 10:*1344, 1395*

Chesapeake Bay 11:1492

chestnuts 6:792

chestnut trees

American 9:1266; 10:1324

Moreton Bay 12:1599, *1600*, 1644

chewing 12:1621

chi (Qi) 1:55; 3:360, 361

chiasma, optic 12:1685

chiasmata 3:339–340

chicken pox 7:948; 12:*1683*

chickens

domestic 4:544

pecking-order 11:1523

lice 8:1033

permaculture 9:*1280*

prairie 4:459

chickpeas 8:1028

Chicxulub 5:659

chiggers 9:1264

chigoes 6:738

childbed fever 8:1101

childbirth *see* pregnancy and birth

child development 3:354–359

attention span 3:358

cognitive development 3:354–355, *359*, 394

differences between the sexes 3:359

imitation 3:358

importance of stimulation 3:356–357

memory development 3:358

motor skills 3:356

nature versus nurture 3:359

nervous system development 3:355–356

newborn babies 3:355

physical growth 3:358

and play 10:1330

pruning of axons and synapses 2:260–261

reading and writing 3:358

social contacts 3:358–359

speech 3:357–358

see also adolescence

children

emotional and behavioral problems 11:*1536*, 1537–1538

growth 3:358

mental disorders 8:1115

see also babies; child development; special educational needs

chilling, requirements of plants 4:549

Chilopoda 3:343–345

Chimaera (ratfish) 6:734

chimpanzees 10:1368–1369

adolescence 1:28

brain 2:260

communication 3:406

with man 3:406

grip 7:869

grooming 10:1370

hunting by 10:1370

intelligence 7:967

movement 10:1370

nests 9:1206

play 10:*1329*

pygmy 10:1368–1369

territories 12:1615

tools 10:1369–1370

understanding language 3:406

China, forests 12:1610

Chinese medicine 1:55; 3:360–361

see also acupuncture

chipmunks

eastern 12:*1608*

winter lethargy 7:891–892

Chiropotes sp. (bearded sakis) 10:1368

chiropractic 1:*56*, 57

Chiroptera 2:173

chitin 3:298, 342; 6:726; 8:1143

chitons 8:*1148*

Chlamydia psittaci 1:89

Chlamydosaurus kingii (frilled lizard) 8:1052

Chlamyphorus truncatus (lesser fairy armadillo) 1:104

chloral 9:1215

chlorella, cultivation 1:125

chlorine

a disinfectant 1:116

in water 5:627

chlorobium chlorophyll 10:1306

chlorofluorocarbons (CFCs) 2:157; 5:623; 10:*1341*

chloroform 1:76; 8:1102

chloromethane 5:627

chlorophyll 3:335; 5:616; 10:*1303*

chlorophyll a 10:1304, *1306*

chlorophyll b 10:*1306*

chlorophyll c 10:1306

chlorophyll d 10:1306

P$_{680}$ 5:617–618

P$_{700}$ 5:618; 10:1306

Chlorophyta 1:47; 10:1381

chloroplasts 3:332, *335*; 8:1023; 10:1303–1304

bundle sheath 10:1305

evolution from symbiotic bacteria 3:392

mesophyll 10:1305

chlorpromazine 9:1212, 1215

chlorpromazine (Thorazine) 11:1466

choanocytes 11:1552, 1553

choanoflagellates, evolution of sponges from 11:1553

choking, prevention 8:1059

cholecystectomy 8:1047; 11:1575

cholecystokinin (CCK) 8:1047; 9:1260

cholera 5:627, 633, *634*; 6:746; 7:948

for biological warfare 2:197

in chickens 7:934–935

vaccine 7:934–*935*

cholesterol 3:362–363; 5:691

and artery disease 3:362, 363, 377; 7:881; 9:1225

bile derived from 8:1044, 1047

and the menopause 8:1110

transport 3:362–*363*

cholesterol esterase 9:1260

cholesterol esters 5:691

cholla, silver 2:273

Choloepus spp. (two-toed sloths) 1:104

Chomsky, Noam 5:662

Chondrichthyes 6:730; 11:1487; 12:1671

see also fish, cartilaginous

chondrin 3:319

chondroblasts 3:319

chondrocytes 3:319–320

Chondrostei 6:734

Chondrus spp. (Irish moss/carrageen) 7:987, 988

Chopra, Deepak 7:943–944

chordates 1:97; 3:364–365; 7:972; 12:1671

chorionic villus sampling (CVS) 3:367; 4:477; 10:1358

choroid 5:685

chromaffin cells 5:640

chromatids 3:*338, 339*, 340

chromatin 3:333

chromatography 1:63, 66–67; 2:181

chromesthesia 11:1516

chromophores 10:1309, 1310

chromoplasts 6:761

chromoproteins **10**:1376

chromosomes 3:333, **366–369**; **7**:*919*; **10**:1403

abnormalities, and genetic diseases **3**:369; **6**:812–813

bacterial **3**:367

chromatids **3**:*338*, *339*, 340, *366*

deletions and duplications **7**:921

extra **9**:1190

and aggression **1**:30

see also aneuploidy; polyploidy

genes on **3**:367

see also genes

haploid and diploid **3**:368

homologous **3**:339–340, 368; **5**:588

karyotyping **3**:*367*

"lampbrush" **5**:589

loss **3**:369; **9**:1190

lymphocytic, and leukemia **8**:1030

maps **7**:920–*921*

mutations *see* mutation

numbers **3**:367–368; **6**:812; **7**:918

prokaryotic **3**:366–367

recombination (crossing over) **3**:368; **7**:919–920

and mutations **9**:1190

sex **3**:368; **6**:812; **7**:906, 918

and X-linked characteristics **9**:1164

and X-linked disorders **8**:1107; **10**:1358

structure **3**:366

translocation, and leukemia **8**:1030

XYY combination **1**:30

see also genes

chrysalids **2**:268, 269

chrysanthemums **2**:217

Chrysemys picta (painted turtle) **4**:459

Chrysina spp. (jewel beetles) **2**:283

Chrysophyta *see* diatoms

Chtridiomycetes **8**:1137

chuckwallas **4**:486

chyle **8**:1063

chylomicrons **3**:362–363

chyme **4**:522; **11**:1564

chymotrypsin **4**:518; **5**:*632*; **9**:1260

cicadas **2**:216

cichlids, parental care **6**:733

Cicindela campestris (tiger beetle) **9**:1208

Ciconia ciconia (white stork) **8**:1134

cigarettes *see* smoking

cilia **3**:338; **11**:1578

ciliates (Ciliophora) **10**:1382

cimetidine **7**:898

Cimolestes **3**:310

Cimolopteryx **12**:1701

cinchona trees **8**:1103

Ciona intestinalis **3**:*365*

ciprofloxacin **2**:196

circadian rhythms **2**:216, 217, 218, 219

and sleep **11**:1511–1512

circalunar cycles **2**:216

circulatory systems 3:370–378

closed **3**:*372*–375

CT scans **4**:475

human

diseases of **3**:376–378

evolution of **3**:378

fetal **7**:878

lymphatic *see* lymphatic systems

open **3**:371–*372*

role of calcium **2**:278

versus diffusion **3**:370–371

vertebrate **3**:375–376

circumcision **10**:1412

cirrhosis **7**:894; **8**:1046

CITES **2**:266; **5**:609

cities *see* urban habitats

citrate **7**:995

citric acid cycle *see* Krebs cycle

citrullinaemia **12**:1668

citrulline **12**:1667

Citrus spp. **6**:792, 795

citrus fruits **6**:792, 795

prevention of scurvy **8**:*1095*

seedless **6**:792

civets **3**:311–312

clades **12**:1602

cladistics **12**:1602

cladograms **12**:1602

Cladonia spp. **8**:1034, *1036*, 1037

Cladoselache **11**:1489

clams **3**:371; **8**:*1148*

deep-sea **8**:1149; **9**:1233

farming of **1**:124

gills **10**:1418–1419

Clarias mossambicus (African catfish) **10**:1419

classification **8**:1042

limitations **11**:1539–1540

see also species; taxonomy

Claviceps purpurea (ergot) **1**:50; **6**:765, 800; **8**:1139

claws **7**:871

cleaning stations, underwater **4**:450–451

Clean Water Act (1972) **12**:1706

clear-cutting **4**:491, 492

clematis **6**:*757*

climate

change **3**:428–429; **4**:493

recorded by fossils **9**:1257

recorded by tree rings **12**:1640

see also global warming

effect of coral reefs on **4**:449

life-regulating **6**:802–*803*

tropical rain forests and **12**:1644

Climate Protocol, Kyoto (1997) **10**:1341

climax vegetation, in temperate forests **12**:1607

climbing plants 3:379–380; 11:*1449*

Cliona spp. **11**:1553

clitoris **10**:1413

clomiphene citrate **5**:709, 711

cloning 3:381–386; 11:1482

DNA **3**:384

humans **3**:*385*; **11**:1558, 1559

sheep **3**:340, 383–384; **11**:1558

therapeutic **3**:384–385, 386; **11**:1558, 1559

Clostridium spp. **5**:700, 702, 703; **9**:1217

C. botulinum **6**:764, 765; **8**:1117; **9**:*1253*; **11**:1462

toxins **9**:1203; **11**:1462

C. perfringens **6**:765; **9**:1253

C. tetani **9**:1203

and food poisoning **6**:765

clotting, blood **2**:241–*242*, 278; **7**:937

clouds, temperature control **6**:802, *803*

clover **8**:1028; **10**:1322

clown fish (anemone fish) **1**:126; **3**:*389*, 390; **4**:450; **7**:890, *970*; **11**:1580

clubfoot **5**:*699*

club mosses **5**:706, *707*; **10**:1326–1327

clubroot disease **10**:1321

Cnemidophorus unipareus (whiptail lizard) **10**:1405

Cnidaria (cnidarians) **1**:94–95

characteristics **7**:980–981

digestion **4**:512; **7**:969–970

nervous system **9**:1204–1205

radial symmetry **7**:969–970

social **11**:1524

stinging cells, used by sea slugs **7**:981

undifferentiated cells **10**:1400

see also corals; jellyfish; sea anemones, and hydras

cnidoblasts **7**:980

CoA (coenzyme A) **12**:1691

coagulation cascade **12**:1620

coal **3**:304; **6**:783

desulfurization **8**:1132

dust **5**:*628*

coastal waters **9**:1236–1237

see also shore habitats

coast disease **9**:1227

coatis (coatimundis) **3**:310, 311; **12**:*1725*

cobalt

deficiency **4**:489

in livestock **9**:1227

cobras **9**:1203; **11**:1518, 1520

tooth structure **11**:*1519*, 1520

cocaine **1**:24; **4**:*555*, 556; **8**:1014

crack **1**:24

during pregnancy **2**:260

coccidiomycosis **7**:948

Coccinella spp. (ladybug) **7**:*957*; **10**:1351

Coccinia rehmanii **11**:1446

coccyx **8**:1069

cochicine **1**:136

cochineal **7**:884

cochlea **4**:*560*

cochlear implants **2**:215; **7**:874; **8**:1093

cockatoos, pink **7**:*962*

cockleburs **2**:217

cockroaches 1:*18*, 139; **3**:**387–388**; **5**:655; **8**:1076; **12**:1612, 1665

resistance to insecticides **9**:1193

coco **8**:1014

cocoa **1**:51; **5**:701; **12**:1644

coco-de-mer **9**:1259

coconut palms **6**:725; **9**:1160, 1259

coconuts **9**:1160, *1259*

Cocos nucifera (coconut palm) **6**:725; **9**:1160, *1259*

cod **12**:*1599*

codeine **1**:51

codons **4**:*536*, 537; **10**:1378

coelacanths **6**:734; **8**:1048–1049, 1050; **12**:1673

coelenterates *see* Cnidaria

coelenteron **7**:981

coelom, in annelids **1**:98, 99; **11**:1496

coelomates **9**:1196

coenzymes **9**:1227

coenzyme A (CoA) **12**:1691

coevolution 2:268; **3**:**389–392**; **5**:657

animals/flowers **2**:268; **3**:389–390; **6**:757–758, 760; **10**:*1336*, 1337

host/parasites **3**:390; **9**:1267

of males and females **11**:1485

cofactors, for enzyme activity **5**:630–631

coffee **3**:295

cognition 3:393–394

cognitive development **3**:*359*, 394

stages **3**:354–355

see also child development

and intelligence, *see also* intelligence

see also learning; memory; perception; problem solving

Cohen, P. P. **12**:1667

Cohen, Stanley **2**:227

coir **6**:725

colchicine **2**:266; **3**:367

Colchicum sp. (autumn crocus) **2**:266

cold-blooded animals 3:396–397

dinosaurs as **4**:531

ectothermy **5**:*632*; **12**:1617–1618

enzymes in **5**:631

metabolism **8**:1122–1123

see also amphibians; fish; reptiles

colds, common 3:395; **7**:929; **8**:1059

cold turkey **1**:24; **4**:558

Coleoptera **2**:177

Coleorrhyncha **7**:884

colitis **4**:519

collagen **3**:298, 319, 419; **6**:726; **8**:1142; **10**:1376

and aging **1**:34

and bone formation **2**:277

Bold words with bold page numbers indicate complete articles; bold numbers preceding colons are volume numbers; numbers following colons indicate page numbers; italic page numbers refer to illustrations or other graphics.

collagen *(continued)*
  in connective tissue **10**:*1377*
  disorder of **3**:420
  in tendons **6**:*726*
  and wounds **10**:1402
collective unconscious **10**:1385
Colle, Giovanni **2**:244
collenchyma **8**:1025; **11**:1560
Collins, Francis **7**:919, *923*
Collip, James Bertram **4**:508
Collip, John **7**:965
Collocalia spp. (cave swiftlets) **3**:328;
  4:574; **9**:*1222*
colon **4**:517, 523
  bacteria in **5**:703
  cancer
    colon **3**:295, 299; **4**:523, 538
    treatment **3**:353
  inflammation (colitis) **4**:519
colonies
  ant **1**:119; **7**:958–959
  bird **9**:1209; **11**:1474; **12**:1614–1615
  see also social organization
colonizers, plant **3**:410; **7**:974–975
coloration
  of cave-dwelling animals **3**:327
  change
    in chameleons **2**:282; **4**:483; **7**:*908*;
      10:1310
    in octopuses and squid **4**:483; **7**:908
    in phasmids **8**:1017
  and courtship **4**:*455*
  cryptic **2**:281–282; **8**:*1076*
  disruptive **2**:282–283
  plant, flowers **6**:761–762
  seeing colors *see* vision, color
  for temperature regulation **3**:397
  warning **4**:483–484
    in frogs **6**:*788*
    in insects **3**:404; **7**:959–960
  see also camouflage and mimicry;
    pigmentation
color blindness **5**:687; **12**:*1687*–1688
color therapy **1**:57
colostrum **5**:676; **7**:998
Coluber constrictor (racer) **11**:1518
Colubridae **11**:1519–1520
Columbia River **10**:1427
comas 3:398–400; **5**:644
comb jellies (sea gooseberries) **1**:95;
  2:207; **7**:969–970
comets
  collision with the Earth **5**:624, *653*
  and extinction of dinosaurs **4**:528; **5**:624
  Halley's **5**:*653*
commensalism **3**:390; **11**:1579, *1580*
communication 3:401–406
  decoding **3**:401
  methods **3**:404–406
    using the tail **12**:1594
    see also pheromones; songs; sounds;
      speech

plant-to-animal **10**:1318
plant-to-plant **10**:1317
primate **3**:*406*
uses **3**:402–404
  for courtship *see* courtship
  for danger **3**:403–404
  for dominance or submission **3**:*402*
  see also parapsychology
communities **10**:1348
  biotic **5**:583
companion cells **12**:1631
competition 3:407–410; **11**:1484
  territorial *see* territories
  see also mating
complement **1**:114; **7**:929–930, 938
complementary therapies
  see alternative medicine
composting **11**:1461
computed axial tomography
  see CT scanning
computed tomography *see* CT scanning
computer modeling, neural networks
  9:1214
Concentricycloidea **4**:569–570
conception **5**:708
concepts, learning **8**:1021
conditioning 3:411–414
  classical **3**:411–412; **8**:*1020*
  conditioned reflexes **3**:*411*; **9**:*1271*, 1272
  counterconditioning **10**:1301
  operant **10**:1387
  operant/instrumental **3**:*412*–413;
    8:1020
  the Skinner box **3**:*412*, 413; **8**:1020
condoms **4**:*440*
condors **6**:752
  California **2**:236, 237; **5**:*607*; **12**:1725
Condylactis gigantea (pink-tipped anemone)
  7:983
Condylura cristata (star-nosed mole) **7**:955
coneflowers, purple **9**:*1277*
cones
  gymnosperm **3**:415; **5**:716
    pollination **10**:*1338*
confidentiality, medical **2**:190
congenital defects
  clubfoot **5**:*699*
  congenital adrenogenital syndrome
    7:889
  prenatal diagnosis **2**:191
  see also genetic diseases
congestive heart failure **10**:1308
Coniferophyta *see* conifers
conifers 3:415–417; **10**:1326,
  1327–1328; **12**:1637, 1638
  cones *see* cones
  deciduous and evergreen **12**:1638
  northern forests *see* taiga biomes
  pollination **10**:*1338*
  shape **12**:1646
  timber **3**:*417*; **12**:1590, 1639
  see also gymnosperms

conjugation, bacterial **1**:110; **8**:1082
conjunctiva **5**:685; **9**:1172
connective tissue 3:298, **418–420**
  fibroblasts **3**:419; **10**:1402
  specialized *see* blood; bone; cartilage
  see also collagen
Connochaetes taurinus (wildebeest)
  8:1134–1135, *1136*; **12**:1662
Conophytum **2**:274
Conraua goliath (goliath frog) **6**:787;
  12:1642
consciousness 3:421–424; **5**:662
conservation 2:186; **3**:425–430;
  12:1724–1725
  captive breeding and *see* captive breeding
    programs
  estimation of biodiversity **2**:183–184
  in the Everglades **5**:649
  and mountain biomes **3**:429; **9**:1168
  and nesting **9**:1209
  plant **2**:252, 254
  reserves *see* national parks; reserves
  uses of cryobiology **4**:473; **12**:1724
  see also extinction
constipation **4**:519
contact inhibition **12**:1625
continental drift **8**:1079; **9**:1255; **12**:1719
continental rise **9**:1231
continental shelves 4:437–439
continental slope **9**:1231
continuous subcutaneous insulin infusion
  (CSII) **4**:507
contraception 4:440–443; **8**:1111
contractile vacuoles **3**:336–337; **5**:666
control systems *see* feedback systems
Convallaria majalis (lily-of-the-valley)
  12:1651
Convention on International Trade in
  Endangered Species *see* CITES
convergence, visual **12**:1685
convergent evolution 2:274; **3**:*380*;
  4:444–446; **5**:656
  and gliding **6**:*749*
Conway, John **2**:150
cooking food **6**:763
cooperative behavior **1**:58, 86
  see also altruism
cooties (human body lice) **8**:*1032*, 1033
copal **3**:417
copepods **1**:*141*; **10**:1314
  estuarine **11**:1492
Copernica prunifera (carnauba wax palm)
  9:1259
copper
  deficiency **4**:489
  and metabolism **8**:1124
copper carbonate **10**:1323
copperheads **11**:1520
copper sulfate **10**:1323
coprophagy *see* feces, consumption
corallite **4**:452
Corallus spp. **11**:1519

coral reef biomes **2**:211; **4**:447–451;
  9:1237, *1239*
  coral/alga symbiosis **4**:449–450
  coral islands **4**:450
  destruction **4**:*450*, 451
  fish **2**:*282*; **4**:450
  Great Barrier Reef **4**:447–448, *449*, 451
  see also corals
corals 4:452–453
  black **4**:*453*
  bleaching **2**:*186*; **11**:1581
  blue **10**:1310
  hard (stony) **4**:449, *452*, 453
  reproduction **4**:453
  skeleton **4**:452; **11**:1497–*1498*
  symbiosis with algae **4**:449–450, 453;
    11:1581
  see also Cnidaria; coral reef biomes
Corchorus spp. (jute) **3**:342
cord grass **11**:1493
Coriolis force **9**:1235
cork **12**:1639
Cormack, Allan **4**:474
cormorants **11**:1472, 1473, 1474, 1578;
  12:1701
  flightless (Galápagos cormorant) **6**:754;
    9:1169; **11**:1473
corms *see* bulbs and corms
cornea
  grafting **12**:1633, *1636*
  laser surgery **8**:*1091*
corn (maize) **1**:78; **4**:*545*; **6**:793
  flowers **6**:758
  genetically modified **6**:810
  hybrid varieties **1**:40; **11**:1481
  products from **9**:1161
  transpiration and water economy **8**:1025
corn starch **9**:1161
  fermentation **5**:702
corolla **6**:758
coronary artery bypass grafting (CABG)
  7:881; **11**:1572
  see also bypass surgery
coronary artery disease (CAD) **3**:362,
  363; **7**:881; **9**:1225
  and ultrafast scanning **4**:475
  see also heart disease
coronary thrombosis **12**:1620
corpus allata **5**:612; **7**:908; **8**:1126
corpus callosum **2**:263, 264; **5**:638; **7**:967
corpus cardiaca **8**:1126
corpus luteum **8**:1109, 1110; **10**:*1413*,
  1414
corpus striatum **2**:259
Correns, Karl **8**:1107
corridors, wildlife **3**:429; **12**:1664, 1718
Cortés, Hernán **12**:1723
cortex (plant) **11**:1448, 1560
corticoids *see* corticosteroids
corticosteroids 2:240; **4**:454;
  5:612
  glucocorticoids **4**:454

mineralocorticoids 4:454
 treatment 4:454
  for asthma 2:153
corticosterone 4:454
corticotropin releasing factor (CRF) 7:905
cortisol *see* hydrocortisone
corynebacteria 2:171
Corypha umbraculifera (talipot palm)
 10:1319
Corythosaurus 4:531
cosmids 12:1679
Cottam, Clarence 4:481
cotton 3:342; 4:510
 fibers 6:726
 organically grown 9:1246, 1248, 1249
 pesticide-resistant 9:1247
 pesticides used on 9:1249
cottonmouths (water moccasins) 11:1520
cotyledons 9:1160; 11:*1476*
 and germination 11:1478
 see also dicotyledons; monocotyledons
cougars 3:323, 324
counterconditioning 10:1301
countercurrent systems
 in gills 6:728
 heat exchange 7:901; 11:1472, 1488;
  12:1618
 in the kidney 7:990
 oxygen exchange 10:1424
countershading 2:283
courtship 4:**455–460**; 11:1540
 by nocturnal species 4:457
 communal 4:460
 evolution 4:458
 flehmen behavior 4:*460*
 functions 4:455–456
 gift giving 4:459; 8:1084
 innate behavior 1:*82*
 and sexual selection 11:*1483*–1484
 using bioluminescence 2:206; 4:457
 using pheromones 4:460
 vocal communication 4:458–459
  songs 4:459
 see also mating
covalent bonds 5:617
Covenant of the Wild, The (Stephen
 Budiansky) 4:544
cowbirds, brown-headed 4:445; 9:1274
cowpox 7:933–934, *936*; 8:1100–1101,
 1130
cows *see* cattle
coyotes 4:*539*, 540, 541; 11:1569
coypus (nutrias) 10:*1436*; 11:1465;
 12:*1705*
crabs
 blue 11:1492
 camouflage 2:282
 edible 4:*467*
 fiddler
  biorhythms 2:*218*
  claw waving 4:457; 7:962
  feeding 4:467

hermit 4:450, 468, *469*; 11:1581
horseshoe/king 1:93, 130, *140*, 141;
 5:650; 8:*1049*
molting 9:1158
movement 1:139
spider 1:137; 4:484
 see also crustaceans
crabs (lice) 8:1033
crack 1:24
cranes 12:1701
 whooping 5:607, 608; 12:1701
Craniata 12:1671
Crassulaceae 2:*274*
crassulacean acid metabolism (CAM)
 2:273; 10:*1305*–1306
Crataegus spp. (hawthorn) 4:482
Cratena pilata (striped nudibranch) 7:981
crayfish 3:327, 371
creationism 2:204; 5:654
creativity 10:1329
creodonts 3:310
creosote bushes 9:1277; 10:*1319*
Crepidula fornicata (slipper limpet) 7:890
Creutzfeldt-Jakob disease (CJD) 1:89;
 4:495; 7:949; 9:1202; 10:1371,
 1372, 1373
 new variant (vCJD) 10:1371, 1372
 prion causing 3:*371*
crickets *see* grasshoppers and crickets
Crick, Francis, and James Watson
 2:202, 221, 227; 4:**461–462**, 537;
 7:918
Crinoidea 4:570
crocodiles *see* crocodilians, crocodiles
crocodilians 4:**463–466**; 8:1050
 alligators
  American 4:459, *463*, 464, *466*; 5:647
   circulatory system 3:374–375
  appearance 4:464
  circulation 4:465
 crocodiles
  American 5:*649*
  Indopacific 4:464
  Nile 4:464
  saltwater 4:465
  swimming 11:1578
 distribution 4:463–464
 evolution 4:464; 9:1255
 excretion 5:665
 eyes 4:464
 hearing by 4:562
 and humans 4:464
 movement 4:465
 nutrition 4:466
 physiology 4:465
 reproduction 4:*466*
 senses 4:464–465
Crocodylus spp. 4:463–464; 5:*649*
Crocus spp. 1:80
crocuses
 autumn 2:266
 Chilean blue 2:266

Crocuta crocuta (spotted hyena) 3:*312*;
 10:1414
Crohn's disease 4:519
Cro-Magnon man 7:917
crop, bird 4:521
crop milk 7:997
crops
 frost-resistant 8:1131
 fruit 10:1328
  see also fruits and fruit plants
 fungal diseases 10:*1320, 1321–1322*
 genetic engineering and 6:809–*811*;
  9:1244
  Flavr Savr tomatoes 2:227; 6:765,
   794, 809
  for nitrogen fixation 9:1219
  resistance to pesticides 9:1247
  see also genetically modified foods
 leaf crops 8:**1013–1014**
 leguminous 9:1219; 10:1321
  see also legumes
 new varieties 11:1481
 origins of growing 1:38; 4:545–546
 pest control 10:1346–1347
  see also biological control; pesticides
 pests of *see* pests
 root and tuber 11:**1445–1446**;
  12:1650
 rotation 1:39–40; 8:1029; 9:1219, 1243
 selective breeding 11:1481
  and polyploidy 10:1408
 squash family 11:1554
 see also agriculture; grains; grasses,
  cereal; Green Revolution
crossing over (recombination) 3:368;
 7:919–920
 and mutations 9:1190
Crossopterygii 12:1673
Crotalus spp. 3:351; 9:1207, 1222;
 11:*1520*
crottle lichen 8:*1035*
croup 5:641
cruel plant 10:1318
crustaceans 1:97, 141; 4:**467–470**
 anatomy 4:*467–468*
 antennae 1:*106*
 chemoreception 12:1595
 courtship 4:457
 excretory systems 5:668
 gas exchange 4:468
  gills 4:468
 hormones 5:612
 larvae 4:469; 10:1314
 limbs 1:139
 locomotion 4:468
 migration 4:469
 nervous system and sensory organs
  4:468–469

touch receptors 12:1627
parasitic 4:467–468
reproduction 4:469
tail 12:1592
waste removal 4:468
 see also barnacles; crabs; lobsters; shrimps
Cruveilhier, Jean 9:1175, *1176*
cryobiology 4:**471–473**
 antifreeze proteins
  in animals 4:472; 10:1332
  in lichens 8:1036
 cryonics 4:472
 cryopreservation 4:472
 cryosurgery 4:473
Cryptobranchidae 11:1454, 1456
Cryptocarpus pyriformis (saltbush) 11:*1459*
Cryptocercus spp. 3:388; 12:1612
cryptosporidiosis 7:948, 949
crypts of Lieberkuhn 5:674
crystal therapy 1:57
CSII (continuous subcutaneous insulin
 infusion) 4:507
Ctenophora *see* comb jellies
CT scanning 1:72; 2:260; 4:**474–475**;
 8:1090
cuckolding 8:1083
cuckoos 1:58–*59*; 4:445
Cuclotogaster heterographus (chicken-head
 louse) 8:1033
Cuculus spp. (cuckoo) 1:58–*59*; 4:445
cucumbers 3:380; 11:1554
 squirting 10:1319
Cucumis spp. 11:1554
Cucurbitaceae *see* squash family
cucurbitacins 11:1555
Cucurbita spp. 11:1554, *1555*
Cucurbitoideae 11:1555
cudbear 8:1035
cuds 4:515, 521; 11:*1453*
Culex spp. (mosquitoes) 7:1004; 10:*1419*
 diseases carried by 7:946, 947
Culpepper, Nicholas 7:888
Culpepper's Herbal 7:888
culture, human 7:917
cultures, of microorganisms
 8:1131–1132
Cuon alpinus (dhole) 3:309; 4:540
Cupressus spp. 3:415
Curacin A 9:1290
curare 9:1183, 1203
 in medicine 9:1183, 1203; 11:1571
Curie, Marie 8:1091; 10:1394, 1395
Curie, Pierre 8:1091; 10:1395
curlews 2:230; 12:1628
Cuscuta spp. (dodder) 3:379; 9:1265;
 10:1321; 12:*1632*
Cushing's syndrome 4:454
cushion stars 4:569

Bold words with bold page numbers indicate complete articles; bold numbers
preceding colons are volume numbers; numbers following colons indicate
page numbers; italic page numbers refer to illustrations or other graphics.

cuticle
arthropod 1:137, *138*; 11:1496, *1497*
insect 11:1505–1506
plant 8:1023; 11:1560; 12:1702
cutin 11:1560
cuttings, plant 3:381; 11:1481
cuttlefish
courtship 4:458
see also mollusks
Cuverian tubules 4:570
Cuvier, Georges 2:201, 202; 5:652, 679;
10:1391
CVS *see* chorionic villus sampling
Cyanea capillata (lion's mane jellyfish)
7:982
cyanobacteria 1:47, 49; 3:332; 5:651;
6:801
evolution into chloroplasts 2:168; 3:392
nitrogen fixing 9:1217
prokaryotes *see* prokaryotes
cyanophytes *see* cyanobacteria
Cyathea spp. 5:706
cybernetics 7:952
Cyborg (Caidin) 2:215
Cycadophyta (cycads) 9:1259; 10:1327
Cycas spp. 9:1259
cyclamens 2:266
cyclo-oxygenase 1 (COX-1) 2:182
Cyclopes didactylus (silky anteater) 1:103
cyclophosphamide 3:353
Cyclorrhapha 6:743
cycloserine 5:630
cyclosis 3:371
cyclosporine 8:1088; 12:1635
Cyclostomata 12:1671
cyclothymia 10:1390
Cycnoches sp. 9:1241
Cygnus spp. 12:1701
Cylindroiulus punctatus 3:346
Cynomys spp. (prairie dog) 5:694; 9:1207;
12:1614
Cyperus spp.
C. congestus 11:1446
C. papyrus 10:1427
cypresses 3:415, 416; 5:648
bald 12:1638
swamp 12:*1703*
Cyprinus carpio (carp) 4:545
Cypripedium spp. (lady's slipper) 9:1240
cysteine 1:*63*
cystic fibrosis (CF) 2:191; 6:805, *812*;
8:1061; 9:1172
effect on the pancreas 9:1261
gene therapy 6:806
cystitis 5:671
Cystophora cristata (hooded seal) 7:998
Cystopteris spp. (bladder fern) 10:*1327*
Cytisus spp. (broom) 10:1319; 11:1477
cytochromes 10:1377
in photosynthesis 7:973
in respiration 8:1119
similar amino acid sequences in 10:1377

cytokines 1:53
cytokinesis 3:339
cytokinins 7:909; 10:1316, 1317
cytology 4:476–477
clinical 4:477
plant 2:254
see also cell biology, plant
cytoprocts 4:511
cytosine 4:533, 535, 537; 5:654; 10:1428
cytotoxic drugs, effects of 2:240

D
D5W, intravenous 8:1039
Dactylopius coccus (cochineal scale insect)
7:884
daffodils 6:759
winter 2:266
Dahlia spp. (dahlia) 9:*1189*; 11:1449;
12:1650
Daisyworld model 6:803
Daltonism *see* blindness, color
Damadian, Raymond B. 8:1068
dams 10:*1426*, *1427*
damselflies
common blue 12:*1719*
see also dragonflies and mayflies
Danaus plexippus (monarch butterfly)
2:*269*, 270; 4:484; 6:810–811;
7:959–960, 1003; 8:*1125*, 1135
dandelions 1:80; 4:*509*; 6:725, 791;
10:1405
roots 11:*1449*
seeds 11:*1477*
danger signals 3:403–404
Daphne spp. 1:80
Daphnia spp. 4:467; 7:1001
dark adaptation 12:1687
Darlingtonia spp. 8:1027
Dart, Raymond 7:915
Darwin, Charles 2:192; 4:478–479;
5:585
and animal experimentation 1:91
and the bombardier beetle 5:677
and carnivorous plants 3:314
and coral reefs 4:448
Descent of Man 7:913
and facial expressions 5:605
and Galápagos finches 4:478; 9:1192
and insect/flower coevolution 2:268;
3:389–390
and instinct 7:963
On the Origin of Species 4:479; 5:653;
7:912–913; 9:1192, 1193
and phototropism 12:1645, *1646*
and seed dispersal 1:79
and sexual selection 11:1483
theory of evolution 4:479; 5:652–653;
7:912–913; 9:1192–1193; 11:1479;
12:1721
survival of the fittest 4:444–445;
10:1345
see also Darwinism

Darwin, Erasmus 7:912
Darwin, Francis 12:1645, *1646*
Darwinian medicine 4:479
Darwinism 7:912–913
neo-Darwinism 2:202; 4:479; 5:654
see also Darwin, Charles; evolution;
natural selection
Dasypus spp. (long-nosed armadillos) 1:104
date palms *see* palms, date
Daubentoniidae 10:1366
Daucus carota (carrot) 11:1446
David, Père 3:309
da Vinci, Leonardo *see* Leonardo da Vinci
da Vinci (surgical robot) 10:1432–1433
Dawson, Charles 6:782; 7:917
daylength
plants and 2:217; 6:759
dormancy 4:*549*
DDT 1:41; 3:318; 4:480–481; 5:584,
622; 7:959; 9:1243; 10:1343–1344;
11:1532
biomagnification 4:481; 9:1280, 1287
effect on birds 2:235–236; 5:584,
622–623, 680; 9:1275, 1287;
10:1343–1344
for lice control 8:1033
pest resistance 4:480–481
deafness 7:*874*–875
and bionic ears 2:215
and communication 7:873; 11:*1545*
hearing restoration 7:875
and learning 11:*1537*, 1538
deamination 5:665
Deane, John 9:1238
death
assisted *see* euthanasia
brain 3:399; 12:1636
criteria 8:1040
and forensic science 6:746, 772–773;
9:1183
and organs for transplants 12:1636
playing dead 2:*206*; 8:1017, 1080
death cap fungus 9:*1188*; 11:*1460*
Death Valley 4:*498*
deception 3:404
see also camouflage and mimicry
decomposition
and the carbon cycle 3:303
in the soil 11:1531
of wood 11:1460–1462; 12:1609
decompression sickness (the bends)
9:1238; 10:1422
deep brain stimulation 4:497
deer
antlers 12:1663
growth and shedding 2:217; 7:911
feet 5:*697*
migration 2:210
mule 3:*350*, 351
muntjac 12:1663
musk 12:1606, 1663
red 2:210; 4:460

intersexual competition 3:*409*
strutting 8:1084
in urban areas 12:1665
vocal communication 8:1083–1084
Deere, John 1:39
defense mechanisms 4:482–486
behavioral 4:486
bioluminescence used for 2:206–207
chemical
in animals 3:345; 4:485–486
in plants 4:482–483
feet used for 5:698
plant 4:*482*–483
safety in numbers 4:*484*
self-amputation *see* autotomy
self sacrifice 4:486
visual *see* camouflage and mimicry
defibrillators, ventricular 2:214
**deficiency-related diseases
4:487–489**
malnutrition 4:*487*–488, 489; 9:1227;
10:1378
mineral deficiency 4:489
vitamin deficiency 4:488–*489*
deforestation 4:490–493; 5:623;
12:*1639*
and the carbon cycle 3:304
effect on the atmosphere 4:491–493
effect on coral reefs 4:451, 491
rain forests 4:493; 5:*624*; 12:1643
by fire 4:*491*
causing extinctions 4:493; 5:*680*
slash-and-burn 4:491
**degenerative brain diseases
4:494–497**
Alzheimer's disease 1:61;
4:*494*–497; 9:1204, 1213; 10:1389;
11:1558
Creutzfeldt-Jakob disease (CJD) 1:89;
4:495; 7:949; 9:1202; 10:1371, *1372*
new variant (vCJD) 10:1371, 1372,
1373
prion causing 10:*1371*
Huntington's chorea 4:495–*496*; 6:805;
9:1202
motor neurone disease 4:495, 496, 497
Parkinson's disease 2:261; 4:494–497;
8:1092; 9:1204, 1213; 11:1558
dehydroepiandrosterone (DHEA) 1:36
Deima 9:1232
Deinonychus 4:531
delirium 10:1389
delta cells 9:1261
delusions 10:1388; 11:1466
dementia 10:1389
senile *see* Alzheimer's disease
see also Creutzfeldt-Jakob disease
demes 9:1194
Demospongiae 11:1553
dendrites 2:255; 9:1198; 12:1626
Dendroaspis polylepis (black mamba)
11:1518, 1520

Dendrobates spp. (poison-dart/poison-arrow frogs) **4**:483–484; **5**:677; **6**:*788*

dendrochronology **12**:1640

Dendrocopus major (great spotted woodpecker) **2**:232

Dendrocygna bicolor (fulvous tree duck) **4**:460

Dendroica pennsylvanica (chestnut-sided warbler) **3**:402

Dendrosicyos socotranus **11**:1555

dengue fever (breakbone fever) **7**:947

denitrification **9**:1218; **11**:1462

dental procedures, anesthetic **1**:*75*

deontological theories **2**:188

dependent personality disorder **9**:1285

deprenyl **9**:1204

depressants **1**:23–24

depression **5**:663; **10**:1390
 manic **8**:1113; **10**:1390

Dermanector spp. (wood tick) **1**:*131*; **9**:*1264*

Dermaptera **4**:563

dermatitis **1**:*53*; **7**:870

dermis **11**:1506, 1508

Dermochelys coriacea (leatherback turtle) **11**:1492

Descartes, René **3**:*422*–423

Descent of Man (Charles Darwin) **7**:913

desensitization (exposure therapy) **1**:122; **10**:1301

desert biomes 2:210–*211*; **4**:**498–501**
 animals **2**:211; **4**:*500–501*
 plants **2**:211; **4**:*499–500*; **11**:*1459*; **12**:1617
  cacti and succulents **2**:273
 soil **11**:1530

desertification 4:**502–505**; **5**:624

Desmana moschata (Russian desman) **7**:955

desmans **7**:955

Desmodus rotundus (common vampire bat) **1**:*60*; **2**:174; **4**:574; **11**:*1526*–1527

detergents **1**:117
 biological **2**:*222*

detoxification, in the liver **8**:1046–1047

detrivores **6**:767

De Usu Partium (Galen) **2**:200

Deuteromycota **8**:1137

deuterostomes **7**:972

developed countries **10**:1348

developing countries **10**:1348

development, cognitive
 see child development

dewlaps, lizard **4**:459

dextrose *see* glucose

DHEA (dehydroepiandrosterone) **1**:36

dholes **3**:309; **4**:540, 541

diabetes 4:**506–508**; **9**:1261
 bronze **4**:508
 diabetes insipidus **4**:506
 diabetes mellitus **2**:165; **4**:506–507; **5**:612
  types I and II **4**:507; **7**:905, 965

and dioxins **4**:532

insulin **4**:507; **7**:965
 from genetic engineering **2**:222; **7**:965; **8**:1131

in pregnancy **4**:507–508

self-monitoring **4**:507

and transplants **12**:1634

see also insulin

Diadema antillarium **3**:403–404

Diagnostic and Statistical Manual of Mental Disorders (DSM) **9**:1283; **10**:1389

dialysis **7**:*992*; **8**:1039–1040

diapause **2**:269; **7**:1005
 in the housefly **6**:745

diaphragm **8**:*1057*, 1058; **10**:1422

diaphragms (contraceptives) **4**:440–*441*

diarrhea **4**:519, 523; **7**:949

diastole **7**:879

diatoms (Chrysophyta) **1**:47; **8**:*1130*; **10**:*1312*, 1313, 1380–1381

Diatrymas **6**:755

diazepam (Valium) **9**:1215

Dicentra spectabilis (Dutchman's breeches) **10**:1337

DICER enzyme **10**:1430, *1431*

Diceros bicornis (black rhinoceros) **11**:*1579*

Dicksonia spp. **5**:706

dicotyledons 1:78; **4**:**509–510**; **10**:1328; **11**:1476
 anatomy of eudicots **4**:509–*510*
 differ from monocotyledons **9**:1161
 germination **11**:1478
 leaf veins **8**:1025
 vascular bundles **12**:1669

Dicrostonyx spp. (lemming) **10**:1334; **12**:1654

Dictyostelium discoideum **9**:1293

Didelphis virginiana (Virginian/Northern opossum) **5**:*650*; **8**:1080; **11**:*1541*

dieldrin **2**:237

diestrus **8**:1111

diet *see* nutrition

diethylstilbestrol (DES) **3**:352

diets, reducing **3**:300

diffusion
 circulatory systems versus **3**:370–371
 passive **9**:1252
 in plants **9**:1252
 for respiration **10**:1418

Digenea **6**:736–737
 see also flukes

digestion **4**:511, 520–521
 absorption of nutrients **4**:518–519
 chemical processes **4**:517–518
 enzymes *see* enzymes, digestive
 extracellular **4**:511, 512
 of fats, and bile **8**:1047
 fermentation in the gut **4**:515
 intracellular **4**:511, 512
 in the stomach **4**:516, 517–518
 vertebrate, *see also* peristalsis
 see also digestive systems

digestive systems 4:**511–519**
 carnivore **4**:516, *520*, 521
 digestive tract 4:**520–523**
 disorders **4**:519, *523*
 herbivore **4**:514–*515*, *520*, 521
 human **4**:*511*, *516*–519, *521*–523
  bacteria in **2**:172
 invertebrate **4**:*512*–513
 mucosal layers **8**:1065
 mucous membranes **9**:1171–1172
 omnivore **4**:516
 protozoan **4**:511
 teeth *see* teeth
 vertebrate **4**:513–516
 see also digestion; liver; pancreas; stomach

Digitalis spp. (foxglove) **1**:80; **2**:*179*; **9**:*1291*

digitoxin **9**:*1291*

digoxin **9**:*1291*

Dikaryomycota **6**:799

dikdiks **12**:*1662*, 1663

dimethyl sulfide (DMS), and cloud formation **6**:802

dimorphism and polymorphism 4:**524–525**
 polymorphism in cnidarian colonies **7**:981
 sexual dimorphism **4**:458, *524*–525
  in birds **4**:459, *524*

dingos **4**:*542*

dinoflagellates **1**:47, 48; **10**:1313, 1347, 1380
 bioluminescence **2**:*207*
 see also zooxanthellae

Dinomastigota **10**:1313

dinosaurs 4:**526–531**
 classification **4**:529–531
 eggs **4**:*526*, 528
 evolution, coevolution **3**:391
 evolution of birds from? **4**:529
 extinction **2**:185; **4**:*528–529*
  due to climate change **4**:528–529
  due to an impacting space object **4**:528, *529*; **5**:624, 659
 fossils **4**:*527*
  see also fossils
 life of **4**:527–528
 warm- or cold-blooded? **4**:531

Diomedea spp. **2**:232; **4**:456; **5**:*658*; **6**:*752*

Dionaea muscipula see Venus's-flytrap

Dioscorea spp. (yam) **3**:380; **9**:1161; **11**:1446

Dioscorides **2**:253

dioxins 4:**532**; **10**:1343

diphtheria **5**:592
 vaccine **7**:935

Diplocarpon rosae **10**:1321

Diplocentridae **11**:1470

Diplocodus **4**:530

Diplopoda **3**:345–346

Dipodomys spp. (kangaroo rat) **4**:501; **5**:669, *670*, 699; **9**:1207; **10**:1436

Diptera *see* flies

disaccharides **3**:297

disasters, environmental
 see environmental disasters

Disa uniflora (flower of the gods orchid) **5**:609

discrete trial teaching (DTT) **2**:163

discrimination **8**:1021

diseases
 of animals *see* animal diseases
 autoimmune *see* autoimmune disorders
 caused by deficiency *see* deficiency-related diseases
 coevolution and **3**:391–392
 environmental 5:**625–628**
 epidemiology 5:**633–635**
 germ theory **1**:117; **2**:202; **8**:1128; **9**:1269; **11**:1570
 hereditary *see* genetic diseases
 incidence rate **5**:634
 infectious 7:**945–950**
  of animals **1**:*88*–90
 prevalence **5**:634
 respiratory *see* respiratory diseases
 vectors **7**:945

disinfectants **1**:115

Dismorphia amphione **2**:286

dispersal **2**:193–194
 seed *see* seeds, dispersal

Dispholidus typhus (boomslang) **11**:1518

displacement activities **11**:1566–1567

displays
 courtship
  in birds **1**:*82*, 84–85
  in dolphins **4**:456
  see also courtship
 threat **8**:1072–1073

dissection **1**:*70*, 72

dissociation, double **9**:1212

dissociative disorders **8**:1114–1115

distemper **1**:89–90; **8**:1061

distribution *see* biogeography; zoogeography

ditches, permaculture and **9**:1281

Ditylenchus dipsaci **10**:1321

diuretics, urea as **12**:*1667*

diversity
 genetic **2**:183–184; **5**:589–590
 see also biodiversity

diverticular disease **9**:1225

diving, undersea **9**:*1238*

diving bells **9**:1238

Bold words with bold page numbers indicate complete articles; bold numbers preceding colons are volume numbers; numbers following colons indicate page numbers; italic page numbers refer to illustrations or other graphics.

dizziness 4:561

DNA 3:*366*; **4**:**533–538**; **8**:1144;
　　10:1428

　cloning 3:384

　discovery 8:1142

　effects of chemotherapy on 3:353

　and evolution 5:654

　fingerprinting 2:224; **4**:*535*; **6**:*773*, 774;
　　9:*1174*

　the genetic code 4:536

　"junk" (noncoding) 4:534; **7**:922–923

　mapping 7:920–921

　markers 7:920

　in mitochondria (mtDNA) 2:168; **3**:385
　　and human origins 7:917

　mutation 4:538

　prokaryotic 2:167; **3**:331

　and protein synthesis 4:*536*, 537;
　　10:1378

　radioactive tagging 2:182

　recombinant 2:170, 223; **8**:1143, 1145
　　see also genetic engineering

　repair 6:806

　replication 4:*534–536*

　　scientific (polymerase chain reaction)
　　　3:384; **4**:*535*; **6**:774; **8**:1145–1146
　　see also meiosis; mitosis

　sequencing 7:920, *921–922*; **8**:*1146*

　splitting 8:1145

　structure 4:*533–534*; **7**:918–919

　　discovery 4:461–462, 537; **8**:1142

　transcription 4:537; **9**:1189; **10**:1378,
　　1428, *1429*

　transposons (transposable elements;
　　jumping genes) **1**:110; **7**:922–923;
　　8:1086; **9**:1190

　typing 2:182

　viral 12:1681

　X-ray crystallography 6:786
　see also chromosomes; genes

DNA ligases 8:1145

DNA polymerase 3:353; **4**:*535*; **8**:1146

Dobzhansky, Theodosius 9:1193

doctrine of signatures 7:887

dodders 3:379; **9**:1265; **10**:1321; **12**:*1632*

dodos 1:19; **5**:*678*; **7**:977

dogfish 6:734; **11**:1489

　embryos 5:*597*

　piked 11:1490

dogs 3:309; **4**:**539–542**

　African wild 3:307, 309; **4**:*540*, 542

　　breeding 11:1524

　　communication 3:404; **4**:542

　　dominance 11:1524

　　hunting 7:979

　breeding, selective 4:*540–541*

　bush 4:540, *541*

　characteristics 4:539–540

　　feet 4:539

　classification 4:542; **12**:1601

　conditioning experiments on 3:411, 412

　diseases 1:89–90

dog-wolf hybrids 4:541–542

domestic 1:37–38; **4**:*540–541*, 544

dominance and submission
　　3:402

endangered 4:541

evolution 4:540

feet 5:*697*

feral 11:1569

fleas 6:738

lice 8:1033

nose, wet 12:1622

panting 11:1506; **12**:*1622*

Pavlov's, and conditioned reflexes
　　9:*1271*, 1272

sense of smell 11:1515

sheepdogs 1:*83*

social behavior 4:540

in space 11:1534

training 3:*413*

Dolly (sheep) 3:*340, 383*–384; **11**:1558

dolphins *see* whales, porpoises,
　　and dolphins

Domagk, Gerhard 8:1103

domestication 1:38; **4**:**543–546**;
　　5:659

　of cats 3:323

　of dogs 4:*540–541*

　of plants 4:545–*546*

　of ungulates 12:1662

dominance 8:1072; **11**:*1522*

　signals 3:*402*

Donald, Anna 8:1096, 1097, 1098

Donald, Ian 8:1090

donepezil 4:496

Donkin, Bryan 6:765

dopamine 1:24; **4**:494, 556; **8**:1092;
　　9:1204, 1213

　and aggression 1:33

　dopamine-producing tissue 2:261

　and schizophrenia 9:1212

dormancy 4:**547–549**

　in animals *see* hibernation

　and buds 4:547–548, *549*

　chapparal plants 3:350

　effect of day length on 4:*549*

　innate and imposed 4:547

　in perennials 4:547

　role of hormones 4:548

　seeds 4:*547*, 548–549; **11**:1478
　　see also germination

　in woody plants 4:547–548

dormice 7:*891*; **8**:*1069*

dormin 4:548

doves 6:776

Down syndrome 3:*369*; **6**:812–813;
　　10:1358; **11**:1536

　testing for 4:477

downwellings 9:1236

dragonflies and mayflies 4:**550–552**

　dragonflies

　　northern limit 12:1718

　　wings 6:750

mayflies 1:*142*
　see also damselflies

dragons, Komodo 7:*977*; **8**:1051;
　　12:1717

Drake, Frank 5:683

Drake equation 5:683, 684

dreaming 2:264; **11**:1512

Drew, Charles 2:*245*; **4**:**553–554**

drips, intravenous 8:1039; **11**:1571

Dromaius novaehollandiae (emu) 5:*698*;
　　6:756

dromedaries 4:501

drones, honeybee 12:1694

dropsy, treatment 9:1291

Drosera spp. (sundew) 3:*314*–316; **5**:696

Drosophila spp. (fruit fly)

　circadian clocks 2:218

　courtship 3:402; **4**:455, 456–457; **7**:962

　early genetic studies on 9:1164, 1193

　embryo development 5:597–598

　memory 8:1105

　mutation 5:599; **6**:746

　nurse cells 5:589

　reproduction 7:958

　for scientific research 1:93; **6**:746

　speciation 5:657

drought 5:624

drought deciduous plants 4:499

drugs

　affecting the emotions 5:603

　antibacterial 5:630

　anticonvulsant 5:639

　antiviral 12:1678

　automated dispensing systems
　　10:*1434*–1435

　calcium antagonists 2:278

　for cancer treatment (chemotherapy)
　　2:219; **3**:296, 352–353

　computer modeling 1:*93*

　corticosteroid *see* corticosteroids

　curare-type 9:1183, 1203; **11**:1571

　delivery 8:*1092*

　dependency on *see* addiction

　depressants 4:556

　design 7:898

　fertility 5:709, 711

　from fungi *see* penicillin

　from plants 1:80; **4**:483

　　ethnobotanical search for 9:1292
　　see also herbal medicine

　illegal

　　cannabis (marijuana) 4:557

　　during pregnancy 2:260

　　ecstasy 4:556, *557*

　　emotion manipulation 5:603

　　heroin 1:*23*–24; **4**:556–557, *558*

　　LSD 4:557
　　see also cocaine; hallucinogens

　　immunosuppressive 12:1635

　　medicinal 4:555, 557

　　mind-altering 1:*23*; **4**:555–557

　　mode of action 9:1291

opiates 4:556–557

origins of treatment 9:1289, 1291

psychedelic 4:557

radioactively labelled 9:1290

resistance to 3:353

sleeping pills 11:1512

stimulants 4:555–556

study of (**pharmacology**) 8:1090;
　　9:**1289–1292**

sulfa 9:1290

synthetic 9:1290

testing and approval 9:1291–1292

test-tube evolution 9:1290–1291

use and abuse 4:**555–558**
　see also addiction; antibiotics

drupes 6:792, 795

drying, food 6:763

Dryopithecus see Proconsul

dry rot fungus 6:799; **11**:1462

*DSM (Diagnostic and Statistical Manual of
　　Mental Disorders)* 9:1283;
　　10:1389

Dubois, Eugene 7:916, 917

ducks 12:1701

　communication in the egg 3:405

　countercurrent heat-exchange system
　　7:901

　courtship 1:85

　ruddy 12:1700

　sea 11:1472

　shoveler 5:695

　steamer 6:754

　torrent 12:1701
　see also tree ducks

duckweed 8:1022

Duesberg, Peter 9:1174

Dugesia 5:685; **6**:735

duikers, West African 5:694

dulse 7:987

　pepper 7:987

duodenum 4:517, 522

　ulcers 1:*71*

durians 10:1318

Durio zibethinus (durian) 10:1318

Dust Bowl 4:*503*

Dutch elm disease 2:178, 184; **9**:1265,
　　1294; **10**:1322; **12**:1640

Dutchman's breeches 10:1337

dwarfism 5:613

dyes

　from lichens 8:1035

　from plants 8:1029

　from snails 8:1149

　for microscopy 7:895

Dynastes hercules (rhinoceros/hercules
　　beetle) 2:*177*

dysentery, amoebic 3:388

dyslexia 11:1536

dysmenorrhea 8:1110

dyspraxia 11:1536

dystrophia myotonica 9:1181

dystrophin 7:895

E

eagles
  bald 2:235
    effects of DDT 2:235–236; 4:481;
      5:680; 9:1287; 10:1343–1344
    territories 12:1614
  harpy 2:234
ears 4:559–562
  and balance 4:560–561
  bionic 2:215
  cartilage in 3:320
  and echolocation 4:562
  fish, lateral line 4:561–562; 6:731
  human 4:559, 562; 7:872, 873–875
  and human evolution 4:561
  nonmammalian 4:561–562
  structure 4:559–560
  wax 12:1702
  see also hearing
Earth
  age of 10:1304
  collision with space objects 4:528, 529;
    5:624, 659; 8:1073
  a living organism see Gaia hypothesis
  origins of life on 6:801; 10:1304
  temperature see temperature, Earth
earthquakes 5:624
Earth Summit 2:183; 10:1341
earthworms 1:96
  aortic arches (hearts) 3:372; 7:876
  clones 3:382
  excretion 5:667; 7:989
  feeding and digestion 4:512–513
  reproduction 10:1407–1408
  respiration 10:1418
  skeleton 11:1496
  and the soil 1:99, 100; 11:1532
  touch receptors 12:1627
  see also annelids
earwigs 4:563–564
earworms, corn 2:270
eating disorders 4:565–566; 8:1114
Ebbinghaus, Hermann 10:1383
ecdysis see molting
ecdysone 7:908, 1005; 8:1126
Echballium elaterium (squirting cucumber)
  10:1318
echidnas 4:445; 9:1162–1163
Echinacea purpurea (purple coneflower)
  9:1277
Echinocactus ingens (ball cactus) 2:273
Echinocereus engelmannii (hedgehog cactus)
  2:272
echinoderms 1:97; 4:567–570; 7:972
  bioluminescence 2:206
  classification 4:569–570
  endoskeleton 4:567; 11:1499
  evolution 4:568
  locomotion 4:567–568
  nervous system 4:569; 9:1205
  tube feet 4:567, 568, 569, 570
  water vascular system 4:567; 12:1670

Echinoidea 4:570
Echinus spp. 4:570; 8:1126; 11:1499
Echis spp. (saw-scaled vipers) 11:1518
Echiura 1:96
echolalia 2:161
echolocation 4:562, 571–574; 12:1657
  by bats 1:19; 2:174–175; 4:562,
    572–573; 7:873; 9:1222
  by birds 9:1222
  by mammals 8:1071
  by shrews 8:1071
  by whales and dolphins 4:572; 7:873;
    8:1135; 12:1708
ecology and ecosystems 5:581–586
  biodiversity 2:184, 185
  biogeochemical cycles 5:584
    see also carbon cycle; nitrogen cycle
  biotic pyramids 5:586; 6:768, 769
  DDT in see DDT
  ecology
    autecology 12:1720
    behavioral 5:643
    community 5:583
    plant 2:254
    population 5:583
    restoration ecology 3:427; 5:583
  ecosystems 5:583–584; 6:766
    feedback in 7:953
    energy flow 5:584
      see also food webs
    isolated ecosystems 11:1540
      see also island habitats
    microecosystems 5:585
    models of 3:348; 5:584–585
    productivity 6:769–770
    see also biomes and habitats
ecstasy 4:556, 557
ECT (electroconvulsive therapy) 8:1113;
  10:1390
ectomorphs 10:1385
Ectopistes migratorius (passenger pigeon)
  5:659; 11:1522
Ectoprocta 1:96
ectothermy 3:396; 12:1617–1618
  see also cold-blooded animals
eczema 11:1508
  treatment 12:1667
edema 8:1065; 12:1667
Edentata 1:103–104
Edge of the Sea, The (Rachel Carson) 3:318
Edwards' syndrome 3:369
Edwin Smith papyrus 9:1213–1214
EEGs see electroencephalograms
eelgrass (tape grass) 6:761; 10:1338
eels 12:1592
  electric 4:485; 6:728
  European, migration 2:210
  moray 11:1576
effector cells 7:938
eggs 5:587–590
  birds' see birds, eggs
  excretion within 5:665

fertilized, see also fertilization
  meiosis 5:587–588, 589–590
  nurse cells and follicle cells 5:589
  oogenesis 5:587, 588
  of plants 5:590
  sperm penetration 5:713–714
Ehler's Danlos syndrome 3:420
Ehrlich, Paul 2:239; 5:591–592;
  8:1103, 1131; 9:1289
ehrlichiosis 7:949
Einstein, Albert 5:703; 7:967; 10:1394
Einthoven, Willem 8:1090
ejaculation 10:1411, 1412
  retrograde 5:710
Elaeis guineensis (oil palm) 3:382
Elaphe obsoleta (rat snake) 11:1517
Elasmobranchii 11:1487; 12:1671
elasmobranchs 6:734
  uterine milk 7:997
  see also rays; sharks; skates
elastin 3:419; 10:1377
Elastol 12:1698
elbows, replacement 8:1092
elderly, the, sleep patterns 2:219
Eldredge, Niles 1:21; 2:203; 5:654
electrical potential, of cells 10:1308
electricity
  for communication 3:405
  in fish 4:485; 6:728, 734
electric shock treatment
    see shock treatment
electrocardiograms (EKGs; ECGs) 7:881;
  8:1090
electroconvulsive therapy (ECT) 8:1113;
  10:1390
electroencephalograms (EEGs) 2:255,
  260; 5:638; 8:1090
  and sleep 11:1509–1510
electromagnetic fields, dangers of 5:627,
  628
electromagnetic spectrum 5:616;
  12:1712
electromyography 4:496
electronetting 12:1721
electron transfer/oxidative
  phosphorylation 2:159, 160; 3:300;
  7:993, 996; 8:1118–1119
electro-osmosis 12:1631
electrophoresis 1:67; 2:181–182
  for DNA analysis 7:921, 922
  gel 8:1145
Electrophorus electricus (electric eel) 4:485
electroporation 6:805–806, 807
Eledone cirrhosa 11:1577
elements, of life 8:1142
eleostearic acid 5:690
elephant birds 6:755
elephantiasis 7:946; 8:1065; 9:1267

Elephant Man 11:1504
elephants and mammoths 5:593–596
  elephants 5:593, 594–596
    African 4:514; 5:593, 595; 8:1074
    Asian 5:593, 595, 596
    differences between African and Asian
      5:595
    duels 4:460
    effect on the environment 5:594
    evolution 5:593
    feeding 5:696
    gestation 8:1074
    heartbeat 7:880
    teeth and tusks 5:594–595; 12:1605
    trunk 5:595; 10:1374
    young 10:1348
  mammoths 5:593; 6:764, 782; 9:1256
elephant snouts 3:405
Elephantus rufescens (rufous elephant shrew)
  7:956
Elephas maximus (Asian elephant) 5:593,
  595, 596
Elion, Gertrude see Hitchings, George,
  and Gertrude Elion
ELISA 5:630
elk (moose) 8:1084; 10:1350; 12:1591,
  1619
elms, Dutch elm disease 2:178, 184;
  9:1265, 1294; 10:1322; 12:1640
El Niño events 2:186; 4:438
Elton, Charles 6:768, 769
elytra 4:563
Elytrigia repens (couch grass) 12:1651
embolisms 3:377
  pulmonary 11:1573
embryology 1:71
embryos 5:597–601
  cryopreservation 4:472, 473
  human 3:385; 5:597, 600; 10:1352,
    1353, 1354
    brain development 2:260
    cartilage formation 3:319–320
    for research 5:600
    stem cells 2:261; 4:497; 5:600;
      11:1557, 1558, 1559
    transplantation 5:711
  invertebrate 5:597–598
  mammalian 8:1074
  muscle development 9:1183
  notocord 5:597
  plant 5:597, 600–601; 11:1476
    development 5:716
    in seeds 11:1476
  transplantation (transfer)
    in animals 11:1481
    in humans 5:711
  transplanted cells between 8:1088
  vertebrate 5:598–600

Bold words with bold page numbers indicate complete articles; bold numbers preceding colons are volume numbers; numbers following colons indicate page numbers; italic page numbers refer to illustrations or other graphics.

eyes *(continued)*
retina **4**:*506*; **5**:686; **9**:*1202*
implants **8**:1093
simple **5**:*685–687*; **12**:1685
surgery, laser **8**:*1091*; **11**:1575
tapetum lucidum **3**:322; **4**:464; **10**:1365
third (pineal; parietal body) **8**:1052;
10:1415, 1416
see also vision
eyespots **5**:685
used as mimicry **2**:271, 283
Eysenck, Hans J. **9**:*1283*

F

F$_1$, F$_2$, and F$_3$ generations **8**:1107
Fabaceae *see* legumes
Fabre, Henri **7**:963
Fabricius, Johann **5**:621; **8**:1042
face-lifting, using Botox **9**:1203
facial expressions
in apes **10**:1368–1369
and emotions **5**:*605*
and play **10**:1329
Factor VIII **2**:225, 242
Factor IX **2**:242; **3**:384
FAD **5**:618; **7**:996
FADH$_2$ **2**:*159–160*; **7**:996
Fagus sylvatica (beech) **12**:1608
fairy rings **9**:*1187*, 1188
Falconidae **2**:235
Falconiformes **2**:235–236
falconry, history **2**:237
falcons **2**:234
peregrine **2**:235, 236, 237; **12**:1665
Falco spp.
F. peregrinus (peregrine falcon) **2**:235,
236, 237; **12**:1665
F. sparverius (American kestrel) **11**:1569
F. tinnunculus (common kestrel) **11**:*1569*
fallopian tubes **5**:715; **10**:*1354*, 1413
damaged **5**:*711*, 712
and sterilization **4**:442–443
Fallopius, Gabriele **4**:560
families (classification) **12**:1600
family size, human **10**:1346
Fannia spp. (housefly) **5**:699
Faraday, Michael **8**:1102
farming *see* agriculture
farsightedness (hyperopia) **5**:687
Fasciola spp. (common fluke) **6**:*735*
fasting **8**:1124
fatal familial insomnia (FFI) **10**:1371, 1373
fats and oils 5:689–692
absorption
from the digestive system **4**:518–519
by the lymphatic system **8**:*1063*
breakdown **8**:1118
and cancer **3**:295
dietary **5**:690; **9**:1226, 1229
digestion **8**:1047; **9**:1260
pollutants in **9**:1244
energy content **2**:279

as energy storage **5**:619, 691; **8**:*1121*
from seeds **11**:1477
function **5**:691–692
hydrogenation **5**:692
metabolism **2**:280
errors **8**:1124
see also Krebs cycle
oil **5**:690
saturated and unsaturated **5**:689
monounsaturated fats **5**:690
polyunsaturated fats **5**:690
uses **5**:691
see also fatty acids; lipids
fatty acids **5**:689–690
essential **5**:692
favism **8**:1028
feathers **2**:*228–229*; **6**:725
feather stars **4**:568, *569*, 570
feces **4**:519
consumption (coprophagy) **4**:515–516;
9:1229; **10**:1393; **11**:1453, 1564
elephant **5**:594
elimination **5**:665
see also waste products
feedback systems **7**:*900*, 952–953
life regulates the environment? **6**:802–*803*
negative **7**:900, 953; **8**:1116; **10**:1308
blood concentration and volume **7**:990
blood glucose **4**:506; **7**:902, 953
blood pressure **7**:902
hormone production **7**:900
temperature control **7**:900–901
positive **7**:900, 953
childbirth **7**:*953*; **10**:1308
milk production **7**:998
see also cybernetics; homeostasis
feeding 5:693–696
behavior for survival **1**:86
by parasites *see* parasites
by phagocytosis **2**:240; **3**:336, *337*;
5:693; **7**:929, 938
cannibalism **8**:1076
carnivores *see* carnivores
communal **11**:1522
deposit **4**:439
filter **4**:439; **5**:695
by crustaceans **4**:467
by sharks **10**:*1314*
herbivores *see* herbivores
heterotrophism **8**:1117, *1124*–1126;
9:1252
omnivores *see* omnivores
prenuptial **8**:1084
scavengers **5**:695
and territoriality **12**:1613
see also digestion; digestive systems;
nutrition
feet 5:697–699
artificial **2**:213
bird
colder than the rest of the body
12:1618

webbed **11**:1472
zygodactyly **6**:775, 778
disorders **5**:*699*
of dogs **4**:539
elephant **5**:595
human **11**:1503
vertebrate **5**:697
Felidae **3**:312–313
see also cats
Feliformia **3**:311–313
Felis spp. **3**:313, 324
F. lynx (lynx) **3**:324; **10**:1350
F. serval (serval cat) **3**:321; **4**:445
F. silvestris catus see cats, domestic
Fenestraria **2**:274, *282*
fennecs **4**:*500*, 501, 539; **9**:1220
Fennecus zerda (fennec) **4**:*500*, 501, 539;
9:1220
feral animals **4**:543; **11**:1569
**fermentation 2:159, 225, 226; 3:301;
5:619, 700–703; 8:1117**
acetone-butanol **5**:702, 703
of amino acids **5**:703
discovery of action **8**:*1127*, 1128;
9:1269
in food and drink production **2**:172;
5:700, 701; **6**:763; **12**:1715
in the gut **5**:703; **11**:1452, 1453
industrial **5**:*702*
to make antibiotics **1**:109
in muscle cells **5**:703
**ferns and fern allies 5:704–707;
10:1326**
classification **5**:705–706, *707*
club mosses **5**:706, *707*; **10**:1326–1327
ferns **5**:706–707; **10**:1327
bladder ferns **10**:*1327*
fork (whisk ferns) **5**:706, *707*; **10**:1326
fossilized **6**:*783*
tree ferns **5**:*704*, 706; **12**:1637–1638
vegetative reproduction **5**:*704*, 706
horsetails **5**:706, *707*; **10**:1327
evolution **10**:1326
field **12**:1651
life cycle **5**:704–705
quillworts **10**:1326–1327
ferredoxins **7**:973
fertility 5:708–712
infertility **5**:710–712
animal **5**:*712*
drugs for **5**:709
fertility trials **7**:896
in vitro fertilization (IVF) **2**:223;
5:*710*, 711, 712
see also captive breeding programs
trials **7**:896
see also contraception; menstrual cycle;
ovulation; reproduction
fertilization 5:713–716
animal **5**:713–*715*
artificial insemination **2**:224; **5**:712;
11:1481

the estrus cycle **5**:714; **10**:1414
see also menstrual cycle
external **8**:1081–*1082*; **10**:1406, 1409
in frogs **5**:*715*
human **5**:*713*, 714–715; **10**:1353, *1354*
see also menstrual cycle
internal **8**:*1081*, 1082; **10**:1406, 1409
plant **5**:715–716; **6**:791–792
avoidance of self-fertilization **6**:761
double **6**:*760*
see also pollination
prevention *see* contraception
self, versus cross-fertilization **7**:889
in vitro (IVF) **2**:223; **5**:*710*, 711, 712
embryo storage **4**:473
see also eggs; sperm
fertilizers 1:40–41; 5:717–718; 9:1219
and the environment **5**:*718*; **10**:1342
and algal blooms **7**:*1001*
organic **9**:1247
fetalization *see* paedomorphosis
feticide, selective **12**:1656
fetus **10**:1355
accepted by the mother's immune
system **7**:941
bone development **2**:248, *249*
brain development **2**:260
circulatory system **3**:375; **7**:878
effects of rubella on **7**:950
exocrine gland development **5**:673
fetal tissue to treat Parkinson's disease
2:261
fishlike characteristics **12**:1594
screening **2**:191, 222
amniocentesis **3**:367; **4**:477; **10**:*1358*
chorionic villus sampling (CVS) **3**:367;
4:477; **10**:*1358*
karyotyping **3**:367
X rays **12**:1713
spleen **8**:1064
see also abortion; embryos
feverfew **7**:*888*
fevers **7**:901, 938
fiber, dietary **3**:299, 342; **9**:1225
fibers 6:725–726
collagenous **6**:*726*
fibrin **2**:242, 278; **12**:1620
fibrinogen **2**:242, 278; **12**:1620
fibroblasts **3**:419; **10**:1402
fibrocartilage **3**:*319*, 320
fibroids **8**:1110
fibroin **10**:1375; **11**:1549
Ficus spp. (fig) **12**:*1643*, 1693
fiddleheads **5**:706
fighting *see* aggression
fight-or-flight reaction **5**:641; **7**:905;
11:1566
figs
pollination by wasps **12**:1693
strangler **12**:*1643*
filarial worms, parasitic **8**:1065
filariasis **7**:946; **8**:1065; **9**:1196

Bold words with bold page numbers indicate complete articles; bold numbers preceding colons are volume numbers; numbers following colons indicate page numbers; italic page numbers refer to illustrations or other graphics.

flowers and flower structure *(continued)*
color **6**:761–762
embryos **5**:601
fragrance **6**:762
insect-trapping **6**:*762*
life cycle **6**:759–761
nectar **6**:762
nocturnal **9**:1220
onset of flowering **6**:759
pollen *see* pollen
pollination *see* pollination
structure **6**:757–759
see also angiosperms
flu *see* influenza
fluconazol **1**:109
flukes **3**:390–391; **6**:*735*, 736–737;
    9:*1267*, 1268
blood **6**:*736*, 737
and disease, *see also* schistosomiasis
excretion **7**:970
life cycle **9**:1265–1266
see also flatworms
fluoride **12**:1604
in water **5**:627; **12**:1604
fluoxetine (Prozac) **9**:1215
fly agaric **9**:*1185*, 1186, 1187
flycatchers, spotted **6**:750
flying foxes, common **2**:174
Fockea **11**:1446
fog harvesters **4**:501
folic acid
antimetabolites and **1**:108
deficiency **1**:74; **2**:246
follicle cells **5**:589; **10**:1413
follicle-stimulating hormone (FSH) **5**:708,
    709, 712; **7**:906; **8**:1108, 1109,
    1110; **10**:1410, 1413
and twins **12**:1655
food
allergies to **1**:53
colorings **3**:317
cravings **8**:1121
diseases carried in **7**:949
from plants
seaweeds **7**:987–988
seeds **11**:1477
see also crops
GM *see* genetically modified (GM) foods
organic 9:1242–1245
pasteurization **1**:115; **2**:226–227; **6**:765;
    8:1128; **9**:1269, *1270*
preservation 1:16; **6:763–765**
spoilage **11**:1462; **12**:1716
technology
fermented foods **5**:*700*, 701; **12**:1715
using microorganisms **8**:1132
see also nutrition
food chains **6**:766–767
Charles Elton and **6**:768, 769
pesticide biomagnification **4**:481;
    9:1280, 1287
see also food webs

food poisoning **6**:765
and cockroaches **3**:388
food webs 6:766–770
energy flow **5**:584
oceanic, continental shelves **4**:437–439
see also food chains
foot and mouth disease (hoof and mouth
    disease) **1**:88; **7**:949
foraminiferans **9**:1232; **10**:1314
Forbes, Edward **9**:1239
forensic science 6:771–774
cause of death **6**:773
collecting evidence **6**:*771–772*
flies and **6**:746
and the polymerase chain reaction
    9:*1174*
serology **6**:774
blood typing **2**:243, *244–245*; **6**:774
DNA fingerprinting **2**:224; **4**:*535*;
    6:*773*, 774; **9**:*1174*
time of death **6**:773; **9**:1183
forests
birds *see* birds, forest
boreal *see* taiga biomes
mimicked by permaculturalists **9**:1281
northern coniferous *see* taiga biomes
organic matter decomposition
    11:1460–1462; **12**:1609
temperate *see* temperate forest biomes
tropical **4**:491
rain forests *see* tropical rain forest
    biomes
types **4**:490–491
see also deforestation
Forficula auricularia (common earwig)
    4:*563*, 564
Forficulina **4**:563
Formica spp. **1**:*118*; **4**:483; **7**:963
fossas **3**:313
Fossey, Dian 6:779–780; **10**:1367
fossil fuels
and carbon **3**:304
cutting consumption of **10**:1340
fossils 6:781–784
amphibian **11**:1456
annelid **1**:99
bacteria **2**:168; **6**:784; **10**:1380
body fossils **6**:781
complete preservation **6**:782–783
dating **6**:783–784
diatom **10**:1313
dinosaur **4**:*527*
earliest **3**:332
earwig **4**:564
formation **6**:781–782
horses **9**:1256
human
"Lucy" **6**:784; **7**:*914*, 915
Piltdown Man hoax **6**:782; **7**:917
lagerstätten **9**:1256
lagomorph **10**:1393
living 8:1048–1050

to map extinction **5**:678–679
and paleobiology **9**:1254–1257
petrifaction **6**:*782*; **12**:1638
plant **6**:*783*
living fossils **8**:1050
preserved in amber **6**:*781*, 782
of pterosaurs **10**:*1391*
and the study of evolution **6**:784
trace fossils **6**:781, 783; **9**:1257
founder effect **9**:1194
fovea **5**:687; **12**:1684
foxes **4**:540
Arctic **9**:*1159*; **12**:1619
bat-eared **4**:540
desert sand **4**:501
fennec **4**:*500*, 501, 539; **9**:1220
kit **4**:501
red **12**:*1671*
in groups or paired **11**:1523
foxgloves **1**:80; **2**:*179*; **9**:*1291*
fractals **3**:*347*, *349*
fractures
osteoporosis and **11**:1502
repair **2**:249
Framingham Heart Study **5**:635
Francis, Thomas **11**:1457
Franklin, Rosalind 2:202, 221; **4**:462,
    537; **6:785–786**
Fratercula cirrhata (tufted puffin) **11**:*1471*
free radicals **1**:*34*, 35, 36; **3**:294, 317
freeze-drying **6**:765
freezing
cells **4**:471–472
food **6**:764
Fregata spp. **4**:*455*
Frere, John **7**:912
freshwater biomes **2**:211
see also lakes and ponds;
    rivers and streams
Freud, Sigmund **1**:*30*, *121*, *122*; **3**:*422*;
    4:*556*; **10**:*1383*, 1384–1385
and phobias **10**:1301
frigate birds **2**:250; **4**:*455*; **11**:1473, 1474
Fringilla teydea (canary) **9**:1273
frogmouths **6**:776
frogs and toads 6:787–790
adaptations **6**:789
avoiding predators **6**:*788*
body shape **6**:787
calls **4**:458–459; **6**:790
courtship **4**:*458–459*
distribution **6**:788
ears **6**:789
estivation **7**:892
evolution **6**:790
excretion **5**:666
eyes **6**:788–789
feeding **6**:790
frogs
breathing **10**:1422
clawed **9**:1290
common **5**:*715*

crab-eating **6**:788
eggs **5**:*589*
embryo formation **5**:*599*
external fertilization by **5**:*715*
flying **5**:699
goliath **6**:787; **12**:1642
leopard **6**:787
mating behavior **11**:*1527–1528*
nests **9**:1206
poison arrow (poison dart frogs)
    4:483–484, 485; **5**:677; **6**:*788*, 790
swimming **11**:1578
tree **5**:699; **6**:787, 790; **11**:*1527*
lungs **8**:*1060*
metamorphosis **8**:1125; **10**:1308
molting **9**:1158
reproduction and development **6**:*790*
direct development **6**:789
spleen **11**:1551
tadpoles **3**:403; **5**:696; **6**:*789*, 790;
    7:1005; **8**:1125
change into frogs **3**:335; **10**:1308
phototaxis **12**:1647
respiratory system **10**:1418
temperature regulation **3**:397; **6**:789
toads
American **3**:403
cane **1**:*51*; **2**:*196*
estivation **7**:892
Malayan/Asian horned **6**:*787*
midwife **6**:*790*
spadefoot **4**:*458–459*, *500–501*;
    5:699; **6**:*790*; **7**:892; **12**:*1673*
Surinam **6**:789
tongue **12**:1621
see also amphibians
Fromm-Reichmann, Frieda **9**:1212
frontal lobes **2**:*259*; **11**:1544
fructose **3**:297, *298*, 301
fructose-1,6-biphosphate **2**:159; **5**:702
fructose-6-phosphate **5**:702; **10**:1304
fruits and fruit plants 6:791–796;
    10:1328
economically important **6**:794–796
fertilization producing **6**:791–792
see also fertilization, plant
fruits
ancient **6**:794
compound **6**:*792*, *794*
and reproduction **6**:791
ripening **7**:*909*
science and **6**:793–794
simple **6**:792, *793*
see also grains
grafting **6**:796
and humankind **6**:793
trees, chilling requirements **4**:549
types of plants **6**:793
fucoxanthin **7**:986
Fucus spp. **7**:988
fugue, psychogenic **8**:1114
fulmars **11**:1474

fumarase **7**:995

fumarate **12**:1667

fungi 6:797–800; 8:1130; **12**:1601, 1670

  alkaloids from **1**:50; **9**:1188

  and aspergillosis **1**:89

  bracket **9**:1187

  breakdown of cellulose **3**:342

  club *see* Basidiomycetes

  and the colonization of land by plants
    11:1581

  decomposition by **6**:797; **11**:1460–1462

  drugs from, penicillin **1**:109; **2**:164;
    6:*741*–742, 799

  evolution **6**:*798*; **9**:1187

  farmed by termites **12**:1611

  hyphae **8**:1137; **9**:1186; **12**:1670

  movement of water and minerals
    12:1632

  parasitic **6**:800; **12**:1670

  plant diseases **10**:*1320, 1321–1322*

  propagation and dispersal **6**:798

  sac *see* ascomycetes

  saprophytic **6**:800; **9**:*1225*;
    11:*1460–1462*

  spores **6**:798–799; **9**:1186

  symbiotic *see* lichens; mycorrhizae

  see also molds and mildews; mushrooms
    and toadstools; yeasts

fungus gnats *see* glowworms

fungus roots *see* mycorrhizae

fur **6**:725

  molting **9**:1159

  trade in **12**:*1591*

furbelows **7**:988

furcula **1**:141

Fusarium fungus **10**:1321

fuschias **6**:762

fuzzy raptor **4**:529

G

Gadus morrhua (cod) **12**:*1599*

Gaia hypothesis 2:203; **6:801–803**

galactose **3**:297

galactosemia **8**:1123

galagos (bush babies) **9**:1294; **10**:1366;
  12:*1686*

Galago senegalensis (lesser northern galago)
  9:*1294*; **12**:*1686*

Galápagos Islands **9**:1169

  finches **2**:*185*; **4**:478; **5**:656–657, 696;
    7:*976*; **9**:1192

  giant tortoises **1**:*33*; **3**:410

  goats on Abingdon Island **3**:410; **6**:770

Galápagos Rift **9**:1233

  bacteria at **5**:651

Galdikas, Dr. Birute **10**:1367

Galen **1**:70, 71; **2**:200, *201*; **8**:1099;
  9:1214, 1289

Galenys pyrenaicus (Pyrenean desman)
  7:955

Gall, Franz Joseph **9**:1214

Gallaudet, Thomas Hopkins **7**:873

gallbladder *see* liver and gallbladder

Gallinago gallinago (common snipe)
  12:1593

Gallodactylus svevicus **10**:*1391*

galls, plant **11**:1562

gallstones (bile stones) **4**:523; **8**:*1047*

Galton, Francis **7**:966, 967

Game of Life **2**:150

gamete intrafallopian transfer (GIFT)
  5:710

gametes **10**:1405

game theory **1**:32, 85–86

gametophytes **5**:590, 600–601; **10**:1325

  in algae **1**:49

  ferns and fern allies **5**:*705*

  in gymnosperms **3**:416; **5**:601

  in mosses, liverworts, and hornworts
    9:1166

  in seed plants **5**:716

gamma-aminobutyric acid (GABA) **5**:639;
  9:1212

gamma rays **10**:1394

ganglia, nerve **2**:258

gangrene **3**:377

gannets **2**:*231*; **11**:1472–1473, 1474

ganzfeld technique **9**:1263

garbage, household **12**:1695, 1696

gardens, botanical 2:251–252

garlic **2**:266

  crow **2**:266

garpike (long-nosed pike) **7**:978

gases, greenhouse *see* greenhouse gases
  and greenhouse effect

gas exchange

  in the lungs **8**:1055–*1056*

  in plants **10**:*1424*; **12**:1629

    see also stomata

  see also respiration, breathing

gasoline

  from seaweeds **7**:988

  pollution from leaking tanks **10**:1342

Gasterosteus aculeatus (three-spined
  stickleback) **4**:456, 485; **7**:*1002*

gastric juice **11**:1564

gastric pits **4**:522

gastrin **5**:610

gastroenteritis **7**:948

gastroliths **4**:466

gastropods **8**:1150

  feet **5**:698

  mucus **9**:*1172*

gastroscopes **8**:1091; **11**:1575

gastrotrichs **1**:95

gastrulation **5**:597–599

gaurs **4**:545

Gause, G.F. **3**:408

Gavialis gangeticus (gharial) **4**:446, 463–*464*

gavials (gharials) **4**:446, 463–464

Gazella thomsoni (Thomson's gazelle)
  4:460; **12**:1662, 1663

gazelles **12**:*1726*

  Thomson's **4**:460; **12**:1662, 1663

GDP (guanosine diphosphate) **7**:995

Gebhart, Gerald **1**:92

geckos **5**:699; **8**:1052, 1053; **9**:1221

geese **12**:1701

  Canada **11**:*1521*

  communication **3**:404

  fixed action patterns **1**:83; **7**:962

  flocks **3**:402

  greylag **7**:962

  Hawaiian nene **11**:*1482*

  migrating **2**:*216*; **8**:1134

    flight **6**:752

Gelsinger, Jesse **6**:807

gemma cups **9**:*1165*

gemmae **9**:*1165*

GenBank **8**:1145

genera **2**:253; **12**:1600

generalization **8**:1021

generalized anxiety disorder (GAD))
  1:122; **8**:1113

"General Sherman" tree **12**:1608

genes **3**:367; **4**:534; **7**:918, *919*

  activation by hormones **7**:*906*

  and aggression **1**:30

  cancer-associated (oncogenes) **1**:35; **3**:294

    silencing **10**:1430

  closing down **10**:1430, *1431*

  codominant **6**:812

  dominant and recessive **6**:812

  evolution and **11**:1526

  exons **4**:538; **6**:805; **7**:920; **10**:1429

  expression **4**:536; **6**:805, 807–808;
    11:1558

  fitness **1**:59

    inclusive **1**:60

  flow (migration) **5**:656; **9**:1194

  introns **4**:538; **6**:805; **7**:920; **10**:1429

  "jumping" *see* transposons

  linked **12**:1597

  mutation *see* mutation

  new combinations engineered
    see genetic engineering

  numbers in the human genome **7**:920

  patenting **7**:923

  promoters **6**:807–808

  regulatory (control genes) **4**:538; **5**:599

  repairing **6**:806

  selection *see* selective breeding

  sex-linked **9**:1164; **12**:1688

  site on DNA, identifying *see* Human
    Genome Project

  structural **4**:538

  switched on and off **5**:632

    by TCDD **4**:532

  transgenic **6**:809; **9**:*1243*, 1244

  tumor-suppressor **3**:294

  see also alleles; chromosomes; Human
    Genome Project

gene therapy 2:222; **6:804–808**;
  8:1093; **9**:1290

  for Parkinson's disease **4**:497

**genetically modified (GM) foods
  (GMFs) 2**:223–224, 225;
  6:809–811; **9**:1244

  Flavr Savr tomatoes **2**:227; **6**:765,
    794, 809

  safety **2**:225; **6**:811

  see also genetic engineering, crops

genetically modified organisms (GMOs)
  see genetic engineering

genetic diseases 6:812–815

  albinism **9**:*1191*

  asthma as **2**:153

  autosomal recessive traits **6**:*812*

  chromosome abnormalities **6**:812–813

  color blindness **5**:687; **12**:*1687–1688*

  of connective tissues **3**:420

  Down syndrome **3**:*369*; **6**:812–813;
    10:1358; **11**:1536

    testing for **4**:477

  errors of metabolism **8**:1123

    phenylketonuria (PKU) **8**:*1123*, 1124;
      10:1358

  gene therapy **6**:805

  genetic counseling **4**:496

  hemophilia **2**:222, 242; **6**:805; **8**:1107

  Huntington's disease (Huntington's
    chorea) **4**:495–*496*; **6**:805; **9**:1202

  Marfan's syndrome **3**:420, *421*

  multiple sclerosis **9**:1175

  neurofibromatosis **11**:1504

  screening for **2**:191, 222; **8**:1093–1094;
    10:1358

  sickle-cell anemia *see* anemia, sickle-cell

  single nucleotide polymorphisms (SNPs)
    7:922

  Tay-Sachs disease **4**:477

  thalassemias **1**:73; **2**:247

  X-linked **8**:1107

  see also cystic fibrosis; muscular
    dystrophy

genetic drift **1**:18; **5**:656; **9**:1194

genetic engineering **2**:181, 221

  for artificial blood **2**:246

  cellulose from **6**:725

  crops **6**:809–811; **9**:1244

    Flavr Savr tomatoes **2**:227; **6**:765,
      794, 809

    for nitrogen fixation **9**:1219

    resistant to pesticides **9**:1247

    see also genetically modified foods

  ethics **2**:187, 225

  of farm animals **1**:*92*

  and food preservation **6**:765

  of growth hormone **2**:224

  for insulin production **2**:*223*

genetic engineering (continued)
  recombinant DNA 2:223; 8:1143
  transgenic organisms, plants 2:223;
    6:809; 9:1243, 1244
  using bacteria 2:170; 8:1131
  versus selective breeding 11:1482
  and viruses 12:1678–1679
  yeasts and 12:1715
  see also gene therapy
genetics 6:821–828; 12:1721
  biochemical 12:1598
  disease see genetic diseases
  dominant and recessive genes 6:812
  and evolution 5:653–656
  Mendelian 8:1106–1107
    and selective breeding 11:1479–1480
  plant 2:254
  population, Hardy-Weinberg law 5:655
  use of colchicine 3:367
  see also genes; genetic engineering;
    heredity; Human Genome Project
genets 3:311–312
genius 7:967
genomes, mapping see Human Genome
    Project
genotypes, genotypic polymorphism 4:525
genus (plural genera) 2:253; 12:1600
Geospiza scandens (cactus ground finch)
    2:185
Geospiza spp. (finches) 2:185
geotropism (gravitropism; gravity affecting
    growth) 10:1316, 1317; 11:1449;
    12:1645–1646
Geotrupes spp. (dung beetles) 11:1464
Gerardia savaglia (black coral) 4:453
Gericke, Dr. William F. 7:924
German measles see rubella
germ cells, primordial 5:587
germination 1:79; 4:548–549; 11:1478
    and tropisms 10:1316, 1317; 12:1647
germ warfare see biological warfare
Gerstmann-Straussler-Scheinker disease
    (GSS) 10:1371, 1373
Gestalt psychology 10:1384
gestation 6:832–834; 10:1352
gharials (gavials) 4:446, 463–464
Ghini, Luca 2:251
Gibberella fujkuroi 7:909
gibberellins 4:548; 7:909
Gibbon, John 11:1572
gibbons 3:406; 10:1368, 1370
GIFT (gamete intrafallopian transfer)
    5:710
gifts, during courtship 4:459; 8:1084
gigantism 5:613
gila monsters 8:1053
Gilbert, Walter 7:919
gills and spiracles 6:835–838
  gills 10:1418–1419
    book 1:140
    caudal 4:552
    crustacean 4:468

dragonfly nymph 4:552
  fish 6:727–728; 10:1419
  slits 3:364
  spiracles 1:140; 10:1419
ginger 12:1650
gingivitis 12:1605
Ginkgo biloba see ginkgo trees
ginkgo trees 5:659; 8:1050; 10:1327
ginseng 7:888; 11:1445, 1446
Giraffa camelopardalis see giraffes
giraffes
  blood pressure 3:374
  evolution of long neck 1:20
    Lamarck's theory 1:21; 9:1191
  feeding by 5:694; 11:1451, 1452
  horns 7:910, 911
  mating 8:1084
  neck vertebrae 11:1498
  nerve cells 3:329
  tongue 12:1622
gizzard 4:514, 521; 11:1564
glaciation 2:194
gladioli, corms 2:266
glands
  endocrine see endocrine systems,
    glands of
  exocrine see exocrine glands
  swollen 3:371; 8:1066
Glasgow Coma Score 3:399
glass, recycling 12:1697
Glaucidium brasilianum (cactus ferruginous
    pygmy owl) 2:273
glaucoma 5:687
  treatment 11:1575
Glaucomys spp. (flying squirrels) 6:749;
    12:1591
Glenny, A. 7:935
glial cells 2:255; 9:1200
Glidden, J.F. 1:40
gliders 8:1080
gliding 6:749
gliomas 3:294
Glisson's capsule 8:1044
global warming 2:157; 3:306,
    428–429; 4:493, 505; 10:1341
  and extinction 2:186
  Gaia hypothesis and 6:802–803
  see also greenhouse gases
    and greenhouse effect
Globodera rostochiensis (golden nematode)
    9:1195
globulins 2:241
glochidia (immature mussels) 8:1149
glomeruli 7:989, 990
Glossinia spp. (tsetse fly) see flies, tsetse
Glossopteris 2:192
glowworms (fungus gnats) 2:205; 3:328
glucagon 3:301; 5:612; 7:902, 904, 953,
    964; 9:1261
glucocorticoids 4:454, 487
glucose 3:297, 298
  alpha- and beta-glucose 3:341

blood 4:506; 7:902, 902–903;
    9:1260–1261
  self-monitoring 4:507
  see also diabetes; glucagon; insulin
  and energy 3:299–300; 8:1117, 1121
  energy from 2:159
  fermentation 5:701–703
  in plants
    production see photosynthesis
    storage, see also starch
    regulation by the liver 8:1047
    storage, as glycogen see glycogen
glucose-6-phosphate 3:300–301; 5:702
glutamate 9:1212
glutamate dehydrogenase 12:1667, 1668
glyceraldehyde-3-phosphate (GALP)
    2:159; 5:702; 8:1118
glycerol 5:689; 8:1118; 12:1715
glycine 1:62, 63
Glycine max see soybeans
glycogen 2:277; 8:1143
  and exercise 3:299
  as glucose storage 3:298, 300–301;
    5:619, 641; 7:902, 904, 964
    in the liver 3:301; 8:1047, 1118, 1124
glycolipids 3:298
glycolysis 2:159, 269–270; 5:618–619;
    7:993, 994; 8:1117–1118
glycoproteins 3:298
glycosuria 4:506
glycylalanine 1:63
glycylalanylcysteine 1:63
gnathostomes 6:730
Gnathostomulida 1:95
gnats
  fungus (glowworms) 2:205; 3:328
  larvae 11:1577–1578
Gnetophyta 10:1328
GnRH (gonadotropin-releasing hormone)
    5:708, 709; 8:1108, 1111; 10:1410
goats
  domestication 4:544
  saliva 11:1452
  see also ruminants
godwits 12:1628
goiter 2:166; 7:905; 9:1227
Goldman, Emma 4:443
Goldschmidt, Richard 8:1086
Golgi, Camillo 3:334
Golgi complex 3:334
gonadotropin-releasing hormone
    see GnRH
gonadotropins (gonadotrophins) 7:907;
    8:1108
  FSH see follicle-stimulating hormone
  human chorionic (HCG) 2:224; 5:613;
    8:1110; 10:1353
  LH see luteinizing hormone
gonads see ovaries; testes
Gondwanaland 8:1079; 9:1255
gonorrhea 1:116; 5:710; 7:949
Gonyaulax spp. 1:48; 2:217

Goodall, Jane 10:1370
good-gene hypothesis (handicap
    hypothesis) 11:1485
"goose bumps" 7:901
Gorgas, William 9:1267
Gorham, Eville 1:15
Gorilla gorilla see gorillas
gorillas 1:28; 10:1365, 1368–1369
  albino 9:1190
  endangered 10:1367
  grip 7:869
  mountain, Dian Fossey and 6:779–780;
    10:1367
  movement 10:1370
  sense of smell 8:1070
  social groups 10:1369; 11:1523
  threat displays 8:1073
goshawks 2:235
Gosling, Raymond 6:786
Gosse, Philip 1:126
Gossypium spp. see cotton
Gould, Stephen Jay 1:21; 2:203; 5:654;
    11:1525
gourds, bottle 11:1554
gout 2:266; 3:300; 8:1124
grafting 12:1633
  corneal grafts 12:1633, 1636
  in plants 6:796; 11:1480
  skin grafts 8:1087, 1088; 11:1507
  see also transplants
grains 6:843–845; 9:1161
  smuts on 8:1139
Gram, Hans Christian 2:168
Gramineae see grasses
grana 3:335; 10:1304
Grant, Peter R. 9:1192
granulation tissue 3:419
granulocytes 2:239, 243; 8:1109
granulomatosus, chronic 2:240
granulosa cells 8:1108
grapefruit 6:795
grapes 6:794, 795
  diseases 10:1320, 1321–1322
grapevines 3:379
grasses 6:846–847; 9:1160
  bent grass 9:1194
  cereal 9:1161; 10:1328
    see also grains
  couch 12:1651
  lawns 11:1568
  pollination 7:890
  rhizomes 12:1651
  see also grassland biomes
grasshoppers and crickets 7:958
  circulatory system 3:371–372
  coloration 12:1618
  crickets
    biological control of 2:196
    cave 3:325
  grasshoppers, temperature regulation
    12:1618
  life cycle 7:1004–1005

molts **8**:1126

nervous system **9**:*1205*

wings **6**:750

grassland biomes 6:851–852; **2**:210

earthworms **1**:100

see also savanna biomes

Graves' disease **2**:166

gravitropism *see* geotropism

grazers **5**:693–*694*

and desertification **4**:503

on grasslands **11**:1464–1465

Great Barrier Reef **4**:447–448, *449*, 451

grebes **11**:1471, 1472, 1473, 1578

Greengard, Paul **9**:1215

greenhouse gases and greenhouse effect
2:157; **3**:304, 306; **4**:492–493;
10:1341; **11**:1542

carbon dioxide **2**:157; **3**:304, 306;
4:492–493; **6**:802; **10**:1341;
11:1542; **12**:1644

tropical rain forests and **12**:1644

see also global warming

Greenland **10**:1331

Green Revolution **1**:40; **5**:718

and pesticides **9**:1287

Griffin, Donald R. **4**:573

grooming **3**:*405*; **8**:1072; **10**:*1370*

ground cover, in temperate forests
12:1609

ground effect **6**:752

ground meristem cells **11**:1448

groupers **6**:732; **12**:*1688*

group therapy **10**:*1384*

grouse

sage **4**:460

of the taiga **12**:1591

growth

appositional **3**:320

in children **3**:358

and hormones **7**:905–906

interstitial **3**:320

plant

acid rain and **1**:16

determinate and indeterminate **1**:36

growth factors

epidermal (EGFs) **11**:1507

intrinsic **10**:1345

growth hormone (GH; somatotropin)
2:219, 222; **7**:906; **8**:1120

genetically engineered **2**:224

and lactation **7**:998

over/under secretion **5**:613

Gruiformes **12**:1701

Grus spp. **5**:607, 608; **12**:1701

GTP (guanosine triphosphate) **7**:995;
12:1668

guanine **4**:533, 535, 537; **5**:654, *665*;
10:1428

a pigment **10**:1311

a product of excretion **12**:1666

guanophores **10**:1310, 1311

guanosine diphosphate (GDP) **7**:995

guanosine triphosphate (GTP) **7**:995;
12:1668

Guara rubra (scarlet ibis) **10**:1311

guard cells **7**:902; **12**:*1630*

guenons **10**:1369

guillemots **11**:1474

guinea pigs **4**:545

Gulf War (1991), oil disaster **12**:1698

gulls **11**:1471

egg incubation **1**:83–84

glaucous-winged **11**:*1458*

herring **5**:657; **11**:1471

instincts **7**:*961*

lesser black-headed **5**:*657*

as pests **11**:1474

ring species **5**:*657*

Gulo gulo (wolverine) **12**:*1654*

gumbo-limbo trees **5**:648

gum disease **12**:1605

guppies **1**:*127*

Gurdon, John **3**:383

gustation *see* taste

guttation **8**:1026; **12**:*1632*

Gymnogyps (*Vultur*) *californianus* (California
condor) **2**:236; **5**:607

Gymnomycota *see* slime molds

Gymnophiona **1**:64; **2**:275

gymnosperms 6:858–859; **10**:1326;
11:1475, 1476; **12**:1637

fertilization **5**:716

wood **11**:1562

see also conifers; Cycadophyta;
ginkgo trees

Gynaephora groenlandica (woolly bear
caterpillar) **4**:472

gynoecium **6**:758

Gyps ruppellii (Ruppell's griffon vulture)
2:*237*

Gyrinusis spp. **2**:284

H

Haber-Bosch process **9**:1217

habit **1**:23

habitats *see* biomes and habitats

habituation **8**:1020; **12**:1627

hadal zone **9**:1231, 1237

hadrosaurs **4**:530–531

Haeckel, Ernst **1**:71; **3**:320; **5**:581

Haemophilus influenzae **2**:171

Haemotopinus vituli (long-nosed cattle
louse) **8**:1033

Hagenback, Carl **12**:1723

hagfish **6**:733; **11**:1499

excretion **6**:732

splenic tissue **11**:1551

tongue **12**:1622

Hahnemann, Samuel **1**:*55*

hair 6:*774*; **860–861**; **8**:1070

defensive **4**:485

loss (baldness) **9**:1256

and touch **12**:1626

see also whiskers

hairs

leaf (trichomes) **8**:1026; **12**:*1629*

root **11**:1447, 1448

Haldane, J.B.S. **2**:181; **5**:654

Haliaeetus leucocephalus (bald eagle)
2:235–236; **4**:481; **5**:680; **12**:1614

Halichondria panicea **11**:*1553*

Haliplanella luciae (striped anemone) **7**:983

hallucinations **10**:1388

with schizophrenia **8**:*1112*; **11**:1466;
12:1597

see also hallucinogens

hallucinogens 4:557; **6**:862; **9**:1186

see also addiction

Halsted, William **3**:296

halteres **6**:743, 744, 750

hamsters **7**:880

molting **9**:1159

pheromones **9**:1294

handedness, left- and right- **7**:*871*

handicap hypothesis (good-gene
hypothesis) **11**:1485

hands 7:869–871; **11**:1498, 1503

artificial **2**:212, 213; **8**:1092–1093

disorders **7**:870

evolution **7**:871

transplants **8**:1088

handwashing, compulsive **8**:*1114*

Hansen, James **10**:1341

Hanson, Joseph **5**:585

Haplochromis spp. **11**:1486

haploid cells **10**:1404

Haplorhini **10**:1365

haptens **1**:110

haptoglobin (Hp) **6**:774

Hardy, Alister **7**:*913*

Hardy-Weinberg law **5**:655

harems *see* mating, polygyny

hares *see* rabbits and hares

Harlow, Harry **5**:604

Haro (robot) **10**:*1435*

Harpia harpyja (harpy eagle) **2**:234

Harris, Thaddeus **5**:621

harvesting machines **1**:*41*

harvestmen **1**:141

Harvey, William **1**:71; **2**:201; **3**:*378*;
8:*1100*

Hashimoto's thyroiditis **2**:165, 166

Hatch-Slack (C_4) cycle **8**:1023

haustoria **10**:1321; **12**:1670

Haversian system **2**:*248*; **11**:1500

Hawaiian islands **9**:1170

Hawk-Dove game **1**:32

hawkmoths, five-spotted **4**:483

hawks **2**:*234*, 235; **5**:687

hawthorn **4**:482

hay fever (allergic rhinitis) **1**:53; **5**:628;
9:1172; **10**:1338

Head Start program **7**:967

Health Interview Surveys **5**:635

hearing 7:872–875; **8**:1070–1071

and aging **1**:35

colored (chromesthesia) **11**:1516

in humans **7**:*872*, 873–875

loss and deafness **7**:873, *874*–875

measurement **7**:874

see also ears; echolocation

heart 3:371; **7:876–881**

and aging **1**:34

artificial **2**:214; **8**:1094; **12**:1636

cardiac pacemakers **2**:214; **7**:879;
8:*1039*, 1092; **12**:1636

heart-lung machines **11**:1571–1572

ventricular assist devices (VADs) **2**:*214*

cardiac muscle **1**:69; **7**:*879*; **9**:*1180*;
11:*1558*

evolution **7**:876–878

heartbeat **7**:879–880

rate **7**:880, 955; **9**:1252

mammalian **7**:878–879

muscle **7**:*879*

in open circulatory systems **7**:876

rheumatic fever and **2**:164

role of calcium **2**:278

sounds **7**:878

surgery, robots used in **10**:1432–1433

transplants **12**:*1635*

heart-lung transplants **8**:1092;
12:1635–1636

see also heart, artificial

valves **7**:*876*

vertebrate **3**:375; **7**:*877*–879

heart attacks **7**:881; **9**:1225

and atherosclerosis **3**:363, 376

clots causing **2**:242

and ultrafast scanning **4**:475

heartburn **11**:1563, 1565

heart disease **8**:1094; **9**:1225

in cats and dogs **1**:90

see also coronary artery disease

heart failure, congestive **10**:1308

heartwood **12**:1639

heat **5**:616; **12**:1616

Heath, Dr. R. G. **5**:604–605

heather **6**:800; **7**:*882*

mycorrhizae **6**:800; **7**:882

**heaths and moorland habitats
7:882**

"heat island" effect **12**:1665

heavy metals, environmental **12**:1696

Hedera spp. **11**:1450

hedgehogs **7**:955–956

hibernation **7**:892

height, *see also* growth

Heimlich maneuver **8**:1059

Heleomyza serrata **3**:328

Helianthus spp.
  H. annuus (sunflower) **1**:*101*, 102
  H. tuberosus (Jerusalem artichoke) **4**:548;
    12:1650
helicase **4**:534
Helicobacter pylori **4**:516, 523; **11**:1565
Heliconius spp. **2**:286; **9**:1293
Helicoverpa spp. **2**:270
Heliopora caerulea (blue coral) **10**:1310
Helix aspersa (common snail) **8**:*1150*
hellbenders **11**:1454
Helmholtz, Hermann von **8**:1102
helping behavior **5**:644
  see also altruism
hemangiomas, strawberry **10**:1359
hematopoiesis **11**:1559
heme **10**:1309–1310
Hemerocallis spp. (day lily) **9**:*1160*
hemerythin **7**:973
hemicelluloses **3**:298
Hemichordata **1**:97; **3**:365; **7**:*1006*
Hemimerina **4**:563, 564
hemipenes **11**:1519
Hemiptera 7:883–885
hemlocks **3**:415
hemocoel **3**:371
hemocyanin **10**:1310, 1376, 1424
hemodialysis **2**:215; **8**:1040
hemoglobin **1**:73; **2**:239; **10**:*1375*,
    1377, 1424
  in animals at high altitudes **1**:18; **8**:*1058*
  artificial **2**:246
  broken down **8**:1047
  and carbon monoxide **10**:1420
  carrying oxygen **7**:973; **8**:1056;
    9:*1252*, 1253
  fetal **10**:1355
  in sickle-cell anemia **1**:74; **4**:538; **9**:1266
  structure **2**:*239*
hemolymph **1**:140; **3**:371; **7**:876
hemophilia **2**:222, 242; **6**:805; **8**:1107
  and HIV-infected blood **1**:45
hemorrhages, cerebral **3**:377
hemorrhoids **4**:519
hemostasis **11**:1573
hemp **6**:726; **9**:1246, 1248
Henseleit, Hans **12**:1666–1667
Henseleit, Kurt **7**:994
Henslow, John Stevens **4**:478
HEPA filter masks **2**:198
heparin **3**:420
hepatic ducts **8**:1044–1045
hepatitis 7:886; 8:1046
  hepatitis A **7**:886, 948; **8**:1046
  hepatitis B **3**:295; **7**:886; **8**:1046
  vaccines against **7**:886
Hepatophyta **9**:1165; **10**:1326
herbaceous perennials *see* perennial plants,
    herbaceous
herbal medicine 1:56; 7:887–888; 8:1103
  Chinese **3**:*361*; **7**:887
  see also drugs, from plants

herbals (catalogs) **2**:253; **7**:888
herbariums **2**:252
herbicides
  dioxins **4**:532
  genetically modified crops resistant to
    6:810
herbivores **5**:693–*694*; **8**:1071, *1072*;
    9:1228–1229
  cellulose digestion **9**:1228; **10**:1380,
    1393; **12**:1661
  see also under cellulose
  digestive systems **4**:514–*515*, *520*, 521;
    11:1563
  in the food web **6**:767
  teeth **4**:517; **7**:979; **8**:1070; **12**:*1603*, 1605
  see also ruminants; vegetarianism
herbs, leaf crops **8**:1013
herds **2**:284; **12**:1662–1663
heredity **6**:812
  and intelligence **7**:968
  and Mendel's experiments **8**:1106–1107
  see also genetics
hermaphrodites 7:889–890;
    10:1407–1408
  permanent and sequential **10**:1408
  plant **7**:889–*890*; **9**:1166
heroin **1**:*23*–24; **4**:556–557, *558*
herons, black **12**:*1701*
Herophilus **1**:70
Herophilus of Chalcedon **2**:200
Herpestes spp. (mongoose) **3**:313; **11**:1520
Herpestidae **3**:313
herpesviruses **12**:1682, 1683
  herpes simplex **7**:949
  herpes zoster **7**:948
Hershey, Alfred **4**:537
Hertwig, Oscar **4**:476
Hertz, Heinrich **12**:1713
Hesperiidae **2**:268
Hesperornis **12**:1701
Hess, W.R. **1**:31
Heteractis magnifica **7**:*970*
Heterocephalus glaber (naked mole rat) **1**:60;
    4:*486*; **10**:1438; **11**:*1523*
heterochromatin **3**:367
heterochrony **9**:1256
Heteroptera **7**:883, 884
heterosis (hybrid vigor) **4**:546; **11**:1480,
    1541
heterosphere **2**:155
heterotrophs **8**:1117, *1124*–1126; **9**:1252
  bacteria as **2**:169
  holozoic **9**:*1224*, 1225
heterozygotes **6**:812; **9**:1193
heterozygous advantage **11**:1482
Hevea brasiliensis (rubber tree) **12**:1644
Hexactinellida **11**:1553
hibernation 3:396, 420; 7:891–893
  estivation **7**:892; **8**:1072
  desert animals **4**:500, 501
  frogs and toads **7**:892, *893*
  heart rate during **7**:880

hibernation induction trigger (HIT) **7**:892
hibiscus **6**:762
high-density lipoproteins (HDLs) **3**:363
hijiki **7**:987
Hilara sartor **4**:459
Hill, William **8**:1091
Himalayas **9**:1170
hip dysplasia, in cats and dogs **1**:90
hip joint replacement **8**:1092
hippocampus **2**:257
  and memory **2**:263; **8**:1105
Hippocampus spp. (sea horse) **6**:729–730,
    733
Hippocrates **2**:187, 200; **3**:293;
    5:636–637; **8**:*1099*; **9**:1214
Hippocratic Oath **2**:189
Hiroshima, atomic bomb **2**:*189*
Hirsutella dipterigina **3**:328
histamines **1**:53; **2**:153, 241; **3**:420;
    4:454; **7**:937, 941
histology 7:894–896
histones **3**:366
histoplasmosis **2**:176
Historia Plantarum (John Ray) **11**:1539
Histrio histrio (sargasso fish) **2**:282
histrionic personality disorder **9**:1285
Hitchings, George, and Gertrude
    Elion 7:897–898; 8:1088
Hitler, Adolf **10**:*1389*
HIV (Human Immunodeficiency Virus)
  see AIDS
hives **1**:53
hoatzins **1**:134; **6**:777
Hodgkin's disease **3**:353, 371
Hoffmanseggia glauca (hog potato)
    11:1445
Hogarth, William, engraving by **9**:*1215*
holdfast **7**:986
Holland, John **2**:151
Holmgren, David **9**:1279
Holocephali **12**:1671
holoplankton **10**:1314
Holostei **6**:734
Holothuria spp. **4**:570
Holothuroidea **4**:570
Holter monitors **7**:881
homeopathy **1**:*55*–56, *57*
homeostasis 7:899–902; 10:*1307*
  blood glucose levels **3**:301; **7**:902
  for blood pressure **7**:902
  for body temperature **7**:900–*901*
  Earth in *see* Gaia hypothesis
  and the excretory system **5**:664, 669;
    7:*902*
  feedback **7**:900
    see also feedback systems
  for fluid balance **7**:901–902
  from endocrine and nervous systems
    7:899–900
  and osmosis **11**:1458
  plant **7**:902
  see also cybernetics

homeotherms **3**:396; **7**:891; **8**:1122;
    12:1616
  endothermic **7**:900–901
hominines **10**:1360–1361
homocystinuria **5**:630
Homoptera **7**:883, 884
homosphere **2**:155
Homo spp.
  H. erectus (Java man) **3**:293; **7**:*915*, 916;
    10:1361
    migration **7**:917; **10**:1361, 1363
    skin color **9**:1227
  H. habilis **2**:258; **7**:916; **10**:1361
  H. neanderthalensis (Neanderthal man)
    7:*912*, 917; **10**:1362
  H. sapiens **10**:1362–1364
    migration **10**:1363
    prehistoric creativity **10**:*1363*–1364
  H. sapiens sapiens **7**:916
    Cro-Magnon man **7**:917
Homotherium **3**:310
homozygotes **6**:812; **9**:1193
honeybees **12**:1693–1694
  antennae **1**:106
  beeswax **12**:*1702*
  comb cells **12**:*1702*
  communication **3**:402, *403*; **12**:1694
  defense **4**:484
  drones **12**:1694
  honey from **12**:1694
  metamorphosis **7**:1006
  pheromones **9**:*1294*
  pollination by **10**:1336–1337
  queen **9**:*1294*; **11**:*1524*; **12**:1694
  royal jelly **12**:1694
  social groups **11**:*1524*
  swarms **12**:1694
  temperature regulation **3**:397
  vision **12**:1687
honeycreepers **11**:1542
honeyguides **3**:403; **6**:761; **11**:1582
hoof and mouth disease (foot and mouth
    disease) **1**:88; **7**:949
Hooke, Robert **2**:226; **3**:*330*; **4**:476;
    8:1100; **12**:1721
hookworms **1**:90
hooves **5**:697; **12**:1659–1660
hops **3**:*380*
hormone replacement therapy (HRT)
    1:61; **2**:250; **8**:1110
hormones 7:903–909
  chemical composition **7**:906–907
  classification **7**:903
  in contraceptives **4**:441, 442
  corticosteroid *see* corticosteroids
  effects on the cell **7**:907
  endocrine
    adrenal **5**:612
    gastrointestinal **5**:610
    hypothalamic **5**:*611*
    invertebrate **7**:908
    pancreatic **5**:612; **7**:904

parathyroid **5**:612

pituitary **5**:*611*

  sex hormones **1**:*26–27*; **5**:612–613

  thyroid **5**:612

environmental **5**:680

from tumors **5**:613

gastrointestinal *see* cholecystokinin;

  gastrin; secretin

gonadotropic *see* gonadotropins

growth *see* growth hormone

and heartbeat **7**:880

hormonal diseases **7**:905

invertebrate **7**:908

and metamorphosis **7**:908, 1005

molting **7**:908; **9**:1158

  in mammals **9**:1159

negative-feedback control **7**:*900*

neurohormones **5**:611

parapineal **5**:613

peptide **7**:*907*

pineal **5**:613

plant **7**:908–*909*

  and dormancy **4**:548

protein **7**:*907*; **10**:1377

in puberty *see* puberty, hormones

receptors, adrenergic **5**:640–641

role in metabolism **8**:1120

sex hormones **1**:*26–27*; **5**:612–613

steroid *see* steroids

stress **5**:641

of the thymus **5**:613

and tumor growth **3**:352

used in blood glucose regulation

  see glucagon; insulin

vertebrate **7**:907–908

hornets **4**:484; **12**:1692–1693

horns 7:910–911; **11**:*1528*; **12**:1663

hornworts **9**:1166; **10**:1326, 1338

horsehair worms **1**:96

horses

  courtship **4**:460

  digestion by **9**:1228

  distribution **2**:194

  domestication **4**:545

  evolution **5**:659; **6**:784; **9**:1255

  fighting **4**:*457*

  fossil **9**:1256

  hooves **5**:697

  lactation **7**:998

  Przewalski's **5**:*712*

  tail **12**:1594

  teeth **12**:*1603*, 1604

  vision **12**:1687

horseshoe worms **1**:96

horsetails *see* ferns and fern allies

Horsley, Victor **5**:638

Horwitz, Susan **9**:1290

hot flashes **8**:1110

Hounsfield, Godfrey **4**:474

HRT *see* hormone replacement therapy

HTLV-I and HTLV-II **8**:1031

Huggins, Charles Brenton **3**:352

human chorionic gonadotropin (HCG)

  2:224; **5**:613; **8**:1110; **10**:1353

human evolution 4:479; **7**:912–917

  Australopithecus see Australopithecus spp.

  bipedalism **1**:22; **7**:871, 914, *916*;

    10:1360, 1361

  and the "aquatic" ape **7**:913

  continuing **9**:1193

  and culture **7**:917

  ears as indicators of **4**:561

  first humans **7**:915–917

  fossil skeletons

    "Lucy" **6**:784; **7**:*914*, 915

    Piltdown Man hoax **6**:782; **7**:917

  from apes **7**:913–915

  Homo see Homo spp.

  Proconsul (Dryopithecus) **7**:914–915

  Ramapithecus **7**:916

  sites of **7**:917

Human Genome Project (HGP)

  2:222; **6**:808; **7**:918–923

humans

  adaptations for upright walking **1**:22

  altruism **1**:60

  evolution *see* human evolution

  life expectancy **10**:1348

  preserved **6**:782–783

  sexual selection in **11**:1486

  sociobiology **11**:1528

Humboldt, Alexander von **2**:192

hummingbirds

  bill **9**:*1275*

  feet **2**:231

  intraspecific competition **3**:*408*

  migration **8**:1136

  nests **9**:1208

  pollination by **1**:78–79; **10**:*1337*–1338

  ruby-throated **12**:1718

  rufous **3**:*408*

  territories **12**:1614

humoral immune response **7**:930–931

"humors," Greek **7**:888; **8**:1099

Humulin **2**:227

humus **11**:1531

hunger, and animal behavior **1**:84

Hunter, John **7**:984; **12**:1633

hunter-gatherers, ancient **10**:1362

Hunter's syndrome **8**:1123–1124

hunting

  by prehistoric humans **10**:1364

  cooperative **1**:58

  see also predation

Huntington, George **4**:495

Huntington's disease (Huntington's

  chorea) **4**:495–*496*; **6**:805; **9**:1202

Hurler's syndrome **8**:1123–1124

Huxley, Thomas **5**:653

hyacinths **1**:80

Hyaena spp. **3**:312

Hyaenidae **3**:312

Hyalophora cecropia (cecropia silkmoth)

  2:270

hyaluronate **3**:298

hyaluronidase **2**:172

Hyatt, John W. **3**:342

hybridization

  animal **11**:1480

    dog-wolf **4**:541–542

    donkey-horse (mules) **4**:546; **11**:1480,

      1540, 1541

    sheep-goat **11**:1540

  plant **6**:794; **11**:1481

    corn **1**:40

hybridomas **12**:1677

hybrid vigor (heterosis) **4**:546; **11**:1480,

  1541

Hydrangea spp. **3**:380; **6**:761

hydras **7**:981–*982*; **10**:*1405*

hydrillas **5**:649

hydrocarbons, atmospheric **5**:626

Hydrochoerus hydrochoeris (capybara)

  10:1436, 1437; **11**:1465

hydrocortisone (cortisol) **2**:219, 240;

  4:454; **7**:905; **11**:1566

  effect on the immune system **11**:1567

Hydrodamalis gigas (Steller's sea cow) **2**:186

hydrogenation, of oils **5**:692

hydrogen peroxide, to kill bacteria **2**:240

hydroids **7**:980, 982

hydrological (water) cycle **9**:*1235*

hydrophytes **12**:1703

hydroponics 7:924–925

hydrothermal vents *see* vents,

  hydrothermal

hydrotropism **12**:1645, 1646

hydroxyapatite (hydroxylapatite) **3**:319;

  10:1302

Hydrozoa **7**:981–982, *983*

Hydrurga leptonyx (leopard seal) **10**:*1334*

hyenas **3**:312; **9**:1223; **10**:1414

Hylobates spp. **3**:406

Hylobatidae **10**:1368

Hylobittacus spp. **8**:1084

Hyman, Flo **3**:420

Hymenomycetes *see* mushrooms

  and toadstools

Hymenomycotina **9**:1185

Hymenoptera **12**:1611

  see also ants; wasps and bees

Hympolimnas misippus **2**:270

Hynobiidae **11**:1456

hyperammonaemia **12**:1668

hyperbaric oxygen therapy (HBOT)

  3:400; **9**:1176

Hyperchiria nausica **2**:284

hyperglycemia **4**:506

hypermetamorphosis **2**:178

hyperopia **5**:687

hyperparasites **9**:1265

hypersensitivity **7**:931, 941–942

hypersensitivity response (HR), in plants

  7:932

hypersplenism **11**:1551

hypertension **3**:374

hyperthermia **12**:1616

hyperthyroidism **7**:*905*

hypertrophy, kidney **10**:1402

hypnosis 1:57; **3**:*421*; **7**:*926*; **9**:*1213*

  hypnotherapy **10**:1387

hypocotyl **5**:601; **11**:1476

hypodonts **11**:1489

hypoglycemia **4**:506, 507

hypomania **10**:1390

hypostasis **6**:773

hypotension **3**:374

hypothalamus **2**:166, 257

  and the adrenal glands **5**:640; **7**:905

  affecting pituitary hormone release

    5:611, 709; **7**:900; **8**:1108

  and aggression **1**:31

  and blood concentration **7**:990

  and body temperature **7**:901; **12**:1619

  and emotion **5**:602, 604, 605

  endorphin production **5**:614

  and hibernation **7**:893

  and lactation **7**:998

  and metamorphosis **8**:1126

  role in childbirth **7**:*953*

  role in puberty **1**:26–27

  and sex hormone release **1**:26–27;

    7:906; **8**:1108

  and stress **11**:1566

hypothermia **12**:1616

hypotheses **11**:*1467*–1468

hypothroidism **7**:905

hypoxia **3**:398

hyraxes, related to elephants **5**:*594*

hysterectomy, laser treatment as an

  alternative to **11**:1575

hysteria **9**:*1213*

hysteroscopes **11**:1575

Hystricognathi **10**:1437, 1438

I

ibises **5**:648; **12**:1700

  scarlet **10**:1311

Ibn An-Nafis **2**:201; **8**:1100

ice ages **3**:428

Iceland moss **8**:1036

iceplants **2**:274

Icerya purchasi (cottony-cushion scale

  insect) **2**:195

ice worms **9**:1233

Ichthyophiidae **2**:275–276

Ichthyostega **6**:790; **11**:1456

icterus *see* jaundice

iguanas **8**:1053

  at high altitude **9**:1169

Bold words with bold page numbers indicate complete articles; bold numbers preceding colons are volume numbers; numbers following colons indicate page numbers; italic page numbers refer to illustrations or other graphics.

iguanas *(continued)*
    marine **8**:*1052*
Iguanodon **4**:527
ileum **4**:519
ileus, paralytic **11**:1574
imaging, medical
    CT scans 1:72; **2**:260; **4**:*474–475*;
        8:1090
    ECGs **7**:*881*; **8**:1090
    EEGs **2**:*255*, 260; **5**:638; **8**:1090;
        11:*1509–1510*
    MRI *see* magnetic resonance imaging
    PET **2**:*260*; **8**:1090–1091
    ultrasound 8:1090; **12**:**1657**
    see also X rays
immune systems 7:**927–932**
    and aging **1**:34
    AIDS and **1**:*43*
    allergic response *see* allergies
    B-cells and T-cells *see* lymphocytes
    development and organization **7**:932
    disorders *see* allergies; autoimmune
        disorders; hypersensitivity;
        immunodeficiency
    evasion by microorganisms **7**:929
    evolution **7**:928
    immunity
        acquired (adaptive) **7**:*929*, 930–932,
            938–941
        active and passive **7**:939
        cell-mediated **7**:931–932, 939
        humoral **7**:930–931, 938–939
        natural (innate) **7**:*927–930*, 937–938
    and the lymphatic system **7**:932, *942*
    memory cells **7**:*929*, 932, 939
    MHC *see* major histocompatibility
        complex
    of plants **7**:932
    primary and secondary immune
        responses **7**:939
    recognition of self-nonself **2**:164;
        7:*939–940*
    see also antibodies; inflammation;
        lymphatic systems
immunization 7:**933–936**
    active and passive **1**:112; **7**:934
    against viral diseases **12**:1677–1678
    history of **7**:933–934, *936*, *984*
    vaccines **5**:635; **7**:934–935; **8**:1102
        cancer **3**:296
        from attenuated (live) organisms **7**:935
        from biotechnology **2**:227
        from inactivated organisms **7**:935
        genetic **7**:935
        schedules **7**:935–936
        subunit **7**:935
        testing **7**:934
        toxoid **7**:935
immunodeficiency **7**:931, 942
    severe combined immunodeficiency
        disease (SCID) **6**:*804*, 808
    see also AIDS

immunoglobulins **7**:931
    IgA **1**:111, 114; **7**:931, 998
    IgD **1**:114; **7**:931
    IgE **1**:52, 53, 111, 114; **7**:931
        and asthma **2**:153
    IgG **1**:52, 66, 111, 114; **7**:931
    IgM **1**:52, 111, *113*, 114; **7**:931
    see also antibodies
immunohistochemistry **7**:895
immunology 7:**937–942**; **8**:1130
    blood typing **2**:243, *244–245*; **6**:774
immunotherapy **3**:296
Impatiens spp. (balsam) **11**:1477
implantation, of fertilized eggs, delayed
    10:1353
implants
    cochlear **2**:215; **7**:874; **8**:1093
    drug **8**:1092
    retinal **8**:1093
imprinting **7**:962; **8**:1019
inbreeding **11**:1480, 1482; **12**:1724
incineration, waste **12**:1696, 1697
incisors **12**:1603, 1605
incubators **8**:1040
incus **4**:573
Indian medicine 7:887–888, **943–944**
Indicator indicator (honeyguide) **3**:403
indigestion **11**:1565
Indigofera spp. **8**:1029
indoleacetic acid (IAA) **7**:909; **12**:1645
indoloids **6**:762
Indriidae **10**:1366
Indri indri (indris) **9**:1221
indrises **9**:1221
"induced fit" hypothesis **5**:631
Industrial Revolution **8**:1101; **10**:*1339*,
    1340
infanticide, human **4**:443
infection
    prevention *see* antisepsis
    and swollen glands **8**:*1066*
infectious diseases 7:**945–950**
    of animals **1**:*88*–90
inferiority complex **10**:1385
infertility *see* fertility, infertility
inflammation **3**:419; **7**:930, 937
    effect of corticosteroids on **4**:*454*
inflorescences **6**:758
influenza 7:**951–953**; **8**:1059
    equine **1**:89
    vaccines **7**:936, 951
    virus, evading the immune system **7**:929
inheritance *see* heredity
inheritance, chromosome theory of **6**:746
injections, drug **8**:1092; **9**:1291, *1292*
inkblot tests, Rorschach **9**:*1211*
ink caps, shaggy **9**:1188
insecticides *see* pesticides
insectivores 7:**954–956**; **8**:1072
    plants *see* carnivorous plants
insects 1:142; **7**:**957–960**
    anatomy **7**:*957–958*

    antennae, types **1**:105
    bioluminescence **2**:178, 205, *206*; **4**:457
    brain **1**:140
    in caves **3**:327
    circulatory system **3**:371–*372*
    classification **7**:960
    coloration **7**:959–960
        butterflies and moths **2**:270–*271*
        in phasmids **8**:1017
    communication **12**:1647
    courtship **4**:456–457
    development, *see also* larvae and pupae;
        metamorphosis
    diapause **2**:269; **6**:745; **7**:1005
    diseases carried by **7**:945–946, *947*
        lice **7**:946, 950; **8**:1032; **9**:1267
    endocrine glands **5**:612
    entomology 5:**620–621**
    evolution **7**:958
    excretion **5**:668–669; **7**:989
    exoskeleton **7**:957–958; **11**:1505–1506
    eyes **5**:*687–688*
        and night vision **9**:1221
    flight **4**:550–551; **9**:1180
    hearing **7**:872, 873
    hemimetabolous **8**:1126
        see also metamorphosis, incomplete
    homometabolous, *see also*
        metamorphosis, complete
    and humans **7**:960
        see also biological control; pesticides
    memory **8**:1105
    molting (ecdysis) **7**:1005; **8**:1126;
        9:1157–1158
    nesting **9**:*1208*
    numbers **7**:958
    pollination by **6**:*761*; **7**:890; **9**:1240;
        10:*1335*, 1336–1337; **12**:*1693*
    reproduction **7**:959
    respiration **10**:*1419*–1420
    social **2**:203; **4**:524; **7**:958–*959*;
        11:*1524*
        pheromones **11**:*1524*
        torpor **12**:1618
    swimming **11**:1577–1578
    taste **12**:*1595*
    temperature regulation **3**:397
    touch receptors **12**:1627
    wings **7**:958
insemination, artificial *see* artificial
    insemination
insight **8**:1021
insomnia **11**:1510
instinct 7:**961–963**; **8**:1019
    fixed action patterns **1**:83; **7**:962
    see also reflexes
insulin 2:222; **4**:*507*; **5**:612; **7**:**964–965**
    in blood glucose regulation **3**:301; **4**:506;
        7:*902*, *904*, 953, 964–965; **9**:1261
    continuous subcutaneous insulin infusion
        (CSII) **4**:507
    discovery **4**:508; **7**:*965*; **8**:1103

    from genetic engineering **2**:*223*
    manufacture **2**:*223*
    structure **7**:*903*
    see also diabetes
integuments
    inverebrate **11**:1505–1506
    plant **11**:1475–1476
intelligence 7:**966–968**
    artificial (AI) **3**:424; **7**:967
    see also cognition
intensive care *see* life support
intercostal muscles **8**:1058
interferon **2**:222; **3**:395; **7**:929, 930
    and multiple sclerosis **9**:1176
interleukins
    IL-1 **7**:*929*, 931, 938; **11**:1508
    IL-2 **7**:929
    IL-4 **7**:929
intermedin *see* melanocyte-stimulating
    hormone
International Species Information System
    (ISIS) **12**:1724
interneurons **9**:1198
interstitial fluid **11**:1458
intestines
    carnivore **4**:*516*
    herbivore **4**:515
    human **4**:517, *521–523*
    large **4**:514, 517, 523; **9**:1172
    mucous membranes **9**:1171
    small **4**:514, 517, *521*, *522*–523; **9**:1171
        transplants **12**:1636
    smooth muscle **9**:1179
intracellular fluid **10**:1307
intravenous therapy **8**:1039
intrinsic factor of Castle **4**:519
intrinsic growth factor **10**:1345
introns **4**:538; **6**:805; **7**:920; **10**:1429
introverts **10**:1385
Inuit **12**:1654
invertebrates 7:**969–972**
    abdomen **1**:13
    asymmetrical **7**:969
    circulatory systems **3**:372–373
    courtship **4**:456–458
    digestive systems **4**:*512–513*
    embryo development **5**:597–598
    endocrine glands **5**:612
    excretory systems **5**:*666–669*; **7**:989
    feet **5**:698
    hormones **7**:908
    immunity **7**:928
    integuments **11**:1505–1506
    memory storage **8**:1105
    molting (ecdysis) **7**:1005; **9**:1157–1158
    mucous membranes **9**:1172
    protostomes **7**:971–972
    pseudocoelomates **7**:971; **9**:1196
    regeneration of body parts
        10:1399–1400, *1401*
    success compared with vertebrates
        12:1674

symmetry
  bilateral **6**:735; **7**:970–971
  radial **7**:969–970
  tails **12**:1592
  taste **12**:1595
  vertebrates are larger than **12**:1673
  vision **5**:688; **12**:1685–1686
iodine **1**:116
  dietary **9**:1227
    and goiter **2**:166; **9**:1227
  from seaweeds **7**:988
ionic bonds **5**:617
Ipomoea spp. (sweet potato) **11**:1445, 1446
IQ tests **7**:966
Iraq, biological weapons **2**:*199*
iridium, in sediments **4**:528; **5**:679
iridology **1**:56
iris (of the eye) **5**:685; **12**:1685
irises (plants) **12**:*1651*
  seeds **10**:*1326*
Irish moss **7**:987
Irish Potato Famine **10**:1322, 1382
iron 7:973
  and iron-deficiency anemia **1**:73; **2**:246;
    4:489; **7**:973
  stored in the spleen **11**:1551
iron lungs **8**:1039
irradiation, food **6**:765
isidia **8**:1035
island habitats 7:974–977
  animals change in size **7**:977
  colonization of **7**:974–975
  coral islands **4**:450
  evolution on **7**:976
    Darwin's finches **5**:656–657; **7**:976;
      9:1192; **11**:1541
    flightless birds **7**:977
  extinction of species *see* extinction,
    on islands
  number of species **2**:193
  problems facing populations on **7**:975
  variety **7**:975
  see also Galápagos Islands
islets of Langerhans **5**:612; **7**:*895*, 904,
  964; **9**:1260, *1261*
  replacement **12**:1634
isocitrate **7**:995
isocitrate dehydrogenase **7**:995
Isoetopsida **10**:1326–1327
isolation
  ecological **11**:1540
  geographic **11**:1541
  reproductive **11**:1540–1541
  see also island habitats
isomaltose **3**:299
isomers, of amino acids **1**:*62*, 63
Isoptera **12**:1611
isotopes, radioactive, for tagging
  see radioactive tagging
IUCN (World Conservation Union), Red
  Data Books and Red Lists **2**:186;
    5:606–607

IUDs (interuterine devices; coils) **4**:440,
  441–*442*, 443
IUSs (interuterine systems) **4**:442
Ivanovsky, Dmitri **12**:1675
IVF *see* fertilization, in vitro
ivy **3**:*380*
  Boston **11**:*1449*
  poison **4**:483
Iwanowski, Dmitri **8**:1130
Ixodes spp. **1**:131, 132

J

jacanas **8**:*1083*; **12**:1700
jackals **4**:540
  simien *see* wolves, Ethiopian
jack-in-the-pulpit **6**:*762*; **7**:890; **10**:1318
jackrabbits **4**:500
  antelope **10**:1392
Jackson, John Hughlings **5**:637–638
Jacobson's organ **8**:1051; **10**:1416;
  11:1515, 1518; **12**:1596
Jaculus spp. (African jerboa) **4**:501
jaguars **2**:284; **3**:324
James, William **10**:1383
Janssen, Zacharias **2**:226
Jarvik, Robert Koffler **8**:1094
Jarvik-7 heart **2**:214; **8**:1094
Jarvik-2000 heart **8**:1094
jasmolic acid **10**:1317
jaundice (icterus) **7**:*886*; **8**:1046, 1047
Java man *see Homo* spp, *H. erectus*
jaws 4:513; **7:978–979**
  of carnivores **3**:307; **7**:*978*, 979
  see also teeth
jays, scrub **1**:58
Jeffreys, J. Gwen **9**:1239
jellyfish, sea anemones, and hydras
  7:980–983
  hydras **7**:981–*982*
    budding **7**:982; **10**:*1405*
    feeding and digestion **4**:*512*; **7**:981
    nerve net **7**:982; **9**:*1205*
    skeleton **11**:1495
    see also Cnidaria
  hydroids **7**:980, 982
  hydrozoans
    by-the-wind sailor **7**:983
    Portuguese man-of-war **7**:*983*;
      9:1182; **11**:1580
    stem cells (interstitial cells) **11**:1558
  jellyfish **7**:*981*
    bioluminescence **7**:982
    cannonball **7**:982
    compass **11**:*1495*
    differences in **7**:982
    lion's mane **7**:982
    skeleton **11**:1495–1496
    touch receptors **12**:1628
  sea anemones **7**:982–983; **9**:1232, *1237*
    reproduction **3**:*381*, 382; **7**:983
    stinging structures **7**:*970*
    symbiosis **3**:*389*, 390; **4**:*469*

Jenner, Edward 7:933, 934, *936*, **984**;
  8:1100, 1130; **11**:1513; **12**:1678
jerboas, African **4**:501
jet lag **2**:219
jiggers **6**:738
Johanson, Donald **6**:784; **7**:*914*
joints
  fibrocartilage in **3**:320
  replacement **8**:1092
  types **11**:1501
Jones, Drs. H. and G. **5**:*708*
Joshua trees **9**:1160
juncos **8**:1134
June bugs **2**:178
Jung, Carl **10**:1385
junipers **3**:415, 416
Jupiter, moons, life on? **5**:682–*683*
Jurassic Park (film) **9**:1174
Jurine, Charles **4**:573
jute **3**:342
juvenile hormone (JH) **7**:908, 1005;
  8:1126

K

Kaiser, Emil **2**:180–181
kakapos **6**:755
Kalahari desert, bushmen **9**:1227
Kalanchoe **2**:274
Kallima inachus (leaf butterfly) **2**:283
Kalm, Pehr **8**:1042
Kampecaris tuberculata **3**:346
Kandel, Eric **9**:1215
kangaroos **8**:1080
  gray **11**:*1465*
  lactation **7**:998
  red **11**:1465
  reproduction **8**:*1078*, 1079;
    10:1352–1353
  tail **12**:*1594*
Kanner, Leo **2**:*162*
Kanzi (chimpanzee) **3**:406
kapok **6**:725
Kaposi's sarcoma **1**:42, 44; **9**:1174
karyotyping **3**:367
kauris **3**:416
keas, play **10**:1329
Keller, Helen **7**:*874*
kelps and seaweeds 7:985–988
  animal feed and fertilizers **7**:988
  classification **7**:985
  colors **7**:985–986
  farming **1**:125
  as food **7**:987–988
  kelp **1**:*48*; **4**:439; **7**:*986*, 987, 988
    translocation **12**:1632
  reproduction **7**:987
  on the shore **7**:986–987
  structure **7**:986–987

useful products from **7**:988
  see also algae
keratin **2**:228; **6**:725–726, *774*; **7**:910;
  10:1375, 1377; **11**:1506
keratinocytes **11**:1558
keratoplasty (corneal grafting) **12**:1633,
  1636
keratotomy, radial **5**:687
kestrels **11**:*1569*; **12**:*1592*
ketacidosis **2**:165
ketoglutarate, alpha- **7**:995; **12**:1665, 1668
ketoglutarate dehydrogenase, alpha- **7**:995
ketone bodies **8**:1124
ketones **3**:300; **4**:506–507
ketosis **3**:300; **4**:506–507
Kevorkian, Dr. J. **5**:645
kidney disease, in cats and dogs **1**:90
kidneys 7:989–992
  aging **1**:34
  artificial **2**:215
  blood supply **7**:*991*
  Bowman's capsule **5**:668, 671; **7**:990
  countercurrent multiplication system
    7:990
  embryonic development **7**:992
  failure **5**:672; **7**:992; **8**:1039–1040
  fluid samples taken from **7**:990
  function **7**:990
    endocrine **7**:990–992
  hypertrophy **10**:1402
  loop of Henle **5**:669, 670–671, *672*;
    7:990, 992
  storage of **4**:472–473
  structure **7**:*989*–990
  transplants **4**:472; **8**:1039, 1065–1066,
    1088; **12**:*1634*, 1636
    first **8**:1088, 1092; **12**:1634
  vertebrate **5**:669
  see also excretory systems
Kilimanjaro, Mount **9**:1167
killdeer **2**:232; **3**:404
  camouflage **2**:*283*
kilocalories **2**:279
kinetic energy **5**:616
kingdoms **12**:1600–1601
kingfishers **2**:230; **5**:699
King, Thomas **3**:383
kinkajous **3**:310, 311
kinorhynchs **1**:95
kin selection **1**:58, 60; **11**:1524, *1525*
Kirby-Bauer test **8**:1129
Kircher, Athanasius **2**:207
Kitasato, Shibasaburo **1**:112; **5**:592
kites, snail **2**:234, 237
kittiwakes **11**:1474
kiwis **6**:*756*
Kleinman, Devra **10**:1367
kleptoparasitism **11**:1472

Bold words with bold page numbers indicate complete articles; bold numbers
preceding colons are volume numbers; numbers following colons indicate
page numbers; italic page numbers refer to illustrations or other graphics.

Knoop, Franz 7:994

koalas 8:*1077*, 1080

kobs 11:1521; 12:1613

Kobus kob (African kob) 11:1521

   K. kob thomasi (Uganda kob) 12:1613

Koch, Robert 1:107, 117; 5:591; 8:1102, 1129

Koch's postulates 8:1129

Koestler, Arthur 9:*1263*

Kohler, Georges 1:113; 2:224

Köhler, Wolfgang 8:1021

Kolff, Willem Johan 2:*212*

Komodo dragons 7:977; 8:1051; 12:1717

Kornberg, Arthur 4:534

Kosmos (Humboldt) 2:192

Koss, Leopold 4:477

Kraepelin, Emil 9:1212

krait 9:1203

Krakatoa, explosion 2:155

Krebs, Hans A. 2:180; 7:*994*; 12:1666–1667

Krebs cycle (citric acid cycle; tricarboxylic acid cycle) 2:*159*–160, 180; 3:300; 5:619, 632; **7:993–996**; 9:1252

krill 4:467

k-selection 10:1352

   in plants 1:101–102

KT event 5:659

kudzu vine 3:379

Kuhne, Fredrich 5:629

Kupffer cells 8:1047

kuru 10:1371

Kurzweil, Raymond 3:*424*

kwashiorkor 4:487; 9:1227; 10:1378

L

labellae 6:745

labia majora 10:1413

labia minora 10:1413

labium 4:551; 6:743

labor 10:*1357*–1358, 1414

   premature 8:1098

La Brea Tar Pits 9:1257

Labroides dimidiatus (cleaner wrasse) 4:450–451

beta-lactamases 9:1291

beta-lactam rings 1:109

lactase 9:1225

   deficiency 8:1124; 12:1715

lactate dehydrogenase 5:703

lactation 7:997–998; 10:1414

   see also mammary glands; milk

lacteals 8:1063

lactic acid 2:159; 3:300; 5:703; 8:1122; 9:1183

Lactobacillus spp. 2:172

   L. bulgaricus 6:763

Lactuca sativa (lettuce) 1:*102*; 2:179

ladybugs 7:*957*, 960; 10:1351

lady's slippers 9:1240

Laennec, René T.H. 8:*1101*, 1102

Lagenieria siceraria (calabash/bottle gourd) 11:1554

lagomorphs *see* rabbits and hares

Lagopus spp. 10:1333

Lagothrix spp. (woolly monkeys) 10:1368

Laing, R.D. 9:1212

lakes and ponds 7:999–1002

   eutrophication 9:1280; 10:1302; 11:1462

   pollution *see* pollution, water

   Rift Lakes (eastern Africa) 7:976–977

   see also rivers and streams

Lamarck, Jean Baptiste de 1:20–*21*; 5:652; 7:912; 9:*1191*–1192; 12:1721

Lama spp. 4:545

lamina propria 9:1171

Laminaria spp. 7:987, 988

lampreys 6:733; 11:1499, 1500

   mouth 6:732

   splenic tissue 11:1551

Lampropeltis spp. 4:484

lamp shells 1:96

Lampyridae 2:*206*

lancelets *see* amphioxus

landfills 12:1696

Landsteiner, Karl 2:*243*, 244; 4:554; 8:1092

Langdon, John 3:369

Langerhans, Paul 7:904, 965

Langton, Christopher 2:149

language 3:394; 11:1544, 1545

   body 3:404, 406

   development in the child 3:357–358; 11:1544

   dolphins and 12:1710

   evolution of 5:662

   sign language 7:873; 11:*1545*

      taught to apes 3:406

   see also speech

Laniarius aethiopicus (boubou shrike) 3:402

Lanius spp. (shrikes) 9:1274

lanolin 12:1702

lantern eyes 2:205

laparoscopes and laparoscopy 8:1091; 11:*1574*

laparotomy 11:1573

lapwings 11:1580

larches 3:415, 417; 12:1591, 1617

   Dahurian 12:1590

Larix spp. *see* larches

Larrea divaricata subsp. *tridentata* (creosote bush) 9:1277; 10:*1319*

Larus spp.

   L. argentatus (herring gull) 5:*657*; 11:1471

   L. glaucescens (glaucous-winged gull) 11:*1458*

larvae and pupae 7:1003–1006; 9:1158

   larvae 7:959, 1003–1004, 1005

   permanent 7:*1006*

marine larvae

   of echinoderms 4:569; 8:*1126*

   nauplius 4:469

   pedogenesis 7:1006

   pupae 7:959, *1005*–1006

   see also chrysalids

   see also metamorphosis

laryngoscopes 8:1091

larynx 1:140; 10:1420; 11:*1543*

Lasallia pustulata (rock tripe) 8:1036

laser surgery 8:1091; 11:1574, *1575*

Lasik 5:687

Lasius spp. (black ant) 1:*119*, 120; 4:483

Lassa fever 10:1438

lateral line 4:*561*–562; 6:731; 12:1628

Lates niloticus (Nile perch) 2:186

latex 11:1562

Lathyrus spp. 8:1029

Latimeria (coelacanth) 6:734; 8:1048–1049, 1050, 12:1673

Latrodectus mactans (black widow spider) 1:133, *139*; 11:1547

laudanum 1:23

Laurencia pinnatifida (pepper dulse) 7:987

laver 7:987

Law of Effect, Thorndike's 3:412

Lazerta galloti 7:977

LD50 test 1:93

LDLs (low-density lipoproteins) 3:363

L-dopa 8:1092; 9:1204

lead

   environmental 5:625, 626; 9:1203

   poisoning 5:625, 626; 9:1203

leaf crops 8:1013–1014

leafhoppers 10:1323

leaf insects and walking sticks 8:1015–1018

   camouflage 2:283, 284; 8:*1015*–1016, *1017*

Leakey, Louis 6:779; 7:915–916

Leakey, Mary 6:784; 7:915

Leakey, Richard 7:916

learning 2:261–262; 8:1019–1021

   of aggressive behavior 1:30–31

   associative 8:1020

   of birdsong 3:402–403; 8:1021

   of concepts 8:1021

   conditioned *see* conditioning

   difficulties 11:1535–1538

   experimental psychology and 10:1386

   habituation 8:1020

   insight and problem solving 8:1021

   laboratory experiments 8:1020

   in octopuses 8:1149

   perceptual 8:1021

   role of play 10:1330

   sensitization 8:1020

   see also cognition; intelligence

leaves and leaf structure 8:1022–1027

   adaptations 8:*1026*, *1027*

   cacti 8:1022

   carotenoids 3:*317*; 10:1306

compound and simple 8:1026

dicotyledon 4:509–510

"drip tips" 12:1643

falling leaves 8:*1022*, *1025*

fossil 9:1257

fractal patterns 3:*348*

hairs (trichomes) 8:1026

leaf crops 8:1013–1014

   movements 10:*1316*

   palmate leaves 8:1026; 9:1258

   pinnate leaves 8:1026; 9:1258

   sclerophyllous 3:350

   sessile leaves 8:1022

   starch storage 3:297

   start of a leaf 8:1023

   tissues 8:*1023*–1025

   variations 8:1026–1027

   variegated 10:1323

   variegated 10:1323

   venation 8:1025

   see also spines; stomata; transpiration and translocation

Lecanora esculenta (manna lichen) 8:1036

lectins 7:928

leeches 1:96, *100*

Leeuwenhoek, Antonie van 1:71; 2:169, 201, 207; 8:1100, 1127; 12:1715

leghemoglobin 7:973

Legionella pneumophila 5:627

Legionnaire's disease 5:627; 7:948

legs

   artificial 2:213; 8:1092

   bones 11:1503

   countercurrent heat exchange 7:901; 11:1472

   regeneration 10:1400

legumes 3:380; **8:1028–1029**

   nitrogen fixation 5:718; 8:1029; 9:1217, *1218*; 10:1322

   proteins from 10:1377

   seeds 3:297; 8:1029

legumin 10:1377

Leguminosae *see* legumes

Leipoa ocellata (mallee fowl) 2:232

leishmaniasis 7:946

leks 4:460

lemmings 10:1334; 12:1654

Lemmus spp. (lemming) 10:1334; 12:1654

lemons 6:795

Lemuridae 10:1366

lemurs

   gentle 9:1221

   mouse 10:1366

   nocturnal 9:1221

   plant pollination by 10:1338

   ring-tailed 10:*1366*

   sportive 10:1366, 1369

   tail 12:1594

   true 10:1366

Lenard, Philipp E. A. 12:1713

Lens culinaris (lentil) 8:1028

lenses, eye 5:685–686; 12:1684

lenticels 11:1562

lentils 8:1028
Leonardo da Vinci 2:201; 7:*871*; 9:1214
leopards 2:284; 3:*313*, 324
  clouded 3:313, 324
  snow 3:*323*, 324; 7:*997*
Leopold, Aldo 5:582, 586
Lepas spp. 4:*470*; 7:*889*
Lepidochora discoidalis (dune beetle) 4:501
Lepidoptera *see* butterflies and moths
Lepilemuridae 10:1366
Lepisosteus osseus (garpike/long-nosed pike) 7:978
Leptinotarsa decemlineata (Colorado potato beetle) 2:*178*
Lepus spp. 10:1393
  L. alleni (jackrabbit) 4:500; 10:1392
  L. americanus (snowshoe hare) 2:281–282; 9:1159; 10:1392
  L. mandshuricus (Manchurian hare) 10:1393
  L. timidus (Arctic/mountain hare) 9:1159
let-7 gene 10:1430
lettuce 1:*102*; 2:179
Leuconia spp. 11:1552
leukemia 2:247; 3:294; **8:1030–1031**
  causes 8:1031
  treatment 8:*1031*; 11:1557
leukocytes 2:239, *240*, 243
  granulocytes 2:239, 243
  mononuclear cells 2:239
leukoplakia 12:1622
levees 12:1705
leven 12:1650
LHRF (luteinizing hormone releasing factor) 4:442
LHRH *see* GnRH
Lialis spp. (snake lizard) 8:1052
lianas 3:379; 11:1555; 12:1643
liberty cap 9:1186
lice 8:1032–1033
  carrying diseases 7:946, 950; 8:1032; 9:1267
  controlled by DDT 8:1033
  fish 4:467–468
lichens 6:800; **8:1034–1037**; 11:1581; 12:1670
  of the tundra 12:1653
licorice 8:1029
Licuala orbicularis 9:1258
life
  artificial *see* artificial life
  beginning 5:600
  elements of 8:1142
  extraterrestrial 5:681–684
  molecules of 8:1142
  origins on Earth 6:801; 10:1304
  origins of 2:181; 5:651
  patenting 2:190
  prehistoric 10:1360–1364
  regulates the environment? 6:802–*803*
  requirements for 5:681
life expectancy, human 10:1348

life spans 1:33, 36
life support 8:1038–1040
  and euthanasia 5:646
ligaments 3:419; 11:1501
  springing 12:1659
light
  energy
    for photosynthesis 5:616
    see also photosynthesis
  and photoperiodism 2:217; 6:759; 10:1317
  phototropism and 10:1316, 1317; 12:*1646*
  production *see* bioluminescence
lightning, and nitrogen fixation 9:*1219*
light therapy 1:57
lignin 12:1639
  breakdown 11:1462
lilacs, dormancy 4:547–548
Liliaceae 9:1160–1161
lilies 2:254; 9:1160–1161
  day 9:*1160*
Lilioceris lilii (lily beetle) 8:*1081*
lily-of-the-valley 12:1651
limbic lobes, and emotion 2:257; 5:604–605
limbs
  artificial 2:212–213; 8:*1092–1093*
  movement of paralyzed 2:213
  self-amputation *see* autotomy
limestone 3:303
  acid rain and 1:17
Limosa spp. (godwit) 12:1628
limpets 3:408; 4:445
  slipper 7:890
  vision 12:1685
Limulus spp. *see* crabs, horseshoe/king
Lincoln, Abraham 3:420
Lind, James 8:*1095*; 12:*1690*
Lindenmayer, Aristid 3:349
linebreeding 11:1482
link reaction 7:993, 994
Linnaeus, Carolus 2:201, 253, 276; 5:621, 652; 7:912; **8:1041–1042**; 11:1539; 12:1600, 1721
Linné, Carl von *see* Linnaeus, Carolus
Linognathus vituli (long-nosed cattle louse) 8:1033
linoleic acid 5:690, 692
linolenic acid 5:*690*, 692
linsangs, spotted 3:312
Liolaemus 9:1169
lions 1:*81*; 3:321, *322*; 5:*643*
  Asiatic 3:324
  feeding 5:*693*; 9:*1224*, 1228
  kin selection 11:*1525*, 1526
  male lions killing young 11:1526
  mating 10:*1406*
  teeth 3:*307*
  territories 12:*1615*

lipase 2:172; 4:517
  pancreatic 9:1260
lipids 5:690
  essential 9:1226
  see also fats and oils
Lipomyces spp. 12:1714
lipopolysaccharide (LPS) 2:169
lipoproteins 10:1376
liposomes 5:691
  used in gene therapy 6:807
Listeria spp. 6:765; 10:*1404*
Lister, Joseph 1:116; 5:701; **8:1043**, 1102, 1128–1129
listerosis 6:765; 7:949
lithium 9:1215
Lithops 2:273, 274, *282*, 284
lithotripsy, extra-corporeal shockwave (ESWL) 8:1091
Lithotrops spp. 6:767
littoral zones 2:211; 7:*1000*–1001
liver and gallbladder 8:1044–1047
  gallbladder 8:*1044*, 1045, *1046*, *1047*
    removal 8:*1047*; 11:1575
    stones in (gallstones; bile stones) 4:523; 8:*1047*
  liver
    artificial 2:215
    cancer 3:295
    detoxification in 8:1046–1047
    diseases 7:894; 8:1046
    erythrocyte destruction 8:1047
    metabolism 8:1046, *1118*, *1119*, *1121*; 12:1667
    regeneration 10:1401
    storage of products 3:*301*; 8:1044, 1045–1046, 1047, *1118*, 1124
    structure 7:894; 8:*1044*, 1045
    sugar regulation 8:1047, *1118*
    synthesis of products 8:1044–1045
    transplant 4:472; 8:1046; 12:1634–1635
liverworts *see* mosses, liverworts, and hornworts
livestock farming, organic 9:1243
living fossils 8:1048–1050; 9:1255
Livistona spp. (fan palms) 9:1259
lizards 8:1051–1053
  agama 3:396; 8:*1053*
  anole 4:459
  asexual reproduction 10:1405
  beaded 8:1053
  courtship 4:459
  defenses 8:1052
  dewlaps 4:459
  exocrine gland secretions 5:677
  flat 8:1052
  frilled 8:1052
  iguanid *see* iguanas

monitor 7:977; 8:1053
  night 8:1053
  parapineal gland 5:613
  self-amputation and regeneration 8:1052–*1053*; 10:1400
  side-blotched, mating strategies 11:*1485*
  snake 8:1053
  in suburbia 11:1569
  tail 12:1593
  temperature regulation 3:396, 397; 8:*1122*
  thorny devil 4:*485*
  tongue 12:1622
  tuatara 8:*1050*; 11:1581–1582
  whiptail 10:1405
  see also chameleons; geckos; gila monsters; iguanas; reptiles; skinks
llamas 1:18; 4:545; 8:*1058*; 9:1169
lobelia, giant 9:1167
lobsters 4:468
  antennae 1:106
  larvae 10:1314
  spiny 1:*13*; 4:469
Locard, Edmond 6:771
lock and key hypothesis
  for enzyme action 5:*631*
  for olfaction 11:1514–1515
locoweed 8:1029
locusts
  pheromones 9:1293–1294
  swarms 5:*620*; 7:959; 9:1294
Lodoicea maldivica (coco-de-mer) 9:1259
logging 12:1643
logistic maps 3:348
Loligo vulgaris (common squid) 2:*205*
Long, Crawford 1:76
"long-day" plants 2:217
long-term potentiation (LTP) 2:263
loofahs 11:1554
loons 9:1209; 11:1471, 1472, 1473, 1578
loop of Henle 5:669, 670–671, *672*; 7:990, 992
Lorenz, Edward 3:347
Lorenz, Konrad 1:30, 31–32, 84; 5:604, 643; 7:*963*
Loret, Erwann 8:*1142*
Loricifera 1:95
lorises
  slender 9:1223
  slow 10:1366, *1367*
Loris tardigradus (slender loris) 9:1223
Lotka-Volterra model 10:1350
lottery routes 12:1718–1719
lotus 11:*1478*
  sacred 12:1650
Lou Gehrig's disease (amyotrophic lateral sclerosis) 9:1181, 1202
Lovaas therapy 2:163

Bold words with bold page numbers indicate complete articles; bold numbers preceding colons are volume numbers; numbers following colons indicate page numbers; italic page numbers refer to illustrations or other graphics.

lovastatin 3:363

love 5:*602*

lovebirds 4:459

Love Canal community 10:1342–1343; 11:1532; 12:1695

Lovelock, James 2:203; 6:801, *802*, 803

low-density lipoproteins (LDLs) 3:363

Loxodonta africana (African elephant) 5:*593, 595*; 8:1074

Loxosceles spp. (recluse spiders) 1:133; 11:1547

LSD 4:557; 8:1139

L-systems 3:349

lucerne 2:*227*

luciferase 2:205, 206

luciferin 2:205, 206

"Lucy" (*Australopithecus afarensis*) 6:784; 7:*914*, 915

lugworms 12:1592

lumbar punctures (spinal taps) 11:1573

lungfish 6:734; 8:1060; 12:1672–1673

    African 10:*1422*

        excretion 6:732

    estivation 7:*892*; 12:1672–1673

    respiration 6:728

    splenic tissue 11:1551

lungs 8:1054–1061; 9:1253

    book 8:1060; 10:*1420*; 11:1547

    cancer 3:294, *295*; 8:1060

        and diet 3:317

        and smoking 3:*295*; 8:1059–1060

        treatment 11:1575

    diseases *see* respiratory diseases

    and respiration *see* respiration

    structure 8:*1054, 1055*; 10:*1420–1423*

        cilia 7:*938*

lupines 8:1029

lupulin 3:380

Luridae 11:1470

luteinizing hormone (LH) 5:708; 7:906; 8:1108, 1109, 1110; 10:*1410*, 1413

luteinizing hormone releasing factor (LHRF) 4:442

luteinizing hormone releasing hormone (LHRH) *see* GnRH

Lycaon pictus see dogs, African wild

Lycoperiscon esculentum see tomatoes

Lycophyta *see* club mosses

Lycopodiophyta *see* club mosses

Lycopodiopsida 10:1326–1327

Lycopodium spp. 5:706

Lyell, Charles 4:478; 5:653

Lygus spp. (lygus bugs) 7:885, *960*

Lymantria dispar (gypsy moth) 2:196, 268–269, 270; 10:1346, *1347*

Lyme disease 1:131; 7:947, 949

lymph 7:942; 8:1062

    buildup in the tissues 8:1065–1066

    circulation 3:371; 8:1062–1063

lymphadenectomy 8:1064

lymphadenitis *see* swollen glands

lymphadenopathy 8:1066

lymphangiosarcomas 8:1066

lymphatic systems 3:371; 8:1062–1066

    and cancer 8:*1064*, 1066

    circulation 8:1062–1063

    disease and 8:1065, *1066*

    fat absorption 8:*1063*

    and the immune system 7:932, 942

    lymph 3:371

    obstruction 8:1065–1066

    tissues 8:1063

        age involution 8:1064

        see also lymph nodes; spleen; thymus gland

lymphedema 8:1065

lymph hearts 8:1062

lymph nodes 3:371; 7:942; 8:*1063, 1065*

    and cancer 8:*1064*

    disorders 8:*1066*

    removal 8:1064

    see also lymphatic systems

lymphocele 8:1066

lymphocytes 2:241; 7:*927, 941, 942*; 8:1063

    B-cells 1:43–44, 52, 53; 2:241, 243; 7:934, 938

        and the immune response 1:112; 7:*929, 930*, 939–940

        memory B-cells 1:114; 7:*929*

    becoming memory cells 7:*929*, 932

    CD-4 1:*43*, 44

    development 2:243; 7:*932*; 11:1559

    and the lymphatic system 7:932

    natural killer (NK) 7:*929*, 938

    T-cells 1:52–53; 2:241, 243; 7:934, 938, 939–940

        and aging 1:34

        cytotoxic (killer T-cells) 1:44; 7:*930*, 931, 938

        inducer 7:*931*–932

        suppressor 7:932

        T-helper cells 2:241; 7:*929*, 934, 938

        and the thymus 7:*930*, 932; 8:1064

lymphoid cells 11:1559

lymphoid tissues 8:1063

lymphomas 3:294; 8:1066

    Burkitt's 8:1066

    non-Hodgkin's 3:371; 8:1066

lynxes 3:324; 10:1350

lyochromes (flavins) 10:1310

lyrebirds 6:778; 9:*1276*

Lysandra coridon (blue chalkhill butterfly) 10:*1403*

lysogenic cycle 12:1681

lysosomes 3:334–335; 7:929

    of protozoans 4:511

lysozome 6:741

lysozyme 7:928

M

Macaca spp. 1:19–*20*; 3:*405*; 5:*604*; 10:1368

macaques *see* monkeys, macaque

macaws 6:778

McCarthy, Maclyn 8:1141–1142

McClintock, Barbara 8:1085–1086; 9:1190

McCormick, Cyrus 1:*39*

McDougall, William 9:1262

mackerel 6:732; 10:1424

    California 4:481

McKinley Park (Alaska) 2:*208*

MacLeod, Colin 8:1141–1142

Macleod, John J.R. 4:508; 7:*965*

Macroclemys temmincki (alligator snapping turtle) 2:283; 12:1623–1624

Macrocystis spp. (kelp) 1:*48*; 7:*986*, 987

macroevolution 9:1255–1256

macrofibrils 3:341

macroglossia 12:1622

macromolecules 8:1142–1144

macronutrients 5:717; 9:1226

    plant 11:1447

    see also carbohydrates; fats and oils; proteins

Macropanesthia rhinoceros (giant burrowing cockroach) 3:387

macrophages 1:52; 2:241; 3:420; 5:*592*; 7:*937*, 938; 8:1059

    and acquired immunity 7:*929*, 931

    chemotaxis 12:1647

    and natural immunity 7:*928*, 929

    and wound healing 10:1402

Macropodus opercularis (labyrinth fish) 9:1206

Macropus spp. (kangaroo) 11:*1465*

macrotrichia 2:267

mad cow disease *see* BSE

Madoqua spp. (dikdik) 12:*1662*, 1663

magainins 9:1290

maggots *see* flies, larvae

Magicicada spp. (cicadas) 2:216

magnesium, deficiency 4:489

magnetic resonance imaging (MRI) 1:72; 2:260; 3:399–*400*; 8:1067–1068,1091, *1104*; 9:*1214*

    functional (fMRI) 2:260; 8:1091

magnetoencephalography (MEG) 2:260

magnolias 2:*193*; 9:*1257*

Magnoliophyta (Anthophyta) 1:77; 10:1328

    see also angiosperms; flowers and flower structure

magpies, nests 9:1208

mahogany trees 5:648

Maiasaura 4:528

maidenhair trees *see* ginkgo trees

Mairan, Jean-Jacques d'Ortous de 2:216

maize *see* corn

major histocompatibility complex (MHC) 7:931, 932, 940

Malacopsylloidea 6:740

Malacosoma spp. 2:269

Malacostraca 4:469–470

malaria 5:621; 6:*744*; 7:946; 9:1265, 1266, 1268

    and sickle-cell anemia 2:247; 4:525; 9:1266

    treatment 6:744; 8:1103; 9:1266

Malawi, Lake 7:976–977

Maldives 7:*974*

mallards, sexual dimorphism 4:*524*

mallee fowl 2:232

malleus 7:873

Mallophaga (chewing lice) 8:1032, 1033

malnutrition *see* deficiency-related diseases

Malpighian capsules 11:1550

Malpighian tubules 5:668–669; 7:989

Malpighi, Marcello 1:71; 2:201, 202; 3:378; 5:621, *671*; 8:1100

Malthus, Thomas 4:479; 5:653; 9:1192; 10:*1345*

maltose 3:299; 4:517

mambas, black 11:1518, 1520

mammals 8:1069–1074; 12:1674

    anatomy and characteristics 8:1069–1070

    armor 4:485

    brain 2:258

    circulatory system 3:*373*, 375

    courtship 4:*460*

    digestive system 4:*520*, 521

    dwellings 8:1072

    ears 7:872

    embryos

        development 5:598–599

        similarity 8:1074

    endothermy 7:900–901; 8:1069

    evolution 8:*1073*; 12:1672

    excretion 5:670–671

    feeding 8:*1071–1072*

    insectivores 7:954–956; 8:1072

    see also carnivores; herbivores

    feet 5:697

    hair 6:*774*; 8:1070

    heart 7:*877*–879

        heart rates 7:880

    hibernation and estivation 7:892–893

    at high altitude 9:1169

    jaws 7:979

    lactation 7:997–998

    licking skin of newborn 12:*1625*, 1626

    lungs 10:1423

    mammary glands 5:676–677; 7:997–998; 8:1070

    marine *see* whales, porpoises, and dolphins

    migration 8:1072

    milk production *see* lactation

    molting 9:1159

    nesting 9:1206–*1207*

    nocturnal 9:1220–1221

    orders of 8:1071

    pancreas 9:1261

    plant pollination by 10:1338

    in polar regions 10:1333; 11:1507

regeneration in **10**:1401

reproduction **8**:1074, 1083

see also estrus

senses **8**:1070–1071

sense of touch **12**:1626

skin **11**:*1506–1507*

sleep **11**:*1511*

social behavior **8**:1072–1074

see also social organization

of the taiga **12**:*1590, 1591*

tail **12**:*1593, 1594*

taste receptors **12**:1596

teeth **8**:1070; **12**:*1603, 1605–1606*

toothless **1**:103

see also marsupials; monotremes;

ruminants

mammary glands **5**:*676–677*; **7**:*997–998*;

8:1070

mammoths **5**:593–594, 679–680

Mammuthus spp. *see* mammoths

Mandelbrot, Benoît **3**:347

Mandelbrot sets **3**:347, *349*

mandibles **4**:467

mandrills **10**:1368; **12**:1594

mangabeys, African **3**:406

manganese, deficiency **4**:489

mange **1**:90

mangroves **9**:1237; **11**:*1494*

mangrove trees **5**:648; **11**:1494

red **12**:*1704*

mania **5**:663; **8**:1113; **10**:1388

Manihot esculenta (cassava) **5**:701; **11**:1446

manna lichen **8**:1036

manorialism **1**:39

Manta birostris (manta ray) **6**:*734*

Mantell, Dr. Gideon **4**:527

Mantell, Mary Ann **4**:527

mantids 4:483; **8**:**1075–1076**

mantises

Chinese **8**:1075

orchid **2**:286

praying **8**:*1075*, 1084

mantle **8**:1147

manure, green **5**:718

maquis **2**:209

Maranta leuconeura (prayer plant) **10**:1316

Marasmius oreades (fairy ring fungus)

9:*1187*, 1188

marasmus **4**:487; **9**:1227; **10**:1378

marble, acid rain and **1**:*17*

Marchantia polymorpha **9**:*1165*

Marchantiophyta **9**:1165; **10**:1326

Marfan's syndrome **3**:420, *421*

margarine **5**:692

Margulis, Lynn **2**:*202*, 203; **3**:332; **5**:585

marijuana *see* cannabis

Mariopteris nervosa **6**:*783*

Marmosa spp. (mouse opossum) **7**:997;

8:1077

marmosets **5**:694; **10**:1367–1368

pygmy **10**:1367

marmots, Alpine **10**:1437

Mars, life on **5**:*682*

marshes **12**:1703–1704

see also salt marshes

Marsh, George Perkins **4**:490

Marsh, Pete **9**:1166

marsupials 5:656; **8**:**1077–1080**;

12:1674

American **8**:1077

birth and development **8**:1078;

10:1352–1353

evolution and distribution **8**:1078–1079;

11:1541; **12**:1717

convergent evolution **4**:446

marsupium **8**:1077–1078

martens **12**:1591

Martes spp., of the taiga **12**:1591

Martins, Carl **7**:994

martins, nests **9**:1209

Masai Mara Game Reserve **3**:427, *430*;

11:*1463*

Masai people **9**:*1194*; **11**:1465

mass flow **12**:1631

mass spectroscopy **1**:68; **6**:*772*

mast cells **1**:53, 114; **3**:420; **7**:941

mastectomy **3**:296

mastication **4**:514; **12**:1621

Mastigophora see flagellates

mastitis **1**:89

mastodons **5**:679–680

Mastomys natalensis (multimammate rat)

10:1438

mating 8:**1081–1084**

attracting a mate **8**:1083–1084; **11**:*1540*

and cannibalism **8**:1076

cuckolding **8**:1083

differences between the sexes

8:1082–1083

females choosing a mate **11**:*1527*–1528

and intersexual selection **11**:1485

and intrasexual selection **11**:1484

monogamy **10**:1406

nonrandom **5**:656

polyandry **3**:409; **8**:*1083*

polygamy **3**:409; **10**:1406

polygyny (harem breeding) **3**:409;

4:460; **8**:1084; **11**:1523

postcopulatory mate guarding **8**:1083

and sperm "competition" **8**:1083

and territories **12**:1613–*1614*

see also courtship; fertilization;

reproduction

matorral **2**:209

Maupertuis, Pierre Louis Moreau de **2**:202

maxillae **4**:467

maxillipeds **4**:467

Maxillopoda **4**:470

see also barnacles

May, Robert **3**:348

mayflies *see* dragonflies and mayflies

Mayotis bechsteri (Bechstein's bat) **2**:*173*

MDMA (ecstasy) **4**:556, *557*

meat, preservation **5**:701

meat eating

versus vegetarianism **9**:1228

see also carnivores

mechanoreceptors

and breathing **8**:1058–1059

and touch **12**:1626

Medawar, Peter 8:**1087–1088**, 1103;

12:1633–1634

Medicago sativa see alfalfa

medical technology 8:**1089–1094**

see also bionics; imaging, medical;

pharmacology; transplants

medication, preoperative **11**:1573

medicine

alternative *see* alternative medicine

Darwinian **4**:479

and diagnosis, remote **10**:1434

evidence-based (EBM) 8:**1095–1098**

genetic **8**:1093–1094

history of 8:**1099–1103**

anatomy and dissection **1**:70–71

anesthesia **1**:76; **8**:1102; **11**:1571

antibiotics **2**:*180*; **6**:741–742, 799;

8:1103

antisepsis **1**:115; **8**:1043, 1101, 1102

discovery of blood circulation **1**:71;

8:*1100*

discovery of insulin **4**:508; **7**:*965*;

8:1103

the first MRI scanner **8**:1068

Greek medicine **8**:*1099*

herbal drugs **8**:1103

immunization **1**:110–111; **7**:933–934,

936, 984; **8**:1130; **11**:1513

nursing **8**:*1102*

surgery **11**:1570–1571

transplants **8**:1087–1088, 1103

robotics in 4:497; **10**:**1432–1435**

telemedicine **8**:*1094*; **10**:*1433*–1434

veterinary **1**:88, *90*

medicines *see* drugs

Mediterranean region, forests **12**:1610

medulla (brain) **2**:256, 259

respiratory center **9**:1252

medusae **7**:980

meerkats **1**:*58*; **3**:313; **11**:1522

Megachiroptera **2**:173–174; **9**:1222

megakaryocytes **2**:243

Megalosaurus **4**:527

Meganeura **4**:552; **6**:748

Megaptera novaeangliae (humpback whale)

1:*97*; **3**:*405*; **4**:*438*, 460; **11**:1580

megasporangium **10**:1336

megaspores **5**:590, 716

megasporocytes **5**:590

Megazostrodon **7**:954

Mege-Mouries, Hippolyte **5**:692

Megophrys nasuta (Asian horned toad) **6**:*787*

meibomian glands **5**:676

meiosis **3**:*339–340, 368*; **10**:1403–1404

in egg cells **5**:587–588, 589–590

see also DNA, replication

melaleuca **5**:649

Melanerpes uropygialis (Gila woodpecker)

2:*273*

melanin **9**:1193; **10**:1310; **11**:1507;

12:*1658*, 1689

absence **10**:1310

melanocytes **10**:*1310*; **11**:1507

melanocyte-stimulating hormone

(MSH/intermedin) **5**:611;

7:907–908

melanomas, malignant **3**:295; **9**:1193

melanophores **2**:282; **10**:1310

melanophore-stimulating hormone (MSH)

10:1310

melatonin **2**:218, 219; **5**:613

Meloe franciscanus **2**:178

melon (cetacean) **4**:572; **12**:1702

melons (plants) **3**:380; **11**:*1554*

Melospiza melodia (song sparrow)

3:402–403, 408

membranes

cell *see* plasma membranes

mucous 9:**1171–1172**

memory 8:**1104–1105**; **9**:1211

declarative (explicit) **2**:261–263

development in the child **3**:358

and emotions **5**:604

and experimental psychology

8:1020–1021

and forgetting **8**:1105

see also amnesia

immediate/sensory **8**:1104, *1105*

improvement **8**:1105

long-term **2**:262–263; **8**:1104, *1105*;

11:1543

nondeclarative (procedural/implicit)

2:262

short-term/working memory **2**:262,

263; **8**:1104, *1105*; **11**:1543–1544

storage **2**:257; **8**:*1104–1105*

see also cognition; conditioning;

learning

memory cells **7**:*929*, 932, 939

Menacanthus stramineus (chicken-body

louse) **8**:1033

menarche **1**:28; **7**:906; **8**:1111

Mendel, Gregor 2:202, 227; **5**:653;

8:**1106–1107**; **11**:1479–1480

Law of Segregation **8**:1106

Ménière's disease **4**:561

meninges **2**:259

meningitis **9**:1202

tuberculous **12**:1648

Menkes syndrome **8**:1124

Bold words with bold page numbers indicate complete articles; bold numbers
preceding colons are volume numbers; numbers following colons indicate
page numbers; italic page numbers refer to illustrations or other graphics.

menopause 8:*1110*
 osteoporosis and the 11:1502
 in primates 8:1111
menorrhagia 8:1110
menstrual cycle 2:219; 7:906;
  8:**1108–1111**; 10:1414
 and cervical mucus 4:442; 9:1172
 cessation *see* menopause
 disorders of 8:1110
 menstruation 8:1108, 1109–1110
  and iron loss 1:73
 and natural methods of contraception
  4:442
 premenstrual syndrome (PMS)
  8:1110–1111
 and puberty 1:27–28; 8:1111
 synchronized 9:1294
 see also fertilization; mating; ovulation;
  reproductive systems
mental disorders 8:**1112–1115**
 difficult diagnosis of 10:1389
 see also phobias; psychology; psychoses;
  psychotherapy; schizophrenia
Menura spp. (lyrebirds) 6:778; 9:*1276*
Mephitis spp. (skunk) 4:486; 11:*1516*
mercaptopurine, 6- 7:898
mercury
 compounds 1:116
 in fish 1:17
mercy killing *see* euthanasia
meristems 8:1023; 11:1560
mermaid's purses 11:*1489*
meroplankton (temporary marine
  zooplankton) 10:*1313*–1314
Merostomata 1:141
Merriam, C. Hart 9:1167
Merrick, Joseph Carey 11:*1504*
Meselson, Matthew 4:534
Mesembryanthemum crystallinum (iceplant)
  2:274
Mesmer, Franz Anton 7:926
mesocarp 6:792, 795
mesogloea 7:981, *982*
mesohyl 11:1552
mesomorphs 10:1385
mesonephric duct 7:992
mesonephros 7:992
mesophyll 8:*1024*
Mesosaurus 2:192; 9:1255
mesosphere 2:154, *155*
Mesothelae 11:1546
mesothelioma 5:628
mesquites, desert 4:499
metabolism 8:**1116–1124**
 anabolism 8:1116, 1119–1120, 1121
 basal metabolic rate (BMR) 2:280;
  8:1121–1122
 catabolism 5:618–619; 8:1116,
  1117–1119
 see also fermentation; respiration
 crassulacean acid (CAM) 2:273;
  10:*1305*–1306

 and enzymes 8:1118
 see also enzymes
 and hormones 8:1120
 see also hormones
 human 8:1120–1124
 inborn errors of 8:1123
 metabolic oxygen consumption
  2:279–280
 metabolic rate and heart rate 7:880
 respiratory quotient (RQ) 2:280
 role of ATP *see* ATP
 role of the liver in 8:*1118,* 1119, *1121*
 and starvation 8:1120
 see also energy; homeostasis
metacarpals 7:869
metagenesis 10:1407
metamorphosis 7:1004; 8:**1125–1126**;
  10:1308
 complete 7:1005–1006; 8:1126
  in butterflies and moths 7:1006
  in fleas 6:739–740
  in flies 6:743
  in insects 7:959; 9:1158
  pupae 7:959, *1005*–1006
 hormonal control 7:908, 1005; 8:1126
 incomplete 7:1004–1005; 8:1126
  in amphibians 7:1005
  in dragonflies and mayflies 4:551
  in earwigs 4:564
  in grasshoppers and crickets
   7:1004–1005; 8:1126
  in insects 7:959; 9:1157–1158
  in phasmids 8:1018
 purpose 8:1125
 tracheal system during 10:1420
 see also larvae and pupae; molting
metanalysis 8:1098
metanephridia 5:666–667; 7:989
metastases 3:294; 8:1064
metatarsals 11:1503
Metatheria *see* marsupials
meteorites
 and extinction of dinosaurs 4:*529*; 5:659
 Gaia hypothesis and 6:802
 life from Mars on 5:682
 meteorite craters 4:*529*; 5:659
metestrus 8:1111
methadone 4:558
methane
 and the carbon cycle 3:303–304
 from landfills 12:1696
 from microorganisms 5:702
 as a fuel 9:1280
 a greenhouse gas 10:1341
methanobacteria 5:702
methionine 5:630
methotrexate 3:353
methyldopa 2:164
methyl isocyanate 5:628
MHC *see* major histocompatibility complex
mice
 chemical signals 3:404

harvest 1:79
house 10:1437; 11:1569
pheromones 9:1294
pygmy 10:1436
micelles 4:519
Michigan, deforestation 4:*492*
Micrathene whitneyi (elf owl) 2:236
microanalysis 1:68
microbiology 8:**1127–1132**
 environmental 8:1132
 famous microbiologists 8:*1127*–1129
 industrial 8:1132
 medical 8:1132
 and vaccination *see* immunization
 see also genetic engineering;
  microorganisms
Microcebus murinus (mouse lemur) 10:1366
Microchiroptera 9:1222
Micrococcus spp. 2:171
Microcosmus (Lynn Margulis) 5:585
microecosystems 5:585
microevolution 9:1255
microfibrils 3:341
Micrographia (Hooke) 3:*330*
micronutrients 5:717; 9:1226–1227
 and hydroponics 7:924–925
 plant 11:1447–1448
  and hydroponics 7:924–925
 see also minerals; trace elements; vitamins
microorganisms 8:1130
 ecological role 5:585
 immune system and 7:928–929
 mating in 8:1082
 study of *see* microbiology
 see also bacteria; protozoa; viruses
micropuncture, kidney 7:990
micropyle 5:*716*; 10:1336; 11:1476
microscopes and microscopy 2:201;
  3:330; 8:1128
 atomic force (AFM) 4:476
 electron 1:71; 3:330; 4:476; 7:894–895
  cryoelectron microscopy 12:1677
  freeze-etch 4:*473*
  freeze-fracture 4:473
  scanning (SEM) 4:476; 7:895; 8:1128;
   12:1721
  transmission (TEM) 4:476; 7:895;
   8:1128; 12:1721
 fluorescence 4:476
 interference 12:1721
 light 1:71; 3:330; 7:*894,* 895; 12:1721
  binocular 11:*1572*
  phase-contrast 4:476; 12:1721
 remote-controlled 10:1434
 use during surgery 8:*1089*; 11:*1572*
microsporangia 3:416
microsurgery 11:*1572*
Microtus ochrogaster (prairie vole) 10:1437
microvilli
 intestinal 4:517, 523
 on taste cells 12:1596
microwhip scorpions 11:1469

Micrurus spp. 4:484
midges 7:1001
 gall 7:1006
Midwest, American, Dust Bowl 4:503
Miescher, Friedrich 4:537
migration 2:210; 8:**1133–1136**
 an adaptive behavior 1:19
 bird 2:210; 5:619; 6:776–777;
  8:1135–1136; 10:1333; 11:1474;
  12:1700
  Arctic tern 8:*1133*; 11:1474
  to the tundra 12:1654
  white storks 8:1134
 butterflies and moths 2:*269*
 caribou 8:1135; 10:1333; 12:1654
 eel 2:210
 elephant 5:594
 and genetic diversity 8:1135
 mammalian 8:1072
 navigation 8:1135–1136
 salmon 8:1133–*1134,* 1135; 10:1426
 spiny lobster 4:469
 squid 8:1136
 vertical 8:1136
 whale 8:1135; 12:1710
mildew *see* molds and mildews
milk
 antibodies in 7:*934*
 and bovine somatotropin/growth
  hormone 4:545
 crop milk 7:997
 fermentation 6:763
 mammalian
  composition 7:998
  purpose 7:998
  production 7:998
  per cow 1:40
  see also lactation
 soybean 8:1028
 uterine 7:997
 see also mammary glands
Miller, Frederick Robert 4:508
Miller, Stanley 2:181, 202; 5:651, *652,*
  682
Miller-Urey experiment 5:651, *652,* 682
millipedes *see* centipedes and millipedes
Milroy's disease 8:1065
Milstein, Cesar 1:113; 2:224
milt 6:732
mimicry *see* camouflage and mimicry
Mimosa pudica (sensitive plant) 10:*1316*
Mimosoidea 8:1029
Mimulus cardinalis (monkey flower) 3:351;
  12:1630
Mimus polyglottos (mockingbird) 9:1274
mind-body problem 3:422, 423
mineralocorticoids 4:454
minerals
 deficiency 4:489
 metabolism, errors of 8:1124
 required by plants 2:277
mining industry, bacteria used in 8:1132

mink 10:*1351*; 12:1591

Minkowski, Oskar 7:965

minnows, fathead 6:733

mint, rusts 10:1321

miracadia 9:1265, 1268

Mirounga spp. (elephant seals) 1:*85*; 3:311

miscarriage 1:14; 10:1354

Mississippi River 10:1427; 12:1704–1705

   basin 10:1426

mistletoe 9:*1265*; 10:1321; 11:1477

Mitchell, Peter 2:*160*

mites 1:132, 141

   carrying disease 1:131

      mange 1:90

   cockroach 3:388

   flour 1:132

   follicle 1:132

   house 2:153; 5:*627*

   spider 10:1320

   velvet 1:*132*

mitochondria 3:332, *333*, 335; 8:1118, 1119

   DNA (mtDNA) 2:168; 3:385

      and human origins 7:917

   evolution of 2:168; 3:392; 5:585

   Krebs cycle and ATP production

      2:159–160; 3:300, 335; 5:619;

      7:996

   link reaction in 7:994

   and the urea cycle 12:1667

mitosis 3:*338*–339

   blocked by drugs 3:353

   interruption leading to polyploidy 2:266

   see also DNA, replication

mnemonics 8:1105

mockingbirds 9:1274

Mode, C.J. 3:389

Moeritherium 5:*593*

Mojave Desert 4:499

molars 12:1603, 1605

molds and mildews 8:1137–1140

   mildews

      downy 8:1138

      powdery 8:*1137*, 1138; 10:*1321*

   molds

      on bread 6:*763*; 8:1138; 9:*1225*

      in cheese 6:763

      see also food, preservation

   rusts and smuts 6:800; 8:1139; 10:1321

   slime molds and water molds

      8:*1139*–1140; 10:1381–1382

molecular biology 8:1141–1146

   DNA

      replication *see* polymerase chain

         reaction

      structure discovered 4:461–462,

         533–534, 537; 7:918–919; 8:1142

      see also DNA

   karyotyping 3:*367*

   monoclonal antibodies 1:113; 2:*221*,

      224, 226

   RFLP analysis *see* restriction fragment

      length polymorphisms

see also genetic engineering; Human

   Genome Project

molecular clock theory 5:654

moles 7:*954*, 955; 11:1532

   golden 7:956

   marsupial 8:1079–1080

   star-nosed 7:955

mollicutes 10:1323

Mollison, Bill 9:1279, 1280

mollusks 1:96; 7:972; 8:1147–1150

   anatomy 8:1147–1149

   aquaculture 1:125

   bivalve *see* bivalves

   circulatory system 3:371, 372–373;

      8:1148

   classification 8:1150

   courtship 4:458

   epidermis 11:1506

   evolution 8:1148

   excretion 5:667

   exoskeletons 11:1497

   and humans 8:1149

   mucus 9:*1172*; 11:1506

   nervous system 8:1147; 9:1205

   range 8:1149–1150

   reproduction 8:1150

   shell 8:*1148*–1149; 11:1497, 1506

   see also octopuses; snails; squid

Moloch horridus (thorny devil) 4:*485*

Molothrus ater (brown-headed cowbird)

   4:445; 9:1274

molting 1:139; 7:908; 8:1126;

   9:1157–1159; 11:1497, 1506

   in insects 7:1005; 8:1126

Monachus spp. 5:*655*

Monera 10:1380; 12:1601

monestrus animals 8:1111

Mongolian spots 10:1359

mongooses 3:313; 11:1520

monkey flowers 3:*351*; 12:1630

monkey puzzle trees 3:416

monkeys 10:1368

   capuchin 3:402; 10:1368

   colobus 10:1368

   dominance hierarchy 8:1083

   feet 5:697

   Goeldi's 10:1368

   grip 7:869

   howler 10:1368; 12:1594, 1615, 1640

   macaque 1:19–20; 3:*405*; 10:1368, 1369

   mating 8:1083

   New World 10:*1367*–*1368*

   Old World 10:1367, 1368

   patas 3:406

   play 10:1329–1330

   proboscis 10:1374

   rhesus 3:*405*; 5:*604*

   spider 12:1594

      marimonda 10:*1368*

   squirrel 8:*1070*

   tail 12:1594

   titi 3:405

vervet/African green 3:403; 11:1523

   washing food 1:19–*20*

   woolly 10:1368

   see also primates

monkshood 6:758

monocarpic plants 1:101; 10:1319

monocotyledons 1:78; 4:*510*;

   9:1160–1161; 10:1328; 11:1476

   different from dicotyledons 9:1161

   germination 11:1478

   leaf veins 8:1025; 9:1160

   vascular bundles 12:1669

   see also grasses; orchids; palms

monocultures 9:1244

monocytes 2:241, 243

monogamy 10:1406

Monogenea 6:736

monomers 8:1142

Mononegavirales 12:1682

mononuclear cells 2:239

Monoplacophora 8:1049, 1150

monosaccharides 3:297; 8:1143

monosodium glutamate (MSG) 2:153;

   12:1621

monotremes 8:1074; 9:1162–1163;

   11:1541; 12:1674

   mammary glands 5:676–677; 7:997

Monstera tenuis (cheese plant) 10:1316

Montague, Mary Wortley 7:984

Monterey Bay Aquarium 1:*129*

Montezuma 12:1723

Monument Valley (Arizona) 2:*211*

mood disorders 8:1113

moon jellies 7:*981*, 982

moors *see* heaths and moorland habitats

moose (elk) 8:1084; 10:1350; 12:1591, *1619*

morality *see* bioethics

Morchella sp. 6:*800*

Morgan, Thomas Hunt 6:746; 8:1085,

   1107; 9:1164; 12:1721

morning glory 12:1646

Moro reflex 10:1397–1398

morphine 1:51; 4:556; 5:614; 9:1215

morphogenesis 3:348–349

morphology, plant 2:254

Morpho spp. (morpho butterfly)

   12:1642

Morris, Robert 9:1263

mortality, density-dependent 10:1347

Morton, W.T.G. 1:76

mosquitoes 7:1004

   antennae 1:106

   control, using microorganisms 8:1132

   diseases from 6:*744*; 7:946, *947*

      see also malaria; yellow fever

   larvae and pupae 7:*1004*; 10:*1419*;

      11:1577–1578

   nocturnally active 9:1222

pitcher plant 3:316

   and threadworms 9:1222

mosses, liverworts, and hornworts

   9:1165–1166

   hornworts 9:1166; 10:1326, 1338

   liverworts 9:*1165*, 1166; 10:1326;

      12:*1670*

   mosses 9:1165–*1166*; 10:1326

      epiphytic 12:*1670*

      sphagnum 11:1532; 12:1703

      of the tundra 12:1653

   movement of water and minerals

      12:1632, 1670

   reproduction 5:716

mother-of-pearl 8:1149

moths *see* butterflies and moths

motion sickness 4:561

   in astronauts 11:1534

motivation 1:83–84; 10:1386

motor neurone disease 4:495, 496, 497

mountain biomes 9:1167–1170

   animals and plants 9:1168–*1170*

   and conservation 3:429; 9:1168

   creation of mountain ranges 9:1170

   mountain zones 2:209; 9:*1167*–1168

Mount St. Helens 1:*16*; 5:624

mouse *see* mice

mouth 4:513–514, *516*

   bacteria in 2:171–172

MRI *see* magnetic resonance imaging

mucin 9:1171

Mucizonia spp. 2:274

mucoproteins 10:1376

Mucor spp. 6:*763*

mucosa-associated lymphoid tissue

   (MALT) 8:1065

mucosal layers 8:1065

mucous membranes 9:1171–1172

mucus 9:1171, *1172*

   cervical 4:442; 9:*1172*

   respiratory-tract 7:928; 9:1171

mud puppies 10:1418; 11:1454

mudskippers 6:*728*, 730

mudsuckers 6:728

muggers 4:463–464

Muir, John 3:426

mules 4:546; 11:1480, *1540*, 1541

Müller, Fritz 3:391

Muller, Hermann J. 2:202; 6:746; 9:1190

Müller, Johannes 2:276; 9:1214

Müller, Paul 4:480, *481*

mullet 11:1492

Mullis, Kary 9:1173–1174

multinucleated cells 5:*592*

multiple personality disorder (MPD)

   8:1114, 1115

multiple sclerosis (MS) 2:165;

   9:1175–1176, 1202–1204

Bold words with bold page numbers indicate complete articles; bold numbers preceding colons are volume numbers; numbers following colons indicate page numbers; italic page numbers refer to illustrations or other graphics.

Multiplicity (film) **3**:*386*

murein **2**:169

Murex spp. **8**:1149

Murray, Joseph **8**:1088

murres (guillemots) **11**:1474

Mus spp. (mouse) **10**:1436, 1437; **11**:1569

Musa spp. (banana plant) **6**:796; **9**:1160;
   10:1338; **11**:*1542*

Musca domestica (housefly) **4**:480; **5**:699;
   6:745; **12**:*1647*

Muscardinus avellanarius (common
   dormouse) **8**:*1069*

muscarine **1**:50

Muscicapa striata (spotted flycatcher) **6**:750

muscular dystrophy **2**:222; **7**:895; **9**:1181
   Duchenne **7**:921; **9**:1181

muscular systems 9:1177–1184
   and aging **1**:34
   atrophy **9**:1184
   capacity for new growth **9**:1183
   diseases **9**:1181
   and exercise
      lactic acid (lactate) accumulation
         2:159; **3**:300; **5**:703; **9**:1183, 1252
      muscle size **9**:*1184*
   fermentation in cells **5**:703
   fibers (cells) **9**:1178, 1181, 1183
   muscle blocks (myotomes) **9**:1179
   muscle contraction **9**:1179–1180,
      1182–1183
   muscle renewal **11**:1558
   muscle structure and function
      9:1180–1183
   muscle wasting **9**:1184; **11**:1533
   pectoral muscles **6**:*748*, 751
   and regeneration **10**:1402
   relaxants for surgery **9**:1183
   role of calcium **2**:278; **9**:1182
   stimulation of paralyzed **2**:213
   types of muscle
      cardiac **1**:69; **7**:*879*; **9**:*1180*; **11**:*1558*
      skeletal **1**:69; **9**:*1178*–1179,
         1180–*1181*
      smooth **1**:69; **9**:1179–1180
   mushroom body **8**:1105

mushrooms and toadstools
   9:1185–1188
   alkaloids **1**:50; **9**:1188
   edible or poisonous? **9**:1188
   fairy rings **9**:*1187*, 1188
   hallucinogenic **9**:1186
   mushrooms **6**:800; **8**:1139
      cap **6**:799
      cultivated **9**:1185
      "magic" **9**:1186
      toadstools **6**:797
   see also fungi
musk ox **10**:1333; **12**:*1653*, 1654
muskrats **10**:1351; **12**:1593
   nests **9**:1206–1207
mussels **8**:*1147*; **11**:1493
   freshwater **8**:1149–1150; **10**:1427

mustard gas **3**:352

Mustela spp. **3**:308; **9**:1159; **10**:1351;
   12:*1591*

Mustelidae **3**:308

musth **5**:595–596

mutagenicity (Ames) test **3**:295

mutagens **9**:1190

mutation 1:*19*; **4**:538; **9:1189–1190**
   adaptive **11**:1542
   bacterial **2**:170
   and cancer **3**:294–295, 333; **9**:1190;
      12:1658
      see also carcinogens
   causes **9**:1189, 1190
      radiation **10**:1394–1395
      X rays **12**:1713
   and evolution **2**:285; **5**:654–656; **7**:913
   frameshift **9**:1190
   in fruit flies **5**:599; **6**:746
   and genetic variation **1**:20
   homeotic **6**:746
   and jumping genes **8**:1086; **9**:1190
   and natural selection **5**:653, 654, 655;
      9:1191
      see also natural selection
   plant **9**:*1189*
      and selective breeding **11**:1481–1482
   point **9**:1190
   and polymorphism **4**:524
   somatic **9**:1189, 1190

Muttaburrasaurus **4**:*527*

mutualism *see* symbiosis, mutualism

myasthenia gravis **9**:1181

Mycobacterium tuberculosis **5**:591; **7**:948;
   8:1059, 1066; **12**:1648

Mycoplasmas (mollicutes) **10**:1323

mycorrhizae **3**:389; **6**:800; **9**:1187–1188;
   10:1322; **11**:1450, 1582;
   12:1590, 1640
   heather **6**:800; **7**:882
   orchid **9**:1241

Mycteria americana (American wood stork)
   12:1700

myelin **3**:362; **9**:*1200*

myelination **3**:355–356

myelin basic protein (MBP) **9**:1175

myeloblasts **2**:243

myeloid cells **11**:1559

myeloid tissue **2**:249

Mygalomorphae **11**:1546

Mylabris tiflensis (toxic oil beetle) **3**:404

myoblasts **9**:1183

myocardial infarction *see* heart attacks

Myocastor coypus (coypu/nutria) **10**:*1436*;
   11:1465; **12**:*1705*

myoclonus **11**:1511

myofibrils **9**:*1178*, 1181

myofibroblasts **10**:1402

myofilaments **9**:1181

myogenic contraction **9**:1179–1180

myoglobin **7**:913–914, 973; **9**:1183;
   10:1375, *1424*

myopia **5**:687

myosin **6**:726, 772; **9**:1178, *1181*, 1182;
   10:1377

Myotis spp. **4**:*573*, 574

myotomes **9**:1179

myriapods, evolution **3**:346

Myripristis violaceous (squirrelfish)
   3:403

Myrmecophaga tridactyla (giant anteater)
   1:*103*, 104; **4**:*445*; **12**:*1621*

mysticetes (Mysticeti) **12**:1707, 1708

Mytilus spp. (mussel) **8**:*1147*; **11**:1493

myxamebae **8**:1139–1140

myxoma virus **3**:391–392

Myxomycota **8**:1139–1140

N

nacre **8**:1149

NAD^+ **5**:702, *703*; **7**:994, 995

NADH **2**:159–160; **5**:618–619, 702;
   7:994, 995

$NADH_2$ **2**:*159*, 160

$NADP^+$, in photosynthesis **5**:618;
   10:1304

NADPH, in photosynthesis **5**:618;
   10:1304

Nageli, Karl von **8**:1107

Nagel, Thomas **3**:424

nails **7**:870–871

Naja naja (hooded cobra) **9**:1203

nalidixic acid **1**:109

Namib Desert, fog harvesters **4**:501

NANB ('non-A non-B') **7**:886

Nannopterum harrisi (Galápagos cormorant)
   6:754; **9**:1169

nanobots **10**:1434

naphthaleneacetic acid, 1- **7**:909

narcissistic personality disorder (ASPD)
   9:1284–*1285*

narcolepsy **11**:1511

narcotics **1**:23

narwhals **12**:1606

Nasalis larvatus (proboscis monkey)
   10:1374

nasutes **12**:*1612*

National Arboretum, U.S. **2**:*252*

National Center for Atmospheric Research
   (NCAR) **2**:155

National Oceanic and Atmospheric
   Administration (NOAA) **2**:155

national parks **3**:*425*, 426, 430
   problems with **3**:428–431
   see also reserves

Natrix natrix (grass snake) **9**:*1157*

naturalistic fallacy **1**:82; **2**:204

natural killer (NK) cells **7**:929, 938

natural selection 1:18, 20;
   9:1191–1194
   Darwin's theory **7**:912–913
      see also Darwinism
   leading to evolution **5**:653, 654, 655;
      7:912–913; **10**:1404

   see also evolution
   mutation and **5**:653, 654, 655; **9**:1191
   and sexual selection **11**:1483
      see also adaptation; competition;
         dimorphism and polymorphism

nature versus nurture
   and animal behavior **1**:83
   in child development **3**:359
   in human behavior **9**:1194
   in intelligence **7**:968
   and twins **12**:1655

nausea **4**:519; **11**:1565

Nautilus **4**:446; **5**:687; **8**:*1048*

NCAR (National Center for Atmospheric
   Research) **2**:155

Nd-YAG lasers **11**:1575

Neanderthals **7**:*912*, 916–917; **10**:1362

nearsightedness (myopia) **5**:687

nectar **6**:762; **12**:1694

Nectarinia reichenovi (golden-winged
   sunbird) **5**:*696*

Necturus maculosus (mud puppy) **10**:1418

Needham, John Turberville **2**:202

neem tree, extracts from **9**:1243, *1248*

Negaprion brevirostris (lemon shark)
   11:1490

nekton **4**:438; **10**:1312

Nelson, Ridley **4**:503

Nelumbo nucifera (Oriental lotus flower)
   11:*1478*

Nematocera **6**:743

nematocysts **7**:970, 980

Nematoda (Nemata; Nemalthelminthes)
   9:1196

nematode worms 1:90, 96; **7**:971;
   9:1195–1196
   causing disease **7**:946; **9**:1196, *1266*
   molting **9**:1157, 1195
   as plant pests **9**:1196; **10**:1321
   in the soil **9**:1195; **11**:1531

Nematomorpha **1**:96

Nemertea **1**:95

nemertines **1**:95; **7**:970–971

neocortex *see* brain, cerebral cortex

neo-Darwinism **2**:202; **4**:479; **5**:654

Neofelis nebulosa (clouded leopard)
   3:313, 324

Neolithic era **10**:1364

Neopilina **8**:1049

neoteny *see* paedomorphosis

Neotoma spp. (wood rat) **10**:1437

Nepenthes spp. **3**:316

Nephila clavipes **11**:1549

nephridia **5**:666

nephritis, in cats and dogs **1**:90

nephrons **5**:669, 671; **7**:989–990

nephrostomes **5**:666

Nereocystis luetkeana (bull kelp) **7**:987

nerve cells *see* neurons

nerve cord *see* spinal cord

nerve gases **9**:1183

nerve nets **2**:255, 258; **7**:982; **9**:*1205*

nerves *see* nervous systems, nerves

nervous systems 1:69; **9**:**1197–1205**

autonomic (ANS) **9**:1197

and the heart **9**:1180

and homeostasis **7**:899

smooth muscle contraction **9**:1179

central (CNS) **9**:1197

disorders **9**:1202–1204

see also prions

and the endocrine system **5**:610; **9**:1201

evolution **9**:1204–1205

and muscle contraction **9**:1182

myelin **3**:362; **9**:*1200*

nerve cells *see* neurons

nerve cord *see* spinal cord

nerve net **2**:255, 258; **7**:982; **9**:*1205*

nerves

communication **9**:1200–1201

glossopharyngeal **12**:1597

impulses **9**:1198–1200

optic **5**:687; **12**:1685

and touch **12**:1626

peripheral (PNS) **9**:1197

poisons **9**:*1203*

sympathetic, epinephrine and

norepinephrine release **5**:640, 641

synapses **1**:69; **9**:1200–1201

see also brain; neurotransmitters; reflexes

nesting 9:**1206–1209**

in birds *see* birds, nests

nettles, stinging **4**:483

neural networks **9**:1214

neural plate **5**:599

neural tube **2**:260

neurobiology **9**:1210–1211

Ramón y Cajal and **10**:1396

neurochemistry **9**:1212–1213

neurofibromatosis **11**:1504

neurohormones **5**:611

neurohypophysis **5**:611

neurons (nerve cells) **9**:1197–1201;

10:1308

association (interneurons) **9**:1198

function **9**:1198–1201

motor **9**:1198

myelination **3**:355–356

receptor **9**:1198

primary **12**:1595

sensory **9**:1198; **12**:1627

structure **2**:255–256; **9**:*1198*

see also synapses

neuropsychiatry **9**:1213, 1215

neuropsychology **3**:424; **9**:*1211–1212*

neuroscience 9:**1210–1215**

neuroses **8**:1113–*1114*; **10**:1389

Neurospora crassa **8**:1140

Neurospora spp. **9**:1225

neurotransmitters **2**:277–278; **9**:1182,

1183, 1200–1201

and aggression **1**:31, 32, 33

in the brain **9**:1212–1213

mind-altering drugs **1**:24; **4**:556

peptide (neuropeptides) **9**:1212–1213

and PMS **8**:1111

see also acetylcholine; dopamine

neurulation **5**:597, *599*

neutrophils **2**:239–*240*; **7**:*928*, 929,

937–938

nevi **10**:1359

Newell, Allen **7**:967

Newton, Isaac **9**:1235

newts *see* salamanders and newts

Ngorongoro Crater **11**:1464–1465

Nhandiroboideae **11**:1555

niches, ecological **3**:408, 409

Nicolson, Garth **3**:*331*

Nicotiana spp. (tobacco) **1**:51, 79; **8**:*1014*;

10:1337

nicotine **1**:51; **4**:555; **8**:1061

patches **8**:1092

nictitating membranes (third eyelids)

3:322, *323*; **5**:687; **8**:1052

night blindness **9**:1291

nighthawks **6**:775, 776

Nightingale, Florence **8**:*1102*

nightjars **6**:775

nightmares **8**:1115

nightshade, deadly **1**:*57*, 80; **9**:1291

night terrors **8**:1115

ninhydrin **1**:63

nitrates

from fertilizers **5**:718

and the nitrogen cycle **9**:1217, 1218

nitric acid, in acid rain **1**:16

nitrification **9**:1217–1218

Nitrobacter **9**:1217, 1218

nitrocellulose **3**:342

Nitrococcus **9**:1217–1218

nitrofurans **1**:108

nitrogen, in fertilizers **5**:718

nitrogenase **9**:1217

nitrogen cycle 9:**1216–1219**

nitrogen fixation **1**:17, 49; **3**:*352*; **5**:718;

8:1132; **9**:1217; **11**:*1531*

nonbiological **9**:*1219*

nitrogen mustard **3**:352; **4**:*538*

nitrogen oxides **2**:156

atmospheric **1**:*15*; **10**:1340

nitrogen dioxide **5**:625

nitric oxide **2**:156

nitrous oxide, for anesthesia **1**:76;

8:1102

Nitrosomonas **9**:1217–1218

nits **8**:1032–1033

NK (natural killer) cells **7**:929, 938

NOAA (National Oceanic and

Atmospheric Administration) **2**:155

nocireceptors **12**:1626

nocturnal life 9:**1220–1223**

courtship **4**:457

echolocation and hearing **9**:*1222*–1223

flowers opening at night **9**:1220

forest birds **6**:776

phasmids **8**:1017

sense of smell **9**:1223

vision **9**:*1221*–1222; **12**:*1686*, 1687

nodes, leaf **8**:1022, 1023

non-A non-B (NANB) **7**:886

enteric **7**:886

nondisjunction, chromosomal **3**:369

non-Hodgkin's lymphoma **3**:371;

8:1066

nonoxynol-9 **4**:441

Nopalea cochinillifera (cochineal cactus)

7:884

noradrenalin *see* epinephrine and

norepinephrine

norepinephrine *see* epinephrine and

norepinephrine

nori **7**:987

green **7**:987

North America

Midwest Dust Bowl **4**:*503*

species from South America **3**:409

Norwalk viruses **7**:948

nose

bacteria in the **2**:171

cartilage **3**:320

mucous membrane **9**:1171

see also smell

nosebleeds, treatment **12**:1619

Nothofagus sp. (southern beech) **9**:*1255*;

12:1610

notochord **3**:364

Notomis mantelli (takahe) **6**:756

Notophthalmus viridescens (red-spotted

newt) **11**:1456

Notoryctes spp. **4**:446

N. typhlops (pouched mole) **8**:1079

nucellus **11**:1475

nuclear accidents *see* power plants, nuclear

nuclear magnetic resonance *see* magnetic

resonance imaging

nuclear transfer (nuclear transplantation;

NT) technique **3**:383, *385*; **11**:1558

nuclear waste **10**:1344

nucleases

semisynthetic **2**:181

see also enzymes, restriction

nucleic acids **8**:1144; **10**:1428

discovery **4**:537

see also DNA; RNA

nucleoid **3**:331, 366

nucleoli **4**:476

nucleoplasm **3**:333

nucleoproteins **10**:1376

nucleosomes **3**:366

nucleotides **4**:535

nucleus **3**:333–334

freeze-etch microscopy of **4**:*473*

polar nuclei **5**:601

synergids **5**:590

nudibranchs (sea slugs) **4**:484; **7**:981

Numenius spp. (curlew) **12**:1628

Nuremberg (Nürnberg) Code **2**:189

nurse cells **5**:589

nursing **8**:*1102*

nuthatches **12**:*1609*

nutrias *see* coypus

nutrients

absorption by digestion **4**:518–519

plant **11**:1446–1447

nutrition 8:*1117*; **9**:**1224–1229**

amino acids **9**:1226

antioxidants **3**:*294*; **12**:1691

ß-carotene **3**:317

autotrophism and heterotrophism **5**:584;

9:1224–1226

a balanced diet **9**:1229

calories 2:**279–280**

carbohydrates **3**:301; **9**:1226, 1229

loading **3**:299

colostrum **5**:676; **7**:998

dioxins in food **4**:532

fats and oils **5**:690

and atherosclerosis **3**:377

fish oils **5**:690

fiber **3**:299, 342; **9**:1225

food coloring, carotenes **3**:317

iodine **9**:1227

iron **7**:973

macronutrients **9**:1226

malnutrition *see* deficiency-related

diseases

micronutrients **9**:1226–1227

and organic foods **9**:1244

poor **9**:1225

reducing diets **3**:300

and root crops **11**:1446

see also carbohydrates; fats and oils;

feeding; food; milk; proteins;

vitamins

nuts **6**:791, 792

Nycticebus coucang (slow loris) **10**:1366,

1367

Nyctimene albiventer (tube-nosed fruit bat)

2:173

Nygmia phaeorrhoea (brown-tail moth)

2:*270*

nymphs

dragonfly and mayfly **4**:551–552

grasshopper and cricket **7**:1004–1005

mantid **8**:1076

see also metamorphosis, incomplete

nystatin **1**:109

O

oak trees

mycorrhizae **9**:1187–1188

oak forests **12**:1608

oak trees *(continued)*
  transpiration **12**:1629
Obelia spp. **11**:1524
obsessive-compulsive disorders (OCDs)
  1:*122*; **8**:*1114*; **9**:1285
occipital lobes **2**:*259*, 261; **12**:1688
ocean floor 9:1230–1233
  chemosynthetic bacteria **3**:305; **5**:651;
    9:1233, 1237
  mining of phosphate **10**:1302
ocean habitats 9:1231, **1234–1239**
  continental shelves 4:437–439
  deep-sea **9**:1230–1231, 1237–1238
    see also fish, deep-sea
  oceans
    carbon in **3**:304–*305*
    creation **9**:1237
    currents **9**:1235–1236
    seawater composition **9**:1237
    tides **9**:1235
    upwellings **4**:438
    see also coral reef biomes; ocean floor;
      shore habitats
oceans, definition **9**:1234
ocelli **1**:140; **6**:743; **12**:1685
ocelots **3**:323, 324
Ochrolechia tartarea (cudbear) **8**:1035
octopuses **8**:*1149*
  "brain" **2**:255
  color change **4**:483; **7**:908
  larvae **8**:1150; **10**:1313–1314
  learning by **8**:1149
  movement **11**:1499, *1577*
  reproduction **8**:1150
  skeleton **11**:1499
  see also cephalopods; mollusks
Octopus vulgaris (common octopus) **8**:1149
Odobenus rosmarus (walrus) **3**:311
Odocoileus hemionus (mule deer) **3**:*350*, 351
Odonata **4**:550
odontocetes (Odontoceti) **12**:1707, 1708
Odontosyllis spp. **2**:216
  bioluminescence **2**:206
oil **5**:690
  see also fats and oils
oilbirds **4**:*574*
oil, environmental
  disposal **11**:1461; **12**:*1698*
  Gulf War oil disaster **12**:1698
  spills **2**:170; **5**:*623*; **9**:1239; **12**:*1698*
    yeasts and **12**:1715
oil palms **3**:382; **9**:1259
Olea europaea (olive tree) **11**:*1480*
oleic acid **5**:*689*, 691
olfaction *see* smell
Oligochaeta **1**:99
oligomanose **1**:*111*
oligosaccharides **3**:297
olives **6**:795
  oil **5**:*691*
olive trees, grafting **11**:*1480*
olms **11**:1454

omasum **4**:*515*; **11**:*1452*, 1453
ommatidia **1**:140; **5**:*688*; **9**:1221; **12**:1686
omnivores **5**:695; **6**:767; **8**:1072
  digestive system **4**:516
  jaws and teeth **3**:311; **4**:517; **7**:979
oncogenes **1**:35; **3**:294
  silencing **10**:1430
Oncorhynchus spp. **8**:1133–1134; **10**:1426,
    1427
Ondatra zibethicus (muskrat) **9**:1206–1207;
    10:1351
onions **2**:265; **8**:1013
On the Origin of Species (Darwin) **4**:479;
    5:653; **7**:912–913; **9**:1192, 1193
ontogeny
  and behavior **1**:84
  recapitulates phylogeny **5**:597
On the Use of the Parts of the Human Body
    (Galen) **1**:70
Onychophora **1**:97; **7**:972; **8**:1049;
    12:*1602*
Onymacris unguicularis **4**:501
oocytes **5**:587, 588–589
oogenesis **5**:587, *588*
  see also eggs
oogonia **5**:587–588
Oomycetes **8**:1140
Oomycota **10**:1381–1382
Oparin, Alexander **2**:181, 202
Oparin-Haldane theory **5**:651
operating rooms **11**:*1571*
  "smart" **10**:1433
Ophiophagus hannah (king cobra) **11**:1518
Ophiuroidea **4**:570
ophthalmoscopes **8**:1102
opiates **1**:23
opioid peptides **5**:614
Opisthocomus hoazin (hoatzin) **1**:134; **6**:777
opisthosoma **1**:130
opium **1**:23; **4**:*556*; **9**:1291
opossums **8**:1080; **11**:1569
  mouse **7**:997; **8**:1077
  Virginian/Northern **5**:*650*; **8**:1080;
    11:*1541*
opsin **12**:1685
optimality theory **4**:458
optimization problems **1**:86
Opuntia spp. **2**:270, 273
orange peel fungus **9**:*1186*
oranges **6**:795, 796
orangutans **7**:*870*; **10**:1367, 1368–*1369*,
    1370
orcas (killer whales) **10**:1350; **12**:1707,
    1708, 1709, 1710
Orchidaceae **9**:1161, 1240
orchids 9:1161, **1240–1241**
  bee or wasp mimicry **2**:*286*; **6**:761
  endangered **5**:609, 642
  epiphytic **9**:1161, 1240
  flower of the gods **5**:609
  Madagascan **3**:390
  mycorrhizae **9**:1241

pollination **3**:390; **6**:761
  root tubers **11**:1449
  saprophytic **9**:1161
orchil **8**:1035
Orcinus orca (killer whale) **10**:1350;
    12:1707, *1708*, 1709, 1710
Orconectes **3**:327
ore, extraction **8**:1132
organ of Corti **4**:561, *562*; **7**:874, *875*
organelles, cytoplasmic **3**:333–335, *336*
  evolution from prokaryotes **2**:168, 203;
    3:332, 392; **10**:1380; **11**:1581
organic foods 9:1242–1245
organic molecules **3**:303
organic products 9:1246–1249
organ networks, in Chinese medicine
    3:360
organochlorines *see* DDT; dioxins
organogenesis **5**:599–600
organophosphates **2**:195
organs, cryopreservation **4**:472–473
Origin of Species (Darwin) **4**:479; **5**:653;
    7:912–913; **9**:1192, 1193
Ormia depleta **2**:196
ornithine carbamoylase **12**:1667
ornithine cycle *see* urea cycle
ornithine transcarbamylase (OTC) **6**:807;
    12:1668
Ornithischia **4**:530–531
Ornithorhynchus anatinus see platypuses,
    duckbill
Orobanche spp. **12**:1632
Orphyrys apifera (bee orchid) **2**:286
orrisroot **12**:1650
orthogenesis **7**:912
orthomyxoviruses **7**:*951*
Orthonectida **1**:95
Orthoptera, *see also* cockroaches;
    grasshoppers and crickets; mantids
Oryctolagus cuniculus (European rabbit)
    3:391–392; **8**:*1072*; **10**:*1353*, 1392
oryxes, Arabian **12**:1725
Oryza sativa see rice
Oscillatoria bacteria **2**:169
oscilloscopes **12**:1627
Oscines **9**:1273
osculum **11**:1552, 1553
osmoregulation **5**:671–672
  in fish **5**:*669*
osmosis **11**:1458–1459
  fish and **5**:*669*; **6**:732; **7**:902
  and water flow in plants **12**:1631, 1670
ospreys **2**:*236*
  effects of DDT **4**:481
  feet **5**:698
  nests **2**:236
ossification, endochondral **3**:319
Osteichthyes **6**:730, 734; **12**:1672–1673
  see also fish, bony
osteoarthritis **1**:136; **7**:870
  in cats and dogs **1**:90
osteoblasts **2**:248, 249; **3**:319

osteoclasts **2**:249, 250
osteocytes **2**:248–249, *250*; **11**:1500
osteomalacia *see* rickets
osteons **2**:*248*
osteopathy 1:57; **9**:1250
  see also chiropractic
osteoporosis **2**:250, *277*, 278; **8**:*1110*;
    11:1502
  in astronauts **11**:1533
osteosarcomas **3**:294
ostracoderms **6**:730; **12**:1672
ostriches **5**:698; **6**:*755*
Ostrom, John **4**:529
Otariidae **3**:311
Otocyon megalotis (bat-eared fox) **4**:540
otoliths **4**:561
otosclerosis **7**:875
otters **11**:*1578*
  sea **4**:439; **7**:*988*
    cracking shells **3**:*308*
Ouija boards **9**:*1262*
Out of Africa hypothesis **7**:917
ova **5**:587
  see also eggs
ovarian cycle **8**:1108–*1109*
ovarian failure, premature **5**:711
ovaries **10**:*1412*, *1413*
  egg cells **5**:715; **8**:1108
  hormone production **5**:613
  and the ovarian cycle **8**:1108–*1109*
  plant
    angiosperm **6**:759
    position **6**:759
  premature ovarian failure **5**:711
ovenbirds **6**:*776*
Ovibos moschatus (musk ox) **10**:1333;
    12:*1653*, 1654
ovipositor **12**:1592
Ovis spp. (sheep) **4**:*460*, 544
ovulation **2**:219; **5**:715; **8**:1109, 1111;
    10:1413
  and cervical mucus **9**:1172
  disorders **8**:1110
  induced **10**:1352
  prediction **4**:442
Owen, Richard **4**:527; **5**:653
owl parrots **6**:755
owls **2**:234, *235*, 236–237
  barn **2**:237; **9**:*1158*, 1222
  burrowing **9**:1206
  elf **2**:236
  feet **5**:698
  forest **6**:776
  great horned **2**:237
  hearing **2**:235
  little **11**:1569
  nocturnal **9**:*1220*, 1221, 1222
  saw-whet **9**:*1220*
  songs **3**:402
  suburban **11**:1569
  tawny **3**:402; **9**:1221
  vision **2**:234–235; **12**:1687

oxaloacetic acid/oxaloacetate 7:995;
  10:1305
oxen, musk oxen 10:1333; 12:*1653*
oxidation 5:617
oxidation-reduction (redox) reactions
  5:618, 700–701; 7:996
oxpeckers 11:*1579*
oxygen 9:1251–1253
  atmospheric
    and combustion 9:*1251*, 1253
    and the origins of life on Earth 6:801;
      10:1304; 12:1658
  cycle 9:1252
  debt 3:300; 9:1183, 1252
  in evolution 12:1658
  gaseous exchange 9:*1252*–1253
    countercurrent 10:1424
  hyperbaric 3:400; 9:1176
  inhibiting photosynthesis 10:1305
  metabolic oxygen consumption
    2:279–280
  in plants 9:1253
  structure and properties 9:1251–1252
  transport by respiratory pigments
    see hemocyanin; hemoglobin;
      myoglobin
  variation of heart rate with oxygen
    requirements 9:1252
  in water, Biological Oxygen Demand
    (BOD) 7:1001
oxyhemoglobin 8:1056; 9:1253
oxyradicals 1:*34*
oxytocin 7:903, 906, 953, 998; 10:1414
Oxyura jamaicensis (ruddy duck) 12:1700
Oxyuranus microlepidotus (taipan) 11:1518
oystercatchers 12:1700
oysters
  farming of 1:124, 125
  fishing for 8:1149
ozone 2:157; 5:625; 10:1304
  depletion 2:*157*; 5:623, 625; 10:1341
    and coral reefs 4:449
  and evolution of life on land 12:1658
  tropospheric and ground-level 1:16;
    5:625; 10:1340

P

pacemaker
  artificial 2:214; 7:879; 8:*1039*, 1092;
    12:1636
  biological (sinoatrial node) 7:879;
    9:1180
Pachycephalosaurs 4:531
Pacinian corpuscles 12:1626
paddlefish 6:734
paddle worms 7:*971*
paedogenesis *see* paedomorphosis
paedomorphosis 4:544; 7:1006; 9:*1256*;
  11:1455
  in cave-dwelling animals 3:327
  and dog breed selection 4:541
Paget's disease 2:181

pain 12:1627
  back 3:320
    treatment 1:57
  natural painkillers 5:614
  reflex 10:1398
paintings, cave 10:*1363*–1364
pair bonding 4:456
Palaemonias ganteri (Kentucky cave shrimp)
  3:326
Palaeocoma egertoni 6:*784*
Palaeotringa 12:1701
paleobiogeography 9:1254, *1257*
paleobiology 9:1254–1257
paleobotany 2:254
paleoecology 9:1254
palisade layer 8:*1024*
Palmae 9:1258
  see also palms
Palmeria palmata (dulse) 7:987
palmitic acid 5:*689*
palms 2:193; 9:1160, *1161*, 1258–1259;
  12:1638
  carnauba wax 9:1259; 12:1702
  coconut 6:725; 9:1160, 1259
  date 6:758, 794; 8:1026; 9:*1258*, 1259
    pollen 10:1336
  leaves 8:1022; 9:1258
  oil 3:382; 9:1259
  rattan 9:1259
  sago 9:1259
  talipot 10:1318
Palpigradi 11:1469
pampas 2:210
Panama Canal 9:1267
Panama, isthmus of 3:409
Panax spp. (ginseng) 7:888; 11:*1445*, 1446
pancreas 9:1260–1261
  anatomy 9:*1260*
  artificial 2:215
  cells 2:*180*
  CT scans 4:475
  endocrine function 5:612; 9:1260–1261
    see also glucagon; insulin
  evolution 9:1261
  exocrine function (digestive enzymes)
    4:518, 522; 5:677; 9:1260
  histology 7:*895*; 9:*1261*
  islets of Langerhans 5:612; 7:*895*, 904,
    964; 9:1260, *1261*
  replacement 12:1634
  nonhuman 9:1261
  transplants 12:1634
pancreatic duct 9:1260
pancreatitis 9:1261
pancreozymin 4:522
pandas
  giant 3:308–309; 5:*656*; 12:1609
    captive breeding 12:1725
    fertility 5:712
  red 3:309
pandemics, influenza 7:951
Pandinus spp. 1:*133*; 11:*1469*

Pandion heliaetus (osprey) 2:*236*; 4:481;
  5:698
Pandionidae 2:236
Pandulus borealis (deep-sea prawn) 1:*106*
Pangaea 4:527
pangolins 1:103; 4:445, 486
panic attacks 1:122; 10:1301
panic disorder (PD) 8:1113
Panorpa spp. 8:1084
panspermia, theory of 5:651–652, 683
Pan spp. *see* chimpanzees
Panthera spp. 3:313, 323–324
  P. atrox 3:324
  P. leo see lions
  P. pardus (leopard) 3:*313*, 324
  P. tigris see tigers
  P. uncia (snow leopard) 3:*323*, 324;
    7:*997*
panthers, Florida 3:323; 10:1343
panting 11:1506; 12:*1622*
Panulirus argus (spiny lobster) 1:*13*;
  4:469
Papanicolaou, George 4:477
Papaver spp. 2:*253*; 9:*1170*
paper, recycling 12:1696
papermaking 3:342
Papilio machaon (common swallowtail)
  2:*267*, 284
Papilionoidea 8:1028–1029
papillae, on the tongue 12:*1597*, 1621
Papio spp.
  P. hamadryas (hamadryas baboon) 1:*86*
  P. sphinx (mandrill) 10:1368; 12:1594
Pap smear test 4:477
Parabuteo unicinctus (Harris's hawk) 2:235
Paracelsus 8:1100; 9:1289
parachuting 6:749
paraffinoids 6:762
parakeets 3:401
paralysis
  infantile *see* poliomyelitis
  movement of paralyzed limbs 2:213
paralytic ileus 11:1574
Paramecium spp. 10:*1382*
  competition 3:408
  digestion 4:511
paramyxoviruses 12:1683
paranoid personality disorder (paranoia)
  9:1284; 10:1388
paraphyly 12:1602
parapineal gland 5:613
parapsychology 9:1262–1263
Parasaurolophus 4:531
parasites 5:695; 9:1264–1268;
  11:1579–1580
  adaptations 9:1267–1268
  of bats 3:328
  blood flukes *see* schistosomiasis

brood 7:963
coevoltionary response to 3:390; 9:1267
crustaceans as 4:467–468
disrupt instinctive patterns 7:963
ecto- and endoparasites 9:1264–1265;
  11:1579–1580
flies as 6:746
flukes *see* flukes
fungi as 6:800; 12:1670
in history 9:1267
hookworms 1:90
host-specific 9:1265
intermediate hosts 9:1268
kleptoparasitism 11:1472
leeches 1:100
lice 8:1032–1033
  carrying diseases 7:946, 950; 8:1032;
    9:1267
  fish 4:467–468
life cycles 9:1265–1266
nematode worms as 9:1195–1196
neutral parasitism 9:1266
nocturnal 9:1222
obligate and facultative 9:1265
of plants 9:*1265*
plants as 9:*1265*; 10:1321; 12:*1632*
self-protection 9:1268
social, slave-making ants 1:120
tapeworms *see* tapeworms
  see also fleas; mites; ticks
parasitoids 2:195–196; 5:695
parasomnias 8:1115
parathyroid gland, hormones 2:278;
  5:612; 7:903
parathyroid hormone (parathormone)
  2:278; 5:612; 7:903
Paratrechina longicornis 7:976
Paré, Ambroise 8:1099–1100; 11:1570
parenchyma 8:1024; 11:1448, 1560
parental care 10:1352
  is altruistic 1:58
parietal lobes 2:*259*
parkinsonism 4:495
Parkinson, James 2:261; 4:497
Parkinson's disease 2:261; 4:494–497;
  8:1092; 9:1204, 1213; 11:1558
parks, national *see* national parks
Parmelia saxatilis (crottle lichen) 8:*1035*
Parnassius apollo (apollo butterfly)
  2:186
parrots 6:*778*; 12:*1642*
  feet 5:698
parsnips 11:1449
parthenocarpy 6:792
Parthenocissus spp.
  P. quinquefolia (Virginia creeper) 3:*380*;
    11:1450
  P. tricuspidata (Boston ivy) 8:*1149*

Bold words with bold page numbers indicate complete articles; bold numbers preceding colons are volume numbers; numbers following colons indicate page numbers; italic page numbers refer to illustrations or other graphics.

parthenogenesis 4:469; 10:1407
  in insects 4:552; 8:1018; 10:1407
  in rotifers 10:1313
particulates, atmospheric 2:154, 155–156;
  5:625
Parus major (great tit) 1:29, 85; 9:1274
Paruvoctus mousiness 9:1223
parvoviruses 6:807; 12:1683
Passer domesticus (house sparrow)
  9:1274–1275
Passeriformes *see* birds, perching
passerines *see* birds, perching
Pasteur, Louis 9:1269–1270
  and antisepsis 8:1101, 1128
  and diseases of silkworms 9:1269–1270
  and fermentation 2:226; 5:629; 8:1127,
    1128; 9:1269; 12:1715
  and germ theory 8:1128; 9:1269
  and the origins of microorganisms 1:116;
    2:202; 5:652; 8:1127–1128
  and pasteurization 1:115; 2:226–227;
    6:765; 8:1128; 9:1269
  and vaccines/immunization 1:107;
    7:934–935; 8:1102; 9:1270;
    12:1678
pasteurization 1:115; 2:226–227; 6:765;
  8:1128; 9:1269, 1270
Patau syndrome 3:369
Patella cochlear (limpet) 3:408
paternity testing, blood groups 2:245
pathophysiology 10:1308
Patient Self-determination Act (1991),
  U.S. 5:646
patriotism 1:60
Pauling, Linus 4:462
Pavlov, Ivan 2:261; 3:411–412; 7:961;
  8:1020; 9:1271–1272; 10:1383, 1398
Pavo cristatus (Indian peacock) *see* peacocks
Payen, Anselme 5:629
PBN (phenylbutyl nitrone) 1:36
PCR *see* polymerase chain reaction
peaches, trees, diseases 10:1321
peacocks 4:459; 5:656
  tail 2:228; 4:525; 11:1483–1484
peanuts 8:1028
  Aspergillus on 11:1462
  growing 11:1530
peanut worms 1:96
pearls 8:1149
pea(s) 8:1028
  blackeye 8:1028
  climbing 3:380; 8:1027
  germination 12:1647
  and Mendelian genetics 8:1106–1107;
    11:1479–1480
  see also legumes
peat
  bogs containing 11:1532
  human remains in 9:1166
pebrine 9:1269–1270
pecans 6:792
pecking-order 11:1523

pectoralis majora 6:748
Pedetes capensis (African spring hare)
  10:1437
Pediculus spp. (body louse) 7:946, 950;
  8:1032, 1033
pedipalps 1:130; 11:1469, 1546, 1547
pedogenesis *see* paedomorphosis
Pelagophycus (elk kelp) 7:987
Pelecaniformes 11:1471–1472
Pelecanus spp. *see* pelicans
pelicans 11:1472–1473, 1494
  brown 12:1706
pellagra 4:488
Pelletier, Pierre-Joseph 1:50–51; 8:1103
pelvic girdle 11:1503
pelvic inflammatory disease 5:712
Penfield, Wilder 5:637
penguins 1:22; 6:754; 11:1473, 1474
  countercurrent heat exchange system
    12:1618
  emperor 6:754; 11:1473, 1474
  swimming 6:753; 11:1578
penicillin 1:108; 2:164; 6:742, 799;
    11:1571
  allergy to 1:110
  bacteria resistant to 1:110
  discovery 1:108; 6:741–742; 8:1103,
    1131, 1138; 9:1290; 11:1461
  manufacture 1:109
  mode of action 1:109; 5:630; 6:799;
    9:1291
Penicillium spp.
  in cheesemaking 6:763
  and penicillin 1:109, 110; 6:799;
    8:1138; 9:1290; 11:1461
penis
  human 10:1409, 1412
  of insects 8:1083
penstocks 10:1426
peppers 1:51
  Brazilian 5:649
pepsin 4:516, 517, 518, 522; 11:1564
pepsinogen 4:517, 518
peptide bonds 1:63
peptides, opioid 5:614
peptidoglycan 3:298
peramorphosis 9:1256
perception 3:393–394; 10:1386
  see also cognition; intelligence
perch, Nile 2:186
perching birds 5:697; 9:1273–1276
percutaneous transluminal coronary
  angioplasty (PTCA) 11:1574
perennial plants 1:101; 9:1277–1278
  herbaceous 4:548; 9:1277
  monocarpic 9:1278
  woody 9:1277–1278
    dormancy 4:547
  see also trees
perfume 11:1515
perianth segments 6:759
pericarp 6:792

perichondrium 2:248, 249; 3:320
pericycle 11:1448
peridontitis 12:1605
periods *see* menstrual cycle, menstruation
Periophthalmus barbarus (mudskipper) 6:728
periosteum 2:248, 249
Peripatopsis spp. 12:1602
Peripatus 8:1049–1050
periphyton 5:642
Perissodactyla *see* ungulates, odd-toed
peristalsis 4:513, 517, 521; 9:1179;
  11:1564
periwinkles 1:80; 4:483; 11:1493
permaculture 9:1279–1282
permafrost 2:208; 12:1652
Perodicticus potto (potto) 10:1366, 1370
peroxides 1:116–117
peroxisomes 3:335
persistent vegetative state (waking coma)
  3:399; 5:646; 8:1038, 1040
personality 10:1385, 1386
personality disorders 8:1115;
  9:1283–1286
  obsessive-compulsive 1:122; 8:1114;
    9:1285
Persoz, François 5:629
pertussis (whooping cough) 7:948
  vaccine 7:935
Perutz, Max 2:246
pesticides 1:41; 2:195; 9:1247,
  1287–1288; 11:1532
  biological/biorational (natural/organic)
    9:1244, 1247
    neem 9:1243, 1248
  biomagnification of 4:481; 9:1280,
    1287
  harmful to birds 2:235–236, 237; 5:584,
    622–623, 680; 9:1275, 1287
  harmful to humans 5:626; 9:1243, 1288
  history of 9:1288
  resistance to 1:19; 4:480–481; 9:1193,
    1247
  see also DDT; herbicides
pests 10:1320–1321
  beetle 2:178
  cockroaches 3:387, 388
  control 10:1346–1347
    using viruses 12:1679
    see also biological control; pesticides
  nematode 9:1196
  phasmids as 8:1017
  plants as *see* weeds
  resistance to pesticides 1:19; 4:480–481
  rodent 10:1437
PET *see* positron emission tomography
petals 6:757
Petaurista elegans (spotted giant flying
  squirrel) 10:1436–1437
"Pete Marsh" 9:1166
petioles 8:1022
petrels 11:1473
  blue 11:1473

flight 6:752
  Wilson's storm 11:1474
Peyer's patches 8:1065
PGAL-dehydrogenase 5:702
pH 1:16; 11:1531
  optimum for enzymes 5:631, 632
Phaeophyta 1:47–48; 10:1381
phages *see* bacteriophages
phagocytes 7:937–938; 11:1551
  chemotaxis 12:1647
  see also macrophages; neutrophils
phagocytosis 2:240; 3:336, 337; 5:693;
  7:929, 938
phalangers, flying 4:446
phalanges 11:1503
phalaropes 5:656; 12:1700
pharmacology 8:1090; 9:1289–1292
  see also drugs
pharming 2:224
Pharomachrus mocino (quetzal) 6:777
pharynx 10:1420; 12:1621–1622
Phascolarctos cinereus see koalas
Phaseolus spp. 8:1028; 10:1316
Phasmida *see* leaf insects and walking sticks
phenol coefficient test 1:117
phenols 1:116
phenotypes, polymorphism 4:524–525
phenylalanine 8:1123, 1124
phenylbutyl nitrone (PBN) 1:36
phenylketonuria (PKU) 8:1123, 1124;
  10:1358
phenylthiocarbamide, tasting 12:1597
pheromones 3:404; 5:677;
  9:1293–1294; 11:1515–1516
  alarm signals 4:485; 11:1515
    in ants 1:119
  apple maggot fly 3:402
  in butterflies and moths 1:106;
    2:269–270; 4:460; 12:1596
    the silk moth 2:270; 4:460; 9:1288, 1293
  used in pest control 9:1288
  communication with other species
    (allomones) 5:677
  courtship 4:460
  human 9:1294
  for pest control 2:196
  primer 9:1294
  social insect
    ant 12:1647
    honeybee 9:1294; 11:1524
  to fight Dutch elm disease 9:1294
phi phenomenon 10:1384
phloem 4:509; 8:1024–1025; 11:1448,
  1561
phobias 1:121–122; 8:1113–1114;
  10:1301
  agoraphobia 10:1301
  arachnophobia 3:414; 5:663
  social 8:1114; 10:1301
  treatment 1:122; 3:414; 10:1301
Phoca hispida saimensis (Saimaa ringed seal)
  3:311

Phocidae **3**:311

phoebe, eastern **2**:193; **12**:*1718*

Phoenicopterus spp. *see* flamingos

Phoenix spp. *see* palms, date

Phoronida **1**:96

phosphates, pollutants **10**:1302

phosphenes **12**:1688

phosphoenol pyruvate **10**:1305

phosphoenolpyruvic acid **8**:1023

phosphofructokinase **5**:702

phosphoglucomutase (PGM) **6**:774

phosphoglycerate, in carbon fixation **10**:1304

phosphoglycerate kinase **5**:*618*

phosphoglyceric acid, 3- **8**:1023

phospholipase **9**:1260

phospholipids **5**:690–691

in the plasma membrane **3**:*331*

see also plasma membranes

phosphonomycin **5**:630

phosphoproteins **10**:1376

phosphorus 10:1302

in fertilizers **5**:718

see also phosphates

phosphorylation

oxidative *see* electron transfer/oxidative phosphorylation

photosynthetic (photophosphorylation) **10**:1304, 1306

substrate **8**:1118

Photinus spp. **3**:404

photoautotrophs **5**:584; **9**:1224

Photobacterium **2**:205

Photoblepharon palpebratus **2**:205

photochemical reactions **2**:156

photocytes **2**:205

photons **10**:1394

photoperiodism **2**:217

plant **6**:759; **10**:1317

photophores **2**:205, 206, 207

photophosphorylation (photosyntheic phosphorylation) **10**:1304, 1306

photoradiation therapy **11**:1575

photoreceptors **5**:685, *688*

in the retina **5**:686; **12**:1685

photorespiration **10**:1305

photosynthesis 3:298–299; **5**:616, 617; **8**:1023; **10**:*1303–1306*

anoxygenic **10**:1303

in bacteria **3**:337

C3 (Calvin) cycle **8**:1023; **10**:1304–1305

C4 (Hatch-Slack) cycle **8**:1023

and the carbon cycle **3**:303

carbon fixation **10**:1304–1305

and chloroplasts **10**:1303–1304

and crassulacean acid metabolism (CAM) plants **2**:273; **10**:*1305*–1306

cytochromes **7**:973

dark reactions **3**:298–299; **10**:1303, *1304*

energy pathways **5**:617–618

equation **10**:1303

and evolution **10**:1304

first development of **10**:1304

inhibited by oxygen **10**:1305

iron-containing enzymes **7**:973

light reactions **3**:298; **5**:617–618; **10**:1303, *1304*

photophosphorylation **10**:1304, 1306

pigments **5**:616; **10**:1306

carotenoids **3**:317; **10**:1306

see also chlorophyll

for primary production **6**:767

phototaxis **12**:1647

phototrophs **8**:1117

phototropism **10**:1316, 1317; **12**:*1646*

negative **10**:1316

Photuris spp. **2**:206, 217; **3**:404

phrenology **5**:662; **9**:1214

Phthiraptera **8**:1032

Phthirus pubis (pubic louse; crabs) **8**:1033

phycobilins **10**:1306

phycocyanin **7**:986

Phycodurus eques (sea dragon) **6**:732

phyletic change **6**:784

Phyllidae (leaf insects) *see* leaf insects and walking sticks

Phyllium bioculatum (Japanese leaf insect) **8**:*1015*

Phyllobates spp. (poison dart frog) **6**:788

Phyllodactylus marmoratus (marbled gecko) **8**:1052

Phyllodoca lamelligera (paddle worm) **7**:*971*

Phyllophaga spp. (June bug) **2**:178

phylloxera, grapevine infestation **6**:794

Phylogenetic Systematics (Hennig) **12**:1602

phylogeny, from DNA **5**:654

Physalia physalis (Portuguese man-of-war) **7**:*983*; **9**:1182; **11**:1524, 1580

Physeter catodon (sperm whale) **4**:572

physiology 10:*1307–1308*

plant **2**:253

phytoalexins **1**:117; **7**:932

phytochromes **2**:217; **6**:759; **10**:1317

Phytophthora infestans (late/potato blight) **8**:*1138*; **10**:1321, *1322*, 1382

phytoplankton *see* plankton, phytoplankton

phytoplasmas **10**:1323

phytotherapy *see* herbal medicine

Piaget, Jean **3**:354, 356, 394

Piaget's theory **3**:354–355

Picea spp. *see* spruces

pickling **5**:701; **6**:764

picornaviruses **12**:*1682*, 1683

piezoelectric effect **12**:1657

pigeons **6**:776; **11**:1569

crop milk **7**:997

digestive system **4**:*514*

passenger **5**:659; **11**:1522

in towns **12**:1665

pigmentation 10:*1309–1311*

plant **6**:761–762

carotenes 3:317; **10**:1306

dyes from lichens **8**:1035

fucoxanthin **7**:986

phycobilins **10**:1306

phycocyanin **7**:986

phytochromes **2**:217; **6**:759; **10**:1317

in seaweeds **7**:986

see also chlorophyll

skin **10**:1310; **11**:1508

in evolution **9**:1227

loss **10**:1310

see also coloration

pigs

diseases **1**:*88*

genetically modified **1**:*92*

stressed **11**:*1567*

teats **7**:*998*

wild **12**:1606, *1610*

pike **6**:732

long-nosed (garpike) **7**:*978*

pili **2**:170

pill, the **4**:441, 443

Piltdown Man hoax **6**:782; **7**:917

pimagedine **1**:36

pineal gland

and biorhythms **2**:217–218

in fish **6**:731

hormones **5**:613

pineal/parietal eyes ('third eye') **8**:1052; **10**:1415, 1416

pineapples **6**:792

pines **3**:416

bristlecone **12**:*1638*, 1640

cones **3**:415

leaves **8**:*1026*, 1027

life cycle **3**:*416*

lodgepole **3**:417

mycorrhizae **11**:1450

needles **8**:*1026*

decay **11**:1460

of the taiga **12**:1591

white **4**:*492*; **12**:1639

Wollemi **3**:417

Pinguicula spp. (butterwort) **3**:316

Pinguinus (Alca) impennis (great auk) **6**:*754*; **12**:1654

Pinker, Stephen **5**:662

pinnae **7**:872

Pinnipedia **3**:308, 311

pinocytosis **3**:336, *337*

Pinus spp. *see* pines

pioneer plants **12**:1643

Pipa pipa (Surinam toad) **6**:789

pipefish **11**:1484

Piper nigrum (pepper vine) **3**:380

Pipistrellus pipistrellus (pipistrelle bat) **2**:176; **7**:*873*

piranhas **3**:*401*; **6**:732

pistils **6**:758, 759, 791

Pisum sativum see pea(s)

pitcher plants **3**:*316*, 379; **8**:1027; **10**:1317

pith **11**:1560

pit organs **11**:1518

Pitts, H. and J. **1**:39

pituitary gland **2**:166, 218; **5**:610, *611*, *613*; **7**:903

antidiuretic hormone (ADH) **5**:671; **7**:990

endorphin production **5**:614

hypothalamus-pituitary connection **5**:*611*, 709; **7**:900; **8**:1108

and the menstrual cycle **8**:1108

and reproduction

lactation **7**:998

role in childbirth **7**:*953*

stress and the **11**:1566

see also growth hormone

PKU (phenylketonuria) **8**:*1123*, 1124; **10**:1358

placebo effect **9**:1292

placenta **8**:1074; **10**:1353, *1356*, 1414

choriovitelline **10**:1352

development **11**:1557

expulsion after birth **10**:1359

hormone production **5**:613

placoderms **6**:730

Placozoa **1**:94

plagiogravitropism **12**:1646

plagiotropism **12**:1646

plague **10**:1438

and biological warfare **2**:198

bubonic **6**:740; **7**:950; **8**:1063; **11**:1569

fleas and **6**:740

pneumonic **7**:950

plagues, of locusts **5**:*620*; **7**:959; **9**:1294

plains, soils **11**:1530

planarians *see* flatworms, planarian

plankton 10:*1312–1314*

bioluminescent **2**:207

in food webs **9**:1231

phytoplankton **1**:48; **3**:305; **4**:438; **9**:1236; **10**:*1312–1313*

algal blooms **1**:48; **7**:*1001*; **10**:1302

diatoms **8**:*1130*; **10**:*1312*, 1313

dinoflagellates **10**:1313

in food webs **6**:767; **9**:1231

freshwater **1**:48

marine **1**:48; **10**:1312–1313

red tides **10**:1347

and pollution **10**:1314

zooplankton **3**:305; **4**:438; **10**:1312, *1313*–1314

copepods **1**:*141*; **10**:1314; **11**:1492

Plantago media (hoary plantain) **7**:*890*

plantains, hoary **7**:*890*

Bold words with bold page numbers indicate complete articles; bold numbers preceding colons are volume numbers; numbers following colons indicate page numbers; italic page numbers refer to illustrations or other graphics.

plants 10:1325–1328

aging (senescence) **1**:36; **10**:1319

alarm signals between **10**:1317

alkaloids **1**:50

anatomy **1**:69–70; **2**:253

annual 1:101–102; **11**:1476

behavior 10:1315–1319

timing process **10**:1317

see also photoperiodism; tropisms

and taxes

biennial 1:101; **2**:179

carnivorous *see* carnivorous plants

cells **3**:*335*–336, *337*

classification **10**:1326–1328

colonization of the land by **11**:1581

communication between **3**:404

death **1**:36

desert **2**:211; **4**:*499*–500; **11**:*1459*;

12:1617

cacti and succulents **2**:273

diseases 10:1320–1324

bacterial **10**:1322–1323

fungal **6**:800; **10**:*1320, 1321–1322*

human control of **10**:*1323*

mollicutes **10**:1323

subviral **10**:1324

viral **10**:1323–*1324*; **12**:1678, 1683

domestication **4**:545–*546*

economic importance **10**:*1328*

see also crops

egg cells **5**:590

evolution *see* evolution, plant

excretion in **5**:670

gas exchange **10**:*1424*; **12**:1629

growth

acid rain and **1**:16

determinate and indeterminate **1**:36

healing of tissues **10**:1316–1317

hormones **7**:908–*909*

life cycles **10**:1325

long-day and short-day **2**:217

medicinal *see* drugs, from plants;

herbal medicine

mountain **9**:1169–*1170*

native or exotic? **2**:194

nonvascular **12**:1670

perennial *see* perennial plants

as pests *see* weeds

as primary producers **6**:766

reflexes in **10**:1397

senescence **10**:1319

stress in **11**:1567

structure, carbohydrates and **3**:298

study of *see* botany

in suburbia **11**:1568

thermoregulation **12**:1617

vascular system *see* vascular systems,

plant

plasma **2**:238, 241; **4**:554

plasma cells **7**:938

plasma membranes

electrical potential across **10**:1308

inhibition of function of **1**:108–109

structure **3**:*331*–332, 362

plasmids **1**:109–110; **3**:337; **8**:1145

and genetically modified foods **6**:*811*

plasmin **2**:242

plasminogen **2**:242

plasmodesmata **8**:1025; **12**:1631, 1683

Plasmodium spp. **7**:946

and malaria **5**:621; **6**:744; **9**:1265

plastics

environmental **10**:1344

recycling **12**:1696

plastids **8**:1023

evolution **2**:168

see also chloroplasts

plastron **12**:1623

Platalea spp. (spoonbills) **5**:648; **10**:1311

Platanista minor (Indus River dolphin)

12:1709

Platanus occidentalis (sycamore) **9**:*1278*

platelets **2**:241, 243

and blood clotting **2**:241–242

disorders **2**:247

Plateosaurus **4**:529–530

plate tectonics **9**:1170; **12**:1719

Plato **3**:422

platyfish **11**:1485–1486

Platyhelminthes **1**:95; **5**:715; **7**:970

see also flatworms; flukes; tapeworms

platypuses

duckbill **2**:204; **8**:1050; **9**:1162, *1163*

mammary glands **5**:676–677; **7**:997

Platyrrhini **10**:1365, 1367–1368

Platysaurus intomedius (flat lizard) **8**:1052

play 3:359; **10**:1329–1330

"playing dead" **2**:*206*; **8**:1017, 1080

Pleocotus auritus **4**:*571*

Plethodontidae **11**:1455

pleuropneumonia **1**:88

Pliny the Elder **2**:200; **5**:637

plovers **11**:1471, 1580; **12**:1699

black-bellied **12**:1654

golden **12**:*1700*

migration **8**:1136; **12**:*1700*

see also killdeer

plows **1**:*37*, 39

plumule **11**:1476

Plutchik, Robert **5**:603

Pluvialis spp. **8**:1136; **12**:*1700*

PMS (premenstrual syndrome)

8:1110–1111

pneumatophores **3**:416

pneumonia **8**:1059

Poaceae *see* grasses

podocarps **3**:416

Poecilia reticulata (guppy) **1**:*127*

pogonophores **1**:96

poikilotherms **3**:396; **7**:891;

8:*1122*–1123; **10**:1415;

12:1616–1617

Poincaré, Henri **3**:347

poison ivy **1**:53

poison oak **1**:53; **4**:483

poisons **1**:51

from legumes **8**:1029

see also poisons; toxins

polar body **5**:589

polar regions 10:1331–1334; **12**:1618

plants **10**:*1332*

poliomyelitis (polio; infantile paralysis)

3:388

vaccines **1**:92; **5**:*635*; **7**:934; **8**:*1129*;

11:1457

causing polio **7**:935

virus **8**:*1129*; **12**:1682

pollen **1**:78; **6**:*761*, 762; **10**:1326,

1335–1336

fossilized **6**:783

pollen tubes **6**:760

pollination 10:1335–1338, 1408

angiosperm **1**:78–79; **6**:761

and animal/plant coevolution **2**:268;

3:389–390; **6**:757–758, 760;

10:*1336*, 1337

cross-pollination **1**:78; **6**:761; **10**:1335

fertilization **6**:760

see also fertilization, plant

formation of pollen grains

10:1335–1336

self-pollination **1**:78; **6**:761; **10**:1335

using animals **1**:78; **6**:761, 762; **10**:1318

bats **9**:1220

birds **1**:78–79

insects **6**:761; **7**:890; **9**:1240;

10:*1335*, 1336–1337; **12**:1693

using mimicry, in the bee orchid **2**:*286*;

6:761

using water **6**:761, 762; **10**:1338

using wind **1**:78; **6**:761; **7**:890; **9**:1241;

10:*1338*

pollution 10:1339–1344

air **2**:156; **10**:*1340*–1341;

12:*1664–1665*

smogs **2**:156; **10**:1340

see also atmosphere

causing global warming

see global warming

chemical

dioxins **4**:532; **10**:1343

environmental hormones **5**:680;

10:1343

and the Love Canal community

10:1342–1343; **11**:1532; **12**:1695

by pesticides **10**:1343–1344; **11**:1532

see also DDT; pesticides

and the soil **11**:1532

toxic chemicals **10**:1342–1343;

11:1532

cleaning up the community **10**:*1343*

and extinction **5**:680

indicator species for **8**:1036

oil *see* oil, environmental

and the ozone layer *see* ozone, depletion

permaculture and **9**:1281

by plastic **10**:1344

and seabirds **5**:*623*; **11**:1474

soil **11**:1532

water **5**:*718*; **10**:1341–*1342*

of lakes **7**:*1001*

and plankton **10**:1314

see also acid rain; waste disposal

Polly (sheep) **3**:384

polyandry **3**:409; **8**:*1083*

polyarthritis **1**:*136*

polychaetes **1**:100

bristle worms **1**:96, *98*

ice worms **9**:1233

proboscis **10**:1374

polydactyly **4**:*525*

Polyergus spp. **1**:120

polyestrus animals **8**:1111

polygamy **3**:409; **10**:1406

polygyny (harem breeding) **3**:409; **4**:460;

8:1084; **11**:1523

polymerase chain reaction (PCR) **3**:384;

4:535; **6**:774; **8**:1145–1146

invention **9**:*1173–1174*

polymers **8**:1142

polymorphism *see* dimorphism and

polymorphism

polypeptides **10**:1375

pancratic **9**:1261

Polyplacophora **8**:1150

polyploidy **2**:266; **3**:369; **9**:1190;

10:*1408*; **11**:1481, *1542*

Polypodiophyta (Pterophyta) **10**:*1327*

polyps **7**:980

coral **4**:447, 448–449, 452, 453;

11:1497–1498

polysaccharides **3**:297; **8**:1143

Polystichum spp. **5**:706

Polyxenus spp. **3**:345, 346

Polyzoa **1**:96

Pomacanthus spp. (angelfish) **2**:283

pomegranates **1**:50–51

wild **6**:794

pomelos **6**:795

pomes **6**:792

ponds *see* lakes and ponds

Pongo pygmaeus see orangutans

pons **2**:256

Pontiac fever **5**:627

poorwills **6**:776

Popillia japonica (Japanese beetle)

7:960

poplars **4**:547–548; **12**:1639

balsam **12**:1590

Popper, Karl **11**:1467

poppies **2**:253; **9**:*1170*

populations 5:*582*–583; **6**:766;

10:1345–1348

birth and death **10**:1347

carrying capacity **10**:1345–*1346*

in communities *see* communities

cycles, in lemmings **10**:1334

density **10**:1346–1347

genetics, genetic diversity 2:183–184;
8:1135; 10:1347–1348
growth 10:1345, *1346*
bacteria in a bottle 10:1347
Malthus's theory 4:479; 5:653;
10:*1345*
see also Green Revolution
human 10:1346
aging 1:*35*
inclusive fitness 1:60
isolation 11:1540, 1541
see also island habitats
size, controlled 7:953
Populus balsamifera (balsam poplar) 12:1590
porcine somatotropin (PST) 2:224
porcupines, tail 12:1594
Porifera 11:1552
Porifera *see* sponges
porphin 10:1309
Porphyra spp. (nori/laver) 7:987
porphyrins 10:1310
porpoises *see* whales, porpoises,
and dolphins
Portuguese man-of-war 7:*983*; 9:1182;
11:1524
commensal fish 11:1580
port-wine stains 10:1359
positron emission tomography (PET)
2:*260*; 8:1090–1091
pospiviroids 10:1324
possums, American 8:1078
posthypnotic suggestion 7:926
post mortem investigations *see* autopsies
post-traumatic stress disorder (PTSD)
1:122; 8:1114, *1115*; 11:1567
posture
upright 11:*1503*
see also body language
postvegetative state 3:399
potassium
deficiency 4:489
in fertilizers 5:717
and nerve impulses 9:1198–1199, 1200
potatoes
and Colorado beetles 2:*178*
crops 11:1446
defense 4:483
disease-resistant 2:225
diseases
blight 8:*1138*; 10:1321, 1322
common scab 10:1322
dormancy 4:548
genetically modified plants 6:810
hog 11:1445
Indian 11:1445
planting 12:1651
rhizomes 12:*1650*
sweet 11:1445, 1446
tuber formation 11:1562; 12:1649,
1650
white/Irish 12:1649
potentiation, long-term (LTP) 2:263

Potos flavus (kinkajou) 3:310, 311
pottos 10:1366, 1370
poultry, lice 8:1033
power lines, and cancer 5:627
power plants, nuclear, accidents at 5:622,
626; 10:*1344*
poxviruses 12:1681, 1682, 1683
prairie dogs 5:694; 9:1207;
12:1614
prairies 2:210
see also grassland biomes
prawns, antennae 1:*106*
prayer plants 10:1316
predation 10:1349–1351
cooperative hunting 1:58
killer whales 10:1350
defense against *see* defense
human encouragement of predators
10:1350–1351
see also biological control
predator-prey relationships
10:1349–1350
in lakes and ponds 7:1001
of ungulates 12:1662–1663
used for biological control
see biological control
see also carnivores; hunting
prednisone 2:240
preen glands (uropygial glands) 11:1472;
12:1699
pregnancy and birth 10:1352–1359
birth 3:355; 10:*1357*–1359, 1414
cesarean sections 10:1357, 1359;
11:1574
a positive feedback system 7:*953*
premature labor 8:1098
see also babies
pregnancy
detecting birth defects *see* fetus,
screening
diabetes in 4:507–508
ectopic 5:711; 10:1359
fetus *see* fetus
human timetable 10:1353–1357
and illegal drugs 2:260
iron deficiency in 7:973
kits to test for 10:1353
milk production *see* lactation
miscarriage 1:14; 10:1354
multiple births *see* twins and multiple
births
prevention *see* contraception
problems of 10:1359
"quickening" 10:1355
Rh typing 2:245
tests 2:224
see also embryos; fertility; fetus
see also abortion
prehistoric life 10:1360–1364
premenstrual syndrome (PMS)
8:1110–1111
premolars 12:1603

prenatal testing *see* genetic diseases,
screening for
Prepona spp. 2:271
preservation, food *see* food, preservation
preservatives, chemical 6:764
pressure receptors 12:1626
priapulids 1:95
prickles 3:380
primary consumers 6:767
primary producers 6:767, 768; 9:1224,
1236
primates 10:1365–1370
adolescence 1:*28*
defense 4:484–485
emotions 5:603–*604*
gestation time 10:1369
grooming 10:*1370*
hunting 10:1370
movement 10:1370
opposable fingers or toes 5:697–698;
10:1365
prosimians 9:1223; 10:1365–1367
simians 10:1367–1369
social organization 10:1369–1370
tail 12:1594
teeth 12:1605–1606
tree shrews as 7:955
see also apes; monkeys
primitive streak 5:598–599, 600
primordia 8:1023
leaf 11:1561
Principles of Geology (Charles Lyell) 4:478;
5:653
*Principles of Humane Animal Experimentation,
The* (Russell and Burch) 1:92
Priodontes maximus (giant armadillo) 1:104
Prionace glauca (blue shark) 11:1488
Prionodon pardicolor (spotted linsang) 3:312
prions (birds) 11:1473
prions (proteins) 10:1371–1373
"Prisoner's Dilemma" 1:59
problem solving 3:394
and insight 8:1021
see also cognition; intelligence
proboscis 10:1374
of butterflies and moths 2:267, 268;
10:1337, 1374
of mosquitoes 9:*1268*; 10:1374
proboscis worms 1:95
procambium 11:1560
Procavia capensis (rock hyrax) 5:*594*
Proconsul 7:871, 914–915
Procyonidae 3:310–311
Procyon spp. *see* raccoons
Prodoxus y-inversus (yucca moth) 2:269;
10:1336
productivity, ecosystem 6:769–770
proestrus 8:1111

profiling, psychological 6:773
progeny testing 11:1480
progeria 1:34
progesterone 5:613; 8:1109
challenge test 5:712
in the contraceptive pill 4:441
effect on cervical mucus 4:442
and the menstrual cycle 10:1413–1414
and milk production 7:998
and puberty 1:*27*
prokaryotes 2:167; 3:331
aerobic respiration 8:1118
become eukaryote organelles 2:168,
203; 3:332, 392; 10:1380; 11:1581
DNA 2:167; 3:331
flagella 3:338
and origins of life 2:168; 3:332; 10:1380
prokaryotic algae 1:47
see also bacteria; cyanobacteria
prolactin 2:219; 5:611, 712; 7:998
prontosil 9:1290
Propalaeotherium 9:1256
propanolol 7:898
Propithecus verreauxi (Verreaux's sifaka)
9:1221
proplastids 10:1306
proprioceptors 4:469; 12:1626
prosimians 9:1223; 10:1365–1367
prosoma 1:130
prosopagnosia 9:1211
Prosopis (mesquite) 4:499
prostaglandin H synthase-1 2:182
prostaglandins 5:692; 7:938, 990–992;
8:1109
and aspirin 9:1291
prostate gland 10:1412
cancer 3:295, 352
surgical robots used for 10:1433
treatment of enlarged 11:1575
prostheses 2:212–215; 7:875;
8:1092–1093
see also implants
prosthetic groups 10:1376
protanopia 12:1688
Proteidae 11:1454
proteins 10:1375–1378
action-producing 10:1377
animal fibers from 6:725–726
antifreeze 4:472; 8:1036; 10:1332
breakdown 8:1118; 9:1226
starvation and 8:1120
complete 10:1377
conjugated 10:1376
deficiency 10:1378
protein-energy malnutrition
4:*487*–488; 10:1378
denaturization 10:1376
dietary 9:1226, 1229; 10:1377

proteins *(continued)*
  metabolism **2**:279, 280
  engineering **2**:180–181
    see also genetic engineering
  functions **10**:1376–1377
  metabolism, errors of **12**:1668
  microbial, in ruminants **11**:1453
  plant **10**:1377
  polymorphism **4**:524
  recycled **10**:1377
  shape **8**:1143; **10**:1375–1376
  single-cell (SCP) **12**:1715
  stored **5**:619
  structure **1**:63; **8**:1143–1144;
    10:1375, *1376*
  synthesis **4**:*536*, 537; **7**:919;
    10:*1377–1378*, 1428–1430
    see also amino acids; enzymes
Proteles cristatus (aardwolf) **3**:312
proteolysis (protein catabolism) **8**:*1119*, 1120
Proteus spp. **3**:*327*; **11**:1454
proteus syndrome **11**:1504
prothoracicicotropic hormone **8**:1126
prothrombin **2**:242
Protista
  movement of water and minerals
    12:1632
  see also algae; kelps and seaweeds
protists 8:1130; **10**:**1379–1382**; **12**:1601
  animal-like **10**:*1382*
    see also protozoa
  fungus-like **10**:1381–1382
  plant-like **10**:*1380–1381*
Protoceratops **4**:*526*, 529, 531
protocerebrums **8**:1105
protochlorophyllide **10**:1306
Protococcus **9**:1165
protoderm **11**:1560
protonephridia **5**:666
Protopterus spp. (African lungfish)
  10:*1422*
protostomes **7**:971–972
Prototheria *see* monotremes
protozoa
  chemoreception **12**:1595, 1625
  digestion by **4**:511
  in digestive systems
    cockroach **3**:388
    termite **11**:*1461*; **12**:1611
  estuarine **11**:1492
  excretion **5**:666; **7**:902
  feeding **5**:693
  infections by **7**:949
    carried by ticks **7**:947
    see also Paramecium spp.; *Plasmodium*
      spp.; *Trypanosoma* spp.
  movement **11**:1578
Prozac (fluoxetine) **9**:1215; **10**:*1390*
pruning, of axons and synapses **2**:260–261
Prusiner, Stanley **1**:89; **10**:1371
Psammechinus miliaris (purple-tipped sea
  urchin) **4**:*439*

Psammomys obesus (North African sand rat)
  4:501
Psephotus pulcherrimus (paradise parrot)
  6:778
Pseudaelurus **3**:312, 324
pseudocoelom **7**:971; **9**:1195, *1196*
pseudocoelomates **7**:971; **9**:1196
Pseudocreobota ocellata (orchid mantis)
  2:286
pseudohermaphroditism **7**:889
pseudopodia (pseudopods) **4**:511; **5**:693,
  698; **11**:1578
pseudoscorpions **11**:1469
Psilocybe spp. **9**:1186
Psilophyta (fork/whisk ferns) **5**:706, *707*;
  10:1326
Psilotum spp. (fork-fern) **5**:706
Psittacosaurus **4**:531
psittacosis **1**:89
Psittacus erithacus (gray parrot) **6**:*778*
psoriasis
  and arthritis **1**:136
  treatment **12**:1667
psychiatry **5**:662–663; **9**:1213
  difficult diagnoses in **10**:1389
  psychiatrists **10**:1384
Psychical Research, Society for (SPR)
  9:1263
psychoanalysis **10**:*1383*, 1384–1385
psychoanalysts **10**:1384
psychologists **10**:1384, *1386*
psychology 10:**1383–1387**
  abnormal **10**:1386
  applied **10**:1386–1387
  cognitive **3**:393, 423; **5**:661–662;
    9:1211; **10**:1385
    see also cognition
  evolutionary 5:**660–663**
  experiments **10**:1385–1386
  Gestalt **10**:1384
  personality types **10**:1385
  psychological profiling **6**:773
  schools of thought **10**:1383–1384
  social **5**:661; **10**:1386
    see also behavior; conditioning; learning;
      parapsychology; psychotherapy
psychopaths *see* antisocial personality
  disorder
psychoses 8:**1112–1113**; **10**:**1388–1390**
psychotherapy **10**:*1387*, *1388*, 1390
  group therapy **10**:*1384*
  for personality disorders **9**:*1286*
  for phobias **10**:1301
  psychoanalysis **10**:*1383*, 1384–1385
Psyllophryne didactyla **6**:787
ptarmigan **11**:1580
  rock **10**:1333
PTCA (percutaneous transluminal
  coronary angioplasty) **11**:1574
Pteranodon **10**:1391
Pteridium spp. (bracken fern) **5**:706; **7**:*882*;
  10:1318

Pteridophyta **5**:705; **10**:1326–1327
  see also ferns and fern allies
Pteridospermales **11**:1475
pterins **10**:1311
pterodactyls **10**:1391
Pterocnemia spp. (rheas) **6**:755, 756
Pterophyta (Polypodiophyta) **10**:*1327*
Pteropus vampyrus (common flying fox)
  2:174
pterosaurs 4:530; **6**:748; **10**:**1391**;
  12:1593
Pterygota **7**:960
Ptilonorhynchus violaceus (satin bowerbirds)
  4:*459*; **12**:*1614*
ptosis **1**:72
PTSD *see* post-traumatic stress disorder
ptyalin **11**:1564
puberty **1**:25, 26; **5**:708
  in animals **8**:1111
  hormones **5**:708; **8**:1108
    female **7**:906; **10**:1412–1413
    male **7**:906; **10**:1410
  and the menstrual cycle **1**:27–28;
    8:1111
    see also adolescence
puerperal fever **8**:1101
puffins **11**:*1471*
Pulicoidea **6**:740
pulmonary tree **8**:1055
pulses **8**:1028
pulvilli **6**:745
pumpkins **11**:1554
punctuated equilibrium **1**:21; **2**:203;
  5:654; **9**:1255
punishment **3**:413; **8**:1020
pupae *see* larvae and pupae
puparia **6**:745
pupfish, Devil's Hole **2**:186
pupils **12**:1685
Purcell, Edward M. **8**:1068
purines
  in DNA **4**:533
  metabolism, errors of **8**:1124
  as pigments **10**:1311
  in RNA **10**:1428
pus **7**:937
pygostyle **12**:1593
pyramids, biotic **5**:*586*
  pyramid of biomass **5**:*586*
  pyramid of energy **5**:586; **6**:*768*
  pyramid of numbers **5**:586;
    6:769
pyrethrum **1**:41; **9**:*1247*
pyrimidines
  in DNA **4**:533
  in RNA **10**:1428
pyrrole **10**:1309
Pyrrophyta **10**:1346, 1380
  see also dinoflagellates
pyruvate (pyruvic acid) **2**:159; **3**:300
pythons **11**:1519
  overcoming prey **11**:1518

reticulated **11**:1518
warming their eggs **3**:*397*

Q

Q fever **7**:947; **8**:1061
Qi (chi) **1**:55; **3**:360, 361
quaternary ammonium compounds (quats)
  1:117
queleas, red-billed **9**:1275
quercetin **10**:1311
Quercusia quercus (great purple hairstreak)
  2:*271*
Quercus spp. *see* oak trees
Quetzalcoatlus **10**:1391
quetzals **6**:777
"quickening" **10**:1355
quillworts **10**:1326–1327
quinazolines **3**:345
quinine **1**:51; **2**:164; **6**:744; **8**:1103
quiver tree **12**:1617

R

rabbits and hares 10:**1392–1393**
  digestion by **4**:*515–516*; **9**:1228–1229;
    11:1453, 1564
  hares
    Arctic/mountain **9**:1159;
      10:1392–1393
    breeding **10**:1352
    European **10**:*1393*
    jackrabbits **4**:500
    Manchurian **10**:1393
    rock **10**:1393
    snowshoe **2**:281–282; **9**:1159;
      10:1350, 1392
  rabbits **8**:*1072*
    breeding **10**:1352, *1353*
    cottontail **10**:*1392*
    European **10**:1393
    fleas **6**:739
    and the myxoma virus **3**:391–392
    tail **12**:1594
    teeth **5**:694
rabies **1**:90; **9**:1202
  and bats **2**:176
  vaccine **9**:1270; **11**:1569
raccoons **3**:*309*, 310, 311; **5**:695; **12**:1609
  fishing **12**:1628
  in suburban habitats **11**:*1568–1569*
racers **11**:1518
radiation and radiation sickness
  10:**1394–1395**
  dangers to humans **5**:626; **10**:1395
    causing leukemia **8**:1031
    radiation sickness **10**:1395
    and use of robots **10**:1432
  ionizing radiation **10**:1395
    for microbial sterilization **1**:116
  radiation therapy (radiotherapy) **3**:296
    photoradiation **11**:1575
  radioactive tagging, for drugs **9**:1290
  see also ultraviolet radiation; X rays

radicle 11:1448, *1476*, 1478
  development 5:601
radioactive tagging 1:68; 2:182
  in food webs 6:767
  to label drugs 9:1290
radioactive waste 10:1344
radioactivity 10:1394–1395
  radioactive-waste disposal 12:1697
radiocarbon dating 3:305; 6:784
radioistope labeling *see* radioactive
    tagging
radiolarians 4:438; 10:1382
radiotelemetry 12:1721
radiotherapy 3:296; 8:1031, 1091
radium 10:1394
radon 5:626, 627
radula 8:1147; 10:1374
Rafflesia spp. 6:*759*
rage, sham 1:31
ragweed 2:217; 10:1317, 1338;
    11:1568
rain
  acid *see* acid rain
  pH 1:16
rain forests
  temperate 12:1610
  tropical *see* tropical rain forest biomes
  see also deforestation
Raleigh, Sir Walter 8:1014
Ramalina spp. 8:1036
Ramapithecus 7:916
Ramón y Cajal, Santiago 10:1396
Ramphastos sulfuratus (keel-billed toucan)
    6:*777*
Rana spp.
  R. cancrivora (crab-eating frog) 6:788
  R. catesbeiana (bullfrog) 1:64; 5:666;
      6:787, 790
  R. pipiens (leopard frog) 6:787
  R. temporaria (common frog) 5:*715*
Rangifer tarandus (Arctic caribou) 8:1135;
    10:1333; 12:*1590*, 1654, 1663
Ranidae 6:787
Ranunculus spp. 1:79; 10:*1332*
Ranvier, node of 9:1200
rape victims 6:773
Raphus cucullatus (dodo) 1:19; 5:*678*;
    7:977
rare species 5:607
  see also endangered species
raspberry plants 10:1405
  raspberries 6:795
ratfish 6:734
ratites, *see also* birds, flightless
Ratner, S. 12:1667
rats 10:1437; 11:1569; 12:*1664*
  fleas 6:740
  kangaroo
    burrows 9:1207
    drumming with feet 5:699
    water conservation 4:501; 5:669, *670*;
        10:1436

learning experiments with 8:1020
  mole 1:60; 4:*486*; 10:1437–1438
    naked 11:*1523*
  multimammate 10:1438
  pheromones 9:1294
  and plague 6:740; 7:950
  sand 4:501; 7:*990*
  whiskers 12:1628
  wood 10:1437
rattans 9:1259
rattlesnakes
  courtship 4:459
  diamondback 9:1207
  heat detectors 9:1222
  rattle 11:1519
  tooth structure 11:*1519*
  venom 11:1518
Rattus spp. (rat) 10:1437; 11:1569;
    12:*1664*
ravens, play 10:1329
Ray, John 11:1539
Raynaud's disease 3:377–378
rayon 3:342
rays 6:732, 734; 11:1500
  excretion 5:670; 6:732
  spleen 11:1551
Ray, Tom 2:152
reading, development 3:358
reasoning, deductive and inductive
    11:1467
recapitulation theory 1:71
receptors
  sensory 12:1626, 1627
  see also chemoreceptors;
    mechanoreceptors
recognition, correct species 3:402–403;
    4:456
rectum 4:517
  cancer 3:295; 4:523
Recurvirostra spp. 2:231; 12:*1699*
recycling 10:*1343*, 1344; 12:*1696*–1697
  and composting 11:1461
Red Data Books (IUCN) 5:606
Redi, Francesco 2:202
Red Lists (IUCN) 2:186; 5:606–607
redox potentials 9:1251–1252
redox reactions 7:996; 9:1251
redpolls, Arctic/hoary 10:*1333*
red tides 10:1347
reduction 5:617
reductionism 3:423
  biological 2:203
redwoods 12:1608
  coastal 3:416; 8:1026; 12:1608
  dawn 3:416
  mycorrhizae 11:1450
Reed, Walter 5:621
reflexes 7:961–962; 9:*1204*;
    10:1397–1398
  in babies 3:355; 5:697; 10:*1397*–1398
  brain-stem 10:1398
  conditioned, *see also* conditioning

conditioned (acquired) 3:*411*; 9:*1271*,
    1272; 10:1398
  knee-jerk 10:1397
  milk-ejection 7:998
  plantar 10:1398
  pupillary 10:1397
  the reflex arc 9:*1204*; 10:1397
  simple and complex 10:1398
reflexology 1:57; 5:614
regeneration 10:1399–1402, 1404
  of body parts 10:1399–*1401*
    limb generation in phasmids 8:1017
  landscape 10:*1399*, 1402
  in planarians 6:735, 737
reiki 1:57
reindeer *see* caribou
reindeer moss 8:*1036*, 1037
reinforcement
  negative 3:413; 8:1020
  positive 8:1020
  theory of 3:412
relapsing fevers 1:131; 7:946
relaxin 10:1354
releasing factors 1:26, 27
religion, and creationism 5:654
Remipedia 4:470
remoras 11:1490
remote operated vehicles (ROVs) 9:1238
REM (rapid eye movement) sleep 2:264;
    11:1510–1511, 1512
Renaissance 2:201; 8:1099–1100
renin 7:901, 990
rennin 2:225; 11:1564
Rensselaer Potter II, Van 2:187
repetitive motion injury 5:628
repletes 1:119
reproduction 10:1403–1408
  asexual 10:1403, *1404*–1405, 1406
    in plants 1:80; 2:266; 10:1405;
        11:1562
    in vertebrates 10:1405
    see also apomixis; binary fission;
      budding; regeneration
  asexual or sexual, in the same animal
      10:*1407*
  in dual-sex organisms *see* hermaphrodites
  hermaphrodites 7:889–890;
      10:1407–1408
  human *see* reproductive systems
  k- and r-selection 1:101–102; 10:1352
  mating behavior *see* mating
  pair bonding 4:456
  plant
    apomixis 10:1405
    sexual 10:1408
    vegetative 1:80; 2:266; 10:1405;
        11:1562
    see also grafting, in plants

reproductive cycles 8:*1111*
  see also estrus; menstrual cycle
sexual 10:*1403*, 1405–*1406*
  benefits to evolution 10:1404
  evolution of 3:390
  single-parent *see* parthenogenesis
  sexual versus asexual 10:1406
  strategies 10:1406
  theories of 2:202
  see also courtship; fertility; fertilization;
    pregnancy; pregnancy and birth
reproductive systems 10:1409–1414
  human
    female 10:*1412*–1414
    male 10:*1409*–1412
  see also fertility; menstrual cycle;
    pregnancy; reproduction
reptiles 10:1415–1416; 12:1673
  anatomy 10:1416
  brain 2:*257*, 258
  circulatory system 3:*373*, 374–375
  courtship 4:459
  eggs 10:1413, 1416
  embryo development 5:598–599
  evolution 10:*1416*
  excretion 5:670; 7:989; 12:1673
  eyes 5:685–686
  hearing 4:562
  heart 7:*877*; 10:1416
  hibernation 7:893
  jaws 7:978
  locomotion 10:1416
  molting 9:1158
  nesting 9:1207
  respiration 10:1422
    lungs 8:*1060*; 10:1416, 1423
  salt glands 11:1459
  skin 11:1506
  stomach 11:1563–1564
  tail 12:1592–1593
  temperature regulation 3:397; 10:1415;
      12:1617
  vision 10:1416
  see also crocodilians; dinosaurs; snakes;
    tortoises and turtles
reserpine 1:51
reserves 3:429
  see also national parks
resilin 1:138; 6:738, 739
resin 11:1562
  insects fossilized in amber 6:*781*, 782
resource partitioning 3:410
respiration
  aerobic 7:993; 9:1252
    efficiency 8:1121
    electron transfer/oxidative
      phosphorylation 2:159, 160; 7:993,
      996; 8:1118–1119

respiration *(continued)*
  energy from *see* energy, from aerobic
      respiration
  glycolysis 2:159, 269–270;
      5:618–619; 7:993; 8:1117–1118
  the **Krebs cycle** 2:*159*–160; 3:300;
      5:619, 632; 7:*993*–**996**; 9:1252
  anaerobic 2:159; 5:619; 8:1117
    in muscles 9:1252
    see also fermentation
  breathing 3:306; 8:*1057*–1059;
      10:1398, 1420
    in birds 10:1423
  and the carbon cycle 3:303
  cutaneous 6:789
  gaseous exchange 9:1252–1253
    at high altitudes 8:*1058*; 9:1170
  in the human body 3:306
  see also respiratory systems
respirators 8:*1038*–1039
respiratory diseases 8:1059–1061
  in animals 8:1061
  see also asthma
respiratory quotient (RQ) 2:280
respiratory systems 10:1417–1424
  of amphibians 10:1418
  of birds 10:1423–1424
  diseases of *see* respiratory diseases
  of fish
    gills 6:727–728; 10:1419
    lungfish 10:*1422*
  human 10:1420–1422
    bacteria 2:171
    mucus 7:928
  of insects 10:*1419*–1420
  of mammals 10:1423
  membranes 8:1065; 9:*1171*
  pigments 10:1424
    see also hemocyanin; hemoglobin;
        myoglobin
  of plants 10:*1424*
    see also stomata
  of reptiles 10:*1422*
  of spiders 10:1420
  see also gills and spiracles; lungs;
      respiration
resting potential 9:*1199*
restriction enzymes *see* enzymes,
    restriction
restriction fragment length polymorphisms
    (RFLPs) 6:774; 7:920; 8:1146
retching 11:1565
rete mirabile
  in birds 11:1472
  in tuna 6:731
reticular formation 2:256–257
Reticulitermes lucifugus 11:*1461*; 12:*1611*
reticulorumen 11:1451
reticulum 4:*515*; 11:1451, *1452*, 1453
retina 4:506; 5:686; 9:*1202*
Retin A 12:1691
retina, implants 8:1093

retinal 12:1685
retinitis pigmentosa 5:687
retinoic acid 5:676
retroviruses 4:537; 6:806; 10:1431;
    12:1681–1682, 1683
  causing leukemia 8:1031
  causing mutation 9:1189
  genetic engineering and 12:1679
  HIV as 1:43
reverse transcriptase (RT) 1:44; 6:806;
    12:1679, 1682
Reynolds, Craig 2:151
RFLPs (restriction fragment length
    polymorphisms) 6:774; 7:920;
    8:1146
Rhacophorus spp. (flying frog) 5:699; 6:749
Rhagioletis pomonella (apple maggot fly)
    3:402
Rh blood typing *see* rhesus (Rh) system
Rhea americana (gray/common rhea) 6:755
rheas 6:755–756
rhesus (Rh) system 2:244, 245; 6:774;
    7:941
rheumatic fever 1:136; 2:164
rheumatism 7:870
Rhinatrematidae 2:276
Rhincodon typus (whale shark) 10:*1314,
    1418*; 11:*1487, 1488*
Rhine, J.B. and Louisa 9:1262
rhinitis, allergic *see* hay fever
rhinoceroses
  black 11:*1579*
  horns 7:911; 12:1663
  white
    endangered 5:*606*
    hunting of 11:1464
  woolly 5:679–680; 6:782
Rhinolophus ferrumequinum (greater
    horseshoe bat) 2:*174*, 175; 3:*325*
rhinotracheitis 8:1061
rhinoviruses 3:395
Rhizanthella sp. 9:1240
Rhizobium 11:*1531*
  leghemoglobin 7:973
  nitrogen fixation 8:*1029*; 9:*1217, 1218*
Rhizocarpon geographicum (map lichen)
    8:1035
rhizoids 9:1165
rhizomes *see* tubers and rhizomes
Rhizophora mangle (red mangrove) 12:*1704*
Rhizopus spp. 8:1138; 9:*1225*
Rhoades, Marcus 8:1085
Rhododendron spp. (rhododendron) 1:77
Rhodophyta 1:46, 48; 10:1381
rhodopsin 10:1311
rhodopsin *see* visual purple
Rhodospirillum spp. 2:171
Rhombozoa 1:95
Rhus spp. 1:53
Rhynchocephala 10:1415
  see also tuataras
Rhynchops spp. (skimmer) 11:1473

rhyncocoels 1:95
ribbon worms 1:95; 7:970–971
rib cage, during breathing 8:*1057*
ribonucleoproteins, small nuclear
    (snRNPs) 10:1429
ribosomes 3:334
  and amino acid/protein synthesis 4:537;
      9:1189; 10:*1378*, 1429, 1430
  bacterial 2:169
  structure 10:1429
ribozymes 10:1431
ribulose diphosphate (RDP) 10:1304,
    1305
rice 1:40; 9:1161
  genetically modified 6:810; 9:1244
rickets 2:250, 278; 4:*489*; 9:*1227*;
    11:1502
rickettsias 7:946, 947; 9:1267
ridges, mid-ocean 9:1231
rifampin 1:109; 12:1648
Riftia pachyptila 5:651
Rift Lakes (eastern Africa) 7:976–977
rigor mortis 6:772; 9:1183
rinderpest 1:89
Ringer, Sydney 2:278
Ringer's solution, lactated 8:1039
ringtails 3:310
Riopa fernandi (Fernand's/fire skink) 8:*1051*
rivers and streams 10:1425–1427
  see also lakes and ponds
RNA 8:1144; 10:1428–1431
  and evolution 5:654; 9:1254; 10:1431
  interference (RNAi) 10:1430
  messenger (mRNA) 3:333; 4:536, 537;
      7:919, 920; 10:*1378*, 1428–1429
    and mutations 9:1189, 1190
  and the origins of life 2:181
  and protein synthesis 4:*536*, 537;
      10:*1378*, 1428–*1430*
  ribosomal (rRNA) 10:1429, 1431
  structure 10:*1428*
  transfer (tRNA) 4:*536*, 537; 9:1189;
      10:1378, 1429, *1430*
RNA polymerase 1:109; 4:537; 10:*1378*,
    1428–1429
RNA world 10:1431
roadrunners 4:501
robins 1:29–30; 8:1136; 12:1614
  American 11:1569
robotics
  and artificial life 2:*149*
  in medicine 4:497; 10:1432–1435
    for surgery 4:497; 10:*1432*–1434
    telemedicine 8:*1094*; 10:*1433*–1434
Roccella spp. 8:1035
rock tripe 8:1036
Rocky Mountains 9:1167–1168
Rocky Mountain spotted fever 1:*131*;
    7:947; 9:*1264*
rodents 10:1436–1438
  coprophagy 11:1564
  and disease 10:1438

evolution 10:1438
  teeth 10:*1436*; 12:1605
Rodolia cardinalis (vedalia beetle) 2:195
rods and cones 5:686–687; 12:1685, 1687
  and night vision 9:1221; 12:1687
Roentgen *see* Röntgen, Wilhelm
Rohm, Otto 2:222
Röntgen (Roentgen), Wilhelm 8:1090,
    1102; 10:1395; 12:1712, *1713*
roots and root systems 11:1447–1450
  absorbency 8:1026
  crops 11:1445–1446
  development 11:1447–1448
  growth 11:1560
  and mycorrhizae 6:800; 9:1187–1188,
      1241; 10:1321; 11:1450
  nodules 8:1029; 11:1531
  oxygen requirements 9:1253
  of plants in dry habitats and deserts
      11:1449–1450
  root cap 11:1560
  root/shoot balance 11:1448
  size 8:*1148*; 11:1450
  storage in 11:1449
  "territorial" 12:1613
  transport by 11:1448
  tropisms 11:1449; 12:1646, *1647*
  types 11:1448–1449
    adventitious 11:*1449*, 1450
    aerial 3:*380*; 11:1450
    buttresses 12:1643
    primary roots 11:1448–1449, 1476
    prop roots 11:1532; 12:*1704*
    tap roots 11:1449
root and tuber crops 11:1445–1446
Rosa spp. *see* rose family
rose family
  fruit crops 6:794–795
  fungal diseases 10:1321
Rosenberg, William 8:1096, 1097, 1098
roses 3:*380*; 4:482
Ross, Ronald 5:621
Rostrhamus sociabilis (snail kite) 2:234, 237
rotifers 1:*95*; 10:1313, 1407
rots
  dry 6:799
  noble 10:*1319*, 1321–1322
  soft 10:1322
Roundup (pesticide) 9:1247
roundworms *see* nematode worms
routes, lottery 12:1718–1719
royal jelly 12:1694
RQ (respiratory quotient) 2:280
r-selection 10:1352
  in plants 1:101
rubber trees 12:1644
rubella 7:875, 950; 10:1354
rubidium 6:784
Rubus spp. 6:795
rugae 11:1564
rumen 4:*515*; 11:1451, *1452*, 1453, 1564
  of a cow, contents 9:1229

Ruminantia 11:1451

ruminants 11:1451–1453

digestion by 3:342; 4:*515*, 521; 8:1071, 1128; 9:*1226*; 11:1453, 1581; 12:1661–1662

feeding behavior 11:1453

saliva 4:515; 11:1452

stomach of 4:515; 11:1451–*1452*, 1564

teeth 11:1452

see also cattle; goats; sheep; ungulates

"runner's high" 5:614

Rupicapra rupicapra (chamois) 9:*1169*

Russell, William M. S. 1:92

rusts 6:800; 8:1139; 10:1321

mint 10:1321

Rutacea 6:795

rye, smut 6:765

S

Sabin, Albert 1:92

sable 12:1591

Saccharomyces spp. (yeasts) 5:701; 12:*1714*, 1715

Saccharum officinarum see sugar cane

Saccorhiza polyschoïdes (furbelow) 7:988

saccule 4:561

Sachs, Julius von 7:924

Sackett, David 8:1098

Sacks, Oliver 9:1211

SAD (seasonal affective disorder) 2:218

Sagan, Carl 5:*684*

Sagan, Dorian 5:585

Sagittariidae 2:236

Sagittarius serpentarius (secretary bird) 2:236

sago palms 9:1259

Sahara Desert 4:499, 504

Sahel Desert 4:504, 505

Saimiri sciureus (squirrel monkey) 8:*1070*

Sainte-Catherine cave (Ariege) 3:326

St. Helens, Mount 1:*16*; 5:624

salamanders and newts 11:1454–1456

cave-dwelling 3:*327*

leg regeneration 10:1400

lungs 8:*1060*

metamorphosis 8:1125

nervous system 9:*1205*

newts

fat store 7:892

palmate 11:*1456*

red-bellied 4:458

red-spotted 11:1456

tail 12:*1593*

paedomorphosis 11:1455

poisonous 11:1454

reproduction 11:1456

respiration 11:1455

salamanders 1:*64*

fire 11:*1455*

giant 11:1454, 1455

lungless 10:*1423*; 11:1455

mole 11:*1454*, 1455

molting 9:1158

tiger 11:*1454*, 1455

torrent 11:1455

temperature regulation 3:397

see also amphibians

Salamandra salamandra (European fire salamander) 11:*1455*

saliva 3:299; 11:1564

human 4:516, 521

ruminant 4:515; 11:1452

salivary glands 4:514, 516

Salix sitchensis (Sitka willow) 10:1317

Salk, Jonas 8:1103, *1129*; 11:1457

Salmo spp. 1:124; 8:*1082, 1134*; 11:1492

salmon

Atlantic, fertilization 8:*1082*

farmed 1:124

migration 6:733; 8:1133–*1134*, 1135; 10:*1427*

nests 9:1206

Pacific 10:1426

and salinity changes 11:1492

sockeye 6:731; 8:1133–1134; 10:*1427*

Salmonella spp. 5:703

and food poisoning 6:765

from cockroaches 3:388

S. typhi 7:948

as a terrorist weapon 2:199

salmon patches 10:1359

salt

concentration in the blood 5:672

as a preservative 6:764

saltbushes 11:*1459*

salt glands 11:1459, 1472

Salt Lake City 7:1002

salt marshes 6:*769*; 9:1237

plant roots in 11:1450

saltpeter 7:988

salts 11:1458–1459

salvarsan (arsphenamine) 5:592; 8:1103; 9:1289

sampling techniques, to estimate biodiversity 3:426

sand dollars 4:568, 570

sand dunes 12:*1649*, 1650

sanderlings 11:1494

sandfish, long belted 7:890

sandpipers 11:1471; 12:1699–1700

broad-billed 12:1700

curlew 12:1700

nests 9:1209

Sanger, Frederick 7:*920*, 921, 965

Sanger, Margaret Higgins 4:443

sanitization 1:115

sap

in plants 12:1631, 1632

polar 10:*1332*

saplings 12:1639

saprophytes 5:696; 9:1224–1225; 11:1460–1462

fungi 6:800; 9:*1225*; 11:*1460*–1462

and the nitrogen cycle 9:1217

orchids 9:1161

sarcodines (Sarcodina) 10:1382

see also amoebas; radiolarians

sarcolemma 9:1181

sarcomas 3:294

sarcomeres 9:1181

Sarcophilus harrisii (Tasmanian devil) 8:*1079*

Sarcopterygii 6:730; 12:1672–1673

Sarracenia spp. (pitcher plants) 3:316; 8:*1027*; 10:1317

satellites (subviral agents) 10:1324

Saurischia 4:529–530

Saurolophus 4:530–531

sauropods 4:529–530

sausages 5:701

Savage-Rumbaugh, Dr. S. 3:406

savanna biomes 2:210; 11:1463–1465; 12:*1663*

see also grassland biomes

saxifrage, golden 6:762

Sayornis phoebe (eastern phoebe) 2:193; 12:*1718*

Say, Thomas 5:*621*

SBGM (self-blood-glucose monitoring) 4:507

scabies 1:131

scabs 7:937; 10:1401, 1402

scala tympani 4:560

scala vestibuli 4:560

scale insects 2:*195*; 7:885

scallops 8:1149; 11:1497

scans *see* imaging, medical

Scaphiopus spp. (spadefoot toad) 4:458–459, 500–501; 6:790

Scaphopoda 8:1150

scapulae 11:1503

scarification, seed 4:547, 549

Scarus spp. (parrot fish) 4:451, 453

scavengers 5:695

scent, marking territories 8:1073

Schachter, Stanley 5:602–603

Schiaperelli, Giovanni 5:682

Schindler, Robert 7:874

Schistocera spp. (locusts) 9:1294

Schistosoma spp. (blood fluke) 6:*736*, 737; 9:1265; 10:1438

schistosomiasis 6:*736*; 10:1438

schizoaffective disorder 10:1390

schizocarps 2:274

schizoid personality disorder 9:1284

schizophrenia 3:398; 8:*1112*–1113; 9:1212; 10:1388, 1389–1390; 11:1466

disorganized 11:1466

and taste 12:1597

schizotypal personality disorder 9:1284

Schjelderup-Ebbe, T. 11:1523

Schleiden, Matthias 3:330–331; 4:476

Schmiederberg, Oswald 9:1289

schooling, fish 3:402; 6:*729*, 730–731

Schwann, Theodor 1:71; 2:202; 3:331; 4:476; 5:629

Schwann cells 3:362; 9:1200

SCID (severe combined immunodeficiency disease) 6:*804*, 808; 9:1290

scientific method 11:1467–1468

see also analytical techniques

Scilla 11:1446

scissor bills (skimmers) 11:1473; 12:1700

Sciurognathi 10:1437, 1438

Sciurus spp. (squirrels) 2:194; 9:1206; 12:*1665*

sclera 5:685

sclereids 11:1448, 1560

sclerenchyma cells 11:1448, 1560

scleroderma 2:*164*, 165

sclerosis

amyotrophic lateral (ALS; Lou Gehrig's disease) 9:1181, 1202

multiple *see* multiple sclerosis

Sclerospongiae 11:1553

Scolecomorphidae 2:276

Scoliopteryx libatrix (herald moth) 3:328

Scolopacidae *see* sandpipers

Scolopendra spp. 3:343

Scolytus scolytus (elm-bark beetle) 2:178

Scomber sp. (mackerel) 6:732

Scopes, John Thomas 7:913

scopolamine 1:51

scorpion flies 8:1084

Scorpionidae 11:1470

scorpions 1:*133*; 11:1469–1470

coloring 11:1470

courtship 4:457

feeding 1:141; 11:1470

imperial 11:*1469*

reproduction 11:*1470*

sand 9:1222–1223

true and false 1:133

venomous 11:1470

whip scorpions 11:1469

see also arachnids

scrapie 1:89; 10:1371, 1373

screamers 12:1701

screening, genetic 2:191, 222; 8:1093–1094; 10:1358; 11:1482

scrofula 8:1066

scrotum 10:1409–1410

scrub disease 1:131

Scudder, John 4:554

scurvy 4:488; 6:764; 8:*1095*; 9:1227; 12:1605, *1690*, *1691*

scutes 12:*1623*

Scyphozoa *see* jellyfish

sea anemones *see* jellyfish, sea anemones, and hydras

Sea Around Us, The (Rachel Carson) **3**:318

seabed *see* ocean floor

seabirds *see* birds, seabirds

sea cabbage **11**:1493

Seacole, Mary **8**:1102

sea cows **2**:186

sea cucumbers **4**:568, 570; **9**:*1230*, 1232

sea dragons **6**:732

sea gooseberries *see* comb jellies

sea grasses **4**:439

sea hares **2**:217

sea horses **6**:729–730, *733*; **11**:1484

sea lettuce **7**:987

sea lilies **4**:568, 569, 570; **9**:1232

sea lions **2**:210; **3**:*311*; **8**:1124; **12**:1615

seals **3**:311; **10**:1334

   elephant **1**:*85*; **3**:311; **11**:*1484*

   flippers **5**:699

   leopard **10**:*1334*

   migration **2**:210

   milk **7**:998

   monk

     Hawaiian **3**:311

     Mediterranean **5**:*655*

   swimming **11**:1578

seamounts **9**:1231

seances **9**:1263

sea pens **9**:1232

Search for Extraterrestrial Intelligence
   (SETI) **5**:683, 684

seas, definition **9**:1234

sea scorpions **1**:132

sea slugs *see* nudibranchs

seasonal affective disorder (SAD) **2**:218

sea spiders **1**:130, 141

sea squirts **3**:*365*, 371

Sea Sweep **12**:1698

sea urchins **4**:570

   alarm signals **3**:403–404

   endoskeleton **4**:567; **11**:*1499*

   feeding **4**:568

   larvae **4**:569; **8**:*1126*; **10**:1314

   metamorphosis **7**:1005; **8**:*1126*

   purple **4**:439

   purple-tipped **4**:*439*

   reproduction **4**:569

   spines **4**:568

   tube feet **4**:567, 569, *570*

   see also echinoderms

seawater, composition **9**:1237

seaweeds *see* kelps and seaweeds

Seba, Albertus **2**:276

sebaceous glands **5**:*673*, 674, 675–676;
   11:1508

sebum **7**:870; **11**:1508

Secale cereale see rye

Sechium edule (chayote/chocho) **11**:1554

secondary consumers **6**:767

secretary birds **2**:236

secretin **4**:518, 522; **5**:610, 612; **9**:1260

sedges **11**:1477

Sedum spp. **2**:*274*

seed drills, invention **1**:39

seed ferns **11**:1475

seed plants *see* angiosperms; gymnosperms

seeds 5:716; **11**:**1475–1478**

   ancient **11**:*1478*

   banks **2**:252; **3**:427; **4**:473

   coat (testa) **10**:1326

   dispersal **1**:79; **10**:1318–1319, *1326*;
     11:*1476–1477*

     active **10**:1319; **11**:1477

     by animals **1**:79; **10**:1318, 1319;
       11:1477

     birds **1**:79; **11**:1477

     and fruit capsules **11**:1477–1478

     "splash cup" **2**:274

   dormancy **4**:547, 548–549; **11**:1478

   evolution **5**:715; **10**:1325, 1326;
     11:1475

   fire and **4**:*548*

   formation **11**:1475–1476

   scarification **4**:547, 549

   structure **1**:*79*

   used by man **11**:1477

   by water **11**:1477

   by wind **1**:79; **6**:725; **10**:1319;
     11:*1477*

   see also germination; grains

seeps, cold **9**:1233

segmentation, metameric, in annelids
   1:98, *99*

Segregation, Law of **8**:1106

Seiurus aurocapillus (ovenbird) **6**:*776*

seizures, epileptic *see* epilepsy

Selaginella spp. (spike moss) **5**:706

Selasphorus rufus (rufous hummingbird)
   3:*408*

selection

   artificial **4**:479

     see also selective breeding

   diversifying (disruptive) **9**:1194

   kin **1**:58, 60; **11**:1524, *1525*

   natural *see* natural selection

   r- and k-selection **1**:101–102; **9**:1278;
     10:1352

   sexual *see* sexual selection

selective breeding 2:223; **5**:659;
   11:**1479–1482**

   of animals **11**:1480

     cattle **1**:40; **11**:1480, *1481*

     dogs **4**:*540–541*

   of humans **7**:923

   of plants **11**:*1480–1482*

   polyploidy **10**:1408; **11**:1481

   see also domestication

selenium **3**:294

self-blood-glucose monitoring (SBGM)
   4:507

selfish behavior **11**:1525–1526

self-organizing systems **2**:150

self-sacrifice **4**:486

sella turcica **5**:611

semen (seminal fluid) **5**:711; **10**:1412

semicircular canals **4**:560

seminal fluid *see* semen

seminal vesicles **10**:1412

seminiferous tubules **10**:*1411*

Semmelweis, Ignatz P. **1**:115; **8**:1101

sensilla **12**:1627

sensitive plant **10**:*1316*

sensitization **8**:1020

sensory bias hypothesis **11**:1485

sensory cortex **2**:259

sensory deprivation **12**:1626

sepals **6**:757, 759

Sepia spp. **4**:458; **7**:978

Sequoiadendron giganteum (giant sequoia)
   3:*415*, 416; **12**:1608

sequoias, giant **3**:*415*, 416; **12**:1608

Sequoia sempervirens (coastal redwood)
   3:416; **8**:1026; **12**:1608

Serengeti **3**:427; **11**:1453, 1463,
   1464–1465; **12**:1663

Sergestes **2**:207

serial killers **9**:*1284*

serology **6**:774

   blood typing **2**:243, *244*–245; **6**:774

   DNA fingerprinting **2**:224, 226; **6**:*773*,
     774

serotonin **3**:420; **4**:556; **9**:1213

   and aggression **1**:32

Serpula lacrymans (dry rot fungus) **6**:799;
   11:1462

servals **3**:321; **4**:445

Sesia apiformis (hornet moth) **2**:*286*

SETI (Search for Extraterrestrial
   Intelligence) **5**:683, 684

severe combined immunodeficiency
   disease (SCID) **6**:*804*, 808; **9**:1290

sewage

   disposal **12**:1695

   pollution from **10**:1342

   treatment **8**:1132; **9**:1219; **11**:1461;
     12:1695–1696

   permaculture and **9**:1281

sex

   change in **7**:890

   of crocodilians depends on temperature
     4:466

   differences between, in child
     development **3**:359

sex hormones **7**:904

   and animal behavior **1**:84

   see also endocrine systems, hormones

sex-linkage

   of disorders **8**:1107; **9**:1181; **10**:1358;
     12:1688

   of traits **9**:1164

sexual assault **6**:773

sexual behavior, *see also* courtship

sexually transmitted infections (STIs)
   7:949–950

   and infertility **5**:710

sexual selection 4:458, 524–525;
   11:**1483–1486**

   and horns **12**:1663

   the peacock's tail and courtship display
     4:525; **11**:*1483–1484*

shade-tolerant plants **12**:1643

shads **4**:573

Shannon, Claude **7**:952

sharks 11:**1487–1490**

   basking **6**:732; **11**:1487

   behavior **11**:1490

   benthic and deep-sea **9**:1232;
     11:1488–1489

   blue **11**:1488

   body form **11**:1488–1489

   bull **11**:1488

   buoyancy **6**:728; **11**:1577

   cat **11**:1488

   chemical reception **12**:1596

   distribution **11**:1488

   evolution **11**:1489

   excretion **5**:670; **6**:732; **7**:*902*

   feeding **11**:1489

   fossil **11**:1489

   goblin **9**:1232

   great white **4**:450; **11**:*1487*, 1489, 1490

   Greenland **9**:1232

   ground **11**:1487

   hammerhead **6**:733; **11**:1489, 1490

   hunting of **11**:1490

   lemon **11**:1490

   mackerel **11**:1488

   megamouth **11**:1489

   nurse, gray **11**:*1500*

   osmotic regulation **11**:1489

   reef **12**:*1672*

   reproduction and life cycle **6**:733;
     11:*1489–1490*

   and salts **11**:1459

   silky **11**:*1490*

   skeleton **11**:1489, *1500*

   spiny **7**:978

   spleen **11**:1551

   swell **11**:*1489*

   swimming **11**:1500, 1577

   teeth **6**:732, 733–734; **12**:*1606*

   thermotaxis **12**:1647

   thresher **11**:1488

   tiger **11**:1489

   vision **6**:731

   "warm-bodied" **11**:1488; **12**:1617

   whale **10**:*1314*, *1418*; **11**:1487, *1488*

   see also dogfish

Sharpey-Schafer, Edward **7**:965

shearwaters **11**:1473, 1474, 1582

sheathbills **11**:1471

sheep

   in Australia **11**:1465

   bighorn **4**:500; **7**:*910*, 911; **11**:*1528*

     flehmen behavior **4**:460

   clones of Dolly the **3**:*340*, 383–384;
     11:1558

cloning **3**:*340, 383*–384; **11**:1558

crossbred **11**:1480

diseases, coast disease **9**:1227

domestication **4**:544

lice **8**:1033

protection from predators **4**:545

saliva **11**:1452

see also ruminants

Sheldon, William **10**:1385

shelducks **12**:1700–1701

shells

molluskan **8**:*1148*–1149; **11**:1497, 1506

tortoise **12**:*1623*

turtle **12**:*1623*

Shên Nung **7**:887, 987; **8**:1014

shepherd's purse **5**:*601*

Sherrington, Charles Scott **9**:1215

shiatsu **1**:57

Shigella **5**:703

shingles **7**:948

shipworm **8**:1149

shock **3**:378

anaphylactic **1**:53

shock treatment

for mental disorders **8**:1113

for nervous diseases **9**:*1212*

shoebills **12**:1701

shorebirds (waders) **12**:1699–*1700*

shore habitats 11:1491–1494

ecological zones **9**:1235

lichens **8**:1037

rocky **9**:1236–1237; **11**:*1493*–1494

seaweed **7**:986–987

see also estuaries; wetlands

"short-day" plants **2**:217

shortening **5**:692

shrews **7**:880, 954, 955

echolocation **8**:1071

elephant **7**:*956*

tree **7**:955

shrikes **9**:1274

boubou **3**:402

shrimps

brine **12**:1592

fairy **1**:106; **12**:1592

ghost **4**:467

Kentucky cave **3**:326

larvae **10**:1314

mud **4**:467

snapping **4**:470

see also crustaceans

shrublands **2**:209

see also chapparal biomes

shrubs **9**:1277–1278; **12**:1637

development of woody stems **11**:*1561*

Sialia sialis (eastern bluebird) **3**:*410*

sickle-cell disease *see* anemia, sickle-cell

siddha **7**:944

sidewinders **11**:*1520*

SIDS (sudden infant death syndrome) **12**:1691

sieve plates **12**:1631, 1632

sieve tubes **12**:1631, 1632, 1669

sifakas **9**:1221

sight *see* vision

sign language **7**:873

taught to apes **3**:406

sign stimuli **1**:83

silage **9**:1280

Silent Spring (Rachel Carson) **1**:41; **3**:318; **4**:481; **5**:584, 680; **9**:1288

silicosis **5**:628

silk **6**:*725*, 726

spider **1**:131; **6**:726

silkworms **6**:*725*

diseases of **9**:1269–1270

silverfish **11**:1580

silver nitrate **1**:116

simian crease **3**:369

simian immunodeficiency viruses (SIVs) **1**:42, 43

simians **10**:1367–1369

Simon, Herbert A. **7**:967

Simon, Theodore **7**:966

Simon-Binet test **7**:966–967

Simpson, James **1**:76; **8**:1102

Singer, Jonathan **3**:*331*

Singer, Peter **1**:91

single-cell protein (SCP) **12**:1715

single nucleotide polymorphisms (SNPs) **7**:922

sinoatrial (SA) node **7**:879

Sinosauropteryx **9**:1254

Siphonaptera **6**:738

Sipuncula **1**:96

sirens (Sirenidae) **11**:1455

sisal **9**:1161

Sistrurus spp. **4**:459

Sitta europea (nuthatch) **12**:*1609*

SIV virus **1**:42, 43

Six Million Dollar Man, The (television series) **2**:215

Sjögren disorder **2**:165

skates **6**:734

skeletal systems 11:1495–1504

appendicular skeleton **11**:1502

axial skeleton **11**:1502

computer models **11**:1501

dermal skeleton **11**:1501

disorders of **11**:*1502*

endoskeletons **11**:1498–1504

adaptations **11**:1498

bird **11**:1498, *1501*

echinoderm **4**:567; **11**:1499

fetal **11**:1500–1501

fish **11**:1499–*1500*

human **11**:*1496*, 1501

invertebrate **11**:1498–1499

of sponges **7**:969; **11**:1498–1499

of squid and octopuses **11**:1499

vertebrate **2**:248; **3**:319; **11**:1499–1504

see also bone

exoskeletons **11**:1496–*1498*

arthropod **1**:138–139; **7**:971–972; **11**:1496–*1497*

coral **4**:452; **11**:1497–*1498*

insect **7**:957–958; **11**:1505–1506

mollusk shells **8**:*1148*–1149; **11**:1497

fossilized *see* fossils, human

human skeletons for study **11**:1501

hydrostatic **11**:*1495*–1496

somatic skeleton **11**:1502

visceral skeleton **11**:1501–1502

skills, learning **3**:394

skimmers (scissor bills) **11**:1473; **12**:1700

skin 11:1505–1508

aging **1**:34; **11**:1507

bacteria **2**:171

birthmarks **10**:1359

cancer **3**:294, 295, 296, 317, 353; **9**:*1193*; **12**:1658

treatment **12**:1713

collagen **6**:726

color **9**:1227; **11**:1507, 1508

in caves **3**:327

loss **10**:1310

and disease **7**:950; **11**:*1508*

excretion via **5**:672

glands **5**:*673*, 675–676

see also sweat glands

grafts **8**:1087, 1088; **11**:1507

human **11**:1507–*1508*

and touch **12**:1626

mammalian **11**:1506–*1507*

mucus secretion **11**:1506

renewal **11**:1558

tissue-engineered **8**:1093

vertebrate **11**:*1506*

see also hair

skin corrosion test **1**:93

skinks **8**:1053

Fernand's/fire **8**:*1051*

tail **12**:1593

tongue **12**:1622

Skinner, B. F. **1**:82; **3**:412–413, 414; **8**:1020; **10**:1383

Skinner boxes **3**:*412*, 413; **8**:1020

skippers (Hesperiidae) **2**:268

skull **11**:1498

of birds **7**:978–979; **11**:1498

boring holes into **11**:1570

of Neanderthal man **7**:*912*, 916

skunks **4**:486; **11**:*1516*

sky, color **2**:155

skydusters **9**:1258

sleep 11:1509–1512

brain function during **2**:264; **11**:*1509*–*1510*

cycle (stages of sleep) **2**:219; **11**:*1510*–1511

deprivation **11**:1510

disorders **8**:1115; **11**:1511

dreaming **2**:264; **11**:1512

sleep apnea **11**:1511

sleeping pills **11**:1512

sleeping sickness **1**:88; **7**:929, 946

sleep talking **8**:1115; **11**:1511

sleepwalking **8**:1115; **11**:1511

slime molds (Gymnomycota) **8**:*1139*–1140; **10**:1381; **12**:1647

communication **9**:1293

slipped disk **11**:*1502*

sloths **1**:*104*

hands **11**:1498

slow learners **11**:1535–1536

sludge worms **1**:*128*

slugs

foot **5**:698

mucus **9**:*1172*

smallpox 11:1513; **12**:*1677*, 1682

biological warfare and **2**:198; **11**:1513; **12**:1679

immunization **7**:933–934, *936*, 984; **8**:1100–1101, 1130; **11**:1513

smear tests **4**:477

smell 8:1070; **11:1514–1516**

disorders of **11**:1516

in mammals **11**:1515

in nocturnal animals **9**:*1223*

and taste **11**:1516; **12**:1597

see also nose; pheromones; taste

smelling salts **11**:1516

smiling **5**:*605*

Smilodon (saber-toothed tiger) **3**:310, 312, 324; **5**:678; **10**:*1349*

Smith, Robert Angus **1**:15

Smith, Susan **7**:961

smog **10**:1340

photochemical **2**:156

smoking **4**:555

and cancer **3**:*295*; **8**:1059–1060; **12**:1622

and free radicals **1**:*34*

historical development **8**:1014

and the lungs **8**:*1061*

and Parkinson's disease **4**:497

passive **8**:1061

smoking, food **6**:763

smuts **8**:1139

snails

common **8**:*1150*

giant African **2**:185

land, lungs **8**:1060

mucus **9**:1172

polymorphism **4**:525

radula **10**:1374

shell **8**:*1148*; **11**:1497

slime **5**:699

see also mollusks

Bold words with bold page numbers indicate complete articles; bold numbers preceding colons are volume numbers; numbers following colons indicate page numbers; italic page numbers refer to illustrations or other graphics.

snakebite, inactivation **7**:934

snakes 11:1517–1520

  advanced **11**:1519–1520

  blind **11**:1518, 1519

  brown tree **2**:186

  coral

    instinctive avoidance of **7**:961

    mimics of **2**:*285*; **4**:484

  courtship **4**:459

  ears **11**:1517

  eyes **11**:1517

  "flying" **11**:1519

  garter **10**:1351; **11**:1519, 1520

  grass **9**:*1157*

  jaws **5**:695; **7**:978, *979*

  mating and reproduction **11**:1519

  milk **4**:484

  mimicry **2**:*285*, 286

  molting **9**:*1157*

  phobia of **1**:122

  pipe **11**:1519

  primitive **11**:1519

  rat **11**:*1517*

  record-holding **11**:1518

  respiration **10**:1422

  sea **10**:1422; **11**:1520

  sense of smell and taste **10**:1416; **11**:*1515*, 1518; **12**:*1596*

  skin **11**:1518

  sunbeam **11**:1519

  tail **12**:1592

  teeth **11**:*1519*; **12**:1606

  tongue **10**:1416; **12**:*1596*, 1622

  venomous **4**:485; **7**:*939*; **11**:1518; **12**:1606

  vine **11**:1519

  see also reptiles

snapdragons

  alleles for color **6**:812

  pollination **1**:78; **10**:1337

snipe, common **12**:1593

Snow, John **5**:*633*, 634

snow blindness **12**:1658

Soal, Samuel **9**:1262

soap **5**:*691*

  and antisepsis **1**:117

social contacts, and child development **3**:358–359

social organization 11:1521–1524

  and altruism **1**:59–60, 86

  in cnidarians **11**:1524

  communal feeding **11**:1522

  and communication **3**:402; **11**:1524

    see also communication

  defending food **11**:1523

  in dogs **4**:540

  dominance **8**:1072; **11**:*1522*, 1523

  grooming **8**:1072; **10**:*1370*

  in insects **2**:203; **7**:958–959; **11**:*1524*; **12**:1611

  in mammals **8**:1072–1074

  modeling **3**:349

phenotypic variation **4**:524

  in primates **10**:1369–1370

  problems associated with **11**:1524

  related individuals **11**:1523–1524

  in rodents **10**:1437–1438

  safety reasons **11**:1521–1522

  sociogenesis **3**:349

  see also sociobiology

sociobiology 5:644; 11:1525–1528

sociogenesis **3**:349

sociopaths *see* antisocial personality disorder

Socrates **2**:187

soda, extracted from seaweed **7**:988

sodium

  deficiency **4**:489

  and nerve impulses **9**:1198–1199, 1200

  pump **9**:1198; **11**:1458–1459

soil ecology 11:1529–1532

  acid rain and **1**:17

  aeration **11**:1532

  and conservation **11**:1532

  contamination **11**:1532

  desert soils **11**:1530

  and disease **11**:1531

  erosion **11**:1530–1531; **12**:1640

  formation **11**:1529–1530

  hydric soils **12**:1703

  life in **11**:1531–*1532*

    ants **11**:1531–1532

    earthworms **1**:99, 100; **11**:1532

    nematodes **9**:1195; **11**:1531

  permaculture and the **9**:1281

  pH **11**:1531

  and plants **11**:1530

  profiles and horizons **11**:1530

  in savannas **11**:1464

  urban soils **12**:1664

  wetland soils **12**:1703

Solander, Daniel **2**:254

Solanum tuberosum (white/Irish potato) **10**:1321; **11**:1446, 1562

solar system, life in **5**:682–*683*

solenodons **7**:956

Solifugae **11**:1469

Solpugida **11**:1469

somatostatin **5**:612; **9**:1261

somatotropin

  bovine *see* bovine growth hormone/bovine somatotropin

  in humans *see* growth hormone

  porcine (PST) **2**:224

somites **5**:599

sonar **4**:574

  for underwater exploration **9**:1238

songbirds **9**:1273, 1274

songs

  bird **2**:232, 233; **3**:402; **4**:459; **9**:1274; **12**:1614, 1615

    learning **3**:402–403; **8**:1021

soredia **8**:1035

sores, canker (aphthous ulcers) **12**:1622

Sotalia fluviatilis (tucuxi) **12**:1710

sounds

  caterpillar **1**:119

  signals **3**:404–405

    courtship **4**:457, 458–459

    see also birds, songs; calls

  see also echolocation

South America, species from North America **3**:409

Southern, Edwin **2**:182; **4**:535

Southern blotting **2**:182; **4**:535

sow bugs **4**:468

soybeans **8**:1028

  and acid rain **1**:17

  herbicide-resistant **6**:810

space medicine 11:1533–1534

space shuttles **11**:*1533*

space sickness **11**:1533

space suits **11**:*1534*

spadix **6**:762

Spallanzani, Lazzaro **2**:202; **4**:572–573; **5**:652; **8**:1127

Spanish moss **5**:642

sparrows

  house **9**:1274–1275

  song sparrows **3**:402–403, 408

  white-crowned **3**:402

  white-throated **8**:1136

Spartina spp. (cord-grass) **11**:1493

Spearman, Charles **7**:967

special educational needs 11:1535–1538

  for autism **2**:162–*163*; **11**:1536–1537

speciation *see* evolution, speciation

species 11:1539–1542; 12:1600

  adaptive radiation **11**:1541–1542

    Galápagos finches **9**:1192; **11**:1541

  biodiversity **2**:185

  classification limitations **11**:1539–1540

  distribution **9**:1257

  early ideas about **11**:1539

  emergent **5**:658

  endangered *see* endangered species

  extinction *see* extinction

  forms of *see* dimorphism and polymorphism

  and geographic isolation **11**:1541

  introduced **2**:195, *196*; **3**:*410*; **5**:607

  keystone **2**:184

  mutation **11**:1542

  names **8**:1042

  new *see* evolution, speciation

  number on islands **2**:193

  number of **2**:185; **5**:650; **9**:1255

  plant **2**:253

  ranges and geographical barriers **12**:1717–1718

  recognition **3**:402–403; **4**:456

  and reproductive isolation **11**:1540–1541

  ring **5**:*657*

  see also classification; taxonomy

Species Plantarum (Carolus Linnaeus) **12**:1600

Species Survival Plan (SSP) **12**:1724

spectacles (brilles) **11**:1517

spectrography **1**:68

speech 11:1543–1545

  the brain and **2**:264; **11**:1543–1544

  child development and **3**:357–358; **11**:1544

  child-directed (CDS) **3**:356–357

  stuttering **11**:1545

  teeth and **12**:1604

  therapy **11**:*1544*, 1545

  the tongue and **12**:1622

  see also language

Speothos venaticus (bush dog) **4**:540, *541*

sperm **10**:*1410*, 1411–1412

  "competition" **8**:1083

  egg penetration **5**:713–714

  formation of **5**:714–715; **10**:*1411*

  and infertility **5**:710–711

  survival **4**:442

spermaceti **12**:1702

spermathecae **11**:1547

spermatids **5**:715; **10**:1411

spermatocytes **5**:714–715; **10**:1411

spermatogonia **5**:714

spermatophores **4**:457, 458, 551; **8**:1083; **11**:1456

Spermatophyta (spermatophytes) **10**:1325

spermicides **4**:440, 441

Spermophilus spp.

  S. parryi (Arctic ground squirrel) **12**:1654

  S. richardsoni (Richardson's ground squirrel) **11**:1532

Sperry, Roger **2**:264

sphagnum mosses **11**:1532; **12**:1703

Spheniscus humboldti (Humboldt penguin) **6**:754

Sphenodon spp. (tuatara lizard) **8**:*1050*; **10**:*1415*; **11**:1581–1582

sphincters

  anal **9**:1180–1181

  cardiac **11**:1564

  pyloric **4**:516–517, 521; **11**:1564, 1565

sphygmomanometers **3**:374

Sphyma lewini (scalloped hammerhead) **11**:1490

spider plants **10**:1405

spiders 1:130, 131–132; **11:1546–1549**

  anatomy **11**:*1547*

  "ballooning" **11**:*1548*

  bird-eating **11**:*1548*

  black widow **1**:133, *139*; **11**:1547

  bolas/angling **1**:131–132

  camouflage **1**:131

  catching prey **11**:1548

  courtship **4**:457; **11**:1548–1549; **12**:1628

  crab **1**:96, 131; **11**:1548, 1549

  digestion by **1**:140

excretion **7**:989; **12**:1666

eyes and vision **11**:1547; **12**:1687

feet **5**:699

funnel-web **1**:133, 139

garden **1**:131; **11**:1548; **12**:*1627*

habitats **11**:1548

jumping **4**:457; **9**:1169; **11**:1547, 1548–1549

legs **1**:139

movement coordination **11**:1547

nocturnal, vision **12**:1687

nursery web **11**:1549

recluse **1**:133

  brown **11**:1547

redback/button **1**:133

reproduction **11**:1547–1548

respiration **11**:1547

silk produced by **1**:131; **6**:726; **11**:1549

spitting **1**:132

tarantula **11**:1548

  red-kneed **11**:*1546*

trap-door **11**:1548

true **11**:1546

underwater **1**:131

venomous **1**:133, *139*, 141; **4**:485; **11**:1547

waste products **5**:*665*

water **11**:1549

web-building **1**:131, 141; **11**:1547, 1548, *1549*; **12**:*1627*–1628

  courtship **4**:457

wolf **11**:1548

see also arachnids

spinach **2**:217; **8**:1014; **10**:1317–1318

Spinacia oleracea (spinach) **2**:217; **8**:1014; **10**:1317–1318

spinal cord **9**:*1201*–1202

  chordate **3**:364

  damaged **9**:1202

  and multiple sclerosis **9**:*1175*

spinal taps (lumbar punctures) **11**:1573

spindle, action of colchicine **3**:367

spine *see* vertebral column

spines

  animal **4**:485

  plant **2**:273; **4**:482; **8**:1022, 1027; **10**:1317

spinnerets **11**:1549

spiracles *see* gills and spiracles

spiroplasmas **10**:1323

spleen 2:243; **8**:1064–1065; **11**:1550–1551

  accessory spleens **8**:1065

  disorders of **8**:1065; **11**:1551

  nonhuman spleens **11**:1551

  removal **8**:1064–1065; **11**:1551, 1570

  see also lymphatic systems

splenectomy (removal of the spleen) **8**:1064–1065; **11**:1551, 1570

splenic cords **11**:1550

splenomegaly **11**:1551

spliceosomes **10**:1429

split-brain syndrome **5**:638

sponges 1:94; **11**:1552–1553

  asconoid **11**:1552

  boring **11**:1553

  bread-crumb **11**:*1553*

  colored **11**:1552

  diffusion in **3**:371

  evolution **11**:1553

  feeding and digestion **7**:969

  leuconoid **11**:1552

  regeneration **10**:1400

  skeleton **7**:969; **11**:1498–1499

  vegetable (loofahs) **11**:1554

sponges (contraceptives) **4**:440–441

spongy layer **8**:*1024*

spontaneous generation **1**:116; **2**:202; **5**:652; **8**:1127; **9**:1269

spontaneous recovery, and conditioning **8**:1021

spoonbills **5**:648; **10**:1311; **12**:1700

spoon worms **1**:96

sporangia

  in cones **10**:1338

  fungal **8**:1138, *1140*

  in mosses and liverworts **9**:1166

spores

  bacterial **2**:170; **11**:1531

  fungal **6**:798–799; **9**:1186

sporophytes **5**:590; **10**:1325

  in algae **1**:49

  fern and fern allies **5**:704–*705*

  gymosperm **3**:416

  in mosses and liverworts **9**:1166

sporozoans (Sporozoa) **10**:1382

  see also Plasmodium

spring hare, African **10**:1437

springtails **1**:141; **8**:1126, **12**:1719

spruces **3**:415, 416, 417; **4**:492

spurges **2**:274

squalene **6**:728

Squalus acanthias (piked dogfish) **11**:1490

Squamata **10**:1415; **11**:1517

squash family 3:380; **11**:1554–1555

squid **8**:*1148*

  bioluminescence **2**:*205*, 207

  color change **4**:483; **7**:908; **10**:1310

  common **2**:*205*

  eyes **5**:685–686; **8**:1149

  giant **4**:574; **8**:1149; **11**:1499

  "jaws" **7**:978

  movement **11**:1499, 1577

  skeleton **11**:1499

  vertical migration **8**:1136

  see also cephalopods; mollusks

squirrelfish **3**:403; **12**:*1613*

squirrels

  desert **8**:1072

  flying **6**:*749*; **10**:1436–1437; **12**:1591

  gray **2**:194; **12**:*1665*

  ground **7**:891, 892; **11**:*1532*; **12**:1654

  red **2**:194

  tree **7**:891–892; **9**:1206

Stadler, Lewis **8**:1086; **9**:1190

Stahl, Franklin **4**:534

staining techniques **7**:895

stamens **1**:78; **6**:758, 759, 791; **10**:1335

Stanley, Wendell **8**:1130

stapes (stirrup) **7**:873, 874

  plastic **7**:875

Staphylococcus spp. **2**:171

  S. aureus **2**:171; **6**:765

  S. epidermidis **2**:171

starch **3**:*297*

  as energy storage **5**:619

starfish **4**:568, 569, 569–570

  crown-of-thorns **4**:*450*, 451, 453, 568

  endoskeleton **11**:1499

  regeneration **10**:1399–1400, *1401*, 1404

  reproduction **10**:1400

  structure **4**:567

  sunflower **9**:*1230*

  tube feet **4**:567

  see also echinoderms

starlings **3**:401, 410; **9**:*1273*, 1275

  communication **3**:402

  introduction to the United States **3**:410

starvation **8**:1120; **9**:1227

  see also deficiency-related diseases

statistical methods, experiments and **11**:1468

statocysts **4**:469

statoliths **4**:469

  in root cells **11**:1449

stearic acid **5**:*689*, 690

Steatornis caripensis (oilbird) **4**:*574*

Stegosaurus **4**:528, 531; **12**:1593

stem cells 11:1556–1559

  adult **11**:1557–1558

  evolution **11**:1558

  hematopoietic (blood) **2**:242–243; **3**:330; **11**:1559

  human embryonic **2**:261; **4**:497; **5**:600; **11**:*1557*, 1558, 1559

  medical uses of **11**:1557

    and gene therapy for SCID **6**:804

    and regeneration of body parts **10**:1400

    therapeutic cloning **3**:385, 386; **11**:1558

  multipotent **3**:340

  pluripotent **3**:340; **11**:1557, 1558–1559

  research **3**:334; **9**:1204

  unipotent **11**:1557–1558

stems and stem systems 10:1318; **11**:1560–1562

  cacti **2**:273

  climbing **3**:379, 380

  tropism **12**:*1647*

  see also bulbs and corms; tubers and rhizomes; vascular systems

Stenonychosaurus **4**:529

steppes **2**:210

stereochemistry **9**:1269

stereotypes, behavioral **12**:1725

sterilization (fertility), human **4**:442–442

sterilization (microbial) **1**:116

Stern, William **7**:966–967

Sterna spp.

  S. albifrons (little tern) **11**:*1474*

  S. hirundo (common tern) **11**:*1472*

  S. paradisaea (Arctic tern) **8**:*1133*; **12**:1654

  S. sumatrana (black-napped tern) **1**:*82*

Sternbergia candida (winter daffodil) **2**:266

Sternorrhyncha **7**:883–884

steroids **3**:362; **7**:906, 907

  gene activation **7**:*906*

  treatment for cancer **3**:352

  see also corticosteroids

stethoscopes, invention **8**:*1101*, 1102

Steward, F.C. **3**:382

Stichopus spp. **4**:570

stick insects **4**:483

  see also leaf insects and walking sticks

sticklebacks **6**:733; **9**:1206; **12**:1615

  three-spined **4**:456, 485; **7**:*1002*

Sticta canariensis (canary sticta) **8**:1037

stigmas **1**:79; **6**:760

Still, Andrew Taylor **9**:1250

stilts **12**:1700

stimulants **1**:24

stimuli, sign stimuli **1**:83

stints, little **12**:1700

stirrup *see* stapes

stolons **5**:706; **10**:1405

stomach 4:514, 516, 517–518, 521–522; **11**:1563–1565

  disorders **4**:523; **11**:*1565*

  mucus **9**:1171

  ruminant **4**:515; **11**:*1451*–*1452*, 1564; **12**:1661

  study of gastric function **4**:517

  tissues of **7**:894

stomata **3**:415–416; **7**:902; **8**:1023–1024; **10**:*1424*; **11**:1560; **12**:1629–*1630*

  effect of water stress on **11**:1567

  night-opening in desert plants **1**:18–19

Stomolophus meleagris (cannonball jellyfish) **7**:982

Stone Age man **10**:1362, 1364

stonecrops, wall-pepper **2**:*274*

Stonehenge **10**:*1362*

stoneplants **2**:285

stones, bile *see* gallstones

stoneworts **1**:47

storks **6**:752; **8**:1134; **12**:1700

  whale-headed **12**:1701

storksbill **11**:1477

Bold words with bold page numbers indicate complete articles; bold numbers preceding colons are volume numbers; numbers following colons indicate page numbers; italic page numbers refer to illustrations or other graphics.

stratification 4:549

stratosphere 2:154, *155*

strawberry plants 6:795

  runners 3:*382*

  stolons 10:1405

streak plating 8:1131

streams *see* rivers and streams

Strepsirhini 10:1365

Streptococcus spp. 2:172

  in food making 6:763

  S. mutans 2:171, 172; **12**:1605

  S. pneumoniae 2:171; **11**:1551

streptomycin 6:742

stress 11:1566–1567

  and the immune system 7:942

  post-traumatic stress disorder (PTSD)
    1:122; **8**:1114, *1115*; **11**:1567

  stress hormones 5:641

stress tests 7:881

stridulation 3:405

Strigidae 2:236–237

Strigiformes 2:236–237

Strigops habroptilus (owl parrot/kakapo)
  6:755

Strix spp. 3:402; **9**:1221

strokes 2:242, 256; **3**:377; **7**:902;
  12:1620

  learning to move after 10:1435

stromatolites 3:332

Strongylocentratus franciscanus (purple sea
  urchin) 4:439

Struthio camelus (ostrich) 5:698; **6**:*755*

strychnine 1:51

stubborn 10:1323

Study of Instinct, The (Tinbergen) 1:84

sturgeons 6:734; **11**:1492

Sturnus vulgaris (starling) 3:401, 410;
  9:*1273*, 1275

stuttering 11:1545

style 1:78

stylets 6:738, 744; **7**:884

suberin 8:1025; **11**:1561

submersibles 9:1233, 1238

submission, signals 3:402

subsoil 11:1530

subspecies 12:1600

substantia nigra 9:1213

subtilisin 2:181

suburban habitats 11:1568–1569

succession

  plant 3:428, *429*; **10**:1402

    in lakes and ponds 7:999

    in tropical rain forests 12:1643

succinate dehydrogenase 7:995

succinyl-CoA 7:995

succinyl-CoA synthetase 7:995

succulents *see* cacti and succulents

suckerfish 11:1490

suckling 7:998

sucrose 5:619

Sudden Infant Death Syndrome (SIDS)
  12:1691

sudiferous glands *see* sweat glands

Suez Canal 8:1126

sugar beet 4:510

sugar cane, a C4 plant 10:1305

sugars 3:297, *298*

Suiformes 11:1451

Sula spp. 2:*231*

sulfa drugs 9:1290

sulfones 1:108

sulfur, desulfurization of coal 8:1132

sulfur dioxide

  atmospheric 1:*16*; **5**:625; **10**:1340

  see also acid rain

sulfuric acid 1:16

sulfur oxides, as pollutants 2:156

sulphonamides 1:108

sunbirds, golden-winged 5:*696*

sunburn 12:*1658*

Suncus etruscus (Savi's pygmy shrew) 7:954

sundews 3:*314–316*; **5**:696

sunflowers 1:*101*, 102; **10**:*1315*

sunsets 2:*154*

superfetation 10:1353

superoxide 2:240

superregenerators 10:1399–1400

suprachiasmatic nucleus (SCN) 2:217,
  218; **11**:1512

surface spreading 12:1631–1632

surfperches 6:733

surgery 11:1570–1575

  anesthesia for 1:75–76; **8**:1102;
    11:1571, *1573*

  and antisepsis 8:1043

  biopsies 4:475

  brain 5:*639*; **11**:*1575*

  cryosurgery 4:473

  development 11:1570–1571

    see also medicine, history of

  elective and nonelective 11:1572–1573

  eye 11:1575

  heart 8:1101; **11**:1571–1572

  keyhole (minimally invasive surgery;
    MIS) **10**:1433; **11**:*1574–1575*

    see also endoscopy

  laser 8:*1091*; **11**:*1574*, *1575*

  microsurgery 11:*1572*

  minimal access *see* surgery, keyhole

  plastic 11:1572

  remotely controlled 8:1094

  robots used in 4:*497*; **10**:*1432*–1434

  spare-part 8:1092

  transplantation *see* transplants

  use of microscopes 8:*1089*

Suricata suricatta (gray meerkat) 1:*58*;
  3:313; **11**:1522

suricates 3:313

surrogate motherhood 5:712

survival of the fittest 9:1191; **10**:1345

suspension feeders, on the ocean floor
  9:1232

Sus scrofa (wild boar) 12:1606, *1610*

sutures 11:1573

Suwa, Gen 7:915

Svedberg, The 10:1376

swales, permaculture and 9:1281

swallowing 12:1621–1622

swallows

  nests 9:1209

  parasites of 11:1524

Swammerdam, Jan 5:621

swamps 12:1704

swans 12:1701

sweat 5:672, 675–676; **12**:1619

  night sweats 8:1110

sweat glands 5:672, 674, *675–676*;
  11:1508

Swietenia spp. (mahogany) 5:648

swiftlets, cave 3:*328*; **4**:574; **9**:*1222*

swifts 2:231

swim bladders 3:405; **6**:*728*, 729;
  11:1577

swimmerets 1:*13*

swimming 11:1576–1578

  fish 6:729–730; **9**:1178–1179;
    11:*1576–1577*

    sharks 11:1500, 1577

  in humans 11:1577

    babies 3:*356*

swollen glands 3:371; **8**:*1066*

sycamores 4:547–548; **9**:*1278*

Syconycteris australis (southern blossom bat)
  2:173–174

Sydenham, Thomas 8:1100

syllogisms 11:1467

Sylvilagus spp. (cottontail rabbits) **10**:*1392*

symbiosis 9:1264; 11:1579–1582

  between plant and animal kingdoms
    9:1252

  commensalism 3:390; **11**:1579, *1580*

    see also epiphytes

  endosymbiosis, prokaryotes as organelles
    2:203; **3**:332, 392; **5**:585; **10**:1380

  mutualism 3:390; **11**:*1579*

    ant/acacia tree 1:118–119; **3**:*390*;
      4:483; **11**:1580–1581

    ant/aphid 4:483; **11**:*1581*

    bird/herbivore 4:485

    clams/bacteria 9:1233

    cockroaches/protozoa 3:388

    and coevolution 3:*390*–391

    cooperative hunting 1:58

    corals/single-celled algae 1:49;
      4:*449–450*, 453

    evolution 11:1581

    facultative 11:1579, 1581–1582

    honeyguides 3:403; **11**:1582

    legumes/soil-bacteria 8:*1029*; **9**:1217,
      1218

    lichens 8:1034; **11**:1581

    microorganisms in the gut 4:517;
      9:*1226*, 1228; **12**:1611

    mycorrhizae 3:389; **6**:800;
      9:1187–1188; **10**:1322; **11**:1450,
      1582; **12**:1590, 1640

  obligatory 11:1579, 1581

  vestimentiferan worms/bacteria
    9:1233

parasitism *see* parasites

symbiotic luminous bacteria 2:205

symmetry

  bilateral 1:75; **7**:970–971

    in flatworms 6:735

  disguising 2:284

  in flowers 6:759

  radial 7:969–970

Symphata 12:1692, 1693

Symphytum officinale (comfrey) 7:888

symplastic pathways 8:1025

synapses 1:69; **12**:1626

  discovery 10:1396

  nerve impulses across 9:1200–1201

  pruning 2:260

synergids 5:590

synesthesia 11:1516

synovia 7:869

syphilis 7:949

  cure for 5:*591*, 592

  Tuskagee Syphilis Study 2:189

syringes, needle-free 8:*1092*

Systema Naturae (Carolus Linnaeus) 5:621;
  8:1041, 1042; **12**:1600

systematics 12:1599–1600

systemic acquired resistance (SAR) 7:932

systemic lupus erythematosus (SLE)
  2:164, 165

systems, nonlinear 3:347–348

systole 7:879

Szent-Györgi, Albert 7:994

T

T$_3$ *see* triiodothryronine

T$_4$ *see* thyroxine

T$_4$ cells *see* T-helper cells

T$_4$ phages 12:*1681*

Tachyglossus aculeatus (short-beaked
  echidna) 9:1162–1163

tacrine (THA) 1:61, 4:496

Tadorna tadorna (shelduck) 12:1701

tadpoles *see* frogs and toads, tadpoles

Taenia spp. (tapeworms) 6:*737*; **9**:1268

tagging

  of animals 12:*1720*, 1721

  radioactive *see* radioactive tagging

taiga biomes 2:208; 4:490–491;
  12:*1589–1591*

  animals 2:208, 210; **12**:*1591*

    birds 6:776–777; **12**:1591

  farming in 12:1590

  light taiga 12:1590

tails 12:1592–1594

  chordate 3:364–365

  invertebrate 12:1592

  regeneration 10:1400; **12**:1593

  shedding (autotomy) 8:1017,
    1052–1053; **10**:1400; **12**:1593

  vertebrate 12:1592–1593

taipans **11**:1518

Taj Mahal **1**:*17*

takahes **6**:756

Takaki, Kanehiro **12**:1690

Takifugu rubripes (Japanese puffer fish)
    1:*50*; **4**:485

tamanduas **1**:103–104

tamaracks **12**:1591

tamarins **10**:1367–1368
    golden lion **10**:*1367*; **12**:1718, 1725

Tamias striatus (eastern chipmunk)
    12:*1608*

tamoxifen **3**:353

Tanacetum parthenium (feverfew) **7**:*888*

tannins **3**:404; **4**:483; **11**:1562

Tansley, Arthur **5**:582

tape grass *see* eelgrass

tapetum lucidum **3**:322; **4**:464; **10**:1365

tapeworms **1**:90; **3**:390–391; **6**:736, *737*;
    9:1267–1268
    excretion **7**:970
    self-fertilization **7**:890

taphonomy **9**:1254, 1256

Taphrina deformans **10**:1321

tapirs **9**:1257

tarantulas **4**:485; **11**:*1546*, 1548

Taraxacum spp. *see* dandelions

Tardigrada **1**:97

Taricha rivularis (red-bellied newt) **4**:458

tarsiers **9**:*1221*, 1222; **10**:1367

Tarsiidae **10**:1367

Tarsius spp. **9**:*1221*

Tasmanian devils **8**:*1079*

Tasmanian tigers (Tasmanian
    wolves/thylacines) **4**:446; **8**:1079

taste 8:1070; **11**:1516; **12:1595–1597**,
    1621
    disorders **12**:1597
    see also smell

taste buds **12**:1596, *1597*, 1622

Tatum, Edward 8:1140; **12:1598**

taxes **12**:1645, 1647

taxis *see* taxes

Taxodium spp. **3**:415, 416; **5**:648; **12**:*1703*

taxol **3**:417; **9**:1290

taxon cycle **12**:1711

taxonomy 12:1599–1602
    Linnaeus and **2**:201, 253; **12**:1600
        see also Linnaeus, Carolus
    plant **2**:254
    see also classification; species

Taylor, Edwin **2**:276

Tay-Sachs disease **4**:477

TB *see* tuberculosis

TCDD **4**:532

T-cells *see* lymphocytes, T-cells

tea **4**:*546*; **8**:*1013*, 1014

TEACCH program **2**:162–163

teaching machines **3**:414

teak **12**:*1644*

Tecophilaea cyanocrocus (Chilean blue
    crocus) **2**:266

Tectaria gemmifera **5**:706

Tectona grandis (teak) **12**:*1644*

tectum **2**:259

Teddy (robot) **10**:1435

teeth 4:517; **12:1603–1606**
    carnassials **3**:307, 321; **4**:517; **12**:1605
    of carnivores **3**:*307*, 309, 310; **4**:517;
        7:979; **8**:1070; **12**:1605
    decay **12**:1604–*1605*
    dental formula **12**:1606
    fillings **12**:1605
    of herbivores **4**:517; **7**:979; **8**:1070;
        12:*1603*, 1605
        ungulates **12**:1660–1661
    heterodont **12**:1674
    human **12**:*1604*
    hypsodont **11**:1452
    mammalian **8**:1070; **12**:1603,
        1605–1606
    milk/deciduous teeth **12**:1603, *1604*
    of omnivores **3**:311; **7**:979; **8**:1072
    pleurodont **8**:1051
    of rodents **10**:*1436*; **12**:1605
    wisdom **12**:1604
    X rays **12**:1712

telekinesis **9**:1262

telemedicine **8**:*1094*; **10**:*1433*–1434

teleological explanations, for traits **2**:204

Teleostei **6**:734

Telicomys **10**:1438

Teliomycetes *see* rusts; smuts

Teliomycotina **9**:1185

temperate forest biomes 2:209;
    12:1607–1610, 1637
    animals and birds **6**:777; **12**:*1609*
    deciduous **2**:209; **12**:1608
    epiphytes **5**:642
    evergreen **2**:209; **12**:1610
    growth and renewal **10**:1402; **12**:1609
    layers **12**:1608–1609
    mixed **4**:491
    rain forests **12**:1610

temperature **5**:616
    affecting sex of crocodilians **4**:466
    body **5**:641
        basal body (BBT), at ovulation **4**:442
    Earth **6**:802, *803*
        see also global warming
    low, for cryobiology **4**:471–475
    regulation *see* thermoregulation

temperature-dependent sex determination
    (TSD) **4**:466; **10**:1416

temporal lobes **2**:*259*

tendons **3**:419; **6**:*726*; **9**:1178; **11**:1501

tendrils **3**:379–380; **8**:1027; **10**:1316;
    11:1554

Tenebrio spp. **2**:178

Tenhaeff, W.H.C. **9**:1263

Tenodera aridifolia (Chinese mantis) **8**:1075

tenrecs **7**:*955*, 956; **9**:1221

Terman, Lewis M. **7**:967

termitaria **12**:1612

termites 12:1611–1612
    castes **12**:1611
    cellulose digestion **1**:140; **10**:1380;
        11:*1461*, 1462; **12**:1611
    evolution **12**:1612
    nests **7**:*959*; **9**:*1208*; **12**:1612
    touch receptors **12**:1627

terns **11**:1474
    Arctic, migration **8**:*1133*; **12**:1654
    black-napped **1**:*82*
    common **11**:*1472*

terpenoids **6**:762

terrapins **12**:1624
    river **12**:1623

territories 12:1613–1615
    a counterproductive stategy **12**:1615
    limiting population density **10**:1346
    territorial behavior **3**:402
        aggression **1**:29–30, 85
    see also competition

terrorists, biological weapons **2**:199

testes **10**:*1409*–1410
    castration **10**:1414

testosterone **5**:708
    and aggression **1**:*31*
    and castration **10**:1414
    daily rhythm **2**:219
    and puberty/adolescence **1**:*26*, 27;
        7:906; **10**:1410
    secretion **5**:612, 613

Testudo elephantopus (Galápagos tortoise)
    1:*33*; **12**:1623

tetanus **2**:172; **9**:1203; **11**:1531
    vaccines **9**:1203

tetany **2**:278; **5**:612

Tetracanthella arctica (springtail) **12**:1719

tetracycline **1**:109

tetraiodothyronine *see* thyroxine

tetrapyrroles **10**:1309–1310

tetras **1**:*125*

tetrasaccharides **3**:297

tetrodotoxin **1**:50; **4**:485

textiles, organic **9**:1248

thalamus **2**:257; **5**:602; **12**:1627

thalassemias **1**:73; **2**:247

Thalassia spp. **10**:1338

thalidomide **5**:698; **8**:1090

Thamnophis spp. (garter snake) **10**:1351;
    11:1520

Thaumatogyllus **3**:326

thecodonts **4**:530

thelarche **8**:1111

T-helper cells **2**:241; **7**:*929*, 934, 938
    AIDS and **7**:940

Theobroma cacao (cocoa) **1**:51; **12**:1644

Theophrastus **2**:253

therapods **4**:529

thermal energy **5**:616

thermal equilibrium **5**:616

thermocline **7**:1002

thermodynamics, laws of **5**:*615*

thermometers, history **8**:1102

thermophilic and thermophobic behavior
    3:397

thermoreceptors **12**:1626

**thermoregulation (temperature
    regulation) 7**:900–*901*;
    12:1616–1619
    in bats **2**:175–176
    behavioral **8**:1051
    in butterflies and moths **2**:271
    in cold-blooded animals **3**:*396*–397;
        8:*1122*; **12**:1616–1618
    under water **3**:397
    in vertebrates **11**:1506
    in warm-blooded animals **12**:1616,
        1617, 1618–1619

thermosphere **2**:154–155, *155*

thermotaxis **12**:1647

thigmotropism **3**:380; **12**:1645, 1646

Thiobacillus spp.
    T. denitrificans **9**:1218
    T. ferrooxidans **7**:973

Thomson, Charles Wyville **9**:1239

thoracoplasty **11**:1570–1571

thorax **1**:13

Thorazine (chlorpromazine) **11**:1466

Thorndike, E.L. **3**:412

thorns **4**:*482*; **11**:*1562*

thoughts, organization of **3**:394

Three Mile Island **5**:626; **10**:1395

threshing machines, development **1**:39

thrombi **12**:1620

thrombin **2**:278

thrombocytopenia **2**:247

thrombophlebitis **12**:*1620*

thromboplastin **2**:242, 278

thrombosis 12:1620
    cerebral **3**:377
    coronary **12**:1620
    deep vein (DVT) **12**:1620
        postoperative **11**:1573
    prevention **12**:1620

thromboxanes **5**:692

thrush (candidiasis) **12**:1716

thrushes, song **4**:459; **9**:1274

thumbs, opposable **7**:869

Thylacinus cynocephalus (Tasmanian
    wolf/Tasmanian tiger) **4**:446; **8**:1079

thylakoids **3**:335; **10**:1304
    membranes **10**:1306

thymidine **7**:896

thymine **4**:533, 535, 537; **5**:654; **10**:1428

thymocytes **8**:1064

thymomas **8**:1064

thymopoietin **11**:1508

> **Bold words with bold page numbers indicate complete articles; bold numbers preceding colons are volume numbers; numbers following colons indicate page numbers; italic page numbers refer to illustrations or other graphics.**

thymosin 7:904

thymus gland 1:34; 7:903–904; 8:1064

  hormones 5:613; 7:904

  lymphocytes in (thymocytes) 7:*930*, *932*; 8:1064

  see also lymphatic systems

Thyone spp. 4:570

thyroid gland 2:*166*

  diseases of 2:165, 166; 7:*905*; 9:1227

  hormones 5:612; 7:900, 903, 907

thyroid-stimulating hormone (TSH) 2:166; 5:612; 7:*900*; 8:1120; 9:1159

thyrotropin-releasing hormone (TRH) 2:166

thyroxine (tetraiodothyronine; T4) 2:166; 7:907; 8:1126; 12:1618

tick birds 4:485

ticks 1:132, 141

  diseases from 1:*131*; 7:*946–947*, 949; 9:*1264*

  northern deer 7:*946*

  wood 1:*131*; 9:*1264*

tidal zones *see* littoral zones

tides 9:1235

Tierra (digital world) 2:*152*

tigers 1:*32*; 2:*284*; 3:313, *321*, 324; 5:*607–608*, 694

  saber-toothed 3:310, 312, 324; 5:678; 9:*1254*; 10:*1349*

Tillandsia usneoides (Spanish moss) 5:642

timber 3:*417*; 12:1590, 1639

  see also wood

timberline 9:1168

Tinbergen, Nikolaas 1:83, 84; 5:643, *644*; 7:963

tine test 12:1648

tinnitus 7:875

tissue culture 3:382; 11:1562; 12:1676

tissue engineering 8:1093

tissues 1:69

  body, water balance 11:1459

  sampling and fixation 7:895

  see also histology

tits, great 1:*29*, 85; 9:1274

Tmesipteris spp. (fork-fern) 5:706

toadfish 3:405

toads *see* frogs and toads

toadstools *see* mushrooms and toadstools

tobacco 10:1337

  cultivation 8:*1014*

  seeds 1:79

  see also smoking

tobacco mosaic diseaese 8:1130; 10:1323, *1324*

Tobamovirus 10:1323

toes

  extra (polydactyly) 4:*525*

  opposable 5:697–698; 10:1365

Tollund man 6:782–783

tomatoes 6:793

  diseases 10:*1322*

  Flavr Savr 2:227; 6:765, 794, 809

freeze-resistant 2:225; 6:765

plants, response to attack 10:1317

tomentum 6:743

tongue 4:514; **12:1621–1622**

  disorders of 12:1622

  and taste 12:*1597*, 1621

tongue worms 1:97

tonsils 8:1065

tools

  ancient man and 10:*1361*, 1362–1363

  chimpanzees and 10:1369–1370

topsoil 11:1530

Torosaurus 4:531

torpor 12:1618

tortoises and turtles 12:1623–1624

  armor 4:485; 12:1623

  and humans 12:1624

  movement 12:1623

  respiration 12:1623

  tortoises, giant 3:410; 12:*1623*, 1624

  turtles 11:*1492*

    alligator snapping 2:283, 286; 12:1623–1624

    courtship behavior 4:459

    eggs 12:1624

    feeding by 12:1623–1624

    green 4:*437*; 8:1134; 11:*1492*; 12:1624

    hawksbill 11:1492; 12:1624

    jaws 7:978; 12:1606

    leatherback 11:1492

    loggerhead 11:1492

    map 12:1623

    migration 8:1134

    nest holes 9:1209

    painted 4:459

    reproduction 12:1624

    sea 12:1623, *1624*

    soft-shelled 12:1623

    terrapin 12:1623, 1624

toucans 6:777

touch 8:1071; **12:1625–1628**

  communication by 3:405

  nerves and 12:1626

tourism, in savannas 11:1464

toxins 1:51

  bacterial 2:169, 172

  from plants 12:1640

  see also alkaloids; venom

Toxocara canis 9:*1266*

toxocariasis 9:*1266*

toxoid vaccines 7:935

trace elements

  deficiency 4:489; 9:1227

  plant 9:1227

trachea 3:320; 8:1054–1055; 10:1420

  arthropod and insect tracheae 1:140; 10:1419–1420

tracheae (plant cells) 12:1631

tracheids 12:1631

Trachurus symmetricus (California mackerel) 4:481

tracks, fossilized 6:783

tractors 1:40

Tradescant, John 2:*254*

transcription 4:537; 9:1189; 10:1378, 1428, *1429*

transduction 1:110; 2:170

transformation 1:110; 2:170

transformist theory, of Lamarck 5:652

transfusions

  blood 2:*244*–245; 11:1571

    Charles Drew and 4:*553*–554

transgenic organisms, plants 2:223; 6:809; 9:*1243*, 1244

translation, in protein synthesis 4:537; 9:1189; 10:1378, 1429–1430

translocation (plant) *see* transpiration and translocation

transmissible spongiform encephalopathies (TSEs) 10:1371

transpiration and translocation 12:1629–1632

  guttation 8:1026; 12:1632

  translocation 11:1448, 1561; 12:1631–1632

  transpiration 7:902; 8:1026; 11:1448, 1561; 12:*1629–1631*, 1669

  see also vascular systems

transplants 8:1092; **12:1633–1636**

  abdominal viscera 12:1636

    small bowel 12:1636

  autotransplants and allotransplants 8:1092; 12:1633

  bone marrow 2:249; 3:353; 4:535; 8:1031; 11:1557; 12:*1633*

  drawbacks 3:384–385

  embryo 5:711

  hand 8:1088

  heart 7:*940*; 8:1088

    from animals 12:1634

  heart-lung 8:1092; 12:1635–1636

  history of 8:1088; 12:1633–1636

  and the immune response 7:932, 940–941; 8:1087–1088

  kidney 4:472; 8:1039, 1065–1066, *1088*; 12:*1634*, 1636

    the first 8:1088, 1092; 12:1634

  liver 4:472; 8:1046; 12:1634–1635

  Medawar, Peter, and 8:1087–1088, 1103; 12:1633–1634

  multivisceral "cluster" 12:1636

  pancreas 12:1634

  and rejection 12:1635

  supply of organs 12:1636

  and therapeutic cloning 3:384–385; 11:1558

  using stem cells 5:600; 11:1557

  xenotransplants 2:189, 225; 8:1092; 12:1634

  see also grafting

transposons (transposable elements; "jumping genes") 1:110; 7:922–923; 8:1086; 9:1190

traveler's disease *see* dysentery, amoebic

Trechus micros (ground beetle) 3:327

tree ducks, fulvous 4:460

treehoppers 2:283

trees 9:*1277–1278*; **12:1637–1640**

  age and aging of 12:*1638*, *1640*

  angiosperm (flowering) 12:1637, 1638

  apical dominance 8:1023

  bark 12:1639

  bonsai 11:*1450*; 12:1639

  deciduous 2:209; 8:*1022*, *1025*; 12:1608, 1638

  decomposition of dead 11:1460–1462; 12:1609

  development 12:1639

    of woody stems 11:*1561*

  diseases 12:1640

    Dutch elm disease 2:178, 184; 9:1265, 1294; 10:1322; 12:1640

  distribution 12:1637

    due to glaciation 2:194

  diversity 12:1637

  dormancy 4:547–548

  effects of acid rain 4:491–492

  eudicot 4:510

  evergreen 2:209; 12:1638

  fossilized 12:1638

  fruit 4:549

  gymnosperm 12:1637, 1638

    see also conifers; Cycadophyta; ginkgo trees

  hardwood 11:1562

  on island habitats 7:977

  life in 12:1640

  monocotyledonous *see* palms

  permaculture and 9:1281–1282

  pests of 12:1640

  record-breaking 12:1608, *1638*, 1640

  rings, annual 12:1639, *1640*

  roots 11:1450; 12:1640

  shade-tolerant 12:1643

  shape 12:*1637*, 1639

  softwood 11:1562; 12:1637, 1639

  structure 12:1639–1640

  of the taiga 12:1591

  of the tundra 12:1653

  see also conifers; forests; timber; wood

Trematoda 6:*735*; 9:1265

trenches, deep-sea 9:1231

trench fever 7:946, 950

trephining 11:1570

Treponema pallidum 2:171

tretinoin cream 12:1691

Treviranus, Gottfried 2:200

Triadobatrachus 6:790

trials

  blind and double-blind 8:1096

  fertility 7:896

  randomized controlled 8:1096, 1097

  see also experiments

Triatoma spp. 7:885

tricarboxylic cycle *see* Krebs cycle

triceps 9:*1179*

Triceratops 4:528, 531

Trichinella spiralis 9:1196

trichinosis 9:1196

Trichodectes oris (sheep-biting louse) 8:1033

trichomes 4:482, 500; 8:1026, *1027*

Trichomonas spp.

  T. *hominis* 9:1266

  T. *vaginalis* 7:950

trichomoniasis 7:950

Trichonympha spp. 11:*1461*, 1462

Trichoplax adhaerens 1:94

Trieste (submersible) 9:1238

Trifolium spp. (clover) 8:1028; 10:1322

triglycerides 5:641, *689, 690, 691*

  see also fats and oils

triiodothryronine (T3) 2:166; 8:1126

trilobites 1:138; 6:783

trimethoprim 1:108

trimethylamine oxide (TMAO; TMO)
  5:665, 670; 11:1459

Triphosa dubitata (tissue moth) 3:328

triplets 12:1656

trisaccharides 3:297

trisomy-21 3:369

tritanopia 12:1688

Triticum see wheat

Triturus helveticus (palmate newt) 11:1456

triungulins 2:178

Trivers, Robert 11:1527

troglodytes 3:325

trogons 6:777

Trombidium spp. 1:*132*

trophic levels 5:586; 6:768

tropical rain forest biomes
  2:*209–210*; 5:*581*; **12:1641–1644**

  animals 5:694; 6:*777–778*; 12:1642

  biodiversity 2:184; 12:1637, 1641–1642

  commercial yield 12:*1644*

  conservation 3:426

  deforestation 4:492, 493; 12:1643

  effects on global climate 12:1644

  layers 12:1642–1643

  plants 5:642; 12:*1643*–1644

  regeneration 10:1402

  soils 11:*1529*

tropic birds 11:1472–1473

tropisms and taxes 12:1645–1647

  taxes 12:1645, 1647

  tropisms 10:1316; 12:1645–1646

    geotropism (gravitropism; gravity
      affecting growth) 10:1316, *1317*;
      11:1449; 12:1645–1646

    phototropism 10:1316, 1317

    plagiotropism 12:1646

    thigmotropism 3:380; 12:1646

tropomyosin 9:1182

troponin 9:1182

troposphere 2:154, *155*

trout

  farmed 1:124

  population densities 3:408

trumpet cells 12:1632

Trychonympha 10:1380

Trypanosoma spp. 9:1265; 10:1382

  T. *brucei* 7:946

  T. *cruzi* 7:885, 946

trypanosomiasis

  African *see* sleeping sickness

  American *see* Chagas' disease

  host response 9:1267

trypsin 4:518, 522; 9:1260

  optimum pH for 5:*631*

Tschermak, Erich 8:1107

tsetse flies *see* flies, tsetse

Tsuga spp. (hemlocks) 3:415

tuataras 8:*1050*; 10:*1415*; 11:1581–1582

tubal ligation 4:442–443

tube feet 4:567, *568, 569, 570*;
  12:1670

tubenoses 11:1474

tuberculin skin test 12:1648

tuberculosis 5:591–592; 7:948; 8:1059;
  12:1648

  bovine 1:88

  renal 5:671

  treatment 12:1648

  vaccine 7:935; 12:1648

  X rays to show 12:*1648*, 1713

tubers and rhizomes 11:1449;
  12:1649–1651

  crops 12:1650

    see also crops, root and tuber

  rhizomes 10:1318; 11:*1560*; 12:1646,
    1649, 1650–*1651*

  tubers 12:1649–*1650*

    root 11:1449; 12:1650

    stem 4:548

Tubifex spp. 1:*128*

tubuloacinar glands 5:674

tucuxis 12:1710

tularemia 2:198; 7:947

Tulippa spp. *see* tulips

tulips 1:*78*

  bulbs 2:*265*

  viral infections 10:*1323*

Tull, Jethro 1:39

tumor promoters 3:295

tumors 3:294

  hormone-secreting 5:613

  in the spleen 11:1551

  see also cancer

tuna 10:1424; 12:1617

  skipjack 6:731

tundra biomes 2:*208*; 10:1332–1333;
  12:1590, 1652–1654

  Alpine and Arctic 12:1653

  animals 2:208, 210; 12:*1653–1654*

  lichens 12:1653

  plants 12:1653

Tunga penetrans (chigger/chigoe/jigger)
  6:738; 9:*1264*

Tunicata (Urochordata) 3:*365*

Turbellaria 6:735–736

Turdus spp. 9:*1274*; 11:1569

Tursiops truncatus (bottlenose dolphin)
  4:572

turtles *see* tortoises and turtles

Tuskagee Syphilis Study 2:189

tusks 12:1606, 1663

twins and multiple births 5:590;
  12:1655–1656

  identical twins 3:383, *384*; 12:*1655, 1656*

  nonidentical/fraternal twins 12:1655, *1656*

    and skin grafts 8:1087, 1088

  Siamese twins 12:1656

Tylopoda 11:1451

Tympanuchus spp. (prairie chicken) 4:459

Typhlonectidae 2:276

typhoid (typhoid fever) 5:627, *634*; 7:948

typhus 9:1267

  tick 7:947

typing, blood 2:243, *244–245*; 6:774

Tyrannosaurus 4:528, 529, 531

tyrosine 10:1310

Tyto alba (barn owl) 2:237; 9:*1158*, 1222

Tytonidae 2:237

U

uakaris 10:1368

Uca spp. (fiddler crab) 2:*218*; 4:457, 467

Ulam, Stanislaw 2:150

ulcers

  mouth 12:1622

  peptic 4:516, 519, 523

    duodenal 1:*71*

    stomach (gastric) 9:1172; 11:*1565*, 1567

Ulmus spp. (elm) 2:184

Uloboridae 11:1547

ultracentrifugation 2:181; 10:1376;
  12:1677

ultradian rhythms 2:219

ultrasound 1:72; 12:1657

  Doppler 8:1090

  for prenatal screening 12:1657

  used by bats *see* echolocation, by bats

ultraviolet radiation 12:1658

  dangers to humans 12:*1658*

  detection by animals 5:688; 10:1337

  effect on corals 4:449

  and evolution 12:1658

  markings on flowers 6:761; 10:1337

Ulva spp. (sea lettuce) 7:987

umbilical cord 10:1356

  stem cells 11:*1556*, 1557

Umbilicaria spp. 8:1036

Umbonia spinosa (treehopper) 2:283

unani 1:044

unconscious 3:422

  collective 10:1385

Undaria pinatifida (wakame) 7:987

undernutrition 9:1227

ungulates 12:1659–1663

  defense 4:484–485

  domestic 12:1662

  even-toed (Artiodactyla) 12:1659, *1660*,
    1661

  evolution 12:*1661*

  feet 5:697; 12:*1659–1660*

  on grasslands 11:1453, 1464–1465;
    12:*1663*

  mammary glands 5:676

  odd-toed (Perissodactyla) 12:1659,
    1660, 1661

  see also horns; ruminants

Union Carbide accident 5:628

Uniramia 1:97

uniramians 1:141–142

United Nations, Conference on
  Environment and Development
  (UNCED) 2:183

universal constructor model 2:150

Upogebia spp. (mud shrimp) 4:467

upwellings 4:438; 9:1236

uracil 4:536; 10:1428

Uraeotyphidae 2:276

uranium 10:1395

urban habitats 12:1664–1665

  cities by lakes 7:1002

urea, medical uses 12:*1667*

urea cycle 12:1666–1668

  discovery 12:1666–1667

  urea 5:665; 12:1666

    formation in the liver 8:1046, *1119*

    in shark tissues 11:1459

uremia 7:992

ureotelic organisms 12:1666, 1667, *1668*

ureter 5:671

urethra 5:671; 9:1172; 10:1412

Urey, Harold 2:181; 5:651, *652*, 682

Uria aalge (common guillemot) 11:1474

uric acid

  causing gout 8:1124

  as a pigment 10:1311

  waste product 5:665; 12:1666

uricotelic organisms 12:1666

urinary tract diseases, in cats and dogs
  1:90

urine

  examination 5:671

  formation 5:671, 672

  retention 11:1574

Urochordata 3:365

Urodela 1:64

urogenital tracts, mucous membranes
  9:1172

Uropygi 11:1469

Ursavus elmensis (dawn bear) 3:309

Ursidae 3:308–309

  see also bears

Ursus spp. **3**:308–309
  U. americanus (American black bear)
    12:1655–1656
  U. arctos (European bear) **11**:1541
  U. maritimus see bears, polar
  U. spelaeus (cave bear) **11**:1541
Urtica dioica (stinging nettle) **4**:483
use-dilution test **1**:117
Ustilaginomycotina **9**:1185
uterus **10**:*1412*, 1413–1414
  endometrial thickness **8**:*1109*
  see also placenta
utilitarianism **2**:188
utricle **4**:561
Utricularia spp. (bladderworts) **3**:314, *315*;
  12:1670

V

vaccines *see* immunization, vaccines
vaccinia virus **12**:1679
vacuoles, cell **3**:*335*, 336–337; **5**:666;
  8:1023
vacuum packing **6**:765
VADs (ventricular assist devices) **2**:*214*
vagina **10**:*1412*, 1413
  mucous membrane **9**:1172
Valium (diazepam) **9**:1215
Vallisneria spp. (eelgrass/tape grass)
  10:1338
vancomycin **5**:630
vaquitas **12**:1709
Varanus komodoensis (Komodo dragon)
  7:*977*; **8**:1051; **12**:1717
Vargula spp., bioluminescence **2**:206
varicocele **5**:711
vasa deferentia **10**:1411
  and vasectomy **4**:443
vascular systems 12:1669–1670
  animal, in echinoderms **4**:567;
    12:1670
  plant **1**:70; **11**:1560–1561; **12**:1669
    aquatic vascular plants **12**:1670
    eudicot **4**:509
    root **11**:1448
    vascular bundles **4**:509
    xylem and phloem **4**:509;
      8:1024–1025; **11**:1448, 1561;
      12:1631–1632, *1669*
  see also stems and stem systems
vasectomy **4**:443
vasopressin **5**:611
vedic medicine **7**:944
vegans **9**:1228
vegetables, biennial **2**:179
vegetarianism **9**:1228
vegetative reproduction, plant **1**:80;
  2:266; **10**:1405; **11**:1562; **12**:1650
vegetative state **3**:399, 400; **5**:646;
  8:1038, 1040
vehicles, and pollution **10**:*1340*
veins **3**:*376*
  hepatic portal **7**:894; **8**:1044

renal **7**:*991*
splenic **11**:1551
veins (leaf) **8**:*1024–1025*
Vejovidae **11**:1470
veld **2**:210
Velella velella (by-the-wind-sailor) **7**:983
Velociraptor **4**:528, 529
velvet worms **1**:97, 138; **8**:1049–1050;
  12:*1602*
venom **4**:485
  snake **7**:*939*; **11**:1518
  spider **1**:133, *139*, 141; **4**:485
  see also toxins
Venter, Craig **7**:*923*
ventilation, mechanical **8**:1038–1039
ventricles **7**:877, *878*, 879
ventricular assist devices (VADs) **2**:*214*
vents, hydrothermal **5**:651, 681; **9**:1230,
  1232–*1233*, 1237, 1239
Venus **5**:683
Venus's-flytrap **3**:314, 316; **5**:696;
  8:*1027*; **10**:1316, 1397;
  12:1625, 1646
  endangered **5**:*609*; **10**:1317
verdins **2**:273
Vermivora bachmanii (Bachman's warbler)
  9:1275
verrucae **5**:699
vertebral column
  chiropractic manipulation **1**:*56*, 57
  disks of cartilage in **3**:*319*, 320
  mammalian **11**:1498
  slipped disks **11**:*1502*
vertebrates 1:94, 97; 12:1671–1674
  abdomen **1**:13
  brain **2**:*257*, 258, 259
  are chordates **3**:365
  circulatory systems **3**:373–376
  cloning **3**:382–383, 385
  colonizing the land **12**:1674
  digestive systems **4**:513–*516*
  embryo development **5**:598–600
  evolution **12**:1672
  excretory systems **7**:989–990
  heart **3**:375; **7**:*877–879*
  immune system **7**:928
  are larger than invertebrates **12**:1673
  molting **9**:1158–1159
  skeleton **11**:1499–1504
  skin **11**:1506
  success **12**:1674
  tails **12**:1592–1593
  taste **12**:1596
  see also amphibians; birds; chordates; fish;
    mammals; reptiles
vertigo **4**:561
Vesalius, Andreas **1**:71; **2**:201; **8**:1099
Vespa spp. (hornets) **12**:1692–1693
Vespula vulgaris (common wasp) **12**:*1692*
vestibular system **4**:*560*
vetches **3**:379
Vibrio spp. **2**:171, 205

V. cholerae **2**:197; **5**:633; **7**:*935*, 948
Vicia spp. **8**:1028
vicodin **4**:557
Victoria, Queen **4**:556
Victoria amazonica **10**:1318
Victoria, Lake, new species of fish **11**:1486
Vigna spp. (blackeye pea) **8**:1028
villi, intestinal **4**:517, 519, *521*, 523;
  8:*1063*; **9**:1171
vinblastine **7**:887
vincoleukoblastine **1**:51
vincristine **7**:887
vinegaroons **11**:1469
vines **6**:795
  pepper **3**:380
  woody *see* lianas
viperfish **7**:979
vipers **11**:1520
  Gaboon **2**:282
  pit **11**:1518, 1520
  saw-scaled **11**:1518
  see also rattlesnakes
Virginia creeper **3**:*380*; **11**:1450
viroids **10**:1324
virology 12:1675–1679
virtual reality **7**:*952*
viruses 8:1130; 12:1680–1683
  attacking cells **12**:1681–1682
  bacteriophages **1**:110; **4**:537; **12**:1675,
    1681
  and cancer **3**:295
  coat **12**:1680
  culturing **12**:1676
  diseases **12**:1682–*1683*
    common cold 3:395
    fighting **12**:1677–1678
    of plants **10**:1323–*1324*; **12**:1678, 1683
  DNA **12**:1681
  extraction and purification
    12:1676–1677
  families **12**:1681
  for gene therapy **6**:806–*807*, *808*
  genetic engineering and **12**:1678–1679
  genetic material **3**:367; **12**:1681
  human immunodeficiency (HIV)
    see AIDS
  indentifying **12**:1677
  mosaic
    cauliflower **10**:1323
    tobacco (TMV) **8**:1130; **10**:1323, *1324*
  origins **12**:1682
  orthomyxoviruses **7**:*951*
  RNA **10**:1430–1431; **12**:1681
    see also retroviruses
  size **12**:1680–1681
  structures analyzed **12**:1677
  types **12**:1680–1681, 1683
  waterborne diseases **5**:627; **7**:948
  as weapons **12**:*1679*
  see also microbiology; prions (proteins)
Viscum album (mistletoe) **9**:*1265*; **10**:1321
Visible Human project **1**:72

vision 8:1071; 12:1684–1688
  and aging **1**:35
  artificial **12**:1688
  binocular/stereoscopic/three-
    dimensional **3**:322; **5**:687; **12**:1687
  bioluminescence used for **2**:205
  in cats **3**:322
  color **12**:1686, 1687
  and the compound eye **1**:140;
    5:687–*688*; **6**:743; **12**:1686
  daytime/photopic **12**:1686–1687
  in fish **6**:731; **12**:*1688*
  human **12**:1684–1685, 1687
    the brain and **2**:*263*; **12**:*1684*
  in invertebrates **5**:688; **12**:1685–1686
  night/scotopic **9**:*1221–1222*; **10**:1311;
    12:*1686*, 1687
  and the simple eye **5**:*685–687*; **12**:1685
  see also coloration; eyes
visual purple (rhodopsin) **10**:1311;
  12:*1685*, 1687
vitamins 9:1229; 12:1689–1691
  absorption from the gut **4**:519
  attacking free radicals **3**:294
  biotin **4**:488; **12**:1691
  as coenzymes **9**:1227; **12**:1691
  deficiency **4**:488–*489*; **9**:1227
  fat-soluble **4**:488–489, 519;
    12:1689–1690
  folic acid **12**:1691
    deficiency **4**:488; **12**:1691
  in foods **9**:1226–1227
  medical uses of **12**:1691
  megadoses **12**:1691
  stored in the liver **8**:1046
  supplements **12**:1691
  vitamin A (retinol) **3**:317; **10**:1311;
    12:1689
    absorption **4**:519
    deficiency **4**:488–489; **9**:1227, 1291;
      12:1689
  vitamin B, from yeast **12**:1715
  vitamin B_1 (thiamine) **4**:488; **12**:1690
    deficiency **9**:1227
  vitamin B_2 (riboflavin) **10**:1310; **12**:1690
    deficiency **12**:1690
  vitamin B_3 (niacin) **5**:630
    deficiency **4**:488
  vitamin B_5 (pantothenic acid)
    12:1690–1691
  vitamin B_6 (pyridoxine) **5**:630–631;
    12:*1689*, 1691
    deficiency **4**:488; **12**:1691
  vitamin B_{12} (cobalamine) **4**:519;
    12:1690, 1691
    deficiency **1**:74; **2**:246, 247; **4**:488;
      12:1691
  vitamin C (ascorbic acid) **3**:294, 395;
    12:1691
    absorption **4**:519
    deficiency **4**:488; **6**:764; **8**:1095;
      9:1227; **12**:*1691*

vitamin D **12**:1658, 1689

absorption **4**:519

and calcium absorption **2**:278; **12**:1691

deficiency **2**:250; **4**:*489*; **9**:*1227*; **11**:1502; **12**:1689

vitamin E (alpha tocopherol) **3**:294; **12**:1690, 1691

absorption **4**:519

deficiency **4**:489

vitamin K **12**:1690

absorption **4**:519

for babies **4**:519

deficiency **2**:242; **4**:489

water-soluble **4**:488, 519; **12**:*1689, 1690–1691*

vitiligo **2**:165; **10**:*1310*

Vitis spp. **3**:380

Viverridae **3**:311–312

viviparity, *see also* gestation

VLDLs (very low-density lipoproteins) **3**:363

vocal cords **11**:*1543*

volcanoes **5**:624

islands **9**:1231

life on the Galápagos Islands **9**:1169

voles, prairie **10**:1437

Vombatus ursinus (wombat) **4**:446; **5**:656; **8**:*1080*

vomeronasal (Jacobson's) organ **8**:1051; **10**:1416; **11**:1515

vomit, fossilized **9**:1257

Vomit Comet **11**:1534

vomiting **4**:519; **11**:1565

induced **11**:1565

see also eating disorders

von Neumann, John **2**:150

von Willebrand's factor **2**:242

Voronoff, Serge **12**:1633

Vries, Hugo de **8**:1107

vulnerable species **5**:606

see also endangered species

Vulpes spp.

V. macrotis (kit fox) **4**:501

V. rupelli (desert sand fox) **4**:501

V. vulpes (red fox) **11**:1523; **12**:*1671*

vultures **2**:235, 236, *237*

flight **6**:750, 752

Old World and New World **4**:446

W

waders *see* waterbirds and waders

wakame **7**:987

waking coma (persistent vegetative state) **3**:399; **5**:646; **8**:1038, 1040

Walker, John **2**:160

walking sticks *see* leaf insects and walking sticks

wallabies **8**:1080

Wallace, Alfred Russel **2**:192; **4**:479; **5**:653; **9**:*1192*–1193

walnuts **6**:792

walruses **3**:311

wapiti **5**:656; **8**:1084, 1133; **12**:1609

warblers

Bachman's **9**:1275

chestnut-sided **3**:402

reed **1**:*59*

resource partitioning **3**:410

Wareing, P.F. **4**:548

warfarin **8**:1096–1097

warm-blooded animals

dinosaurs as **4**:531

endothermy **7**:900–901; **8**:1069

fish as **6**:731; **11**:1488

pterosaurs as **10**:1391

warnings *see* calls, alarm; coloration, warning

warts

genital **7**:949

plantar (verrucae) **5**:699

Warwick, Kevin **2**:215

Washingtonia spp. **9**:1258

Washoe (chimpanzee) **3**:406

wasps and bees 12:1692–1694

bees **12**:1692, *1693–1694*

Africanized **12**:1693

bumblebees **7**:893

carpenter **12**:*1693*

cuckoo **12**:1693

hibernation **7**:893

mimics of **2**:*286*

orchid **9**:1240

pollen baskets **6**:*761*

pollination by **6**:*761*; **9**:1240; **10**:1336–1337; **12**:*1693*

sting **1**:53

temperature regulation **3**:367; **12**:1618

vision **12**:1687

see also honeybees

wasps **12**:*1692*–1693

common **12**:*1692*

ichneumon **12**:1692

parasitic **12**:1692

pollination by **6**:761; **12**:1693

social **12**:1692–1693

sting **1**:53

waste disposal 12:1695–1698

agricultural **12**:1697–1698

algae and **1**:48

animal waste for fertilzers **5**:718

oil spills *see* oil, environmental

radioactive **10**:1344; **12**:1697

recycling **10**:*1343*, 1344; **12**:*1696*–1697

and composting **11**:1461

see also pollution; sewage

waste products

animal **5**:*665*–666

see also excretion; feces

water

balance in the body **11**:1459

diseases carried in **5**:627; **7**:948–949

need, in humans **8**:1120

recycling, using microorganisms **8**:1132

storage in desert plants **2**:272

transportation in plants *see* transpiration

water stress in plants **11**:1567

waterbirds and waders 12:1699–1701

water boatmen **11**:1577

water bugs, giant **7**:885

water cycle (hydrological cycle) **9**:*1235*

water dogs **11**:1454

water fleas **4**:467, 468

waterfowl **12**:1699, 1700–1701, 1706

water hyacinths **5**:648

water lilies, Amazon **10**:1318

watermelons **11**:1554

water molds **8**:1140; **10**:1382

water scorpions **7**:885

water striders/water skippers **7**:885

Watson, James *see* Crick, Francis, and James Watson

Watson, John B. **1**:82; **3**:423; **7**:963; **10**:1383

waxes 5:690; 12:1702

carnauba wax **9**:1259

earwax **5**:676

weasels **3**:308; **9**:1159; **10**:1353

weather changes **5**:624

see also global warming

weavers, nests **9**:1208–*1209*

Weaver, Warren **7**:952

weeds

genes from transgenic plants spreading to **9**:*1243*, 1244

in suburbia **11**:1568

weevils **7**:*969*

boll **2**:178

Wegener, Alfred **2**:192

weightlessness, effects on the body **11**:1533

Weizmann, Chaim **5**:*703*

Weldon–Stupak Bill **3**:386

Wells, Horace **8**:1102

Welwitschia mirabilis **10**:*1305*

Went, F. W. **12**:1645

Wepfer, Johann Jacb **9**:1214

Werner's syndrome **1**:34

Wernicke, Carl **9**:1214

Wernicke's area **11**:1544

Wertheimer, Max **10**:1384

Weschler, David **7**:967

Weschler-Bellevue Scale **7**:967

West Nile virus **7**:947

wetlands 2:184; 12:1703–1706

coastal **12**:*1704*, 1706

Everglades 5:647–649; **12**:*1703*

sewage treatment in **12**:1696

see also bogs; mangroves; shore habitats

whales, porpoises, and dolphins 12:1707–1710

anatomy **12**:1707–1708

behavior **12**:*1707*, 1709

blowholes **10**:*1417*, 1423; **12**:1707, 1708, *1710*

distribution **12**:1710

dolphins

bottlenose **4**:572, 573; **12**:1707

Chinese river (baiji) **12**:1709

communication **3**:*404*, 405

courtship displays **4**:*456*

endangered **12**:1709

Indus River **12**:1709, 1710

intelligence **12**:1709–1710

sonic weapons **4**:574

swimming **11**:1578

teeth **12**:1606

testes **10**:1410

echolocation **4**:572; **7**:873; **8**:1135; **12**:1708

endangered **12**:1709

evolution **12**:1708

feeding **12**:1709

intelligence **12**:1709–1710

navigation and strandings **12**:1710

porpoises, endangered **12**:1709

reproduction **12**:1709

senses **12**:1708–1709

whales

baleen **4**:438; **5**:*695*; **12**:1606, 1708, *1709*, 1710

beaked **12**:1606

blue **3**:405; **4**:438; **8**:1069; **12**:1707, 1708, 1709, 1710

bowhead **12**:1710

bryde's **12**:1710

diving **10**:1423

fin whales **12**:1709, 1710

gray **8**:1134; **10**:*1417*; **12**:1709, 1710

humpback **1**:97; **3**:405; **4**:*438*, 460; **11**:1580; **12**:1709, 1710

killer (orcas) **10**:1350; **12**:1707, *1708*, 1709, 1710

migrations **8**:1135; **12**:1710

minke **12**:1710

northern bottlenose **12**:1709

pilot **12**:1707

respiration **10**:1423

right **12**:1709, 1710

rorqual **12**:1710

sei **12**:1710

"skyhopping" **8**:1135

sounds **3**:405; **12**:1709

spermaceti **12**:1702

sperm whales **4**:572, 574; **12**:1707, 1708, 1709, 1710

whales, porpoises, and dolphins
(continued)
swimming 11:1578; 12:1593
toothed 4:572, 574; 12:1606,
1707–1708, 1710
whaling and 12:1710
wheat 1:101
new varieties 1:40; 4:546
origins of 6:793
and polyploidy 10:1408
rusts of 6:800
selective breeding 11:1479
wheel animals see rotifers
Whipple, Allen 4:554
whippoorwills 2:216; 6:776;
9:1221–1222
whip scorpions 11:1469
whiskers 1:106; 8:1070; 12:1628
whisk ferns (fork-ferns) 5:706, 707;
10:1326
whistling thorns 11:1562
White, Tim 7:915
Whitney, Eli 1:39
whooping cough see pertussis
widow birds, long-tailed 11:1486
Wiener, Norbert 7:952
wildcats 3:324
wildebeest
grazing 12:1662, 1663
migration 8:1134–1135, 1136
wildfires see fires
wildfowl 11:1578
Wilkins, Maurice 6:785–786
Williams, Cicely 10:1378
Williams, Daniel Hale 8:1101
Willis, Thomas 9:1214
willows 1:78; 9:1292
Sitka 10:1317
Wilmut, Ian 3:340, 383, 385
Wilson, Edward O. 5:644, 661, 680;
11:1525; 12:1647, 1711
Wilson, Ernest Henry 'Chinese' 2:254
Wilson's disease 8:1124
wilting
plant 12:1630, 1631
prevention 8:1026; 12:1670
wilts, fusarium 10:1321
winds
as an energy source 10:1340–1341
and environmental disasters 5:624
wine 5:701; 6:763
wings 6:747
of bats 2:173, 175; 6:748, 750, 751
of birds 6:747–748, 777
of insects 7:958
butterflies and moths 2:267–268, 269
dragonflies 6:750
earwigs 4:563
flies 6:743
grasshoppers and crickets 6:750
see also flight
wisteria 3:379

witch hazel 7:887
Withering, William 9:1291
Wolffian duct 7:992
wolverines 12:1654
wolves 4:539–540
dog-wolf hybrids 4:541–542
domesticated 4:541
dominance interactions 3:402; 11:1522
Ethiopian 4:541–542
howling 4:542
maned 4:445
red 4:541, 542
social behavior 4:540
territories 12:1613
timber/gray 3:309, 428; 4:539, 541;
10:1350; 11:1522, 1524
wombats 4:446; 5:656; 8:1080
wood 6:725
decomposition of 11:1460–1462;
12:1609
development of woody stems 11:1561
fossilized 12:1638
hardwood 11:1562
knotholes 11:1562
softwood 11:1562; 12:1639
see also timber; trees
woodlands, English 4:493
wood lice, molt 9:1158
woodpeckers 6:775
competition 3:410
drumming 4:459
feet 5:698; 9:1273
Gila 2:273
great spotted 2:232
nests 9:1209
tongue 12:1621, 1622
woody perennials see perennial plants,
woody
wool 6:725, 726
World Health Organization (WHO) 5:634
World War I
biologial weapons 2:198
lice 8:1033
World War II
biologial weapons 2:198
lice 8:1033
worms
parasitic
in cats and dogs 1:90
see also hookworms; nematode worms;
tapeworms
wounds 7:937
healing 3:419; 10:1401–1402
see also inflammation
wracks 7:988
wrasse 4:445, 450–451; 11:1582
wrens
cactus 2:273; 9:1206
flightless 6:756
nests 9:1206, 1208
Wright, Orville and Wilbur 6:751
Wright, Sewell 5:654

writing, development 3:358
Wucheraria 9:1222
Wundt, Wilhelm 3:423; 10:1383
Wyeomyia smithii 3:316

X

Xanthium strumarium (cocklebur) 2:217
Xanthopan morgani praedicta (hawk moth)
2:268
xanthophylls 3:317
xanthopterin 10:1311
xenacanths 11:1489
Xenicus lyalli (flightless wren) 6:756
Xenopsylla cheopis (rat flea) 6:740
xenotransplantation 2:189, 225; 8:1092
xerophthalmia 12:1689
xerophytes 12:1630
at high altitude 9:1169
see also cacti and succulents
Xerosicyos 11:1555
Xestobium rufovillosum (death-watch beetle)
2:178
Xiphophorus spp. (platyfish) 11:1485–1486
X rays 5:626; 12:1712–1713
dangers of 12:1713
mutations 6:746; 12:1713
discovery 8:1090, 1102, 10:1395;
12:1713
imaging using 1:72; 10:1394
of the chest 12:1648
in CT scanning 4:474–475
of the stomach 11:1563, 1565
X-ray crystallography 1:68; 2:182
of viruses 12:1677
X-ray diffraction 1:68; 6:786; 8:1146
see also radiation and radiation sickness
xylem 4:509; 8:1024; 11:1448, 1561;
12:1631, 1669
Xysticus sp. 11:1549

Y

YACs (yeast artificial chromosomes)
12:1715
yaks 1:18; 4:545; 8:1058
yams 3:380; 9:1161; 11:1446
Mexican 1:80
yeast artificial chromosomes (YACs)
12:1715
yeasts 5:700; 12:1714–1716
as animal fodder 12:1715
baker's 5:701; 12:1715, 1716
dietary supplements 12:1715–1716
dried 12:1716
fermentation by 2:159; 11:1461
in food production 5:701;
12:1714–1715
food spoilage 12:1716
health problems from 12:1716
reproduction 8:1082; 12:1714
yellow fever 7:947; 9:1268; 12:1678
and the Panama Canal 9:1267
and the Suez Canal 8:1126

yellow jackets 12:1692–1693
Yellowstone National Park 3:425, 426;
5:623
yellowwoods 3:416, 417
Yersin, Alexandre 7:950
Yersinia pestis 6:740; 7:950; 8:1063
yews, drugs from 3:417; 9:1290
yin and yang 3:360
yogurt 5:701
yolk 5:588–589
Yucca Mountain (Nevada) 10:1344;
12:1697
yuccas 9:1160
and coevolution 10:1336
see also Joshua trees

Z

Zaglossus spp. (echidnas) 9:1162–1163
Zalophus californianus (California sea lion)
3:311; 8:1124
Zasloff, Michael A. 9:1290
Zea mays (corn/maize) see corn
zebras 3:391, 392; 8:1074
communication 3:401
competing males 3:407
courtship 4:460
grazing 12:1663
plains/Burchell's 12:1663
social groups 11:1523
zeitgebers 2:216–217
Zener, Karl 9:1262
Zener cards 9:1262
ZEUS (robotic surgical system) 10:1432,
1433
zidovudine (azidothymidine, AZT) 1:44,
109; 9:1292; 12:1678
ZIFT (zygote intrafallopian transfer) 5:710
zinc
and Alzheimer's disease 1:61
deficiency 4:489
Zion, Elie de 9:1271
Z lines 9:1181
zona pellucida 5:589
Zonotrichia spp. 3:402; 8:1136
zoogeography 12:1717–1719
zooids 11:1524
zoology 12:1720–1721
zoonoses 1:90
zooplankton see plankton, zooplankton
zoos 12:1722–1726
zooxanthellae 4:449–450, 453
zorros, small-eared 4:539
Zostera marina (eelgrass) 6:761
zoysia 12:1651
zucchini 11:1554, 1555
zygodactyly 6:775, 778
zygomorphic flowers 6:759
Zygomycota 6:799; 8:1137–1138
Zygoptera 4:550
zygosporangia 6:799
zygote intrafallopian transfer (ZIFT) 5:710
zygotes 11:1557